UNDERSTANDING AGGRESSIVE BEHAVIOR IN CHILDREN

ANNALS OF THE NEW YORK ACADEMY OF SCIENCES

Volume 794

UNDERSTANDING AGGRESSIVE BEHAVIOR IN CHILDREN

Edited by Craig F. Ferris and Thomas Grisso

The New York Academy of Sciences
New York, New York
1996

Photograph on softcover by Eugene Richards in *Cocaine True, Cocaine Blue*, Aperture (1994).

Library of Congress Cataloging-in-Publication Data

Understanding aggressive behavior in children / edited by Craig F. Ferris and Thomas Grisso.
      p.   cm. -- (Annals of the New York Academy of Sciences ; v. 794)
   Includes bibliographical references and indexes.
   ISBN 1-57331-012-3 (alk. paper). -- ISBN 1-57331-013-1 (pbk. : alk. paper)
   1. Aggressiveness (Psychology) in children--Congresses.
I. Ferris, Craig F.   II. Grisso, Thomas.   III. Series.
Q11.N5 vol. 794
[RJ506.A35]
500 s--dc20
[155.4'18232]   96-34935
                                                                           CIP

BC/PCP
Printed in the United States of America
ISBN 1-57331-012-3 (cloth)
ISBN 1-57331-013-1 (paper)
ISSN 0077-8923

ANNALS OF THE NEW YORK ACADEMY OF SCIENCES
Volume 794
September 20, 1996

UNDERSTANDING AGGRESSIVE BEHAVIOR IN CHILDREN[a]

Editors and Conference Organizers
CRAIG F. FERRIS AND THOMAS GRISSO

CONTENTS

[a] This volume is the result of a conference, entitled **Understanding Aggressive Behavior in Children,** held in New York City on September 29 to October 2, 1995 by the New York Academy of Sciences.

Financial assistance was received from:

- E. H. HENROTTE
- LILLY RESEARCH LABORATORIES
- PFIZER CENTRAL RESEARCH

Introduction: An Interdisciplinary Approach to Understanding Aggressive Behavior in Children

THOMAS GRISSO[a]

Department of Psychiatry
University of Massachusetts Medical School
55 Lake Avenue North
Worcester, Massachusetts 01655

This volume presents papers that demonstrate the unusual scope of the scientific search to understand the development of aggressive behavior in children. The trajectory of recent scientific advances in this area—in neuroscience, behavioral science, medicine, psychology, sociology, and ethics—allows us to imagine a not-too-distant day when we will be able to understand, prevent, and modify the development of harmful aggressive behavior in children. The authors in this book do not tell us how, but their combined efforts identify a stage in our process toward that goal.

This book also seeks to demonstrate and change a hard reality: if we maintain our present course in our search for causes of aggression in children, we will surely fail. This assertion can be described in no better way than with an extrapolation of the image constructed by Joan McCord later in this book. Why is the sapling outside your window the way it is? What has determined its odd shape, its slow rate of growth, the way it leans, its anemic look despite the luxuriant foliage of your neighbor's tree? Whatever your answer, it will be inadequate (for your understanding of the tree, and for devising well-placed efforts to assist its growth) if you take into account less than everything that influences development.

You may know all that is humanly knowable about floral morphology and chemical processes, but you will not understand this tree if you know nothing about its ecological history. By the same token, you may know precisely the amount and rate of nutrients it received since it germinated, all toxicants against which it struggled, and variants in its exposure to sunlight. These facts will not explain the tree's condition, however, if they are considered in ignorance of the molecular processes with which it was endowed.

My colleague, Craig Ferris, whom I assisted in developing the symposium that produced the papers in this volume, has identified the matter succinctly: "Development is 100% environment and 100% heredity." No aspect of an organism's development is understandable from either perspective alone. Ultimately the answer to the development of aggressive behavior in children requires that we consider dynamic interactions. Biology and environment taken separately are never causes of anything in an organism's development. At any finite moment of growth, they are always a single cause.

[a] Tel: (508) 856-6580; fax: (508) 856-6426; e-mail: tgrisso@bangate1.ummed.edu.

1

INTEGRATING THE FIELD

Despite this simple and uncontroversial fact, the scientific study of the development of aggressive behavior has too often proceeded as if it were not so. Studies in the neuroscience of aggression have progressed largely without reference to the roles of social nurture and neglect in the expression of biological potentials. At the same time, behavioral scientists are making significant strides in identifying the effects of parenting and other social conditions on the development of aggressive behaviors, but they proceed largely without an awareness of the biological factors with which external events interact. This limits our ability to account for the substantial unexplained variance found in all studies that attempt to provide psychosocial explanations of behavior.

It was for this reason that the New York Academy of Sciences valued the development of the conference in 1995 that produced the contributions in this volume. The purpose of the conference was to begin the process of integrating the various domains of science that are studying the development of aggressive behavior in children.

The conference participants were chosen on the basis of their national recognition as leaders in their various fields of research on aggression. Yet many of them had never read each others' works. Neuroscientists studying the biochemistry of aggression listened to behavioral scientists describing the multidimensional scaling of temper tantrums in children and the social phenomenon of bullying in the schoolyard. Behavioral scientists heard about studies of brain plasticity and neuro-adaptation. As the groups listened, they began to develop insights into the potential relationships between their disparate views of the problem of aggression.

That I, a clinical psychologist, am writing this introduction illustrates the extraordinary range of interests included within this effort to communicate across disciplines. My own research is cited by none of this book's experts, and I knew only a few of them prior to the conference. My academic and clinical life is devoted to very applied questions about our social, clinical, and legal responses to youths who commit acts of violence. I deal with the "end product" of the developmental processes described in this book. My world is the one you see in the headlines of your morning paper: the twofold increase in juvenile homicide in the past decade, the law's attempts to respond to it, and the mental health profession's efforts to save youths from themselves.

In their research, clinical practice, and consultation to policy makers, people like me translate what the contributors to this volume produce, in an attempt to use science to guide society in its efforts to prevent and control children's harmful aggression. My colleagues are the consumers of whatever science can tell us about the development of children's aggressive behavior.

That information, however, will be of practical use only if it describes the biology of aggression within a psychological and sociological context. A case example helps to make this point.

To assist a local court, I recently performed a clinical evaluation of a 15 year old who had brutally stabbed and killed his girlfriend. For more than a year he had been engaged in body building with the aid of massive doses of anabolic steroids. My review of the research, as well as my consultation with psychopharmacologists, warned me that it was only "possible," not "known," that steroids would have had any predictable hormonal effect on his aggressive act. Yet is was quite clear to me that steroids had had other biological roles in interaction with social factors. Within a year, the boy had developed physically from average musculature to a body-builder's physique. Beaten up and ignored by his peers throughout childhood, he had now been adopted by more popular peers as their friend and bodyguard because of his frequent demonstrations of how ruthlessly and successfully his new physique allowed him to fight. He became a heavy drinker to try to combat the depressions that accompanied the periods between cycles of steroid use. This negatively influenced his relationship with his mother and perpetuated his repeat of another cycle of steroids.

As a consumer of scientific information for application in the real world, one can never separate biological influences from their psychosocial and environmental context. Basic scientists have that luxury, but they must begin to relinquish it as they come nearer to identifying the answers to questions within their isolated domains. If they do not, they will not reach their ultimate goal.

That was the purpose of the conference at which the papers in this volume were given. We sought to begin the process of integrating disparate scientific discoveries in ways that would hasten the day when society might be able to effectively reduce the development of harmful aggression in children.

CONCEPTUALIZING THE INTEGRATION TASK

In 1993, the National Research Council of the National Academy of Sciences issued a comprehensive review and a call for research on aggression.[1] In its report, called "Understanding and Preventing Violence," the Council reviewed current research within three areas, identifying these as three "perspectives on violence": the biological, the psychosocial developmental, and the social environmental.

The biological perspective is represented, for example, by the extraordinary advances in recent years in testing hormonal mechanisms; neurotransmitters, such as serotonin; and neuroanatomical and neurophysiological abnormalities as correlates of aggression. Knowledge in this area is moving forward rapidly, through the combined efforts of researchers who study humans—frequently encountering difficulties in measurement and controls—and those studying animals—offering greater control but uncertainty about cross-species generalizability.

The psychosocial developmental perspective focuses on the learning of aggressive and nonaggressive behaviors, and on the development of cognitive and perceptual processes by which children interpret and respond to their world. Included here are studies of temperament, persistent psychological traits, and possible relationships between children's aggressive behaviors and exposure to psychosocial variables, such as abuse by family members and peer reinforcement.

The social environmental perspective examines the relationship between aggression, and features of the physical environment and the broader social ecology of which children are a part. Research is identifying the importance of some variables that are economic and political in nature: for example, poverty and its potential relationship to aggression through mediators as diverse as poor nutrition, lead paint, and drug traffic. Other environmental factors include social ecological phenomena: neighborhood cohesion or chaos, policing, and youth gangs.

As research becomes increasingly sophisticated in all of these perspectives, the need for integration of their discoveries is ever more apparent. No matter how great their advances, they will remain in a primitive state until their interrelationships are known. None of them alone is capable of achieving the understanding we need. At first this may simply require research that combines variables identified with the various perspectives. Eventually a paradigmatic breakthrough may be needed to achieve true integration. Anything less may leave us with a fragmented

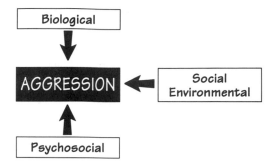

FIGURE 1. Three perspectives on aggression.

patchwork of information, of little use in guiding effective interventions to alter the course of the development of aggression.

The conference that produced this collection of papers sought to begin the process of integrating various perspectives in this field in several ways. FIGURE 1 illustrates the book's most basic objective: bringing the perspectives together around their common interest. No integration can occur until researchers studying the development of aggression have been exposed to the ways in which others outside their own perspective are attempting to study the same problem.

Publishing works from these various perspectives together is one way to try to achieve this objective. Each of the papers is valuable in its own right, demonstrating the latest scientific advances in its area of research. The value of their publication in a single volume, however, is lost if readers use this reference only as a review of work by colleagues identified with their own perspective. Each of the three perspectives has different pieces of a map that lead to the destination we all seek. We will not get there without allowing ourselves to discover the pieces that have been found in perspectives other than our own.

One problem in bringing all of these perspectives into one place, of course, is that of cross-disciplinary translation. The three perspectives tend to speak different languages, due to differences in their theories, concepts, methods, and technical terms. In this volume, the problem is somewhat mitigated by the fact that the authors prepared their papers for the conference knowing that they would be communicating with scientists outside their own specific areas of research.

Learning about other perspectives, however, is only the first step toward our overall goal. We want to encourage the proposition that the dark arrows in FIGURE 1 can provide only simplistic, incomplete information about aggression. The direct effects of neither neurobiological mechanisms nor social learning phenomena hold much promise for explaining the development of aggression, nor do social environmental factors, such as guns, drugs, and poverty. Even the additive effects of their explanatory power will fall well short.

Instead, we want to encourage the proposition illustrated in FIGURE 2. If a particular perspective wants to know its relation to aggression, it cannot get there on its own road. Its causal pathway to aggression ultimately lies through another perspective's territory. Psychosocial factors may have an effect on aggression, not only directly, but by altering biological mechanisms that contribute to aggression. Biochemical factors may influence cognition and temperament, thereby increasing

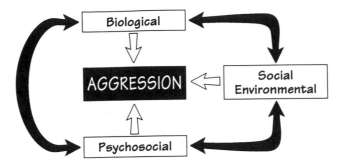

FIGURE 2. Perspectives as mediators of the effects of variables in other perspectives.

the risk of aggression. A primary factor in one perspective may influence aggression through mediating factors associated with another perspective.

In these papers, for example, we learn that disrupting a child's early attachments—a psychosocial factor—can influence aggression by affecting biogenic amine neurotransmitters. We are asked to consider the proposition that social environmental stressors can cause changes in adrenal steroids, which play a role in aggressive behavior. We are offered the concept of brain plasticity: that psychosocial factors can effect development of neuroanatomical sites associated with aggression. Reversing the direction, biological factors are examined for their influence on the learning of aggressive behaviors.

Each of these papers was chosen because the results that it describes provide a potential link to results in other papers arising from different research perspectives. As presented here, the authors' works derive their special significance from the interdisciplinary context of the whole collection.

Many of the authors in this volume have already begun to struggle with the potential interaction of biological, psychosocial, and environmental factors in the development of aggressive behavior. They offer our best hope for stimulating the new generation of cross-disciplinary research needed in this field.

FIGURE 3 illustrates an additional possibility that all perspectives must consider when attempting to understand how aggressive behavior develops. We tend to

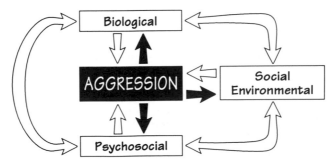

FIGURE 3. Perspectives as mediators of the effects of aggression on further aggression.

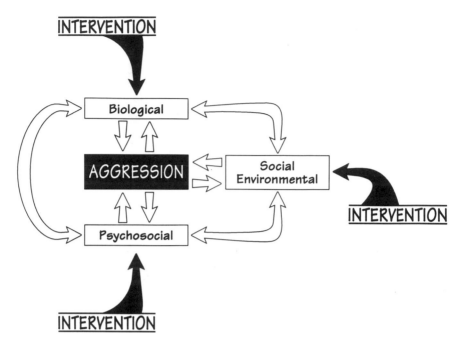

FIGURE 4. Perspective-related interventions to reduce the development of aggression.

think of aggression as the effect—the dependent variable. Yet aggression can also be a causal component, exerting an influence on biological or psychosocial factors that offer further explanations for aggression. For example, troubled neighborhoods, or one's own aggressive behavior, create stressful interpersonal and social conditions, which in turn can cause changes in adrenal steroids. Aggression increases the chance of head injury, which may further increase aggression due to neurophysical changes.

The ultimate purpose for understanding the development of aggressive behavior is preventive intervention during childhood development. As illustrated in FIGURE 4, the three perspectives for understanding the development of aggressive behavior also represent three avenues for intervention. In the context of the diagram of interactions, we are encouraged to consider that interventions related to a particular perspective may have a preventive influence on aggression through their effect on variables in other domains. For example, Ritalin may reduce the aggression of an attention-deficit hyperactivity-disordered child, but the reduction in aggressive behavior may also produce a change in the family's response to the child. Whether that response is positive (*e.g.*, interpersonally rewarding) or negative (*e.g.*, the child is suddenly ignored) may influence the continued benefits of the biological intervention. Considering interventions in this cross-perspective manner can help us to develop more effective interventions.

As research develops possibilities for intervention, hard ethical questions are inevitable. They require balancing our concern for reducing harmful aggression against our concern for the autonomy of individuals, families, and groups. These issues are addressed in a paper (see Blustein) that was invited for the conference.

Intervention is the most visible context for these ethical issues. Yet we must also recognize how more fundamental steps in the scientific process—for example, what and whom we choose to study—can have far-reaching ethical implications for society's eventual responses to aggression. Understanding how society might use our research is every bit as important as understanding aggression itself.

Among the papers in this volume that represent the biological perspective, none focus specifically on genetics. In preparing the conference, we believed that specific attention to genetic contributions to aggression would not be a productive use of the unique opportunity that this project provided. In one sense, all of development is an expression of genetic potential. In another sense, there is no credible evidence for a link between genes and aggressive or violent behavior. Moreover, as a practical matter for the conference, we felt that attention to genetic structure would take precious time away from the main purpose of the conference: to explore aggression as a consequence of neuroadaptation to psychosocial and environmental factors, and as a consequence of biological effects on psychosocial development.

We hope that this volume will help us to realize the power of multiple perspectives in interaction, aimed at understanding aggressive behavior in children. We can move nearer to that goal if these papers are read as an exercise. We invite readers to discover for themselves the potential connections between the diverse areas of research represented in this book. We can learn much more about the development of aggression in children through the fusion of these research perspectives than by their results considered in isolation.

REFERENCE

1. NATIONAL RESEARCH COUNCIL. 1993. Understanding and preventing violence. National Academy Press. Washington, DC.

Development and Expression of Hormonal Systems Regulating Aggression[a]

NEAL G. SIMON,[b] SUZANNE E. McKENNA,
SHI-FANG LU, AND ATHENA COLOGER-CLIFFORD

Department of Biological Sciences
Lehigh University
Bethlehem, Pennsylvania 18015

The ability of testosterone (T) to facilitate the display of intermale aggressive behavior in nonprimate mammals is one of the most widely recognized relationships in behavioral neuroendocrinology.[1,2] The wealth of evidence supporting this biobehavioral effect of T has led to numerous investigations regarding the potential role of testicular androgens in human aggression. These studies, however, yielded equivocal results over the past thirty years, even as various aspects of research in this area became more sophisticated.[3,4] Although an in-depth review of this work is beyond the scope of this chapter, a basic feature of many investigations with humans has been the expectation that serum T level will be positively correlated with either prior, ongoing, or potential aggressiveness. The focus on serum T may be a significant, and perhaps principle, factor in the mixed results of human studies, because it does not recognize that intracellular events constitute critical steps in the production of hormonal effects,[5] including behavioral facilitation. The advances in understanding the mechanism of action of steroids such as T[6] have expanded significantly the process that must be investigated to develop a comprehensive model of the neuroendocrine regulation of aggressive behavior. Examples include metabolism, steroid-receptor binding, nuclear acceptor site interactions, transcriptional regulation, and protein synthesis.

Our research over the past ten years has employed a murine model to begin characterizing the cellular processes that mediate T-dependent intermale aggression. These investigations have had four goals. The first was to define the pathways in the adult central nervous system (CNS) through which T could promote the display of aggressive behavior. This involved identifying sex and strain differences in the response to T and its major metabolites, estradiol (E_2) and dihydrotestosterone (DHT).[7,8] The second involved describing the perinatal hormonal conditions that establish these pathways by delineating the specific effects of E_2 and DHT on the sexual differentiation of each system. The third was to use these biobehavioral findings as the basis for biochemical and immunochemical studies of steroid recep-

[a] Support for parts of the research was provided by Grants from the National Institutes of Health (1R15 HD31696), the Harry Frank Guggenheim Foundation, the Howard Hughes Medical Institute, and the National Science Foundation (IBN-9512015) to N. G. Simon.

[b] Address correspondence to N. G. Simon, Ph.D., Department of Biological Sciences, Lehigh University, 111 Research Drive, Room B217, Bethlehem, PA 18015-4732. Tel: (610) 758-3680; fax: (610) 758-4004; e-mail: ngsø@lehigh.edu.

tor function to identify the cellular mechanisms involved in the hormonal regulation of aggression. The fourth, and broadest goal, was to integrate these results to describe the molecular processes that regulate sensitivity/insensitivity to the aggression-promoting property of gonadal steroids. Given the evolutionary conservation of steroid-receptor systems and their regulation,[9] findings with animal models may help facilitate the development of alternative hypotheses concerning how T may or may not influence the expression of certain forms of aggression in humans.

There are three pathways through which T can promote the display of aggression in the adult male brain:[2,10] androgen-sensitive, which responds to T itself or its 5α-reduced metabolite, DHT; estrogen-sensitive, which uses E_2 derived by aromatization of T; and a synergistic or combined pathway, where both the androgenic and estrogenic metabolites of T are used to facilitate behavioral expression. Not all of these activational systems are present in every male. Rather, the functional pathway is determined by genotype, as seen through castration-replacement studies where gonadectomized males were treated with specifically acting androgens or estrogens and then tested for aggression.[10] These experiments showed that CF-1 males, for example, have both an androgen- and estrogen-sensitive regulatory pathway. CFW males have only an estrogen-responsive system, whereas CD-1 males evidence both an androgenic and a synergistic pathway.[11,12] The most commonly recognized system uses E_2 as the active aggression-promoting agent, which supports the aromatization hypothesis.[13] Regardless of the functional system, they share a basic feature of high sensitivity, that is, after the postcastration decline in fighting behavior, it takes an average of only 2-3 days of hormone treatment with the appropriate steroid at physiological doses to restore aggression to levels seen in intact males.

Additional insights into these neuroendocrine regulatory systems were obtained through studies with adult females. Interestingly, the female CNS does have an androgen-sensitive pathway, which can be activated by chronic exposure to T, DHT, or methyltrienolone (R1881), a nonaromatizeable androgen.[14,15] This system differs from that seen in males, however, because of its low sensitivity, that is, it takes about 20 days of androgen exposure after ovariectomy to induce male-like fighting behavior. An even more dramatic difference is that the adult female brain is completely insensitive to the aggression-promoting property of estrogens.[15,16] Thus, although both sexes are capable of using androgen to activate aggression, there is a relative sexual dimorphism in target tissue sensitivity. By contrast, there is an absolute sexual dimorphism in the capacity to respond to the aggression-activating property of estrogen.

The presence of robust differences in gonadal steroid sensitivity between males and females in adulthood points to a pivotal role of hormonal events during sexual differentiation in the establishment of these regulatory pathways. Resolving the specific processes and their timing involved consideration of several factors. First, because the regulatory pathways are independent, there was a need to examine the development of each separately. This was accomplished by characterizing the potential role of the metabolites of T in the establishment of male-typical androgen-sensitive and estrogen-sensitive regulatory systems. Second, it was our view that narrowing the time when each of the systems was established was critical. This necessitated assessments of hormonal effects both late in prenatal development and early in the postnatal period. Our findings from a series of studies[17-21] are summarized in FIGURE 1.

The estrogen-responsive system is organized by an effect of E_2 on neural tissue between day 1 and day 4 postpartum. Several observations supported this concept. One was the males delivered by cesarean section and castrated immediately were

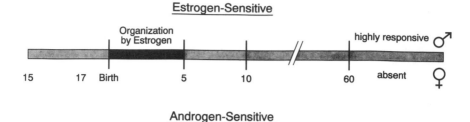

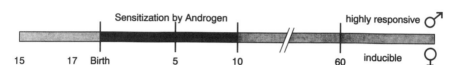

FIGURE 1. Development and expression of neuroendocrine regulatory pathways. A summary of the major hormonal events and their timing in the establishment of estrogen-sensitive and androgen-sensitive regulatory systems for offensive, male-typical aggressive behavior.

incapable of responding to the aggression-promoting property of E_2 as adults. If gonadectomy occurred on day 10, however, the estrogen-sensitive system was fully competent.[21] Consistent with this finding was that the administration of diethylstilbestrol (DES), a synthetic, specifically acting estrogen, on day 1, or the aromatizeable androgen T on day 1-3, masculinized the subsequent response to E_2, whereas R1881, a nonaromatizeable androgen, was ineffective.[18,20] Lastly, the fact that adult female mice are completely insensitive to the induction of male-like aggression by E_2 demonstrates that the prenatal hormonal environment does not contribute to the development of an estrogen-sensitive regulatory pathway.

Resolving the hormonal processes involved in the development of the androgen-responsive system was more complicated, primarily because of controversies surrounding the potential role of prenatal androgens in sensitization of the neural substrate for aggression.[17,22] Our work indicates that maximal sensitization is accomplished by direct androgenic stimulation in the period shortly after birth. Using newborn females as an experimental model, the administration of R1881 and T, but not DES, led to a male-like response to androgen in adulthood.[20] This indicated that the androgenic metabolites of T masculinized the response to the aggression-promoting property of androgen. Also supporting this perspective were results with mice that showed that the greater the duration of androgen exposure in females or the later that males are castrated during the postnatal period, the shorter the duration of androgen exposure required during adulthood to induce aggression.[23,24] Whether prenatal androgen exposure contributes to the masculinization of the androgen-sensitive system is unclear. Primary support for a prenatal effect came from the description of the uterine position phenomena,[22] which suggested that variation in endogenous androgen exposure *in utero* altered subsequent sensitivity to the aggression-promoting property of androgen later in life in Rockland-Swiss female mice. More recently, no effect of uterine position on T sensitivity or hypothalamic androgen binding was noted in CF-1 female mice.[17,19] This raised the possibility that uterine position effects, if present, may be genetically constrained. Given these conflicting results, the conservative view would seem to be that it is direct androgenic stimulation early in postnatal development that masculinizes the androgen-sensitive regulatory pathway for aggression.

In sum, the use of specifically acting androgens and estrogens has allowed characterization of multiple neuroendocrine pathways through which T can promote aggressive behavior and the necessary hormonal events during sexual differentiation that establish subsequent behavioral sensitivity in the adult male central nervous system. These observations provided a framework for investigating the role of androgen receptor (AR) and estrogen receptor (ER) in the regulation of aggression. Given that variation in steroid receptor function is a prominent factor in syndromes of hormone insensitivity, these studies are critical for understanding the cellular processes mediating behavioral responsiveness.

A number of excellent reviews on the mechanism of action of steroids are available.[5,25,26] Although recent evidence has established both genomic and nongenomic effects of steroids, the time frame for the activation of aggressive behavior in mice and other rodents by hormone treatment following castration, 2-3 days, is consistent with the latter, and our efforts have focused on these aspects of hormone function. The major events in the production of genomic effects are steroid-receptor (S-R) binding, activation of the S-R complex that enhances affinity for nuclear acceptor sites, S-R binding to genomic acceptor sites, up- or down-regulation of target genes by S-R, and subsequent changes in protein synthesis, which are in turn linked to behavioral expression. In fact, research into these processes in relation to the steroidal regulation of aggression is at a relatively early stage.

Regarding the androgen-sensitive system, studies with adults examined sex and strain differences in AR binding through equilibrium binding assays and the distribution, density, and regulation of AR through immunochemical studies.[10,27] Scatchard analyses of saturation data from combined hypothalamic-preoptic-septal cytosol showed that there were differences among CF-1, CFW, and CD-1 male mice in receptor concentration and in the affinity of ligand-receptor binding. Although the results were consistent for both [^{3}H]DHT or [^{3}H]R1881, neither of these parameters appeared to be systematically related to observed differences in behavioral sensitivity. These findings suggested that insight into the androgen-sensitive system likely would require a method that permitted analyses on a cellular basis. In this context, immunochemical investigations have permitted the construction of detailed AR distribution maps. Major regions exhibiting positive immunoreactivity include the bed nucleus of the stria terminalis (BNST), the lateral septum (LS), the medial preoptic area (MPO), and the medial amygdala (MAMYG). Interestingly, the results showed that whereas there was no sex difference in AR distribution, there was a major sexual dimorphism in AR density, with males exhibiting far more intense immunostaining in all regions.[27]

An abundant literature has demonstrated in both peripheral and neural tissue from males that AR expression is decreased by castration and up-regulated by androgen replacement therapy.[28–30] These observations raised the possibility that neural AR regulation might differ between males and females and that this could be a contributing mechanism to variation in behavioral sensitivity. Such studies can involve assessments of AR mRNA regulation using *in situ* hybridization, which potentially provides a direct index of changes in transcriptional activity and/or an examination of alterations in the level of AR itself under differing hormonal conditions, which would reflect changes in protein synthesis. To date, we have chosen the latter approach because of inconsistencies in studies that focused on AR message. For example, androgenic stimulation reportedly down-regulates AR mRNA in rat prostate and three human cell lines, LNCap, T47D, and MGM323,[31] whereas no effect was observed in rat testis and micropunched brain regions.[22] In rat Sertoli cells, transient down-regulation of AR mRNA was followed by up-regulations,[33] and in amphibians, up-regulation of AR message by androgens has been described.[34] Whereas these are intriguing findings that require further investigation, measurements that assess changes in protein expression seem to have greater utility, at least until issues surrounding cell and tissue specificity of AR mRNA regulation and stability are better understood.

The effects of castration and castration plus testosterone propionate (TP) implants on AR in several brain regions were compared in adult male and female CF-1 mice, and the results for BNST are shown as an example of typical findings (see FIG. 2). Gonadectomy led to a rapid loss of immunostaining, whereas the TP implant led to nearly a twofold increase in AR density in both sexes. To confirm these results, a Western blot analysis was conducted. Because this technique involves denaturation of all proteins, it avoids a potentially controversial feature of immunochemical studies, that is, whether an antibody fully recognizes both liganded and unliganded forms of the receptor. The results (not shown) were consistent with the immunochemical observations.

The findings of the immunochemical and Western analyses demonstrated that the regulation of AR is comparable in both male and female neural tissue. In both sexes, AR can be over induced and basal levels are androgen dependent. This suggests that one factor contributing to the sexual dimorphism in sensitivity to the aggression-promoting property of androgen may normally be the presence or absence of androgen, with its associated effects on AR density.

Potential cellular processes mediating sensitivity to the aggression-promoting property of estrogen also have been examined. Initial studies involved equilibrium binding assays, and genetic differences were found among CF-1, CD-1, and CFW males in [^{3}H]DES binding.[10] Interestingly, the CF-1 strain exhibited significantly higher affinity [^{3}H]DES-ER binding, whereas the CFW strain had the highest ER concentration in hypothalamic-preoptic-septal cytosol. Although caution in interpreting these findings is appropriate (see below), both the affinity of ligand-receptor interactions and the number of binding sites can influence target tissue sensitivity to steroids.[35,36] Another study examined the dissociation kinetics of activated ER,[37] which provides information on the stability of liganded ER complexes. Rapid dissociation has been linked to diminished sensitivity of juvenile rabbit and aged rat uterine tissue.[38,39] Further, mutant ER that exhibit rapid dissociation kinetics have diminished transcriptional activity.[40] Our findings showed that neural ER exhibited biphasic dissociation kinetics and that the rates were similar in both males and females. The slower k_{-2} component, which reflects activated ER, was consistent with that reported in peripheral tissues. Differences in dissociation kinetics of activated ER, therefore, do not appear to be a contributing factor in the sexual dimorphism in the response to estrogen.

Immunochemical studies of neural ER revealed a comparable distribution in males and females. Major regions exhibiting immunoreactivity included MPO, ventomedial nucleus (VMN), arcuate nucleus (ARC), BNST, and MAMYG. The absence of sex differences in this aspect of ER function suggested that a different level of analysis would be needed to identify potential sources of variation in ER sensitivity. One area of interest involved nuclear binding interactions, particularly at the level of the nuclear matrix. This dynamic substructure has been implicated in the regulation of gene expression due to its role in DNA organization, replication, and transcription; heteronuclear RNA synthesis and processing; the preferential association of actively transcribed genes; and the association of transcription factors and steroid receptors (SR).[41,42] Further, a recent report described the

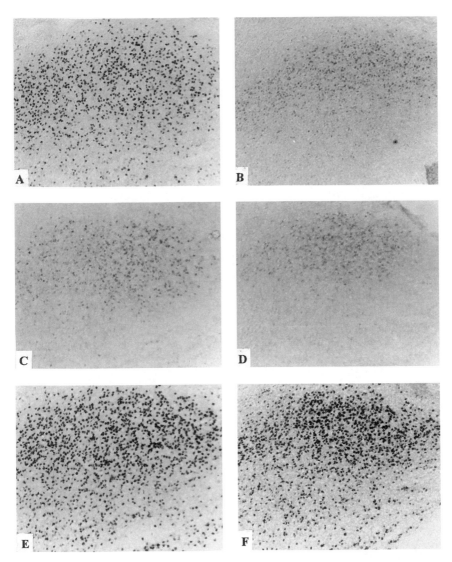

FIGURE 2. Representative sections through the BNST showing immunoreactivity for AR under varying hormonal status. The conditions were (A) intact male, (B) intact female, (C) castrated male, (D) castrated female, (E) castrated male + TP, and (F) castrated female + TP (magnification × 105; reduced here by 35%).

existence of tissue-specific NM proteins, suggesting that the unique NM protein content may be responsible for modulating transcription factor access, thus providing a mechanism for tissue-specific gene regulation.[43] Interestingly, some of these tissue-specific NM proteins were hormonally regulated, strengthening the potential link between the NM and hormonal regulation of gene expression.

Using equilibrium binding assays, we recently demonstrated estrogen-dependent ER binding to NM prepared from hypothalamic-preoptic-septal tissue from female mice.[44,45] These results were confirmed and extended by Western blot analysis.[45] The colocalization of transcriptionally active genes and ER on the nuclear matrix suggests that this kind of analysis may reveal a functionally important site for the estrogenic (and also perhaps androgenic) regulation of hormone-responsive genes.

Although the demonstration of specific ER-NM binding establishes a new level of analysis for receptor-acceptor site interactions in neural tissue, resolving the basis for the sexual dimorphism in response to estrogen requires understanding how ER can produce such dramatically different effects in male and female neural tissue. This problem recently was approached from the perspective of ER structure and function. More precisely, ER contains two transcriptional activating functions, AF1 and AF2, which are respectively located within the N-terminal and C-terminal domains of the receptor.[46] The relative effect of these activating functions is cell- and promoter-specific, as shown through studies with transfected cell lines.[47] These findings raise the intriguing possibility that sex-typical responses to estrogen may be a product of differential effects of AF1 and AF2. Support for this concept can be found in studies that compared the effects of tamoxifen and estradiol on estrogen-regulated responses in mice. Tamoxifen is an estrogen antagonist that blocks ligand-dependent responses, that is, those mediated primarily through AF2, and in some instances promoting constitutive, AF1-regulated transcription. This compound suppressed estrogen-induced lordotic behavior and progestin-receptor induction in ovariectomized female mice but had no effect when given alone.[48] In castrated males, however, tamoxifen restored aggression as effectively as DES (unpublished observations). These findings suggest that, at least in mice, female-typical responses to estrogen may be mediated through AF2, whereas male-typical aggression may involve a predominant role for AF1. Although additional work will be needed to fully explore this concept, the possibility of differential effects of the two activating functions should not be surprising because (1) the neuroanatomical substrates for aggression in males and lordosis in females differ and, as noted above, (2) the effects of AF1 and AF2 can vary by tissue, cell, and promoter.

SUMMARY

There are multiple pathways involved in the regulation of male-typical aggression by T, and the functional pathway is determined by genotype. Target-tissue sensitivity to the aggression-promoting properties of T and its estrogenic and androgenic metabolites is determined by a complex sequence of events in which steroid receptors play a critical role. To date, it appears that the relative density of AR may be an important factor in the biobehavioral effects of androgens. Regarding sensitivity to estrogens, characterization of ER-NM interactions, and understanding of the contribution of the two activating functions within ER, appears to be necessary to comprehensively describe the cellular basis for responsiveness to the aggression-promoting effect of this T metabolite. In broader terms, these observations indicate that understanding the relationship between T and the expression of aggression in humans will require models that incorporate cellular aspects of steroid hormone action, including metabolism, receptor function, and gene regulation.

ACKNOWLEDGMENTS

We recognize the expert technical assistance of Yu Wang, Eugene Nau, and Jarrett Burton. Our thanks go to Dr. G. Prins for generously providing the anti-AR polyclonal antibody.

REFERENCES

1. GANDELMAN, R. 1980. Gonadal hormones and the induction of intraspecific fighting in mice. Neurosci. Biobehav. Rev. **4:** 130–140.
2. SIMON, N. G., S. F. LU, S. E. MCKENNA, X. CHEN & A. C. CLIFFORD. 1993. Sexual dimorphisms in regulatory systems for aggression. *In* The Development and Expression of Sex Differences in Behavior. M. Haug *et al.*, Eds. 389–408. Kluwer Academic Press. the Netherlands.
3. ALBERT, D. J., M. L. WALSH & R. H. JONIK. 1993. Aggression in humans: What is its biological foundation? Neurosci. Biobehav. Rev. **17:** 405–425.
4. ARCHER, J. 1991. The influence of testosterone on human aggression. Br. J. Psychol. **82:** 1–28.
5. O'MALLEY, B. W., S. Y. TSAI, M. BAGCHI, N. L. WEIGEL, W. T. SCHRADER & M.-J. TSAI. 1991. Molecular mechanism of action of a steroid hormone receptor. Recent Prog. Horm. Res. **47:** 1–26.
6. CHANG, C., A. SALTZMAN, S. YEH, W. YOUNG, E. KELLER, H-J. LEE, C. WANG & A. MIZOKAMI. 1995. Androgen receptor: An overview. Crit. Rev. Eukaryotic Gene Expression **5:** 97–125.
7. NAFTOLIN, F., K. RYAN, I. DAVIS, V. REDDY, F. FLORES, Z. PETRO, M. KUHN, R. WHITE & Y. TAKAOKA. 1975. The formation of estrogens by central neuroendocrine tissues. Recent Prog. Horm. Res. **31:** 295–319.
8. CELOTTI, F., R. MELCANGI, P. NEGRI-CESI & A. POLETTI. 1991. Testosterone metabolism in brain cells and membranes. J. Steroid Biochem. Mol. Biol. **40:** 673–678.
9. BEATO, M. 1989. Gene regulation by steroid hormones. Cell **56:** 335–344.
10. SIMON, N. & R. WHALEN. 1986. Hormonal regulation of aggression: Evidence for a relationship among genotype, receptor binding, and behavioral sensitivity to androgen and estrogen. Aggressive Behav. **12:** 255–266.
11. FINNEY, H. & M. ERPINO. 1976. Synergistic effect of estradiol benzoate and dihydrotestosterone on aggression in mice. Horm. Behav. **7:** 391–400.
12. SIMON, N. & D. MASTERS. 1988. Activation of intermale aggression by combined estrogen-androgen treatment. Aggressive Behav. **14:** 291–295.
13. BRAIN, P. F. & M. HAUG. 1991. Hormonal and neurochemical correlates of various forms of animal "aggression." Psychoneuroendocrinology **17:** 537–550.
14. SCHECHTER, D., S. HOWARD & R. GANDELMAN. 1981. Dihydrotestosterone promotes fighting behavior in female mice. Horm. Behav. **5:** 233–237.
15. SIMON, N., R. WHALEN & M. TATE. 1985. Induction of male-typical aggression by androgens but not by estrogens in adult female mice. Horm. Behav. **19:** 204–212.
16. SIMON, N. & R. GANDELMAN. 1978. The estrogenic arousal of aggressive behavior in female mice. Horm. Behav. **10:** 118–127.
17. SIMON, N. G. & A. COLOGER-CLIFFORD. 1991. In utero contiguity to males does not influence morphology, behavioral sensitivity to testosterone, or hypothalamic androgen binding in CF-1 female mice. Horm. Behav. **25:** 518–530.
18. KLEIN, W. & N. SIMON. 1991. Timing of neonatal testosterone exposure in the differentiation of estrogenic regulatory systems for aggression. Physiol. Behav. **50:** 91–93.
19. COLOGER-CLIFFORD, A., N. SIMON & B. JUBILAN. 1992. Genotype, uterine position, and testosterone sensitivity in older female mice. Physiol. Behav. **51:** 1047–50.
20. SIMON, N. & R. WHALEN. 1987. Sexual differentiation of androgen-sensitive and estrogen-sensitive regulatory systems for aggressive behavior. Horm. Behav. **21:** 493–500.

21. SUAREZ, A., A. COLOGER-CLIFFORD & N. SIMON. 1992. Sexual differentiation of an estrogen-sensitive regulatory system for aggression. Eastern Psychol. Assoc. **63:** 48.

22. VOM SAAL, F. & F. BRONSON. 1980. Sexual characteristics of adult female mice are correlated with their blood testosterone levels during prenatal development. Science **208:** 597–599.

23. MOTELICA-HEINO, I., D. A. EDWARDS & J. ROFFI. 1993. Intermale aggression in mice: Does hour of castration after birth influence adult behavior? Physiol. Behav. **53:** 1017–1019.

24. VOM SAAL, F. S., R. GANDELMAN & B. SVARE. 1976. Aggression in male and female mice: Evidence for changed neural sensitivity in response to neonatal but not adult androgen exposure. Physiol. Behav. **17:** 53–57.

25. BRANN, D. W., L. B. HENDRY & V. B. MAHESH. 1995. Emerging diversities in the mechanism of action of steroid hormones. J. Steroid Biochem. Molec. Biol. **52:** 113–133.

26. YAMAMOTO, K. R. 1985. Steroid receptor regulated transcription of specific genes and gene networks. Annu. Rev. Genet. **19:** 209–252.

27. LU, S., N. G. SIMON, G. NAU & J. BURTON. 1994. Testosterone enhances androgen receptor immunoreactivity in mouse brain. Soc. Neurosci. **20:** 376.

28. MERNARD, C. S. & R. E. HARLAN. 1993. Up-regulation of androgen receptor immunore-activity in the rat brain by androgenic-anabolic steroids. Brain Res. **622:** 226–236.

29. PRINS, G. S. & L. BIRCH. 1993. Immunocytochemical analysis of androgen receptor along the ducts of the separate rat prostate lobes after androgen withdrawal and replacement. Endocrinology **132:** 169–178.

30. WOOD, R. I. & S. W. NEWMAN. 1992. Intracellular partitioning of androgen receptor immunoreactivity in the brain of the male Syrian hamster: Effects of castration and steroid replacement. J. Neurobiol. **24:** 925–938.

31. HACKENBURG, R., T. HAWIGHORST, A. FILMER, E. P. SLATER, K. BOCK, M. BEATO & K-D. SCHULZ. 1992. Regulation of androgen receptor mRNA and protein level by steroid hormones in human mammary cancer cells. J. Steroid Biochem. Mol. Biol. **43:** 599–607.

32. ABDELGADIR, S. E., P. B. CONNOLLY & J. A. RESKO. 1993. Androgen regulation of androgen receptor message ribonucleic acid differs in rat prostate and selected brain areas. Mol. Cell. Neurosci. **4:** 532–537.

33. BLOK, L. J., A. P. THEMMEN, A. H. PETERS, J. TRAPMAN, W. M. BAARENDS, J. W. HOOGERBRUGGE & J. A. GROOTEGOED. 1992. Transcriptional regulation of androgen receptor gene expression in sertoli cells and other cell types. Mol. Cell. Endocrinol. **88:** 153–164.

34. VARRIALE, B. & I. SERINO. 1994. The androgen receptor mRNA is up-regulated by testosterone in both the harderian gland and thumb pad of the frog, *Rana esculenta*. J. Steroid Biochem. Mol. Biol. **51:** 259–265.

35. ARAI, K. & G. P. CHROUSOS. 1995. Syndromes of glucocorticoid and mineralocorticoid resistance. Steroids **60:** 173–179.

36. FRENCH, F. S., D. B. LUBAHN, T. R. BROWN, J. A. SIMENTAL, C. A. QUIGLEY, W. G. YARBROUGH, J-A. TAN, M. SAR, D. R. JOSEPH, B. A. J. EVANS, I. A. HUGHES, C. J. MIGEON & E. M. WILSON. 1990. Molecular basis of androgen insensitivity. Recent Prog. Horm. Res. **46:** 1–40.

37. CHEN, X. & N. G. SIMON. 1991. Dissociation kinetics of hypothalamic estrogen recep-tors. Soc. Neurosci. **17:** 571.

38. BELISLE, S., G. BELLABARBA, J-G. LEHOUX, P. ROBEL & E. BAULIEU. 1986. Effect of aging on the dissociation kinetics and estradiol receptor nuclear interactions in mouse uteri: Correlation with biological effects. Endocrinology **118:** 750–758.

39. CHILTON, B., N. WILLIAMS, A. COBB & W. LEAVITT. 1987. Ligand-receptor dissocia-tion: A potential mechanism for the attentuation of estrogen action in the juvenile rabbit uterus. Endocrinology **120:** 750–757.

40. PAKDEL, F. & B. S. KATZENELLENBOGEN. 1992. Human estrogen receptor mutants with altered estrogen and antiestrogen ligand discrimination. J. Biol. Chem. **267:** 3429–3437.

41. BARRACK, E. R. 1987. Steroid hormone receptor localization in the nuclear matrix: Interaction with acceptor sites. J. Steroid Biochem. **27:** 115–121.
42. GETZENBERG, R. H. 1994. Nuclear matrix and the regulation of gene expression: Tissue specificity. J. Cell. Biochem. **55:** 22–31.
43. GETZENBERG, R. H. & D. S. COFFEY. 1990. Tissue specificity of the hormonal response in sex accessory tissues is associated with nuclear matrix protein patterns. Mol. Endocrinol. **4:** 1336–1342.
44. McKENNA-REPSHER, S. E. & N. G. SIMON. 1994. Estrogen receptor interactions with nuclear matrix of limbic tissue in the female mouse. Soc. Neurosci. **20:** 376.
45. McKENNA-REPSHER, S. E. & N. G. SIMON. 1995. Immunodetection of estrogen receptor in nuclear matrix of the female mouse brain. Soc. Neurosci. **21:** 191.
46. LEES, J. A., S. E. FAWELL & M. G. PARKER. 1989. Identification of two transactivation domains in the mouse oestrogen receptor. Nucleic Acids Res. **17:** 5477–5488.
47. BERRY, M., D. METZGER & P. CHAMBON. 1990. Role of the two activating domains of the oestrogen receptor in the cell type and promoter-context dependent agonistic activity of the anti-oestrogen 4-hydroxytamoxifen. EMBO J. **9:** 2811–2818.
48. McKENNA, S. E., N. G. SIMON & A. COLOGER-CLIFFORD. 1992. An assessment of agonist/antagonist effects of tamoxifen in the female mouse brain. Horm. Behav. **26:** 536–544.

Gonadal and Adrenal Hormones

Developmental Transitions and Aggressive Behavior[a]

ELIZABETH J. SUSMAN,[c] DOUGLAS A. GRANGER,
ELISE MUROWCHICK,[b] ANGELO PONIRAKIS, AND
BRENDA K. WORRALL

Department of Biobehavioral Health
[b]Department of Human Development and Family Studies
College of Health and Human Development
The Pennsylvania State University
210 East Health and Human Development
University Park, Pennsylvania 16802-6508

Hormones and antisocial behavior are coupled in the theories guiding both animal and human model research. Testosterone (T) is the hormone most often linked with aggressive behavior in humans.[1] Elevated circulating T levels have been reported in some adult perpetrators of violent crime and antisocial youth.[1,2] In children and adolescents, the testosterone-aggression link is not consistently reported across studies. The inconsistency of aggressive behavior and T links has led to the conclusion that gonadal hormones are only one of a myriad of influences on aggressive behavior during adolescence. Behaviorally oriented developmental studies show that factors influencing the expression of aggression include cognition[3] and environmental circumstances. The peer and family context also can encourage aggressive and coercive behavior.[4,5] Stressful life circumstances and antisocial behavior, for instance, may influence the activity of the hypothalamic-pituitary-gonadal (HPG) axis.[6] The question posed here is whether chronicity of aggressive and impulsive behavior problems affects hormone concentrations in adolescents during the developmental reproductive transitions of puberty and pregnancy. Reproductive transitions provide excellent periods of development in which to examine hormone-behavior relations because there are rapid changes in both hormones (*e.g.*, sex steroids) and mental health problems, particularly in females. First, we present an overview of models that have been used to conceptualize hormone-behavior relations. Then, we consider evidence indicating that hormones and behavior have reciprocal influences during adolescence.

[a] The research reported here was supported by the Intramural Programs of the National Institute of Mental Health and the National Institute of Child Health and Human Development and Grants from the National Institute of Child Health and Human Development: RO1 HD26004 and P20 HD29356.

[c] Tel: (814) 863-7256; fax: (814) 863-7525; e-mail: ejs5@psu.edu.

18

MODELS OF THE DEVELOPMENT OF
HORMONE-BEHAVIOR INTERACTIONS

Historically, hormones have been considered causes, consequences, and mediators of behavior and development.[7] The classic experimental approach employed to decipher hormone effects on behavior involves removing the physiological source of the hormone (ablation), administering known concentrations of exogenous hormones (replacement), and measuring the effects of the replaced hormone on behavior. This research strategy has revealed that hormones influence behavior by shaping and reshaping brain function and structure. For instance, during the prenatal and early neonatal periods, studies reveal that exposure to gonadal steroids organize the brain in such a way that subsequent behavior patterns will be affected.[8]

The first study to show the activational influences of circulating T and aggressive behavior in adolescents was done with Swedish 15- to 17-year-old males.[9] Testosterone was related to self reports of physical and verbal aggression in response to hypothetical provocation. Using causal modeling statistical techniques, it was shown that there was a direct and longitudinal effect of T on provoked aggressive behavior.[10] Studies of T and aggressive behavior in younger children and pubertal age adolescents are less conclusive.[11-16] The inconsistent T and aggressive behavior associations may reflect problems in measuring T in prepubertal children. Brain and Susman[2] offer a developmental explanation and assert that the findings linking T and antisocial behavior in adults but not in youth indicate that T levels may be a consequence and not a cause of aggressive behavior in adults.

In this decade it has been realized that the traditional one-hormone, one-behavior coordinate model is limited in its ability to address the complexity of environmental and biobehavioral processes. First, individuals arrive at the pubertal or pregnancy transition with diverse developmental histories. A history of aggressive behavior or emotional problems, for example, may contribute to the probability that developmental changes in hormones will influence a behavior. Some aggressive behavior patterns emerge before puberty[17] but may reflect childhood behaviors that are relatively stable across time.[18] Hormonal, social, and cognitive developmental changes at puberty may potentiate aggressive behavior patterns. Second, the empirical findings relating aggression and T in humans do not always support the association between the two.[1] Third, circulating T levels may not be the appropriate level of analysis with respect to physiologically relevant behavioral effects. For instance, a product of T metabolism may be the critical molecule in mediating aggression and hormones.

BEHAVIORAL EFFECTS ON HORMONE CONCENTRATIONS

The effects of experience with hormones remains a central focus in behavioral endocrinology. For instance, mice pups isolated and housed in a clean bedding area for 15 minutes per day for 14 days showed elevated concentrations of corticosterone that persisted for 14 days, suggesting that they did not habituate to the stressful situation.[19] Studies employing avian species (*e.g.*, red-winged blackbirds, cowbirds, and chickens) also reveal that environmental challenges affect hormone levels.[20] Excessively high or low levels of cortisol concentrations affect neural development in subhuman primates[21] (olive baboons). Contemporary theorists now posit that environment-hormone interactions are responsible for phenotypic differences in developmental outcomes even between individuals having the same genetic constitution[6] (*i.e.*, identical twins). The conclusion is that similar developmental and evolutionary consequences may occur in humans as well. Rose[22] was one of the first to show that short- and long-term stressors appear to affect hormone concentrations. Until recently, similar effects on adrenal androgens and gonadal steroid hormone concentrations received only minimal research attention.[23]

Response to stress reflected in higher concentrations of glucocorticoids has been shown to influence levels of gonadal hormones in both animals and humans. Higher concentrations of cortisol in subhuman primates are related to lower concentrations of T.[24] In human adolescents, antisocial behavior was associated with a profile of lower gonadal steroid and higher adrenal androgen concentrations.[14,16] Higher adrenal androgen concentrations were interpreted as an index of higher stress. In adult prison inmates, as cortisol concentrations increased, the correlation between T and violent behavior decreased.[25] The hypothesis derived from the accumulated findings is that aspects of the adrenocortical responses to stress (*i.e.*, cortisol) moderate the effects of T on behavior.

What are the mechanisms that lead to short- or long-term behavioral effects on hormone concentrations? Studies conducted to date have primarily examined concurrent relations between hormone concentrations and behavior. The longer-term influences of behavior on the hormonal milieu remain to be explored. Aggressive or assertive behavior may have an immediate effect on gonadal or adrenal hormones in humans, but these fluctuations reflect temporary changes that are not representative of usual (baseline) endocrine status. Concurrent relations between hormones and behavior are likely to reflect an emotional component. Emotions are likely to precipitate a hormone change, primarily cortisol and epinephrine. Is it possible that aggressive and antisocial behavior change hormone concentrations in both the short- and long-term case? Sapolsky[24] showed that social stress, dominance, and aggression affect T and cortisol levels in subhuman primates and support the hypothesis that social experiences affect both cortisol and sex steroids. In humans, some aggressive and assertive behavior may be associated with attempts to gain social status through dominance and leadership. If successful in these pursuits, T is expected to increase. If unsuccessful, T is expected to decrease because of the negative status associated with failure or rejection. Aggressive adolescents are often actively rejected by peers.[26] Thus, if this hypothesis were true, aggressive behavior problems should be related to lower levels of T. It is further expected that the longer the duration of social stress, the lower the concentrations of gonadal steroids. Alternatively, the links between aggressive behavior and T may involve entirely different emotional and social processes.

To examine the effects of aggressive and antisocial experiences on human adolescents, we tested the hypothesis that aggressive and antisocial behavior affects subsequent concentrations of gonadal hormones, T and estradiol (E_2); and adrenal hormones, cortisol, dehydroepiandrosterone (DHEA), dehydroepiandrosterone sulphate (DHEAS), and androstenedione ($\Delta4$-A). Two studies of pubertal age adolescents report consistent associations between adrenal androgens and aggressive behavior and affect.[11,16] Affective states also are proposed as influences on hormone concentrations. Cortisol concentrations are known to be elevated during states of depression.[27] With noted exceptions,[28] anxiety is less consistently related to hormone concentrations, but anxiety in combination with aggressive behavior predicted lower concentrations of T in pubertal age boys.[29] Thus, we examine the combined influence of both aggressive behavior and emotional regulation on hormone concentrations.

METHOD

Sample

Two samples were included. One sample consisted of boys and girls experiencing the reproductive transition of puberty. The second sample consisted of adolescents experiencing the reproductive transition of pregnancy.

Pubertal-age Sample

The pubertal age sample consisted of 108 healthy adolescents: 56 10- to 15-year-old boys (mean age = 12.7, SD = 1.32 years) and 52 9- to 15-year-old girls (mean age = 11.9, SD = 1.55 years).[14,16] The adolescents were seen three times over the course of a year. Assessments of adrenal and gonadal hormones and pubertal status (Tanner stage) and behavioral measures were obtained. Adolescents and their parents completed measures of behavior problems, moods, and cognitive status.[14,16]

Pregnant Adolescent Sample

The pregnant sample consisted of primarily Caucasian rural adolescents: 77 13- to 19-year-olds (mean age = 17.4, SD = 1.4 years). They were assessed at three times of measurement: at less than 16 weeks gestation, 32–34 weeks, and two weeks postpartum. Plasma and saliva were collected for hormone determinations. Adolescents completed measures of personality, behavior problems, and social support.

Pubertal-age Adolescents

The measures included here consisted of a broadband subscale, Externalizing Behavior Problems, from the Child Behavior Checklist[30] (CBCL). The Impulse Control subscale from the Offer Self Image Questionnaire for Adolescents[31] also was included. Anxiety (total number of anxiety symptoms) was assessed using the anxiety subscale from the Diagnostic Interview Schedule for Children (DISC).[32] The hormone assessments consisted of plasma concentrations of T, E_2, DHEA, DHEAS, $\Delta4$-A, and cortisol.

Pregnant Adolescents

To test similar hypotheses in the pregnant adolescent sample, an antisocial factor score was created based on indices of anger, hostility, number and severity of oppositional and conduct disorder problems, and negative life events that reflect antisocial behavior (*e.g.*, getting expelled from school). The Beck Depression Inventory[33] (BDI) and the State-Trait Anxiety Inventory[34] (STAI) also were administered. Hormone assessments included plasma concentrations of T, E_2, $\Delta4$-A, and cortisol.

RESULTS

Puberty

The statistical model for considering the concurrent and longer-term effects of behavior on hormones consisted of linear regression. The regression model preserves the continuous quality of the distributions and allows for analysis of both concurrent and longitudinal behavioral influences on hormone concentrations. Chronological age was entered first, followed by externalizing behavior problems or impulse control at three occasions of measurement at six-month intervals (time 1, time 2, and time 3). Anxiety symptoms at time 3 on the DISC were entered last into the regression models to examine whether concurrent anxiety contributes an emotional component to antisocial behavior. The hormone outcome–dependent measures were T, E_2, DHEA, DHEAS, $\Delta 4$-A, and cortisol at time 3 of measurement. The regression statistics appear in TABLE 1.

Age

For both boys and girls, chronological age was a significant predictor of T, E_2, and $\Delta 4$-A. Older age was predictive of higher concentrations of T, E_2, and $\Delta 4$-A. For girls, chronological age was a significant predictor of DHEA and DHEAS. Older girls had higher concentrations of DHEA and DHEAS.

Testosterone

For impulse control, a different pattern of findings emerged in boys and girls. In girls, greater impulse control at the second time of measurement predicted higher T concentrations at the third time of measurement. Neither externalizing behavior problems nor impulse control predicted T in boys.

Estradiol

Neither externalizing behavior problems nor impulse control predicted E_2.

DHEA

Anxiety and DHEA at the third time of measurement were significantly related in boys. Higher anxiety was associated with higher DHEA. Neither externalizing behavior problems nor impulse control predicted DHEA in boys or girls.

DHEAS

Greater numbers of externalizing behavior problems at the third time of measurement were related to lower concentrations of DHEAS in girls. For boys,

TABLE 1. Regression of Adrenal and Gonadal Hormones on Externalizing Behavior Problems, Impulse Control, and Anxiety

Predictor	Time of Measurement	Beta[a] Males	Females	t[b] Males	Females	p Males	Females
			Testosterone				
Age	1	.62	.42	5.20	2.95	.0001	.01
EBP[c]	1	−.05	.21	−.24	.81	.81	.42
EBP	2	.10	−.34	.38	−1.38	.71	.18
EBP	3	−.04	.29	−.20	1.29	.84	.21
Anxiety	3	.09	−.16	.78	−1.12	.44	.27

Boys: $R^2 = .42$; $F(5,45) = 6.54$; $p = .001$; Girls: $R^2 = .28$; $F(5,40) = 3.12$; $p = .02$.

Predictor	Time of Measurement	Males	Females	Males	Females	Males	Females
Age	1	.61	.51	4.83	4.08	.0001	.0002
IC[d]	1	−.03	−.17	−.20	−1.11	.84	.27
IC	2	−.24	.53	−1.4	3.29	.16	.0023
IC	3	−.10	.11	−.56	.69	.58	.50
Anxiety	3	.15	−.25	1.19	−1.74	.24	.09

Boys: $R^2 = .45$; $F(5,37) = 6.17$; $p = .0003$; Girls: $R^2 = .48$; $F(5,36) = 6.55$; $p = .0002$.

Predictor	Time of Measurement	Males	Females	Males	Females	Males	Females
			Estradiol				
Age	1	.40	.42	3.05	2.94	.003	.005
EBP	1	.09	.26	.37	.99	.71	.33
EBP	2	.07	−.30	.22	−1.21	.83	.23
EBP	3	−.06	.13	−.25	.57	.80	.57
Anxiety	3	.21	−.04	1.58	−.26	.12	.79

Boys: $R^2 = .26$; $F(5,46) = 3.26$; $p = .01$; Girls: $R^2 = .24$; $F(5, 40) = 2.58$; $p = .04$.

Predictor	Time of Measurement	Males	Females	Males	Females	Males	Females
Age	1	.40	.47	2.85	3.23	.01	.003
IC	1	.02	−.07	.09	−.37	.93	.71
IC	2	−.23	.26	−1.23	1.39	.22	.17
IC	3	.01	.14	.06	.78	.95	.44
Anxiety	3	.28	−.17	1.93	−1.0	.06	.33

Boys: $R^2 = .29$; $F(5,38) = 3.09$; $p = .02$; Girls: $R^2 = .29$; $F(5,36) = 2.94$; $p = .03$.

neither externalizing behavior problems nor impulse control predicted concentrations of DHEAS at the third time of measurement.

Androstenedione

For boys, higher anxiety at the third time of testing was significantly related to higher concentrations of Δ4-A. Neither externalizing behavior problems nor impulse control predicted Δ4-A in boys or girls.

TABLE 1. *Continued*

Predictor		Beta		t		p	
			DHEA				

	Time of Measurement	Males	Females	Males	Females	Males	Females
Age	1	.20	.44	1.48	3.10	.15	.004
EBP	1	−.06	−.02	−.25	−.06	.80	.95
EBP	2	.52	.33	1.71	1.35	.09	.19
EBP	3	−.40	−.37	−1.53	−1.64	.13	.11
Anxiety	3	.34	.02	2.47	.16	.02	.87

Boys: R^2 = .22; F (5,46) = 2.57; p = .04; Girls: R^2 = .26; F (5, 40) = 2.77; p = .03.

	Time of Measurement	Males	Females	Males	Females	Males	Females
Age	1	.14	.40	.92	2.78	.36	.01
IC	1	.06	.04	.29	.19	.77	.42
IC	2	−.18	.15	−.87	.79	.39	.18
IC	3	−.06	−.38	−.27	−2.09	.79	.21
Anxiety	3	.31	.05	1.96	.32	.05	.27

Boys: R^2 = .15; F (5,38) = 1.35; p = .26; Girls: R^2 = .30; F (5,36) = 3.04; p = .02.

			DHEAS				

	Time of Measurement	Males	Females	Males	Females	Males	Females
Age	1	.18	.38	1.15	2.8	.26	.01
EBP	1	.13	.32	.49	1.30	.63	.20
EBP	2	−.07	.08	−.20	.36	.85	.72
EBP	3	−.10	−.51	−.33	−2.41	.74	.02
Anxiety	3	.15	−.20	.96	−1.44	.34	.16

Boys: R^2 = .07; F (5,44) = .67; p = .64; Girls: R^2 = .37; F (5,39) = 4.53; p = .002.

	Time of Measurement	Males	Females	Males	Females	Males	Females
Age	1	.04	.45	.22	3.15	.83	.003
IC	1	.42	.30	1.98	1.75	.06	.09
IC	2	−.31	−.17	−1.49	−.94	.15	.36
IC	3	−.13	−.05	−.60	−.28	.57	.78
Anxiety	3	.05	−.22	.28	1.37	.78	.18

Boys: R^2 = .14; F (5,36) = 1.18; p = .34; Girls: R^2 = .36; F (5,35) = 3.97; p = .006.

Cortisol

For girls, greater numbers of externalizing behavior problems at the second time of measurement predicted higher concentrations of cortisol. In addition, higher anxiety at the third time of measurement predicted higher concentrations of cortisol. Neither externalizing behavior problems nor impulse control predicted cortisol in boys.

TABLE 1. *Continued*

		Beta		t		p	
Predictor							

Androstenedione

Time of Measurement		Males	Females	Males	Females	Males	Females
Age	1	.32	.64	2.44	4.99	.02	.0001
EBP	1	.27	.01	1.23	.04	.23	.97
EBP	2	.07	−.05	.27	−.25	.79	.81
EBP	3	−.10	.09	−.43	.42	.67	.67
Anxiety	3	.31	.15	2.35	1.16	.02	.25

Boys: R^2 = .32; F (5,45) = 4.16; p = .003; Girls: R^2 = .40; F (5,40) = 5.37; p = .0007.

Time of Measurement		Males	Females	Males	Females	Males	Females
Age	1	.34	.65	2.31	5.32	.03	.0001
IC	1	.03	.002	.14	.02	.89	.99
IC	2	−.08	.29	−.43	1.81	.67	.08
IC	3	−.02	−.15	−.09	−.98	.93	.33
Anxiety	3	.30	.10	2.01	.67	.05	.51

Boys: R^2 = .24; F (5,37) = 2.33; p = .06; Girls: R^2 = .49; F (5,36) = 7.0; p = .0001.

Cortisol

Time of Measurement		Males	Females	Males	Females	Males	Females
Age	1	.26	−.01	1.70	−.09	.10	.93
EBP	1	−.06	−.28	−.24	−1.12	.81	.27
EBP	2	.16	.69	.46	2.83	.65	.01
EBP	2	−.20	−.40	−.70	−1.76	.49	.09
Anxiety	3	.07	.46	.44	3.24	.66	.003

Boys: R^2 = .09; F (5,44) = .83; p = .54; Girls: R^2 = .31; F (5,38) = 3.44; p = .01.

Time of Measurement		Males	Females	Males	Females	Males	Females
Age	1	.27	−.14	1.64	−.86	.11	.40
IC	1	−.21	−.02	−1.001	−.10	.32	.92
IC	2	.01	.13	.06	.61	.96	.55
IC	3	.06	−.16	.27	−.80	.79	.43
Anxiety	3	.13	.37	.74	1.96	.46	.06

Boys: R^2 = .10; F (5,36) = .79; p = .56; Girls: R^2 = .16; F (5,34) = 1.26; p = .30.

[a] Beta weights are standardized regression coefficients.
[b] *t*-test.
[c] EBP = externalizing behavior problems.
[d] IC = impulse control.

Pregnancy

A similar linear regression approach to assessing the longer-term effects of behavior on hormone concentrations was used with the pregnant adolescent sample. Gestational age was entered first into the regression model, if it correlated with the hormone, followed by the antisocial factor for the three longitudinal measurements of antisocial behavior (≤ 16 weeks gestation, 32–34 weeks gestation, and two weeks postpartum). Anxiety or depression scores at the third time of measurement were entered last. Depression and anxiety symptoms are expected to rise in the postpartum period. Depressed and anxious affect may show stronger associations with hormone concentrations in the postpartum period than when hormone levels are affected by the physiology of pregnancy. The hierarchical regression model consists of entering the week's gestation, the antisocial factor at three occasions of measurement, followed by either the BDI or the STAI. The hormone outcome–dependent measures were concentrations of T, E_2, Δ4-A, and cortisol.

Testosterone, Estradiol, and Androstenedione

Concentrations of T, E_2, and Δ4-A in the pregnant adolescents did not appear to be affected by antisocial behavior or depressed or anxious affect.

Cortisol

The effect of antisocial behavior and emotional regulation on cortisol revealed a stronger and different pattern of findings. Greater antisocial behavior during the third trimester of pregnancy (32–34 weeks gestation) predicted lower cortisol concentrations in the postpartum period, beta = $-.82$, t = -2.29, p = .03. By contrast, greater antisocial behavior during the postpartum period was associated with higher cortisol concentrations in the postpartum period, beta = .63, t = 2.19, p = .04. Lower anxiety during the postpartum period was related to higher cortisol concentrations, beta = $-.40$, t = -2.41, p = .02.

DISCUSSION

The findings revealed by analyses of hormone-behavior connections during the reproductive transitions of puberty and pregnancy showed scattered instances of behavioral effects on hormone concentrations. The majority of associations were concurrent relationships. Interestingly, when time-lagged effects were revealed, they were primarily observed for girls. That is, levels of impulse control predicted later T levels, and externalizing behavior problems predicted subsequent cortisol levels for adolescent girls. Antisocial behavior during pregnancy was associated with postpartum cortisol levels. These findings provided some support for our hypothesis that individual differences in behavior problems and antisocial behavior may influence hormone concentrations. Our findings regarding behavioral effects on hormones are supported by a long-term longitudinal study of antisocial boys. Children and young adolescents with a history of disruptive behavior problems and anxiety since age six had lower concentrations of T at age 13 than adolescents with only disruptive behavior problems or nondisruptive children.[29] We propose here, as in the past,[14,16] that behavior problems activate the interaction between the adrenal and gonadal axes.

In the younger adolescents, we expected to find that a history of antisocial behavior would lead to lower concentrations of T and E_2, but this prediction found little support in healthy children. Individual differences in T and E_2 concentrations may reflect the day-to-day experiences of both pubertal age and pregnant adolescents, which may negate the longer-term effects of behavior on hormones. Eccles and colleagues[35] showed that T levels within boys across days were more variable than levels between individuals. Day-to-day variability in concentrations of T may explain why our results were not consistent across time. Future studies would benefit from gathering information about the daily routine of the participants while simultaneously gathering multiple assessments of hormone concentrations and behavior.

The higher concentrations of T predicted by impulsive behavior in girls may reflect a dimension of behavior that is the female equivalent of aggressive or dominance behavior. Socializing pressures are toward suppressing aggressive behavior, whereas aggression is more tolerated in boys. Girls may be able to inhibit aggressive behavior but may act impulsively in other domains. Inoff-Germain *et al.*[36] suggest that because of earlier organizational influences of hormones and socialization processes, early adolescent girls may be generally better able to inhibit their behavioral responses than boys. The self-report measure of impulse control assesses feelings of impulse control versus their actual behavior. Girls who report impulsive urges and who act on these urges may also be dominant in social situations, which could explain the effects of high impulse control and higher T.

The negative associations between antisocial behavior and DHEAS were consistent with other findings from the NIMH-NICHD study[37] and those of Brooks-Gunn and Warren.[11] Lower concentrations of DHEAS may indicate activation of the hypothalamic-pituitary-adrenal (HPA) axis related to stressful experiences and emotions. The prediction of cortisol concentrations by externalizing behavior problems and the antisocial factor is consistent with an accumulating body of findings showing that atypical concentrations of cortisol are aspects of the pathophysiology of depression and other mental health disorders,[27] compromised infant health,[39] behavior problems,[15] and internalizing behavior problems.[28] The majority of studies have examined the simultaneous associations between behavior and cortisol. A recent study by Granger *et al.*[38] supported these findings. Adrenocortical responses to a social conflict task were associated with clinic-referred children's subsequent behavioral problems. Specifically, higher levels of HPA responsivity to conflict were associated with six-month outcomes characterized by high levels of internalizing behavior problems. The prediction of cortisol by externalizing behavior problems six and 12 months earlier in the current study and the prediction of behavior problems in the Granger *et al.*[38] suggest that the interaction between behavior problems and shorter-term cortisol reactivity may lead to chronically high cortisol concentrations, which are known to have adverse effects on development. What is unique about the current findings is that cortisol could be predicted by behavior, even though pubertal-age and pregnant adolescents are undergoing rapid hormone, morphological, and social changes.

The prediction of cortisol by antisocial behavior in pregnant adolescents supports the longstanding but untested hypothesis that behavior during pregnancy can have an effect on the endocrine milieu. In turn, changes in the endocrine milieu can have deleterious consequences on the health of the mother and developing fetus. Cortisol associated with maternal stress stimulates expression of CRH by cultured amnion, chorion, decidual and cytotrophoblast cells.[40] Prolonged CRH release may decrease immunity,[42] thereby increasing the opportunity for placental infections.

Overall, our findings indicate that individual differences in hormone concentrations should be pursued as possible influences for possible short- and long-term effects on behaviors. The relation between experience and hormone concentrations undoubtedly reflects a more complex process than merely a one-to-one relationship between a hormone and a behavior. A caveat to our conclusions is that the results were based on a large number of analyses with some results perhaps reflecting chance findings. In addition, we are hampered by the small effect size of the statistical associations in hormone-behavior research as well as a relatively small sample. Nonetheless, there is sufficient support for further research, testing the longer-term effects of experience on the development of the adrenal and gonadal axes.

The effects of behavior on hormone concentrations may have life-span implications. The wide variation in timing of pubertal maturation may be accounted for partially by both aggressive behaviors and other behaviors causing a delay in puberty. Even subtle variations in timing of puberty related to experiences may, in turn, predispose some adolescents to behavior problems, including aggression and violent behavior. Late maturing males experience difficulty in attaining dominance positions and peer popularity because of their immature physical status. To cope with their immature physical status, late maturing boys may turn to aggressive behavior or other less adept ways of coping with later maturational status. Heavy drinking in late-maturing boys, for instance, was a coping strategy adopted that persisted into adulthood.[41] In pregnancy, the effects of behavior on changing the endocrine milieu may have lifetime consequences on neural and behavioral development in children.

REFERENCES

1. ARCHER, J. 1991. The influence of testosterone on human aggression. Br. J. of Psychol. **82:** 1–28.
2. BRAIN, P. & E. J. SUSMAN. Hormonal aspects of antisocial behavior and violence. *In* Handbook of Antisocial Behavior. D. M. Stoff, J. Breiling & J. Maser, Eds. Lawrence Erlbaum Associates. Hillsdale, NJ. In press.
3. GUERRA, N. G. & R. G. SLABY. 1989. Evaluative factors in social problem solving by aggressive boys. J. Abnorm. Child Psychol. **17:** 277–289.
4. COIE, J. D. & M. R. JACOBS. 1993. The role of social context in the prevention of conduct disorder. Dev. Psychopathol. **5:** 263–275.
5. PATTERSON, G. R. 1990. Depression and aggression in family interaction. Lawrence Erlbaum Associates. Hillsdale, NJ.
6. MCEWEN, B. S. 1992. Steroid Hormones: Effect on brain development and function. Horm. Res. **37:** 1–10.
7. BRAIN, P. F. 1994. Hormonal aspects of aggression and violence. *In* Understanding and Preventing Violence: Biobehavioral Influences. A. J. Reiss, K. A. Miczek & J. A. Roth, Eds.: 173–244. National Academy Press. Washington, D.C.
8. PHOENIX, C. H., R. W. GOY, A. A. GERALL & W. C. YOUNG. 1959. Organizing action of prenatally administered testosterone propionate on the tissues mediating mating behavior in the female guinea pig. Endocrinology **65:** 369–382.
9. OLWEUS, D., A. MATTSSON, D. SCHALLING & H. LOW. 1980. Testosterone, aggression, physical, and personality dimensions in normal adolescent males. Psychosom. Med. **42:** 253–269.
10. OLWEUS, D., A. MATTSON, D. SCHALLING & H. LOW. 1988. Circulating testosterone levels and aggression in adolescent males: A causal analysis. Psychosom. Med. **50:** 261–272.
11. BROOKS-GUNN, J. & M. WARREN. 1989. Biological and social contributions to negative affect in young adolescent girls. Child Dev. **60:** 40–55.
12. CONSTANTINO, J. N., D. GROSZ, P. SAENGER, D. W. CHANDLER *et al.* 1993. Testosterone and aggression in children. J. Am. Acad. Child Adolesc. Psychiatry **32:** 1217–1222.

13. GRANGER, D. A., J. R. WEISZ, J. MCCRACKEN, D. KAUNECKIS & S. IKEDA. 1994. Testosterone and conduct problems. J. Am. Acad. Child Adolesc. Psychiatry **33:** 908.
14. NOTTELMANN, E. D., E. J. SUSMAN, L. D. DORN, G. E. INOFF-GERMAIN, G. B. CUTLER, JR., D. L. LORIAUX & G. P. CHROUSOS. 1987. Developmental processes in American early adolescents; Relationships between adolescent adjustment problems and chronological pubertal stage and puberty-related serum hormone levels. J. Pediatr. **110:** 473–480.
15. SCERBO, A. S. & D. J. KOLKO. 1994. Salivary testosterone and cortisol in disruptive children: Relationship to aggressive, hyperactive, and internalizing behaviors. J. Am. Acad. Child Adolesc. Psychiatry **33:** 1174–1184.
16. SUSMAN, E. J., G. E. INOFF-GERMAIN, E. D. NOTTELMANN, G. B. CUTLER, JR., D. L. LORIAUX & G. P. CHROUSOS. 1987. Hormones, emotional dispositions and aggressive attributes in young adolescents. Child Dev. **58:** 1114–1134.
17. CAMPBELL, S. B. & L. J. EWING. 1990. Follow-up of hard to manage preschoolers: Adjustment at age 9 predictors of continuing symptoms. J. Child Psychiatry **31:** 871–889.
18. SERBIN, L. A., A. E. SCHWARTZMAN, D. S. MOSKOWITZ & J. E. LEDINGHAM. 1991. Aggressive, withdrawn, and aggressive/withdrawn children in adolescence: Into the next generation. *In* The Development and Treatment of Childhood Aggression. D. J. Pepler & K. H. Rubin, Eds.: 55–70. Lawrence Erlbaum Associates, Publishers. Hillsdale, NJ.
19. D'AMATO, F. R., S. CABIB, S. PUGLISI-ALLEGRA, F. R. PATTACCHIOLI, G. CIGLIANA, S. MACCARI & L. ANGELUCCI. 1992. Effects of acute and repeated exposure to stress on the hypothalamo-pituitary-adrenocortical activity in mice during postnatal development. Horm. Behav. **26:** 474–485.
20. BELETSKY, L. D., G. H. ORIANS & J. C. WINGLFIELD. 1992. Year-to-year patterns of circulating levels of testosterone and corticosterone in relation to breeding density, experience, and reproductive success of the polygynous red-winged blackbird. Horm. Behav. **26:** 420–432.
21. SAPOLSKY, R. M. & M. J. MEANY. 1986. Maturation of the adrenocortical stress response: Neuroendocrine control mechanisms and the stress hyporesponsive period. Brain Res. **396:** 64–76.
22. ROSE, R. M. 1980. Endocrine responses to stressful psychological events. *In* Advances in Psychoneuroendocrinology. E. J. Sachar, Ed.: **3:** 251–276. The Psychiatric Clinics of North America. W. B. Saunders Company. Philadelphia.
23. BOOTH, A., G. SHELLEY, A. MAZUR, G. THARP & R. KITTOK. 1989. Testosterone and winning and losing in human competition. Horm. Behav. **23:** 556–571.
24. SAPOLSKY, R. M. 1991. Testicular function, social rank, and personality among wild baboons. Psychoneuroendocrinology **16:** 281–293.
25. DABBS, J. M., G. J. JURKOVIC & R. L. FRADY. 1991. Salivary testosterone and cortisol among late adolescent male offenders. J. Abnorm. Child Psychol. **19:** 469–478.
26. POPE, A. W., K. L. BIERMAN & G. H. MUMMA. 1991. Aggression, hyperactivity, and inattention-immaturity: Behavior dimensions associated with peer rejection in elementary school boys. Dev. Psychol. **27:** 663–671.
27. CHROUSOS, G. P. & P. W. GOLD. 1992. The concepts of stress and stress system disorders. J. Am. Med. Assoc. **267:** 1244–1252.
28. GRANGER, D. A., J. R. WEISZ & D. KAUNECKIS. 1994. Neuroendocrine reactivity, internalizing behavior problems, and control-related cognitions in clinic-referred youth. J. Abnorm. Psychol. **103:** 267–276.
29. SCHAAL, R., R. E. TREMBLAY, R. SOUSSIGNAN & E. J. SUSMAN. Testosterone in pubescent males; Links with concurrent social dominance and long-term records of antecedent physical aggression. J. Am. Acad. Child Adolesc. Psychiatry. In press.
30. ACHENBACH, T. M. & C. EDELBROCK. 1979. The Child Behavior Profile: 2. Boys aged 12–16 and girls aged 6–11 and 12–16. J. Consult. Clin. Psychol. **47:** 223–233.
31. OFFER, D., E. OSTROV & K. I. HOWARD. 1984. The Offer Self-image Questionnaire for Adolescents: A manual. Michael Reese Hospital. Chicago, IL.
32. COSTELLO, A. J., C. EDELBROCK, R. KALAS, M. K. DULCAN & S. H. KLARIC. 1983. Diagnostic Interview Schedule for Children. National Institute of Mental Health.

33. BECK, A., C. WARD, M. MENDELSON, J. MOCK & J. ERBAUGH. 1961. An inventory for measuring depression. Arch. Gen. Psychiatry **4:** 561–571.

34. SPIELBERGER, C. D., G. JACOBS, S. RUSSELL & R. S. CRANE. 1970. STAI Manual. Consulting Psychologist Press. Palo Alto, CA.

35. ECCLES, J., C. L. MILLER, M. L. TUCKER, J. BECKER, W. SCHRAMM, R. MIDGLEY, W. HOLMES, L. PASCH & M. MILLER. 1988. March. Hormones and affect at early adolescence. Paper presented at a symposium at the second biennial meeting of the Society for Research on Adolescence, Alexandria, VA.

36. INOFF-GERMAIN, G. E., G. S. ARNOLD, E. D. NOTTELMANN, E. J. SUSMAN, G. B. CUTLER, JR. & G. P. CHROUSOS. 1988. Relations between hormone levels and observational measures of aggressive behavior of early adolescents in family interactions. Dev. Psychol. **24:** 129–139.

37. NOTTELMANN, E. D., G. INOFF-GERMAIN, E. J. SUSMAN & G. P. CHROUSOS. 1990. Hormones and behavior at puberty. In Adolescence and Puberty. J. Bancroft & J. M. Reinisch, Eds.: 88–123. Oxford University Press. New York.

38. GRANGER, D. A., J. R. WEISZ, J. T. MC CRACKEN, S. C. IKEDA & P. DOUGLAS. 1996. Reciprocal influences among adrenocortical activation, psychosocial processes and the behavioral adjustment of clinic referred children. Submitted for publication.

39. GUNNAR, M. R., J. ISENESEE & L. S. FURST. 1987. Adrenocortical activity and the Brazelton Neonatal Assessment Scale: Moderating effects of the newborn's biomedical status. Child Dev. **58:** 1448–1458.

40. JONES, S. A., A. N. BROOKS & J. R. CHALLIS. 1989. Steroids modulate corticotropin-releasing hormone production in human fetal membranes and placenta. J. Clin. Endocrinol. Metab. **68:** 825–30.

41. ANDERSON, T. & D. MAGNUSSON. 1990. Biological maturation in adolescence and the development of drinking habits and alcohol abuse among young males: A prospective longitudinal study. J. Youth Adolesc. **19:** 33–42.

42. GRANGER, D. A., K. H. SCHMEELK & S. D. IKEDA. 1996. Interleukin-1 receptor antagonist is induced in vitro by, and correlated in vivo with, corticotropin-releasing factor. Submitted for publication.

The Time Course of Angry Behavior in the Temper Tantrums of Young Children[a]

M. POTEGAL,[b] M. R. KOSOROK, AND R. J. DAVIDSON

Departments of Psychology and Biostatistics
University of Wisconsin
Madison, Wisconsin

There are great differences of opinion regarding the duration and time course of emotions, including anger. Investigators focusing primarily on emotions elicited in the laboratory by experimental manipulations (*e.g.*, viewing of emotion-eliciting slides), and often involving analysis of facial expression, have suggested that emotions in general last for only a few seconds.[1,2] Other investigators relying mostly on diary methods or retrospective accounts of real-life episodes have concluded that emotions last for considerably longer periods, generally on the order of minutes to hours.[3-5] In the case of anger, Frijda *et al.*[3] have suggested that successive angry expressions can succeed one another continuously for as long as the conflict provoking them lasts. These investigators further remark that "some emotions may have particular, built-in time courses . . . [that cannot] be stopped at will by the subject once overt expression has been allowed to go beyond a certain point. . . . Anger need not be very intense to have this sort of inertia. . ." (p. 200). Potegal[6] has presented a related discussion of a putative "neural flywheel" in the aggressive arousal of humans and other animals.

The variation found in empirical studies of anger duration mirrors that in theoretical disputes. The earliest of five surveys in the literature found a unimodal distribution of anger durations in American college women, with the mode being 10–20 min, but with almost as many subjects reporting durations of 5 minutes or less.[7] Subsequent surveys have generated bimodal distributions of anger. The shorter mode in Japanese and American surveys varies from "a few minutes" to "less than 10 minutes."[5,7-10] The longer mode in all surveys was a day or more. One possible source of variance in these surveys is differences in the intensity of the reported anger. In adults, higher intensities of self-reported anger are associated with longer durations (ref. 10, p. 267). Similarly, Gates' data (ref. 7, Table VI) suggests that modal duration increases systematically with intensity of anger. The inertial metaphors cited above imply that higher intensities of anger are associated with longer durations because it requires more time for the anger to dissipate (*cf* the counter arguments of ref. 10).

[a] Early stages of this project were supported by the Harry Frank Guggenheim Foundation, later stages by a National Research Service Award (F33 NS 09638-01) to M. Potegal from the National Institute of Neurological Disorders and Stroke.

[b] Address for correspondence: Psychology Department, Brogden Building, University of Wisconsin, 1202 W. Johnson St., Madison, WI 53706. Tel: (608) 263-5072 or -9461; fax: (608) 265-2875; e-mail: potegal@psyphy.psych.wisc.edu.

The conclusion that substantial numbers of individuals typically experience episodes of anger with durations between 5 and 15 minutes is consistent with experimental demonstrations of the persistence of aggressive arousal over a delay imposed between provocation and test. Kornadt[11] and Konecni[12] found increases in projective and overt behavioral measures of aggressiveness, respectively, in subjects up to 13 minutes after they had been provoked by insult and/or frustration, whereas Doob and Climie[13] and Buvinic and Berkowitz[14] failed to find such effects after delays of 20 or 60 minutes. Note that all of the foregoing studies estimate overall durations of anger persistence; little effort has been expended to characterize the details of anger's trajectory over time. Although it is intuitive to assume that anger declines monotonically, Frijda et al.[3] indicate that some individuals report multiple peaks in their experience of anger. Detailed studies in other animals of the time course of aggressive behavior following a brief provocation have also suggested a more complex course with several phases.[15,16]

If little is known about the time course of anger in adulthood, even less is known about its development. This is rather surprising, because young children are less likely to mask their emotions and are therefore potentially good subjects for studies of emotional behavior. The laboratory allows for the controlled manipulation and observation of behavior, but the relevance of data so generated to the emotional behavior of children in the natural environment of the home remains a concern. At the other extreme are spontaneous agonistic interactions between individuals. Dawe[17] reported that the average duration of "quarrels" between preschool children was a quite brief 23 seconds; there was some tendency for quarrel duration to increase with age between 25 and 60 months. However, such agonistic interactions between individuals always involve strategies and negotiations that can profoundly alter the nature and time course of the individual experience.[18] Our approach to these issues begins with the observation that temper tantrums are an almost ubiquitous venue for anger in young children. Because many parents have discovered through trial and error that one way to deal with a child's tantrum is to let her/him "work it out" without interference, the time course and sequence of behaviors in tantrums may be less controlled by the behavior of others than is the course of events in other real world anger/aggressive interactions. Goodenough's[19] classic monograph, "Anger in Young Children" appears to be the sole extended treatment of this subject in English. She reported a range of tantrum durations from less than 1 minute to 75 minutes, with the modal duration estimated at 2 minutes.

As mentioned above, there is more to the time course of anger than its persistance. Parens et al.[20] have noted a temporal structure in tantrums consisting of ascending and descending phases of emotional intensity upon which secondary fluctuations are superimposed. Their report, and the accompany figure, are similar to the description by Frijda et al.[3] of the multipeaked time course of emotion in adults. Parens et al.[20] do not identify the behaviors upon which their estimates of emotional intensity are based.

In an initial survey carried out in the United Kingdom, Einon and Potegal[21] identified stamping/jumping, pushing/pulling, hitting, kicking, and throwing things as behaviors common to tantrums. Behaviors of lower incidence and possibly more deliberate aggressiveness included biting, pinching, scratching, and hair pulling. We now report that these behaviors exhibit a common time course, different from crying and several other tantrum behaviors, and we propose that they collectively reflect anger. We address the following two questions: How does the time course of anger vary with tantrum duration? and Are different angry behaviors associated with different overall levels of anger?

METHOD

Subject Selection

We obtained the names of parents of children between 18 and 60 months old from newspaper announcements of Madison-area births collated by the Waisman Center for Human Development and Mental Retardation. Birth announcements are released by the hospitals to the newspaper automatically unless the parents object; hence these lists represent a large sample of Madison-area in-hospital births. In order to highlight changes in tantrum characteristics with age, we selected noncontiguous age groups of children; that is, children who were 18–24, 30–36, 42–48, and 54–60 months old. Data were gathered in two steps.

Step 1: Telephone Interview

A group of undergraduates were trained in asking a series of questions about the incidence, frequency, duration, and general behavioral characteristics of tantrums and their relation to mealtimes, sleeping and awakening, and illness. Almost all of the parents who were reached by telephone consented to be interviewed. In general, parents (especially mothers) were interested and cooperative in responding to our questions; many volunteered additional information, and some asked for a copy of the results. By the end of stage 1, we had interviewed the parents of 1219 children, of whom 991 were classed as "tantrumers."

Step 2: Descriptive Narratives and Questionnaires

At the end of the telephone interview, parents were asked to provide a written description of one of their child's tantrums. The narrative/questionnaire packet sent to them included two "representative" tantrum narratives, which we wrote to indicate to parents the level of detail we wished reported. An ordered checklist of tantrum behaviors on the back of the narrative form was included to clarify and confirm events described in the narrative. The returned narratives varied from one paragraph descriptions to three pages of detailed notes carefully numbered in order of events with the corresponding clock times recorded. In most cases, once the narrative had been received, the parent was called back to verify details. Eight returned packets included no narrative or were dropped from the study because the narratives were fragmentary, inconsistent, and/or could not be clarified by the follow-up call. One narrative described a 77 min tantrum, almost twice as long as any other, with a unique behavioral pattern. This tantrum was not included. The data base for this report was 330 tantrum narratives.

The age × sex distribution of the children represented in the narrative subsample was almost identical to that in the original telephone survey. The age-related distributions of mean tantrum frequency and duration in children represented in the narratives was also quite similar to those in the survey (details to be reported elsewhere). By these criteria, the children whose tantrums were reported in the narratives appeared representative of those in the preceding telephone survey. Review of job, education, and racial self-identification information provided by parents suggested that respondents were largely middle class (*e.g.*, mean educational level of both parents was college graduate) and, with the exception of two Asian families, white.

Defining Tantrums

Tantrums were defined as beginning with the first occurrence of a major tantrum element: arching back/stiffening limbs, getting down, shouting, screaming, crying, pushing/pulling, stamping, hitting, kicking, throwing, running away; or by an aggressive behavior: biting, pinching, scratching, pulling hair. Because of their low individual rates of occurrence, the four latter behaviors were collapsed into an "aggressive behavior" category. The tantrum was defined as over when the last of these behaviors had stopped. Verbal protests (without raising the voice) were noted and whining was scored, but neither were used as tantrum markers.

Forty of the narratives contained gaps of 0.5–7.0 min during which no tantrum behaviors were reported to have occurred. This presented the problem of distinguishing one tantrum with a pause from two tantrums with an interval between them. After detailed examination of these cases, the following rules were adopted: For tantrums of overall duration < 10 min, a pause of ≥ 2.5 min with no tantrum behaviors was interpreted as separating two distinct tantrums. For tantrums > 10 minutes, the criterion pause was 3 minutes. In all cases with two tantrums, only the first was included in the present analysis. The data reported here consist of tantrums (one each) had by 152 girls and 178 boys 18-62 months old. Mean tantrum duration ($\pm$ SD) = 4.7 $\pm$ 5.9 minutes (range: 0.5–39.5 min).

Constructing "Tantrugrams"

An intermediate step in data processing was the conversion of each written narrative into a tantrugram, a time × behavior matrix in which time was partitioned into consecutive 0.5 min units, and behavior in each of 15 different categories was scored as occurring or not occurring within each unit. The following rules were used in this conversion: If a parent's estimate of a given behavior duration was a range, for example, 1-2 min, then the behavior was scored as occurring for the mean value of the range, for example, 1.5 minutes. In some cases a behavior was reported as occurring throughout a period but there was no indication whether it was continuous or intermittent. Based on our general experience, screaming and shouting were scored as continuous, whereas angry behaviors were scored in the first, last, and alternate units of the period in such cases. Hitting and kicking included both directed striking and vigorous flailing in the air with arms and legs, respectively. "Down" was scored for any substantial lowering of the body; in most cases the child dropped to the floor, but also included were instances of sitting, squatting, and kneeling. This work was carried out by pairs of trained undergraduate raters each of whom prepared a tantrugram for a given narrative. The two raters then resolved discrepancies by discussion or by referral to a supervisor. The supervisor subsequently reviewed and corrected the final tantrugram.

Statistical Analysis of Behavior Time Course

To provide an adequate statistical base for evaluating the time course of 13 tantrum behaviors (verbal protest and arch/stiff were excluded from this analysis) while allowing for the possibility that tantrums of different duration may have had different dynamics, tantrums were first partitioned into four duration groups: 0.5–2.0 min (n = 135), 2.5–4.0 min (n = 89), 4.5–10.5 min (n = 70), and 11–39.5

min (n = 36). Under the working assumption that processes within a duration group are roughly homogeneous, the momentary probability of each behavior within successive time epochs for each group was estimated by calculating a Poisson rate parameter, λ, for each epoch across the group from the expression

$$\lambda = \frac{-\log(1 - p)}{T},$$

where p, the probability of the behavior, is estimated by the fraction of corresponding epochs (*e.g.*, the first epoch in each tantrum) during which the behavior occurred. T = the duration of the epoch. Momentary Poisson rates (MPR) are used in our analysis as estimates of behavior magnitude or intensity rather than the directly derived probabilities, because λs derived from epochs of different durations are comparable, whereas probabilities are not. As seen in FIGURES 1 and 2, epochs for the first 3 minutes were set equal to the minimum 0.5 min units originally used to score behavior. To offset the reduction in the number of tantrums still occurring at longer durations, epochs on the right side of the graphs for the last two duration groups were made progressively longer to include a larger sample of data from each remaining tantrum. Standard errors and p values were obtained by bootstrap calculations from the MPR. (In the bootstrap procedure, original data sets are sampled with replacement multiple times to obtain new, random data sets of the same size as the original. Statistical quantities derived in this way from the new data sets are free of parametric assumptions and all approximations and are at least as accurate estimates of true population values as those obtained in the conventional way.[22])

RESULTS

Differences between the Time Courses of Angry Behaviors and Other Acts

FIGURE 1 shows a grouping of tantrum behaviors by two gross features of the time course. The behaviors in A, the upper part of the FIGURE, are all characterized by a peak MPR occurring somewhere in the middle of the tantrum. The behaviors in B, the lower part of the FIGURE, are all characterized by an MPR peak at the beginning of the tantrum. In most cases this peak is followed by a monotonic decline. Note that stamping, pushing/pulling, hitting, and throwing things, all behaviors that intuitively reflect anger most directly, appear in B. The only exception appears to be kicking, and its time course may be explained by its coupling to down: a large portion of kicking happens once the child has thrown her/himself to the floor. Thus, in general, angry behaviors have reached their most probable level within the first 30 seconds of tantrum onset and decline steadily thereafter.

In principal components and multidimensional scaling analyses of these data to be reported elsewhere, we have found that, in fact, the parameters of the angry behavior time courses cluster together in parameter space and that the parameters of other behaviors (*e.g.*, screaming, shouting, and down) are at considerable distances. It thus seems reasonable to suppose that a distinct process or set of processes influences or drives angry behaviors. We refer to these processes as anger and consider it a latent variable. What follows are analyses of some of the characteristics of this latent variable.

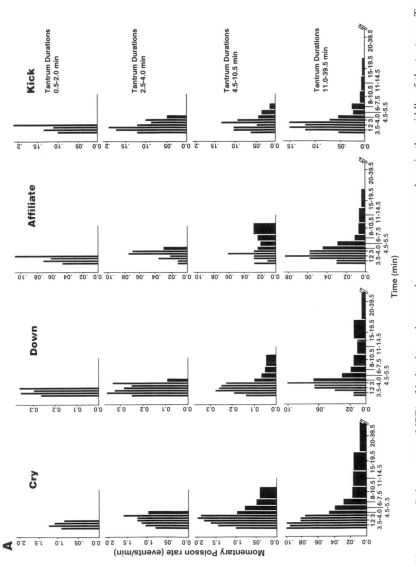

FIGURE 1A. Momentary Poisson rates (MPR) of behaviors whose peak rates occur somewhere in the middle of the tantrum. Tantrums have been collapsed into four groups according to duration.

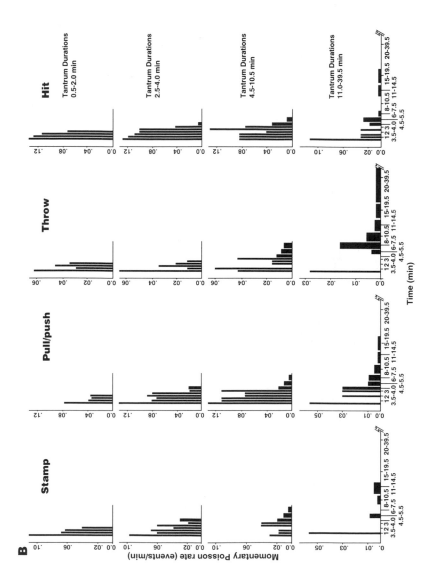

FIGURE 1B. MPR of behaviors whose peak rates occur at the beginning of the tantrum.

The Time Course of Total Anger

The total level of anger in a time epoch is best estimated by combining individual angry behaviors. Unlike probabilities, individual MPRs are additive; we therefore estimate total anger levels by summing the latter. As might be expected from the plots of the individual behaviors, FIGURE 2 shows that the general shape of the time course for each duration group is an initial peak followed by a more-or-less monotonic decline. From the viewpoint of acute tantrum dynamics, one might expect that greater initial anger would be associated with longer tantrums inasmuch as a higher level of initial anger might take longer to dissipate. The plots in FIGURE 2 suggest instead that the longer the tantrum, the lower the initial MPR. That is,

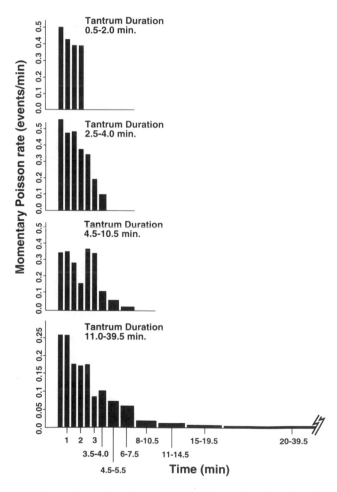

FIGURE 2. Total angry behavior. Summed MPR of stamping, throwing, hitting, kicking, pulling/pushing, and (collectively) scratching, biting, pinching, and hair pulling in four duration groups.

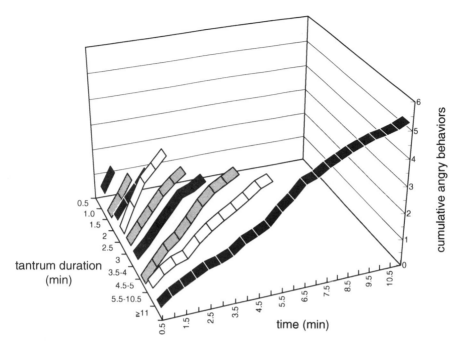

FIGURE 3. Cumulative mean number of angry behaviors in tantrums of nine different durations. The shortest tantrums, 0.5 min long, are not shown. Note that some of the data at the ends of grouped tantrums are truncated (*e.g.*, for tantrums 4.5 to 5.0 min long, the last 30 s of anger in the 5.0 minute tantrums are not shown).

less initial anger is associated with longer tantrum duration. This impression was confirmed by a low but significantly negative Pearson product moment correlation of the number of angry behaviors in the first 0.5 min of the tantrum with the overall tantrum duration across all subjects ($r = -.13$, $p < .02$). Similarly, when tantrums are grouped by duration into 10 groups with durations from 0.5 to $\geq$ 11.0 min (Ns, the number of subjects, ranges between 25 and 35 for each group), an ANOVA with age as a factor shows that mean rates of anger over the whole tantrum decline systematically with duration [$F(9, 289) = 4.95$, $p < .0001$]. As noted in the DISCUSSION section below, we interpret this finding as showing temperament differences, with children prone to greater distress having longer tantrums with more crying and less anger.

Regardless of the explanation of the inverse relationship, it is still reasonable to ask if the time courses of anger in tantrums of different duration are systematically related. For this analysis we again partitioned tantrum duration more finely into 10 duration groups, but this time we excluded tantrums in which no anger was expressed (Ns ranges from 17 to 30). FIGURE 3 displays the time courses of total anger in these groups as cumulative functions. (Because of the smaller N in each group, the anger versus time plots for these groups were more variable than the plots in FIGURES 1 or 2; the patterns in these more finely partitioned data are better displayed by cumulative plots.) FIGURE 3 clearly shows that growth rates decline systematically with increasing tantrum duration, forming a fan of time courses. Although not shown as clearly, there is also a strong trend for the starting point of the plots to decline with increasing tantrum duration. Based on the assumption that the number of tantrums in each time interval and each duration group are Poisson distributed, a χ^2-test comparing the mean anger rate in corresponding time units across the plots demonstrated a highly significant difference among these plots ($p < .0001$). Having demonstrated that the plots differ, we then tested whether they are systematically related. Using a nonparametric, rank-based procedure, we compared the observed ordering of mean anger rate in corresponding time units across the plots to the order generated by a 1000 random permutations of these anger rates; the null hypothesis of a random ordering of rates as a function of duration was rejected ($p < 0.01$). The decline in the cumulative growth rate of anger in tantrums of progressively longer duration shown in FIGURE 3 is thus significantly systematic.

Occurrence of Individual Angry Behaviors as a Function of Total Anger MPR

Inspection of FIGURE 1B suggests that there may be some differences among the time courses of individual angry behaviors. Similarly, although all these behaviors clustered in the same locus within the time course parameter space, their individual 95% confidence regions did not overlap. One possible explanation for these differences is that angry behaviors are differentially coupled to or gated by total anger levels. In other words, some angry behaviors may become more probable and others less probable at different levels of total anger. This hypothesis was examined by collapsing all time epochs with the same total anger MPR and computing the proportion of total MPR (the MPRP) accounted for by individual behaviors for each level of total anger. As FIGURE 4 shows, the MPRP of stamping clearly declines as total anger MPR increases. The MPRP of throwing remains constant, whereas hitting, kicking, and pulling/pushing all increase with increasing total anger MPR (see slopes in TABLE 1). The null hypothesis, that there is no systematic relationship between individual and total behavior MPR can be rejected for all behaviors except throwing. Because the MPR of the individual behaviors sum to the total MPR, these plots are not fully independent. However, the bootstrap procedures for estimating statistical significance take this non independence into account; the relative relationship among the slopes is displayed veridically.

The graphs in FIGURE 4 also contain several points that appear to be statistical "outliers." Reanalyses following removal of these outliers did not significantly change any of the reported results. Changes with total MPR account for 20–25% of the variance in stamping, kicking, and pulling/pushing and considerably less in throwing and hitting (TABLE 1). This indicates that much of the variation in the time course of the angry behaviors comes from sources other than the link with overall levels.

Scaling the Angriness of Behavior

The analyses associated with FIGURE 3 further suggest an approach to scaling the angriness of each angry behavior according to its relative contribution to different overall levels of anger (*i.e.*, stamping reflects less anger, because it is most common at the lowest overall levels of anger). We formed an index of angriness for each behavior by calculating the value of the total MPR at each point on the graph weighted by the individual behavior MPRP at that point [*e.g.*,

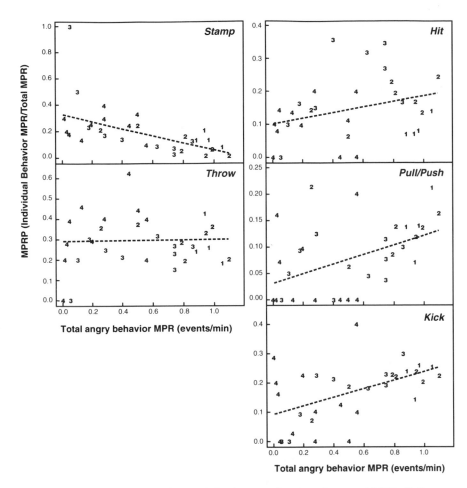

FIGURE 4. MPR of individual angry behaviors as a function of summed MPR of all angry behaviors. Tantrums are grouped into four durations groups, as in FIGS. 1 and 2. Numeric symbols indicate the duration group from which each data point was drawn: 1 = 0.5–2.0 min; 2 = 2.5–4.0 min; 3 = 4.5–10.5 min; 4 = 11–39.5 min.

for stamping: weight = $\Sigma(\text{total}_{mpr} \cdot \text{stamp}_{mprp})/\Sigma\text{stamp}_{mprp}]$. Weights for each behavior are shown in TABLE 1.

DISCUSSION

These results extend the conclusions of Einon and Potegal[21] that there are at least two emotional/behavioral processes with different trajectories at work in temper tantrums (*cf* ref. 23). With the exception of kicking, angry behaviors are characterized by an initial peak in MPR followed by a more or less monotonic

TABLE 1. Characteristics of Angry Behavior MPRs

Angry Behavior	MPRP Slope	Percent Variance Explained	Anger Weight
Stamp	$-.26^a$	25	0.35
Throw	.01	0.1	0.52
Hit	$.08^a$	9.1	0.58
Kick	$.14^a$	26	0.61
Pull/push	$.09^a$	21	0.65

[a] Significantly different from 0.0, $p < .05$.

decline. Although the various angry behaviors appear to differ somewhat in their time courses, multidimensional scaling analysis indicates that they cluster together in a time course parameter space. It is thus plausible to suppose that each of these is a reflection of a common underlying process (or processes) identifiable as anger.

As expected from its constituents, total MPR, the measure of overall anger level, exhibits an initial peak followed by a decline. We have heard anecedotally from some parents that they can see their child becoming visibly more angry at the beginning of a tantrum. Our finding that peak MPR occurs in our first sampling unit suggests that this rising phase of anger must generally happen within 30 seconds. In the future it would be of great interest to chart the rise using observation techniques with a finer time resolution than that provided by narrative reports. For the present, we note that in the preface to their edited volume, The Dynamics of Aggression,[18] Potegal and Knutson remark that there seem to be two temporal patterns of agonistic encounters. Those in which the intensity/riskiness/effortfulness of the behaviors of the antagonists escalate relatively slowly are characteristic of confrontations between strangers in which the outcome of the encounter is in doubt. Those in which the combatants know each other and in which there is a clear asymmetry in dominance/force show a rapid escalation and slower de-escalation (e.g., ref. 24). Tantrums clearly fall in the latter category.

As noted above, it is plausible to suppose that more intense outbursts of emotion should persist for longer times. In our data, parents' judgments of tantrum intensity are significantly correlated with the overall duration of the tantrum. It is thus difficult to explain the observed negative correlation between the initial MPR of angry behaviors and the ultimate duration of the tantrum in terms of acute tantrum dynamics. It also seems implausible that children plan the duration of their tantrum at its outset and adjust their initial anger levels accordingly. These data may be more plausibly interpreted in terms of temperament. Einon and Potegal[21] found that longer tantrums were characteristic of distress-prone children who were less likely than the average child to act aggressively within the tantrum or towards other children outside the tantrum. They were almost twice as likely to be picked on by other children. Thus, longer tantrums may have a lower initial anger because they are had by children more disposed to distress then to anger.

The demonstrated ordering in the plots of cumulative anger suggests that they form a family of related functions. A conventional approach to such an observation is to assume that the differences in the time course of anger observed in tantrums of different durations can be accounted for by variations in the parameter(s) of a single general process of anger operating in all tantrums regardless of duration. A simple example would be an exponential decay of anger; children with high time constants of decay would express anger only briefly, whereas children with low time constants would express anger persistently. The conventional approach involves transformations of the axes to fit the various plots; the challenge under this approach is to identify transformations that preserve the function and that are orderly (*i.e.*, the transformations accounting for plots of successively longer tantrums form a reasonable sequence). A novel alternative to this standard parametric approach is the hypothesis of a single general anger trajectory. Under this hypothesis, the angry behavior in tantrums of different durations would fall along successive, partially overlapping segments of a single trajectory. The challenge under this interpretation is to reconstruct the trajectory and to specify the respective starting points along the trajectory for the angry behavior of tantrums of each duration. Although these approaches are mathematically isomorphic, they have different emphases. The general trajectory approach emphasizes the commonality of the anger process across tantrums; it implies that if a shorter tantrum were to become protracted, the time course of anger expressed toward its end would resemble that in a longer tantrum. Modeling that contrasts these two approaches is currently underway.

In the shortest duration tantrums shown in FIGURES 1B and 2, anger does not appear to taper off but ends abruptly. The general trajectory model stipulates that the shortest tantrums begin at the highest levels of anger, thus implying that they must involve an abrupt drop in anger. If the termination of anger in shorter tantrums is indeed relatively abrupt, it may be that anger is somehow actively inhibited or suppressed, that is, the emotion is regulated. Three- and four-year-olds have been experimentally shown to suppress mild negative responses in the presence of strangers.[25] In tantrums, distress mounts as anger decreases; perhaps sadness somehow displaces anger in some cases. As Miller and Sperry[26] noted of displays of anger by two-year-olds, an entire tantrum often ends abruptly with the resumption of some other activity (parents commonly report that the aftermath of tantrums is "as if nothing happened.") Thus, anger may be transformed or dissolved as a secondary consequence of a switch in the child's attention. If anger in short tantrums routinely ends abruptly, it brings into question the limits if not the adequacy of inertial metaphors for anger. However, it is also possible that the apparently abrupt endings are artifacts of partitioning time into units that are long relative to total tantrum duration. Tantrum observations with greater temporal resolution are needed to definitively establish the existence of abrupt terminations of anger.

There may also be emotion regulatory processes in which anger is actively prolonged by children (*e.g.*, ref. 27). Parental reports suggest that some children intensify their anger reactions in order to prolong the conflict, make sure that parents have noticed their anger, and get what they want. There are other children who refuse to be jollied out of their negative mood and "hold onto" their anger even when it serves no extrinsic purpose. The influence of such emotion regulatory processes on the trajectory of anger remains to be determined.

There was some agreement between the calculated anger weights and a scale included in the narrative/questionnaire packet on which parents rated the "angriness" of various tantrum behaviors. We foresee the anger weights being used in comparing the angriness of tantrums among different children and across different tantrums of the same child. They will also be useful in other situations in which a quantitative estimate of anger magnitude is desired. However, there remain questions about the extent to which the change in individual behavior probability with increasing overall anger MPR represents different degrees of anger *per se* or reflects factors such as the effortfulness/energy expenditure of various responses, the willingness to flout parental rules against the display of certain behaviors (*e.g.*, when asked about biting, parents sometimes replied "We don't allow that"), and/or still other mechanisms.

As indicated above, some psychophysiological investigators believe that emotions in general last for only a few seconds.[1,2] Robinson and Pennebaker[28] note the caveat that estimates of emotion duration are constrained by the behavioral/biological systems being measured and that in the psychophysiological domain events typically last a few seconds. Continuous episodes of angry behaviors (*e.g.*, a flurry of hitting) within individual tantrums are usually quite brief and rarely last more than a minute or two. On the other hand, the probability envelope of these behaviors can persist for many minutes. Do these envelopes represent the repeated elicitation or the continuous activation of emotion? The apparently continuous decline in angry behavior in grouped data can be accounted for by an underlying continuous process that controls the probability of this behavior; as the probability drops the behavior appears more and more intermittent. A scheme of this sort has been shown to account for the temporal pattern of aggressive behavior in other animals.[29] The hypothesis of a continuous process is more parsimonious than the alternative account in which anger is reignited *de novo* at progressively longer intervals. A different aspect of the trajectory of anger that is completely unrepresented in our data is the (presumptive) decline in the intensity of acts, for example, the force of blows or the speed of grabbing things. Other observational techniques will be required to develop such data and determine whether they share a time course with behavior probabilities.

ACKNOWLEDGMENTS

Many University of Wisconsin undergraduate psychology students participated in data collection and analysis. Special thanks are due Sara Woboril for her organization and supervision of their work.

REFERENCES

1. EKMAN, P. 1977. Biological and cultural contributions to body and facial movement. *In* Anthroplogy of the Body. J. Blacking, Ed.: 34–84. Academic Press. London.
2. LEVENSON, R. W. 1988. Emotion and the autonomic nervous system: A prospectus for research on autonomic specificity. *In* Social Psychophysiology and Emotion: Theory and Clinical Applications. H. L. Wagner, Ed.: 17–42. Wiley. New York.
3. FRIJDA, N. H., B. MESQUITA, J. SONNEMANS & S. H. M. VAN GOOZEN. 1991. The duration of affective phenomena or emotions, sentiments, and passions. *In* International Review of Studies of Emotion. K. T. Strongman, Ed. Vol. 1: 187–226. Wiley & Sons. Chichester.
4. GILBOA, E. & W. REVELLE. 1994. Personality and the structure of affective response. *In* Emotions: Essays on Emotion Theory. S. H. M. van Goozen, N. E. Van de Poll & J. A. Sergeant, Eds.: 135–159. Lawrence Erlbaum Assoc. Hillsdale, NJ.
5. SCHERER, K. R. & H. G. WALLBOTT. 1994. Evidence for universality and cultural variation of differential emotion response patterning. J. Pers. Soc. Psychol. **66:** 310–328.
6. POTEGAL, M. 1992. Aggression and aggressiveness in female golden hamsters. *In* Of Mice and Women: Aspects of Female Aggression. K. Bjorkqvist & P. Niemela, Eds.: Academic Press. San Diego.
7. GATES, G. S. 1926. An observational study of anger. J. Exp. Psychol. **9:** 325–336.
8. MELTZER, H. 1933. Students' adjustments in anger. J. Soc. Psychol. **4:** 285–309.

9. UEDA, T. 1962. A study of anger in Japanese college students through the controlled diary method (2). J. Nara Gakugei Univ. **10**: 342–348.
10. FRIDHANDLER, B. M. & J. R. AVERILL. 1982. Temporal dimensions of anger: An exploration of time and emotion. *In* Anger and Aggression. J. R. Averill, Ed. Springer Verlag. New York.
11. KORNADT, H.-J. 1974. Toward a motivational theory of aggression and aggression inhibition: Some considerations about an aggression motive and their application to TAT and catharsis. *In* Determinants and Origins of Aggressive Behavior. J. de Wit & W. W. Hartup, Eds.: 567–578. Mouton. The Hague.
12. KONENCI, V. J. 1975. Annoyance, type and duration of post annoyance activity and aggression: The "cathartic effect." J. Exp. Psychol. **104**: 76–102.
13. DOOB, A. N. & R. J. CLIMIE. 1972. Delay of measurement and effects of film violence. J. Exp. Soc. Psychol. **8**: 136–142.
14. BUVINIC, M. L. & L. BERKOWITZ. 1976. Delayed effects of practiced vs. unpracticed responses after observation of movie violence. J. Exp. Soc. Psychol. **12**: 283–293.
15. POTEGAL, M. 1992. Time course of aggressive arousal in female golden hamsters and male rats. Behav. Neural Biol. **58**: 120–124.
16. POTEGAL, M. & J. POPKEN. 1985. The time course of attack priming effects in female golden hamsters. Behav. Processes **11**: 199–208.
17. DAWE, C. 1937. An analysis of two hundred quarrels of preschool children. Child Dev. **5**: 139–157.
18. POTEGAL, M. & J. KNUTSON. Preface. *In* The Dynamics of Aggression: Biological and Social Processes in Dyads and Groups. M. Potegal & J. Knutson, Eds.: ix–xvii. Lawrence Erlbaum Associates. Hillsdale, NJ.
19. GOODENOUGH, F. 1931. Anger in Young Children. University of Minnesota Press. Minneapolis, MN.
20. PARENS, H., E. SCATTERGOOD, W. SINGLETARY, & A. DUFF. 1987. Aggression in our children. Jason Aronson. Northvale, NJ.
21. EINON, D. F. & M. POTEGAL. 1994. Temper tantrums in young children. *In* The Dynamics of Aggression: Biological and Social Processes in Dyads and Groups. M. Potegal & J. Knutson, Eds.: 157–194. Lawrence Erlbaum Associates. Hillsdale, NJ.
22. EFRON, B. & R. TIBSHIRANI. 1986. The bootstrap (with discussion). Stat. Sci. **1**: 54–77.
23. CAMRAS, L. 1991. View II: A dynamical systems perspective on expressive development. *In* International Review of Studies on Emotion. K. T. Strongman, Ed.: 16–28. John Wiley & Sons. New York.
24. CAIRNS, R. C., V. SANTOYO & K. A. HOLLY. 1994. Aggressive escalation: Toward a developmental analysis. *In* The Dynamics of Aggression: Biological and Social Processes in Dyads and Groups. M. Potegal & J. Knutson, Eds.: 227–254. Lawrence Erlbaum Associates. Hillsdale, NJ.
25. COLE, P. M. 1986. Children's spontaneous control of facial expression. Child Dev. **57**: 1309–1321.
26. MILLER, P. & L. L. SPERRY. 1987. The socialization of anger and aggression. Merrill-Palmer Q. **33**: 1–31.
27. THOMPSON, R. A. 1994. Emotion regulation: A theme in search of definition. *In* The Development of Emotion Regulation: Biological and Behavioral Considerations. N. Fox, Ed.: **59**: 25–52. Monographs of the Society for Research in Child Development. University of Chicago Press. Chicago.
28. ROBINSON, R. J. & J. W. PENNEBAKER. 1991. Emotion and health: Towards an integrative perspective. *In* International Review of Studies on Emotion. K. T. Strongman, Ed.: 247–267. John Wiley & Sons. Chichester.
29. POTEGAL, M. & K. COOMBES. 1995. Attack priming and aggressive arousal in female Syrian golden hamsters *Mesocricetus auratus*. Anim. Behav. **49**: 931–947.

Autonomic Nervous System Factors Underlying Disinhibited, Antisocial, and Violent Behavior

Biosocial Perspectives and Treatment Implications[a]

ADRIAN RAINE[b]

Department of Psychology
S.G.M. Building
University of Southern California
Los Angeles, California 90089-1061

INTRODUCTION

Psychophysiological research has enormous potential to illuminate the etiology of antisocial and violent behavior because it lies at the interface between clinical science, cognitive science, and neuroscience.[1] There have been numerous reviews of the psychophysiology of antisocial behavior in the past decades,[2-5] with the most recent ones being Raine,[6] Fowles,[7] McBurnett and Lahey,[8] Raine,[9] and Raine.[10] Consequently, this chapter will attempt to highlight some of the most important issues and questions surrounding past research, and to give attention to newly emerging ideas that have received little or no previous discussion. Nevertheless, the interested reader is referred to the above reviews for a more in-depth analysis of specific issues surrounding autonomic psychophysiology and antisocial behavior.

AROUSAL

Electrodermal correlates of antisocial and aggressive behavior have recently been reviewed by Raine.[6,9,10] In the past 15 years arousal has been assessed by measurement during an initial "rest" period of either skin conductance levels (SCLs) or nonspecific fluctuations (NSFs). Five of 11 studies have found significant effects, with three of these five finding differences for NSFs. Only two of the five found effects for SCL, although another of these studies found trends for lower SCLs.[11] NSFs may produce stronger support for skin conductance (SC) under-arousal in antisocial children relative to SCLs, because the latter are more influenced by factors such as local peripheral conditions of the skin and the thickness and hydration of the stratum corneum,[12] factors that are unrelated to autonomic arousal.

[a] This paper was written while the author was supported by NIMH Grant no. RO1 MH46435-02 and an NIMH Research Scientist Development Award (1 KO2 MH01114-01).
[b] Tel: (213) 740-7348; fax: (213) 740-0897; e-mail: raine@almaak.usc.edu.

Data on resting heart rate level (HRL) provides striking support for under-arousal in antisocial and aggressive children. Indeed, the findings for HRL on noninstitutionalized antisocial children is probably the strongest and best replicated finding in the field of psychophysiology of antisocial behavior. A detailed review of these studies and theoretical and methodological considerations are given by Raine.[6] Fourteen studies on noninstitutionalized conduct-disordered, delinquent, and antisocial children and adolescents showed that there were significant effects in the predicted direction of lower resting heart rates in antisocial children. Effect sizes were substantial and averaged 0.84. Findings could not easily be attributed to a number of possible artifacts.[6]

ORIENTING

Key findings from nine studies that have assessed SC orienting to neutral stimuli in antisocial groups have been reviewed by Raine,[6] and McBurnett and Lahey[8] also review SC orienting specifically in conduct disordered and delinquent children. Five out of nine studies find evidence for an orienting deficit as indicated by reduced frequency of SCRs to orienting stimuli. Frequency measures of SC orienting appear to produce stronger findings in these studies, perhaps because frequency measures tend to be more reliable than amplitude measures; this, in turn, may be because amplitude is more affected by non-ANS factors, such as the number and size of sweat glands.[12] Raine and Venables[13] theorized that reduced orienting in antisocial children indicate that these children were characterized by a fundamental deficit in the ability to allocate attentional resources to events in the environment.

The general conclusion that antisocial and aggressive individuals are characterized by orienting deficits needs to be qualified at two levels. First, although antisocial children have attentional deficits in paradigms in which they must passively attend or respond in anticipation of an aversive stimulus, the event-related potential literature indicates that they have *better* attention to events of interest.[10,14] Antisocial and aggressive children may therefore fail in school because they do not allocate attentional resources to processing scholastic information, especially when they are passive recipients of such information. Conversely, they appear to have the cognitive capacity to attend well to stimuli and events that are attention grabbing (*e.g.*, gangs, drugs) and may be particularly sensitive to the type of salient and immediate rewards associated with an antisocial and violent way of life.[15,16] This in turn has implications for possible interventions (see below).

Second, reduced SC orienting appears to be specific to aggressive, criminal, and antisocial individuals with schizoid or schizotypal features. For example, Raine and Venables[13] found that SC nonresponding characterized antisocial adolescents who had schizoid tendencies (introversion, psychosis, and anxiety), whereas Raine[17] found that reduced SC orienting characterized criminals with high schizotypal personality scores. This conclusion is supported by two other studies.[6,10] In addition, there is some evidence that schizotypal antisocial children may represent that subgroup of antisocial children who are particularly characterized by prefrontal dysfunction.[6,10] The implication is that whereas it was earlier suggested that underaroused, disinhibited children may be predisposed to aggressive behavior, it is possible that a schizoid subgroup of inhibited children (whose features of shyness, anxiety, and withdrawal have been found by Olin[18] to be childhood precursors of schizotypal personality disorder) may also become violent in adulthood.

PROSPECTIVE PSYCHOPHYSIOLOGICAL RESEARCH ON AUTONOMIC ACTIVITY AND ANTISOCIAL BEHAVIOR

One of the major difficulties in trying to draw conclusions on the psychophysiological basis of criminal behavior is that most studies conducted to date have been nonprospective and have used institutionalized populations. In addition, most studies report results from only one of the three most commonly measured psychophysiological response systems (electrodermal, cardiovascular, or cortical). Prospective longitudinal research allows us to make more powerful statements about predispositions for criminal behavior and to elucidate cause-effect relationships. However, because prospective research is more difficult to execute, there have been few such studies.

A nine-year prospective study of crime development by Raine[11] has shown that low arousal and orienting measured by both skin conductance and heart rate at age 15 years in normal unselected schoolboys predicted criminal behavior at age 24 years. Measures of arousal correctly classified 74.7% of all subjects as criminal/noncriminal, a rate significantly greater than chance (50%). Group differences in social class, academic ability, and area of residence were not found to mediate the link between underarousal and antisocial behavior. This is the first study providing evidence for underarousal in an antisocial population in all three psychophysiological response systems. Furthermore, these findings are not in isolation, with three other prospective studies also finding similar effects (see ref. 10 for full details).

SPECIFICITY OF AUTONOMIC UNDERAROUSAL AND POOR ORIENTING TO VIOLENT OFFENDERS

An important question concerns whether low arousal acts as a generalized predisposition to antisocial behavior, or more specifically predisposes to aggressive, violent behavior. Few if any studies have addressed this issue. The fact that some studies find heart rate particularly low in violent offenders[19,20] constitutes suggestive evidence for the specificity of this effect for violence. Furthermore, Kindlon et al.[21] have recently shown that low resting heart rate from ages 9–12 years is associated with increased fighting from ages 5–12 years, whereas Gottman[22] showed that wife batterers with low heart rates were more likely to be violent towards those outside of the family and showed a more sadistic aggressive personality than those with high heart rates.

To further explore this issue, data from the prospective study by Raine et al.[11] have been reanalyzed. Five of the 17 15-year-old schoolboys who became criminal by age 24 had convictions for violence (assault or wounding), and these were compared to the other 12 nonviolent offenders and 84 controls on resting heart rate. Results of this analysis for resting HR (measured at the start and end of a rest period prior to an orienting paradigm) are shown in FIGURE 1. Effect sizes between each of the two offender groups relative to normal controls are shown above the bars.

The violent group had the lowest heart rates of all, with the nonviolent offender group being intermediate between violent offenders and controls. The averaged effect size of 1.0 for the violent group is slightly higher than that of 0.85 obtained for previous studies on heart rate (HR) reviewed above. Despite the lack of statistical power due to small N size, HRLs for the violent offender group were

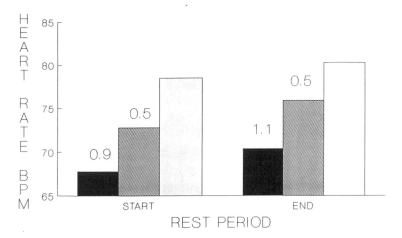

FIGURE 1. 15-year-olds who become violent criminal offenders by age 24 years have significantly lower resting heart rates than noncriminals, with nonviolent criminal offenders lying in the middle. Values above bars indicate effect size. ■, violent; ▨, criminal nonviolent; ▦, controls.

significantly lower than the normal control group at the end of the rest period ($p < 0.05$, two-tailed), with a trend ($p < 0.08$) for the start of the rest period. Conversely, nonviolent offender versus control comparisons were not significant. Similar analyses for nonspecific SC responses and SCL did not produce statistically significant differences between violent offenders and controls, but in all cases the violent offenders had the lowest values of all, with the nonviolent offenders in between violent and control groups. With respect to SC orienting, the same profile was again obtained (*i.e.*, violent offenders having the fewest number of SC-orienting responses), with a substantial averaged effect size of 0.75.

The above analysis is clearly limited by lack of statistical power, and as such strong conclusions cannot be drawn. Taken together with the findings of the above review, however, they suggest that reduced autonomic activity, in general, and low resting HRL at age 15, in particular, may be a particularly strong characteristic of the adolescent who becomes the violent offender.

INTERPRETATIONS OF LOW AROUSAL: FEARLESSNESS AND STIMULATION-SEEKING THEORIES

How is low arousal in aggressive, antisocial adolescents to be interpreted? Two main theoretical interpretations have been proposed. Fearlessness theory indicates that low levels of arousal are markers of low levels of fear.[6,23] For example, particularly fearless individuals, such as bomb disposal experts, who have been decorated for their bravery, have particularly low heart rate levels and reactivity,[24,25] as did British paratroopers decorated in the Falklands war.[26] A fearlessness interpretation of low arousal levels assumes that subjects are not actually at "rest," but that instead the rest periods of psychophysiological testing represents a mildly stressful paradigm, and that low arousal during this period indicates lack of anxiety and fear. Lack of fear would predispose to antisocial and violent behavior inasmuch as such behavior (*e.g.*, fights and assaults) requires a degree of fearlessness to execute, whereas lack of fear, especially in childhood, would help explain poor socialization because low fear of punishment would reduce the effectiveness of conditioning. Fearlessness theory receives support from the fact that autonomic underarousal also provides the underpinning for a fearless or uninhibited temperament (see below).

A second theory explaining reduced arousal is the stimulation-seeking theory.[6,23,27,28] This theory argues that low arousal represents an aversive physiological state, and that antisocial individuals seek out stimulation in order to restore their arousal levels back to an optimal or normal level. Antisocial behavior is viewed as a form of stimulation seeking, in that committing a burglary, assault, or robbery could be stimulating for some individuals.

One direction for future research is to assess why not all underaroused individuals become antisocial. For example, in the discriminant function analysis conducted by Raine,[11] 23% of those who were predicted to become criminal by virtue of having low arousal did not, in fact, have an official conviction for a criminal offense. Some of these false positives may have been due to an error, in that these underaroused subjects were "successful offenders" who did indeed commit offenses, but were not caught by the police. Alternatively, whether or not an underaroused individual turns to crime to obtain their "arousal jag" in life may be a function of their social milieu. For example, those brought up in delinquent neighborhoods and exposed to delinquent peers or have antisocial parents as models may turn to crime to increase arousal levels, whereas those who have high IQ and are brought up in an environment free of crime may obtain their stimulation from a career in politics or academic research. Answering the question of why do not all underaroused individuals become antisocial is important because it can help inform intervention and prevention research.

DISINHIBITED TEMPERAMENT AND REDUCED AUTONOMIC ACTIVITY

The above prospective research highlights the potential importance of underarousal as a psychophysiological predisposition for aggressive and antisocial behavior. A series of recent findings indicates that underarousal may also predispose to a disinhibited temperament, which in itself may act as one early predispositional factor for criminal and violent behavior. Specifically, uninhibited children have been found to have lower HRLs. Low HR and increased vagal tone measured at age 4 was correlated with disinhibited behavior at age 5.5 years, whereas those with relatively low fetal heart rates had lower levels of motoric activity and crying at age 4 months.[29,30] Similarly, Fox[31] found that 5-month-old infants with high vagal tone (associated with increased heart rate variability and low HRLs and indicating increasing parasympathetic tuning of the autonomic nervous system) were more sociable and exploratory at 14 months. Stifter and Fox[32] also found that increased vagal tone at 5 months was associated with high activity levels and a lack of fear to a novel stimulus.

A confirmation and extension of the link between heart rate and disinhibition has been provided in the Mauritius longitudinal study.[33] A cohort of 1795 Mauritian children were tested longitudinally at ages 3, 8, and 11 years. Subjects were rated on theoretically relevant behaviors of inhibition such as approach-avoidance, fearfulness, verbalizations, crying behavior, and sociability. An inhibition index was calculated and used to classify children as extremely inhibited, middle, or extremely uninhibited at each age. Lower heart rate and skin conductance measured at age 3 was associated with disinhibition at age 3 (p <0.0001), whereas those who remained stably disinhibited from ages 3 to 8 years were also found to have lower resting heart rates (p <0.0001) and lower SC levels (p <0.003). Importantly, group differences in autonomic arousal were independent of ethnicity, gender, height, weight, respiratory complaints, and crying behavior.

A disinhibited temperament appears to be underpinned by lower heart rate and skin conductance arousal. The interesting possibility is that reduced autonomic arousal may, in infancy, predispose to exploratory behavior and fearlessness; in childhood, to externalizing behavior problems; in adolescence, to aggression and delinquency; and in adulthood, to violence and crime. Recent findings by Caspi[34] provide some initial support for this notion by showing that children characterized by an undercontrolled temperament at age 3 years are significantly more likely to become conduct disordered at age 15 years. Furthermore, they are more likely at age 18 to score higher on personality measures of aggression and danger seeking.[35] The question of whether underarousal underlies this link between early temperament and antisocial personality in adulthood remains to be seen.

AUTONOMIC PROTECTIVE FACTORS AGAINST CRIME DEVELOPMENT

All psychophysiological research to date has attempted to ask the question What psychophysiological factors predispose to crime? and consequently has focused exclusively on risk factors for crime development. A potentially more important question to be posed, however, is What psychophysiological factors protect a child predisposed to crime from becoming criminal? The first lines of early research in this area are outlined below.

The principle finding to emerge from the first work in this area is that higher autonomic activity during adolescence may act as a protective factor against crime development. Raine, Venables, and Williams[36,37] report on a 14-year prospective study in which autonomic measures of arousal, orienting, and classical conditioning were taken in 101 unselected 15-year-old male schoolchildren. Of these, seventeen antisocial adolescents who desisted from adult crime (desistors) were matched on adolescent antisocial behavior and demographic variables with 17 antisocial adolescents who had become criminal by age 29 (criminals) and 17 nonantisocial, noncriminals (controls). Desistors had significantly higher heart rate levels and higher SC arousal (measured by nonspecific SC responses, see FIG. 2). Desistors also showed significantly higher conditioning, higher orienting, and faster SC recovery times than both criminals and controls (FIG. 3). Findings suggest that individuals predisposed to adult crime by virtue of showing antisocial behavior in adolescence may be protected from crime by heightened levels of autonomic arousal and reactivity. Such protection was specific to autonomic arousal, in that groups did not differ in terms of resting EEG.

Findings from a second study of adults provides some support for this initial finding on adolescents. Brennan, Raine, Venables, and Mednick[38] report on a study of protective factors in 50 men predisposed to crime by virtue of having a seriously criminal father who had been imprisoned. Twenty-four of these men developed a criminal record and were imprisoned themselves, whereas the other

HEART RATE

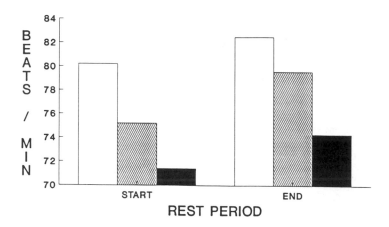

REST PERIOD

NON-SPECIFIC SKIN CONDUCTANCE RESPONSES

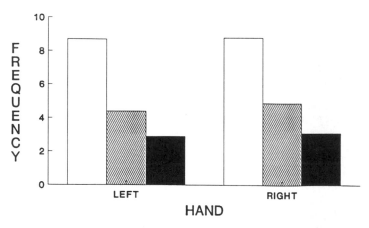

HAND

FIGURE 2. Adolescents who desist from adult crime (desistors) but who are just as antisocial at age 15 as those who become criminal at age 24 (criminals) are characterized by significantly higher resting heart rate and increased SC arousal (frequency of nonspecific SC responses) measured at age 15 years.[36] □, desistors; ▨, normal subjects; ■, criminals.

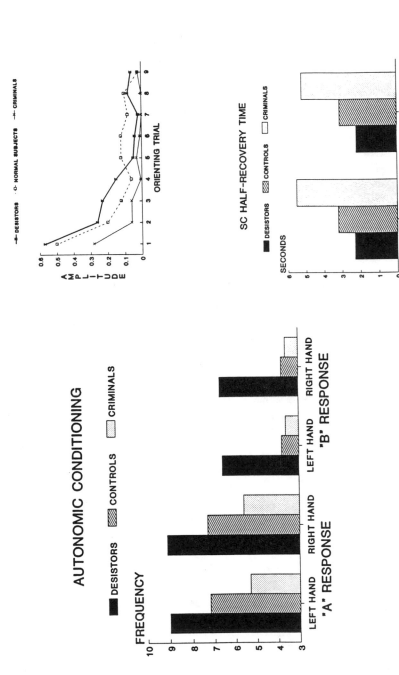

FIGURE 3. Adolescents who desist from adult crime (desistors) but who are just as antisocial at age 24 (criminals) are characterized by significantly better classical conditioning, higher SC orienting, and faster SC half-recovery times measured at age 15 years.[37]

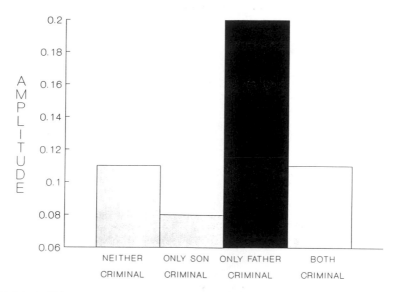

FIGURE 4. Skin conductance orienting. Those at risk for crime by virtue of having a severely criminal father, but who themselves desist from crime (black bar), are characterized by significantly increased SC orienting relative to noncriminal sons with noncriminal fathers (neither criminal), criminal sons with noncriminal fathers (only son criminal), and criminal sons with criminal fathers (both criminal).[38]

group of 26 did not show any criminal offending. SC and HR measures of reactivity to 14 orienting tones were measured at age 35 years. The group that desisted from crime was found to have significantly higher levels of SC and HR orienting relative to those who exhibited criminal behavior, and also relative to a noncriminal control group who had noncriminal fathers (FIG. 4).

With regard to interpretation of findings from these initial studies, desistors can be viewed as being characterized by heightened attentional abilities (better orienting), greater responsivity to environmental stimuli in general (fast recovery), greater sensitivity to cues predicting punishment in particular (better classical conditioning), and higher fearfulness (high heart rate levels). The importance of research on psychophysiological protective factors such as these is that they offer suggestions on possible intervention and prevention strategies for crime development (see below).

BIOSOCIAL PSYCHOPHYSIOLOGICAL RESEARCH ON ANTISOCIAL BEHAVIOR

One of the major challenges for future psychophysiological research on antisocial behavior is to integrate psychophysiological mechanisms with social and psychological processes that are of importance to antisocial and violent behavior in children and adolescents. Biological factors do not operate in a vacuum, and it is quite possible that the interplay between psychophysiological and social risk factors for antisocial behavior are more important than either factor in isolation. Despite this, there has been surprisingly little biosocial research on antisocial behavior, and in particular there has been little psychophysiological biosocial research. A review of research from a broad social psychophysiological perspective on antisocial behavior may be found in Raine.[5] The section below aims to develop and extend this perspective.

Interactions between Social and Psychophysiological Processes

If social factors do impact on the links between psychophysiology and antisocial behavior, what is the nature of such interactions? Few people have investigated this issue, but the evidence available to date suggests that stronger and more consistent psychophysiology-antisocial behavior relationships may be found in those individuals who come from benign home backgrounds.[5,39] Evidence for this view is derived from both studies of resting HR and studies of SC activity.

With respect to resting HR, although HRL is generally lower in antisocial individuals, it is a particularly strong characteristic of antisocial adolescents from higher social classes and those from intact homes. For example, Raine and Venables[13] found lower HRL to be associated with antisocial behavior in adolescents from high social classes, but not in those from lower social classes. Similarly, Wadsworth[19] found that lower HRL at age 11 years predicted criminal behavior in adulthood in those from intact homes but not in those from broken homes. Maliphant[40] found particularly strong links between lower resting HRL and antisocial behavior in girls from privileged middle-class backgrounds attending private schools in England.

Regarding SC activity, a similar pattern of findings has emerged. Reduced SC conditioning characterizes antisocial adolescents from high but not low social classes.[41] Similarly, schizoid criminals from intact home environments show reduced SC orienting, whereas schizoid criminals from broken homes do not.[17] Similarly, criminals without a childhood history broken by parental absence and disharmony show poorer SC conditioning,[42] whereas "privileged" (high socioeconomic status) offenders who commit crimes of evasion show reduced SC arousal and reactivity.[43] Again, reduced SC arousal and reactivity in these studies is found particularly in antisocial individuals from benign home backgrounds.

One explanation for this pattern of results is that where the "social push" towards antisocial behavior is lower (high socioeconomic status, intact homes), psychophysiological determinants of antisocial behavior assume greater importance.[41] Conversely social causes of criminal behavior may be more important explanations of antisociality in those exposed to adverse early home conditions. In support of this proposition, Satterfield[44] found that in the higher social classes, biological high-risk subjects were up to 28 times more likely to be criminal than biologically low-risk subjects, whereas such rates were much lower in the lower social classes (sevenfold increase in crime in biologically at-risk subjects).

Although this biosocial perspective may be a plausible initial hypothesis, there are several other possible ways in which social and psychophysiological risk factors for antisocial behavior may interact. For example, it may be that antisocial behavior is greatest in those who have both psychophysiological and social risk factors. Future research in this area needs to (a) explore this latter possibility,

(b) attempt to confirm or refute the stronger psychophysiology-antisocial links in those from benign home backgrounds, and (c) map out precise biosocial interactions for violent crime, in particular, as opposed to antisocial behavior, in general.

STRESS AND LEARNING AS POSSIBLE DETERMINANTS OF REDUCED AUTONOMIC ACTIVITY

Elsewhere it has been suggested that dysfunction to the prefrontal cortex early in life may be one important determinant of reduced autonomic activity in antisocial individuals.[23] It is also possible that the environmental influence of experiencing environmental stress in early childhood results in reduced autonomic arousal. For example, coming from a broken home by age four years is associated with lower resting HR at age 11 years.[19] Experiencing stress, such as maternal separation or physical abuse at a very early stage in life, could conceivably inoculate the individual, making them more resistant to later life stress. At a prenatal level, it has been long known that stress during pregnancy in rodents results in offspring that are less emotionally reactive to stressful stimuli.[45,46] Children who have criminal parents have been found to have lower resting HR in at least two studies;[20,47] although this may reflect a genetic link, it is possible that parental criminality is a marker for high family stress that results in lower HR in the children. Antisocial individuals may have lower resting HR and be less fearful in a rest period prior to an experimental stimulation because, relative to the very harsh situations they have experienced throughout their lives, such an event is not particularly stressful. Conversely, highly socialized individuals who have generally been protected from life's stressors may be more reactive to a mild stressor.

It is also possible that the psychophysiological fearlessness observed in antisocial subjects, is, in part, a learnt phenomenon. For example, Fenz and Epstein[48] have argued that the low HR observed in experienced parachute jumpers is a learned response, whereas there have also been reports that watching violent films results in lowering of the HR by as much as 10–15 beats per minute.[49] Although the relatively high heritability of HR levels suggests that fearlessness in antisocial individuals may be partly genetically mediated, we must not discount the possibility that stressful experiences, desensitization experiences, and learning experiences may also contribute in important ways to the development of this psychophysiological trait. As such, the reduced resting heart rate shown in antisocial subjects may be modifiable.

TREATMENT AND PREVENTION IMPLICATIONS

What are the implications of the findings that disinhibited, aggressive, and antisocial children are characterized by autonomic underarousal? It was discussed above that some individuals may use violence to compensate for low arousal. It was also suggested that adolescents who are predisposed to becoming criminal, but who desist from adult crime, are characterized by particularly high levels of arousal. It is possible that such individuals could be trained to increase their arousal levels through biofeedback techniques. For example, there have been initial reports of the possible efficacy of using biofeedback to increase 15–18 Hz EEG activity in hyperactive children,[50,51] whereas a more recent pilot work has indicated that this technique shows short-term behavioral improvement with children with conduct problems.[52] However, this technique has not, to date, been applied to adolescents with low arousal who are showing tendencies towards aggression and antisocial behavior, and its efficacy still remains to be tested. In the context of a multimodal treatment package, it may nevertheless prove to be a useful addition.

It is clear that not everyone with low arousal becomes violent. Others with low arousal may alternatively obtain excitement and stimulation legally, for example, by joining the army, becoming a police officer, a politician, or a successful academic. What determines whether an individual with low arousal will become a violent offender or a successful academic is currently unknown. It seems reasonable to hypothesize, however, that individual factors, such as IQ and psychosocial/environmental factors (parental influences, peer influences, and school influences), could critically determine which route an underaroused violence-prone individual takes in life. Antisocial and violent individuals, although possessing important cognitive deficits, are also thought to have information-processing advantages over normal individuals in some circumscribed areas, such as selective attention and visuo-spatial constructive abilities.[39] Early interventions in the school or clinic could conceivably attempt to identify these "islets of abilities" in aggressive and antisocial adolescents, with a view to further developing these latent abilities, which, if fully developed, could provide the excitement and stimulation that antisocial adolescents often crave but rarely get in a traditional school curriculum not geared to their abilities and aptitudes, and that consequently results in boredom, low self-esteem, and rebellion.[53] It is critical that future research turns more towards examining the potential interaction between biological and environmental factors in furthering our understanding and preventing aggressive behavior in children.

SUMMARY

This paper reviews the autonomic psychophysiological correlates of antisocial and aggressive behavior in children and adolescents, outlines a biosocial perspective, and draws implications for treatment and prevention. Findings of studies on resting skin conductance and heart rate indicate that antisocial individuals are characterized by underarousal; these findings suggest that aggressive children may be stimulation seekers who are relatively fearless. Autonomic underarousal also typifies infants and young children with a disinhibited temperament that is thought to be a predisposition to juvenile delinquency and adult aggressive behavior. Deficits in the orienting response, a measure of attention allocation, also predisposes to later antisocial and criminal behavior. Initial studies have shown that particularly high levels of orienting, arousal, and conditionability may protect against crime development in those predisposed to such an outcome. From a biosocial standpoint, it is hypothesized that the psychophysiological correlates of antisocial and violent behavior may be greatest in those from more benign home backgrounds where the psychosocial push forward is relatively weaker. Alternatively, early environmental stress may underlie autonomic underarousal and hyporeactivity in antisocial individuals. Finally, it is possible that biofeedback, in combination with a multimodal treatment program, may be one benign intervention technique that may increase arousal and reduce aggression in underaroused antisocial children.

REFERENCES

1. DAWSON, M. E. 1990. Psychophysiology **27:** 243–255.
2. HARE, R. D. 1978. Electrodermal and cardiovascular correlates of psychopathy. *In* Psychopathic Behavior: Approaches to Research. R. D. Hare & D. Schalling, Eds.: 107–144. Wiley. New York.
3. MEDNICK, S. A., V. POLLACK, J. VOLAVKA & W. F. GABRIELLI. 1982. Biology and Violence. *In* Criminal Violence. M. Wolfgang & N. A. Weiner, Eds.: 21–80. Sage. Beverly Hills.
4. SIDDLE, D. A. T. & G. TRASLER. 1981. The Psychophysiology of psychopathic behavior. *In* Foundations of Psychosomatics. M. J. Christie & P. G. Mellett, Eds.: 283–303. Wiley. Chichester.
5. RAINE, A. 1988. Antisocial behavior and social psychophysiology. *In* Social Psychophysiology and Emotion: Theory and Clinical Application. H. Wagner, Ed.: 231–253. Wiley. London.
6. RAINE, A. 1993. The Psychopathology of Crime: Criminal Behavior as a Clinical Disorder. Academic Press. San Diego.
7. FOWLES, D. C. 1993. Electrodermal activity and antisocial behavior. *In* Electrodermal Activity: From Physiology to Psychology. J. C. Roy, W. Boucsein, D. C. Fowles & J. Gruzelier, Eds.: Plenum. New York.
8. McBURNETT, K. & B. B. LAHEY. 1994. Biological correlates of conduct disorder and antisocial behavior in children and adolescents. *In* Progress in Experimental Personality and Psychopathology Research. D. C. Fowles, Ed. Springer. New York.
9. RAINE, A. Autonomic nervous system activity and violence. *In* Neurobiologic Approaches to Clinical Aggression Research. D. Stoff & R. Cairns, Eds. Lawrence Erlbaum. In press.
10. RAINE, A. Psychophysiology and antisocial behavior. J. D. Master, J. Brieling & D. Stoff, Eds. Wiley. New York. In press.
11. RAINE, A., P. H. VENABLES & M. WILLIAMS. 1990a. Arch. Gen. Psychiatry **47:** 1003–1007.
12. VENABLES, P. H. & M. J. CHRISTIE. 1973. Mechanisms, instrumentation, recording techniques, and qualification of responses. *In* Electrodermal Activity in Psychological Research. W. F. Prokasy & D. C. Raskin, Eds. Wiley. New York.
13. RAINE & VENABLES. 1984. Psychophysiology **21:** 424–433.
14. RAINE. 1989. Int. J. Psychophysiol. **8:** 1–16.
15. SCERBO, A., A. RAINE, M. O'BRIEN, C. J. CHAN, C. RHEE & N. SMILEY. 1990. J. Abnorm. Child Psychol. **18:** 451–463.
16. QUAY, H. C. 1993. Dev. Psychopathol. **5:** 165–180.
17. RAINE, A. 1987. Int. J. Psychophysiol. **4:** 277–287.
18. OLIN, S. S., A. RAINE & S. A. MEDNICK. Childhood Behavior Precursors of Schizotypal Personality Disorder. In press.
19. WADSWORTH, M. E. J. 1976. Br. J. Criminology **16:** 245–256.
20. FARRINGTON, D. P. 1987. Implications of biological findings for criminological research. *In* The Causes of Crime: New Biological Approaches. S. A. Mednick, T. E. Moffitt & S. A. Stack, Eds.: 42–64. Cambridge University Press. Cambridge.
21. KINDLON, D. J., R. E. TREMBLAY, E. MEZZACAPPA, F. EARLS, D. LAURENT & B. SCHAAL. 1995. J. Am. Acad. Child Adolesc. Psychiatry **34:** 371–377.
22. GOTTMAN, J. M., N. S. JACOBSON, R. H. RUSHE, J. W. SHORT, J. BABCOCK, J. J. LA TAILLADE & J. WALTZ. 1995. J. Family Psychol. **9:** 227–248.
23. RAINE, A. autonomic nervous system activity and violence. *In* The Neurobiology of Clinical Aggression. D. M. Stoff & R. F. Cairns, Eds. Lawrence Erlbaum. In press.
24. COX, D., R. HALLAM, K. O'CONNOR & S. RACHMAN. 1983. Br. J. Psychol. **74:** 107–117.
25. O'CONNOR, K., R. HALLAM & S. RACHMAN. 1985. Br. J. Psychol. **76:** 187–197.
26. McMILLAN, T. M. & S. J. RACHMAN. 1987. Br. J. Psychol. **78:** 375–383.
27. EYSENCK, H. J. 1964. Crime and Personality. 1st edit. Methuen. London.
28. QUAY, H. C. 1965. Am. J. Psychiatry **122:** 180–183.
29. KAGAN, J. 1989. Am. Psychol. **44:** 668–674.

30. SNIDMAN, N., J. KAGAN & A. McQUILKIN. 1991. Psychophysiology **28:** 51.
31. FOX, N. A. 1989. Dev. Psychol. **25:** 364–372.
32. STIFTER, C. A. & N. A. FOX. 1990. Dev. Psychol. **26:** 582–588.
33. SCERBO, A., A. RAINE, P. H. VENABLES & S. A. MEDNICK. 1993. J. Abnorm. Child
     Psychol. **18:** 451–463.
34. CASPI, A., B. HENRY, R. O. McGEE, T. E. MOFFITT & P. A. SILVA. 1995. Child Dev.
     666: 55–68.
35. CASPI, A. & P. A. SILVA. Child Dev. In press.
36. RAINE, A., P. H. VENABLES & M. WILLIAMS. 1995. Am. J. Psychiatry. **152:** 1595–1600.
37. RAINE, A., P. H. VENABLES & M. WILLIAMS. Dev. Psychol. In press.
38. BRENNAN, P., A. RAINE, P. H. VENABLES & S. A. MEDNICK. 1994. Psychophysiology
     31: 30.
39. RAINE, A. & S. A. MEDNICK. 1989. Rev. Epidemiol. Sante Publique **37:** 515–524.
40. MALIPHANT, R., F. HUME & A. FURNHAM. 1990. J. Child Psychol. Psychiatry **31:**
     619–628.
41. RAINE, A. & P. H. VENABLES. 1981. Pers. Individ. Differ. **2:** 273–283.
42. HEMMING, J. H. 1981. Pers. Individ. Differ. **2:** 37–46.
43. BUIKHUISEN, W., E. H. M. BONTEKOE, C. D. PLAS-KORENHOFF & S. BUUREN. 1985.
     Int. J. Law and Psychiatry **7:** 301–313.
44. SATTERFIELD, J. H. 1987. Childhood diagnostic and neurophysiological predictors of
     teenage arrest rates: An eight-year prospective study. *In* The Causes of Crime: New
     Biological Approaches. S. A. Mednick, T. E. Moffitt & S. Stack, Eds. Cambridge
     University Press. Cambridge.
45. KEELEY, K. 1962. Science **143:** 44–45.
46. ADLER, R. & P. M. CONKLIN. 1963. Science **142:** 411–412.
47. VENABLES, P. H. 1987. Autonomic and central nervous system factors in criminal
     behavior. *In* The Causes of Crime: New Biological Approaches. S. A. Mednick,
     T. Moffitt & S. Stack. Eds.: 117–133. Cambridge University Press. Cambridge.
48. FENZ, W. D. & S. EPSTEIN. 1967. Psychosom. Med. **29:** 33–51.
49. CARRUTHERS, M. & P. TAGGART. 1973. Br. Med. J. **2:** 383–389.
50. LUBAR, J. F., M. O. SWARTWOOD, J. N. SWARTWOOD & P. H. O'DONNELL. 1995.
     Biofeedback Self-Regul. **20:** 83–99.
51. LUBAR, J. O. & LUBAR, J. F. 1984. Biofeedback Self-Regul. **9:** 1–23.
52. OTMER, S., S. F. OTMER & C. S. MARKS. 1996. Manuscript under review.
53. RAINE, A. & J. J. DUNKIN. 1990. **68:** 637–644.

Ethopharmacology of Aggression: Impact on Autonomic and Mesocorticolimbic Activity[a]

KLAUS A. MICZEK[b] AND WALTER TORNATZKY

Departments of Psychology, Psychiatry, and Pharmacology
Tufts University
Medford and Boston, Massachusetts

The rationale for studying aggressive behavior in nonhuman animal species builds on the premise that these behavior patterns have evolved. Aggressive behavior is present in all vertebrate species, and its occurrence should not be considered accidental or abnormal.[1] Yet, it is debatable whether or not a linear "scala naturae" applies to the evolution of social systems that extend from invertebrates to fish, birds, and mammals, including humans.[2] An important contribution of quantitative ethology to aggression research is the focus on the detailed facets of the ontogeny, structure, and function of aggressive behavior.[3,4] Two particularly neglected aspects of neurobiological research of aggressive behavior are the adaptive and maladaptive changes in autonomic and mesocorticolimbic aminergic and peptidergic systems that are induced by these behavior patterns.

QUANTITATIVE ETHOLOGY

A prerequisite to understanding the initiation, execution, and termination of aggressive interactions is a detailed account of each salient behavioral element as it occurs during the course of a social confrontation. Aggressive behavior patterns like all behavior consist of patterns in time. The sequential characteristics of aggressive behavior become apparent only upon closer scrutiny of the moment-to-moment interactions with each act, gesture, and display following another with predictable probability. "Investigations of behavior deal with sequences that, in contrast to bodily characteristics, are not always visible."[5]

Quantitative ethological studies in rodents and primates have shown that aggression occurs in "bursts" composed of highly predictable sequences composed of pursuits, threats, and attacks. In one series of studies, the onset, duration, and termination of more than 20,000 aggressive acts showed the social confrontations between a resident rat confronting an intruder. More than 85% of all aggressive acts followed each other within a few seconds and represented constituent parts of aggressive bursts, whereas the remaining aggressive acts were separated by longer intervals that constituted the "gaps" or interburst intervals.[6]

[a] The experimental research from the authors' laboratory was supported by USPHS research Grants AA 05122 and DA 02632.

[b] Address correspondence to K. A. Miczek, Ph.D., Research Building, Tufts University, 490 Boston Ave., Medford, MA 02155. Tel.: (617) 627-3414; fax: (617) 627-3939; e-mail: kmiczek@pearl.tufts.edu.

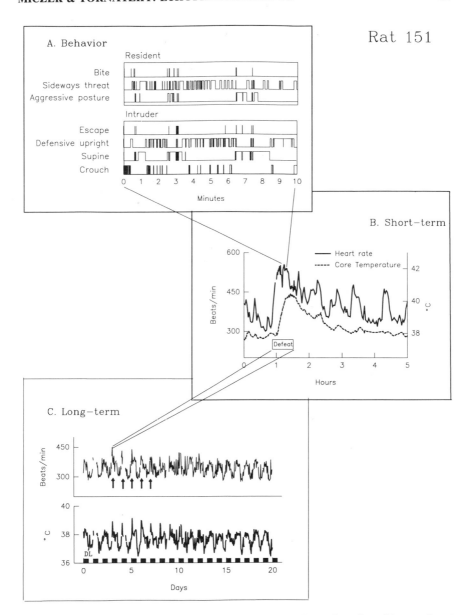

FIGURE 1. **A:** Agonistic behavior during the physical confrontation of a resident rat threatening and attacking an intruder. Bite, sideways threat, and aggressive posture are shown for the resident. Similarly, salient behavioral elements (escape, defensive upright, supine and crouch) of the intruder's behavior are identified as upward deflections from a timeline (in minutes). **B:** Short-term effects of being attacked and threatened on the intruder's heart rate (HR) and core-temperature (T_c) before, during, and after defeat (in hours) as obtained through telemetry. Defeat consisted of PRE = intruder in the resident's home cage, separated by an opaque divider for 10 min; DEF = physical interactions leading to defeat, maximally for 10 min or until intruder has been attacked 20 times; and POST = 10 min of intruder

At the mammalian level, the behavioral repertoire of aggressive interactions consists of several salient acts, postures, gestures, displays (including vocal, visual, and olfactory signals) that are emitted in a temporally organized fashion. This repertoire, often referred to as agonistic behavior, comprises offensive aggressive acts as well as defensive, submissive, and flight responses to aggression (FIG. 1 and ref. 7). There is considerable variation in these sequences, and the transition from one aggressive act to the next is not fixed, but rather it is characterized by a certain probability. A lag sequential analysis provides the means to quantify transition probabilities of one behavioral element to the next one.[8]

Research methodologies have been developed for the quantitative study of animal aggression. These methodologies have also been adapted for research with children.[9] The cardinal features are the accurate video and audio recording of aggressive encounters that permit the moment-to-moment analysis of all acts, gestures, and postures in real time as well as in slow motion in an unbiased manner (e.g., ref. 10). Additionally, vocal signals are recorded and analyzed, as they are synchronized with aggressive acts. These methodological advances allow an unambiguous assessment of the initiation, execution, and termination of aggressive interactions, and, additionally, permit an adequate measurement of nonaggressive behaviors so that the behavioral specificity of any potential intervention can be determined. An essential advantage of comprehensive quantitative ethological measurements of aggressive as well as nonaggressive behaviors in the same context is the comparative assessment of interventions targeting aggressive behavior versus other components in the individual's behavioral repertoire. The assessment of concurrent autonomic and neurochemical changes through telemetry and *in vivo* microdialysis makes it possible to characterize the comprehensive reaction pattern of the individual in anticipation of and in reaction to a salient social confrontation (see FIGURES 1 and 5).

AGGRESSION IMPACTS ON PHYSIOLOGICAL AND NEUROCHEMICAL FUNCTIONS

Aggressive interactions occur between individuals who are highly aroused and excited. Autonomic functions have been the focus on investigations into aggressive and emotional behavior for many decades (e.g., ref. 11). One aspect of this research has emphasized the large and long-lasting consequences of aggressive behavior on the "internal milieu" of autonomic and endocrine activity, even to the degree of causing pathological consequences (e.g., ref. 12). In order to characterize the consequences of aggression and to understand the underlying brain mechanisms, it is necessary to monitor behavioral, autonomic, and neural events in anticipation, during, and after aggressive encounters in all combatants. In experimental prepara-

---

activity in the resident's cage after the defeat with the resident removed; thereafter, the intruder was placed into his own home cage. Sampling period for HR and T_c: 20 s during resident-intruder confrontation, and 5 min in the intruders home cage. **C:** Long-term effects of five consecutive defeats on the magnitude and rhythmicity of heart rate and core temperature as mean values per hour (sampling period: 5 min). Black horizontal bars denote dark periods of the light cycle; arrows point to the intruder's defeats. (Tornatzky & Miczek.[15] With permission from *Physiology and Behavior*.)

tions with male and female laboratory rats, it is possible to detect how submissive and defensive reactions and ultrasonic distress calls are more readily displayed with increasing experience in aggressive encounters.[13-17] This experience-dependent behavioral augmentation suggests sensitized defensive responses.

Large and sustained increases in telemetered heart rate, blood pressure, and core temperature, as well as elevations in plasma levels of the stress hormones corticosterone and ACTH (FIG. 1), accompany these behavioral reactions of the intruder rat to the threats and attacks by an aggressive opponent.[13,18,19] It is particularly noteworthy that neither autonomic nor behavioral responses showed evidence for habituation after repeated weekly confrontations over a three-month period. FIGURE 2 portrays the anticipatory and reactive tachycardia and hyperthermia accompanying the first and the fifth social confrontation.[19]

Ultradian Rhythms Entrain as a Result of Aggressive Encounters

When the subordinate animal is in the presence of an aggressive animal, the ensuing behavioral constraints can lead, in some animals, to pathological changes in cardiovascular, endocrine, and immune system functioning, and eventual death.[20-26]

Even transient daily aggressive episodes, occurring during the course of five consecutive days, resulted in disrupted circadian rhythmicity of heart rate and core temperature in the rat that was the target of aggression (FIG. 1 C and ref. 15). Circadian rhythmicity was quantified by cosinor analysis, a powerful technique that fits a cosinor function by the least-squares method to the time series of heart rate and core temperature data.[27-30] FIGURE 3 illustrates the decrease in circadian amplitude that persisted for 10 days after the last defeat. Recently, even a single defeat was shown to be sufficient to induce these long-term changes in circadian amplitude.[31]

Ultradian rhythms of heart rate or core temperature that have periods shorter than the 24-hour light cycle also emerge during and after repeated defeats in aggressive encounters (FIG. 3A). A prominent feature of the circadian and ultradian rhythms of heart rate and core temperature in the defeated animal is their desynchronization.[30] Desynchronization of physiological rhythms may indicate maladaptive adjustment to adverse environmental demands.[15,30,32,33]

In rats and mice, physiological reactions in winners and losers of aggressive encounters can be differentiated, in that losers show a more prolonged elevation in plasma corticosterone levels than winners.[34-36] In dominant tree shrews the day/night variation of telemetered heart rate was not changed after the second day of continuous cohabitation with a subordinate conspecific, whereas the heart rate of the subordinate remained elevated for many days.[20] The degree to which animals can exert behavioral control over the stressful situation seems to influence the physiological consequences of those situations.[37]

With the aid of nonlinear multioscillatory cosinor analysis, it is possible to quantify the synchronization and the intensity of circadian and ultradian components of heart rate and core temperature rhythms.[30,38] Such analysis reveals profound changes in the thermoregulatory and cardiovascular rhythms of rats who attack and threaten an opponent in repeated encounters.[39] If these aggressive confrontations occur at the same time every day, the heart rate and temperature readings of the resident animal begin to rise prior to the encounter and peak with the arrival of the intruder. In FIGURE 4 it can be seen that the hemicircadian rhythm typically peaks between 3 and 5 hours after lights off (08.00 h). When the

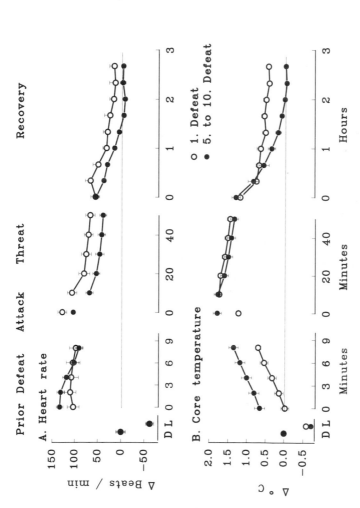

FIGURE 2. The effects of the first and repeated defeats on the intruder rat's time course of autonomic reactions before, during, and after a social confrontation. The deviations of (A) heart rate and (B) core temperature from the subject's baseline means recorded on the previous day during the dark portion of the light cycle (C) are given. The mean and SEM of the reactions of 7 rats are portrayed for consecutive 2-, 10-, and 20-min intervals recorded prior to defeat, during the threat encounter, and during recovery in the intruder's home cage, respectively. Reactions during the light portion of the cycle (L) and during the 10 min after the beginning of the attack encounter are based on the means during these periods. The reactions of every intruder prior to and after the first defeat are compared with the mean of its own reactions during confrontations 5 to 10. (Tornatzky & Miczek.[19] With permission from *Physiology and Behavior*.)

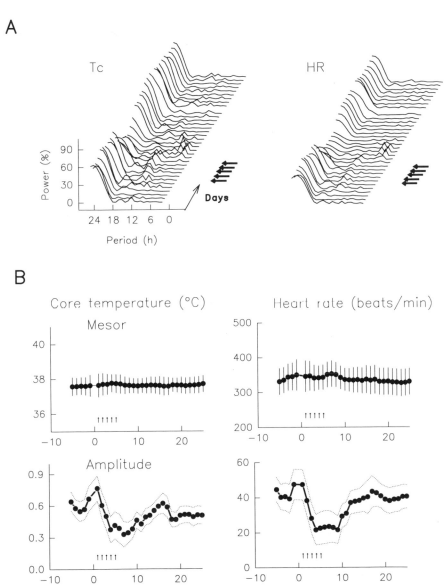

FIGURE 3. Changes in ultradian and circadian rhythmicity of the heart rate (HR) and core temperature (T_c) time series during the experiment exemplified for rat 151. **A:** Circadian and ultradian rhythm. The spectral content for HR and T_c expressed as a proportion of the variability explained by the cosine best fitting a 3-day data span were computed for periods ranging from 1 to 24 h. Daily values were obtained by shifting the starting point of the time series by 1 day. **B:** Circadian rhythm. The HR and T_c mesor and amplitude of the best fitting 24 h cosinor are plotted together with the 95% confidence limits for the consecutive days. The occurrences of the defeats are indicated by arrows. (Tornatzky & Miczek.[15] With permission from *Physiology and Behavior*.)

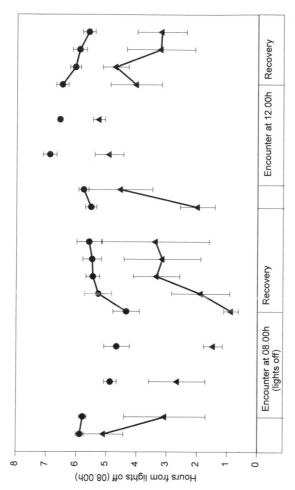

FIGURE 4. Deviation of circadian (circles) and hemicircadian (triangles) phases in telemetered core temperature (T_c) from lights off at 08.00 h. Data points represent the result of multioscillator cosinor analysis of a 3-day period (mean ± SEM). The encounters consisted of a 3-week period when resident rats (n = 4) were provoked by an intruder male for 20 minutes at the specified time point once a day for 5 days a week. The acrophases calculated for the time period of the encounters are based on data recorded during the last 72 hours of the week, when no experimental manipulation was scheduled.

resident confronts an intruder daily at 08.00 h, the peak of the hemicircadian rhythm advances to 08.00 h, and the large variability in this rhythm is reduced. When the aggressive encounter occurs at 12.00 h (*i.e.*, 4 hours after lights off), the peak of the rhythm does not move, but again the variability is reduced. A similar, though less pronounced change can also be seen with the circadian rhythm. As the circadian and ultradian rhythms were altered against a background of a stable circadian Zeitgeber (*i.e.*, the light cycle), the changes could be interpreted as evidence for physiological preparation for the aggressive episode. The precise synchronization of the resident's thermoregulatory and cardiovascular activity to the anticipated social confrontation suggests a successful adjustment to environmental demands. Neural mechanisms for these physiological systems may be modulated by salient life events, such as aggressive encounters, resulting in the anticipatory homeostatic responses. It is important to identify the central neurochemical mechanisms that underlie these shifts and reorganizations within the ultradian and circadian framework.

Aggressive Behavior Causes Neuroadaptive Changes: Tolerance and Sensitization

Neurobiological studies of aggressive behavior patterns have implicated a wide range of fast-acting excitatory and inhibitory amino acids such as glutamate and GABA, slower acting catecholamine and indolamines, acetylcholine, and neuropeptides, as well as long-acting steroids (*e.g.*, refs. 40, 41). Although none of these substances can be considered the single "aggressive neurohumor" (*e.g.*, ref. 42), all of them modulate aggressive behaviors.[40,41,43] Significant neuroadaptive changes are induced by critical and stressful life experiences (*e.g.*, refs. 44, 45), and being the target of aggressive behavior is one such critical behavioral event that renders the individual tolerant as well as sensitized with regard to several neurotransmitter systems. It has become apparent during the last decade how tolerance- and sensitization-like processes in brain opioid peptides and catecholamines are initiated by repeated aggressive behavior and particularly by being subjected to aggressive behavior.

Defeat in a social confrontation can result in naloxone-reversible analgesia that shows cross-tolerance to opiate analgesia.[46-48] This opiate-like analgesia appears to be due to the activation of neural endogenous opioid activity, inasmuch as microinjections of naloxone into the periaqueductal gray area (PAG) and the arcuate nucleus of the hypothalamus block the analgesic effect of social defeat.[49] After having been defeated repeatedly in confrontations with an aggressive resident, intruder rats become tolerant to the defeat-induced analgesia and when challenged with the opioid receptor antagonist, naloxone, exhibit opiate withdrawal-like symptoms.[50] By contrast, potentiated opiate analgesia is seen when the mouse or rat is in the process of being threatened by an aggressive oponent; however, within 24 h after the social defeat, tolerance to opiate analgesia develops.[13] When subjected to threats by an aggressive opponent, but protected from potentially injurious attacks, male as well as female rats exhibit potentiated opiate analgesia that is reversed by mu- and delta-receptor-specific antagonists acting in the PAG,[51] (Vivian and Miczek, in preparation). Specific ligand binding to mu opioid receptors is seen after being defeated in a single aggressive encounter.[52] These results point to a profound impact of the stress arising from social confrontations on the synthesis and release of enkephalins as well as on the regulation of mu and delta opioid receptors.

The expression of c-fos, an immediate early gene (IEG), is a valid marker of neuronal activation. The protein cFOS, the product of this IEG, increases in different brain regions in response to a variety of "stressors," among which is also social stress. During the acute experience of social stress in an experimental preparation with laboratory rats, even while the threatened intruder was protected from potentially injurious attacks, cFOS-labeled cells in the PAG were significantly increased. Even when exposed with a 24-h delay to the cues of a previous defeat, the number of cFOS-staining cells in the PAG is markedly increased.[53] Three hours after the social confrontation, when cFOS expression has subsided, it is possible to detect large increases in the density of enkephalin-containing axons in the PAG. These results highlight the long-lasting regulatory changes in PAG neurons, some of which contain enkephalin that are initiated by social confrontations.

More recently, our studies on early intermediate gene expression were extended to another animal species, the mouse. After being threatened, but protected from potentially injurious attack bites, mice without fighting experience contained increased FOS-positive cell nuclei in the PAG, locus caeruleus, and raphe nuclei in comparison to saline-treated or unstressed mice.[54] The expression of early intermediate cFOS can be engendered within 60 min of an aggressive encounter. It would be intriguing to learn how pain-inhibiting enkephalinergic processes are activated by the cFOS expression in socially stressed individuals.

In addition to the opioid potentiation and tolerance-like processes, it is apparent that as little as one encounter with an attacking and threatening opponent can render the individual sensitized to mesocorticolimbic dopamine-mediated psychomotor effects. It has now been recognized that seemingly divergent neuroplastic changes can occur concurrently, with sensitization developing to one effect of a drug and habituation or tolerance to other effects.[55] The mesocorticolimbic dopamine system is the target of many sensitizing agents such as psychomotor stimulant drugs and environmental stressors (e.g., ref. 56). In an ongoing series of experiments with laboratory mice, it has become evident that amphetamine and cocaine challenges produce a larger motor activation in individuals who have been subjected to a confrontation with an aggressive opponent several days previously. The peak time for this sensitizing response to amphetamine and cocaine is around one week after the social stress experience. By contrast, when the psychomotor challenge is conducted immediately after the confrontation, the activating effects of cocaine and amphetamine are blunted. The method of pharmacologically challenging an individual represents a reversible and neurochemically selective probe for uncovering neuroadaptive changes that are initiated by highly significant events such as the threat of being attacked. Direct evidence for the activation of the mesocorticolimbic dopamine system is now being accrued by *in vivo* microdialysis measurements.

BRAIN DOPAMINE AND AGGRESSIVE BEHAVIOR

When confronted with an aggressive opponent, dopamine, dihydroxyphenylacetic acid (DOPAC), and homovanillic acid (HVA) are significantly elevated in the nucleus accumbens, as measured concurrently by *in vivo* microdialysis in laboratory rats.[57] These increments are severalfold larger and longer lasting than those produced by exploring an unfamiliar environment, so-called novelty stress (FIG. 5). Due to the significant role of forebrain dopamine in motor activation, it is noteworthy that the socially stressed intruder rat is behaviorally restricted in its movements, that is, exhibits crouch postures and orients to the threatening

A.

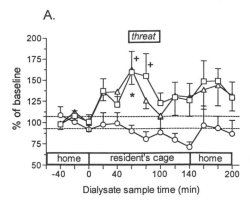

B.

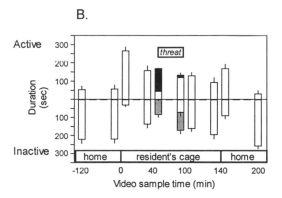

FIGURE 5. Social defeat stress. **A:** Dopamine concentrations in the nucleus accumbens, prefrontal cortex, and lateral striatum of socially defeated rats before, during, and after the threat of being subjected to aggressive behavior. Dopamine concentrations are expressed as percent of baseline values, as obtained in the undisturbed home cage of the animal. Samples were gathered every 20 min. Plus signs denote $p < 0.05$ compared to baseline values; asterisks denote $p < 0.05$ compared to values obtained from rats in the novel cage. -□-, nuclear accumbens; -△- prefrontal cortex; ○, striatum. **B:** Behavior samples from socially defeated rats before, during, and after the threat of being defeated.[57] ■, tracking; ▨, crouching.

opponent, whereas its dopamine in the nucleus accumbens septi and medial prefrontal cortex is greatly elevated. The dissociation between motor activation on the one hand, and increased dopamine activity in the nucleus accumbens and intracellular dopamine metabolism on the other is confirmed by voltametric studies of dopamine signals during defensive behavior.[58] The increased extracellular dopamine concentrations, presumably reflecting increased release, in mesocorticolimbic terminations of dopaminergic projections appear time locked with the exposure to a range of aversive events, and this activation is particularly large and long lasting during behavioral responses to significant events such as the threats of an aggressive opponent. These observations extend previous postmortem studies of limbic dopamine that were limited to a single measurement at a specific time point after the behavior had already occurred.[59,60]

In current *in vivo* microdialysis studies of aggressive rats, large and long-lasting increases in dopamine are measured in nucleus accumbens in the immediate period before, during, and after episodes of threat and attack toward an intruding opponent.[61] The behavioral history of aggressive behavior is established in a series of confrontations with an intruder, and, at the time of the ongoing dialysate sampling, the aggressive rat is autonomically and behaviorally activated prior to the imminent aggressive encounter. It is tempting to interpret the synchrony between the increased dopamine release and the behavioral and autonomic activation in the initiation of aggressive behavior as anticipatory or preparatory events.

It is informative to examine the increased dopamine release in the mesocorticolimbic systems of aggressive resident rats and intruder rats that react to aggressive threats in a broader behavioral context. Rapid increases in the extracellular dopamine in the region of the nucleus accumbens are also seen in male and female rats that are about to initiate copulatory behavior or in female hamsters that display an immobile lordotic posture when rendered sexually receptive.[62–65] These increases in accumbens dopamine are maintained for the duration of the entire copulatory series, accompanying both the phasic elements of copulation as well as the tonic modes of behavior. Most information on increased extracellular dopamine in the nucleus accumbens has been gathered in the context of self-administration of drugs of abuse, such as cocaine, heroin, and alcohol (e.g., refs. 66–68). The considerable evidence on increased dopamine release in the mesocorticolimbic system in anticipation and during responses to significant events, both intensely rewarding and aversive, point to an important role of this forebrain mechanism in focusing on these events and in engaging in appropriate response strategies.[69] Aggressive behavior as well as the response to aggression share with a range of other significant behavioral events a large and long-lasting activation of the mesocorticolimbic dopamine system. The implications for pharmacotherapeutic interventions are that dopaminergic drugs, including those acting on receptor subtypes, exert considerably pervasive effects.

The mesocorticolimbic dopamine measurements during aggressive behavior, responses to aggression, and a broad range of significant life events ranging from sexual behavior, food intake, and drug self-administration should prompt a reevaluation of the pharmacotherapeutic management of aggressive individuals with drugs that target dopamine transmission.[41,70] It has become evident from studies with laboratory rodents and primates that the suppression of aggressive behavior by the typical dopamine-receptor blocking neuroleptic drugs is embedded in a profile of a pervasive suppression of a broad range of active behavior. Early preclinical studies have already demonstrated that phenothiazines and butyrophenones lack behavioral specificity in decreasing aggressive behavior when compared to nonaggressive behavior. In a recently developed experimental protocol, it is possible to assess concurrently the "cost" of behavioral sedation in comparison to the "benefit" of antiaggressive effects after pharmacological intervention.[71] In this procedure with laboratory mice, newer dopaminergic receptor antagonists, Sch23390 and raclopride, which selectively target either D_1 or D_2 subtypes, potently reduced conditioned performance, whereas the same doses decreased attack bites and threats only moderately, if at all (FIG. 6). More detailed analysis of the drug effects show a disruption of the temporal and sequential patterning by D_2 receptor antagonists rather than an inhibition of motor activity. It is noteworthy that under the same conditions indirect and direct dopamine receptor agonists also disrupt conditioned performance and decrease aggressive behavior.[71,72] The mechanism by which dopamine agonists and antagonists at the D_2 receptor subtype decrease aggressive behavior comprise not only the slowing of motor functions but also disorganizing effects on temporally and sequentially organized behavioral sequences.

As previously concluded,[41] the available preclinical data from various experimental preparations in laboratory rodents and primates have highlighted the importance of brain dopamine systems and the dopamine D_2 receptor subtype in several types of aggressive behavior and, at the same time, have demonstrated no specific-

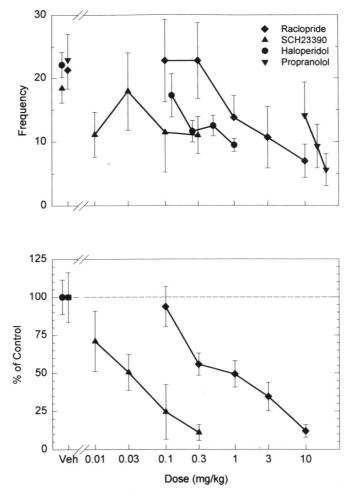

FIGURE 6. Top: The dose-dependent effects of Sch23390, raclopride, haloperidol, and propanolol on the frequency of attacks by resident mice toward intruding opponents during 5-min confrontations. Bottom: The dose-dependent effects of Sch23390 and raclopride on conditioned performance as maintained by a fixed interval schedule of reinforcement according to the protocol by Miczek and Haney.[71]

ity of these systems in the neurobiological mechanisms for aggressive and defensive behaviors.

BENZODIAZEPINE-GABA$_A$ RECEPTORS AND AGGRESSION

GABA systems have been studied for their role in aggressive behavior for several decades in several rodent species.[73–79] Historically, GABA systems have not been the target of intensive developments for potentially pharmacotherapeutic agents with ultimate application in pathologically aggressive individuals. This is not altogether surprising, inasmuch as GABA is ubiquitous in the brain, being the neurotransmitter for about one third of all synapses. This implies that any substance affecting GABA will lack specificity.

The discovery of different types of GABA receptors and of allosteric changes in the $GABA_A$ receptor complex due to modulatory action by benzodiazepines, barbiturates, picrotoxin, neuroactive steroids, and alcohol fundamentally altered the possibilities for specific roles of GABA systems through modifying aggressive behavior (e.g., refs. 80, 81). The most established lines of evidence implicating the $GABA_A$ receptor complex in the modulation of aggressive behavior derive from the closely similar profiles of effects by benzodiazepines, barbiturates, and alcohol on dominance and territorial and maternal aggressive behavior (see, for review ref. 82). Decreased binding by the benzodiazepine antagonist, flumazenil, and decreased muscimol-activated chloride flux characterized the cortical tissue of mice that had been selected to be highly aggressive for more than 30 generations.[83] Full agonists at the benzodiazepine receptor exert a significant and behaviorally specific effect on aggressive and emotional behaviors.[82] In isolated mice, acute administration of benzodiazepines increases aggressive behavior toward an opponent, and higher doses decrease this behavior.[84,85] In dominant rats, a similar dose-dependent biphasic pattern of effects by chlordiazepoxide and diazepam on the frequency of attacks and threats are observed.[86,87] Dominant monkeys, when confronting a rival male, display more frequent aggressive threats and vocal responses after administration of chlordiazepoxide.[88] This biphasic pattern of increasing aggressive behavior at low doses and decreasing it at higher doses characterizes benzodiazepines, barbiturates, and alcohol in various animal species and situations (FIG. 7; see, for review, ref. 89).

During the last decade it has become apparent that C21 steroids can modulate the $GABA_A$ receptor complex. Neuropharmacological evidence demonstrates the positive allosteric modulation of naturally occurring metabolites of progesterone, such as allopregnanolone (5α-pregnan-3α-ol-20-one).[90–92] For example, allopregnanolone and the synthetic steroid, alphaxalone, enhance muscimol binding and muscimol-activated chloride flux.[93–95] Allopregnanolone and alphaxolone also share with benzodiazepines, barbiturates, and ethanol similar anxiolytic, analgesic, anticonvulsant, and anesthetic effects in various animal tests.[96–106]

In current experimental work with $GABA_A$-active steroids, allopregnanolone showed a profile of effects on aggression that is quite similar to those for benzodiazepines and ethanol.[107] Acute administration of lower doses of allopregnanolone to male resident mice produced increases in attack and threat behavior toward an intruder, whereas reduced aggressive behavior resulted from the sedative doses of this steroid.[108] Although emphasizing considerable differences in potency, FIGURE 7 highlights the similarities in the dose effect curves of ethanol, diazepam, and allopregnanolone in mice and rats. It appears that, so far, drugs that positively modulate the $GABA_A$ receptor complex engender characteristic dose-dependent biphasic effects on aggressive behavior.[107]

CONCLUSIONS

An understanding of aggressive behavior at the neurobiological level needs to take into account the salient behavioral features. Here, the burst-like, episodic

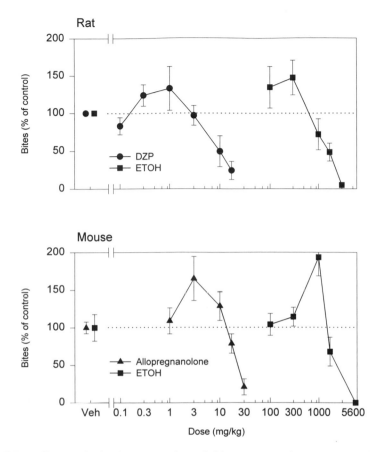

FIGURE 7. Changes in the frequency of attack bites, expressed as a percent of control (100% = control, dashed horizontal line), as a function of dose of diazepam (DZN) and ethanol (ETOH) in resident rats confronting an intruder (top), and of allopregnanolone and ethanol (ETOH) in resident mice confronting an intruder (bottom). Vertical lines in the data points indicate ±1 SEM. (Miczek *et al.*[107] With permission from Plenum Publishing.)

temporal characteristics of aggressive behavior are highlighted as well as the sequential structure of aggressive episodes, as revealed in quantitative ethological studies with laboratory rodents. The impact of aggressive episodes on the rhythmicity of autonomic functions emphasizes the disruptive effects on circadian rhythms and the emergent prominence of ultradian rhythms that entrain to the time of the aggressive encounter. In fact, aggressive and defensive responses profoundly alter autonomic activities as well as ongoing neurochemical events throughout the neuroaxis, but prominently in the mesocorticolimbic system. The response to a single aggressive episode is capable of initiating early intermediate gene expression in brain regions that are important in opioid-mediated pain inhibition. Particularly informative are the large and long-lasting increases in mesocorticolimbic dopamine systems that accompany the preparation for and response to aggressive encounters. These systems appear activated during an individual's focus on salient life events that are either intensely rewarding or aversive, and in the organization of appropriate behavior patterns, among which aggressive and defensive behaviors are but examples. Pharmacological modulation of forebrain dopamine systems and their receptor subtypes potently affects aggressive behaviors in concert with several other biologically important activities. The pharmacological tools for modulating different sites on the $GABA_A$ receptor complex have been expanded from benzodiazepines, barbiturates, and ethanol to neuroactive steroids that share a common profile of increasing and decreasing aggressive behavior in a dose-dependent manner, and potentiating each others effects. It now appears possible to develop a pharmacological intervention strategy that targets the perception of provocative events, the initiation of aggressive behavior, the patterning and execution of these behaviors, or the termination of aggressive episodes.

ACKNOWLEDGMENTS

We are grateful to Drs. J. F. DeBold, J. Cole, M. Haney, D. Harper, E. Nikulina, J. T. Sopko, J. Tidey, A. M. M. van Erp, J. A. Vivian, and E. M. Weerts for their excellent assistance.

REFERENCES

1. SCOTT, J. P. 1958. Aggression. The University of Chicago Press. Chicago.
2. WILSON, E. O. 1974. Sociobiology. The Belknap Press. Cambridge.
3. HUNTINGFORD, F. A. & A. K. TURNER. 1987. Animal Conflict. Chapman and Hall. London.
4. ARCHER, J. 1988. The Behavioural Biology of Aggression. Cambridge University Press. Cambridge.
5. EIBL-EIBESFELDT, I. 1970. Ethology. The Biology of Behavior. Holt, Rinehart and Winston. New York.
6. MICZEK, K. A., E. M. WEERTS, W. TORNATZKY, J. F. DeBOLD & T. M. VATNE. 1992. Psychopharmacology **107:** 551–563.
7. SCOTT, J. P. & E. FREDERICSON. 1951. Physiol. Zool. **24:** 273–309.
8. VAN HOOFF, J. A. R. A. M. 1982. Categories and sequences of behavior: Methods of description and analysis. *In* Handbook of Methods in Nonverbal Behavior Research. K. R. Scherer & P. Ekman, Eds.: 362–439. Cambridge University Press. Cambridge.
9. SACKETT, G. P. 1987. Observing Behavior: Application of Observational/Ethological Methods. University Park Press. Baltimore.
10. MICZEK, K. A. 1982. Ethological analysis of drug action on aggression, defense and defeat. *In* Behavioral Models and the Analysis of Drug Action. M. Y. Spiegelstein & A. Levy, Eds.: 225–239. Elsevier. Amsterdam.
11. CANNON, W. B. 1953. Bodily Changes in Pain, Hunger, Fear and Rage (2nd ed). Charles T. Banford. Boston.
12. SAPOLSKY, R. M. 1992. Neuroendocrinology of the stress response. *In* Behavioral Endocrinology, J. B. Becker, S. M. Breedlove & D. Crews, Eds.: 287–325. MIT Press. Cambridge, MA.
13. MICZEK, K. A., M. L. THOMPSON & W. TORNATZKY. 1991. Subordinate animals: Behavioral and physiological adaptations and opioid tolerance. *In* Stress: Neurobiology and Neuroendocrinology. M. R. Brown, G. F. Koob & C. Rivier, Eds.: 323–357. Marcel Dekker. New York.

14. MICZEK, K. A., W. TORNATZKY & J. A. VIVIAN. 1991. Ethology and neuropharmacology: Rodent ultrasounds. *In* Animal Models in Psychopharmacology. B. Olivier, J. Mos & J. L. Slangen, Eds.: 409–427. Birkhauser. Basel.
15. TORNATZKY, W. & K. A. MICZEK. 1993. Physiol. Behav. **53:** 983–993.
16. TORNATZKY, W. & K. A. MICZEK. 1995. Psychopharmacology **121:** 135–144.
17. HANEY, M. & K. A. MICZEK. 1993. J. Comp. Psychol. **107:** 373–379.
18. MEEHAN, W. P., W. TORNATZKY & K. A. MICZEK. 1995. Physiol. Behav. **58:** 81–88.
19. TORNATZKY, W. & K. A. MICZEK. 1994. Psychopharmacology **116:** 346–356.
20. VON HOLST, D. 1985. Coping behaviour and stress physiology in male tree shrews. *In* Experimental Behavioral Ecology and Sociobiology (Vol. 31). B. Hoelldobler & M. Lindauer, Eds. **31:** 461–470. Gustav Fischer. Stuttgart.
21. DESJARDINS, C., J. A. MARUNIAK & F. H. BRONSON. 1973. Science **182:** 939–941.
22. ELY, D. L. 1981. Physiol. Behav. **26:** 655–661.
23. LUCIANO, D. & R. LORE. 1975. J. Comp. Physiol. Psychol. **88:** 917–923.
24. SPENCER, S. R. & G. N. CAMERON. 1983. Behav. Ecol. Sociobiol. **13:** 27–36.
25. BARNETT, S. A. 1975. The Rat. A Study in Behavior. University of Chicago Press. Chicago.
26. SACHSER, N. & C. LICK. 1991. Physiol. Behav. **50:** 83–90.
27. NELSON, W., Y. L. TONG, J.-K. LEE & F. HALBERG. 1979. Chronobiologia **6:** 305–323.
28. MINORS, D. S. & J. M. WATERHOUSE. 1988. Psychoneuroendocrinology **13:** 443–464.
29. HALBERG, F. 1980. Implications for biological rhythms for clinical practice. *In* Neuroendocrinology. D. T. Krieger, Eds.: 109–117. Sinauer Associates. Sunderland, Mass.
30. HARPER, D. G., W. TORNATZKY & K. A. MICZEK. 1996. Physiol. Behav. **59:** 409–419.
31. MEERLO, P., S. F. DE BOER, J. M. KOOLHAAS, S. DAAN & R. H. VAN DEN HOOFDAKKER. 1996. Physiol. Behav. **59:** 735–739.
32. WOLLNIK, F. 1992. Pharmacol. Biochem. Behav. **43:** 549–561.
33. REILLY, T. 1990. Biomed. Eng. (Berlin) **18:** 165–179.
34. BRONSON, F. H. 1973. Physiol. Behav. **10:** 947–951.
35. BRAIN, P. F. 1980. Adaptive aspects of hormonal correlates of attack and defense in laboratory mice: A study in ethobiology. *In* Progress in Brain Research: Adaptive Capabilities of the Nervous System. P. S. McConnell, G. T. Boer, H. J. Romijn & N. E. van der Poll, Eds. **53:** 391–414. Elsevier North-Holland Biomedical. Amsterdam.
36. SCHUURMAN, T. 1980. Hormonal correlates of agonistic behavior in adult male rats. *In* Progress in Brain Research: Adaptive Capabilities of the Nervous System. P. S. McConnel, G. J. Boer, H. J. Romijn & N. E. van der Poll, Eds. **53:** 415–420. Elsevier Biomedical Press. Amsterdam.
37. HENRY, J. P., P. M. STEPHENS & D. L. ELY. 1986. J. Hypertens. **4:** 687–697.
38. TEICHER, M. H. & N. I. BARBER. 1990. Comput. Biomed. Res. **23:** 283–295.
39. COLE, J. C., W. TORNATZKY, D. G. HARPER & K. A. MICZEK. 1995. Soc. Neurosci. Abstr. **21:** 700.
40. MICZEK, K. A., M. HANEY, J. TIDEY, J. VIVIAN & E. WEERTS. 1994. Neurochemistry and pharmacotherapeutic management of violence and aggression. *In* Understanding and Preventing Violence: Biobehavioral Influences on Violence. A. J. Reiss, K. A. Miczek & J. A. Roth, Eds. **2:** 244–514. National Academy Press. Washington, DC.
41. MICZEK, K. A., E. M. WEERTS, M. HANEY & J. TIDEY. 1994. Neurosci. Biobehav. Rev. **18:** 97–110.
42. EICHELMAN, B. & N. B. THOA. 1973. Biol. Psychiatry **6:** 143–164.
43. EICHELMAN, B. 1992. Arch. Gen. Psychiatry **49:** 488–492.
44. ANTELMAN, S. M., A. J. EICHLER, C. A. BLACK & D. KOCAN. 1980. Science **207:** 329–331.
45. KALIVAS, P. W. & J. STEWART. 1991. Brain Res. Rev. **16:** 223–244.
46. MICZEK, K. A., M. L. THOMPSON & L. SCHUSTER. 1982. Science **215:** 1520–1522.
47. MICZEK, K. A., M. L. THOMPSON & L. SHUSTER. 1986. Analgesia following defeat in an aggressive encounter: Development of tolerance and changes in opioid receptors. *In* Stress-induced Analgesia. D. D. Kelly, Ed. **467:** 14–29. Annals of the New York Academy of Sciences. New York.
48. MICZEK, K. A. & J. T. WINSLOW. 1987. Psychopharmacology **92:** 444–451.

49. MICZEK, K. A., M. L. THOMPSON & L. SHUSTER. 1985. Psychopharmacology 87: 39–42.
50. MICZEK, K. A. & M. L. THOMPSON. 1984. Analgesia resulting from defeat in a social confrontation: The role of endogenous opioids in brain. In Modulation of Sensorimotor Activity during Altered Behavioural States. R. Bandler, Ed.: 431–456. Alan R. Liss. New York.
51. HANEY, M. & K. A. MICZEK. 1995. Psychopharmacology 121: 204–212.
52. KÜLLING, P., H.-R. FRISCHKNECHT, A. PASI, P. G. WASER & B. SIEGFRIED. 1988. Brain Res. 450: 237–246.
53. COHEN, C. A., K. A. MICZEK & R. M. KREAM. Brain Res. In press.
54. NIKULINA, E. M., J. E. MARCHAND, K. A. MICZEK & R. KREAM. 1995. Soc. Neurosci. Abstr. 21: 1954.
55. STEWART, J. & A. BADIANI. 1993. Behav. Pharmacol. 4: 289–312.
56. SORG, B. A. & P. W. KALIVAS. 1991. Brain Res. 559: 29–36.
57. TIDEY, J. W. & K. A. MICZEK. 1996. Brain Res. 721: 140–149.
58. LOUILOT, A., M. LEMOAL & H. SIMON. 1986. Brain Res. 397: 395–400.
59. HANEY, M., K. NODA, R. KREAM & K. A. MICZEK. 1990. Aggressive Behav. 16: 259–270.
60. PUGLISI-ALLEGRA, S. & S. CABIB. 1990. Aggressive Behav. 16: 271–284.
61. VAN ERP, A. M. M. & K. A. MICZEK. 1995. Soc. Neurosci. Abstr. 19: 1702.
62. PFAUS, J. G., G. DAMSMA, G. G. NOMIKOS, D. G. WENKSTERN, C. D. BLAHA, A. G. PHILLIPS & H. C. FIBIGER. 1990. Brain Res. 530: 345–348.
63. MAS, M., J. L. GONZALEZ-MORA, A. LOUILOT, C. SOLE & T. GUADALUPE. 1990. Neurosci. Lett. 110: 303–308.
64. FUMERO, B., J. R. FERNANDEZVERA, J. L. GONZALEZMORA & M. MAS. 1994. Brain Res. 662: 233–239.
65. MEISEL, R. L., D. M. CAMP & T. E. ROBINSON. 1993. Behav. Brain Res. 55: 151–157.
66. PETTIT, H. O. & J. B. JUSTICE JR. 1989. Pharmacol. Biochem. Behav. 34: 899–904.
67. WEISS, F., Y. L. HURD, U. UNGERSTEDT, A. MARKOU, P. M. PLOTSKY & G. F. KOOB. 1992. Neurobiol. Drug Alcohol Addiction 654: 220–241.
68. DI CHIARA, G. & R. A. NORTH. 1992. Trends Pharmacol. Sci. 13: 185–193.
69. LE MOAL, M. & H. SIMON. 1991. Physiol. Rev. 71: 155–234.
70. MICZEK, K. A. 1987. The psychopharmacology of aggression. In Handbook of Psychopharmacology, Volume 19: New Directions in Behavioral Pharmacology. L. L. Iversen, S. D. Iversen & S. H. Snyder, Eds.: 183–328. Plenum. New York.
71. MICZEK, K. A. & M. HANEY 1994. Psychopharmacology 115: 358–365.
72. TIDEY, J. W. & K. A. MICZEK. 1992. Behav. Pharmacol. 3: 553–565.
73. PUGLISI-ALLEGRA, S., S. SIMLER, E. KEMPF & P. MANDEL. 1981. Pharmacol. Biochem. Behav. 14,S1: 13–18.
74. MANDEL, P., G. MACK & E. KEMPF. 1979. Molecular basis of some models of aggressive behavior. In Psychopharmacology of Aggression. M. Sandler, Ed.: 95–110. Raven Press. New York.
75. CLEMENT, J., S. SIMLER, L. CIESIELSKI, P. MANDEL, S. CABIB & S. PUGLISI-ALLEGRA. 1987. Pharmacol. Biochem. Behav. 26: 83–88.
76. HAUG, M., M. L. OUSS-SCHLEGEL, J. F. SPETZ, D. BENTON, P. F. BRAIN, P. MANDEL, L. CIESIELSKI & S. SIMLER. 1987. Biog. Amines 4: 83–94.
77. POTEGAL, M. 1986. Psychopharmacology 89: 444–448.
78. DEPAULIS, A. & M. VERGNES. 1985. Physiol. Behav. 35: 447–453.
79. HAUG, M., S. SIMLER, L. KIM & P. MANDEL. 1980. Pharmacol. Biochem. Behav. 12: 189–193.
80. GRANT, K. A. 1994. Behav. Pharmacol. 5: 383–404.
81. MACDONALD, R. L. & R. W. OLSEN. 1994. Annu. Rev. Neurosci. 17: 569–602.
82. MICZEK, K. A., E. M. WEERTS, J. A. VIVIAN & H. M. BARROS. 1995. Psychopharmacology 121: 38–56.
83. WEERTS, E. M., L. G. MILLER, K. E. HOOD & K. A. MICZEK. 1992. Psychopharmacology 108: 196–204.
84. RODGERS, R. J. & A. J. WATERS. 1985. Neurosci. Biobehav. Rev. 9: 21–35.

85. MICZEK, K. A. & J. M. O'DONNELL. 1980. Psychopharmacology **69:** 39–44.
86. MICZEK, K. A. 1974. Psychopharmacologia **39:** 275–301.
87. OLIVIER, B., J. MOS & K. A. MICZEK. 1991. Eur. Neuropsychopharmacol. **1:** 97–100.
88. WEERTS, E. M. & K. A. MICZEK. Psychopharmacology. In press.
89. MICZEK, K. A., J. F. DEBOLD & A. M. M. VAN ERP. 1994. Behav. Pharmacol. **5:** 407–421.
90. MAJEWSKA, M. D., N. L. HARRISON, R. D. SCHWARTZ, J. L. BARKER & S. M. PAUL. 1986. Science **232:** 1004–1007.
91. GEE, K. W., W. C. CHANG, R. E. BRINTON & B. S. MCEWEN. 1987. Eur. J. Pharmacol. **136:** 419–423.
92. GEE, K. W., M. B. BOLGER, R. E. BRINTON, H. COIRINI & B. S. MCEWEN. 1988. J. Pharmacol. Exp. Ther. **246:** 803–812.
93. LOPEZ-COLOME, A. M., M. MCCARTHY & C. BEYER. 1990. Eur. J. Pharmacol. **176:** 297–303.
94. MORROW, A. L., P. D. SUZDAK & S. M. PAUL. 1987. Eur. J. Pharmacol. **142:** 483–485.
95. SIMMONDS, M. A., J. P. TURNER & N. L. HARRISON. 1984. Neuropharmacology **23:** 877–878.
96. CRAWLEY, J. N., J. R. GLOWA, M. D. MAJEWSKA & S. M. PAUL. 1986. Brain Res. **398:** 382–385.
97. BRITTON, K. T., M. PAGE, H. BALDWIN & G. F. KOOB. 1991. J. Pharmacol. Exp. Ther. **258:** 124–129.
98. NORBERG, L., G. WAHLSTROM & T. BACKSTROM. 1987. Pharmacol. & Toxicol. **61:** 42–47.
99. BITRAN, D., R. J. HILVERS & C. K. KELLOGG. 1991. Brain Res. **561:** 157–161.
100. WIELAND, S., N. C. LAN, S. MIRASEDEGHI & K. W. GEE. 1991. Brain Res. **565:** 263–268.
101. BELELLI, D. & K. W. GEE. 1989. Eur. J. Pharmacol. **167:** 173–176.
102. GYERMEK, L., G. GENTHER & N. FLEMING. 1967. Int. J. Neuropharmacol. **6:** 191–198.
103. SEEMAN, P. 1972. Pharmacol. Rev. **24:** 583–655.
104. KUBLI-GARFIAS, C., M. CERVANTES & C. BEYER. 1976. Brain Res. **114:** 71–81.
105. MENDELSON, W. B., J. V. MARTIN, M. PERLIS, R. WAGNER, M. D. MAJEWSKA & S. M. PAUL. 1987. Psychopharmacology **93:** 226–229.
106. MAJEWSKA, M. D. 1987. Integr. Psychiatry **5:** 258–273.
107. MICZEK, K. A., J. F. DEBOLD, A. M. M. VAN ERP & W. TORNATZKY. 1996. Alcohol, GABA$_A$-benzodiazepine receptor complex, and aggression. *In* Recent Developments in Alcoholism. Alcohol and Violence. M. Galanter, Ed. 13. Plenum Publishing. New York. In press.
108. DEBOLD, J. F., H. BARROS, S. SO & K. A. MICZEK. 1995. Alcoholism Clin. Exp. Res. **19:** 11A.

Discussion: Biological Correlates of Aggression

BURR EICHELMAN[a] AND ANNE C. HARTWIG

Department of Psychiatry and Behavioral Science
3401 North Broad Street, Floor 2
Temple University School of Medicine
Philadelphia, Pennsylvania 19140

The role of a discussion paper may be one of integration that emphasizes findings presented within other papers and that may offer a different perspective as these findings coalesce. It can point out the voids in research germane to the topic under discussion. It might address areas of clinical and social intervention that require attention of the clinical and political spheres. Briefly, this discussion will address all three areas from the perspective of a clinician-researcher and an attorney-bioethicist who attended the conference sponsored by the New York Academy of Sciences.

In determining the format for the discussion, we have chosen to formulate the discussion using four questions. Three of these might be asked by a mother, Mrs. Smith, whose 10-year-old daughter has "tantrums" characterized by throwing objects, shouting, and hitting her mother whenever denied specific goals, such as playing with a friend. Her eleven-year-old brother never manifests this type of behavior when "frustrated." The fourth question reflects social concerns about the ethics of research, clinical intervention, and public policy related to the preceding questions.

Mrs. Smith asks:

1. What do we know from animal models and biological correlates of aggression that might help to explain why my aggressive daughter behaves this way? Findings gleaned from animal research underscore the principle that aggressive behavior in most circumstances is multifaceted in origin. Clearly, there is a genetic "disposition" component that can be selectively bred for within rodent model systems[1] or demonstrated within the domesticated breeds of dogs,[2] from the pacific collie to the vicious pit bull. As yet, this has not been well demonstrated in humans, but Scandinavian studies show a genetic loading for criminal behavior.[3] So, we can certainly tell Mrs. Smith that there might be a genetic predisposition operating in placing her one daughter more "at risk" for displaying a disposition marked with tantrums.

We know more, however. We know that the genetic material of animals and humans creates an organism that has many component systems that affect aggressive behavior. The symposium reviewed portions of the neural substrate for aggressive behavior. This substrate, as noted by N. G. Simon, is organized and influenced by both classes of sexual hormones: estrogens and androgens. It is altered by stress and the hormonal system that modifies stress, including neuromodulators, such as corticotropin-releasing hormone[4] and the pituitary-adrenal axis, as described by Susman in this volume. It is affected by multiple neurotransmitters,

---

[a] Tel: (215) 707-3364; fax: (215) 707-1557; e-mail: eich@astro.ocis.temple.edu.

including serotonin, norepinephrine, dopamine, acetylcholine, and gamma-amino butyric acid (GABA); and the opioid system,[5] as described within by several conference presentations (cf Coccaro, Fuller, and Miczek). Additionally, neuromodulators such as vasopressin (cf Ferris in this volume) also play a modulatory role. We also know that this neurochemical/neuropeptide/neuroendocrine "orchestra" is played through many anatomical sites, including the limbic system; the frontal lobes, in humans; and the periaqueductal gray of the brain stem.

Consequently, we can reply to Mrs. Smith that we know that the net effect of multiple neurochemical elements acting throughout multiple brain regions within an organism genetically prepared to function aggressively can produce both "functional" as well as "dysfunctional" episodes of aggressive behavior. Yet, for her daughter, we also know what we do not know, that is, we do not have the neuroscience knowledge or technology to measure or locate any specific "abnormality" that is diagnostic or singularly explanatory regarding the etiology of any form of nonictal aggressive behavior.

2. What do we know from animal research that might help her to stop this behavior? From a biological perspective, animal research suggests that each chromosomal contribution, each neurotransmitter, each neuromodulator, and each contributing neuroanatomical region can become a handle for the modulation of aggressive behavior. This is not to exclude or minimize the power of learning strategies or more basic operant conditioning, elaborated much more fully in other sections of this volume, but to recognize that biological "handles" for behavior modification also exist. Within child and adolescent psychiatry these have been employed predominantly from an empirical and pragmatic approach. Agents modifying various neurotransmitters as well as electrical kindling have shown promise in the modification of certain forms of dysfunctional aggressive behavior in adults[6] as well as in children and adolescents.[7]

However, in answering Mrs. Smith, we must candidly reply that we only have "half-proofs" of the successes of specific pharmacologic agents; most have never been decisively tested in double-blind, controlled studies from lack of research funding and support as well as because of significant issues of consent and subject cooperation. In the future, this field may make increased use of alternative research strategies, such as using n = 1 research paradigms[8] rather than depending upon traditional large-sample studies.

3. What do we know from animal research that might prevent this type of behavior in my next child or my daughter's children? From a biological perspective, we do not know anything specific that we can tell Mrs. Smith. However, we do know that injury to various neurotransmitter systems (e.g., catecholaminergic and serotonergic) or brain regions[5] can increase the propensity for dysfunctional aggressive behavior in animals. We know that intrauterine and perinatal anoxia as well as alcohol exposure modify brain development in humans and that a continued search for intrauterine neurotoxins continues in order to explain the pathogenesis of attention deficit disorder, with its concomitant comorbid association with dysfunctional aggressive behavior. We also know that perinatal stress has far-reaching effects on stress management in children, as reported by King in this volume and that disruption of social attachment produces a protracted change in brain function and aggressive behavior in primates (as reported by Kraemer at this meeting). We know from animal studies[9] that stress-induced changes in brain chemistry and behavior can be quite durable.

Thus, we can respond to Mrs. Smith and advise her to reduce her stress during her next pregnancy, to avoid exposure to harmful drugs and potential neurotoxins, and to obtain the best prenatal care to assure a healthy pregnancy and well-supervised delivery. We also have learned from animal studies that perinatal stress, particularly through maternal-infant separation, markedly increases the risk of subsequent dysfunctional behavior in the offspring. Perhaps we should advise Mrs. Smith to carry her child to term in an environment/society that treasures its young and provides a supportive, nutritional, and medically supervised environment with reduced stress and protection against maternal separation for its most precious "product," its children. We doubt that our present culture will meet these criteria for many children born this month in this country.

We ask:

4. What ethical questions does a symposium such as this raise and what responses, if any, are required? Certainly, it begins with an implicit negative value being assigned to aggressive behavior, at least to "dysfunctional" aggressive behavior. In the United States, there appears to be a universal acceptance and approval of violence. Whether one describes the "aggressive business approach of corporation X or salesperson Y," when one watches the latest professional hockey match, or when one watches the "successes" of violence on our television screens, it is clear that much of our society venerates aggressive behavior. As a society, we must come to terms with whether the rates of adolescent violence, including homicide, in this country are simply the "spin off" of our successful cultural assertiveness, or whether these rates bear witness to a social illness, even with some biological, environmental, and stress-induced underpinnings.

If we accept this latter position, then the scientific literature suggests to us as a society that we know pitifully little about the biological matrix that supports and modifies mammalian, but particularly human, aggressive behavior. In order to know more, we would need to appropriate additional resources for research, which may or may not be immediately productive. However, both biological and social research does bring to bear considerable scientific support for immediate changes in social policy that would channel societal support to ensure healthier pregnancies, deliveries, and stress-reduced perinatal periods, which would minimize for our children the risks of disrupting early attachment bonds and producing a hostile and excessively stressful environment for the developing child. We already understand, without further research, that this strategy is valuable; we lack national commitment.

Finally, from a legal and moral perspective, we must also deal with issues of responsibility. Except in cases of extreme psychosis or unconsciousness, our legal system purportedly holds individuals responsible for their violent behavior. Examination of the biology of aggressive behavior and the role of biological elements in enhancing or diminishing aggressive behavior need not remove the responsibility for aggressive behavior. The driver who destroys another automobile due to an epileptic seizure or an insulin reaction remains financially responsible for the hazardous operation of his or her vehicle even if there is a biological understanding of elements of his or her behavior and clinical treatments that would reduce the risk of such an "accident" recurring. Thus, the use of biological agents, such as lithium or serotonin-enhancing agents for particularly disturbed clinical populations of dysfunctionally aggressive individuals, should neither be denied on the basis of abrogating responsibility for behaviors, nor serve as excuses for the just consequences of antisocial violence.

In summary, we can only answer Mrs. Smith's questions generally, pointing to the hazy understanding of the biological matrix and its contribution to the origins of childhood and adolescent aggressive behavior. The material in this volume offers optimism that our understanding will increase, but our knowledge is presently only in its nascent stages. However, we do know, and this symposium underscores, the importance and social need to protect, nurture, and support the gestation, birth, and development of our next generation through the provision of a safe uterine environment, reduced maternal stress, safe delivery, and protected maternal-infant bonding in a stress-limited environment. This will maximize the opportunity for the biological basis of social (and aggressive) behaviors to develop "as programmed" and with a reduced probability of biologic dysfunction that could lead to increased dysfunctional aggressive behaviors.

REFERENCES

1. LAGERSPETZ, K. M. J. & K. Y. H. LAGERSPETZ. 1971. Changes in the aggressiveness of mice resulting from selective breeding, learning, and social isolation. Scand. J. Psychol. **12:** 241–248.
2. SCOTT, J. P. & J. FULLER. 1965. Genetics and the Social Behavior of the Dog. University of Chicago Press, Chicago, IL.
3. MEDNICK, S. A., W. F. GABRIELLI, JR. & B. HUTCHINGS. 1984. Genetic influences in criminal behavior: Evidence from an adoption cohort. Science **224:** 891–893.
4. POST, R. M. 1981. Lidocaine-kindled limbic seizures: Behavioral implications. *In* Kindling 2. J. A. Costa, Ed. Raven Press. New York.
5. EICHELMAN, B. 1992. Aggressive behavior; From laboratory to clinic quo vadit? Arch. Gen. Psychiatry **49:** 488–492.
6. EICHELMAN, B. 1988. Toward a rational pharmacotherapy for aggressive behavior. Hosp. Community Psychiatry **39:** 31–39.
7. ZAVODNICK, J. F. 1995. Pharmacotherapy. *In* Conduct Disorders in Children and Adolescents. G. Pirooz Sholevar, Ed. American Psychiatric Press. Washington, D.C.
8. GUYATT, G., D. SACKETT, D. W. TAYLER, J. CHONG, R. ROBERTS & S. PUBSLEY. 1986. Determining optimal therapy: randomized trials in individual patients. N. Engl. J. Med. **314:** 889–892.
9. LAMPRECHT, F., B. EICHELMAN, N. B. THOA, R. B. WILLIAMS & I. J. KOPIN. 1972. Rat fighting behavior: Serum dopamine-β-hydroxylase and hypothalamic tyrosine hydroxylase. Science **177:** 1214–1215.

Neurotransmitter Correlates of Impulsive Aggression in Humans

EMIL F. COCCARO[a]

Clinical Neuroscience Research Unit
Department of Psychiatry
Medical College of Pennsylvania and Hahnemann University
3200 Henry Avenue, 8th Floor
Philadelphia, Pennsylvania 19129

Human aggression constitutes a multidetermined act that often results in physical (or verbal) injury to others or oneself (or objects).[1] It appears in several forms and may be defensive, premeditated (*e.g.*, predatory), or impulsive (*e.g.*, nonpremeditated) in nature. Defensive aggression is generally seen within the normal range of human behavior. However, premeditated and impulsive aggressive behaviors are commonly viewed as pathological. Research into the etiologic determinants of premeditated and impulsive human aggression have focused on various sociologic, psychologic, and biogenetic factors. Most notably among the biogenetic factors is evidence of an abnormality in central 5-HT system function. Evidence of abnormalities in other central neurotransmitter systems is also available for catecholaminergic and peptidergic systems.

SEROTONIN

There are now numerous studies that suggest a role for 5-HT in impulsive aggressive behavior in humans and nonhuman primates. These studies involve data from CSF 5-HIAA, platelet-receptor binding, and psychopharmacologic challenge. First, Asberg *et al.*[2] reported an inverse relationship between violent/lethal suicidal behavior and basal lumbar cerebrospinal fluid (CSF) 5-HIAA concentration in depressed patients. This was soon followed by Brown *et al.*,[3,4] who reported an inverse correlation between lumbar CSF 5-HIAA concentration and a life history of aggression ($r = -0.78$) in 24 male naval recruits,[3] and then a similar correlation between CSF 5-HIAA and psychopathic deviance (Minnesota Multiphasic Personality Inventory (MMPI); $r = -0.77$) in 12 male naval recruits with borderline personality disorder.[4] In both samples, a history of a suicide attempt correlated inversely with CSF 5-HIAA and directly with aggression scores. Linnoila *et al.*[5] have reported reduced CSF 5-HIAA concentration in both impulsive violent offenders and impulsive arsonists compared to premeditated violent offenders, suggesting that it is nonpremeditated (impulsive) aggression, specifically, that correlates with reduced central 5-HT function in these individuals. Limson *et al.*[6] also reported an inverse correlation between CSF 5-HIAA and a life history of aggression in abstinent alcoholics and controls; however, the magnitude of this correlation was much smaller ($r = 0.31$) than that reported by Brown *et al.*[3,4]

---

[a] Tel: 215-842-4208; fax: 215-842-4321; e-mail: coccaroef@allegheny.edu.

Kruesi et al.[7] also reported a modest inverse correlation between age-corrected CSF 5-HIAA and "aggression against persons" ($r = -0.39$) in a group of behaviorally disruptive disordered children and adolescents. In nonhuman primates,[8,9] two studies report an inverse correlation between cisternal CSF 5-HIAA and an ordinal ranking of aggression[8] and observation of escalated aggression (i.e., chasing/attacking opponents) and risk taking[9] (i.e., long leaps in the trees where risk of dying upon a fall is great). Over the past decade, however, there have also been negative CSF 5-HIAA/aggression studies. Roy et al.[10] reported an inverse correlation between CSF 5-HIAA and outwardly-directed hostility in nonpsychiatric subjects of both genders. However, this relationship was largely due to higher CSF 5-HIAA levels in the older subjects, and no relationship was noted once age was controlled for. Gardner et al.[11] reported no relationship between CSF 5-HIAA and life history of aggression in females with severe borderline personality disorder.

Less work has been completed in this area with either brain or platelet measures of 5-HT receptor elements. Brain studies have been exclusively performed in violent suicide victims. More often than not, these studies report reduced numbers of the presynaptic 5-HT transporter,[12] and higher numbers of postsynaptic 5-HT-2a receptors,[13] in violent suicide victims. Platelet studies have found decreased numbers of 5-HT transporter sites in aggressive conduct disordered subjects[14,15] and in aggressive institutionalized psychiatric subjects.[16] In addition, an inverse correlation between platelet 5-HT uptake and Barratt "impulsivity" have been reported in aggressive adult males.[17] Increased numbers of platelet 5-HT-2a receptor binding sites have also been reported in people attempting suicide, regardless of diagnosis, in at least two studies.[18,19]

Physiological studies of the 5-HT system in this area include pharmacochallenge studies with 5-HT probes. Coccaro et al.[20] found an inverse relationship between measures of aggression/history of suicide attempt and PRL[d,1-FEN] response in male personality disorder (PD) subjects and an inverse relationship between history of suicide attempt and PRL[d,1-FEN] only in male depressed patients. Subsequent studies with fenfluramine challenge have generally been positive with (1) reduced PRL[d,1-FEN] responses and elevated aggression scores in nondepressed suicidal individuals;[21] (2) an inverse correlation between PRL[d,1-FEN] responses and assaultiveness in the continuing series of subjects[22] initiated by Coccaro et al.;[20] (3) an inverse relationship between PRL[d,1-FEN] and overt aggression in nonhuman primates;[23] and (4) O'Keane et al.,[24] reporting reduced PRL[d-FEN] responses in impulsive violent offenders with antisocial personality disorder. Additional positive results in this area come from studies involving other 5-HT probes and include (1) an inverse relationship between assaultiveness and PRL[m-CPP] in antisocial personality disordered subjects with a comorbid history of substance abuse[25] and (2) an inverse correlation between PRL[Buspirone] and irritability in a small group of male and female PD subjects.[26] A few published studies have either had negative results or have suggested a direct relationship between hormonal responses to 5-HT probes and aggression. Fishbein et al.[27] reported a positive correlation between PRL[d,1-FEN] responses and Barratt impulsivity in a series of drug (mostly cocaine) -abusing patients. Curiously, Bernstein and Handlesman[28] have recently reported a similarly positive correlation between PRL[m-CPP] responses and Buss-Durkee "irritability" and Barratt "risk taking" in cocaine addicts but an inverse correlation between PRL[m-CPP] and Buss-Durkee "aggression" measures in alcoholics, suggesting that stimulant abuse might alter the biological substrate, such that different relationships between indices of 5-HT and aggression are observed. With regard to studies in children and adolescents, Halperin *et al.*[29] have reported greater PRL[d,1-FEN] responses in aggressive attention deficit/hyperactivity disorder (ADHD) subjects compared with their nonaggressive counterparts. In contrast to Halperin *et al.*, however, Stoff *et al.*[30] found no difference in PRL[d,1-FEN] responses between behavioral disruptive disordered children and normal controls. Given the difficulty in controlling for intersubject differences in development in studies of children and adolescents, more research in this group will be needed before a clear interpretation of these data can be made.

CATECHOLAMINES: NOREPINEPHRINE

Evidence supporting a role in aggression for other neurotransmitter systems such as for catecholamines (*i.e.*, norepinephrine (NE)) is more limited than that for 5-HT. However, there are a number of animal studies that support the hypothesis that the NE system has a direct (*e.g.*, as opposed to an inverse) role in aggression. Indices of increased NE function in the brain correlate positively with the number of shock-induced aggressive episodes in rodents.[31] Moreover, agents that enhance the efficiency of central NE function (*i.e.*, tricyclic monoamine oxidase inhibitor (MAOI) antidepressants) increase shock-induced fighting in rodents.[32] The picture is not as clear in human studies, particularly from the standpoint of synaptic mechanisms. For example, some clinical data support a positive relationship between NE and aggression, and others support a negative relationship. Supporting a positive relationship are (1) clinical data supporting the anti-aggressive effects of beta-blockers (although some effective ones do not readily cross the blood-brain barrier[33]); (2) clinical data that agents that enhance central NE function are also associated with agitation and irritability, particularly in subsets of (borderline) personality-disordered individuals;[34] (3) a positive correlation between CSF (and plasma) NE and the "extroversion" factor of the Eysenck Personality Questionnaire in a group of pathological gamblers;[35] and (4) a positive correlation between CSF 3-methoxy-4-hydroxyphenylglycol (MHPG) and a history of aggression in naval recruits.[3] The last two observations are limited in relevance, however, because extroversion is not closely related to aggression and because CSF MHPG actually explains very little variance in aggression scores once CSF 5-HIAA is accounted for. In contrast to these data, at least two reports demonstrate a reduction of CSF MHPG, but not homovanillic acid (HVA), in violent offenders[5] and impulsive arsonists[36] compared with healthy volunteers. In addition, we have observed an inverse correlation between plasma MHPG and a life history of aggression in a large group of male PD subjects. Is it possible that indices of presynaptic NE function are inversely related to aggression and that indices of postsynaptic NE function are directly related? Animal studies suggest that NE-mediated facilitation of aggression is mediated through stimulation of postsynaptic alpha-2 NE receptors in the hypothalamus.[37] Recently, we reported a positive relationship between GH[CLON] responses (a postsynaptic index) and Buss-Durkee irritability in personality-disordered and healthy volunteer subjects.[38] This is supportive of the proposed hypothesis but it does not easily explain why presynaptic indices would be reduced. However, Ordway *et al.*[39] reported increased presynaptic alpha-2 NE agonist binding in the locus caeruleus (LC) in the brains of violent (but not nonviolent) suicide victims compared with that in sudden accident victims. Accordingly, it is possible that increased presynaptic alpha-2 NE activity at the LC cell bodies results in reduced NE outflow in terminal NE fields and leads to both a reduction in presynaptic NE indices (*e.g.*, CSF MHPG/

plasma MHPG) and an increase in postsynaptic alpha-2 NE responsiveness. In addition to increased sensitivity of typical postsynaptic alpha-2 NE receptor sensitivity at NE synapses, it is also possible that there may be increased sensitivity of alpha-2 NE heteroceptors terminating on presynaptic 5-HT neurons. This leads to at least two possible outcomes when aversive (e.g., provocative) stimuli cause NE terminals to fire: (1) a larger postsynaptic alpha-2 NE signal in NE pathways leading to heightened arousal in response to provocation (i.e., greater fight/flight response) and/or (2) greater alpha-2 NE heteroceptor inhibition of 5-HT firing and/or release at 5-HT/NE synaptic interfaces. The importance of concomitant arousal in impulsive aggressive behavior cannot be underestimated as an interactive factor with 5-HT in impulsive aggressive behavior. This is because animal studies indicate that reductions in 5-HT activity do not lead to impulsive aggressive behavior in the absence of heightened arousal.[40]

CATECHOLAMINES: DOPAMINE

Like NE, animal data tend to support a positive relationship between central dopamine (DA) function and aggression. Treatment with dopaminergic agents induces aggressive behavior in rodents,[41,42] whereas destruction of presynaptic dopamine terminals with neurotoxins increases the effect of these agents.[43] Moreover, foot-shock induced aggression in rats is enhanced, or decreased, by treatment with dopamine-2 (D_2) agonists[44,45] or D_2 antagonists,[45] respectively. Similar studies in humans are not available, though correlational studies suggest that there is a relationship between DA and aggression in humans. An inverse relationship between impulsive aggression and CSF HVA concentration has been suggested by Roy et al.[10] and Limson et al.[6] Inasmuch as CSF HVA concentrations are highly correlated with CSF 5-HIAA concentrations, it is possible that reductions in CSF HVA may simply be reflecting a primary abnormality in CSF 5-HIAA. If reduced CSF HVA reflects reduced DA output, however, an inverse relationship between CSF HVA and indices of impulsive aggression could be consistent with the heightened postsynaptic DA receptor activity exploited in animal studies.[44,45] Also consistent with these animal studies is the observation that treatment with the neuroleptic, flupenthixol, reduces the incidence of suicide attempts in highly suicidal-prone personality-disordered patients in a placebo-controlled study.[46] Although there are no studies of DA receptor sensitivity in impulsive-aggressive individuals, Pichor et al.[47] reports that depressed patients with a history of suicidal behavior have blunted, rather than enhanced, growth hormone responses to the DA agonist, apomorphine. More research in this area is needed.

PEPTIDES: OPIATES

A positive correlation between CSF opioid binding protein and the Buss-Durkee subscale "assaultiveness" ($r = 0.77$, n = 18, $p < 0.0002$) in healthy male volunteers[48] has been the only study related to "other-directed aggression" reported to date to provide evidence for a role of endogenous opiates in aggression. A small number of studies also suggest that individuals who engage in self-injurious behavior have elevated circulating levels of met-enkephalins.[49] Psychopharmacological studies suggest that opiate antagonists (naloxone, naltrexone) can diminish self-injurious behavior in some humans[50] and nonhumans.[51] It is possible that self-injurious individuals have greater pain sensitivity and that self-injurious behavior is a mechanism that can release endogenous opiates for further analgesia. On the other hand, individuals with self-injurious behavior have been reported to feel numb before self-injury and appear to hurt themselves in order to "feel something" even if the feeling is painful.[52] Of interest, reports of increased numbers of opiate receptors in the brains of young suicide victims[53] and of the antisuicidal efficacy of naltrexone[54] suggests that a positive relationship may exist between self-directed aggression, at least, and opiate function.

PEPTIDES: VASOPRESSIN

We have recently noted a positive correlation between life history of aggressive behavior and CSF levels of vasopressin in patients with personality disorder. Although CSF vasopressin was not correlated with CSF 5-HIAA, it was inversely correlated with the prolactin response to d-fenfluramine challenge. This is consistent with animal data[55] that suggest a positive relationship between brain vasopressin levels and aggression, and observations that treatment with serotonergic agents reduce brain vasopressin levels and aggressive responding. If replicated, this would represent another way in which central 5-HT systems may interact with other neurotransmitter systems to modulate aggressive behavior.

CONCLUSION

There is emerging data implicating the role of a variety of neurotransmitters in the mediation of impulsive aggressive behavior in humans. Although most data have suggested a strong role for serotonin, no complex behavior can be explained on the basis of any one neurotransmitter. Undoubtedly, future research will find that the mediation of impulsive aggressive behavior in humans is influenced by a number of neurotransmitters that interact with each other, the environment, and, in children, with developmental factors. Knowledge of the various biological systems involved will be instrumental in our understanding of which pharmacologic and nonpharmacologic interventions will have the greatest success.

REFERENCES

1. Buss, A. H. 1961. The Psychology of Aggression. J. Wiley & Sons. New York.
2. Asberg, M., L. Traksman & P. Thoren. 1976. 5-HIAA in the cerebrospinal fluid: A biochemical suicide predictor? Arch. Gen. Psychiatry 33: 1193–1197.
3. Brown, G. L., F. K. Goodwin, J. C. Ballenger, P. F. Goyer & L. F. Major. 1979. Aggression in humans correlates with cerebrospinal fluid amine metabolites. Psychiatry Res. 1: 131–139.
4. Brown, G. L., M. H. Ebert, P. F. Goyer, D. C. Jimerson, W. J. Klein, W. E. Bunney & F. W. Goodwin. 1982. Aggression, suicide, and serotonin: Relationships to CSF amine metabolites. Am. J. Psychiatry 139: 741–746.
5. Linnoila, M., M. Virkkunen, M. Scheinin, A. Nuutila, R. Rimon & F. K. Goodwin. 1983. Low cerebrospinal fluid 5-HIAA concentration differentiates impulsive from nonimpulsive violent behavior. Life Sci. 33: 2609–2614.
6. Limson, R., D. Goldman, A. Roy, D. Lamparski, B. Ravitz, B. Adinoff & M. Linnoila. 1991. Personality and cerebrospinal fluid monoamine metabolites in alcoholics and controls. Arch. Gen. Psychiatry 48: 437–441.

7. KRUESI, M. J. P., J. L. RAPOPORT, S. HAMBERGER, E. HIBBS, W. Z. POTTER, M. LENANE & G. L. BROWN. 1990. CSF metabolites, aggression, and impulsivity in disruptive behavior disorders of children and adolescents. Arch. Gen. Psychiatry **47:** 419–462.
8. HIGLEY, J. D., P. T. MEHLMAN, D. M. TAUB, S. B. HIGLEY, S. J. SUOMI, M. LINNOILA & J. H. VICKERS. 1992. Cerebrospinal fluid monoamine and adrenal correlates of aggression in free-ranging rhesus monkeys. Arch. Gen. Psychiatry **49:** 436–441.
9. MEHLMAN, P. T., J. D. HIGLEY, I. FAUCHER, A. A. LILLY, D. M. TAUB, J. VICKERS, S. J. SUOMI & M. LINNOILA. 1994. Low CSF 5-HIAA concentrations and severe aggression and impaired impulse control in non-human primates. Am. J. Psychiatry **151:** 1485–1491.
10. ROY, A., B. ADINOFF & M. LINNOILA. 1988. Acting out hostility in normal volunteers: Negative correlation with levels of 5-HIAA in cerebrospinal fluid. Psychiatry Res. **24:** 187–194.
11. GARDNER, D. L., P. B. LUCAS & R. W. COWDRY. 1990. CSF metabolites in borderline personality disorder compared with normal controls. Biol. Psychiatry **28:** 247–254.
12. STANLEY, M. S., J. VIGGILIO & S. GERSHON. 1992. Tritiated imipramine binding sites are decreased in the frontal cortex of suicides. Science **216:** 1337–1339.
13. STANLEY M. & J. J. MANN. 1983. Increased serotonin-2 binding sites in frontal cortex of suicide victims. Lancet **1:** 214–216.
14. STOFF, D. M., L. POLLOCK, B. VITIELLO, D. BEHAR & W. H. BRIDGER. 1987. Reduction of ^{3}-H-imipramine binding sites on platelets of conduct disordered children. Neuropsychopharmacology **1:** 55–62.
15. BIRMAHER, B., M. STANLEY, I. GREENHILL, J. TWOMEY, A. GAVRILESCU & H. RABINOVITCH. 1990. Platelet imipramine binding in children and adolescents with impulsive behavior. J. Am. Acad. Child Adolesc. Psychiatry **29:** 914–918.
16. MARAZZITI, D., A. ROTONDO, S. PRESTA, M. L. PANIOLI-GUADAGNUCCI, L. PALEGO & L. CONTI. 1993. Role of serotonin in human aggressive behavior. Aggressive Behav. **19:** 347–353.
17. BROWN, C. S., T. A. KENT, S. G. BRYANT, R. M. GEVEDON, J. L. CAMPBELL, A. R. FELTHOUS, E. S. BARRATT & R. M. ROSE. 1989. Blood platelet uptake of serotonin in episodic aggression. Psychiatry Res. **27:** 5–12.
18. BIEGON, A., A. GRINSPOON, A. BLUMENFELD, A. BLEICH, A. APTER & R. MESTER. 1990. Increased serotonin 5-HT$_2$ receptor binding on blood platelets of suicidal men. Psychopharmacol. **100:** 165–167.
19. PANDY, G. N., S. C. PANDEY, P. G. JANICAK, R. C. MARKS & J. M. DAVIS. 1990. Platelet serotonin-2 receptor binding sites in depression and suicide. Biol. Psychiatry **28:** 215–222.
20. COCCARO, E. F., L. J. SIEVER, H. KLAR, G. MAURER, K. COCHRANE, T. B. COOPER, R. C. MOHS & K. L. DAVIS. 1989. Serotonergic studies in affective and personality disorder patients. Arch. Gen. Psychiatry **46:** 587–599.
21. LOPEZ-IBOR, J. J., F. LANA & J. SAIZ RUIZ. 1990. Conduct as autoliticas impulsivas y serotonina. Actas Luso Esp. Neurol. Psiquiatr. **18:** 316–325.
22. SIEVER, L. & R. L. TRESTMAN. 1993. The serotonin system and aggressive personality disorder. Int. Clin. Psychopharmacol. **8**(Suppl. 2): 33–39.
23. BOTCHIN, M. B., J. R. KAPLAN, S. B. MANUCK & J. J. MANN. 1993. Low versus high prolactin responders to fenfluramine challenge: Marker of behavioral differences in adult male cynmolgus macaques. Neuropsychopharmacology **9:** 93–99.
24. O'KEANE, V., E. MOLONEY, H. O'NEILL, A. O'CONNOR, C. SMITH & T. G. DINAN. 1992. Blunted prolactin responses to d-fenfluramine in sociopathy: Evidence for subsensitivity of central serotonergic function. Br. J. Psychiatry **160:** 643–646.
25. MOSS, H. B., J. K. YAO & G. L. PANZAK. 1990. Serotonergic responsivity and behavioral dimensions in antisocial personality disorder with substance abuse. Biol. Psychiatry **28:** 325–338.
26. COCCARO, E. F., S. GABRIEL & L. J. SIEVER. 1990. Buspirone challenge: Preliminary evidence for a role for central 5-HT-1a receptor function in impulsive aggressive behavior in humans. Psychopharmacol. Bull. **26:** 393–405.

27. FISHBEIN, D. H., D. LOZOVSKY & J. H. JAFFE. 1989. Impulsivity, aggression, and neuroendocrine responses to serotonergic stimulation in substance abusers. Biol. Psychiatry 25: 1049–1066.
28. BERNSTEIN, D. P. & L. HANDLESMAN. 1995. The neurobiology of substance abuse and personality disorders. In Neuropsychiatry of Behavior Disorders. J. J. Ratey, Ed.: 120–148. Blackwell Scientific Publications, Inc. Oxford, England.
29. HALPERIN, J. M., V. SHARMA, L. J. SIEVER, S. T. SCHWARTZ, K. MATIER, G. WORNELL & J. H. NEWCORN. 1994. Serotonergic function in aggressive and nonaggressive boys with attention deficit hyperactivity disorder. Am. J. Psychiatry 151: 243–248.
30. STOFF, D. M., A. P. PASTIEMPO, J. H. YEUNG, T. B. COOPER, W. H. BRIDGER & H. RABINOVICH. 1992. Neuroendocrine responses to challenge with d,l-fenfluramine and aggression in disruptive behavior disorders of children and adolescents. Psychiatry Res. 43: 263–276.
31. STOLK, J. M., R. L. CONNOR, S. LEVINE & J. D. BARCHUS. 1974. Brain norepinephrine metabolism and shock induced fighting behavior in rats: Differential effects of shock and fighting on the neurochemical response to a common footshock stimulus. J. Pharmacol. Exp. Ther. 190: 193–209.
32. EICHELMAN, B. & J. BARCHUS. 1975. Facilitated shock-induced aggression following antidepressant medication in the rat. Pharmacol. Biochem. Behav. 3: 601–604.
33. YUDOFSKY, S. C., J. M. SILVER & S. E. SCHNEIDER. 1987. Pharmacologic treatment of aggression. Psychiatr. Ann. 17: 397–406.
34. SOLOFF, P. H., A. GEORGE, R. S. NATHAN, P. M. SCHULZ & J. M. PEREL. 1986. Paradoxical effects of amitriptyline in borderline patients. Am. J. Psychiatry 143: 1603–1605.
35. ROY, A., J. DEJONG & M. LINNOILA. 1989. Extraversion in pathological gamblers: Correlates with indexes of noradrenergic function. Arch. Gen. Psychiatry 46: 679–681.
36. VIRKKUNEN, M., A. NUUTILA, F. K. GOODWIN & M. LINNOILA. 1987. Cerebrospinal fluid metabolite levels in male arsonists. Arch. Gen. Psychiatry 44: 241–247.
37. BARRETT, J. A., H. EDINGER & A. SIEGEL. 1990. Intrahypothalamic injections of norepinephrine facilitate feline affective aggression via alpha-2 adrenoceptors. Brain Res. 525: 285–293.
38. COCCARO, E. F., T. LAWRENCE, R. TRESTMAN, S. GABRIEL, H. M. KLAR & L. J. SIEVER. 1991. GH responses to IV clonidine challenge correlates with behavioral irritability in psychiatric patients and in healthy volunteers. Psychiatry Res. 39: 129–139.
39. ORDWAY, G. A., P. S. WIDDOWSON, K. S. SMITH & A. HALARIS. 1994. Agonist binding to alpha-2-adrenoceptors is elevated in the locus coeruleus from victims of suicide. J. Neurochem. 63: 617–624.
40. MARKS, P., M. O'BRIEN & G. PAXINOS. 1977. 5,7-DHT-induced muricide: Inhibition as a result of exposure of rats to mice. Brain Res. 135: 383–388.
41. LAMMERS, A. J. J. C. & J. M. VANROSSUM. 1968. Bizarre social behavior in rats induced by a combination of a peripheral decarboxylase inhibitor and DOPA. Eur. J. Pharmacol. 5: 103–106.
42. SENAULT, B. 1970. Comportement d'agressivite intraspecifique induit par l'apomorphine chez le rat. Psychopharmacologia 18: 271–287.
43. THOA, N. B., B. EICHELMAN & K. Y. NG. 1972. Shock-induced aggression: Effects of 6-hydroxydopamine and other pharmacological agents. Brain Res. 43: 467–475.
44. DATLA, K. P., A. P. SEN & S. K. BHATTACHARYA. 1992. Dopaminergic modulation of footshock induced aggression in paired rats. Indian J. Exp. Biol. 30: 587–591.
45. NIKULINA, E. M. & N. S. KAPRALOVA. 1991. The role of dopamine receptors in controlling mouse aggressivity: The genotype dependence. Zh. Vyssh. Nervn. Deyat. Im. I. P. Pavlova 41: 734–740.
46. MONTGOMERY, S. A. & D. MONTGOMERY. 1982. Pharmacological prevention of suicidal behavior. J. Affect. Dis. 4: 219–298.
47. PITCHOT, W., M. HANSENNES, A. GONZALEZ-MORENO & M. ASSEAU. 1992. Suicidal behavior and growth hormone response to apomorphine test. Biol. Psychiatry 31: 1213–1219.

48. POST, R. M., D. PICKAR, J. C. BALLENGER, D. NABER & D. R. RUBINOW. 1984. Endogenous opiates in cerebrospinal fluid: Relationship to mood and anxiety. *In* R. M. Pos & J. C. Ballenger, Eds.: 356–368. Williams & Wilkins. Baltimore.
49. COID, J., B. ALLOLIO & L. H. REES. 1983. Raised plasma metenkephalin in patients who habitually mutilate themselves. Lancet **2:** 545–546.
50. KONECKI, P. E. & S. C. SCHULZ. 1989. Rationale of clinical trials of opiate antagonists in treating patients with personality disorders and self-injurious behavior. Psychopharmacol. Bull. **25:** 556–563.
51. KRAEMER, G. W. & A. S. CLARKE. 1990. The behavioral neurobiology of self-injurious behavior in rhesus monkeys. Prog. Neuro-Psychopharmacol. Biol. Psychiat. **14:** S141–S168.
52. GARDNER, D. L. & R. W. COWDRY. 1985. Suicidal and parasuicidal behavior in borderline personality disorder. Psychiatr. Clin. N. Am. **8:** 389–403.
53. GROSS-ISSEROFF, R., K. A. DILLON, M. ISRAELI & A. BIEGNON. 1990. Regionally selective increases in mu opioid receptor density in the brains of suicidal victims. Brain Res. **530:** 312–316.
54. SONNE, S., R. RUBEY, K. T. BRADY, R. MALCOLM & T. MORRIS. 1993. Naltrexone for self-injurious thoughts and actions. New Research Abstracts (NR 138), 146th Meeting of the American Psychiatric Association, San Francisco.
55. FERRIS, C. F. & Y. DELVILLE. 1994. Vasopressin and serotonin interactions in the control of agonistic behavior. Psychoneuroendocrinology **19:** 593–601.

Fluoxetine Effects on Serotonin Function and Aggressive Behavior

RAY W. FULLER[a]

Lilly Research Laboratories
Eli Lilly and Company
Lilly Corporate Center
Indianapolis, Indiana 46285

INTRODUCTION

Serotonin is one neurotransmitter known to influence aggressive behavior (see discussion below), so there has been interest in drugs that modify serotonergic function as one potential means of treating patients with pathologic aggression.[1,2] Serotonin (5-hydroxytryptamine) is synthesized in nerve terminals from the amino acid L-tryptophan by way of the intermediate 5-hydroxy-L-tryptophan. After being stored in intraneuronal vesicles or granules, serotonin is released at nerve impulse into the synaptic cleft to act on postsynaptic target neurons. Serotonin in the synaptic cleft is inactivated by being transported back into the presynaptic nerve endings through specific transporters on the neuronal membrane. Inhibitors of that transporter thus prolong the action of serotonin on postsynaptic neurons, that is, enhance serotonergic neurotransmission. Fluoxetine is one selective inhibitor of serotonin uptake that has been used clinically in the treatment of diseases, such as depression, obsessive-compulsive disorder, and bulimia.[3–5] Fluoxetine has also been a useful pharmacologic tool for investigating the operation of serotonin neurons and their physiological roles.

SELECTIVE INHIBITION OF SEROTONIN UPTAKE

Fluoxetine differs from the tricyclic antidepressant drugs, among the earliest known inhibitors of serotonin uptake, in some important ways. First, fluoxetine inhibits serotonin uptake without inhibiting the uptake of other monoamines, such as norepinephrine and dopamine.[6,7] Second, fluoxetine lacks significant affinity for numerous neurotransmitter receptors that the tricyclic drugs have high affinity for, including the muscarinic cholinergic receptor, the histamine H_1 receptor, and the α_1 and α_2 adrenergic receptors.[8] Antagonism of these receptors by the tricyclic drugs not only produces unwanted adverse effects but also complicates interpretation of the mechanism of the drugs' therapeutic actions. Fluoxetine and some other compounds like it (*e.g.*, sertraline, paroxetine, fluvoxamine, citalopram, and indalpine) selectively inhibit serotonin uptake, so most of their pharmacologic effects appear to be mediated by enhanced serotonergic neurotransmission.[9]

[a] Tel: (317) 276-4164; fax: (317) 276-5546.

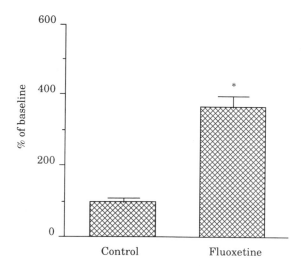

FIGURE 1. Extracellular serotonin concentration in rat hypothalamus at baseline and 60 minutes after the injection of fluoxetine hydrochloride (10 mg/kg i.p.). Mean values ± standard errors for 5 rats per group are shown. Asterisk indicates significant difference (p < 0.05).

INCREASE IN EXTRACELLULAR SEROTONIN CONCENTRATION AFTER UPTAKE INHIBITION

Earlier evidence indicated that inhibition of the serotonin transporter by fluoxetine resulted in increased concentrations of serotonin in the synaptic cleft.[10–12] The introduction of the technique of brain microdialysis,[13] whereby small molecules that diffuse into a semipermeable dialysis fiber surgically implanted into a brain region can be measured quantitatively by liquid chromatographic analysis, has facilitated the study of extracellular serotonin concentrations following administration of an uptake inhibitor to rats. Fluoxetine and other selective inhibitors of serotonin uptake increase extracellular serotonin concentrations in various brain regions.[14] FIGURE 1 shows the concentration of extracellular serotonin in rat hypothalamus after the injection of fluoxetine at a dose previously shown to inhibit serotonin uptake selectively.[6,7] The increase in extracellular serotonin concentration after fluoxetine is maintained throughout the duration of uptake inhibition (more than 24 hours).[15]

Within the first hour after administration of fluoxetine, serotonin neurons in raphe nuclei decrease their firing rate.[16] Serotonin turnover measured by various methods is decreased.[17,18] These adaptive responses are believed due to activation of presynaptic autoreceptors by the increased concentration of extracellular serotonin, and they serve to limit that increase in extracellular serotonin.[19] Serotonin uptake inhibitors given systemically only increase extracellular serotonin to 3 to 5 times the basal concentration, whereas serotonin-releasing drugs, such as fenfluramine[20] and p-chloroamphetamine[21] (also, K. W. Perry and R. W. Fuller, unpublished data), which release serotonin independently of serotonin neuron firing, can produce much larger increases in extracellular serotonin concentrations.

The increase in extracellular serotonin after chronic administration of fluoxetine is somewhat larger than after a single dose, due apparently to the desensitization of autoreceptors that limit the increase initially.[22]

FUNCTIONAL CORRELATES OF INCREASED SEROTONERGIC TRANSMISSION

Accompanying the increases in extracellular serotonin after fluoxetine is given to rats are numerous changes indicative of increased activation of postsynaptic receptors. Overt changes in appearance or behavior of rats in the usual laboratory setting are not observed; for example, fluoxetine and other serotonin uptake inhibitors do not cause the "serotonin behavioral syndrome" seen after high doses of serotonin-releasing drugs, many direct-acting serotonin agonists, or serotonin precursors given with monoamine oxidase inhibitors.[23,24] In fact, fluoxetine blocks the above effects of the serotonin-releasing drug, p-chloroamphetamine, by preventing its transporter-dependent release of serotonin.[25] However, specific behaviors and functions influenced by serotonergic input are changed by fluoxetine. For example, fluoxetine decreases rapid-eye-movement sleep,[26] activates the pituitary-adrenocortical axis,[27,28] reduces food intake[29] (particularly carbohydrate intake[30]), and decreases alcohol intake in rats.[31] The diversity of effects relates to the widespread projections of serotonin neurons to parts of the brain involved in controlling various physiological functions.[32,33] Relevant to this volume are findings that fluoxetine reduces aggressive behavior, not unexpected given the extensive evidence that serotonin is an important endogenous modulator of aggression.[2,34,35]

ROLE OF SEROTONIN IN AGGRESSIVE BEHAVIOR

Eichelman[35] has pointed out the congruence of animal research and human research implicating serotonin as a modulator of aggression, and a few examples will be mentioned to show that the congruence has continued since that review article was written. Much of the human research has involved measurement of cerebrospinal fluid concentrations of the serotonin metabolite, 5-hydroxyindoleacetic acid (5-HIAA), in individuals who have displayed aggressive or violent behavior. Much of the animal research has involved giving drugs that increase serotonin function to produce decreases in aggressive behavior in specific experimental settings.

Virkkunen et al.[36] have described studies supporting the idea that most impulsive offenders who have a tendency to behave aggressively while intoxicated have a low concentration of 5-HIAA in the cerebrospinal fluid. The low concentration of 5-HIAA suggests diminished serotonin function. Citalopram, a selective inhibitor of serotonin uptake, has been reported to decrease the frequency of aggressive incidents in schizophrenic subjects.[37] Amino acid mixtures designed to lower tryptophan availability for brain serotonin synthesis were found to increase aggression in a laboratory study in human male volunteers.[38]

Mutant mice lacking one specific serotonin receptor, the 5-HT$_{1B}$ receptor, showed increased aggressive behavior.[39] Adolescent male rhesus macaques with low cerebrospinal fluid concentrations of 5-HIAA exhibited more violent forms of aggressive behavior and more loss of impulse control.[40] Male cynomolgus monkeys with diminished prolactin elevation in response to fenfluramine, presumably indicating diminished central serotonergic function, displayed more aggressive gestures in response to threatening slides of human beings.[41]

Consistent with the growing body of data implicating serotonin in the control of aggressive behavior, several investigative groups have shown that fluoxetine decreases aggressive behavior in animals. Various species and types of aggressive behavior have been studied.

REDUCTION OF AGGRESSIVE BEHAVIOR IN ANIMALS BY FLUOXETINE

Muricidal aggression is probably the most widely studied type of aggressive behavior in rats. Some strains of rats spontaneously kill mice when the mice are placed into their cages, and this spontaneous muricidal aggression has been shown to be decreased by fluoxetine. A decrease in spontaneous muricide after fluoxetine treatment was reported by Gibbons et al.,[42] Kostowski et al.,[43] and Stark et al.[44] In addition, muricidal aggression induced by treatment with p-chlorophenylalanine, an inhibitor of serotonin synthesis, was reduced by fluoxetine.[43,45,46] Muricidal aggression induced by social isolation or by olfactory bulb ablation was reduced by fluoxetine,[47] as was muricidal aggression induced by electrolytic lesions of the dorsal and median raphe nuclei where cell bodies of serotonin neurons are present.[46] Besides muricidal aggression, intraspecies aggression induced by footshock in rats has also been inhibited by fluoxetine.[48]

Ferris and Delville[49] reported that fluoxetine inhibited territorial aggression in hamsters. Wagner et al.[50] showed that fluoxetine reduced alcohol-induced increases in aggression in mice, an effect potentiated by a tryptophan-supplemented diet. In vervet monkeys, fluoxetine decreased aggressive behavior while increasing positive social interactions and promoting dominance acquisition in previously nondominant males, after the originally dominant male had been removed from the troop.[51]

REDUCTION OF AGGRESSIVE BEHAVIOR AND ANGER/HOSTILITY IN HUMANS BY FLUOXETINE

The possibility that serotonin uptake inhibitors might be useful in reducing aggressive behavior in humans has been suggested based on the animal studies and the knowledge about serotonin's apparent role in aggressive behavior,[35,52] but only a few small clinical studies have been done to test this idea. In three patients with personality disorder, fluoxetine reduced impulsive aggressive behaviors.[53] In five borderline personality disorder patients, fluoxetine decreased depression and impulsivity scores and one but not another measure of hostility.[54] In 21 mentally retarded individuals, aggressive and self-injurious behavior was reduced to some degree in all but two after fluoxetine treatment.[55] Retrospective analysis of a large clinical trial database in depression revealed that events suggestive of aggression had occurred at more than four times the frequency in placebo-treated patients than in fluoxetine-treated patients.[56]

Recent studies have also suggested that fluoxetine reduces feelings of anger as well as aggressive behaviors. Fava et al.[57] found that 44% of depressed outpatients reported having anger attacks, intense spells of anger associated with autonomic signs, and a feeling of being out of control. After treatment with fluoxetine, 71%

of the patients who previously reported anger attacks no longer had them. The authors concluded that fluoxetine treatment appears to be beneficial in reducing anger and hostility in a subgroup of highly irritable and hostile depressed patients. Salzman et al.[58] studied fluoxetine in a small group of volunteers with borderline personality disorder. The investigators reported that the most striking finding was a clinically and statistically significant decrease in anger among the fluoxetine recipients.

POTENTIAL MEDICAL BENEFITS OF
REDUCED ANGER/HOSTILITY

Dembroski et al.[59] presented evidence that anger and hostility are the critical features of type A behavior that predispose individuals to risk of coronary atherosclerotic disease. Indeed, hostility as measured by the Cook-Medley Hostility Scale of the Minnesota Multiphasic Personality Inventory has been reported to predict higher rates both of coronary heart disease and of all-cause mortality.[60] Recently, Barefoot et al.[61] reported an association between hostility scores and angiographically confirmed coronary artery disease in asymptomatic men who were nonsmokers. Williams and Williams[62] have reviewed the medical risks of anger/hostility and suggested strategies for reduction of anger and hostility, hence aggressive behavior. The possibility that reduction of anger and hostility may have lasting medical benefit in addition to improving social relationships deserves further consideration and investigation.

SUMMARY

Fluoxetine inhibits serotonin uptake selectively and increases extracellular concentrations of serotonin in brain regions. The enhanced serotonergic neurotransmission resulting from increased action of that extracellular serotonin on postsynaptic receptors on target neurons results in various functional changes, reflecting the wide distribution of serotonin nerve terminals in brain regions that regulate numerous physiological functions. One consequence of fluoxetine administration in animals is a reduction of aggressive behavior, consistent with a larger body of data implicating serotonin as an important neurotransmitter modulator of aggression. In humans, preliminary data suggest that fluoxetine may also decrease aggressive behavior and feelings of anger or hostility. Further investigation of the potential usefulness of fluoxetine and other drugs that increase serotonergic function as a means of reducing anger, hostility, and aggressive behavior seems warranted.

ACKNOWLEDGMENTS

I thank Kenneth W. Perry and Susan K. Hemrick-Luecke for generating and graphing the microdialysis data, and Joan C. Hager for assistance in preparing the manuscript.

REFERENCES

1. OLIVIER, B., M. TH. TULP & J. MOS. 1991. Serotonergic receptors in anxiety and aggression: Evidence from animal pharmacology. Hum. Psychopharmacol. **6:** S73–S78.

2. MICZEK, K. A., E. WEERTS, M. HANEY & J. TIDEY. 1994. Neurobiological mechanisms controlling aggression: Preclinical developments for pharmacotherapeutic interventions. Neurosci. Biobehav. Rev. **18:** 97–110.

3. WOOD, A. 1993. Pharmacotherapy of bulimia nervosa—experience with fluoxetine. Int. Clin. Psychopharmacol. **8:** 2295–2299.

4. HARRIS, M. G. & P. BENFIELD. 1994. Fluoxetine. A review of its pharmacodynamic and pharmacokinetic properties, and therapeutic use in older patients with depressive illness. Drugs & Aging **6**(1): 64–84.

5. FULTON, B. & D. MCTAVISH. 1995. Fluoxetine—an overview of its pharmacodynamic and pharmacokinetic properties and review of its therapeutic efficacy in obsessive-compulsive disorder. CNS Drugs **3:** 305–322.

6. FULLER, R. W., K. W. PERRY & B. B. MOLLOY. 1975. Effect of 3-(p-trifluoromethyl-phenoxy)-N-methyl-3-phenylpropylamine on the depletion of brain serotonin by 4-chloroamphetamine. J. Pharmacol. Exp. Ther. **193:** 796–803.

7. WONG, D. T., F. P. BYMASTER, J. S. HORNG & B. B. MOLLOY. 1975. A new selective inhibitor for uptake of serotonin into synaptosomes of rat brain: 3-(p-trifluoromethyl-ylphenoxy)-N-methyl-3-phenylpropylamine. J. Pharmacol. Exp. Ther. **193:** 804–811.

8. WONG, D. T., F. P. BYMASTER, L. R. REID & P. G. THRELKELD. 1983. Fluoxetine and two other serotonin uptake inhibitors without affinity for neuronal receptors. Biochem. Pharmacol. **32:** 1287–1293.

9. FULLER, R. W. & D. T. WONG. 1987. Serotonin reuptake blockers *in vitro* and *in vivo*. J. Clin. Psychopharmacol. **7:** 36S–43S.

10. GEYER, M. A., W. J. DAWSEY & A. J. MANDELL. 1978. Fading: A new cytofluorimetric measure quantifying serotonin in the presence of catecholamines at the cellular level in brain. J. Pharmacol. Exp. Ther. **207:** 650–667.

11. MARSDEN, C. A., J. CONTI, E. STROPE, G. CURZON & R. N. ADAMS. 1979. Monitoring 5-hydroxytryptamine release in the brain of the freely moving unanaesthetized rat using *in vivo* voltammetry. Brain Res. **171:** 85–99.

12. GUAN, X. M. & W. J. MCBRIDE. 1988. Fluoxetine increases the extracellular levels of serotonin in the nucleus accumbens. Brain Res. Bull. **21:** 43–46.

13. UNGERSTEDT, U. & A. HALLSTROM. 1987. *In vivo* microdialysis—A new approach to the analysis of neurotransmitters in the brain. Life Sci. **41:** 861–864.

14. FULLER, R. W. 1994. Uptake inhibitors increase extracellular serotonin concentration measured by brain microdialysis. Life Sci. **55:** 163–167.

15. RUTTER, J. J. & S. B. AUERBACH. 1993. Acute uptake inhibition increases extracellular serotonin in the rat forebrain. J. Pharmacol. Exp. Ther. **265:** 1319–1324.

16. CLEMENS, J. A., B. D. SAWYER & B. CERIMELE. 1977. Further evidence that serotonin is a neurotransmitter involved in the control of prolactin serotonin. Endocrinology **100:** 692–698.

17. FULLER, R. W., K. W. PERRY & B. B. MOLLOY. 1974. Effect of an uptake inhibitor of serotonin metabolism in rat brain: Studies with 3-(p-trifluoromethylphenoxy)-N-methyl-3-phenylpropylamine (Lilly 110140). Life Sci. **15:** 1161–1171.

18. FULLER, R. W. & D. T. WONG. 1977. Inhibition of serotonin uptake. Fed. Proc. Fed. Am. Soc. Exp. Biol. **36:** 2154–2158.

19. RUTTER, J. J., C. GUNDLAH & S. B. AUERBACH. 1995. Systemic uptake inhibition decreases serotonin release via somatodendritic autoreceptor activation. Synapse **20:** 225–233.

20. SABOL, K. E., J. B. RICHARDS & L. S. SEIDEN. 1992. Fluoxetine attenuates the DL-fenfluramine-induced increase in extracellular serotonin as measured by *in vivo* dialysis. Brain Res. **585:** 421–424.

21. KALEN, P., R. E. STRECKER, E. ROSENGREN & A. BJORKLUND. 1988. Endogenous release of neuronal serotonin and 5-hydroxyindoleacetic acid in the caudate-putamen

of the rat as revealed by intracerebral dialysis coupled to high-performance liquid chromatography with fluorimetric detection. J. Neurochem. **52:** 1422–1435.

22. RUTTER, J. J., C. GUNDLAH & S. B. AUERBACH. 1994. Increase in extracellular serotonin produced by uptake inhibitors is enhanced after chronic treatment with fluoxetine. Neurosci. Lett. **171:** 183–186.

23. GREEN, A. R. & D. J. HEAL. 1985. The effects of drugs on serotonin-mediated behavioural models. *In* Neuropharmacology of Serotonin. A. R. Green, Ed.: 326–365. Oxford University Press. Oxford, England.

24. ORTMAN, R. 1985. The 5-HT syndrome and the drug discrimination paradigm in rats: Application in behavioral studies on the central 5-HT system. Pharmacopsychiatry **18:** 198–201.

25. GROWDEN, J. H. 1977. Postural changes, tremor, and myoclonus in the rat immediately following injections of p-chloroamphetamine. Neurology **27:** 1074–1077.

26. SLATER, I. H., G. T. JONES & R. A. MOORE. 1978. Inhibition of REM sleep by fluoxetine, a specific inhibitor of serotonin uptake. Neuropharmacology **17:** 383–389.

27. FULLER, R. W., H. D. SNODDY & B. B. MOLLOY. 1976. Pharmacologic evidence for a serotonin neural pathway involved in hypothalamus-pituitary-adrenal function in rats. Life Sci. **19:** 337–346.

28. GIBBS, D. M. & W. VALE. 1983. Effect of the serotonin reuptake inhibitor fluoxetine on corticotropin-releasing factor and vasopressin secretion into hypophysial portal blood. Brain Res. **280:** 176–179.

29. GOUDIE, A. J., E. W. THORNTON & T. J. WHEELER. 1976. Effects of Lilly 110140, a specific inhibitor of 5-hydroxytryptamine uptake, on food intake and on 5-hydroxytryptophan-induced anorexia. Evidence for serotonergic inhibition of feeding. J. Pharm. Pharmacol. **28:** 318–320.

30. WURTMAN, J. J. & R. J. WURTMAN. 1977. Fenfluramine and fluoxetine spare protein consumption while suppressing caloric intake by rats. Science **198:** 1178–1180.

31. ROCKMAN, G. E., Z. AMIT, Z. W. BROWN, C. BOURQUE & S.-O. OGREN. 1982. An investigation of the mechanisms of action of 5-hydroxytryptamine in the suppression of ethanol intake. Neuropharmacology **21:** 341–347.

32. TÖRK, I. 1990. Anatomy of the serotonergic system. Ann. N.Y. Acad. Sci. **600:** 9–35.

33. JACOBS, B. L. & A. C. AZMITIA. 1992. Structure and function of the brain serotonin system. Physiol. Rev. **72:** 165–229.

34. OLIVIER, B., J. MOS, J. VAN DER HEYDEN, J. SCHIPPER, M. TULP, B. BERKELMANS & P. BEVAN. 1987. Serotonergic modulation of agonistic behaviour. *In* Ethopharmacology of agonistic behaviour in animals and humans. B. Olivier, J. Mos & P. F. Brain, Eds.: 162–186. Martinus Nijhoff Publishers. Dordrecht, the Netherlands.

35. EICHELMAN, B. S. 1990. Neurochemical and psychopharmacologic aspects of aggressive behavior. Annu. Rev. Med. **41:** 149–158.

36. VIRKKUNEN, M., D. GOLDMAN, D. A. NIELSEN & M. LINNOILA. 1995. Low brain-serotonin turnover rate (low CSF 5-HIAA) and impulsive violence. J. Psychiatry & Neurosci. **20:** 271–275.

37. VARTIAINEN, H., J. TIIHONEN, A. PUTKONEN, H. KOPONEN, M. VIRKKUNEN, P. HAKOLA & H. LEHTO. 1995. Citalopram, a selective serotonin reuptake inhibitor, in the treatment of aggression in schizophrenia. Acta Psychiatr. Scand. **91:** 348–351.

38. PIHL, R. O., S. N. YOUNG, P. HARDEN, S. PLOTNICK, B. CHAMBERLAIN & F. R. ERVIN. 1995. Acute effect of altered tryptophan levels and alcohol on aggression in normal human males. Psychopharmacology **119:** 353–360.

39. SAUDOU, F., D. A. AMARA, A. DIERICH, M. LEMEUR, S. RAMBOZ, L. SEGU, M. C. BUHOT & R. HEN. 1994. Enhanced aggressive behavior in mice lacking 5-HT1B receptor. Science **265:** 1875–1878.

40. MEHLMAN, P. T., J. D. HIGLEY, I. FAUCHER, A. A. LILLY, D. M. TAUB, J. VICKERS, S. J. SUOMI & M. LINNOILA. 1994. Low CSF 5-HIAA concentrations and severe aggression and impaired impulse control in nonhuman primates. Am. J. Psychiatry **151:** 1485–1491.

41. KYES, R. C., M. B. BOTCHIN, J. R. KAPLAN, S. B. MANUCK & J. J. MANN. 1995. Aggression and brain serotonergic responsivity: Response to slides in male macaques. Physiol. Behav. **57:** 205–208.

42. GIBBONS, J. L., M. GLUSMAN, G. A. BARR, W. H. BRIDGER & S. F. LEIBOWITZ. 1978. Serotonergic mechanisms in aggression. Soc. Neurosci. Abstr. **4:** 493.

43. KOSTOWSKI, W., L. VALZELLI, W. KOZAK & S. BERNASCONI. 1984. Activity of desipramine, fluoxetine and nomifensine on spontaneous and p-CPA-induced muricidal aggression. Pharmacol. Res. Commun. **16:** 265–271.

44. STARK, P., R. W. FULLER & D. T. WONG. 1985. The pharmacologic profile of fluoxetine. J. Clin. Psychiatry **46:** 7–13.

45. BERZSENYI, P., E. GALATEO & L. VALZELLI. 1983. Fluoxetine activity on muricidal aggression induced in rats by p-chlorophenylalanine. Aggressive Behav. **9:** 333–338.

46. MOLINA, V., L. CIESIELSKI, S. GOBAILLE, F. ISEL & P. MANDEL. 1987. Inhibition of mouse killing behavior by serotonin-mimetic drugs: Effects of partial alterations of serotonin neurotransmission. Pharmacol. Biochem. Behav. **27:** 123–131.

47. MOLINA, V., S. GOBAILLE & P. MANDEL. 1986. Effects of serotonin-mimetic drugs on mouse-killing behavior. Aggressive Behav. **12:** 201–211.

48. DATLA, K. P., S. K. MITRA & S. K. BHATTACHARYA. 1991. Serotonergic modulation of footshock induced aggression in paired rats. Indian J. Exp. Biol. **29:** 631–635.

49. FERRIS, C. F. & Y. DELVILLE. 1994. Vasopressin and serotonin interactions in the control of agonistic behavior. Psychoneuroendocrinology **19:** 593–601.

50. WAGNER, G. C., H. FISHER, N. POLE, T. BORVE & S. K. JOHNSON. 1993. Effects of monoaminergic agonists on alcohol-induced increases in mouse aggression. J. Stud. Alcohol Suppl. **11:** 185–191.

51. RALEIGH, M. J., M. T. MCGUIRE, G. L. BRAMMER, D. B. POLLACK & A. YUWILER. 1991. Serotonergic mechanisms promote dominance acquisition in adult male vervet monkeys. Brain Res. **559:** 181–190.

52. CHARNEY, D. S., J. H. KRYSTAL, P. L. DELGADO & G. R. HENINGER. 1990. Serotonin-specific drugs for anxiety and depressive disorders. Annu. Rev. Med. **41:** 437–446.

53. COCCARO, E. F., J. L. ASTILL, J. L. HERBERT & A. G. SCHUT. 1990. Fluoxetine treatment of impulsive aggression in DSM-III-R personality disorder patients [letter]. J. Clin. Psychopharmacol. **10:** 373–375.

54. CORNELIUS, J. R., P. H. SOLOFF, J. M. PEREL & R. F. ULRICH. 1990. Fluoxetine trial in borderline personality disorder. Psychopharmacol. Bull. **26:** 151–154.

55. MARKOWITZ, P. I. 1992. Effect of fluoxetine on self-injurious behavior in the developmentally disabled: A preliminary study. J. Clin. Psychopharmacol. **12:** 27–31.

56. HEILIGENSTEIN, J. H., C. M. BEASLEY JR. & J. H. POTVIN. 1993. Fluoxetine not associated with increased aggression in controlled clinical trials. Int. Clin. Psychopharmacol. **8:** 277–280.

57. FAVA, M., J. F. ROSENBAUM, J. A. PAVA, M. K. MCCARTHY, R. J. STEINGARD & E. BOUFFIDES. 1993. Anger attacks in unipolar depression, Part 1: Clinical correlates and response to fluoxetine treatment. Am. J. Psychiatry **150:** 1158–1163.

58. SALZMAN, C., A. N. WOLFSON, A. SCHATZBERG, J. LOOPER, R. HENKE, M. ALBANESE, J. SCHWARTZ & E. MIYAWAKI. 1995. Effect of fluoxetine on anger in symptomatic volunteers with borderline personality-disorder. J. Clin. Psychopharmacol. **15:** 23–29.

59. DEMBROSKI, T. M., J. M. MACDOUGALL, R. B. WILLIAMS, T. L. HANEY & J. A. BLUMENTHAL. 1985. Components of type A hostility and anger in relationship to angiographic findings. Psychosom. Med. **47:** 219–233.

60. SIEGLER, I. C., B. L. PETERSON, J. C. BAREFOOT & R. B. WILLIAMS. 1992. Hostility during late adolescence predicts coronary risk factors at mid-life. Am. J. Epidemiol. **136:** 146–154.

61. BAREFOOT, J. C., J. C. PATTERSON, T. L. HANEY, T. G. CAYTON, J. R. HICKMAN, JR. & R. B. WILLIAMS. 1994. Hostility in asymptomatic men with angiographically confirmed coronary artery disease. Am. J. Cardiol. **74:** 439–442.

62. WILLIAMS, R. B. & V. A. WILLIAMS. 1993. Anger Kills: Seventeen Strategies for Controlling the Hostility That Can Harm Your Health. Times Books. New York.

Serotonin Diminishes Aggression by Suppressing the Activity of the Vasopressin System

CRAIG F. FERRIS[a]

Program in Neuropsychiatric Sciences
Department of Psychiatry
University of Massachusetts Medical Center
55 Lake Avenue North
Worcester, Massachusetts 01655

The search for biological mechanisms and anatomical substrates underlying the interactions between functionally opposed neurotransmitter systems is an important aspect of the neurobiology of aggression. Two such neurotransmitter systems that have been implicated in the control of aggressive behavior are arginine vasopressin (AVP) and serotonin (5-HT). In the case of the former, microinjection of an AVP receptor antagonist into the anterior hypothalamus of male golden hamsters blocks their offensive aggression, that is, initiated attacks and bites toward a smaller intruder placed into their home case.[1] Adult male hamsters show diminished aggression in a neutral arena when one or both combatants are treated with AVP receptor antagonist in the anterior hypothalamus.[2] Interestingly, male golden hamsters have androgen-sensitive AVP receptor binding in the ventrolateral hypothalamus,[3] an area shown to be critical for aggressive responding in other species.[4] Castration results in a loss of AVP binding in the ventrolateral hypothalamus[3] concomitant with a diminution in aggressive responding.[5] Microinjection of AVP into the ventrolateral hypothalamus results in a dose-dependent decrease in the attack latency of a resident toward an intruder.[5] The facilitation of aggression by AVP is not limited to the golden hamster. Injection of AVP into the amygdala or septum of castrated rats enhances aggression,[6,7] whereas the intracerebroventricular administration of AVP in prairie voles increases their aggression toward male intruders.[8]

In the case of 5-HT, there is a vast literature showing that this classical neurotransmitter can diminish aggressive behavior in animals and humans.[9,10] In animal studies, depleting 5-HT levels in the hypothalamus of resident rats by neurotoxin microinjection increases their offensive aggression toward intruders.[11,12] Conversely, resident rats treated with eltoprazine, a $5\text{-HT}_{1A/1B}$ receptor agonist, show a dose-dependent decrease in offensive aggression toward intruders.[13] The importance of 5-HT_{1B} receptors in mediating the effects of 5-HT on aggression is underscored by the discovery that homozygous mutant mice lacking the 5-HT_{1B} receptor have enhanced offensive aggression.[14]

Because activation of 5-HT_1 receptors decreases aggressive responding, it is not unexpected that the general elevation of extracellular levels of 5-HT in the central nervous system (CNS) by selective 5-HT reuptake inhibitors, for example, fluvoxamine, fluoxetine, and sertraline, also diminishes aggressive behavior.[15–20]

---

[a] Tel: (508) 856-5530; fax: (508) 856-6426; e-mail: craig.ferris@banyan.ummed.edu.

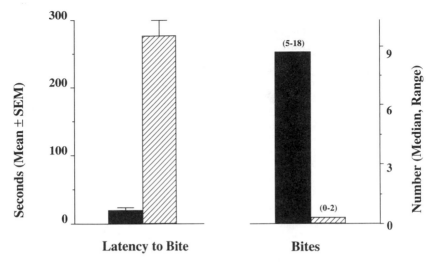

FIGURE 1. Intraperitoneal injection of fluoxetine inhibits offensive aggression in experienced fighters. Vertical lines denote SEM. ■, vehicle; ▨, fluoxetine.

In a recent experiment, a resident/intruder paradigm was used to evaluate the role of 5-HT in the control of offensive aggression in hamsters. On the day of testing, male hamsters experienced in attacking smaller intruders were given an intraperitoneal (ip) injection of fluoxetine (20 mg/kg, n = 8). One hour later, a smaller male intruder was placed into the home cage of these fluoxetine-treated residents. The resident was scored for latency to bite the intruder, total number of bites, and total contact time with the intruder over a 10-min test period. Each resident was tested with both fluoxetine and vehicle, with one week between treatments. Fluoxetine significantly diminished their offensive aggression, as shown in FIGURE 1. Following treatment with vehicle, animals had a mean latency to bite intruders of less than 20 seconds and a mean of 10 bites per 10 minutes. Following treatment with flouxetine, these same animals showed a significant increase in the latency to bite. The contact time did not differ between treatments, as the experienced fighters spent approximately three minutes of the test period smelling and exploring the intruder.

Although several studies have reported elevations in CNS levels of 5-HT as a result of fluoxetine treatment,[21–25] the neural substrates and mechanism(s) of action of fluoxetine on aggressive behavior remain unclear. Interestingly, ip administration of fluoxetine blocks aggression, facilitated by the microinjection of AVP into the ventrolateral hypothalamus[16] (FIG. 2). In a more recent study, the effect of fluoxetine on AVP-facilitated aggression was tested in the anterior hypothalamus. Ten male hamsters were tested for offensive aggression in response to vehicle microinjection in the absence of fluoxetine and AVP microinjection in the presence and absence of fluoxetine. The treatment schedule was counterbalanced, and animals were tested once every five days over a fifteen-day period. On the day of testing, animals were pretreated with ip injections of vehicle or fluoxetine (10 mg/kg). Approximately 60–90 minutes later, the hamsters were microinjected in the anterior hypothalamus with either AVP (0.09 μM in saline) or saline vehicle

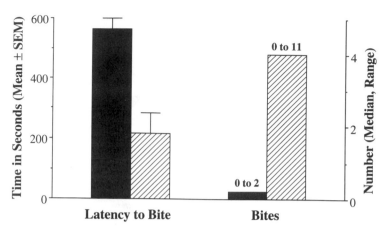

FIGURE 2. Intraperitoneal injection of fluoxetine (Fluox) blocks offensive aggression facilitated by the microinjection of arginine vasopressin (AVP) into the ventrolateral hypothalamus. Vertical lines denote SEM. ■, Fluox + AVP; ▨, vehicle + AVP.

in a volume of 100 nanoliters. Two minutes later a smaller male intruder was introduced, and the resident was scored for total bites (FIG. 3). When injected with saline vehicle into the anterior hypothalamus following ip vehicle treatment, resident animals showed a mean number of approximately five bites over a 10-min test period. When the same animals were microinjected with AVP into the anterior hypothalamus following ip vehicle treatment, the number of bites increased by twofold. However, treatment with fluoxetine essentially abolished the effect of AVP. This study raises the possibility that 5-HT may act to diminish aggression by interfering with action of AVP to facilitate aggression.

In preliminary studies, the effect of fluoxetine on AVP release was tested by sampling the anterior hypothalamus for interstitial levels of AVP by microdialysis.

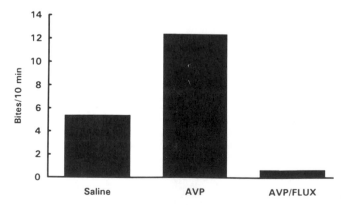

FIGURE 3. Intraperitoneal injection of fluoxetine blocks biting attacks facilitated by the microinjection of AVP into the anterior hypothalamus.

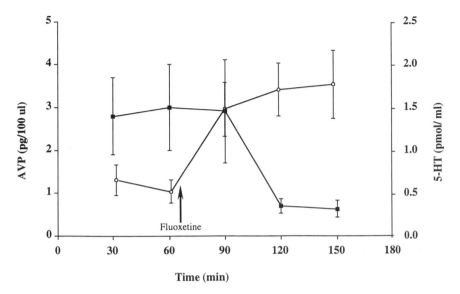

FIGURE 4. Intraperitoneal injection of fluoxetine elevates serotonin (5-HT) and lowers AVP levels in dialysate collected from the anterior hypothalamus of conscious male hamsters. Vertical lines denote SEM. ■, AVP; ○, 5-HT.

Male hamsters were anesthetized and stereotaxically implanted with a micro-dialysis probe aimed at the anterior hypothalamus. On the following day the microdialysis probe of conscious animals was perfused with sterile saline at a rate of 2 μL/minute. Dialysate samples were collected at 30-min intervals prior to and following the ip injection of fluoxetine (10 mg/kg). Each sample was split and assayed for 5-HT, using HPLC and electrochemical detection, and AVP by radioimmunoassay. Within 30 min of fluoxetine treatment, there was a dramatic rise in 5-HT levels in the anterior hypothalamus (FIG. 4). By 60 min postfluoxetine treatment, there was a concomitant decrease in AVP levels.

The studies reported here indicate that 5-HT can diminish offensive aggression in the male golden hamster and other species. Treatment with fluoxetine, a selective serotonin reuptake inhibitor, significantly decreases offensive aggression in experienced fighters while leaving other behaviors like social interest, sexual activity, and motor activity intact. The action of 5-HT to inhibit aggressive responding may, in part, be due to inhibition of the AVP system. The inhibition may be at the level of the act and pre- and postsynaptic sites. These animal studies examining the interaction between AVP and 5-HT are particularly exciting inasmuch as a recent clinical study indicates a similar reciprocal relationship between these neurotransmitters in human studies.[25] Personality-disordered subjects with a history of fighting and assault show a negative correlation for prolactin release in response to d-fenfluramine challenge, an indication of a hyposensitive 5-HT system. Moreover, these same subjects show a positive correlation between cerebrospinal fluid levels of AVP and aggression. Thus, in humans, a hyposensitive 5-HT system may result in enhanced CNS levels of AVP and the facilitation of aggressive behavior.

REFERENCES

1. FERRIS, C. F. & M. POTEGAL. 1988. Vasopressin receptor blockade in the anterior hypothalamus suppresses aggression in hamsters. Physiol. Behav. **44:** 235–239.
2. POTEGAL, M. & C. F. FERRIS. 1990. Intraspecific aggression in male hamsters is inhibited by intrahypothalamic VP-receptor antagonist. Aggressive Behav. **15:** 311–320.
3. DELVILLE, Y. & C. F. FERRIS. 1995. Sexual differences in vasopressin receptor binding within the ventrolateral hypothalamus in golden hamsters. Brain Res. **681:** 91–96.
4. KRUK, M. R. 1991. Ethology and pharmacology of hypothalamic aggression in the rat. Neurosci. Biobehav. Rev. **15:** 527–538.
5. DELVILLE, Y., K. M. MANSOUR & C. F. FERRIS. 1996. Testosterone facilitates aggression by modulating vasopressin receptors in the hypothalamus. Physiol. Behav. **60:** 25–29.
6. KOOLHAAS, J. M., T. H. C. VAN DEN BRINK, B. ROOZENDAL & F. BOORSMA. 1990. Medial amygdala and aggressive behavior: Interaction between testosterone and vasopressin. Aggressive Behav. **16:** 223–229.
7. KOOLHAAS, J. M., E. MOOR, Y. HIEMSTRA & B. BOHUS. 1991. The testosterone-dependent vasopressinergic neurons in the medial amygdala and lateral septum: Involvement in social behaviour of male rats. *In* Vasopressin. S. Jard & R. Jamison, Eds.: 213–219. INSERM/John Libbey Eurotext Ltds. Paris-Londres.
8. WINSLOW, J., N. HASTINGS, S. CARTER, C. HARBAUGH & T. INSEL. 1993. A role for central vasopressin in pair bonding in monogamous prairie voles. Nature **365:** 545–548.
9. COCCARO, E. F. 1989. Central serotonin and impulsive aggression. Br. J. Psychiatry **155:** 52–62.
10. OLIVIER, B. & J. MOS. 1992. Rodent models of aggressive behavior and serotoninergic drugs. Prog. Neuro-Psychopharmacol. Biol. Psychiat. **16:** 847–870.
11. ELLISON, G. 1976. Monoamine neurotoxins: Selective and delayed effects on behavior in colonies of laboratory rats. Brain Res. **103:** 81–92.
12. VERGNES, M., A. DEPAULIS, A. BOEHRER & E. KEMPF. 1988. Selective increase of offensive behavior in the rat following intrahypothalamic 5,7-DHT-induced serotonin depletion. Behav. Brain Res. **29:** 85–91.
13. SIJBESMA, H., J. SCHIPPER & E. R. DE KLOET. 1990. The anti-aggressive drug eltoprazine preferentially binds to 5-HT$_{1A}$ and 5-HT$_{1B}$ receptor subtypes in rat brain: Sensitivity to guanine nucleotides. Eur. J. Pharmacol. **187:** 209–223.
14. SAUDOU, F., D. J. AMARA, A. DIERICH, M. LEMEUR, S. RAMBOZ, A. SEGU, M-C. BUHOT & R. HEN. 1994. Enhanced aggressive behavior in mice lacking 5-HT$_{1B}$ receptor. Science **265:** 1875–1878.
15. COCCARO, E. F., J. J. ASTILL, J. L. HERBERT & A. G. SCHUT. 1990. Fluoxetine treatment of impulsive aggression in DSM-III-R personality disorder patients. J. Clin. Psychopharmacol. **10:** 373–375.
16. DELVILLE, Y., K. M. MANSOUR & C. F. FERRIS. 1995. Serotonin blocks vasopressin-facilitated offensive aggression: Interactions within the ventrolateral hypothalamus of golden hamsters. Physiol. Behav. **59:** 813–816.
17. SANCHEZ, C. & J. HYTTEL. 1994. Isolation-induced aggression in mice: Effects of 5-hydroxytryptamine uptake inhibitors and involvement of postsynaptic 5-HT$_{1A}$ receptors. Eur. J. Pharmacol. **264:** 241–247.
18. FERRIS, C. F. & Y. DELVILLE. 1994. Vasopressin and serotonin interactions in the control of agonistic behavior. Psychoneuroendocrinology **19:** 593–601.
19. GUAN, X-M. & W. J. MCBRIDE. 1988. Fluoxetine increases the extracellular levels of serotonin in the nucleus accumbens. Brain Res. Bull. **21:** 43–46.
20. KAVOUSSI, R. J., J. LIU & E. F. COCCARO. 1994. An open trial of sertraline in personality disordered patients with impulsive aggression. J. Clin. Psychol. **55:** 137–141.
21. AUERBACH, S. B., M. J. MINZENBERG & L. O. WILKINSON. 1989. Extracellular serotonin and 5-hydroxyindoleacetic acid in hypothalamus of unanesthetized rats measured by *in vivo* dialysis coupled to high-performance liquid chromatography with

electrochemical detection: Dialysate serotonin reflects neuronal release. Brain Res. **499:** 281–290.

22. CHEN, N. H. & M. E. REITH. 1994. Effects of locally applied cocaine, lidocaine, and various uptake blockers on monoamine transmission in the ventral tegmental area of freely moving rats: Microdialysis study on monoamine interrelationships. J. Neurochem. **63:** 1701–1713.

23. JORDAN, S., G. L. KRAMER, P. K. ZUKAS, M. MOELLER & F. PETTY. 1994. *In vivo* biogenic amine efflux in medial prefrontal cortex with imipramine, fluoxetine, and fluvoxamine. Synapse (NY) **18:** 294–297.

24. HAUG, M., L. WALLIAN & P. F. BRAIN. 1990. Effects of 9-OH-DPAT and fluoxetine on activity and attack by female mice towards lactating intruders. Gen. Pharmacol. **21:** 845–849.

25. COCCARO, E. F., R. J. KAVOUSSI, M. E. BERMAN & C. F. FERRIS. 1996. Cerebrospinal fluid vasopressin: Correlates with indices of aggression and serotonin function in human subjects. Arch. Gen. Psychiatry. Submitted for publication.

Perinatal Stress and Impairment of the Stress Response

Possible Link to Nonoptimal Behavior

JEAN A. KING[a]

Program in Behavior Neuroscience
Department of Psychiatry
University of Massachusetts Medical School
Worcester, Massachusetts 01655

INTRODUCTION

Determining the role of perinatal stress in the development of nonoptimal behavioral outcome has engaged both social scientists and neuroscientists. In both human studies and animal models, functioning of the hypothalamic-pituitary-adrenal (HPA) axis has been used as a neurophysiological indicator of stress responsivity.[1,2] During development this axis undergoes rapid changes,[3,4] a number of which provide different "windows of vulnerability" that significantly alter the brain's cytoarchitecture,[5] providing the possible basis for the development of nonoptimal behavior, like aggression. Despite this progress, however, there has been little integration across disciplines, mainly due to the exclusive use of humans or animals in the respective studies. Here we will attempt an integration by considering development of the stress response, perinatal stress, and possible impairment of the stress response in aggression.

DEVELOPMENT OF THE STRESS RESPONSE

Stress is any condition (perceived or real) that threatens homeostasis. From an evolutionary point of view, the body's response to this threat (or the stress response) is believed to have developed as an alarm system for animals caught in a potentially dangerous situation, and thus the name "the fight or flight reaction." The body's defense mechanism to combat stress is made up of a group of endocrine and neuroendocrine factors. It is generally accepted that the HPA axis is a major hormonal pathway mediating the stress response and that subtle changes in the components of the axis can have long-term effects on behavior and development. The axis is initiated when parvocellular neurons in the paraventricular nucleus of the hypothalamus release corticotropin-releasing factor (CRF) into the median eminence. CRF traverses the hypothalamic-pituitary portal system to the anterior pituitary gland where it stimulates the release of ACTH (adrenocorticotropic hormone). ACTH then stimulates the adrenal gland to release glucocorticoids.

Proper functioning of the cascade may be impairment during development. Glucocorticoids act as major regulators of carbohydrate and lipid metabolism,

---

[a] Tel: (508) 856-4979; fax: (508) 856-6426; e-mail: jking@bangate.ummed.edu.

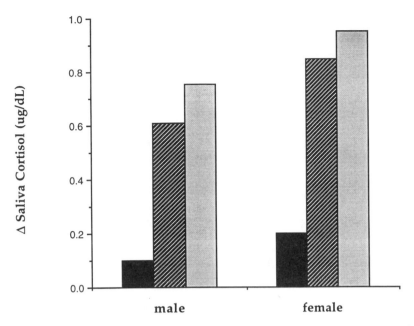

FIGURE 1. Changes in cortisol levels (μg/dL) taken before and after NBAS administration among healthy, preterm, term, and post-term male and female infants at 24–72 hours of age. The difference in cortisol changes between preterm and term infants increased significantly with age in both males and females. ■, preterm; ▨, term, □, post-term.

cardiovascular tone, and muscle contraction. Glucocorticoids also act as negative feedback in the cascade of the HPA axis. This negative feedback is particularly dynamic during development. de Kloet and others,[4] and Sapolsky and Meaney[3] have suggested that at some period during development the levels of corticosteroid receptors and corticosterone-binding globulin (CBG) decrease in such a way that the axis is mostly inhibited. This hypothesis, therefore, explains decreased release of ACTH and glucocorticoids under stressful conditions. This period of adrenocortical quiescence is referred to as the stress hyporesponsive period (SHRP). SHRP occurs during the first two weeks of postnatal life in rats, when similar stressors to those used in adult animals fail to elicit a comparable HPA response. SHRP in development has also been shown to be a defining "window" for factors that establish risk and resilience to various behavioral outcomes, including aggression.[6]

Although some researchers have explored the phenomenon of SHRP and its relationship to long-term behavioral outcome in animals, virtually no one has used this valuable framework to assess the possible existence of this phenomenon in humans. Much recent work has focused on the stress response in humans.[1,7,8] In order to integrate physiological functioning and behavioral measures in newborn human infants, these researchers have assessed HPA functioning through changes in cortisol levels and biobehavioral measures. The Brazelton Neonatal Behavioral Assessment Scale (NBAS)[9] is an assessment involving several behavioral measures. NBAS thereby provides a framework where reflexes that can be used as indicators of behavioral organization and intensity of reaction have been correlated with HPA functioning.[8] Although controversy still exists as to whether basal functioning[10] or HPA reactivity (release of cortisol over basal levels[8]) is the real indicator of optimal biobehavioral functioning early in development, it is generally agreed that physiological functioning and stressful stimuli are highly correlated immediately postpartum.

These studies have been confirmed by data generated regarding changes in the level of cortisol in healthy preterm neonates after administration of NBAS compared to healthy term and post-term infants (FIG. 1). NBAS performed on neonates, housed in the healthy newborn nursery at Crawford Long Hospital (Atlanta, GA) within 48 hours after birth, showed marked changes in saliva cortisol that increased with maturity.[11] Other researchers[1] have found that these changes were sexually dimorphic, with boys having higher cortisol responses to NBAS than girls. Furthermore, others have also shown a graded stress response in human infants at this time.[8] However, when studies are performed on sick neonates, many more neonates had higher serum cortisol levels than their well counterparts, suggesting that the magnitude of response of the HPA axis may be dependent on factors other than an inherent immaturity,[12] such as hyporesponsivity to stressors. In a recent study in human infants at two, four, and six months of age, both basal

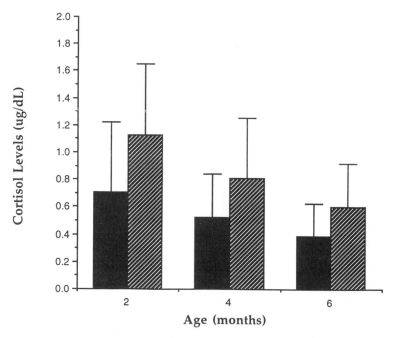

FIGURE 2. Mean ($\pm$ SE) baseline and inoculation salivary cortisol levels in healthy infants (optimal birth condition) at 2, 4, and 6 months of age (n = 64). Baseline saliva cortisol was collected in the waiting room prior to visit, and inoculation saliva cortisol was collected 20 minutes poststress ($p < 0.001$ or better for main effect of age on baseline cortisol levels). ($p < 0.003$ or better for inoculation ANOVA age $\times$ group effect.) Data from Ramsay and Lewis.[13] ■, baseline; ▨, inoculation.

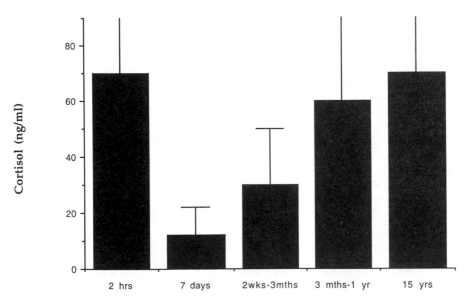

FIGURE 3A. Mean (± estimated SD from data) plasma cortisol levels in healthy unstressed infants. Cortisol levels (ng/mL) (n = 174; 83 boys and 91 girls) were taken between 8:00–10:00 A.M. Mean cortisol levels at 7 days and 2 weeks–3 months were significantly lower (p ≤ 0.05) than 2 h postdelivery. Plasma rose steadily after 3 months to relatively constant mean levels (75 ng/mL) at 1 year.[14]

cortisol levels and levels of postinoculation stress were significantly decreased in an inverse age-dependent manner (FIG. 2 and ref. 13). A similar age-dependent profile for cortisol levels have been demonstrated in animal models and human infants (FIG. 3A and ref. 14; FIG. 3B and ref. 3). These levels reflect an initial high level of postpartum cortisol that decreases significantly in early life, followed by a slight increase that plateaus with maturity.

Taken together, the data suggest that the human neonatal stress response may parallel some aspects of the response in animal development, in that lower basal levels and increased reactivity may correlate with differential levels of maturity. More importantly, the stress hyporesponsive period may act as a window of vulnerability for nonoptimal behavioral outcome.

PERINATAL STRESS AND THE STRESS RESPONSE: AGGRESSION

The premise that early stress can affect the animal's ability to respond to stress through changes in plasticity of the nervous system has been linked to certain molecular events[5] and neuroendocrine manifestations that may persist long after the termination of the stressor,[15] thereby supporting future abnormal behavioral outcome. For instance, perinatal administration of nicotine has been shown to modulate the HPA axis and has been identified as a potent stressor with long-term effects.[15] Early work by Kershbaum[16] suggested that nicotine impacted the HPA axis at the level of the adrenal glands, resulting in increased corticosterone

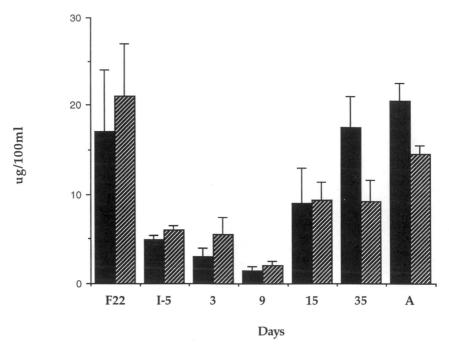

FIGURE 3B. Mean (± SEM) corticosterone levels in male and female rats at various ages: F, fetal: A, adult (90–120 days of age). (Sapolsky & Meany.[3] With permission from *Brain Research Reviews*.) ■, males; ▨, females.

levels. These studies were confirmed by Balfour *et al.*, who showed that nicotine administration to unstressed rats increased the levels of plasma corticosterone, which remained high for one hour after injection. In fact, acute administration of nicotine, when monitored in a time-dependent manner, caused an early rise in ACTH secretion that was followed by an increase in nicotine-induced corticosterones.[2,17–19] Furthermore, at the hypothalamic level, nicotine has been shown to modulate CRF release in a dose-dependent fashion.[20] The receptors responsible for modulating nicotine-induced ACTH release are apparently exclusively nicotinic, inasmuch as muscarinic agonists do not alter ACTH release.[21] These studies suggest that nicotine may be a stimulatory agent in the secretion of CRF, ACTH, and corticosterones, or the principal molecules of the entire HPA axis in adult animals. Recent work has confirmed that prenatal exposure to nicotine also acts as a potent effector of this axis, causing increased basal release of ACTH postpartum.[2] This early exposure to nicotine has been shown to affect the HPA axis permanently. Animals challenged in adulthood with nicotine have a differential response, depending on dosage.[22] It is important to note that although all these studies were done in animals, cigarette smoking in humans has also been shown to elevate levels of cortisol and ACTH in plasma.[23] In fact, recent data suggest that 17% of women in the United States smoke during pregnancy. Because nicotine has been shown to freely cross the placenta and concentrate in fetal tissue,[24] the perinatal effects of this stressor may be of significance.

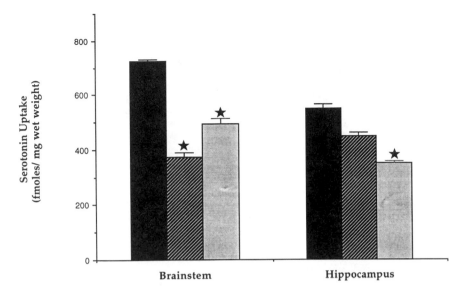

FIGURE 4. Changes in serotonin high-affinity uptake (fmol/mg wet weight) in the brain stem and hippocampus of 21-day-old neonates treated prenatally with nicotine, ACTH 1-39, or saline (n = 4 per subgroup). *p < 0.05 compared to saline controls: ± represents SE of the mean. ■, prenatal saline; ▨, prenatal ACTH 1-39; ▢, prenatal nicotine.

Overexposure to nicotine may be associated with aggression. Aggression has been linked to several neurochemical factors, including testosterone,[6] vasopressin,[25] and serotonin.[26] Interestingly, all of these factors have also been linked to nicotine exposure. In an animal study, researchers showed that prenatal exposure to nicotine altered a rise in testosterone levels in male fetuses[27] and adult male rats.[28] An impairment of the vasopressin system, the hormonal system implicated in aggression, was also reported in rats treated with nicotine prenatally.[29] Furthermore, recent work has also shown that serotonin uptake sites are significantly decreased in the hippocampus and brainstem of neonates administered with nicotine prenatally (ref. 11; FIG. 4). Taken together, these studies of animals prenatally exposed to nicotine exhibit a neurochemical profile akin to that observed in behavioral paradigms associated with aggression.

PERINATAL NICOTINE LEVELS AND AGGRESSION IN HUMANS

Most youngsters seen in mental health clinics are referred for aggressive types of behavior, including conduct disorder. As researchers search for reliable predictive factors of aggression, many are recognizing that early life may be a window of resilience as well as of vulnerability for development of long-term behavioral patterns. In a study looking at prenatal exposure to nicotine and conduct disorder in children, Weitzmann[30] analyzed data of parental reports from a population-based National Longitudinal Survey for children aged 4–11 years. After controlling for the primary demographic factors, that is, family structure, parental psychopathology, and other factors, including alcohol use, researchers still found evidence that there were increased behavioral problems in children prenatally exposed to nicotine.[30,31] The above data are supported by a study performed outside the United States.[32] Using a Finnish cohort, researchers found an interesting association between criminal behavior and prenatal exposure to nicotine.[32] In one of the most recent longitudinal studies of 177 clinic-referred boys, Wakschlag and colleagues[31] assessed subjects five times in a six-year period with the objective of controlling for parental antisocial behavior in establishing a link between nicotine and prenatal exposure, and development of conduct disorder. These researchers reported that prenatal nicotine exposure dramatically increased the risk of conduct disorder in boys through a direct interaction. This behavior was not mediated by known factors like perinatal outcome, demographic variables, parental psychopathology, or family support.[31]

CONCLUSION

Although the role of psychosocial factors on behavioral outcome has been well documented, the role of perinatal stresses, like nicotine, on development of nonoptimal behavior has been less clear. Animal models suggest an importance of the early perinatal environment and a correlation with plasticity of the neuroendocrine system implicated in stress responsivity. Thus, by focusing on this finding, clinical studies may begin to address these factors in humans with hypotheses that take into account a hyporesponsive period of stress. This approach may enable clinicians to look more carefully at unnecessary stressful procedures early in development when the stress-response axis is hyporesponsive and less adaptive. In addition, the link between early perinatal stressors and nonoptimal stress responses, involving behaviors like aggression, may provide a framework to address effective therapies. Here we have presented evidence suggesting that by integrating not only sociological and neuroscience studies but also animal model studies with human patient observations, we may begin to get a clearer picture of the precise links between perinatal stress and the stress response, or hyporesponsiveness.

REFERENCES

1. DAVIS, M. & E. EMORY. 1995. Sex differences in neonatal stress reactivity. Child Dev. **66:** 14–27.
2. KING, J. A. & F. L. STRAND. 1988. Increased ACTH plasma levels with prenatal and postnatal nicotine administration in rats. Ann. N.Y. Acad. Sci. **529:** 301–303.
3. SAPOLSKY, R. M. & M. J. MEANY. 1986. Maturation of the adrenocortical stress response: Neuroendocrine control mechanisms and the stress hyporesponsive period. Brain Res. Rev. **11:** 65–76.
4. DE KLOET, E. R., P. ROSENFELD, J. A. M. vanEckelen, W. SLETANTO & S. LEVINE. 1988. Stress, glucocorticoids and development. Prog. Brain Res. **73:** 101–120.
5. MEANY, M. J., R. M. SAPOLSKY & B. S. McEWEN. 1985. The development of the glucocorticoid receptor system in the rat limbic brain. I. Ontogeny and autoregulation. Dev. Brain Res. **18:** 159–164.
6. KLEIN, W. P. & N. G. SIMON. 1991. Timing of neonatal testosterone exposure in the differentiation of estrogenic regulatory systems for aggression. Physiol. Behav. **50:** 91–93.
7. FIELD, T., D. SANDBERG, R. GARCIA, N. VEGA-LAHR, S. GOLDSTEIN & L. GUY.

1985. Pregnancy problems, postpartum depression and early mother-infant interactions. Dev. Psychol. **21:** 1152–1156.

8. GUNNAR, M. R., J. ISENSEE & S. FUST. 1987. Adrenocortical activity and the Brazelton Neonatal Assessment Scale: Moderating effects of the newborn's biochemical status. Child Dev. **58:** 1448–1458.

9. BRAZELTON, T. B. 1978. Introduction. *In* Organization and Stability of Newborn Behavior: A Commentary on the Brazelton Neonatal Behavior Assessment Scale (pp 1–13). A. J. Sameroff, Ed.: Monog. Soc. Res. Child Dev. **43:** 5–6.

10. SPANGLER, G. & R. SCHEUBECK. 1993. Behavioral organization in newborns and its relation to adrenocortical and cardiac activity. Child Dev. **64:** 622–633.

11. KING, J. A. & E. EMORY. Perinatal stress in human infants. In preparation.

12. ECONOMOU, G., S. ANDRONIKOU, A. CHALLA, V. CHOLEVAS & P. D. LAPATSANIS. 1993. Cortisol secretion in stressed babies during the neonatal period. Horm. Res. **40:** 217–221.

13. RAMSAY, D. S. & M. LEWIS. 1984. Developmental change in infant cortisol and behavioral response to inoculation. Child Dev. **65:** 1491–1502.

14. SIPPELL, G. W., H. G. DORR, F. BIDLINGMAIER & D. KNORR. 1980. Plasma levels of aldosterone, corticosterone, 11-deoxycorticosterone, progesterone, 17-hydroxy-progesterone, cortisol and cortisone during infancy and childhood. Pediatr. Res. **14:** 39–46.

15. KING, J. A., M. DAVILLA-GARCIA, E. C. AZMITTA & F. L. STRAND. 1991. Differential effects of prenatal and postnatal ACTH or nicotine exposure on 5-HT high affinity uptake in the neonatal rat brain. Int. J. Dev. Neurosci. **9:** 281–286.

16. KERSHBAUM, A., D. J. PAPPAJOHN, S. BELLET, M. HIRABAYASHI & H. SHAFIHA. 1968. Effect of smoking and nicotine on adrenocortical secretion. J. Am. Med. Assoc. **203:** 275–278.

17. ANDERSSON, K., R. SIEGEL, K. FUXE & P. ENEROTH. 1983. Intravenous injections of nicotine induce very rapid and discrete reductions of hypothalamic catecholamine levels associated with increased ACTH, vasopressin and prolactin secretion. Acta Physiol. Scand. **118:** 35–40.

18. CAM, G. R. & J. R. BASSETT. 1984. Effect of prolonged exposure to nicotine and stress on the pituitary-adrenocortical response. Pharmacol. Biochem. Behav. **20:** 221–226.

19. KING, J. A. & F. L. STRAND. 1988. Nicotine depression of neonatal motor activity. Peptides **9:** 39–44.

20. WEIDENFELD, J., N. SIEGAL, R. CONFORTI, R. MIZRACHI & T. BRENNER. 1983. Effect of intracerebroventricular injection of nicotinic acetylcholine receptor antibodies on ACTH, corticosterone and prolactin secretion in male rat. Brain Res. **265:** 152–156.

21. HILLHOUSE, E. W., J. BURDEN & M. T. JONES. 1975. The effect of various putative neurotransmitters on the release of corticotrophin releasing hormone from the hypothalamus of the rat *in vitro*. I. The effect of acetylcholine and noradrenaline. Neuroendocrinology **17:** 1–11.

22. POLAND, R. E., P. LUTCHMANSINGH, D. AU, C. HSIEH, S. AFRANE, S. LYDECKER & J. T. MCCRACKEN. 1994. Exposure to threshold doses of nicotine in utero: II. Neuroendocrine response to nicotine in adult male offspring. Dev. Brain Res. **83:** 278–284.

23. WILKINS, J. N., H. E. CARLSON, H. VAN VUNAKIS, M. A. HILL, E. GRITZ & M. E. JARVIK. 1982. Nicotine from cigarette smoking increases circulating levels of cortisol, growth hormone and prolactin in male chronic smokers. Psychopharmacology **78:** 305–308.

24. LUCK, W., H. NAU & R. HANSEN. 1985. Nicotine and cotinine transfer to the human fetus, placenta and amniotic fluid of smoking mothers. Dev. Pharmacol. Ther. **8:** 384–395.

25. FERRIS, C. F., J. F. AXELSON, A. M. MARTIN & L. F. ROBERGE. 1989. Vasopressin immunoreactivity in the anterior hypothalamus is altered during the establishment of dominant/subordinate relationships between hamsters. Neuroscience **29:** 675–683.

26. COCCARO, E. F. 1989. Central serotonin and impulsive aggression. Symposium of the XVIth Collegium Internationale Neuro-psychopharmacologicum: Serotonin in behavioral disorders. Br. J. Psychiatry **155:** 52–62.

27. LICHTENSTEIGER, W. & M. SCHLUMPF. 1985. Modification of early neuroendocrine
     development by drugs and endogenous peptides. Prog. Neuroendocrinol. **1:** 153–166.
28. SEGARRA, A. C. & F. L. STRAND. 1989. Perinatal administration of nicotine alters
     subsequent sexual behavior and testosterone levels of male rats. Brain Res. **480:**
     151–159.
29. ZBUZEK, V. K. & V. ZBUZEK. 1992. Vasopressin system is impaired in rat offspring
     prenatally exposed to chronic nicotine. Ann. N.Y. Acad. Sci. **654:** 540–541.
30. WEITZMAN, M., S. GORTMAKER & A. SOBOL. 1992. Maternal smoking and behavior
     problems of children. Pediatrics **90:** 342–349.
31. WAKSCHLAG, L. S., B. LAHEY, R. LOEBER, S. GREEN & B. LEVENTHAL. 1985. Maternal
     smoking during pregnancy increases offspring's risk of conduct disorder. Arch. Gen.
     Psychiatry. Submitted.
32. RANTAKALLIO, P., E. LAARA, M. ISOHANNI & I. MOILAMEN. 1992. Maternal smoking
     during pregnancy and delinquency of the offspring. Intl. J. Epidemiol. **21:** 1106–1113.

Developmental Factors Influencing Aggression

Animal Models and Clinical Correlates

JOSEPH GARTNER[a] AND
PATRICIA M. WHITAKER-AZMITIA

Department of Psychiatry and Behavioral Science
State University of New York
Stony Brook, New York 11794-8101

The human brain develops by tremendous overgrowth followed by periods of rearrangement and regression. Most of the neurons of the brain are born and differentiated prenatally. Outgrowth of axons and synaptogenesis continues up to approximately two years of age. At two years of age, the brain contains the highest concentration of neurotransmitters and their receptors. At this time, and continuing up to approximately five or six years of age, selections are made regarding which synaptic connections are kept and which are eliminated. Most of this selection is based simply on what synapses are being used.

For example, changes in sensory input at this time will have important consequences in selecting synapses and connections that remain for life. The impact of extraordinary early sensory experience provides several clear-cut examples of environmental extremes leading to permanent changes in brain function. Prolonged and severe isolation in children produces marked delays in intellectual and language function that remain permanent unless the isolation is reversed prior to puberty.[1,2] This may be a case of too few synapses being chosen. Another example of excessive synaptic loss may be seen in children with impairment of language after transient hearing loss from middle ear infection. Conversely, excess retention or formation of synapses may also occur when there is a need to recover lost functions. This may be seen in children undergoing cerebral lobectomy at a relatively young age, who have little gross language impairment because of the ability of the alternate hemisphere to take over these functions.

But what about the case of more subtle environmental influences? Does the environment actually change the brain circuitry and chemistry? Does this altered brain chemistry then result in observed behaviors? There is evidence from animal studies that this could indeed be true. Animal studies have been used to model several human conditions—specifically abuse and neglect, the influence of gender, and the role of specifically identified genetic changes. Thus, aggression produced in animals by environmental factors during development could prove useful in understanding aggression in children produced by similar factors.

---

[a] Author to whom correspondence should be addressed. Tel: (516) 444-1619; fax: (516) 444-7534.

ABUSE AND NEGLECT

Lower socioeconomic status, increased rates of abuse, coercive family interactions, and neglect or maltreatment have all been shown to contribute to aggressive behaviors. The degree of the socioeconomic problem appears related to the degree of aggressive behavior, with more severe disorders associated with greater adversity.[3–5] Antisocial and aggressive behavior in the family, caused by environmental and genetic factors, contributes to a child's aggressive behavior. Regardless of the genetic-environmental background, the stability of severe aggressive and conduct-disordered behavior is remarkable, paralleling that of IQ.[6] It is likely that prolonged rather than short-term exposure to multiple adverse experiences is the rule for the most impaired children. Once antisocial behavior is established in childhood, the risk for adult antisocial behavior increases dramatically as the number of symptoms increase and age of onset decreases.[7]

Maltreated children develop insecure attachments with their caretakers.[8] They also show greater aggressivity, avoidance, and withdrawal in peer settings.[9,10] Whereas socially aggressive children more often attribute hostile intention to others, even in ambiguous situations,[11,12] maltreated children more often display aggressive behavior and tend to justify their behaviors as more permissible.[13] Impairment of empathy for the pain of others is also found in maltreated children,[14] and others have noted language problems, particularly in putting feelings into words. Both of these characteristics are hypothesized to be intermediary factors in the expression of aggressive behavior.[15]

Human infants suffering the most profound kinds of isolation are found to have extreme developmental delays in language, intellectual, and social functioning.[1] After discovery and treatment, children may recover to near normal or normal intellectual, language, and social functioning if the severe deprivation has not continued too long. However, even lesser degrees of neglect are associated with aggressivity and poor peer relationships.[16–18] Physical abuse is also found to have occurred at high rates in violent adolescents.[19,20] It is likely that individual characteristics and the nature of the stress combine to produce differing behavioral and biologic adaptations.

There is good evidence that aggressive responses can be learned in animals[21] as well as in humans.[22] Learned aggression has been demonstrated for aggressive children in the context of prolonged coercive (negative-negative) family interactions.[23–28] Interactions between family variables and wider neighborhood and social-environmental characteristics on aggression are being elucidated.[29,30]

Animal studies also show the need for appropriate maternal interactions for normal behavioral development to take place. Rat pups call for their mothers with ultrasonic vocalizations, which results in the mother's retrieving the pup. When repeatedly isolated from its mother, the pup stops the vocalization,[31] in effect learning that nuturing will not be provided. As well, removal from the mother causes deficits in play-fighting, which appears to be a normal and necessary developmental stage in rats.[32]

However, both animal and human studies show the sometimes beneficial effects of peer support. Interventions targeting the peer relations of maltreated children find benefits to these children in their aggressive and avoidance behavior.[33] Interestingly, when abused children are confronted with a peer in distress they display aggressive behavior at higher rates than neglected or nonmaltreated children.[19] Socialization processes may mediate the relation between socioeconomic status behavioral and peer problems.[29,30,34] In animal models, rats reared in isolation during the peak time for synaptic remodeling show an increase in defensive (footshock induced) aggression as adults, which is not seen if the animals are allowed an hour of play-fighting daily with litter-mates.[35] This may be related to the question of whether or not appropriate social experience will prevent or reverse aggressiveness. In another example of this, it is found that removing pups from their cages but placing the litter together in a relatively confined space for 15 minutes, every day for the first 21 days of life, causes increased coping responses and responses to stress as an adult.[36,37] In a study of nonhuman primates, reconciliation after aggressive behaivor improves in a situation where an aggressive strain is allowed to play with a more passive strain.[38] However, in a study of two mice strains, with one significantly more aggressive than the other, raising the strains together did not lead to a lessening of aggression.[39] Clearly, peer support is not always effective.

It has been shown by a number of investigators that maltreated and stressed children display differences in their autonomic and endocrine responses to threat and that these alterations in functioning may persist over time.[40–42] Studies of aggressive behavior–disordered children have demonstrated many alterations in various physiologic, endocrine, and neurotransmitter measurements; alterations in stress-induced and resting heart rate; orthostatic changes; and altered cortisol levels, and dopaminergic and serotonergic functioning.[43–47] There are animal studies finding similar changes. Glucocorticoid receptors rapidly develop from postnatal days 1 to 16, and thus glucocorticoids increased by stress may influence development of the brain at this time.[48] Changes in ACTH and cortisol responses have also been reported.[49] As well, isolation appears to increase production of nerve-growth factor (NGF)[50] and decrease the number of serotonin receptors.[51] Depleting the developing brain of substance P causes a greater propensity for isolation-induced aggression in the adult.[52] All of these factors, glucocorticoids, NGF, and substance P, have effects on the development of the serotonin system. Thus, this neurotransmitter system may play a key role in the appearance of aggressive symptoms. Oxytocin may also play an important role and lack of appropriate peer relations may be related to changes in this neuropeptide. Separation of infant rats from their mothers causes a loss of hippocampal oxytocin receptors.[53]

GENDER

Overt physical and verbal aggression is more common in males than females. The brain-organizing effects of masculinizing hormones are well known and thought to account for several trait differences between males and females, including differing rates of language acquisition and visual-spatial abilities,[54] motor activation, and aggression.[55,56] The association between concentrations of these hormones and aggression over the course of development seem to be equivocal in most studies of adults and adolescents.[57,58] In one study of disruptive behavior–disordered children, there was no relationship,[59] and in another there was a moderate positive relationship.[60] Interestingly, in postmortem studies of human brains, women had a higher density of serotonin innervation of cortex than men, a finding that the authors suggest may underly a number of gender-specific behaviors, including aggression.[61]

There are also animal models that illustrate the role of gender in the appearance of aggression. Testosterone injections in females on the second day of life can increase the aggressive behaviors of some strains of mice, to the level seen in their male littermates.[62] In a transgenic animal model, described below, aggression is observed only in the males and is abolished by castration. The aggression is reinstated by treatment with 17 beta-estradiol.[63]

GENETIC CHANGES

Twin, adoption, and family studies of adult criminals, juvenile delinquents, and aggressive and antisocial individuals all show a high degree of environmental influence that is predominantly of the shared variety (individuals sharing the same environment share similar risk status).[64] Other genotype-environmental studies indicate environmental variables themselves (such as family environment) show substantial genetic influence during childhood.[65] A number of other studies have noted that contributions to conduct disorder, aggressivity, and adult antisocial behavior are derived from both genetic and genetic-environmental factors.[64,65] Together, this kind of information suggests the possibility that the correlation between childhood environmental factors and outcome may be derived in part from genetic factors.

Very few specific gene changes have thus far been reported to occur in aggressive disorders. However, one interesting study has reported a Dutch family with a mutation of the gene for monoamine oxidase (MAO) that has a high degree of aggressive behavior.[66] An animal study modeling this observation used gestational exposure to MAO inhibitors. The animals thus treated were aggressive and difficult to handle. Neurochemical studies in the animals showed markedly decreased serotonin terminal density in the cortex.[67]

Advances in gene technology have given rise to a number of animals that either have had a specific gene removed ("knockout") or extra copies of a gene inserted. If the resultant animal is aggressive, it may be assumed that the gene deleted or inserted is in some way important for development and/or regulation of a part of the brain that influences aggression. Using the knockout technology, animals have been produced that have no MAO-A. As in the human cases, these animals were reported to be highly aggressive.[68]

Although there are no comparable human studies, other genetically altered animals have been produced that are highly aggressive. A surprisingly large number of these animals are shown to have deficits in serotonin. This includes mice deficient for alpha-calcium calmodulin-dependent kinase II, who show decreased fear response and an increase in defensive aggression associated with decreased serotonin release.[69] Animals expressing an extra copy of the gene for transforming growth factor–alpha are very aggressive in the resident-intruder test and show decreased serotonin activity. Interestingly, the aggression is reversed by serotonergic drugs, such as tryptophan or the selective serotonin reuptake inhibitors (SSRIs).[70] Finally, mice that express no serotonin 5-HT_{1b} receptors are faster to attack an intruder than are control mice.[71] All of these studies point to potentially interesting targets for genetic studies in humans.

SUMMARY

Clearly, models of developmentally induced aggression in animals can give us important insights into the factors inducing aggression in children. Several such models have been produced, and the neurochemical substrates eliciting the aggressive behavior have been identified. In many cases, the serotonergic system is involved. In the future, these animal models may also prove useful in identifying appropriate treatments.

REFERENCES

1. SKUSE, D. 1984. Extreme deprivation in early childhood. II Theoretical issues and a comparative review. J. Child Psychol. Psychiatry **25**: 543–572.
2. YULE, W. & M. RUTTER. 1987. Language development disorders. Clinics in Developmental Medicine. Vol. 101/102. MacKeith Press/Blackwell Scientific. London.
3. LOEBER, R., B. LAHEY & C. THOMAS. 1991. Diagnostic conundrum of oppositional defiant disorder and conduct disorder. J. Abnorm. Psychol. **100**(3): 379–390.
4. LOEBER, R. *et al.* 1995. Which boys will fare worse? Early predictors of the onset of conduct disorder in a six-year longitudinal study. J. Am. Acad. Child Adolesc. Psychiatry **34**(4): 499–509.
5. TREMBLAY, R. *et al.* 1991. Disruptive boys with stable and unstable high fighting behavior patterns during junior elementary school. J. Abnorm. Child Psychol. **19**(3): 285–300.
6. LOEBER, R. 1982. The stability of antisocial and delinquent child behavior: A review. Child Dev. **53**(6): 1431–1446.
7. ROBINS, L. N. 1991. Conduct disorder. J. Child Psychol. Psychiatry **32**(1): 193–212.
8. AINSWORTH, M., M. C. BLEHAR, E. WATERS & S. WALL. 1978. Patterns of attachment: A psychological study of the Strange Situation. Erlbaum. Hillsdale, NJ.
9. PRINO, C. & M. PEYROT. 1994. The effect of child physical abuse and neglect on aggressive, withdrawn, and prosocial behavior. Child Abuse & Neglect **18**(10): 871–884.
10. GEORGE, C. & M. MAIN. 1979. Social interaction of young abused children: Approach, avoidance, and aggression. Child Dev. **50**: 306–318.
11. RIEDER, C. & D. CICCHETTI. 1989. An organizational perspective on cognitive control functioning and cognitive-affective balance in maltreated children. Dev. Psychol. **25**: 382–393.
12. DODGE, K., R. MURPHY & K. C. BUCHSBAUM. 1984. The assessment of intention-cue skills in children: Implications for developmental psychopathology. Child Dev. **55**: 163–173.
13. SMETANA, J. G. & M. KELLY. 1989. Social Cognition in Maltreated Children. *In* Child Maltreatment: Theory and Research on the Causes and Consequences of Child Abuse and Neglect. D. Cicchetti & V. Carlson, Eds.: 620–646. Cambridge University Press. Cambridge.
14. MAIN, M. & C. GEORGE. 1985. Response of abused and disadvantaged toddlers to distress agitates: A study in the day care setting. Dev. Psychol. **21**: 407–412.
15. CICCHETTI, D. & M. BEEGHLY. 1989. Symbolic development in maltreated youngsters: An organizational perspective. *In* Atypical Symbolic Development. M.B. D. Cicchetti, Ed. San Francisco. Jossey-Bass.
16. CICCHETTI, D. 1989. How research on child maltreatment has informed the study of child development: Perspectives from developmental psychopathology. *In* Child Maltreatment: Theory and Research on the Causes and Consequences of Child Abuse and Neglect. D. Cicchetti & V. Carlson, Eds.: 377–431. Cambridge University Press. New York.
17. MUELLER, E. 1989. Peer relations in maltreated children. *In* Child Maltreatment: Theory and Research on the Causes and Consequences of Child Abuse and Neglect. D. Cicchetti & V. Carlson, Eds.: 529–578. Cambridge University Press. New York.
18. WIDOM, C. S. 1989. The Cycle of Violence. Science **244**: 160–166.
19. FARRINGTON, D. P. 1978. The family backgrounds of aggressive youths. *In* Aggression and Antisocial Behavior in Childhood and Adolescence. L. A. Hersov & D. Shaffer, Eds.: 73–93. Pergamon. Oxford.
20. LEWIS, D. O., C. MALLOUH & V. WEBB. 1989. Child abuse, delinquency, and violent criminality. *In* Child Maltreatment: Theory and Research on the Causes and Conse-

quences of Child Abuse and Neglect. D. Cicchetti & V. Carlson, Eds.: 707–721. Cambridge University Press. Cambridge.

21. HAMBURG, D. A. 1971. Psychobiological studies of aggressive behavior. Nature **230:** 19–23.

22. BANDURA, A. 1973. Aggression: A Social Learning Analysis. Prentice Hall. Englewood Cliffs.

23. PATTERSON, G. 1974. A basis for identifying stimuli which control behaviors in natural settings. Child Dev. **45**(4): 900–911.

24. PATTERSON, G. 1976. The aggressive child: Victim and architect of a coercive system. *In* Behavior modification and families. E. J. Mash *et al.*, Eds.: 276–316. Brunner/ Mazel. New York.

25. PATTERSON, G. 1977. Accelerating stimuli for two classes of coercive behaviors. J. Abnorm. Child Psychol. **5**(4): 335–350.

26. BADEN, A. & G. HOWE. 1992. Mothers' attributions and expectancies regarding their conduct-disordered children. J. Abnorm. Child Psychol. **20**(5): 467–485.

27. HOWING, P. *et al.* 1990. Child abuse and delinquency: The empirical and theoretical links. Soc. Work **35**(3): 244–249.

28. WAHLER, R. & J. DUMAS. 1986. Maintenance factors in coercive mother-child interactions: The compliance and predictability hypotheses. J. Appl. Behav. Anal. **19**(1): 13–22.

29. DODGE, K., G. PETTIT & J. BATES. 1994. Socialization mediators of the relation between socioeconomic status and child conduct problems. Child Dev. **65**(2 Spec. No): 649–665.

30. KUPERSMIDT, J. *et al.* 1995. Childhood aggression and peer relations in the context of family and neighborhood factors. Child Dev. **66**(2): 360–375.

31. GOODWIN, G. A., V. A. MOLINA & L. P. SPEAR. 1994. Repeated exposure of rat pups to isolation attenuates isolation-induced ultrasonic vocalization rates: Reversal with naltrexone. Dev. Psychobiol. **27**(1): 53–64.

32. JANUS, K. 1987. Early separation of young rats from the mother and the development of play fighting. Physiol. Behav. **39**(4): 471–476.

33. HOWES C. & M. P. EPINOSA. 1985. The consequences of child abuse for the formation of relationships with peers. Child Abuse & Neglect **9:** 397–404.

34. HAAPASALO, J. & R. TREMBLAY. 1994. Physically aggressive boys from ages 6 to 12: Family background, parenting behavior, and prediction of delinquency. J. Consult. Clin. Psychol. **62**(5): 1044–1052.

35. POTEGAL, M. & D. EINON. 1989. Aggressive behaviors in adult rats deprived of play-fighting experience as juveniles. Dev. Psychobiol. **22**(2): 159–172.

36. MEANEY, M. J., J. B. MITCHELL, D. H. AITKEN, S. BHATNAGAR, S. R. BODNOFF, L. J. INY & A. SARRIEAU. 1994. The effects of neonatal handling on the development of the adrenocortical response to stress: Implications for neuropathology and cognitive deficits later in life. Psychoneuroendocrinology, **16:** 85–103.

37. COSTELA, C., P. TEJEDOR-REAL, J. A. MICO & J. GIBERT-RAHOLA. 1995. Effect of neonatal handling on learned helplessness model of depression. Physiol. Behav. **57:** 407–410.

38. DE WAAL, F. B. & D. L. JOHANOWICZ. 1993. Modification of reconciliation behavior through social experience: An experiment with two macaque species. Child Dev. **64**(3): 897–908.

39. HOFFMANN, H. J., R. SCHNEIDER & W. E. CRUSIO. 1993. Genetic analysis of isolation-induced aggression. II. Postnatal environmental influences in AB mice. Behav. Genet. **23**(4): 391–394.

40. URSIN, H. & M. OLFF. 1993. Psychobiology of coping and defence strategies. Neuropsychobiology **28**(1–2): 66–71.

41. VAN DER KOLK, B. & R. FISLER. 1991. The biologic basis of posttraumatic stress. Primary Care **20**(2): 417–432.

42. ITO, Y., M. H. TEICHER, C. A. GLOD, D. HARPER, E. MAGNUS & H. A. GELBARD. 1993. Increased prevalence of electrophysiological abnormalities in children with psychological, physical, and sexual abuse. J. Neuropsychiatry Clin. Neurosci. **5:** 401–408.

43. KINDLON, D. *et al.* 1995. Longitudinal patterns of heart rate and fighting behavior in 9-through 12-year-old boys. J. Am. Acad. Child & Adolesc. Psychiatry **34**(3): 371–377.
44. VAN GOOZEN, S., W. MATTHYS, P. COHEN-KETTENIS & H. VAN ENGELAND. The role of cognitive, emotional, and biological factors in antisocial behavior of CD/ODD and normal boys. Poster presentation at the conference entitled Understanding Aggression in Children. Sept. 29–Oct. 2, 1995.
45. KRUESI, M. *et al.* 1990. Cerebrospinal fluid monoamine metabolites, aggression, and impulsivity in disruptive behavior disorders of children and adolescents. Arch. Gen. Psychiatry **47**(5): 419–426.
46. KRUESI, M. *et al.* 1992. A 2-year prospective follow-up study of children and adolescents with disruptive behavior disorders. Prediction by cerebrospinal fluid 5-hydroxyindoleacetic acid, homovanillic acid, and autonomic measures? Arch. Gen. Psychiatry **49**(6): 429–435.
47. RAINE, A. & F. JONES. 1987. Attention, autonomic arousal, and personality in behaviorally disordered children. J. Abnorm Child Psychol. **15**(4): 583–599.
48. CINTRA A., B. SOLFRINI, L. F. AGNATI, J. A. GUSTAFSSON & K. FUXE. 1991. Strongly glucocorticoid receptor immunoreactive neurons in the neonatal rat. Neuroreport **2**(2): 85–88.
49. SUCHECKI, D., D. Y. NELSON, H. VAN OERS & S. LEVINE. 1995. Activation and inhibition of the hypothalamic-pituitary-adrenal axis of the neonatal rat: Effects of maternal deprivation. Psychoneuroendocrinology **20**(2): 169–182.
50. ALOE, L., E. ALLEVA & R. DE SIMONE. 1990. Changes of NGF level in mouse hypothalamus following intermale aggressive behaviour: Biological and immunohistochemical evidence. Behav. Brain Res. **39**(1): 53–61.
51. ST. POPOVA, J. & V. V. PETKOV. 1990. Changes in 5-HT1 receptors in different brain structures of rats with isolation syndrome. Gen. Pharmacol. **21**(2): 223–225.
52. BIGI, S., L. DE ACETIS, R. DE SIMONE L. ALOE & E. ALLEVA. 1993. Neonatal capsaicin exposure affects isolation-induced aggressive behavior and hypothalamic substance P levels of adult male mice (Mus musculus). Behav. Neurosci. **107**(2): 363–369.
53. NOONAN, L. R., J. D. CALDWELL, L. LI, C. H. WALKER & C. A. PEDERSEN. 1994. Neonatal stress transiently alters the development of hippocampal oxytocin receptors. Brain Res. **80**(1–2): 115–120.
54. HINES, M. 1982. Prenatal gonadal hormones and sex differences in human behavior. Psychol. Bull. **92**(1): 56–80.
55. ERHARDT, A. A. & J. MONEY. 1967. Progestin-induced hermaphroditism: IQ and psychosexual identity in a sample of 10 girls. J. Sex Res. **3:** 83–100.
56. ERHARDT, A. A., R. EPSTEIN & J. MONEY. 1968. Fetal androgens and female gender identity in the early treated adrenogenital syndrome. Johns Hopkins Med. J. **122:** 160–167.
57. HALPERN, C. *et al.* 1993. Relationships between aggression and pubertal increases in testosterone: A panel analysis of adolescent males. Soc. Biol. **40**(1–2): 8–24.
58. ALBERT, D., ML. WALSH & RH. JONIK. 1993. Aggression in humans: What is its biological foundation? Neurosci. Biobehav. Rev. **17**(4): 405–425.
59. CONSTANTINO, J. *et al.* 1993. Testosterone and aggression in children. J. Am. Acad. Child & Adolesc. Psychiatry **32**(6): 1217–1222.
60. SCERBO, A. & D. KOLKO. 1994. Salivary testosterone and cortisol in disruptive children: Relationship to aggressive, hyperactive, and internalizing behaviors. J. Am. Acad. Child Adolesc. Psychiatry **33**(8): 1174–1184.
61. ARATO, M., E. FRECSKA, K. TEKES & D. J. MACCRIMMON. 1991. Serotonergic interhemispheric asymmetry: Gender difference in the orbital cortex. Acta Psychiatr. Scand. **84**(1): 110–111.
62. SANDNABBA, N. K., K. M. LAGERSPETZ & E. JENSEN. 1994. Effects of testosterone exposure and fighting experience on the aggressive behavior of female and male mice selectively bred for intermale aggression. Horm. Behav. **28**(3): 219–231.
63. HILAKIVI-CLARKE, L. & R. GOLDBERG. 1995. Gonadal hormones and aggression-maintaining effect of alcohol in male transgenic transforming growth factor-alpha mice. Alcoholism Clin. Exp. Res. **19**(3): 708–713.

64. PIKE A. & R. PLOMIN. 1996. Importance of non-shared environmental factors for childhood and adolescent psychopathology. J. Am. Acad. Child Adolesc. Psychiatry **35**(5): 560–570.
65. PLOMIN, R. 1995. Genetics and children's experiences in the family. J. Child Psychol. Psychiatry Allied Discip. **36**(1): 33–68.
66. BRUNNER, H. *et al.* 1993. Abnormal behavior associated with a point mutation in the structural gene for monoamine oxidase A. Science **262**(5133): 578–580.
67. WHITAKER-AZMITIA, P. M., Z. XINI & C. CLARKE. 1994. Effects of gestational exposure to monoamine oxidase inhibitors in rats: Preliminary behavioral and neurochemical studies. Neuropsychopharmacology **11**(2): 125–132.
68. CASES, O. *et al.* 1995. Aggressive behavior and altered amounts of brain serotonin and norepinephrine in mice lacking MAO-A. Science **268**(5218): 1763–1766.
69. CHEN, C., D. G. RAINNIE, R. W. GREENE & S. TONEGAWA. 1994. Abnormal fear response and aggressive behavior in mutant mice deficient for alpha-calcium-calmodulin kinase II. Science **266**(5183): 291–294.
70. HILAKIVI-CLARKE, L. A. & R. GOLDBERG. 1993. Effects of tryptophan and serotonin uptake inhibitors on behavior in male transgenic transforming growth factor alpha mice. Eur. J. Pharmacol. **237**(1): 101–108.
71. RAMBOZ, S., F. SAUDOU, D. AMARA *et al.* 1996. 5-HT1b receptor knock out— Behavioral consequences. Behav. Brain Res. **73**: 305–312.

Social Attachment, Brain Function, and Aggression[a]

GARY W. KRAEMER[b,d] AND A. SUSAN CLARKE[c]

[b]Department of Kinesiology and Harlow Primate Laboratory
University of Wisconsin
Madison, Wisconsin

[c]Asher Center for the Study and Treatment
of Depressive Disorders
Department of Psychiatry and Behavioral Sciences
Northwestern University Medical School
and Harlow Primate Laboratory
University of Wisconsin
Madison, Wisconsin

INTRODUCTION

Can advances in psychobiology help us to understand why the incidence of violence among youth in our society is increasing; why any particular child is more aggressive than they ought to be, given what we know about their culture, family, social environment, and socioeconomic status; or, whether one child is more likely than others, with a similar background, to commit an act of violence in the future?

It has been suggested that low brain serotonin (5-HT) system function is associated with violence in humans.[1-3] If pathologically aggressive behavior is directly related to the (mal)function of a brain neurotransmitter system in humans, the clinical implications would be profound. The clinician could infer that patients with relatively low measures of 5-HT system function are prone to violence toward others or themselves. It could also be inferred that whatever causes low 5-HT system function, whether of genetic or environmental origin, or both, is ultimately the cause of violence.

The idea that low brain 5-HT system function is related to violence among humans is based on correlations among indirect measures of 5-HT system activity and various forms of aggressive behavior, however. Although measures of 5-HT function may be inversely correlated with violence in clinical populations, this finding does not permit us to reason that violence is usually associated with low 5-HT function. There is no indication of what proportion of humans could be counted as having low 5-HT function and yet never engage in violent behavior or come to the attention of the medical or justice systems. A causal relationship between brain 5-HT function and aggression in humans has not been demonstrated,

[a] Research and manuscript preparation was supported by the John D. and Catherine T. MacArthur Foundation (G. W. Kraemer, A S. Clarke), the Harry Frank Guggenheim Foundation (A. S. Clarke), and NIMH R03-51704 (A. S. Clarke).

[d] Address correspondence to Gary W. Kraemer, Harlow Primate Laboratory, University of Wisconsin, 22 N. Charter St., Madison, WI 53715. Tel: (608) 263-5076; fax: (608) 263-4356; e-mail: kraemer@uakari.primate.wisc.edu.

121

nor can the relationship be tested experimentally for a variety of ethical and practical reasons.

Perhaps because of this, there is considerable interest in determining whether correlations between measures of 5-HT system function and aggression can be observed in animals, and particularly, nonhuman primates.[4] Further basic research using animals could then be directed at elucidating the underlying neurobiological causes of violence. Such information could then be used to guide approaches to the neurobiological treatment of violent individuals.[4]

One aim of this report is to review studies of nonhuman primates that are pertinent to this issue. Another aim is to present the results of a longitudinal experiment in which the neurobiological and behavioral effects of a social environmental factor that produces increased aggression in rhesus monkeys were studied. Privation of maternal care, or privation of social experience per se, increases the probability that a rhesus monkey will exhibit aggression that is less predictable, of greater frequency and/or duration, and more severe than that observed in mother-reared socialized monkeys.[4-7] The question this report addresses is whether inordinate aggression known to be promoted by a social environmental factor (maternal privation) is associated with reduced 5-HT system function and/ or changes in other neurotransmitter and neuroendocrine systems in monkeys. Determining what environmental and neurobiological factors are significantly correlated with unusual aggression in monkeys can inform debates on whether understanding of the psychobiology of brain function helps us to understand the causes of violence among humans.

Background: Serotonin and Aggression

Reduced effect of the brain 5-HT system is associated with increased aggression in animals.[8] The 5-HT system may regulate sensory-motor gating in such a way that nonaggressive behavioral responses to stressors are more readily accessible if this system is active, and this would be one of its functions.[8] Brain 5-HT system activity cannot be measured directly in humans, however. The idea that violent humans may have low functional 5-HT system activity is primarily based on finding a negative correlation between 5-hydroxyindoleacetic acid (5-HIAA) in cerebrospinal fluid (CSF) and measures of violent behavior.[1-3] 5-HIAA is the major metabolite of 5-HT. Thus, if one assumes that the concentration of metabolite in CSF is proportional to the amount of 5-HT released,[9] then relatively low CSF 5-HIAA concentration can be taken as an indicator of low activity of the brain 5-HT system.

It is well to note, however, that measures of neurotransmitter metabolite are not measures of the effect that released neurotransmitter is having on postsynaptic cells. For the moment, though, let us assume that CSF 5-HIAA is a good measure of brain 5-HT system activity. If aggression is inversely correlated with brain 5-HT system activity, is this because the activity of the system is affected by engaging in aggression, or does the activity of the system determine whether aggression will be exhibited in the first place?

Regulators of 5-HT Function and Aggression

In human and nonhuman primates, one's stature in the social dominance hierarchy is usually an important regulator of whether one is the exhibitor or recipient of aggression. In vervet monkeys, pharmacological agents thought to increase 5-HT system output promote acquisition of dominance, whereas agents that reduce 5-HT system activity reduce the likelihood of attaining dominant status.[10,11] This suggests that variation in 5-HT system activity could determine whether one is dominant or subordinate, and hence be a factor in whether one is likely to exhibit or be the recipient of aggression. Determining what usually regulates brain 5-HT function thus becomes a significant issue.

The developmental expression of the 5-HT system appears to be under substantial genetic control in rhesus monkeys.[12,13] Levels of CSF 5-HIAA within and across individuals are significantly correlated across time,[11,14,15] and CSF 5-HIAA levels usually decline from birth to adolescence.[14,15] Thus, CSF-5-HIAA levels appear to be constitutional or trait-like in one respect, but there is a trajectory of change over time. Environmental influences on this system may be most evident in change in developmental trajectory.[15]

CSF 5-HIAA levels are affected by social environmental factors in some primate species but not others. One factor is whether an individual is currently in a dominant or subordinate position in a social group. Subordinate talapoin monkeys exhibit elevated levels of 5-HIAA by comparison to dominant individuals.[16] On the other hand, CSF 5-HIAA levels do not differ significantly among dominant and subordinate vervet monkeys.[11] Another factor is whether an individual has been deprived of social interaction per se or maternal care in infancy. Thus, rhesus monkeys reared in social isolation, or with peers but not mothers, have higher levels of 5-HIAA than mother-reared socialized monkeys.[15,17]

What may seem puzzling, then, is that pharmacological treatments that presumably augment the effect of 5-HT on postsynaptic cells promote acquisition of dominance in vervet monkeys,[10] whereas elevated levels of 5-HIAA (increased 5-HT system function?) are associated with subordination or social privation (often a precursor of being relegated to subordinate status) in other species.[6,18,19] Also, it seems that having relatively high or low 5-HT system function might be a determinant of whether one becomes dominant or subordinate, but there is also evidence that being dominant or subordinate affects 5-HT system function. It is also true that the dominant or subordinate status of an individual is not directly related to the amount of aggression that that individual exhibits or measures of 5-HT system function in any simple or linear manner.[5] When differences in the level of 5-HIAA are found in group comparisons, they are related to prior rearing history and social status rather than day-to-day variation in aggressive encounters.[11,15,16] Findings of this sort illustrate the limitations of simplistic and overgeneralized inferences from constructs of "dominance," to presumed indices of 5-HT system function (metabolite levels), and then to probable levels of aggression across species.

Consideration of factors, such as gender, social developmental history, and social status, makes the proposed 5-HIAA-aggression relationships more salient, however. Raleigh and McGuire[11] measured aggression and CSF 5-HIAA over 4 months in male or female vervet monkeys that were either dominant or subordinate. Among subordinate male and female vervet monkeys, 5-HIAA was inversely correlated with aggression.[11] Herein, data will be presented indicating that the total duration of aggression over a 6-week period was inversely related to CSF 5-HIAA in mother-reared rhesus monkeys housed in a laboratory. Paradoxically, Mehlman et al.[20] report that male rhesus monkeys living in a natural environment that were subordinate, less involved in affiliative or prosocial behaviors, and more likely to be wounded if they did become aggressive, were also likely to have low levels of 5-HIAA by comparison to more dominant, social, and less wounded conspecifics.

In summary, participation in aggressive encounters seems to be inversely correlated with CSF 5-HIAA in nonhuman primates if one assesses groups delineated by one or more of the following factors: gender, rearing condition, current environment, social dominance or subordination, species, and if one uses measures of aggression occurring over time. It is well to reflect on the limitations of this finding, however. If one considers only juvenile subordinate male vervet monkeys living in a seminatural environment (outdoor pens), then aggression is likely to be inversely related to CSF 5-HIAA in this group. This does not mean, however, that the relatively low CSF 5-HIAA of the most aggressive juvenile subordinate male vervet monkey will be lower than the least aggressive juvenile dominant male. Also, among rhesus monkeys studied by Mehlman et al.,[20] it appears that "impulsivity" and then being the victim of aggression of more dominant monkeys is associated with low 5-HIAA. Hence, relative 5-HIAA levels alone do not tell us whether a "generic" monkey is inordinately aggressive or victimized, or likely to be so in the future. The next question, though, is, What is happening when we observe aggression that is unusual and attributable to unusual circumstances? Are measures of 5-HT system function helpful in understanding the biological basis of aggression when such aggression is extraordinary by nonhuman primate standards?

Clinically Significant Aggression in Humans and Monkeys

Clinicians concerned about or confronted with increases in juvenile and adolescent aggression per se, or engaged in diagnosing and treating clients that are presented by the court system, are not as concerned about usual aggression as they are about unusual aggression. Aggression among monkeys usually occurs in definable social contexts and has a level of duration and severity appropriate to the context.[4,5,7,21] It is exhibited in competition for dominance, resources, territory, and in protection of offspring, to cite a few examples. What about human aggression that comes to clinical or judicial attention because it is intrusive on, rather than part of, the usual societal order?

Here, the term "usual behavior" with a focus on aggression needs to be highlighted in a more global and developmental context. What is developmentally usual is that a rhesus monkey is born, cared for by its biological mother, plays with peers, learns the social rules, and becomes an adequate member of its society. Interactions with the mother are critical in the offspring's learning of the "when" and "how," and "how vigorously" to defend and aggress. A mature member of rhesus society is usually prepared to engage in aggression or defense when those behaviors are called upon by social or environmental circumstances. When can we begin to refer to aggression as being unusual? The following characteristics are suggested as being characteristic of unusual aggression in rhesus monkeys and perhaps in humans: (1) It is not predictable. It occurs out of the usual social context or in the absence of antecedent social signals. In monkeys, usual social aggression and defense is preceded and accompanied by facial (threat face, ear retraction, flushing), somatic (piloerection), and vocal (barking) displays of "threat." Unusual aggression may not be preceded or accompanied by these signals. (2) It is out of proportion and does not terminate appropriately. Unusual aggression may escalate to severe or lethal wounding and persist even after the recipient acknowledges the threat or responds to the attack with submissive gestures. (3) It does not contribute to retention or attainment of increased social status (dominance). The object of aggression is either not threatening (an infant, for example), or, for all practical purposes, is invincible (a clearly dominant male, for example).

Monkeys observed in their free-ranging environment and mother-reared monkeys observed in the laboratory exhibit aggression that is understandable to most human observers. This behavior is consonant with a social context; it is regulated in effort, severity, and persistence; and it is directed toward antagonists. Maternally deprived monkeys exhibit aggression that is not predictable, out of proportion in severity and duration, and directed towards improbable objects.[7,19,22,23] One could anthropomorphically refer to the latter form of unusual aggression as "violence." It is not clear that violence among monkeys can be attributed to the (mal)function of only one brain neurochemical system, however.

System Malfunction versus Brain Disorganization

The idea that some human psychiatric disorders might be attributable to malfunction in one neurochemical system has been prominent in biological psychiatry theorizing in the past. For example, too much brain dopamine (DA) activity or too little norepinephrine (NE) activity have been cited as probable causes of schizophrenia or depression, respectively.[24,25] Claims that low serotonin function might be a cause of increased aggression appear to be in this genre. The idea that psychiatric disorders might be attributable to disorganization of function among brain systems has been propounded more recently.[26,27] It is not entirely clear how disorganization should be measured, however, but it ought to be at least the contrapositive of organization.

Organization implies that indices of activity in individual systems should be within normal limits and that measures of activity among systems that are mechanistically linked should be correlated. Overall, it seems that demonstrable covariance in dependent measures of system activity is critical, inasmuch as individual measures might be within normal limits while usual covariance is nonexistent. Ideally one would measure the level of activity in multiple systems and the covariance among their activity levels. With both sets of information, one should be able to ascertain whether levels of activity and interrelationships among several brain neurochemical systems account for the behavior of interest.

Multivariate Measures of Organization

CSF measures of activity in brain 5-HT, NE, and DA systems are usually correlated. This suggests that the development and actions of these systems in the brain are usually interrelated as well.[15,17,28] For example, there are significant and substantial intercorrelations among CSF NE, 5-HIAA, and homovanillic acid (HVA) beginning within two months after birth and thereafter in groups of mother-reared rhesus monkeys tracked from birth to preadolescence.[5,15] Thus, 5-HIAA levels usually covary with measures of activity in other biogenic amine systems. Also, measures of NE and/or DA system activity covary with developmental changes in the exhibition of social behavior and behavioral responses to stressors, such as separation from companions.[17,29,30]

It is important to note that measures of biogenic amine system activity do not always intercorrelate significantly. For example, the interrelationships cited above, as developing soon after birth in mother-reared monkeys, do not materialize in socially isolated rhesus monkeys.[15] This finding suggests, first, that the usual correlations among measures observed in mother-reared monkeys are not attributable to necessarily interlocked neurochemical or transport mechanisms and, second, that important aspects of neurobiological organization are attributable to infant-mother attachment and do not occur if the infant monkey has no mother.[31]

These findings and results presented herein indicate that the neurobiological effects of social environmental factors that adversely affect social development in rhesus monkeys are not restricted to one neurochemical system. Furthermore, once changes in multiple systems are observed, usually significant interrelationships among measures of the activity of different systems are absent as well. What this report highlights is that once the usual interrelationships among neurobiological systems degrade, the usual relationship of activity in any particular system to behavior also degrades.

Summary and Research/Clinical Problem

(1) Propensity to engage in inordinate aggression (violence) is inversely correlated with CSF 5-HIAA in humans, that is, among humans that have come to the attention of either medical or judicial systems that sanction collection of biological data on humans. It is not clear whether humans with low 5-HIAA are more violent per se, however; nor are the data required to resolve the issue likely to be collected by random sampling of human populations, for both ethical and practical reasons.

(2) Data collected in research on nonhuman primates where aggression and CSF 5-HIAA were measured parallels findings on studies of human clinical populations to some extent, but there certainly is not a perfect marriage. The relationship between CSF 5-HIAA and aggression varies among subgroups of monkeys delineated on the basis of dominance versus subordination, prior social rearing history, gender, and species. After these cofactors are considered, an inverse relationship between CSF 5-HIAA and aggression is evident for some subgroups of monkeys.

(3) The nonhuman primate conditions cited in point 2 seem to parallel the human condition cited in point 1. A more traditional way to explain the cross-species congruity might be that, among social primates, social factors might affect the regulation of the 5-HT system, or vice versa. A newer, and perhaps, more heuristically useful explanation is that the "5-HIAA-aggression correlation" is prominent or insignificant in one species (group) or another because of the way in which multiple neurochemical systems are usually interrelated (organized) in individuals.

More specifically, correlations between 5-HIAA and aggression may exist in some brain organizational states, not because variation in psychosocial experience has specific effects on the brain 5-HT system, but because correlations between measures of neurobiology and behavior (5-HIAA and aggression) occur when neurobiological systems are organized in the usual way, and not otherwise. Unusual aggression might be attributable to the general disorganization of neurobiological function, rather than shifts in the activity of any particular system.

(4) Researchers seeking developmental and multivariate data in human populations face both ethical and practical constraints. Use of a compelling nonhuman primate model may provide information about the way in which multivariate assessment of both behavioral- and neurochemical-dependent measures could contribute to an understanding of how human biological-behavioral interrelationships might be assessed and interpreted in clinical studies of humans. Multiple

measures of behavior and neurobiological status can be obtained in research in nonhuman primates. Such data can be used to test the "aggression-low 5-HIAA" versus "aggression-disorganization" hypothesis.

METHODS

Subjects, Early Rearing Conditions, and Maintenance

The subjects were 48 infant rhesus monkeys (*Macaca mulatta*). At birth, the infants were randomly assigned to one of two rearing conditions, either mother-reared (N = 13 males, 11 females) or peer-reared (N = 13 females, 11 males). Peer-reared infants were reared in single cages in a multianimal nursery for the first month of life, during which time they were provided with daily peer socialization (30 min with two other peers) and object stimulation (rotated toys), and were trained to self-feed formula (Similac) from bottles mounted in their cages. At six weeks of age, peer-reared infants were placed into peer groups of three monkeys each. Sexes were balanced across peer groups to the extent possible within the constraint of placing those closest in age together. The infants were maintained in their rearing conditions for the first six months of life. Cerebrospinal fluid and blood samples were collected monthly from the infants under anesthesia beginning at one month of age (see ref. 32). With the exception of the monthly sample collections, during this phase the infants were otherwise undisturbed.

At approximately seven months of age, the mother-reared infants were separated from their mothers and placed into mixed-sex peer groups of three animals each. To effect a comparable social transition, the peer-reared infants were separated from their rearing partners and placed in a new peer group (*i.e.*, each peer-reared monkey was placed with two unfamiliar peer-reared infants). Throughout their early rearing and this phase of the study, all animals were housed in multianimal rooms maintained at a constant temperature (21°C) and on a 12 : 12 h light/dark cycle. The monkeys were fed commercial monkey biscuits and fruit once daily, and had water available *ad libitum*.

Behavior

The behavioral data reported herein were collected from the monkeys beginning two weeks after rearing partner separations and continuing thereafter for six weeks. This phase was preparatory for a later study in which several of the groups were to be treated with pharmacological agents. Therefore, over this six-week time period all subjects were removed from their housing cage once in the morning and given several milliliters of water through nasogastric intubation. This was the route chosen for later administration of drugs, so this phase counts as a training or pretreatment condition to acclimate the monkeys to the procedure. A 30-minute video recording was made of each group four days per week in the afternoon. Later, by video tape replay, each monkey was observed for five minutes (300 seconds) per session. Behavioral data were collected by trained observers using a previously described computerized scoring system.[30]

The intent in analysis of behavior was to focus on relevant general aspects of social behavior and not detailed analysis of individual behaviors. Therefore, the behavioral data were collapsed into four categories collectively comprising approximately 90% of the behavior exhibited in social groups (behaviors not included were eating, drinking, self-care behaviors, *e.g.*, self-grooming, and "disturbance behaviors," *e.g.*, self-directed behavior and stereotypies). The behavioral categories were as follows: *activity*, including locomotion and environmental exploration (manual manipulation of objects); *social*, collectively including the range of prosocial behaviors, such as grooming, body or manual touching of others, and maintaining proximity (< 10 cm) to others; *inactivity*, not active and not social (basically this is sitting quietly with no other scorable behavior evident); *aggression*, biting, fur pulling, and scratching.

Neurochemical/Neuroendocrine Measures

CSF and blood samples were collected at the end of weeks three and six of behavioral observation. Samples were collected from the cisterna magna by syringe through spinal puncture under ketamine hydrochloride anesthesia (10 mg/kg) within 10 minutes of initial disturbance between 1300–1500 hours. Samples were frozen in dry ice and stored at −70°C until an assay was performed in duplicate by multichannel HPLC for NE; the NE metabolite 3-methoxy-4-hydroxyphenylglycol (MHPG); and the dopamine metabolites 3,4-dihydroxy-phenylacetic acid (DO-PAC), HVA, and 5-HIAA, as described in Schmidt *et al.*[33] For the purposes of this report, MHPG and DOPAC data will not be presented, inasmuch as NE, HVA, and 5-HIAA data represent the parent compound or the major metabolite of the NE, DA, and 5-HT systems, respectively. Hypothalamic-pituitary-adrenal (HPA) axis activity was measured through assay of plasma adrenocorticotrophic hormone (ACTH) and cortisol concentrations in blood plasma. Sample preservation and assay details are described in Clarke *et al.*[34]

RESULTS

Effects: Main Effects of Rearing

TABLE 1 shows that, by comparison to mother-reared monkeys, peer-reared monkeys exhibited significantly higher levels of activity, lower levels of inactivity, and lower levels of NE, HVA, ACTH, and cortisol. Though not statistically different ($p < 0.05$), the mean levels of 5-HIAA and aggression were higher in peer-reared monkeys by comparison to mother-reared monkeys. One should also note the large standard deviation by comparison to the mean for each group. This occurs because aggression is exhibited by some mother- or peer-reared monkeys and not by others. However, in peer-reared monkeys the duration of aggression varies dramatically once it is exhibited. The way in which this variation plays out across rearing groups and in relation to other measures is presented in subsequent tables showing intercorrelations among measures.

Relationships

TABLES 2 and 3 show the intercorrelations among the behavioral and neurochemical measures for mother- and peer-reared monkeys. In mother-reared monkeys 9 out of the 21 intercorrelations among the variables were significantly dif-

TABLE 1. Main Effects of Rearing on Behavioral and Neurochemical Measures[a]

	Mother	Standard Deviation	Peer	Standard Deviation	p value
Activity	144.87	18.18	181.88	25.53	0.0001
Social	65.23	28.23	54.34	17.57	0.1153
Inactive	47.63	15.63	27.85	12.65	0.0001
Aggressive	8.67	18.14	11.60	35.54	0.7280
NE	481.27	178.42	391.87	54.58	0.0233
HVA	343.40	67.64	299.31	50.77	0.0140
5-HIAA	68.95	18.72	77.37	14.56	0.0886
ACTH	54.71	17.93	38.78	13.50	0.0011
Cortisol	36.37	6.56	29.77	5.73	0.0005

[a] Value and standard deviation of behavior duration (activity, social, inactive, measured over six weeks; mean out of possible 300 seconds/session); total duration of aggression (seconds); and cerebrospinal fluid concentrations of norepinephrine (NE, pg/mL), homovanillic acid (HVA, ng/mL), 5-hydroxyindoleacetic acid (5-HIAA, ng/mL), plasma adrenocorticotrophic hormone (ACTH, pg/mL), and cortisol (μg/dL) in mother- and peer-reared juvenile rhesus monkeys. Significance (p value) of between-groups comparisons, peer- versus mother-reared, determined by analysis of variance.

ferent from zero. Of these 9 correlations, 5 were significantly different from correlations among the same measures observed in peer-reared monkeys. Most importantly, aggression in mother-reared monkeys was negatively correlated with both CSF NE and 5-HIAA levels and positively correlated with prosocial behavior. By contrast, only 2 of 21 correlations were significantly different from zero in peer-reared monkeys, and neither of these were significantly different from those observed in mother-reared monkeys. Aggression in peer-reared monkeys was not correlated with any of the other social or neurochemical variables.

FIGURES 1 and 2 show the scatter plots for 5-HIAA and aggression in mother- and peer-reared monkeys, respectively. Inspection of these plots indicates that aggression among mother-reared monkeys was exhibited primarily by individuals

TABLE 2. Behavioral and Neurochemical Intercorrelations in Mother-reared Monkeys (N = 24)[a]

	NE	HVA	H-IAA	Inactive	Activity	Social
NE						
HVA	0.38					
H-IAA	*0.55	*0.63				
Inactive	**−0.58	−0.20	−0.27			
Activity	−0.16	0.05	−0.04	−0.04		
Social	*−0.57	−0.24	*−0.46	**0.59	0.23	
Aggressive	**−0.43	−0.10	**−0.58	0.33	0.28	**0.57

[a] Correlations (Pearson's product) of behavior duration (activity, social, inactive, measured over six weeks; mean out of possible 300 seconds/session); total duration of aggression (seconds); and cerebrospinal fluid concentrations of norepinephrine (NE, pg/mL), homovanillic acid (HVA, ng/mL), 5-hydroxyindoleacetic acid (5-HIAA, ng/mL), plasma adrenocorticotrophic hormone (ACTH, pg/mL), and cortisol (μg/dL) in mother-reared juvenile rhesus monkeys (N = 24; * = significantly different from zero, p < 0.05; ** = significantly different from peer-reared monkeys, p < 0.05).

TABLE 3. Behavioral and Neurochemical Intercorrelations in Peer-reared Monkeys (N = 23)[a]

	NE	HVA	H-IAA	Inactive	Activity	Social
NE						
HVA	0.26					
H-IAA	0.24	*0.71				
Inactive	0.16	−0.25	−0.37			
Activity	0.02	0.17	0.39	*−0.54		
Social	−0.26	−0.14	−0.19	0.17	0.02	
Aggressive	0.04	−0.03	−0.14	−0.15	0.07	−0.08

[a] Correlations (Pearson's product) of behavior duration (activity, social, inactive, measured over six weeks; mean out of possible 300 seconds/session); total duration of aggression (seconds); and cerebrospinal fluid concentrations of norepinephrine (NE, pg/mL), homovanillic acid (HVA, ng/mL), 5-hydroxyindoleacetic acid (5-HIAA ng/mL), plasma adrenocorticotrophic hormone (ACTH, pg/mL), and cortisol (µg/dL) in peer-reared juvenile rhesus monkeys (N = 23; * = significantly different from zero, $p < 0.05$). Data from Monkey AP 41 were excluded from computation of correlation coefficients.

with CSF 5-HIAA levels less than the mean value for the group, and most prominently in three monkeys with values less than 50 ng/mL. It should also be noted that three mother-reared monkeys with CSF 5-HIAA values less than 50 ng/mL were not conspicuously aggressive. By contrast, inspection of the CSF 5-HIAA data for the peer-reared monkeys indicates that there are no individuals with values less than 50 ng/mL. The most aggressive monkey (identification number AP 41) falls in the upper end of the spectrum for this group. For values on any other measure, AP 41 does not stand out. Specifically, among all variables examined, the only measure on which AP 41 was clearly exceptional is aggression.

DISCUSSION

Catecholamines, HPA Axis, and Aggression

Peer-reared monkeys had lower levels of CSF NE and HVA than their mother-reared counterparts. This suggests that maternal privation reduces the baseline

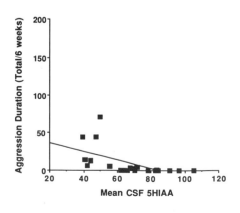

FIGURE 1. Scatter plot of total duration of aggression (seconds) and cerebrospinal fluid concentrations of 5-hydroxyindoleacetic acid (5-HIAA, ng/mL) in mother-reared juvenile rhesus monkeys. Pearson's product correlation = −0.58; $p < 0.05$ difference from zero.

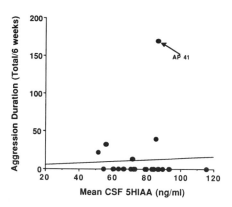

FIGURE 2. Scatter plot of total duration of aggression (seconds) and cerebrospinal fluid concentrations of 5-hydroxyindoleacetic acid (5-HIAA, ng/mL) in peer-reared juvenile rhesus monkeys. Pearson's product correlation = -0.03; not significantly different from zero.

activity of the NE and DA systems in juvenile rhesus monkeys. It also appears that maintenance of below normal baseline activity in these systems eventually results in postsynaptic receptor supersensitivity. So when the catecholamine (CA) systems are activated by either drugs that promote release of CA neurotransmitters or social stressors, the behavioral response to the stressor or drug is exaggerated and inordinate.[5] A similar explanation has been forwarded for NE/DA activation of irritable aggression in rodents.[35] It is also noteworthy that levels of ACTH and cortisol were lower in peer- by comparison to mother-reared monkeys. Other studies indicate that peer-reared monkeys have a blunted HPA axis response (increase in ACTH and/or cortisol) to psychosocial stressors.[32] Thus, the exaggerated behavioral response to stressors in peer-reared monkeys, perhaps mediated in part by brain CA receptor systems, is not paralleled by comparably enhanced or even normal neuroendocrine responses. This suggests that the usual organization of responses to stressors among brain neurochemical and neuroendocrine mechanisms fails to materialize in peer-reared monkeys.

5-HIAA, Rearing, and Aggression

Peer-reared monkeys did not, as a group, have levels of CSF 5-HIAA that differed significantly from mother-reared monkeys. There was considerable overlap of distributions across rearing groups (see FIGURES 1 and 2). One conspicuous rearing difference, however, was that no peer-reared monkey had values of less than 50 ng/mL, whereas six of the mother-reared monkeys fell in this range. For the moment let us refer to having levels of 5-HIAA of less than 50 ng/mL as having "low CSF 5-HIAA" if you are a rhesus monkey. Three of the six mother-reared monkeys with levels of 5-HIAA less than 55 ng/mL account for the overall magnitude of the negative correlation between 5-HIAA and aggression in this group. Hence, finding "low 5-HIAA" in a mother-reared monkey would not be a good indicator of whether the monkey was unusually aggressive, and, indeed, aggression is correlated with prosocial behavior in mother-reared monkeys (TABLE 2).

From a behavioral standpoint the peer-reared monkeys in this study were generally more active (and less inactive) than their mother-reared counterparts. They did not differ from mother-reared monkeys in general levels of prosocial behavior, nor were they significantly more aggressive as a group than the mother-reared monkeys. There are two conclusions that are relevant from the clinical point of view.

(1) Privation of social rearing and/or social experience produces unusual patterns of aggression in monkeys, but it does not produce reductions in CSF 5-HIAA, a measure that has been associated with unusual aggression and violence in humans. The fact that aggression duration in peer-reared monkeys is not correlated with any other neurochemical or social behavioral measure provides one numeric indication of why aggression among these monkeys is viewed as being unpredictable.

(2) Exceptionally aggressive individuals are more likely to surface in peer-reared groups than in mother-reared groups. In this study, monkey AP 41 is the example cited. AP 41's level of measured aggression, duration is almost four standard deviations removed from like-reared peers and even further removed from the mean level of measured aggression in mother-reared monkeys. Nevertheless, AP 41's measures of neurochemical or neuroendocrine activity were not exceptional or strikingly different from less aggressive monkeys in any regard.

ATTACHMENT

Primate brains are set up so that mechanisms that usually control behavior come into existence as a result of early attachment and later social interactions, and fail to organize otherwise.[31] Thus, brain function, meaning the cohesive patterning of neural activity producing purposeful behavior, normally depends on social attachment in nonhuman and presumably human primates.[31] This does not mean that the brain cannot regulate bodily functions or initiate behavior if attachment does not occur. It does imply that the brain of the unattached infant cannot regulate behavior in the usual way. The idea is that neural systems that would usually interconnect as a result of social experience fail to connect if the individual does not have the experience.[5,27,31,36]

Although the development of any one neurochemical system, considered in isolation, may seem to be more attributable to genetic endowment than experience, it seems likely that the development of interrelationships among measures of biogenic amine system activity depends on experience. Data presented herein indicate that maternal privation in monkeys produces changes in the levels of some neurochemical measures and degradation of the usual interrelationships among measures. In the absence of usual rearing and social interaction, the usual correlations among biological and behavioral measures do not develop in rhesus monkeys.[5,27,31] Therefore, the behavioral effects of social deprivation (unpredictable aggression, for example) might be best understood as reflecting the disorganization of the usual interactions among neurobiological regulatory systems. One implication of this is that CSF 5-HIAA may be a good measure of 5-HT system effects in the organized system, but not in the disorganized system. Thus, we can define usual relationships among neurobiological measures and behavior in monkeys, but when the unusual case arises what we find is that the relationships are absent. The individual does not conform to the usual neurobiological rules any more than they conform to the usual social rules.

CONCLUSION: UNUSUAL BEHAVIOR AND BRAIN FUNCTION

The idea that a range of behavior disorders might be attributable to reduced function in one neurotransmitter system is appealing for a variety of reasons. As outlined in the introduction, a clear association between a measure of neurotransmitter function and a psychiatric disorder would allow us to both predict future behavior and perhaps to rationally treat a disorder based on objective biological measures. Indeed, there may be disorders associated with low 5-HT system function, but the relationship between measures of 5-HT and violence may only apply to certain subgroups and not to the larger problem of societal violence that we seem to be facing.

What this research shows most clearly is that exposure to psychosocial risk factors, such as maternal privation, produces biological changes in offspring and increases the probability of violence. The biological changes are not restricted to one neurochemical or neuroendocrine system. The result is that an individual's behavior is less predictable and less related to measures of any single measure of neurobiological function than it would be in the usual case. Given this situation it is unlikely that tinkering with increasingly specific pharmacological fixes of what seems to be a general disorganization of brain function will be successful. Devising social strategies to intervene before brain organizational processes fail deserves a high priority.

REFERENCES

1. BROWN, G. L., F. K. GOODWIN, J. C. BALLENGER, P. F. GOYER & L. F. MAJOR. 1979. Aggression in humans correlates with cerebrospinal fluid amine metabolites. Psychiatry Res. **1:** 131–139.
2. COCCARO, E. F. 1992. Impulsive aggression and central serotonergic system function in humans: An example of a dimensional brain-behavior relationship. Int. Clin. Psychopharmacol. **7**(1): 3–12.
3. LINNOILA, V. M. & M. VIRKKUNEN. 1992. Aggression, suicidality, and serotonin. J. Clin. Psychiatry **53**(Supplement): 46–51.
4. HIGLEY, J. D., M. LINNOILA & S. J. SUOMI. 1994. Ethological contributions: Experiential and genetic contributions to the expression and inhibition of aggression in primates. Handbook of aggressive and destructive behavior in psychiatric patients. M. Hersen, R. T. Ammerman & L. Sission, Eds.: 17–32. Plenum Press. New York.
5. KRAEMER, G. W. & A. S. CLARKE. 1990. The behavioral neurobiology of self-injurious behavior in rhesus monkeys. Prog. Neuro-psychopharmacol. Biol. Psychiatry **14**(Supplement): 141–168.
6. CAPITANIO, J. P. 1985. Early experience and social processes in rhesus macaques (Macaca mulatta): II. Complex social interaction. J. Comp. Psychol. **99:** 133–144.
7. HARLOW, H. F., M. K. HARLOW & S. J. SUOMI. 1971. From thought to therapy: Lessons from a primate laboratory. Am. Sci. **59:** 538–549.
8. SOUBRIE, P. 1986. Reconciling the role of central serotonin neurons in human and animal behavior. Behav. Brain Sci. **9:** 319–364.
9. EBERT, M. H. & M. J. PERLOW. 1977. Utility of cerebrospinal fluid measurements in studies of brain monoamines. Structure and function of brain monoamine systems. E. Usdin, N. Weiner & M. B. H. Youdin, Eds.: 963–984. Marcel Dekker. New York.
10. RALEIGH, M. J., M. T. McGUIRE, G. L. BRAMMER, D. B. POLLACK & A. YUWILER. 1991. Serotonergic mechanisms promote dominance acquisition in adult male vervet monkeys. Brain Res. **559**(2): 181–190.
11. RALEIGH, M. J. & M. T. McGUIRE. 1994. Serotonin, aggression, and violence in vervet monkeys. The neurotransmitter revolution. R. Masters & M. T. McGuire, Eds.: 129–145. Southern Illinois University Press. Carbondale, Illinois.
12. CLARKE, A. S., C. KAMMERER, K. GEORGE, D. KUPFER, W. T. McKINNEY, A. SPENCE & G. W. KRAEMER. 1995. Evidence of heritability of norepinephrine, HVA, and 5HIAA values in cerebrospinal fluid of rhesus monkeys. Biol. Psychiatry **38:** 572–577.

13. HIGLEY, J. D., W. W. THOMPSON, M. CHAMPOUX, D. GOLDMAN, M. F. HASERT, G. W. KRAEMER, J. M. SCANLAN, S. J. SUOMI & M. LINNOILA. 1993. Paternal and maternal genetic and environmental contributions to cerebrospinal fluid monoamine metabolites in rhesus monkeys (Macaca mulatta). Arch. Gen. Psychiatry 50: 615–623.

14. HIGLEY, J. D., S. J. SUOMI & M. LINNOILA. 1992. A longitudinal study of CSF monoamine metabolite and plasma cortisol concentrations in young rhesus monkeys: Effects of early experience, age, sex, and stress on continuity of individual differences. Biol Psychiatry 32: 127–145.

15. KRAEMER, G. W., M. H. EBERT, D. E. SCHMIDT & W. T. MCKINNEY. 1989. A longitudinal study of the effects of different rearing environments on cerebrospinal fluid norepinephrine and biogenic amine metabolites in rhesus monkeys. Neuropsychopharmacology 2: 175–189.

16. YODYINGYUAD, U., C. DE LA RIVA, D. H. ABBOT, J. HERBERT & E. B. KEVERNE. 1985. Relationship between dominance hierarchy, cerebrospinal fluid levels of amine transmitter metabolites (5-hydroxyindoleacetic acid and homovanillic acid) and plasma cortisol in monkeys. Neuroscience 16(4): 851–858.

17. HIGLEY, J. D., S. J. SUOMI & M. LINNOILA. 1991. CSF monoamine metabolite concentrations vary according to age, rearing, and sex, and are influenced by the stressor of social separation in rhesus monkeys. Psychopharmacology 103: 551–556.

18. ANDERSON, C. O. & W. A. MASON. 1974. Early experience and complexity of social organization in groups of young rhesus monkeys (Macaca mulatta). J. Comp. Physiol. Psychol. 87: 681–690.

19. ANDERSON, C. O. & W. A. MASON. 1978. Competitive social strategies in groups of deprived and experienced rhesus monkeys. Dev. Psychobiol. 11: 289–299.

20. MEHLMAN, P. T., J. D. HIGLEY, I. FAUCHER, A. A. LILLY, D. M. TAUB, J. VICKERS, S. J. SUOMI & M. LINNOILA. 1995. Correlation of CSF 5-HIAA concentration with sociality and the timing of emigration in free-ranging primates. Am. J. Psychiatry 156(6): 907–913.

21. BERNSTEIN, I. S. & C. EHARDT. 1986. The influence of kinship and socialization on aggressive behavior in rhesus monkeys (Macaca mulatta). Anim. Behav. 34: 739–747.

22. HARLOW, H. F. 1969. The age-mate or peer affectional system. Advances in the study of behavior. E. B. Foss, Ed.: 2: 333–383. Academic Press. New York.

23. MASON, W. A. 1985. Experiential influences on the development of expressive behaviors in rhesus monkeys. The development of expressive behavior: Biology environment interactions. G. Zivin, Ed.: 117–152. Academic Press. New York.

24. SCHILDKRAUT, J. J. & S. S. KETY. 1967. Biogenic amines and emotion. Science 156: 21–30.

25. SNYDER, S. H. 1973. Amphetamine psychosis: A "model" schizophrenia mediated by catecholamines. Am. J. Psychiatry 130: 61–67.

26. SIEVER, L. J. 1987. Role of noradrenergic mechanisms in the etiology of the affective disorders. Psychopharmacology: The third generation of progress. H. Y. Meltzer & M. Lipton, Eds.: 493–504. Raven Press. New York.

27. KRAEMER, G. W. 1982. Neurochemical correlates of stress and depression: Depletion or disorganization? Behav. Brain Sci. 5: 110.

28. AGREN, H., I. N. MEFFORD, M. V. RUDORFER, M. LINNOILA & W. POTTER. 1986. Interacting neurotransmitter systems. A non-experimental approach to the 5HIAA-HVA correlation in human CSF. J. Psychiatr. Res. 20: 175–193.

29. KRAEMER, G. W. 1985. The primate social environment, brain neurochemical changes and psychopathology. Trends Neurosci. 8: 339–340.

30. KRAEMER, G. W., M. H. EBERT, D. E. SCHMIDT & W. T. MCKINNEY. 1991. Strangers in a Strange Land: A psychobiological study of mother-infant separation in rhesus monkeys. Child Dev. 62: 548–566.

31. KRAEMER, G. W. 1992. A psychobiological theory of attachment. Behav. Brain Sci. 15(3): 493–511.

32. CLARKE, A. S. 1993. Social rearing effects on HPA axis activity over early development and in response to stress in young rhesus monkeys. Dev. Psychobiol. 26: 433–447.

33. SCHMIDT, D. E., M. ROZNOSKI & M. H. EBERT. 1990. Qualitative and quantitative high performance liquid chromatographic analysis of monoamine neurotransmitters and metabolites in cerebrospinal fluid and brain tissue using reductive electrochemical detection. Biomed. Chromatogr. 4(5): 215–220.
34. CLARKE, A. S., D. J. WITTWER, D. H. ABBOTT & M. L. SCHNEIDER. 1994. Long-term effects of prenatal stress on HPA axis activity in juvenile rhesus monkeys. Dev. Psychobiol. 27: 257–270.
35. HEGSTRAND, L. & B. EICHELMAN. 1983. Increased shock induced fighting and super-sensitive beta-adrenergic receptors. Pharmacol. Biochem. Behav. 19: 313–320.
36. KRAEMER, G. W. 1995. The significance of social attachment in primate infants: The caregiver-infant relationship and volition. Motherhood in human and nonhuman primates: Biological and social determinants. C. R. Pryce, R. D. Martin & D. Skuse, Eds.: 152–161. S. Karger. Basel.

The Role of Early Environmental Events in Regulating Neuroendocrine Development

Moms, Pups, Stress, and Glucocorticoid Receptors

DARLENE FRANCIS, JOSIE DIORIO,
PATRICIA LaPLANTE, SHELLEY WEAVER,
JONATHAN R. SECKL, AND MICHAEL J. MEANEY[a]

Developmental Neuroendocrinology Laboratory
Douglas Hospital Research Centre
Departments of Psychiatry, and Neurology and Neurosurgery
McGill University
Montreal, Canada
and
Molecular Endocrinology Laboratory
Department of Medicine
University of Edinburgh
Edinburgh, Scotland, UK EH4 2XU

OVERVIEW

The adrenal glucocorticoids and catecholamines constitute a frontline of defense for mammalian species under conditions (stressors) that threaten homeostasis. Glucocorticoids are the end product of the hypothalamic-pituitary-adrenal (HPA) axis and along with the catecholamines serve to mobilize the production and distribution of energy substrates during stress. The increased secretion of pituitary-adrenal hormones in response to stress is stimulated by the release of corticotropin-releasing hormone (CRH) and/or arginine vasopressin (AVP) from neurons in the paraventricular nucleus of the hypothalamus. In this way a neural signal associated with the stressor is transduced into a set of endocrine and sympathetic responses.

The development of the HPA response to stressful stimuli is altered by early environmental events. Animals exposed to short periods of infantile stimulation or handling show decreased HPA responsivity to stress, whereas maternal separation, physical trauma, and endotoxin administration enhance HPA responsivity to stress. In all cases these effects persist throughout the life of the animal and are accompanied by increased hypothalamic levels of the mRNA for CRH and often that for AVP.

The inhibitory regulation of the synthesis for these ACTH-releasing factors is

[a] Address correspondence to Michael J. Meaney, Developmental Neuroendocrinology Laboratory, Douglas Hospital Research Centre, 6875 Boulevard LaSalle, Montreal, Quebec H4H 1R3, Canada. Tel: (514) 762-3048; fax: (514) 762-3034; e-mail: dfranc@po-box.mcgill.ca.

achieved, in part, through a negative feedback loop whereby circulating glucocorticoids act at various neural sites to decrease CRH and AVP gene expression. Such inhibitory effects are initiated through an interaction between the adrenal steroid and an intracellular receptor (either the mineralocorticoid or glucocorticoid receptor). We have found that these early environmental manipulations regulate glucocorticoid receptor gene expression in the hippocampus and frontal cortex, regions that have been strongly implicated as sites for negative-feedback regulation of CRH and AVP synthesis. When the differences in glucocorticoid receptor density are transiently reversed, so too are those in the HPA responses to stress.

These findings reflect the influence of the early postnatal environment on the differentiation of hippocampal neurons. This effect involves an altered rate of glucocorticoid receptor gene expression, resulting in changes in the sensitivity of the system to the inhibitory effects of glucocorticoids on the synthesis of CRH and AVP in hypothalamic neurons. Changes in CRH and AVP levels, in turn, determine the responsivity of the axis to subsequent stressors; increased releasing factor production is associated with increased HPA responses to stress. Thus, the early environment can contribute substantially to the development of stable individual differences in HPA responsivity to stressful stimuli. These data provide examples of early environmental programming of neural systems. One major objective of our research is to understand how such programming occurs within the brain.

THE HYPOTHALAMIC-PITUITARY-ADRENAL STRESS RESPONSE

The HPA response to stress is a basic adaptive mechanism in mammals. The increased secretion of CRH and cosecretagogues, such as AVP and oxytocin, into the hypophysial-portal system of the anterior pituitary during stress enhances the synthesis and release of proopiomelanocortin-derived peptides, adrenocorticotropin (ACTH), and β-endorphin.[1-3] Elevated ACTH levels, in turn, increase the synthesis and release of adrenal glucocorticoids. The highly catabolic glucocorticoids, in concert with the adrenomedullary catecholamines, produce lipolysis, glycogenolysis, and protein catabolism, resulting in increased blood glucose levels.[4,5] These actions assist the organism during stress by increasing the availability of energy substrates.

However, prolonged exposure to elevated glucocorticoid levels can present a serious risk, leading to a suppression of anabolic processes; muscle atrophy; decreased sensitivity to insulin; and a risk of steroid-induced diabetes, hypertension, hyperlipidemia, hypercholesterolemia, arterial disease, amenorrhea, impotency, and the impairment of growth and tissue repair, as well as immunosuppression.[4-6] It is in the organism's best interest to limit these costly metabolic stress responses.

The responsivity of the HPA axis to stress is, in part, determined by the ability of the glucocorticoids to regulate ACTH release (*i.e.*, glucocorticoid negative feedback). Circulating glucocorticoids feedback onto the pituitary and specific brain regions to inhibit the secretion of releasing factors from hypothalamic neurons and ACTH from pituitary corticotrophes.[7-13] In addition to pituitary and hypothalamic sites, there is now considerable evidence for the importance of the limbic system, the hippocampus, and the frontal cortex in the regulation of HPA activity.[9-11,14] Indeed, the hippocampus contains the highest density of corticosteroid receptors in the brain.[13]

ENVIRONMENTAL REGULATION OF HPA DEVELOPMENT

We have outlined the effects of early postnatal events on the development of HPA responsivity to stress in several recent reviews (e.g., refs. 15, 16). The focus here is on the mechanisms underlying the effect of early environment on the differentiation of corticosteroid receptor systems in the rodent forebrain. We will limit our summary of the neuroendocrine studies to simply a rationale for the focus on these systems.

As described above, circulating glucocorticoids act at central corticosteroid receptor sites to inhibit subsequent HPA responsivity; this is the neural basis for glucocorticoid negative feedback. Glucocorticoid receptor systems in the rodent forebrain show considerable plasticity during the first week of life. Ultimately the development of these systems is, in part at least, regulated by the early environment, and we view this as a feature of normal development (see below). In this manner the early environment can regulate the sensitivity of critical forebrain structures to circulating glucocorticoids, and thus alter feedback efficacy.

Postnatal stimulation or handling increases glucocorticoid receptor expression in the hippocampus and frontal cortex, two brain regions that have been implicated in feedback regulation of HPA activity. By contrast, prolonged periods of maternal separation (MS), lasting 180 minutes, produce decreased glucocorticoid receptor levels in the hypothalamus, frontal cortex, and hippocampus. Similarly, early endotoxin exposure decreases glucocorticoid receptor expression in the hypothalamus, hippocampus, and frontal cortex. In all cases these effects persist well into adult life, and at least in the case of handling, throughout life.[17]

The effects of handling are almost completely the opposite of those of maternal separation. This suggests that the differentiation glucocorticoid receptor systems in selected brain regions are sensitive to a variety of environmental signals during the postnatal period. These signals can act to permanently increase or decrease glucocorticoid receptor expression within specific neural structures that regulate CRH/AVP synthesis in PVNh neurons. These cells furnish the neural signal by which stress activates the pituitary-adrenal unit. Thus, the early environment can determine the responsiveness of the HPA axis to stress throughout the lifetime of the animal. We feel that these findings reflect a natural state of neural plasticity through which HPA responsiveness to stress in adulthood can be either enhanced or dampened as a function of early environmental events.

In each case there is evidence for altered glucocorticoid negative feedback sensitivity. MS and nonhandled (NH) animals show decreased glucocorticoid inhibition of ACTH release, whereas handling increases negative feedback efficacy. Glucocorticoids are known to regulate the synthesis and release of hypothalamic CRF and AVP.[43-47] Indeed, this process is considered as a basis for delayed glucocorticoid negative feedback effects.[9] Thus, we proposed that the increased synthesis of CRF and AVP in the NH and MS animals occurs in response to a decreased tonic, glucocorticoid negative feedback signal.[15,16] The forebrain glucocorticoid receptor system is, therefore, an important and common target for early environmental regulation. In altering feedback sensitivity, the early environment establishes the efficacy of tonic glucocorticoid inhibition over hypothalamic CRF/AVP neurons, altering readily releasable pools of these releasing factors in the terminals of PVNh neurons, and thus HPA responsivity to stress. We would predict that handled (H) and NH/MS rats should differ in HPA responses to any form of stress.

BIOLOGICAL SIGNIFICANCE

We believe that the effects of early environment on the development of HPA responses to stress reflect a naturally occurring plasticity whereby the early environment is able to "program" rudimentary, biological responses to threatening stimuli. The activation of adrenocortical/sympathoadrenal responses to stress is both essential for survival and metabolically costly. Increased glucocorticoid responses to stress are associated with enhanced immunosuppression (see ref. 6 for a review) and increased risk for neuropathology in later life.[17-21] Although it is clearly in the animal's best interest to activate these neuroendocrine systems in response to threat, exaggerated or unnecessary activity can also be damaging: hence the importance of an appropriate response to the existing threat.

Like humans, the Norway rat inhabits a tremendous variety of ecological niches, each with varied sets of environmental demands. The plasticity observed in these developmental studies could allow animals to adapt defensive systems to the unique demands of the environment. Because most mammals usually spend their adult life in an environment that is either the same or quite similar to that in which they were born, developmental "programming" of CNS responses to stress in early life is likely to be of adaptive value to the adult. Such programming affords the animal an appropriate level of adrenal hormone response, minimizing the need for a long period of adaptation in adult life. The results of our studies suggest that this neonatal programming occurs by way of the forebrain neurons that govern HPA activity.

The various environmental paradigms used in these studies differ considerably, and yet each alters the development of forebrain glucocorticoid receptor systems. This has led us to wonder whether there is some common element to these manipulations. Do these procedures alter some naturally occurring event that is relevant to glucocorticoid receptor development? Might such variation be associated with an epigenetic factor, such as variation in maternal care? Levine first suggested that the handling manipulation map onto naturally occurring individual differences in early life experiences involving maternal care.[22] Handling results in changes in mother-pup interactions. We (Woodside *et al.*, unpublished) have examined the effect of handling on the amount of time the mother spends with her offspring. Typically, a nesting bout begins when the mother approaches the litter, gathers the pups under her, suckles, and terminates when the mother licks the pups and leaves the nest (the termination of a nest bout is associated with an increase in the mother's body temperature[23,24]). Overall, we found that mothers of H pups spend the same amount of time with their litters as mothers of NH pups. However, mothers of H litters have shorter but more frequent nest bouts and spend significantly more time manipulating their pups, especially licking of pups (also see refs. 25 and 26) than mothers of NH pups. This latter effect is likely due to the fact that mothers of H litters are getting on and off her pups more frequently, and licking is associated with the termination of each bout. H pups show increased ultrasonic vocalizations,[27] and such calls elicit maternal care (*e.g.*, retrieval). Several aspects of the mother-pup interactions are of known importance in neural development, especially maternal licking. Handling ultimately results in an increase in mother-pup contact, whereas both maternal separation and endotoxin exposure (Shanks, unpublished) result in diminished mother-pup contact. Long periods of maternal separation clearly alter the amount of time the mother is in contact with her pups, and mothers of endotoxin-treated pups also spend less time in contact with their offspring, perhaps due to the increased body temperature of the pups that serves to limit maternal contact.[28] The question, then, is whether some aspect of this altered pattern of maternal behavior may serve as a critical stimulus for the environmental effects on the development of glucocorticoid receptor systems. In support of this idea, Hennessy et al.[29] found that the strain of the mother determined the nature of the handling effect on adrenal glucocorticoid responses to novelty in mice. The question is then, How does this maternal mediation occur?

In studies currently in progress, we have used a procedure described by Michael Meyers[30] in order to examine the relationship between maternal behavior and HPA development. Handling has been shown to alter the frequency with which mothers lick and groom pups as well as nest-bout timing. In extended descriptive studies we also found that handling increases arched-back nursing: nonhandled mothers more frequently adopt a "blanket" posture lying over pups. We examined maternal behavior in a cohort of primiparous dams whose pups were unmanipulated, looking for naturally occurring individual differences in maternal behavior (note these pups were neither handled nor nonhandled; nonhandled pups are completely undisturbed for the first two weeks of life, whereas the litters in this study underwent routine cage cleaning). Three behaviors served to divide the mothers into two groups: arched-back licking, nesting, and licking and grooming. There was a close correlation between these behaviors, especially between arched-back nursing, and licking and grooming ($r = +.91$). Thus, one group of mothers showed well-built nests, as well as a high frequency of licking and grooming, and arched-back nursing. The variability here is considerable. On measures of licking and grooming, and arched-back nursing, these mothers resembled mothers of handled pups: the question is, What of the HPA response to stress in the offspring?

The offspring were tested as adults and the groups classified as either high NAL (high nest rating, and high frequency of both licking and grooming frequency and arched back nursing) or low NAL. Pups of high NAL mothers showed significantly lower plasma ACTH and corticosterone responses to restraint stress compared with pups of low NAL mothers. The next question is whether some aspect of the differences in maternal behavior is critical for the difference in HPA responses to stress. The magnitude of the plasma corticosterone responses was significantly and negatively correlated with the frequency of both licking and grooming ($r = -.60$) and arched-back nursing ($r = -.61$). Plasma corticosterone responses to restraint were not correlated with nest rating.

These findings would seem to support the Levine hypothesis that alterations in maternal behavior mediate the handling effect. Exactly how maternal licking and grooming or arched-back nursing might affect HPA development is unclear, but the focus on maternal-pup interactions is, in our minds, exciting.

Under natural conditions there is considerable variation in the amount of time that mothers spend away from their litters.[31] This variation derives, in part, from the social status of the mother. Dominant female rats build their nests in proximity to food/water and have ready access to these resources. Subordinate females are forced to locate their nests further from food and water and gain access to these resources only in the absence of competition from dominant animals. Accordingly, Calhoun found that it is not uncommon for a subordinate dam to be off her litter for 2–3 hours at a time. This is exactly the period of time that was used in the Plotsky and Meaney[32] maternal separation study and that produced significantly increased hypothalamic CRH mRNA expression and HPA responses to stress. In this manner, the behavior of the mother towards her offspring could alter the differentiation of limbic and cortical neurons that govern behavioral and endocrine responses to stress. Interestingly, in primates at least, the offspring tend to assume the rank of their mothers. In both the rat and old world monkey, subordinate animals show increased HPA activity.[33-35] The increased HPA activity of the subordinate could be adaptive in several respects. It could assist the animal in meeting the metabolic demands associated with the stress of social subordination. We assume that these animals are not biologically more or less fit based on their HPA responses to stress. These animals are simply different, and the differences can be at least partially understood in terms of the early environmental events, and perhaps in differences in maternal care.

THE MECHANISM OF ACTION OF HANDLING ON GLUCOCORTICOID RECEPTOR DEVELOPMENT

The handling paradigm provides a model for understanding the mechanisms by which environmental stimuli can regulate neural development. This model is somewhat unique, inasmuch as many other paradigms, involving alterations in either environmental or hormonal conditions, have focused on changes in either synapse formation or neuron survival.[36] By contrast, handling affects neurochemical differentiation in the hippocampus, specifically altering the sensitivity of hippocampal cells to corticosterone, through an effect on glucocorticoid receptor gene expression and thus receptor density. Indeed, this effect seems to occur independently of processes, such as neuron survival, inasmuch as adult H and NH rats do not appear to differ in hippocampal morphology.[17] Such variations in neuronal differentiation likely underlie important individual differences in tissue sensitivity to hormonal signals and thus represent a biochemical basis for environmental programming of neural systems.

The handling effect on the development of glucocorticoid receptor density in the hippocampus shows the common characteristics of a developmental effect. First, there is a specific "critical period" during which the organism is maximally responsive to the effects of handling. Second, the effects of handling during the first 21 days of life on glucocorticoid receptor density endure throughout the life of the animal. Finally, there is substantial specificity to the handling effect. Handling alters the glucocorticoid, but not mineralocorticoid, receptor gene expression. Interestingly, glucocorticoid and mineralocorticoid receptors are coexpressed in virtually all hippocampal neurons. Thus, the handling effect on gene expression is really quite specific.

Temporal Features of the Handling Effect

Handling during the first week of life was as effective as handling during the entire first three weeks of life in reducing adrenal steroid responses to stress[37] and in increasing hippocampal glucocorticoid receptor density.[38] Handling over the second week of life was somewhat less effective, whereas animals handled between days 15 and 21 did not differ from NH animals in glucocorticoid receptor binding. Thus, in terms of both HPA activity and glucocorticoid receptor binding, the sensitivity of the system to environmental regulation wanes progressively over the first three weeks of life. Moreover, in comparison to same-aged NH animals, H animals exhibited significantly increased hippocampal glucocorticoid receptor density as early as day 7 of life, and the magnitude of the effect did not increase thereafter.[38] Thus, glucocorticoid receptor binding capacity appears to be especially sensitive to environmental regulation during the first week of life.

Note, however, that this does not preclude the possibility of other periods of environmental regulation. Mohammed et al.[39] have reported that environmental enrichment during the postnatal period results in increased hippocampal glucocorticoid receptor mRNA expression. Ader and Grota[40] had previously reported that handling during the postweaning period also reduced the magnitude of HPA responses to stress. Thus, there may exist a period during the postweaning period when HPA development is once more sensitive to environmental events. If this is indeed true, it will be interesting to compare the biological bases for the handling effects during these two periods.

The temporal pattern for the handling effect on hippocampal glucocorticoid receptor levels corresponds to the normal developmental changes in glucocorticoid receptor density occurring over the early postnatal life (see ref. 16 for a review). Glucocorticoid receptor density is low on postnatal day 3 ($\sim$30% of adult values) and increases steadily towards adult values, which are achieved by about the third week of life. A comparable pattern occurs for glucocorticoid receptor mRNA levels.[41–43] It is during this period of ontogenetic variation that environmental events can influence the development of the receptor population. In contrast to the glucocorticoid receptor, mineralocorticoid receptor density varies minimally with age: hippocampal mineralocorticoid receptor density in early postnatal life is largely indistinguishable from that of adult rats[16,44,45] and, as mentioned above, handling has no effect on hippocampal mineralocorticoid receptor binding.[45,46] Thus, it is tempting to consider the relationship between the developmental pattern in hippocampal glucocorticoid receptor density and both the sensitivity of this receptor system to environmental stimuli and the timing of the critical period for these stimuli on glucocorticoid receptor development. However, the developmental pattern for glucocorticoid receptor binding in regions not affected by handling, such as the hypothalamus, amygdala, and septum,[47] is identical to that of the hippocampus (references cited above) and the frontal cortex.[48] Thus, it is unlikely that the handling effect on glucocorticoid receptor density in the hippocampus and the frontal cortex can be explained simply by the status of the glucocorticoid receptor system during the first weeks of life.

The Role of Thyroid Hormones

Handling during the first week of life activates the hypothalamic-pituitary-thyroid axis, leading to increased levels of circulating thyroxine (T_4) and increased intracellular levels of the biologically more potent T_4 metabolite, triiodothyronine (T_3[49]). Moreover, the pituitary-thyroid axis is a major regulator of HPA development.[16] Thus, we[50] examined whether the effects of handling might be mediated by increased exposure to thyroid hormones. Neonatal treatment with either T_4 or T_3 resulted in significantly increased glucocorticoid receptor binding capacity in the hippocampus in animals examined as adults. Like the handling manipulation, neither T_4 nor T_3 treatment affected hypothalamic or pituitary glucocorticoid receptor density. Moreover, administration of the thyroid hormone synthesis inhibitor, propylthiouracil (PTU), to H pups for the first two weeks of life completely blocked the effects of handling on hippocampal glucocorticoid receptor binding capacity. These data are consistent with the idea that the thyroid hormones might mediate, in part at least, the effects of neonatal handling on the development of the forebrain glucocorticoid receptor system.

Systemic injections of neonatal rat pups represent a rather crude manipulation, particularly with procedures involving thyroid hormones. Although these data might implicate the thyroid hormones, there is no indication that the hippocampus is actually the critical site of action. To examine whether thyroid hormones might act directly on hippocampal cells, we used an *in vitro* system, using primary cultures of dissociated hippocampal cells.[51] The hippocampal cells were taken from embryonic rat pups (E20), and beginning on the fifth day after plating, the cultures were exposed to 0, 1, 10, or 100 nM T_3. These cells express both mineralocorticoid and glucocorticoid receptor binding.[52] Indeed, both receptors as well as their mRNAs (on Northern blots) can be detected using material from a 60 mm dish. The cells were cultured in 10% fetal calf serum stripped of thyroid hormones. The results of several experiments have failed to detect any effect of thyroid hormones on glucocorticoid receptor density in cultured hippocampal cells.[49] These *in vitro* data suggest that the effects of the thyroid hormones on the glucocorticoid receptor binding occurs at some site distal to the hippocampal cells, or that thyroid hormones interact at the level of the hippocampus with some other hormonal signal that is obligatory for the expression of the thyroid hormone effect.

The Role of Serotonin

Thyroid hormones have pervasive effects throughout the developing central nervous system, and one such effect involves the regulation of central serotonergic neurons (*e.g.*, ref. 53). Thyroid hormones increase serotonin (5-HT) turnover in the hippocampus of the neonatal rat.[54] Handling also increases hippocampal 5-HT turnover,[54,55] and thus both manipulations increase serotonergic stimulation of hippocampal neurons. There is also direct evidence for an effect of 5-HT on glucocorticoid receptor density in the neonatal rat. 5,7-Dihydroxytryptamine (5,7-DHT) lesions of the raphe 5-HT neurons dramatically reduce the ascending serotonergic input into the hippocampus. Rat pups administered 5,7-DHT on day 2 of life showed reduced hippocampal glucocorticoid receptor density as adults.[54]

Serotonin also had a profound effect on glucocorticoid receptor density in cultured hippocampal cells.[52,56] In hippocampal cells cultured in the presence of increasing concentrations of 5-HT, there was a twofold increase in glucocorticoid receptor binding. The effect of 5-HT was dose related, with an EC_{50} of 4–5 nM, and the maximal effect was achieved at 10 nM concentrations. A minimum of four days of treatment was required for the maximal effect of 5-HT. Shorter periods of exposure were ineffective, suggesting that the effect of 5-HT involves the increased synthesis of receptors. In support of this idea, we (O'Donnell and Meaney, unpublished) found that the effect of 5-HT on glucocorticoid receptor density in cultured hippocampal cells was blocked by either actinomycin D or cycloheximide and was paralleled by an increase in glucocorticoid receptor mRNA levels.

The effect of 5-HT on glucocorticoid receptor expression appears to occur uniquely in the neuronal cell population. We found no effect of 5-HT on glucocorticoid receptor binding in hippocampal glial-enriched cell cultures. This finding is not surprising, inasmuch as our initial studies were performed with cultures constituted largely (~85%) of neuron-like cells.[52] Moreover, the composition of the cultures was unaffected by 5-HT treatment. We also examined the potential involvement of the glial cells by using a conditioned-medium experiment in which glial-enriched cultures were treated for five days with 5-HT, and the medium was then used to feed neuronal cultures. This procedure had no effect on glucocorticoid receptor density, suggesting that the effect was not due to a 5-HT-induced glial secretory product.

The effects of 10 nM 5-HT on glucocorticoid receptor density in cultured hippocampal cells was completely blocked by the $5-HT_2$ receptor antagonists, ketanserin and mianserin.[52,56] Moreover, the $5-HT_{2A}$ agonists DOI, TFMPP, and quipazine were also effective in increasing glucocorticoid receptor binding in hippocampal culture, although not as effective as 5-HT. Selective agonists or antagonists of the $5-HT_{1A}$ or $5-HT_3$ receptors had no effect on glucocorticoid receptor binding. Using [^{125}I]7-amino-8-iodo-ketanserin as a radioligand, we found high-affinity $5-HT_{2A}$ binding sites in our cultured hippocampal cells. Teitler's group[57,58] reported that the ketanserin-labeled $5-HT_2$ site exists in two states: an agonist state ($5-HT_{2AH}$) with a high, nanomolar affinity for 5-HT and an antagonist state ($5-HT_{2AL}$) with a low, micromolar affinity for 5-HT. In both states the receptor shows a high affinity for antagonists, such as ketanserin. The $5-HT_{2AH}$ site binds with high affinity to DOI, TFMPP, and quipazine, and Teitler et al.[57] have reported a K_d of ~5 nM for 5-HT. This K_d closely approximates the EC_{50} (4–5 nM) for the effect of 5-HT on glucocorticoid receptors in cultured hippocampal cells. Taken together, these findings suggest that this effect of 5-HT appears to be mediated through a high-affinity, $5-HT_{2A}$-like receptor.

We have confirmed radiolabeled ketanserin binding in both the hippocampal cell cultures and in neonatal rat hippocampus (using in vitro autoradiography). However, although we[59] found ample $5-HT_{2A}$ receptor mRNA expression in the neonatal rat dorsal hippocampus, there was no evidence for $5-HT_{2C}$ receptor mRNA (consistent with earlier findings from studies with adult rats). Thus, although it is not particularly easy to pharmacologically discriminate between the $5-HT_{2A}$ and $5-HT_{2C}$ receptors, these findings would suggest the involvement of the $5-HT_{2A}$ receptor.

We then began to examine the nature of the secondary messenger systems involved in this serotonergic effect on glucocorticoid receptor binding. Mitchell et al.[52] found that low nanomolar concentrations of 5-HT ($EC_{50} = 7$ nM) produce a fourfold increase in cAMP levels in cultured hippocampal cells, with no effect on cGMP levels. This increase in cAMP is blocked by ketanserin and at least partially mimicked by quipazine, TFMPP, and DOI. Indeed, there is a rather good correlation (+0.97) between the effects of these 5-HT receptor agonists on cAMP and glucocorticoid receptor levels.

Treatment with the stable cAMP analogue, 8-bromo-cAMP, or with 10 μM forskolin produces a significant increase in glucocorticoid receptor density in cultured hippocampal neurons.[56] The effect of 8-bromo cAMP is concentration related, and the maximal effect of 8-bromo-cAMP (~190%) is comparable to that for 5-HT (~200%). Interestingly, as with 5-HT, the effects of 8-bromo cAMP on glucocorticoid receptor density were not apparent until at least four days of treatment and served to increase glucocorticoid receptor mRNA levels.

Taken together, these findings suggest that changes in cAMP concentrations may mediate the effects of 5-HT on glucocorticoid receptor synthesis in hippocampal cells. We[56] also found that the cyclic nucleotide–dependent protein kinase inhibitor, H8, completely blocked the effects of 10 nM 5-HT on glucocorticoid receptor binding in hippocampal cell cultures. By contrast, the protein kinase C inhibitor, H7, had no such effect. These data suggest that activation of protein kinase A might, at some point, be involved in the serotonergic regulation of hippocampal glucocorticoid receptor development.

In these studies we are working with intact cells over long incubation periods, and there is ample possibility for an interaction between second messenger systems. This issue also arises, because the $5-HT_{2A}$ receptor has been linked not to cyclic nucleotide but to phospholipase C-related second messenger systems. In *vivo* and *in vitro*, 5-HT$_{2A}$ agonists increase both diacylglycerol (DAG) levels and inositol phosphate metabolism (notably IP$_1$) in hippocampal membranes.[60] There are numerous examples in the literature of such "cross-talk" between second messenger systems, and the stimulation of inositol phosphate metabolism by way of phorbol esters has been shown to alter cAMP levels (*e.g.*, ref. 61). However, in contrast to other compounds, such as glutamate or carbachol, we found that stimulation of IP metabolism by 5-HT in hippocampal slices was rather modest in animals during the first week of life.[62] Interestingly, the effect of 5-HT on IP metabolism in hippocampal slices was decreased in the handled animals on day 7 of life, whereas the stimulation of DAG was slightly enhanced. However, the overall pattern of 5-HT stimulation was rather weak. This may be due to differences in receptor coupling at this time of life. In the neonatal rat hippocampus the stimulation of IP metabolism occurred by way of 5-HT$_{2C}$ and not by 5-HT$_{2A}$ receptors during the first weeks of life.[63] Because there is little 5-HT$_{2C}$ receptor expression in the dorsal hippocampus, this may explain the weak stimulation of phospholipase C-related second messenger systems.

Together these data suggest that we should perhaps attend to the idea that 5-HT is directly stimulating cAMP formation in hippocampal neurons. This idea is a bit difficult to reconcile with the involvement of a 5-HT$_{2A}$ receptor. However, a number of 5-HT receptors have been cloned, and these receptors directly stimulate adenylyl cyclase activity. These include the 5-HT$_4$, 5-HT$_6$, and 5-HT$_7$ receptors (see ref. 64 for a review). The mRNAs for each of these receptors is expressed in the rat hippocampus. Moreover, the 5-HT$_7$ receptor binds ketanserin with high affinity. Interestingly, antidepressants increase glucocorticoid receptor mRNA in cortical and hippocampal cell cultures.[65,66] Both the 5-HT$_6$ and 5-HT$_7$ receptors bind various antidepressants with high affinity, and the 5-HT$_7$ receptor shows a high affinity for ketanserin.

Because there are no unequivocally selective ligands for these receptors, we are attempting to construct a pharmacological profile examining the effects of various agonists on cAMP formation in hippocampal slices from neonates and both cAMP and glucocorticoid receptor levels in hippocampal cell cultures. On the basis of these studies, we hope to see if any of these receptors are implicated in the environmental regulation of glucocorticoid receptor expression and whether the effects of 5-HT might be mediated through the direct activation of cAMP.

In Vivo *5-HT Effects on Glucocorticoid Receptor Expression*

Our *in vivo* studies[55] of 5-HT activity have provided some insight into why the hippocampus is selectively affected by handling. In rat pups handled for the first seven days of life, and sacrificed immediately following handling on day 7, 5-HT turnover was significantly increased in the hippocampus, but not in the hypothalamus or amygdala (regions where handling has no effect on glucocorticoid receptor density).

These data suggest that handling selectively activates certain ascending 5-HT pathways and that it is this feature of the handling effect, together with the existence of a developing glucocorticoid receptor system, that underlies the sensitivity of this receptor system in specific brain regions to regulation by environmental events during the first week of life. In current studies we are examining whether or not handling alters different ascending 5-HT neuronal populations using c*fos* mRNA as a marker for neuronal activation. The expression of c*fos* has been shown to increase in raphe neurons in response to several forms of environmental stimulation. To date we have found that handling increases c*fos* expression (5 × levels in NH animals) in about 20% of raphe neurons (Goldberg, Diorio & Meaney, unpublished). The hippocampus receives extensive 5-HTergic input that is derived from the raphe (see ref. 67 for a review). The next question is whether these activated neurons project to the hippocampus. It will also be interesting to know the distribution of thyroid hormone receptors within the raphe nuclei.

The *in vitro* data suggested that 5-HT acts at a receptor with a pharmacological profile similar to that of the $5-HT_{2A}$ receptor to alter hippocampal glucocorticoid receptor density (but see above). Clearly one concern here is the relationship between our *in vitro* results and the *in vivo* condition. In light of these thoughts, it was reassuring to find that effects of postnatal handling of rat pups on hippocampal glucocorticoid receptor binding are blocked by concurrent administration of ketanserin.[54] Moreover, ketanserin treatment also blocks the effects of T3 on hippocampal glucocorticoid receptor density.[49] This finding also supports the idea that thyroid hormones mediate the handling effect by serving to increase 5-HT activity.

We have also examined the effects of handling on cAMP levels in hippocampal tissue in neonatal rats and found that handling stimulates a fourfold increase in cAMP levels (Meaney *et al.*, submitted). These increases in cAMP are almost completely abolished by concurrent treatment with either ketanserin or the thyroid hormone synthesis inhibitor, PTU. Thus, to date the results from these *in vivo* studies certainly appear consistent with our earlier *in vitro* experiments.

The regulation of gene transcription by cAMP[68-75] has been shown to be mediated by various transcription factors, including cyclic nucleotide response element binding proteins (CREBs), cyclic nucleotide response element binding modulators (CREMs), most of which seem to be antagonists for CREBs, and the activating transcription factor family (ATF-1, ATF-2, ATF-3). In addition to the CREB/CREM-ATF family, nerve growth factor inducible factors (NGFI-A and NGFI-B) as well as activator protein-2 (AP-2) have also been shown to be inducible by cAMP.[70,81] The promoter region of the human and mouse glucocorticoid receptor gene has been cloned, and at least partially sequenced,[76,77] and contains numerous binding sites for most of these transcription factors, providing a mechanism whereby cAMP might increase glucocorticoid receptor expression.

We[78] have used a variety of techniques to study potential handling-induced changes in the expression of these transcription factors in the neonatal rat hippocampus. Using *in situ* hybridization we found that handling resulted in no change in NGFI-B mRNA expression, a significant (*i.e.*, 2 to 3-fold) increase in AP-2 mRNA expression, and a very substantial (*i.e.*, 8 to 10-fold) increase in NGFI-A mRNA levels. The increase in NGFI-A expression occurred across all hippocampal cell fields and in virtually every neuron. The increase in AP-2 and NGFI-A mRNAs is apparent immediately following the termination of handling, persists for at least three hours, and is associated with an increase in both AP-2 and NGFI-A immunoreactivity, indicating that the increase in mRNA expression is reflected in changes in protein levels.

In preliminary studies using immunocytohistochemistry, we have found that although handling produces no marked increase in either CREB or phosphorylated CREB staining, CREM staining is substantially decreased. Sassone-Corsi *et al.*[79] have argued that most CREM isoforms (save for CREM tau) work as CREB antagonists at the CRE binding sites. Hence, a reduced CREM signal could serve to enhance CREB-regulated gene transcription. Note that the constitutive expression of CREB and phosphoCREB in the neonatal rat hippocampus is intense, such that changes in CREM seem to be occurring against the background of a very substantial CREB signal.

TABLE 1. A Summary of the Results of Immunocytohistochemical Studies Examining the Effects of Handling on the Expression of Various Transcription Factors in the Dorsal Hippocampus[a]

Transcription Factor	Basal	Stimulated (Handling)
CREBir	high	high
pCREBir	moderate	moderate
CREMir	moderate	low
NGFI-Air	low	high
NGFI-Bir	low	low
c*fos*ir	low	low
AP-2ir	low	high
SP-1ir	ND	ND
cJUNir	low	moderate

[a] In all cases, except for pCREB, the effects are maximal at 120 minutes following handling and endure for at least 4 hours. For the modest change in pCREB, the effect was apparent immediately following handling. high: strong staining throughout all cell fields; moderate: clearly detectable staining in all cell fields; low: detectable, but not apparent in all cell fields. ND: no detectable staining.

To date these studies have indicated that at least three cAMP-related transcription factor signals are potentially altered by neonatal handling (see TABLE 1): NGFI-A, AP-2, and CREB through a decrease in CREM expression (see TABLE 1). Moreover, in a very recent study we used Western blotting and found that the handling-induced increases in AP-2 and NGFI-A expression are blocked by ketanserin. In current studies we are attempting to define the molecular targets for the early environmental effects. First, we are assuming that one target for regulation is the promoter region of the glucocorticoid receptor gene. To this end we are attempting to identify relevant binding sites upstream from the 5' untranslated region of the rat glucocorticoid receptor gene encoding regions.

Preliminary work (as well as unpublished data from M. Jacobson & K. Yamamoto) and studies with other species[76,77] suggest the presence of multiple promoters for the glucocorticoid receptor gene upstream of 5' differentially transcribed untranslated exons and hence a rather complicated pattern of regulation. This is not surprising. The glucocorticoid receptor gene is expressed in virtually every cell type in the body, and thus tissue specificity for glucocorticoid effects depends upon tissue-specific regulation.

SO HOW DO THESE EFFECTS RESULT IN THE LONG-TERM DIFFERENTIATION OF HIPPOCAMPAL NEURONS?

There are two very intriguing features of the 5-HT effect that bear directly on the question of the hippocampal cell cultures as a model for neural differentiation. First, the effects of 5-HT on glucocorticoid receptor levels in hippocampal cell cultures are restricted to the first three weeks in culture. Thus, cultures treated with 10 nM 5-HT for seven days at any time during the first three weeks in culture show a significant increase in glucocorticoid receptor density; however, the effect is lost after this point. Cultures treated with 10 nM 5-HT for seven days during the third to the fourth week following plating show no increase in glucocorticoid receptor binding. Second, and most exciting, the increase in glucocorticoid receptor binding capacity following exposure to 10 nM 5-HT persists following 5-HT removal from the medium; for as long as the cultures can be studied, there is a sustained increase in glucocorticoid receptor levels well past the removal of 5-HT from the medium. We have gone as long as 50 days and seen no decrease in the magnitude of the 5-HT effect. Thus, the effect of 5-HT on glucocorticoid receptor density observed in hippocampal culture cells mimics the long-term effects of early environmental events.

Thus, we arrive at the most interesting feature of these effects: the finding that these effects persist well beyond the period of the treatment. There are at least two possible explanations for this finding. First, *in vivo*, the increase in 5-HT turnover associated with the handling procedure might be accompanied by an increase in 5-HT innervation of the hippocampus that persists throughout the life of the animal. The increased 5-HT innervation could then serve to maintain the handling effect. This possibility seems unlikely. The effect in cell cultures persists in the absence of 5-HT in the medium. Moreover, handling does not seem to permanently alter 5-HT innervation into the dorsal hippocampus using either electrochemical[55] or immunocytohistochemical (Desjardins and Meaney, unpublished) measures of 5-HT content.

Alternatively, handling could result in a "structural" change in the glucocorticoid receptor gene (and/or the promoter region), which sustains a difference in basal transcription rates throughout the life of the animal. There is considerable research to be done on this topic, including a verification of differences in transcription rates (which is currently in progress). However, this remains an interesting possibility and one that might explain the persistence of the handling effect, an effect that may represent a rather intriguing example of receptor imprinting occurring in response to an environmental signal.

As a matter of speculation, we offer the reader one possibility. DNA methylation is a very active process in early development that appears to be associated with the inactivation of genes, a process whereby gene expression is rendered tissue specific.[80] Thus, the early postnatal period is an active period of DNA methylation. Methylated sites are inactivated. CpG islands represent a potent target for methylation, and the glucocorticoid receptor promoter is rich in such sites. Some of these sequences may serve as binding sites for enhancers, such as the cAMP-inducible transcription factors discussed above. If, during early development, the binding of these factors is enhanced, then methylation at these sites could be attenuated by the presence of the protein-DNA binding. This would then leave these sites as unmethylated and available in later life. This would afford a greater number of potential sites in the promoter for enhancing gene expression. Clearly this is highly speculative. However, handling does increase NGFI-A expression and might also increase CREB binding (through a decrease in CREM expression). At the very least, this hypothesis allows us to imagine how such differentiation processes emerge in neuronal populations.

REFERENCES

1. ANTONI, F. A. 1986. Hypothalamic control of ACTH secretion: Advances since the discovery of 41-residue corticotropin-releasing factor. Endocr. Rev. **7:** 351–370.
2. RIVIER, C. & P. M. PLOTSKY. 1986. Mediation by corticotropin-releasing factor of adenohypophysial hormone secretion. Annu. Rev. Physiol. **48:** 475–489.
3. WHITNALL, M. H. 1993. Regulation of the hypothalamic corticotropin-releasing hormone neurosecretory system. Prog. Neurobiol. **40:** 573–629.
4. BAXTER, J. D. & J. B. TYRRELL. 1987. The adrenal cortex. *In* Endocrinology and

Metabolism. P. Felig, J. D. Baxter, A. E. Broadus & L. A. Frohman, Eds.: 385–511. McGraw-Hill. New York.

5. BRINDLEY, D. N. & Y. ROLLAND. 1989. Possible connections between stress, diabetes, obesity, hypertension and altered lipoprotein metabolism that may result in atherosclerosis. Clin. Sci. **77:** 453–461.

6. MUNCK, A., P. M. GUYRE & N. J. HOLBROOK. 1984. Physiological functions of glucocorticoids in stress and their relations to pharmacological actions. Endocr. Rev. **5:** 25–44.

7. DALLMAN, M. F., S. AKANA, C. S. CASCIO, D. N. DARLINGTON, L. JACOBSON & N. LEVIN. 1987. Regulation of ACTH secretion: Variations on a theme of B. Recent Prog. Horm. Res. **43:** 113–173.

8. DALLMAN, M. F., S. F. AKANA, K. A. SCRIBNER, M. J. BRADBURY, C. D. WALKER, A. M. STRACK & C. S. CASCIO. 1993. Stress, feedback and facilitation in the hypothalamo-pituitary-adrenal axis. J. Neuroendocrinol. **4:** 517–526.

9. DE KLOET, E. R. 1991. Brain corticosteroid receptor balance and homeostatic control. Front. Neuroendocrinol. **12:** 95–164.

10. FELDMAN, S. & N. CONFORTI. 1980. Participation of the dorsal hippocampus in the glucocorticoid negative-feedback effect on adrenocortical activity. Neuroendocrinology **30:** 52–55.

11. JACOBSON, L. & R. M. SAPOLSKY. 1991. The role of the hippocampus in feedback regulation of the hypothalamic-pituitary-adrenal axis. Endocr. Rev. **12:** 118–134.

12. KELLER-WOOD, M. & M. F. DALLMAN. 1984. Corticosteroid inhibition of ACTH secretion. Endocr. Rev. **5:** 1–24.

13. McEWEN, B. S., E. R. DE KLOET & W. H. ROSTENE. 1986. Adrenal steroid receptors and actions in the nervous system. Physiol. Rev. **66:** 1121–1150.

14. DIORIO, D., V. VIAU & M. J. MEANEY. 1993. The role of the medial prefrontal cortex (cingulate gyrus) in the regulation of hypothalamic-pituitary-adrenal responses to stress. J. Neurosci. **13:** 3839–3847.

15. BHATNAGAR, S., N. SHANKS & M. J. MEANEY. Effects of chronic stress on hypothalamic-pituitary-adrenal and immune responses to acute stress in handled and nonhandled rats. Dev. Psychobiol. In press.

16. MEANEY, M. J., D. O'DONNELL, V. VIAU, S. BHATNAGAR, A. SARRIEAU, J. W. SMYTHE, N. SHANKS & C-D. WALKER. 1994. Corticosteroid receptors in rat brain and pituitary during development and hypothalamic-pituitary-adrenal (HPA) function. *In* Receptors and the Developing Nervous System. P. McLaughlin & I. Zagon, Eds.: 163–202. Chapman and Hall. London.

17. MEANEY, M. J., D. H. AITKEN, S. BHATNAGAR, CH. VAN BERKEL & R. M. SAPOLSKY. 1988. Postnatal handling attenuates neuroendocrine, anatomical, and cognitive impairments related to the aged hippocampus. Science **238:** 766–768.

18. KERR, D. S., L. W. CAMPBELL, S.-Y. HAO & P. W. LANDFIELD. 1989. Corticosteroid modulation of hippocampal potentials: Increased effect with aging. Science **245:** 1505–1509.

19. MEANEY, M. J., D. H. AITKEN & R. M. SAPOLSKY. 1991. Environmental regulation of the adrenocortical stress response in female rats and its implications for individual differences in aging. Neurobiol. Aging **12:** 31–38.

20. ISSA, A., W. ROWE, S. GAUTHIER & M. J. MEANEY. 1990. Hypothalamic-pituitary-adrenal activity in aged cognitively impaired and cognitively unimpaired aged rats. J. Neurosci. **10:** 3247–3254.

21. SAPOLSKY, R. M. 1990. Glucocorticoids, hippocampal damage and the glutaminergic synapse. Prog. Brain Res. **86:** 13–23.

22. LEVINE, S. 1975. Psychosocial factors in growth and development. *In* Society, Stress and Disease. L. Levi, Ed.: 43–50. Oxford University Press. London.

23. LEON, M., P. G. CROSKERRY & G. K. SMITH. 1978. Thermal control of mother-infant contact in rats. Physiol. & Behav. **21:** 793–811.

24. JANS, J. Latent inhibition in nonhandled rats reared on different nest surface temperatures. Dev. Psychobiol. In press.

25. LEE, M. H. S. & D. I. WILLIAMS. 1974. Changes in licking behaviour of rat mother following handling of young. Anim. Behav. **22:** 679–681.

26. LEE, M. H. S. & D. I. WILLIAMS. 1975. Long term changes in nest condition and pup grouping following handling of rat litters. Dev. Psychobiol. **8:** 91–95.
27. BELL, R. W., W. NITSCHKE, T. H. GORRY & T. ZACHMA. 1971. Infantile stimulation and ultrasonic signaling: A possible mediator of early handing phenomena. Dev. Psychobiol. **4:** 181–191.
28. JANS, J. & B. C. WOODSIDE. 1990. Nest temperature: Effects on maternal behavior, pup development, and interactions with handling. Dev. Psychobiol. **23:** 519–534.
29. HENNESSY, M. B., J. VOGT & S. LEVINE. 1982. Strain of foster mother determines long-term effects of early handling: Evidence for maternal mediation. Physiol. Psychol. **10:** 153–157.
30. MEYERS, M. M., S. A. BRUNELL, H. N. SHAIR, J. M. SQUIRE & M. A. HOFER. 1989. Relationship between maternal behavior of SHR and WKY dams and adult blood pressures of cross-foctered F1 pups. Dev. Psychobiol. **22:** 55–67.
31. CALHOUN, J. B. 1962. The ecology and sociology of the Norway rat. H.E.W. Public Health Service. Bethesda, Maryland.
32. PLOTSKY, P. M. & M. J. MEANEY. 1993. Early, postnatal experience alters hypothalamic corticotropin-releasing factor (CRF) mRNA, median eminence CRF content and stress-induced release in adult rats. Mol. Brain Res. **18:** 195–200.
33. BLANCHARD, C., R. R. SAKAI, B. S. McEWEN, S. M. WEISS & R. J. BLANCHARD. Stress: Behavioral, brain and neuroendocrine correlates. Brain Behav. Sci. In press.
34. SAPOLSKY, R. M. 1982. The endocrine stress response and social status in the wild baboon. Horm. Behav. **16:** 279–292.
35. SAPOLSKY, R. M. 1993. The physiology of dominance in stable vs. unstable social hierarchies. *In* Primate Social Conflict. W. Mason & S. Mendoza, Eds.: 171–204. SUNY Press. New York.
36. PURVES, D. 1988. A Torphic Theory of Development. University of Chicago Press. Chicago, IL.
37. LEVINE, S. & G. W. LEWIS. 1958. The relative importance of experimenter contact in an effect produced by extrastimulation in infancy. J. Comp. Physiol. Psychol. **52:** 368–369.
38. MEANEY, M. J. & D. H. AITKEN. 1985. The effects of early postnatal handling on the development of hippocampal glucocorticoid receptors: Temporal parameters. Dev. Brain Res. **22:** 301–304.
39. MOHAMMED, A. H., B. G. HENRIKSSON, S. SODERSTROM, T. EBENDAL, T. OLSSON & J. R. SECKL. 1993. Environmental influences on the central nervous system and their influences for the aging rat. Behav. Brain Res. **57:** 183–191.
40. ADER, R. & L. J. GROTA. 1969. Effects of early experience on adrenocortical reactivity. Physiol. & Behav. **4:** 303–305.
41. BOHN, M. C., D. DEAN, S. HUSSAIN & R. GIULIANO. 1994. Development of mRNAs for glucocorticoid and mineralocorticoid receptors in rat hippocampus. Dev. Brain Res. **77:** 157–162.
42. VAN EEKELEN, J. A. M., W. JIANG, E. R. DE KLOET & M. C. BOHN. 1988. Distribution of the mineralocorticoid and glucocorticoid receptor mRNAs in the rat hippocampus. J. Neurosci. Res. **21:** 88–94.
43. O'DONNELL, D., S. LAROCQUE, J. R. SECKL & M. J. MEANEY. Developmental changes in hippocampal glucocorticoid and mineralocorticoid receptor messenger RNA expression in relation to morphological changes in cell size. Submitted.
44. ROSENFELD, P., W. SUTANTO, S. LEVINE & E. R. DE KLOET. 1988. Ontogeny of type I and type II corticosteroid receptors in the rat hippocampus. Dev. Brain Res. **42:** 113–118.
45. SARRIEAU, A., S. SHARMA & M. J. MEANEY. 1988. Postnatal development and environmental regulation of hippocampal glucocorticoid and mineralocorticoid receptors in the rat. Dev. Brain Res. **43:** 158–162.
46. MEANEY, M. J., D. H. AITKEN, S. SHARMA, V. VIAU & A. SARRIEAU. 1989. Postnatal handling increases hippocampal type II, glucocorticoid receptors and enhances adrenocortical negative-feedback efficacy in the rat. Neuroendocrinology **51:** 597–604.
47. MEANEY, M. J., R. M. SAPOLSKY & B. S. McEWEN. 1985. The development of the

glucocorticoid receptor system in the rat limbic brain: I. Ontogeny and autoregulation. Dev. Brain Res. **18:** 159–164.

48. MEANEY, M. J. & D. H. AITKEN. 1985. [³H]Dexamethasone binding in rat frontal cortex. Brain Res. **328:** 176–180.

49. SHARMA, S., J. B. MITCHELL & M. J. MEANEY. Interaction between thyroid hormones and central serotonin in the development of glucocorticoid receptor systems in the rat. Submitted.

50. MEANEY, M. J., D. H. AITKEN & R. M. SAPOLSKY. 1987. Thyroid hormones influence the development of hippocampal glucocorticoid receptors in the rat: A mechanism for the effects of postnatal handling on the development of the adrenocortical stress response. Neuroendocrinology **45:** 278–283.

51. BANKER, G. A. & M. W. COWAN. 1977. Rat hippocampal neurons in dispersed cell culture. Brain Res. **126:** 397–425.

52. MITCHELL, J. B., W. ROWE, P. BOKSA & M. J. MEANEY. 1990. Serotonin regulates type II, corticosteroid receptor binding in cultured hippocampal cells. J. Neurosci. **10:** 1745–1752.

53. SAVARD, P., Y. MERAND, T. DI PAOLO & A. DUPONT. 1984. Thyroid hormone regulation of serotonin metabolism in developing rat brain. Brain Res. **292:** 99–108.

54. MITCHELL, J. B., L. J. INY & M. J. MEANEY. 1990. The role of serotonin in the development and environmental regulation of hippocampal type II corticosteroid receptors. Dev. Brain Res. **55:** 231–235.

55. SMYTHE, J. W., W. ROWE & M. J. MEANEY. 1994. Neonatal handling alters serotonin turnover and serotonin type 2 receptor density in selected brain regions. Dev. Brain Res. **80:** 183–189.

56. MITCHELL, J. B., K. BETITO, W. ROWE, P. BOKSA & M. J. MEANEY. 1992. Serotonergic regulation of type II corticosteroid receptor binding in cultured hippocampal cells: The role of serotonin-induced increases in cAMP levels. Neuroscience **48:** 631–639.

57. TEITLER, M., R. A. LYON, K. H. DAVIS & K. H. GLENNON. 1987. Selectivity of serotoninergic drugs for multiple brain serotonin receptors. Biochem. Pharmacol. **36:** 3265–3271.

58. TEITLER, M., S. LEONHARDT, E. L. WEISBERG & B. J. HOFFMAN. 1992. 4-[¹²⁵I]Iodo-(2,5-dimethoxy)phenylisopropylamine and [³H]-ketanserin labelling of 5-hydroxytryptamine2 (5-HT2) receptors in mammalian cells transfected with rat 5-HT2 cDNA: Evidence for multiple states and multiple 5-HT2 receptors. Mol. Pharmacol. **42:** 328–335.

59. HOLMES, M., S. LAROCQUE, J. R. SECKL & M. J. MEANEY. Developmental changes in 5-HT2A receptor binding and receptor mRNA expression in the rat forebrain. Mol. Brain Res. Submitted.

60. SANDERS-BUSH, E., M. TSUTSUMI & K. D. BURRIS. 1990. Serotonin receptors and phosphatidylinositol turnover. Ann. N.Y. Acad. Sci. **600:** 224–236.

61. YOSHIMASA, T., D. R. SIBLEY, M. BOUVIER, R. J. LEFKOWITZ & M. G. CARON. 1987. Cross-talk between cellular signalling pathways suggested by phorbol-ester-induced adenylate cyclase phosphorylation. Nature **327:** 67–70.

62. PARENT, A. R., S. SHARMA, R. QUIRION & M. J. MEANEY. Developmental profile of diacylglycerol and inositol phosphate production induced by the stimulation of muscarinic, glutamate, metabotropic, serotonin and endothelin receptors in the hippocampus of neonatally handled rats. J. Pharmacol. Exp. Ther. Submitted.

63. IKE, J., H. CANTON & E. SANDERS-BUSH. 1995. Developmental switch in the hippocampal serotonin receptor linked to phosphoinositide hydrolysis. Brain Res. **678:** 49–54.

64. LUCAS, J. J. & R. HEN. 1995. New players in the 5-HT receptor field: Genes and knockouts. Trends Pharmacol. Sci. **16:** 246–262.78.

65. PEPIN, M. C., S. BEAULIEU & N. BARDEN. 1989. Antidepressants regulate glucocorticoid receptor messenger RNA concentrations in primary neuronal cultures. Mol. Brain Res. **6:** 77–83.

66. PEPIN, M. C., M. V. GOVIDAN & N. BARDEN. 1992. Increased glucocorticoid receptor gene promoter activity after antidepressant treatment. J. Pharmacol. Exp. Ther. **41:** 1016–1024.

67. TÖRK, I. 1990. Anatomy of serotonergic systems. Ann. N.Y. Acad. Sci. **600:** 9–35.
68. DE GROOT, R. P. & P. SASSONE-CORSI. 1993. Hormonal control of gene expression: Multiplicity and versatility of cyclic adenosine 3′,5′-monophosphate-responsive nuclear regulators. Mol. Endocrinol. **5:** 145–153.
69. HABENER, J. 1990. Cyclic AMP response element binding proteins: A cornucopia of transcription factors. Mol. Endocrinol. **4:** 1087–1094.
70. IMAGAWA, M., R. CHIU & M. KARIN. 1987. Transcription factor AP-2 mediates induction by two different signal-transduction pathways: Protein kinase C and cAMP. Cell **51:** 251–260.
71. MONTMINY, M. R., G. A. GONZALEZ & K. K. YAMAMOTO. 1990. Regulation of cAMP-inducible genes by CREB. Trends Neurosci. **12:** 184–188.
72. SHENG, M. & M. E. GREENBERG. 1990. The regulation and function of c-*fos* and other early immediate genes in the nervous system. Neuron **4:** 477–485.
73. VALLEJO, M. 1994. Transcriptional control of gene expression by cAMP-response element binding proteins J. Neuroendocrinol. **6:** 587–596.
74. WALTON, K. M. & R. P. REHFUSS. 1992. Molecular mechanisms of cAMP-regulated gene expression. Mol. Neurobiol. **4:** 197–201.
75. YAMAMOTO, K. K., G. A. GONZALES, W. H. BRIGGS III & M. R. MONTIMY. 1988. Phosphorylation-induced binding and transcriptional efficiency of nuclear factor CREB. Nature **334:** 494–498.
76. LECLERC, S., B. XIE, R. ROY & M. V. GOVINDAN. 1991. Purification of a human glucocorticoid receptor gene promoter-binding protein. J. Biol. Chem. **266:** 8711–8719.
77. STRAHLE, U., A. SCHMIDT, G. KELSEY, A. F. STEWART, T. J. COLE, W. SCHMID & G. SCHUTZ. 1992. At least three promoters direct expression of the mouse glucocorticoid receptor gene. Proc. Natl. Acad. Sci. **89:** 6731–6735.
78. MEANEY, M. J., J. DIORIO, J. YAU, L. DONALDSON & J. R SECKL. Neonatal handling stimulates cAMP formation and altered expression of transcription factors involved in cAMP-regulated gene expression: The role of serotonin. Submitted.
79. DELMAS, V., F. VAN DER HOORN, B. MELLSTROM, B. JEGOU & P. SASSONE-CORSI. 1993. Induction of CREM activator proteins in spermatids: Down-stream targets and implications for haploid germ cell differentiation. Mol. Endocrinol. **7:** 1502–1514.
80. STROBL, J. S. 1990. A role for DNA methylation in vertebrate gene expression. Mol. Endocrinol. **4:** 181–183.
81. VACCARINO, F. M., M. D. HAYWARD, H. N. LE, D. J. HARTIGAN, R. S. DUMAN & E. J. NESTLER. 1993. Induction of immediate early genes by cyclic AMP in primary cultures of neurons from rat cerebral cortex. Mol. Brain Res. **19:** 76–82.

Chaos and Order in the Parenting of Aggressive Children

Personal Narratives as Guidelines

ROBERT G. WAHLER[a]

Clinical Psychology Program
College of Arts and Sciences
The University of Tennessee
307 Austin Peay Building
Knoxville, Tennessee 37996-0900

The parent-child relationship is a social foundation for the child's emerging disposition and ecosystem coping skills. Out of genetically determined capacities, the infant's personal style and specific ways of responding to others is shaped and organized through a multitude of interactions with these caregiving adults. Depending on the genetic base and the quality of the interactions, children find their place in reference to other adults and peers with varying degrees of satisfaction. Some children are reasonably content and generate the same emotions in others, and some children find themselves unhappy and/or they spread distress among family members, teachers, and peers.

These conclusions about the importance of parent-child interactions are commonplace and easily documented.[1–3] What is not so clear, however, is the nature of this process by which child and parent engage one another in ways that either promote or detract from the child's future interpersonal adjustment.[4] Most would agree that the process is transactional, in the sense that both members of this dyad exercise control,[5,8] and most would agree that each member's behavior is influenced by heritability factors unique to each one's biological makeup.[9–11] However, when we turn to the specific ways in which these people influence one another, the complexities are daunting (*e.g.*, refs. 4 and 12). At first, when the child is quite young, the transactional process is fairly straightforward and based on the infant's ability to detect conditional probabilities between its behavior and the behavior of a parent.[13,14] In turn, the parent who is usually geared to any social overture by the baby will be quick to respond in a positive manner to most of these events, particularly if they were elicited by the parent (*e.g.*, parent touches baby's face; baby smiles; parent smiles and laughs). When this turn-taking process begins, it is usually one sided because the infant has yet to learn to sustain the cooperative process. Parents act as if their baby is tracking the sequence of conditional probabilities and, thus, they are sure that their baby appreciates the overall turn-taking enterprise.[15,16] Eventually, as long as the parents continue to orchestrate the turn taking, they will be rewarded by the baby's true participation in these social transactions.[17] By the time most infants are 4 or 5 months old, the turn taking will become specific to family participants (*e.g.*, parents) as long as these people continue to offer consistent and appropriate contingencies.[18,19]

[a] Tel: (423) 974-2531; fax: (423) 974-3330.

Although it is clear that social contingencies constitute the foundation of cooperative transactions between child and parent, the contingencies per se do not describe this foundation. Rather, it is more accurate to view these turn-taking contingencies as parts of a social context generated over time through joint efforts of the dyad.[20,21] In effect, the quality of this holistic contingency pattern is recognized by the child, and this recognition seems to determine the power of any particular contingency within that contextual pattern. Depending on context quality, a stimulus, such as mothers' smile, could function on various occasions as either positive or negative reinforcer, or as an insignificant event, meaning that the child judges each stimulus within its historical context. The terms *reciprocity*,[22] *synchrony*,[23] *momentum*,[24] *coordination*,[25] and *predictability*[26] have been used to describe this critical nature of social context. All five terms depict parent and child who are sensitive to one another and who then respond in timely and appropriate ways to words and actions as these events occur. Because of this orchestration, the participants create a continuity in which their mutual contributions to the contingency patterns generate an unbroken stream of activity.

In all of the studies cited above, a child's disposition to comply with maternal instructions was a function of the historical context generated by dyadic contingencies. Thus, in the studies by Isabella *et al.*,[23] Parpal and Maccoby,[22] and Westerman,[25] mothers who were appropriately responsive to their children's ongoing activities obtained higher probabilities of child compliance than dyads in which this continuity was not established. In a similar vein, Ducharme and Worling,[24] and Wahler and Dumas[26] showed that mothers who were selective in their instructions or who were consistent in matching their children's affect also obtained high probabilities of compliance after establishing these particular dyadic histories.

As the above studies suggest, transactions between parent and child are figural events set within a context describing the historical orchestration of these transactions. If that orchestration is synchronous, the immediate transactions will function as positive reinforcers promoting cooperative exchanges. On the other hand, a context summarizing asynchronous or disjointed interactions will lend negative or, at best, neutral valence to the particular things said and done by members of the dyad.

In the creation of synchronous or asynchronous social context, children and their parents can be realistically portrayed as coarchitects. Some children, by virtue of their behavioral dispositions early in life, can pull or elicit negative responses from their parents—and from other adults as well.[27–29] These "difficult" infants and preschoolers clearly have the power to disrupt the turn-taking strategies of many parents and, thus, create the social chaos in which aggression can thrive. By contrast, a child's early disposition to be responsive or "easy" elicits positive parental reactions along with the cooperative turn taking that comprises a synchronous relationship. Of course, not all parents are negatively swayed by a child's difficult temperament, and not all parents step into a cooperative dance with their responsive children. Just as children contribute to or detract from the turn-taking continuity, some adults are better prepared to be parents than are others.[30–32]

Regardless of who disrupts the interaction synchrony, it is up to a parent to repair discontinuity in the dyadic relationship. Based on that adult's greater knowledge and responsibility, the parent must rise to this occasion and generate the necessary discipline and affection required to induce that turn-taking dance promoting child compliance. If the parent fails to do so, and the child's temperament is difficult, these two people are apt to engage one another in disputes that become "coercion traps" (after ref. 33). Coercion traps are persistently recurring exchanges of irritating verbal behaviors, such as complaints, demands, threats, and whining, usually following instructions from a parent that specify an expected change in the child's behavior (*e.g.*, "It's time to eat;" "Stop that!"). In the course of such aversive exchanges, the already difficult child gains learning experiences promoting an escalating sequence of aggression ranging from whining and arguing to yelling and hitting.[34–36]

Coercion traps can be avoided or terminated when the parent addresses the more fundamental problem caused by relationship asynchrony. Through the adult's focus on why he or she cannot seem to make the right response at the right time, new developments in parental responsiveness are likely to emerge.[4] Sometimes the synchrony problem is a direct function of the child's difficult nature and is thus correctable by teaching the parent to be responsive through timely use of discipline, listening, and social approval. In other words, the parent's lack of responsiveness was due to his or her failure to monitor the contingency patterns comprising the child-care context. In other cases that are marked by a multiplicity of parent problems, teaching responsive child care is not sufficient. Parents who have marital problems, who are in conflict with friends and relatives, and who are socioeconomically disadvantaged represent these more chronically troubled individuals. These parents' monitoring failures and the ensuing asynchrony with their children can be influenced by the just described problems, many of which occur outside the child-care domain.[6,35,37]

It would appear that parents' success in generating synchrony with their children depends on parental perception of the proximal child-care context as well as the distal context surrounding the child-care domain. Clearly, distal events, such as marital dysfunction, can blend into the parent-child relationship, even though the two are not directly connected. One would think that an objective parent could keep these domains separate and therefore contain turmoil within its relevant domain—a logical and effective problem-solving strategy. As we know, however, human performance is not always rational, and parents may perceive child behavior within its distal context from time to time. For example, a mother who would normally judge her child's smile in a context of her youngster's just-noted discovery of a squirrel on the windowsill does not appreciate this context because she and her husband have had another in a series of quarrels. Instead, mother perceives the smile in this distal context and she responds accordingly: "What's so funny? Would you quit being so silly!?" Of course, some parents keep the two contexts separate, even when disorder reigns in one of them, and the question of how they do so is just as important as our wonder about parents who perceive an overlap. It is as if some parents carry a guideline allowing them to perceive order across their ecosystems, whereas others do not possess such a guideline.

THE FRAMING OF PROXIMAL AND DISTAL CONTEXT THROUGH PERSONAL NARRATIVES BY PARENTS

There is growing evidence that a parent's autobiographical narrative serves as a guidance function in the narrator's personal relationships, including those with children. These "life stories"[38] are particularly relevant to one's ability to integrate the proximal and distal contexts, in such a way that the two are perceived as interrelated but not confounded. Apparently this guidance function has less to do with the factual basis of story content and more to do with the coherence of what is told.[39,40] In other words, the stories are like folktales amounting to theories about the narrators' behavioral development that could be taken as models describing traits or dispositions. Thus, if the theory is coherent, it offers a prototype for future behavior—a guideline allowing the theorist to systematically explore the fit between his or her traits and the ecosystem context in which these traits will be expressed. If the quality of fit is known, the explorer has a distinct advantage in future negotiations that will establish relationships with spouse, children, and friends.

Research based on the adult attachment interview[39] supports the coherence quality of personal narratives as bases for predicting the adult storyteller's parenting strategy. Through prompting by an interviewer's questions about family of origin and other historical experiences, the adult provides reliable narrative episodes that are then used to classify the adult's frame of reference about his or her earlier relationship experiences. As expected, the adult parent uses this frame as a guide within the child-care arena. For example, adults who provide clear and nonblame-oriented stories of their own early relationships with parents are classified as "autonomous," and they tend to enjoy synchronous interactions with their infants.[41–43] By contrast, adults who provide sketchy stories in which the themes depict avoidance, anger, and ambivalence are classified as 'dismissing" or "preoccupied," and their social exchanges with their children tend to be asynchronous.

In a meta-analysis of studies focused on the adult attachment interview and parental responsivity, several further conclusions are warranted with regard to the correlational findings just presented.[44] First, because some of the coherence measures of personal narratives by parents were taken before these people became parents, it appears reasonable to infer that the personal narratives indeed functioned as guidelines influencing the parents' style of responding to their infants. Second, cognitive abilities of the parents, such as general intelligence and long-term memory, were not related to the coherence of their personal narratives. Thus, it appears that differences in story coherence have less to do with intellect/memory, and more to do with the specific process of constructing one's autobiography. Logically, one would think that experiences in the narrator's family of origin would be instrumental facets of this process.[45] Although this is an intriguing hypothesis, we have yet to see a consistent body of supporting evidence.[46]

Adaptive and maladaptive parenting appear to be complex functions of a parent's knowledge about children along with the ability and willingness to study and use context when generating contingencies during child-care interactions. Certainly it is true that one's knowledge base can lead a parent to an appreciation and use of proximal context in a creation of synchrony and useful teaching experiences for the child. Inasmuch as distal context will often overlap with the proximal in varying degrees across parents, however, its influence in contingency arrangements must also be considered. The parent's knowledge base is again critical, but the component information here is much more extensive than that used in understanding proximal context. because distal context comprises a broad array of events, many of which seem irrelevant to the child-care domain, the parent needs an idiosyncratic coding system to identify the keystone pattern. That system is "carried" by the parent in the form of his or her autobiographical narrative, a coding template used to guide to misguide the parent's response to context.

If the above summary is valid, it would follow that a technology for promoting adaptive parenting might be developed. Part of that technology is already available in the form of well-established "parent training" programs developed through the seminal work of Patterson and colleagues (e.g., ref. 47), Forehand and colleagues (e.g., ref. 48), and Webster-Stratton and colleagues (e.g., ref. 49). Of course, parent training is largely devoted to helping parents to observe and understand the proximal context so relevant to child-care activities. Given this prerequisite understanding, it has proven possible to help parents alter their tactics of discussion, praise, listening, and discipline in ways that promote adaptive child care. Unfortunately, parent training is not apt to promote parental awareness of distal context and its impact on parenting. Possibly because of this omission, treatment outcomes have not been favorable for parents whose ecosystems are marked by socioeconomic disadvantage, marital distress, social isolation, and coercive extrafamily relationships.[50-53]

We turn now to speculations on ways to enhance parental awareness of distal context, including a means of helping parents with the difficult task of integrating this sphere of context with the proximal sphere that is more directly relevant to child care. As one might guess, parents' personal narratives become the vehicle through which awareness and integration are promoted.

PERSONAL NARRATIVES AS GUIDELINES IN SYSTEMIC INTERVENTIONS

Parents, like other adults, develop personal narratives to convey knowledge about themselves, about their impressions of others, and about their understanding of social rules.[54,55] The narratives are in story format comprised of protagonist and other characters whose actions are woven into a plot with a beginning, middle, and end. If a guidance function for the narrator is contained within these stories, a listener ought to be able to discern a pattern or script based on the narrator's conveyed knowledge about story characters and the rules behind their social exchanges (see ref. 56). Over a sample of stories by one narrator, the listener should derive a picture of the narrator's role; the roles assigned to child, spouse, and other people in the narrator's ecosystem; and the narrator's conception of rules governing relationships among the various characters. Based on this picture, the listener is now in a position to assist the narrator in much the same way that an editor assists a writer. Depending on how the listener responds, the narrative could remain as it stands or its structure and content could undergo revision.

It is interesting to note that "good" listening runs in the same professional psychotherapy circles as it does in family domains. Thus, a therapist's listening skills are demonstrated through this propensity to pick out subtle changes in the client's verbal content, how things are said, and a host of nonverbal cues (*e.g.*, ref. 57). Of course, one's ability to identify another person's intentions is not worth much in itself, because it is the listener's response that really matters. A sensitive listener will have impact on a narrative if he or she also knows what to do upon hearing a story, whether that "doing" be a reflection, a correction, or nothing at all. Sensitive therapists are good therapists because of their responsiveness, as seen in the timing and nature of their interpretations, reflections, and limit setting.[58]

A speaker may consider a listener to be responsive simply because the latter correctly identifies and acknowledges the speaker's intentions.[59] However, although such listener strategies make for a positive relationship between speaker and listener, the speaker's personal narrative is left untouched and even stabilized. Certainly this outcome would be desirable when the narrative serves the speaker well in terms of its guidance properties. If this is not the case, however, and the listener decides to question the narrative structure and/or content, the relationship quality in this dyad is put at risk. People do not like to be corrected or to have their conclusions doubted, and the listener who does so may be viewed by the speaker as hostile instead of helpful. Of course, the developmental and clinical concept responsiveness is far more than a picture of parents, friends, and clinicians simply engaging in these intrusive tactics. A responsive listener is also a listener whose sense of timing is a paramount feature of what this person says and does. Although such a listener may certainly challenge a speaker's personal narrative, this is only a small part of the more crucial synchrony generated between the two. The responsive listener's intrusive comments and questions are perceived as helpful because of a context comprised of the full range of supportive, confirmatory, and neutral reactions, most of which are delivered at the appropriate time (see ref. 60).

When a responsive listener wonders about what is said, the questions usually have to do with issues of clarity of the narrative and the affective content of human experiences described therein. Thus, the responsive listener will ask for clarity primarily when the narrative content centers on the speaker's personal views, interpersonal exchanges, and psychological adjustment. In the process of such listener-speaker exchanges, the speaker will modify his or her personal narrative accordingly. As clarity is enhanced, however, story coherence will be affected if the new information is not consistent with the existing plot and cast of characters. Under these conditions, listener and speaker are apt to engage in a synthesis of the story content so that plot and characters are changed to enhance the story coherence. We think that this synthesis process is the keystone of change in one's personal narrative, and its product is similar to the insight phenomena generated in successful psychodynamic and behavioral systems treatment strategies (refs. 61–63).

Through synthesis, narrator and listener are able to achieve important story modifications in which coherence is improved and relationships are described as balanced and diverse in affect. Because a single coherent theme is still present, the relationship quality depicted is indeed more complex, and the combination of coherence and complexity suggests a harmony not present in the early story. When characters are portrayed as in harmony, their social exchanges are motivated by reciprocal influences that range from bidirectional to systemic, all woven together into a single coherent theme. Because the narrator has expanded the relationship determinants, no single affect predominates, and, instead, the characters are motivated by a range of emotions more true to real life than the narrow picture presented earlier. As a result, the narrator presumably carries a more useful set of guidelines for social exchanges with others.

COHERENCE OF A PARENT'S PERSONAL NARRATIVE AND SYNCHRONY IN PARENT-CHILD INTERACTION: A CASE ILLUSTRATION

Degree of synchrony in a parent-child relationship can be measured through molecular analyses of matches and mismatches between a child's various responses and the parent's reactions. In this operation, matches have to do with affect valences of response and reaction in which positives should be aligned with positives and negatives with negatives. A mismatch occurs when a negative parent reaction follows a positive child response and vice versa. As shown in research with parents and their normal or conduct-problem children, the proportion of mismatches (asynchrony) is significantly higher in parent-conduct problem-child dyads than in normal dyads,[64,65] and the mismatch index correlates with the rate of child-aversive behavior.[26,66]

Mismatches in a parent's reaction to child responses often seem to occur because of parental perseveration of one particular reaction. This process can be viewed by examining conditional probabilities of a parent's positive and negative reactions in various time windows following the child's positive and negative responses. Thus, a perseverative reaction would be seen through its repetition despite changes in the child's responding. Sensitive/responsive parents are likely to react appropriately to a child response, look for new responses by the child, and then offer new and appropriate reactions. If the parent routinely repeats a reaction, however, the more likely it is that its appropriate nature will be lost because of changes in the child's responding.

The perseveration index, although it has not been systematically used in parent-child interaction research, has heuristic value in understanding insensitive/unresponsive parenting: if it is indeed true that these parents are confounded by the chaotic nature of context, this confounding ought to be reflected in the perseveration of their reactions. As we see it, perseveration describes a sequential process in which a parent (1) has no plan of action in how to react to child's negative and positive responses, (2) finds a reaction that "works" in the sense that it affects the child, and (3) depends on that reaction as a guide regardless of what the child says and does. Thus, perhaps parents become asynchronous with their children because of this perseverative style rather than insensitivity per se. In other words, parental insensitivity might be a summary label for a process in which the parent is periodically aimless, led by the child and prone to depend on habit, repeatedly using a sometimes appropriate reaction. An earlier example of the mother who reacted inappropriately to her child's positive comment about a squirrel on the windowsill could have been due to a perseveration of an earlier reaction to some negative response from the child.

We suspect that perseveration of a parent's reaction is most apt to be prompted by the child's negative responses. Because negative social events are usually more salient than positive stimuli,[67] the parent's in kind or matching negative reactions could be keystone experiences when that parent is confounded by context. Thus, a parent who "holds a grudge" or is in a "bad mood" may be preoccupied with an earlier negative matchup with the child. Keeping in mind that perseveration might be a function of contextual confounding, the parent's "replaying" of this negative matchup could be due to some unrelated but also negative matchup between the parent and another adult. The "grudge" held against an offending child by this parent is in actuality a more generally construed grudge in which the child might be a minor player. Of course, this grudge scenario should be mediated by the parent's personal narrative and, more specifically, by its poor coherence. Were this parent to sort out the story characters and themes through the feedback of a helpful listener, the real life players and their thematic rules in the parent's story might become more coherent, helping this parent to integrate the proximal and distal context of his or her personal ecosystem. This done, the parent's tendency to perseverate should lessen and synchronous interactions between child and parent ought to increase. The following case study provides and illustration of one parent's perseverative reactions to her conduct-problem child, her personal narratives about life with this child, and covariations between the coherence of her narratives and her perseverative reactions.

Rudy (age 8) and his single mother were referred to our clinic because of her concern about his "violent nature." According to the mother, he was stubborn,

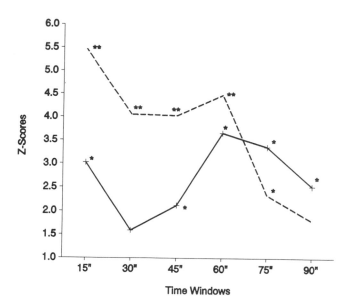

FIGURE 1. Z-scores of conditional probabilities in six time-windows for mother reactions to child behavior. Computations were based on five hours of home observations during baseline. __, Mother negative reactions to child negative responses. _ _, Mother positive reactions to child positive responses. ** = p < 0.01; * = p < 0.05.

argumentative, and prone to extreme temper outbursts in which he would destroy property and sometimes hit her. She outlined her concerns by pointing out her despair at Rudy's growing tendency to be equally defiant and aggressive at school and in other community settings. When she was asked about her role in the boy's conduct problem, mother simply noted, "He just sweeps me along; I can't do nothing with him." When Rudy was asked about his conflict with his mother he was largely unresponsive but did voice his belief that she did not like him.

The clinical treatment protocol offered to the mother and Rudy was described to them as comprising five phases: (1) clinic discussion and home observations—essentially a baseline phase to sample the mother's personal narratives and the mother-child home interactions; (2) parent training, in which the mother would learn the use of time-out, praise, and reflective listening; (3) a follow-up phase identical to phase 1; (4) synthesis teaching, in which discussions between the mother and the clinician were geared to promoting greater coherence in her personal narratives; and (5) a follow-up phase, identical to phase 1.

Baseline Levels of the Mother's Perseveration and Coherence

FIGURE 1 depicts conditional probabilities (as Z-scores) of the mother's positive and negative reactions following Rudy's positive and negative social approaches to her in their home. Selection of these 90-second episodes was based on sequences in which Rudy's initial positive or negative response was not repeated during the episode. In other words, all of Rudy's responses after the 15-second interval were neutral in affect. These coded records were based on direct observations using the standardized observation codes (see ref. 68). The 15-second time-window shows the likelihood of the mother's matching Rudy's positive and negative responses. Notice that her conditional probabilities of both matches were statistically above base rate, and her matching of his positive responses was more likely than her matching of negatives. Although not depicted in FIGURE 1, it is important to remember that Rudy's social approaches to the mother in the following time-windows were neutral. Thus, the mother's continued offering of positive and negative reactions to Rudy followed his neutral responses in windows 30 through 90 seconds. Although her perseveration in positive reaction could be considered appropriate (*i.e.*, Rudy's neutral approach followed by the mother's positive reaction), her continued propensity to react negatively when Rudy behaved in neutral ways was clearly inappropriate.

The mother's personal narratives about life with Rudy were transcribed and coded for coherence through a coding procedure described in Wahler, Armstrong, and Meginnis.[69] According to the scoring format, the coherence dimension was anchored at the high end by a rating of 5 and at the low end by 0. Most of the mother's narratives were focused on Rudy, but themes about her ex-husband (Rudy's father), her mother, and her friends also appeared from time to time. Across the five discussion sessions, the mother's average coherence score was 2.2, reflecting the ambiguity of her stories.

Parent Training Levels of the Mother's Perseveration and Coherence (FIGURE 2)

During the parent training course, the mother's negative reactions to Rudy's negative behavior dropped to her base rate, while her positive matches in these 15-second windows remained well above her base rate. Thus, the mother proved to be an adept learner (by using the time-out for Rudy's negative responses and affirming his positive responses with praise). Notice also that her positive reactions were not as persistent over the time-windows and reached her base rate during the 75-second window. By contrast, a clear increase in the mother's conditional probabilities of offering inappropriate negative reactions began in the 60-second window and continued through the 90-second window. Of course, because Rudy was not behaving negatively during any of these later windows, the mother's high probability run of negative reactions was clearly inappropriate. Inasmuch as parent training was limited in time (5 weeks), no further sessions were devoted to teaching parenting skills.

The mother's personal narratives during the clinic discussion sessions within the parent training phase, although more optimistic in tone, continued to be tangential, blame oriented, and in other respects low in coherence (average 2.5 on the 0 to 5 scale). She was pleased with the changes in Rudy: home observations not depicted in the FIGURES showed a downward trend in his negative behavior and progressively higher probabilities of his compliance. Despite these obvious improvements, the mother tended to downplay her role in the changes; she also tended to point to signs of negativism in Rudy's overall attitude.

Postparent Training Levels of the Mother's Perseveration and Coherence (FIGURE 3)

In a 5-week return to baseline between the conclusion of parent training and the forthcoming synthesis teaching, the mother's perseverative reactions to Rudy's

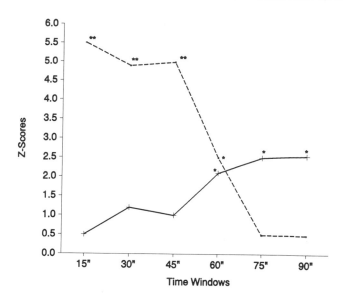

FIGURE 2. Z-scores of conditional probabilities in six time-windows for mother reactions to child behavior. Computations were based on five hours of home observations during parent training. __, Mother negative reactions to child negative responses. ___, Mother positive reactions to child positive responses. ** = p < 0.01; * = p < 0.05.

negative and positive behavior were much the same as in her previous baseline pattern. Once again she was well above her base rate in positive and negative matches in the 15-second time-window just following Rudy's positive and negative responses. Although she had ceased to do so during the parent training phase, the mother promptly matched Rudy's negative responses and persisted in reacting this way over all subsequent time-windows, despite Rudy's cessation of negative responding during these 90-second episodes. To her credit, the mother continued to affirm Rudy's positive responses with her own positive attention, and she gradually reduced her positive perseveration over the time-windows. As one might expect from the mother's increased probability of negative reactions, Rudy's overall rate of negative behavior now resembled his earlier baseline rate.

This disappointing picture of the mother's parent training benefits makes sense, in view of the continued low coherence of her personal narratives. A summary of the mother's story communications over the five discussion sessions in our clinic yielded an average coherence score of 1.9. Most noteworthy in the content of these ambiguous narratives was the mother's dysphoric view of Rudy and her life in general.

Synthesis Teaching Levels of the Mother's Perseveration and Coherence

Over a five-week period in which the clinician prompted the mother's consideration of new perspectives in her story themes, changes occurred in the mother's home interactions with Rudy, as well as in the coherence levels of her stories.

Notice in FIGURE 4 the complete absence of the mother's negative reactions to Rudy's negative behavior during any of the time-windows following the boy's efforts to provoke her. In addition, she remained likely to react positively to his positive overtures, with declining perseveration over the longer time-windows. Equally impressive were the mother's enhanced coherence scores in her coconstructed personal narratives (4.6 average over five sessions).

Follow-up Levels of the Mother's Perseveration and Coherence

In the five-week follow-up phase, the mother continued to meet in weekly clinic sessions with her therapist who simply listened to and acknowledged her weekly stories (in accordance with the previous baseline protocols). Although the coherence level declined during this phase (3.9 average over five sessions), the mother continued to present her narratives with a coherence quality above that of all phases prior to synthesis teaching. Finally, notice in FIGURE 5 that the mother's negative reactions to Rudy remained at her base rate, while she continued to be above her base rate in positive reaction—with even less perseveration.

This case illustration, although not meeting all standards of scientific proof, lends promise to the hypothesis about guidance functions of personal narratives. These stories do seem to serve as coding templates for parents who wrestle with the demands of child care within ecosystems fraught with other demands that sometimes blend into the child care domain. Certainly parent training in child care has its place as a crucial educational tool promoting quality home relationships. It

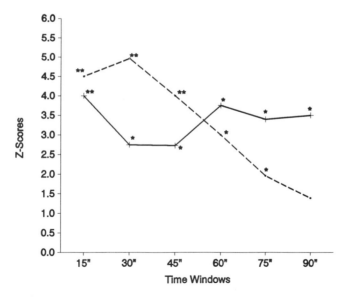

FIGURE 3. Z-scores of conditional probabilities in six time-windows for mother reactions to child behavior. Computations were based on five hours of home observations during postparent training. __, Mother negative reactions to child negative responses. _ _, Mother positive reactions to child positive responses. ** = $p < 0.01$; * = $p < 0.05$.

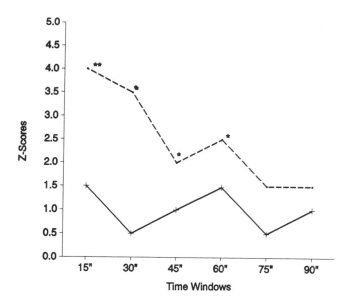

FIGURE 4. Z-scores of conditional probabilities in six time-windows for mother reactions to child behavior. Computations were based on five hours of home observations during synthesis teaching. __, Mother negative reactions to child negative responses. _ _, Mother positive reactions to child positive responses. ** = $p < 0.01$; * = $p < 0.05$.

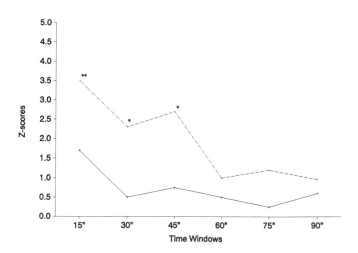

FIGURE 5. Z-scores of conditional probabilities in six time-windows for mother reactions to child behavior. Computations were based on five hours of home observations during follow-up. __, Mother negative reactions to child negative responses. _ _, Mother positive reactions to child positive responses. ** = $p < 0.01$; * = $p < 0.05$.

is also obvious that this focused training may not always be a sufficient means of promoting the parent's sense of order in a chaotic ecosystem. The study of parent personal narratives, along with ways to help parents to synthesize their story themes, holds promise in this respect.

SUMMARY

Parenting is viewed as a difficult task comprised of judgments about what to do and when to do it. Because these judgments must be rendered in an ever-changing stream of social activity, it is difficult for any parent to maintain adequate performance, particularly when the changes are stressful. In the midst of such chaos, parents can maintain good judgment as long as they are able to monitor their children from a big picture perspective in which specific child behaviors are viewed as figural stimuli set within a relevant context. This perspective is attained through the parent's use of personal narrative about life within and outside the child-care domain. Difficult children and other ecosystem stressors challenge this perspective by biasing a parent's perceptual context, making it difficult for the parent to render objective judgments about child behavior. This paper has reviewed evidence for the personal narrative model of parent monitoring, evidence for adaptive and maladaptive parent-monitoring guidelines, and speculations on a clinical strategy geared to developing new guidelines through changes in the parent's personal narrative.

REFERENCES

1. AREND, R., F. GOVE & L. A. SROUFE. 1979. Continuity of individual adaption from infancy to kindergarten: A predictive study of ego-resiliency and curiosity in pre-schoolers. Child Dev. 50: 950–959.
2. BAUMRIND, D. 1989. Rearing competent children. In Child development today and tomorrow. W. Damon, Ed. Josey-Bass. San Francisco.
3. ERICKSON, M., B. EGELAND & L. A. SROUFE. 1985. The relationship between quality of attachment and behavior problems in preschool in a high-risk sample. In Growing Points in Attachment Theory and Research. I. Bretherton & E. Waters, Eds.: 147–186. Monographs of the Society for Research in Child Development, 50(1–2), Serial No. 209. University of Chicago Press. Chicago, IL.
4. DIX, T. 1991. The affective organizing of parenting: Adaptive and maladaptive processes. Psychol. Bull. 110: 3–25.
5. BELL, R. Q. 1977. Socialization findings re-examined. In Child effects on adults. R. Q. Bell & R. V. Harper, Eds.: 53–84. Erlbaum. Hillsdale, NJ.
6. BELSKY, J. 1984. The determinants of parenting: A process model. Child Dev. 55: 83–96.
7. LYTTON, H. 1990. Child and parent effects in boys' conduct disorder: A reinterpretation. Dev. Psychol. 26: 683–697.
8. SAMEROFF, A. J., R. SEIFER & M. ZAX. 1982. Early development of children at risk for emotional disorder. Monogr. Soc. Res. Child Dev. 47(7, Serial No. 199).
9. PLOMIN, R. & D. DANIELS. 1987. Why are children in the same family so different from one another? Behav. Brain Sci. 10: 1–59.
10. TELLEGEN, A., D. T. LYKKEN, T. J. BAUCHARD JR., K. J. WILCOX, N. L. SEGAL & S. RICH. 1988. Personality similarity in twins reared apart and together. J. Per. Soc. Psychol. 54: 1031–1039.
11. MCGUE, M., S. BACON & D. T. LYKKEN. 1993. Personality stability and change in early adulthood: A behavioral genetic analysis. Dev. Psychol. 29: 96–109.

12. MACCOBY, E. E. 1992. The role of parents in the socialization of children: A historical overview. Dev. Psychol. **28:** 1006–1017.
13. DUNHAM, P. & F. DUNHAM. 1990. Effects of mother-infant social interactions on infants' subsequent contingency task performance. Child Dev. **61:** 785–793.
14. WATSON, J. S. 1972. Smiling, cooing, and "the game." Merrill-Palmer Q. **18:** 323–340.
15. EMDE, R. 1985. The affective self: Continuities and transformations from infancy. *In* Frontiers in Infant Psychiatry–II. J. Call, E. Galenson & R. Tyson, Eds. Basic Books. New York.
16. SCHAFFER, H. R. 1977. Mothering. Harvard University Press. Cambridge, MA.
17. SROUFE, L. A. & M. J. WARD. 1984. The importance of early care. Women in the Workplace: The Effects on Families. *In* D. Quarm, K. Borman & S. Gideonse, Eds. Ablex. Norwood, NJ.
18. SROUFE, L. A. & E. WATERS. 1976. The ontogenesis of smiling and laughter: A perspective on the organization of development in infancy. Psychol. Rev. **83:** 173–189.
19. STERN, D. N. 1977. The first relationship: Infant and mother. Harvard University Press. Cambridge, MA.
20. GREENBERG, M. & K. CZNIC. 1988. Longitudinal predictors of developmental status and social interaction in premature and full-term infants at age two. Child Dev. **59:** 554–570.
21. SROUFE, L. A., E. WATERS & L. MATAS. 1974. Contextual determinants of infant affective response. *In* The Origins of Fear. M. Lewis & L. Rosenblum, Eds. Wiley. New York.
22. PARPAL, M. & E. E. MACCOBY. 1985. Maternal responsiveness and subsequent child compliance. Child Dev. **56:** 1326–1334.
23. ISABELLA, R. A., J. BELSKY & A. VON EYE. 1989. Origins of infant-mother attachment: An examination of interactional synchrony during the infant's first year. Dev. Psychol. **25:** 12–21.
24. DUCHARME, J. M. & D. E. WORLING. 1994. Behavioral momentum and stimulus fading in the acquisition and maintenance of child compliance in the home. J. App. Behav. Anal. **27:** 639–647.
25. WESTERMAN, M. A. 1990. Coordination of maternal directives with preschoolers' behavior in compliance-problem and healthy dyads. Dev. Psychol. **26:** 621–630.
26. WAHLER, R. G. & J. E. DUMAS. 1986. Maintenance factors in coercive mother-child interactions: The compliance and predictability hypotheses. J. Appl. Behav. Anal. **19:** 13–22.
27. ANDERSON, K. E., H. LYTTON & D. M. ROMNEY. 1986. Mothers' interactions with normal and conduct disordered boys: Who effects whom? Dev. Psychol. **22:** 604–609.
28. HALVERSON, C. & M. WALDROP. 1970. Maternal behavior towards own and other preschool children: The problem of ownness. Child. Dev. **41:** 839–845.
29. OLWEUS, D. 1980. Familial and temperament determinants of aggressive behavior in adolescent boys: A causal analysis. Dev. Psychol. **16:** 644–660.
30. BELSKY, J., C. HERTZOG & M. ROVINE. 1986. Children of parents with unipolar depression: A controlled 1-year followup. J. Abnorm. Child Psychol. **14:** 149–166.
31. COX, M., M. OWEN, J. LEWIS, C. RIEDEL, L. SCALF-MCIVER & A. SUSTER. 1985. Intergenerational influences on the parent-infant relationship in the transition to parenthood. J. Fam. Issues, **6:** 543–564.
32. ELDER, G., A. CASPI & G. DOWNEY. 1986. Problem behavior and family relationships: Life course and intergenerational themes. *In* Human Development: Interdisciplinary Perspectives. A. Sorensen, F. Weinert & L. Sherrod, Eds.: 293–340. Erlbaum. Hillsdale, NJ.
33. PATTERSON, G. R. 1982. Coercive family process. Castalia. Eugene, OR.
34. PATTERSON, G. R. 1976. The aggressive child: Victim and architect of a coercive system. *In* Behavior Modification and Families. I. Theory and Research. E. J. Mash, L. A. Hamerlynck & L. C. Handy, Eds.: 131–158. Brunner/Mazel. New York.
35. WAHLER, R. G. & J. E. DUMAS. 1989. Attentional problems in dysfunctional mother-child interactions: An interbehavioral model. Psychol. Bull. **105:** 116–130.

36. WELLS, K. C. & R. FOREHAND. 1985. Conduct and oppositional disorders. *In* Handbook of Clinical Behavior Therapy with Children. P. H. Bornstein & A. E. Kazdin, Eds.: 218–265. Dorsey. Homewood, IL.

37. EMERY, R. 1982. Marital turmoil: Interpersonal conflict and the children of discord and divorce. Psychol. Bull. **92:** 310–330.

38. MCADAMS, D. P. 1989. The development of a narrative identity. *In* Personality Psychology: Recent Trends and Emerging Directions. D. Buss & N. Cantor, Eds.: 160–174. Springer-Verlag. New York.

39. GEORGE, C., N. KAPLAN & M. MAIN. 1985. Adult attachment interview. Unpublished manuscript. University of California, Berkeley.

40. HENRY, B., T. E. MOFFETT, A. CASPI, J. LANGLEY & P. A. SILVA. 1994. On the "remembrances of things past": A longitudinal evaluation of the retrospective method. Psychol. Assessment **6:** 92–101.

41. BENOIT, D. & K. C. H. PARKER. 1994. Stability and transmission of attachment across three generations. Child Dev. **65:** 1444–1457.

42. FONAGY, P., H. STEELE & M. STEELE. 1991. Maternal representations of attachment during pregnancy predict the organization of infant-mother attachment at one year of age. Child Dev. **62:** 891–905.

43. WARD, M. J. & E. A. CARLSON. Associations among adult attachment representations, maternal sensitivity, and infant-mother attachment in a sample of adolescent mothers. Child Dev. In press.

44. VAN IJZENDOORN, M. H. 1995. Adult attachment representations, parent responsiveness, and infant attachment: A meta-analysis on the predictive validity of the adult attachment interview. Psychol. Bull. **117:** 387–403.

45. LYONS-RUTH, K. 1995. Broadening our conceptual framework: Can we reintroduce relational strategies and implicit representational systems to the study of psychopathology? Dev. Psychol. **31:** 432–436.

46. FOX, N. A. 1995. Of the way we were: Adult memories about attachment experiences and their role in determining infant-parent relationships: A commentary on van Ijzendoorn. Psychol. Bull. **117:** 404–410.

47. PATTERSON, G. R., J. B. REID & T. J. DISHION. 1992. A social learning approach: Antisocial boys. Castalia. Eugene.

48. FOREHAND, R. & R. J. MCMAHON. 1981. Helping the noncompliant child: A clinician's guide to parent training. Guilford. New York.

49. WEBSTER-STRATTON, C. 1990. Long term follow-up of families with young conduct problem children: From preschool to grade school. J. Clin. Child Psychol. **19:** 144–149.

50. DUMAS, J. E. & C. WEKERLE. 1995. Maternal reports of child behavior problems and personal distress as predictors of dysfunctional parenting. Dev. Psychopathol. **7:** 465–479.

51. DUMAS, J. E. & R. G. WAHLER. 1983. Preditors of treatment outcome in parent training: Mother insularity and socioeconomic disadvantage. Behav. Assess. **5:** 301–313.

52. GRIEST, D. L. & K. C. WELLS. 1983. Behavioral family therapy with conduct disorders in children. Behav. Ther. **14:** 37–53.

53. WEBSTER-STRATTON, C. & M. HAMMOND. 1990. Preditors of treatment outcome in parent training for families with conduct problem children. Behav. Ther. **21:** 319–337.

54. GERGEN, K. J. & M. M. GERGEN. 1988. Narrative and the self as relationship. *In* Advances in Experimental Social Psychology. L. Berkowitz, Ed.: **21:** 17–56. Academic Press. San Diego, CA.

55. SMITH, E. R. 1984. Model of social inference processes. Psychol. Rev. **91:** 392–413.

56. ABELSON, R. P. 1981. Psychological states of the script concept. Am. Psychol. **36:** 715–729.

57. STILES, W. B. 1987. Some intentions are observable. J. Counseling Psychol. **34:** 236–239.

58. SILBERSCHATZ, G. & J. T. CURTIS. 1993. Measuring the therapists' impact on the patients' therapeutic process. J. Consult. Clin. Psychol. **61:** 403–411.

59. MILLER, D. T. & W. TURNBULL. 1986. Expectancies and interpersonal process. Annu. Rev. Psychol. **37:** 233–256.

60. STILES, W. B. 1992. Describing talk: A taxonomy of verbal response modes. Sage. Newbury Park, CA.
61. CRITS-CHRISTOPH, P., A. COOPER & L. LUBORSKY. 1988. The accuracy of therapists' interpretations and the outcome of dynamic psychotherapy. J. Consult. Clin. Psychol. 56: 490–495.
62. SILBERSCHATZ, G., P. B. FRETTER & J. T. CURTIS. 1986. How do interpretations influence the process of psychotherapy? J. Consult. Clin. Psychol. 54: 646–652.
63. WAHLER, R. G., P. G. CARTOR, J. FLEISCHMANN & W. LAMBERT. 1993. The impact of synthesis teaching and parent training with mothers of conduct-disordered children. J. Abnorm. Child Psychol. 21: 425–440.
64. DUMAS, J. E. & R. G. WAHLER. 1985. Indiscriminate mothering as a contextual factor in aggressive-oppositional child behavior: "Damned if you do and damned if you don't." J. Abnorm. Child Psychol. 13: 1–17.
65. DUMAS, J. E. 1986. Indirect influence of maternal social contacts on mother-child interactions: A setting event analysis. J. Abnorm. Child Psychol. 14: 205–216.
66. WAHLER, R. G., A. J. WILLIAMS & A. CEREZO. 1990. The compliance and predictability hypotheses: Some sequential and correlational analyses of coercive mother-child interactions. Behav. Assess. 12: 391–407.
67. GOTTMAN, J. M. 1993. A theory of marital dissolution and stability. J. Family Psychol. 7: 57–75.
68. CEREZO, M. A. 1988. Standardized observation codes. In Dictionary of Behavioral Assessment Techniques. M. Herson & A. Bellock, Eds.: 442–445. Pergamon Press. New York.
69. WAHLER, R. G., J. ARMSTRONG & K. MEGINNIS. 1995. Coding of personal narratives and listener responses. Unpublished manual. Psychology Department. University of Tennessee, Knoxville.

Aggressive Symptoms and Salivary Cortisol in Clinic-referred Boys with Conduct Disorder

KEITH McBURNETT,[a,d] BENJAMIN B. LAHEY,[b]
LISA CAPASSO,[a] AND ROLF LOEBER[c]

[a]Child Development Center
University of California, Irvine
4621 Teller Street, Suite 108
Newport Beach, California 92660

[b]University of Chicago
Chicago, Illinois

[c]University of Pittsburgh
Pittsburgh, Pennsylvania

Summarizing a review of 61 multivariate studies of child problem behavior, Quay[1] noted that the one pattern that emerged almost without exception was the aggressive, disruptive, and noncompliant syndrome befitting the term undersocialized aggressive conduct disorder (CD). The many replications of the syndrome do not include covert types of antisocial and rule-breaking behavior such as stealing, lying, and truancy from home, which factor instead with the less robust pattern that Quay called socialized CD. Since that review, different methods continue to validate the distinction between an aggressive pattern and a covert or delinquent pattern, including large-scale factor analysis (*e.g.*, ref. 2), two quantitative meta-analyses of factor-analytic studies of child conduct problems,[3,4] and a distillation of longitudinal studies of the development of juvenile antisocial behavior.[5] Aggression shows the kind of longitudinal stability characteristic of other enduring behavioral traits, and it is one of the best-validated predictors of the development of anti-social syndromes.[6-8]

Drawing on the wealth of this kind of data, the third edition of the Diagnostic and Statistical Manual of Mental Disorders (DSM-III)[9] used aggression to distinguish subtypes of CD. Later editions, however, diminished the use of aggression as a subtyping criterion. The current DSM-IV[10] discards aggression entirely and instead uses age of onset of CD (by age 10, or later) to distinguish a childhood-onset type from an adolescent-onset type. This method takes advantage of empirical observations that early onset conduct problems are more strongly associated with aggression (as well as with persistence, progressive versatility, comorbid attention-deficit/hyperactivity disorder, and male gender) than conduct problems that appear for the first time in adolescence.[7,11,12] These later-emerging behavior problems are far more likely to consist predominantly of covert antisocial behavior and drug and alcohol use. They often seem to represent a stage of experimentation or rejection of parental values lasting no more than a few months to a few years. Compared to prior CD nosologies, the age-of-onset scheme can be safely assumed to have an advantage in reliability. There are insufficient data at present, though,

---

[d] Tel: (714)833-9088; fax: (714)833-8008; e-mail: kmcburne@uci.edu.

to compare the validity of the DSM-IV method to approaches based on operationalizing aggression.

Strong support for the validity of aggression as a behavioral construct and as a subtyping criterion for CD comes from its association with low activity or reactivity in several biological systems.[13–15] Theoretical interpretations of this relationship are numerous, but among the most influential are (a) autonomic hyporeactivity does not provide the biological substrate for normal development of conditioned emotional responding to signals of aversive stimulation (*i.e.*, threat of punishment) and passive avoidance learning, and (b) hypoactivity and hyporeactivity are indicators that the neural control system referred to in Gray's[16,17] theory as the behavioral inhibition system is weak or deficient. These theories are particularly applicable to electrodermal activity (EDA),[18,19] but in one form or another they may help explain other psychophysiological and biochemical differences found in aggressive and antisocial individuals.

In recent years, investigators have linked low levels of the stress hormone cortisol to chronic aggressive and antisocial behavior. Virkkunen[20] reported that in habitually violent adult male offenders, those who had the DSM-III subtype of undersocialized aggressive CD in childhood excreted only about half the amount of free cortisol in 24-hour urine as those with no such history. In this same sample of prisoners, analyses using their concurrent adult diagnoses found that the mean 24-hour urinary free cortisol in prisoners diagnosed as antisocial personality disorder (APD) with habitually violent tendencies was about half that found in five other experimental groups: APD without habitual violence, intermittent explosive disorder, other violent offenders, recidivistic arsonists, and psychiatric personnel. Vanyukov and colleagues[21] found a negative correlation between the number of CD symptoms and the concentration of cortisol in the saliva of preadolescent boys. They also found that boys whose fathers qualified for a diagnosis of CD before age 18 and a diagnosis of APD as adults had lower cortisol than boys whose fathers had CD before age 18 but did not progress to APD, as well as boys whose fathers never had CD or APD. McBurnett[22] compared children with DSM-III-R CD but no DSM-III-R anxiety disorder to children diagnosed with CD and a comorbid anxiety disorder and to children without either diagnosis. The children with CD but not anxiety had more contacts with police, more suspensions from school, and more nominations by their classmates for being "meanest" and for "fights most" than children with both CD and an anxiety disorder.[23,e] The concentration of cortisol in saliva in the CD group that was free from anxiety was significantly lower than in the CD plus anxiety group. When these same subjects were reclassified according to DSM-IV criteria,[26] those with childhood-onset CD were found to have significantly lower levels of salivary cortisol than subjects with adolescent-onset CD and subjects without CD.[f] Together, the data from these three samples suggest that lower cortisol is associated with a chronic syndrome

---

[e] Other analyses with this subject sample point to a specific association between low cortisol and aggression. Across all subjects (n = 67), cortisol was significantly and inversely related to peer nominations for "meanest" (−.39), nominations for "fights most" (−.40), and number of aggressive CD symptoms reported by parents (−.41), but insignificantly to number of nonaggressive symptoms (−.08).[24,25]

[f] Although the mean difference in salivary cortisol between childhood-onset and adolescent-onset subtypes was large and statistically significant, the results of this particular analysis must be viewed cautiously until replicated because of the small cell size for adolescent-onset disorder (n = 4). Cell sizes for the comparison between childhood-onset CD and clinic-referred children without CD were far more adequate.

of aggressive antisocial behavior that begins early in life and persists into adulthood.

Three other studies of cortisol in antisocial youth failed to find any association between diagnostic group status and cortisol.[27-29] However, because none of those studies separated the disruptive subjects into subgroups, their designs could not discern whether low cortisol might be associated narrowly with chronic, aggressive CD. We report here a reanalysis of the original data from McBurnett et al.[22] along with new follow-up diagnostic and cortisol data across a four-year interval, designed to address the specificity of cortisol with aggressive and nonaggressive symptoms of CD. The diagnostic and experimental methodology and the validity of salivary cortisol as a physiological index are described in greater detail in the original report. These data were collected at the Georgia Children's Center at the University of Georgia as part of the Developmental Trends Study.[30]

METHOD

Subjects

The subjects were 67 males, mean age 9.6 years at the outset (age range, 7–12 years), who were referred to the Georgia Children's Center for Psychological Assessment for psychodiagnostic evaluation and entered into a larger longitudinal study of the development of CD. All subjects assented to the procedures, and their primary guardians (in nearly all cases, their mothers) provided fully informed consent for their child's participation and their own participation as behavioral informants for their child.

Diagnostic Procedure

Children were diagnosed at four annual intervals. Symptom information was derived from clinical interviews of children, their parent, and their teacher, using the Diagnostic Interview Schedule for Children (DISC).[31] A summary table was constructed for each case listing all reported symptoms and their frequency, duration, and age of onset in separate columns for each of the three DISC informants. Two clinicians following a written set of "best-estimate" diagnostic guidelines independently assigned child diagnoses by determining which DSM-III-R criteria were fulfilled by the tabled information. The kappa reliability of the initial symptom report (comparing the primary interviewer's tallies to an independent rater's tallies in one quarter of the cases) was never lower than .65 for any of the individual DSM-III-R CD symptoms across each of the four years, with a median kappa of 1.0. The lowest kappa obtained for the cross-diagnostician CD diagnosis in the four years was .92.

Cortisol Collection and Assay

A single sample of saliva was collected from the child during the second year and fourth year clinic visits. Subjects refrained from eating at least one hour before providing saliva. Flow was stimulated by chewing sugarless gum. After removing the gum, subjects placed a specimen tube to their lower lip and allowed saliva to flow directly into the tube as they were able to produce it (under the supervision of a research assistant who prevented subjects from hacking or depositing sputum). Most subjects required approximately 2–5 minutes to generate 5 cc of saliva.[g] The tubes were capped and frozen at $-80°C$ until all samples for the year were collected, at which time they were thawed, centrifuged, and radioimmunoassayed using a commercially prepared kit. In year 2, 63 subjects provided saliva. Only 38 of these subjects provided saliva in year 4, and four additional subjects were included who had not given saliva in year 2. The reasons for these variations in participation were several, including family relocations, child refusal, and rescheduling some of the evaluations at remote locations to accommodate special circumstances.

Cortisol Data Considerations

The time of collection could not be controlled and was allowed to vary across the morning to midafternoon hours. Cortisol levels rise and fall along a predictable diurnal rhythm, but changes in level are interspersed with relative plateaus lasting several hours. Data from Puig-Antich and colleagues[32] graphically shows that across the same hours in which we collected saliva, the mean cortisol level in a group of hospitalized children was virtually flat, except for a brief small spike at lunchtime. Consistent with that study, we found no significant relationship of salivary cortisol concentration and time of collection (in year 2, $n = 63$, $r = .14$, $p = .26$; year 4, $n = 42$, $r = -.008$, $p = .96$). We also found no significant relation between child age and cortisol concentration (year 2, $r = .19$, $p = .13$; year 4, $r = .13$, $p = .41$). We repeated all regression analyses using time of collection as a covariate, age of child as a covariate, and both as covariates, and each time the variance in cortisol accounted for by CD symptoms was similar. In order to validly use parametric statistics, we transformed the cortisol concentration values, which were positively skewed and leptokurtic in raw form, using Blom's[33] procedure. This method preserves the rank order of subject scores but modifies the scale difference between scores in order to produce a normal score distribution.

Three scores based on DSM-III-R CD symptoms were computed for each subject: the sum of all CD symptoms reported by any informant (parent, teacher, or child) over the four-year period, and the sums of aggressive and nonaggressive CD symptoms similarly reported. The aggressive symptoms were the following: often initiates physical fights, has used weapons, has been physically cruel to people, has stolen while confronting a victim, has forced someone into sexual activity, and the DSM-IV item of bullies. The nonaggressive symptoms included the following: has set fires; has destroyed property; has broken into someone else's house, building, or car; tells lies; has stolen without confronting the victim; has run away from home overnight; has been cruel to animals; is truant from school; and the DSM-III item of vandalism. CD symptoms were used in regression models to predict cortisol collected in years 2 and 4, and the mean of these cortisol values. For this latter composite, we used the single available cortisol value for the 25 subjects who provided saliva in only one year, and the mean cortisol across the two years for the other 42 subjects, on the assumption that this was the best

---

[g] For the last several years, we have found it easier to use a different method of saliva collection adapted from Megan Gunner at the University of Minnesota. Children place a dry sterile cotton dental roll in their mouth and chew it until it is saturated. The cotton is then compressed in a 10 cc syringe, and the saliva is forced out into a crytotube to be frozen. This method filters the saliva well enough to obviate the need for centrifuging.

TABLE 1. Correlations of Salivary Cortisol, Four-year Aggressive and Covert CD Symptom Totals, and Ages of Onset of Aggressive and Covert CD Symptoms (Pearson's r/Probability)

	Cortisol in Year 2	Cortisol in Year 4	Four-year Aggressive CD	Four-year Covert CD	Age of First Aggressive Symptom	Age of First Covert Symptom
Cortisol in year 2	1.0/0.0					
Cortisol in year 4	.19/.26	1.0/0.0				
Four-year aggressive CD	−.42/.001	−.37/.02	1.0/0.0			
Four-year covert CD	−.20/.12	−.19/.22	.68/.0001	1.0/0.0		
Age of first aggressive symptom	.36/.01	.32/.07	−.36/.005	−.14/.29	1.0/0.0	
Age of first covert symptom	.14/.33	.09/.65	−.16/.25	−.20/.13	.24/.10	1.0/0.0

large estimate of a stable trait level of daytime hypothalamic-pituitary-adrenal (HPA) axis arousal available from the data.

RESULTS

TABLE 1 presents the correlations among predictor and criterion variables. The total number of aggressive symptoms over the four annual assessments was significantly and inversely associated with salivary cortisol collected in years 2 and 4. The age at which children were reported to exhibit their first aggressive CD symptom was significantly associated with salivary cortisol in year 2.

TABLE 2 shows the results of the regression models in which the four-year total of CD symptoms was the predictor. The total number of CD symptoms over four years was significantly and inversely associated with cortisol from year 2 and with the cortisol composite across years 2 and 4, but the variance in cortisol accounted for by CD symptoms was small. Visual inspection of the plots of cortisol-by-CD symptoms suggested a curvilinear relationship, which was confirmed by a

TABLE 2. Prediction of Salivary Cortisol from Four-year CD Symptom Total

Criterion	r^2[a]	b weight[b]	SE b[c]	Beta[d]	F	p
Year-2 cortisol	.07	−.04	.02	−.27	4.87	.03
Year-4 cortisol	.06	−.05	.03	−.24	2.34	.13
Mean cortisol	.06	−.03	.02	−.24	3.93	.05

[a] Total variance in criterion accounted for (coefficient of determination).
[b] Nonstandardized multiple regression coefficient.
[c] Standard error of b weight.
[d] Standardized multiple regression coefficient.

TABLE 3. Quadratic Prediction of Salivary Cortisol from Four-year CD Symptom Total

Criterion	r^2	b weight	SE b	Beta	t/F^a	p
Year-2 cortisol						
Linear	.07	−.16	.05	−1.07	−3.02	.004
Quadratic	.03	.01	.003	.84	2.39	.02
Joint	.15				5.47	.007
Year-4 cortisol						
Linear	.06	−.20	.09	−.98	−2.29	.03
Quadratic	.02	.008	.005	.79	1.86	.07
Joint	.13				2.97	.06
Mean cortisol						
Linear	.06	−.18	.05	−1.23	−3.55	.001
Quadratic	.01	.007	.002	1.05	3.03	.004
Joint	.18				6.80	.002

[a] Value of t or F statistic.

significant quadratic term in polynomial regression models (TABLE 3). Substantially more variance in cortisol could be explained by the quadratic models than by linear models.

TABLE 4 shows the results of the simple and multiple regression models for aggressive and nonaggressive CD symptoms, including the independent variance accounted for by each predictor after holding the other predictor constant. The aggressive CD symptoms, but not the covert CD symptoms, were significantly negatively associated with all three cortisol measures, and more of the variance in cortisol was accounted for by the purer measure of aggression than had been the case before separating the CD symptoms. Covert symptoms did not predict cortisol. The cortisol-by-aggression plot appeared to be curvilinear, and the exis-

TABLE 4. Multiple and Partial Regression Models Predicting Cortisol from Four-year Aggressive and Nonaggressive CD Symptom Totals

Model	Model Parameters						Unique Parameters		
Year-2 Cortisol Predicted by:	r^2	b weight	SE b	Beta	t/F	p	r^2	F	p
Aggressive	.18	−.14	.04	−.50	−3.30	.002	.147	11.07	.01
Nonaggressive	.04	.03	.03	.12	.80	.426	.008	.59	NS
Both	.19			−.27	6.92	.002			
Year-4 Cortisol Predicted by:									
Aggressive	.13	−.15	.07	−.40	−2.11	.041	.099	4.53	.05
Nonaggressive	.04	.02	.05	.06	.32	.753	.003	.14	NS
Both	.14			−.24	3.08	.057			
Mean Cortisol Predicted by:									
Aggressive	.17	−.14	.04	−.53	−3.57	.001	.161	16.1	.01
Nonaggressive	.03	.04	.03	.19	1.24	.220	.019	1.9	NS
Both	.19			−.24	7.47	.001			

TABLE 5. Quadratic Prediction of Salivary Cortisol from Four-year Total Aggressive Symptoms of CD

Criterion	r^2	b weight	SE b	Beta	t/F	p
Year-2 cortisol						
Linear	.18	−.30	.09	−.08	−3.48	.001
Quadratic	.09	.02	.01	.71	2.27	.03
Joint	.24				9.67	.0002
Year-4 cortisol						
Linear	.13	−.37	.14	−1.00	−2.70	.01
Quadratic	.06	.02	.01	.69	1.85	.07
Joint	.20				5.01	.01
Mean cortisol						
Linear	.17	−.37	.08	−1.37	−4.64	.0001
Quadratic	.07	.02	.007	1.03	3.47	.0009
Joint	.30				13.79	.0001

tence of a statistically significant quadratic component was confirmed in the polynomial regression model (TABLE 5).

TABLES 6 and 7 present similar regression models as in TABLES 2 and 4 but instead of using symptom totals as predictors, the ages at which CD symptoms first appeared are the predictor variables. Both the age at which CD symptoms first appear, and the age at which aggression first appears, are significant predictors of year 2 salivary cortisol and of the years 2 and 4 cortisol composite, but the onset of aggression accounted for more variance alone than the total CD symptom count. Onset of covert symptoms did not predict cortisol. When the sample was limited to children with at least one aggressive CD symptom during the four years (to permit direct comparison of the different onset ages on the same subjects), the age of the first CD symptom accounted for 9.8%, 2.5%, and 8% of the variance in the respective cortisol measures. The age of onset of the first aggressive CD symptom, in comparison, accounted for 13.3%, 10.3%, and 18.4%, respectively.

DISCUSSION

These results suggest that in clinic-referred boys of elementary and middle-school age, CD and aggression are associated with low salivary cortisol. Because covert symptoms of CD show no such relationship, the link between CD and cortisol appears to be a function of the more specific inverse relationship between aggression and cortisol. This seems also to be the case for age of onset: the age at which CD symptoms first appear is associated with salivary cortisol, but this appears to be a diluted representation of the more specific link between the first

TABLE 6. Prediction of Salivary Cortisol by Age of Onset of Any CD Symptom

Criterion	r^2	b weight	SE b	Beta	F	p
Year-2 cortisol	.10	.10	.04	.32	6.45	.01
Year-4 cortisol	.06	.08	.06	.24	2.3	.14
Mean cortisol	.11	.09	.04	.33	7.10	.01

TABLE 7. Multiple and Partial Regression Models Predicting Cortisol from Age of First Aggressive and Nonaggressive CD Symptoms

Model	Model Parameters						Unique Parameters		
Year-2 Cortisol Predicted by:	r^2	b weight	SE b	Beta	t/F	p	r^2	F	p
Aggressive	.26	.18	.05	.52	3.58	.001	.26	12.96	.01
Nonaggressive	.01	−.01	.04	−.05	−.33	.75	.00	.11	NS
Both	.27				6.53	.004			
Year-4 Cortisol Predicted by:									
Aggressive	.16	.18	.08	.44	2.12	.05	.18	4.48	.05
Nonaggressive	.004	−.05	.07	−.17	−.81	.43	.03	.66	NS
Both	.19				2.20	.13			
Mean Cortisol Predicted by:									
Aggressive	.28	.20	.05	.54	3.89	.0004	.28	15.14	.001
Nonaggressive	.002	−.02	.04	−.08	−.56	.58	.006	.31	NS
Both	.28				7.63	.002			

appearance of aggression and cortisol. Children who are more aggressive throughout their childhood years, and children who start behaving aggressively at younger ages, have lower cortisol.

Without having additional cortisol samples on these same subjects, we cannot determine the extent to which these effects represent a lower tonic cortisol level or a muted HPA response to the stress and novelty of the clinical-experimental setting. Sampling of cortisol across times and situations is needed in future research to delineate the deviations in HPA activity in aggressive children. We could see from the plots that children with very low levels of cortisol were almost always highly aggressive, and thus we would interpret low cortisol in childhood to be a risk factor for chronic aggression.

The data provide support for the notion that psychobiological diversity accompanies the diagnosis of CD, and that subtyping based on behavioral characteristics, such as aggressiveness, may be used to establish more psychobiologically homogeneous subgroups. This approach is promising, but practical difficulties must be confronted (*e.g.*, difficulty gaining accurate multiinformant history, lack of accepted methods for operationalizing behavioral constructs). As the current study and those reviewed herein show, biobehavioral relationships may not be apparent unless studied with focused experimental designs and statistical treatments (transformations, polynomial models).

The findings have implications for using age of CD onset as a subtyping criterion, which, although not directly related to biological differences, does appear to demarcate subgroups that are different from each other in physiological activity/reactivity.[13-26] The age at which aggression first appears may be a more valid criterion for establishing homogeneous subtypes than the age of onset of any CD symptom (insofar as cortisol concentration may be considered a validating criterion). However, the validity of dichotomous subtypes based on age of onset depends also on the particular cutoff age selected. It may be possible to select a cutoff age for onset of CD that will account for more of the variance in cortisol (and in other external validators) than the same cutoff age for onset of aggression, and vice versa. Future analyses could address this issue using receiver-operating characteristics or similar statistical approaches.

REFERENCES

1. QUAY, H. C. 1986. Classification. *In* Psychopathological Disorders of Childhood. H. C. Quay & J. S. Werry, Eds.: 1–34. John Wiley & Sons. New York.
2. ACHENBACH, T. M. *et al.* 1989. Replication of empirically derived syndromes as a basis for taxonomy of child/adolescent psychopathology. J. Abnorm. Child Psychol. **17**(3): 299–323.
3. LOEBER, R. & K. SCHMALING. 1985. Empirical evidence for overt and covert patterns of antisocial conduct problems: A meta-analysis. J. Abnorm. Child Psychol. **13**(2): 337–352.
4. FRICK, P. J. *et al.* 1993. Oppositional defiant disorder and conduct disorder: A meta-analytic review of factor analyses and cross-validation in a clinic sample. Clin. Psychol. Rev. **13**(4): 319–340.
5. LOEBER, R. 1988. Behavioral precursors and accelerators of delinquency. *In* Explaining Criminal Behavior. W. Buikhuisen & S. A. Mednick, Eds.: 51–67. Brill. Leiden.
6. LOEBER, R. *et al.* 1995. Which boys will fare worse? Early predictors of the onset of conduct disorder in a six-year longitudinal study. J. Am. Acad. Child Adolesc. Psychiatry **34**(4): 499–509.
7. LOEBER, R. 1988. Natural histories of conduct problems, delinquency, and associated substance abuse: Evidence for developmental progressions. *In* Advances in Clinical Child Psychology. B. B. Lahey & A. E. Kazdin, Eds.: 73–124. Plenum Press. New York.
8. OLWEUS, D. 1979. Stability of aggressive reaction patterns in males: A review. Psychol. Bull. **86**(4): 852–875.
9. AMERICAN PSYCHIATRIC ASSOCIATION. 1980. Diagnostic and Statistical Manual of Mental Disorders, Third Edition. APA. Washington, DC.
10. AMERICAN PSYCHIATRIC ASSOCIATION. 1994. Diagnostic and Statistical Manual for Mental Disorders, Fourth Edition. 1990. APA. Washington, DC.
11. MOFFITT, T. E. 1990. Juvenile delinquency and attention deficit disorder: Boys' developmental trajectories from age 3–15. Child Dev. **61**: 893–910.
12. MOFFITT, T. E. 1993. Adolescence-limited and life-course-persistent antisocial behavior: A developmental taxonomy. Psychol. Rev. **100**: 674–701.
13. LAHEY, B. B. *et al.* 1993. Neurophysiological correlates of conduct disorder: A rationale and a review of research. J. Clin. Child Psychol. **22**(2): 141–153.
14. LAHEY, B. B. *et al.* 1995. Psychobiology. *In* Conduct disorders in children and adolescents. G. P. Sholevar, Ed.: 27–44. American Psychiatric Press. Washington, DC.
15. McBURNETT, K. & B. LAHEY. 1994. Psychophysiological and neuroendocrine correlates of conduct disorder and antisocial behavior in children and adolescents. *In* Progress in Experimental Personality and Psychopathology Research. D. C. Fowles, P. Sutker & S. Goodman, Eds.: 199–232. Springer Publishing Company. New York.
16. GRAY, J. A. 1982. The neuropsychology of anxiety: An inquiry into the functions of the septo-hippocampal system. Oxford University Press. Oxford.
17. GRAY, J. A. 1987. The psychology of fear and stress. 2d Ed. Cambridge University Press. Cambridge.
18. FOWLES, D. C. 1980. The three arousal model: Implications of Gray's two-factor learning theory for HR, electrodermal activity, and psychopathy. Psychophysiology **17**: 87–104.
19. FOWLES, D. C. & K. A. MISSEL. 1994. Electrodermal hyporeactivity, motivation, and psychopathy: Theoretical issues. *In* Progress in Experimental Personality and Psychopathology Research. D. C. Fowles, P. Sutker & S. H. Goodman, Eds. Springer. New York.
20. VIRKKUNEN, M. 1985. Urinary free cortisol secretion in habitually violent offenders. Acta Psychiatr. Scand. **72**(1): 40–44.

21. VANYUKOV, M. M. *et al.* 1993. Antisocial symptoms in preadolescent boys and in their parents: Associations with cortisol. Psychiatry Res. **46:** 9–17.
22. McBURNETT, K. *et al.* 1991. Anxiety, inhibition, and conduct disorder in children: II. Relation to salivary cortisol. J. Am. Acad. Child Adolesc. Psychiatry **30:** 192–196.
23. WALKER, J. L. *et al.* 1991. Anxiety, inhibition, and conduct disorder in children: I. Relations to social impairment and sensation seeking. J. Am. Acad. Child Adolesc. Psychiatry **30:** 187–191.
24. LAHEY, B. B. & R. LOEBER. 1991. A preliminary developmental-psychobiological model of conduct disorder. *In* Relationships among the externalizing disorders. Session at the Annual Meeting of the Society for Research in Child and Adolescent Psychopathology. Zandvoort, Holland.
25. McBURNETT, K. *et al.* 1990. Association of cortisol with peer nominations of popularity, aggression, and social inhibition in clinic-referred children. Presented at the 24th Annual Meeting of the Association for the Advancement of Behavior Therapy. San Francisco.
26. McBURNETT, K. & L. J. PFIFFNER. Estimating developmental risk for psychopathy, using subtypes, comorbidities, and biological correlates of conduct disorder. *In* Psychopathy: Theory, Research, and Implications for Society. R. D. Hare, D. Cooke & A. Forth, Eds. In press.
27. KRUESI, M. J. *et al.* 1989. Urinary free cortisol output and disruptive behavior in children. J. Am. Acad. Child Adolesc. Psychiatry **28**(3): 441–443.
28. SCERBO, A. S. & D. J. KOLKO. 1994. Salivary testosterone and cortisol in disruptive children: Relationship to aggressive, hyperactive and internalizing behaviors. J. Am. Acad. Child Adolesc. Psychiatry **3**(8): 1174–1184.
29. TARGUM, S. D. *et al.* 1990. Measurement of cortisol and lymphocyte subpopulations in depressed and conduct-disordered adolescents. J. Affect. Dis. **18:** 91–96.
30. LAHEY, B. B. *et al.* 1990. Comparisons of DSM-III and DSM-III-R diagnoses for prepubertal children: Changes in prevalence and validity. J. Am. Acad. Child Adolesc. Psychiatry **29:** 620–626.
31. COSTELLO, A. J., C. EDELBROCK, R. KALAS & M. DULCAN. 1984. The NIMH Diagnostic Interview Schedule for Children (DISC): Development, reliability, and comparison between clinical and lay interviewers. University of Massachusetts Medical Center. Worcester, MA.
32. PUIG-ANTICH, J. *et al.* 1989. Cortisol secretion in prepubertal children with major depressive disorder. Arch. Gen. Psychiatry **46:** 801–809.
33. BLOM, G. 1958. Statistical Estimates and Transformed Beta Variables. Wiley. New York.

Stress Hormones, Genotype, and Brain Organization

Implications for Aggression[a]

E. RONALD DE KLOET,[b] S. MECHIEL KORTE,
NYNKE Y. ROTS, AND MENNO R. KRUK

Division of Medical Pharmacology
Leiden/Amsterdam Center for Drug Research
University of Leiden
P.O. Box 9503
2300 RA Leiden, the Netherlands

INTRODUCTION

It is generally accepted that aggressive behavior is a specific feature of a more general pattern of stress reactions displayed by animals and humans in response to a changing environment, but how stress and aggression are related is not precisely known. Another fundamental question in stress and aggression research is why some individuals suffer from pathology, while others are healthy under seemingly similar conditions. Of great significance for the study of these questions are the seminal observations of Henry[1] and Engel,[2] which indicate that individuals with an extreme difference in stress reaction coexist in a normal population. In response to a psychosocial challenge, the extremists display either a fight/flight response[3] or a conservation-withdrawal response. Individual differences in endocrine reactions that are associated with differences in aggressive coping styles have also been reported in other species than rodents, for example, tree shrews,[4] monkeys,[5] and humans.[6,7]

In this contribution we will briefly review recent findings of studies with genetically selected mouse and rat lines that have substantiated the notion of coexistence of extreme differences in individual reaction patterns to stress. Next, we will address the issue that these individual differences not only depend on genotype, but also on the persistent effects of early experience related to mother-pup interaction. We focus on stress hormones, in particular on the corticosteroids, which, during ontogeny, program stress-reaction patterns for life. We conclude that the conceptual understanding of the underlying mechanism of hormone action in the nervous system has reached a sufficiently advanced level that new approaches are possible for studying the pathology of stress and aggression.

[a] Research performed in the Division of Medical Pharmacology, LACDR, Leiden, was supported by the Netherlands Organization for Scientific Research (NWO), Grants 546-092, 554-545, 551-057 (to S. M. Korte), and 564-025. The support by the Harry Frank Guggenheim Foundation (to M. R. Kruk) and by the Netherlands Heart Foundation (to S. M. Korte) is gratefully acknowledged.

[b] Tel: 31-71 527 6210; fax: 31-71 527 6292; e-mail: e.kloet@lacdr.LeidenUniv.nl.

GENETIC SELECTION FOR AGGRESSION AND SEROTONIN

Research by Bohus, Koolhaas, and colleagues[8–10] has further substantiated the notion of the coexistence of two extremes in stress-reaction patterns. The Dutch researchers used for their studies two mouse lines genetically selected for aggressive behavior, that is, the aggressive short-attack latency (SAL) and the nonaggressive long-attack latency (LAL) mice. The SAL mice feature the fight/ flight reaction mode. They are characterized by vigorous offensive aggression when confronted with an intruder, which turns into flight during confrontation with a physically stronger resident. By contrast, the LAL mice react with immobility and withdrawal.[11]

Additional observations suggest that the variation in attack latency of the SAL and LAL mice seems to be a reflection of a more fundamental difference in the way these animals react upon their environment. Previously, it was shown that the SAL mice were more active in avoidance of an aversive experience (e.g., electric shock) than LAL mice.[12] By contrast, the nonaggressive LAL animals show a passive behavioral response during threatening conditions.[12,13] Furthermore, the SAL, rather than the LAL mice, rely, under stable living conditions, on behavioral routines; they perform worse and show a more impaired adaptation when conditions are changing. The SALs make, therefore, more errors than LAL mice in solving problems encountered during changes in maze configurations.[11] Accordingly, it is predicted that the SAL mice will be more successful in coping with challenge when settled in a territory under stable conditions, whereas the LAL mice have an advantage during migration.[14] These LAL mice appear more flexible in adaptation to stress. If LAL mice choose passive behavior as an option to cope, this response is not an expression of "loss of control," but in fact a behavior that is essential for survival.

Active and passive animals also can be distinguished in neural and endocrine reaction patterns. The active behavioral response (fight/flight) pattern is characterized by high sympathetic activity, but the corticosteroid level is low, provided the subjects are successful. The passive behavioral strategy is characterized by high parasympathetic activity, and corticosteroids (CORT) remain high in subjects suffering from psychosocial defeats.[9,15] The testosterone level is generally high in active and low in passive animals.[16,17]

Recently, we have studied the serotonergic 1A (5-HT1A) receptor in the brains of SAL and LAL mice. The aggressive SAL mice had a level of 5-HT1A mRNA about twice as high in the dorsal hippocampus as observed in the LAL mice. Ligand binding studies showed that increased postsynaptic 5-HT1A receptor expression was also reflected on the protein level in view of the increased 5-HT1A receptor number in the dorsal hippocampus, lateral septum, and frontal cortex. However, no difference in presynaptic 5-HT1A receptors in the dorsal raphe nucleus of SAL and LAL mice was found.[18] Thus, postsynaptic 5-HT1A receptor expression is high in SAL mice having a low CORT tone.

In rats, attacks, quite similar to the attacks of SAL mice, can be induced by pharmacological or electrical stimulation of a hypothalamic area that partly overlaps with the tuberoinfundibular hypothalamus.[19] Interestingly, such attacks can be selectively inhibited by the dopaminergic antagonist, haloperidol, serotonergic agonists, and the serotonin reuptake inhibitor, fluvoxamine.[19,20] Moreover, the same serotonergic drugs dose-dependently suppress the active coping component (biting and kicking) in "spontaneous" intermale aggression while leaving the rest of the social interactions unaffected.[20,21]

Taken together, these data collected from studies with SAL and LAL mice suggest that genetic selection for aggressive behavior coselects for an active coping style, a relatively low corticosteroid hormone exposure, but high limbic 5-HT1A receptor expression. In agreement with previous pharmacological studies using partial 5-HT1A agonists (serenics, *e.g.*, eltoprazine) or 5-HT reuptake inhibitors with antiaggressive properties,[22] the findings suggest a specific role for the limbic 5-HT1 receptors in regulation of aggression.

GENETIC SELECTION AND DOPAMINE

Aggressive SAL mice show a greater enhancement of stereotyped behavior in response to apomorphine than nonaggressive LAL mice.[23] This observation is of particular interest, inasmuch as a series of experiments was recently completed using rats genetically selected for apomorphine susceptibility. In 1985, Alexander Cools of the Catholic University of Nijmegen, the Netherlands, initiated a breeding program based on pharmacogenetic selection of Wistar rats, using as a criterion stereotypic gnawing induced by the mixed dopamine (D1/D2) receptor agonist, apomorphine. Apomorphine-unsusceptible (apo-unsus) rats, which virtually lacked a gnawing response accounted for about 25% of the total population. Another 25% were apomorphine-susceptible (apo-sus), showing vigorous gnawing in response to the drug. The remainder of the population consisted of rats with an intermediate gnawing score. In each generation the most outspoken apo-sus and apo-unsus rats enrolled a particular breeding procedure to maintain genotypic heterogeneity.[24]

Psychopharmacological studies suggested that the two rat lines represent the extremes in dopamine responsiveness coexisting in a normal rat population.[24] Rats of the two selected lines have considerable variation in behavioral and locomotor responses to stress. Apo-sus rats show fleeing behavior after decisive psychosocial defeat and increased locomotor activity in response to novelty.[24] Along with enhanced apomorphine susceptibility, coselection occurs in the apo-sus rats for an active behavior response adopted during coping with stress. Apo-sus rats show, therefore, many of the characteristics displayed by the SAL mice.

Apo-sus rats have significantly higher tyrosine hydroxylase mRNA (THmRNA) and D2 receptor binding and D1 receptor mRNA levels (D2 receptor mRNA and D1 receptor binding were not different) in the nigrostriatal and tuberoinfundibular pathway, thus providing a neurochemical basis to the line differences.[25] Prolactin release in response to stress is significantly lower in apo-sus rats than their apo-unsus counterparts, which is in line with the prediction from the increased tuberoinfundibular dopamine activity.[26] These findings suggest that the high susceptibility for apomorphine-induced stereotypy is reflected by increases in measures for central dopamine activity. The observations also suggest coselection for differential neuroendocrine reactivity in the two genetically selected lines.

Recent studies showed that under basal morning conditions apo-sus rats had a larger number of corticotropin-releasing hormone (CRH) gene transcripts in paraventricular nucleus (PVN) and a higher corticotropin (ACTH) level in plasma relative to their apo-unsus counterparts.[26,27] However, similar concentrations of circulating CORT were observed in both lines. Subsequently, the line difference in sensitivity of the hypothalamic-pituitary-adrenal (HPA) axis to stress was tested by exposing rats to a novel environment. A relatively enhanced ACTH response was observed in apo-sus rats, suggesting that the sensitivity of the ACTH response to stress was increased. Stress-induced CORT secretion did not show a line difference. In fact, the apo-sus adrenal required much higher ACTH levels to maintain the same total CORT level under basal and stress conditions. Thus, it appears that the apo-sus adrenal is hyporesponsive to ACTH.[26,27]

Stress-induced ACTH levels in apo-sus rats remained elevated longer as compared to apo-unsus animals. Also the plasma total and free CORT levels were significantly elevated for longer time intervals after stress. This reduced the ability of apo-sus animals to terminate stress-induced ACTH, and free CORT responses are indicative of CORT feedback resistance relative to their apo-unsus counterparts. The possible site of this CORT resistance was evaluated by conducting humoral challenge tests of pituitary and adrenocortical function. There was no line difference in the CORT response to exogenous CRH and ACTH, suggesting that the feedback resistance of apo-sus rats resides in the brain.[26,27]

In conclusion, genetic selection of rats for extreme differences in susceptibility of the dopamine system coselects for active versus passive behavioral responses during a challenge. In the neuroendocrine realm, coselection also occurs for extreme differences in stress-induced prolactin and ACTH as well as for corticosteroid feedback efficacy. Accordingly, the increased susceptibility to dopaminergic stimulation during stress is associated with decreased prolactin release and impaired containment of the HPA axis by corticosteroids due to adrenocortical hyporesponsiveness and neuroendocrine feedback resistance.

GENOTYPE, STRESS, AND AGGRESSION

Rat lines were also selected on the basis of fear-conditioned behavior. Roman high avoidance (RHA) rats show rapid acquisition of an avoidance response as opposed to the poorly performing Roman low avoidance (RLA) animals. RHA animals show an enhanced locomotor response to novelty, greater exploration, and more activity and aggression than do RLA rats.[28] RHA animals lack a stress-induced increase in plasma prolactin, have an enhanced ACTH response to stress, but display hyporesponsiveness of the adrenals relative to RLAs.[29] Thus, the selection criterion of avoidance behavior allows coselection for divergence in HPA and prolactin responses to stress.

Upon closer inspection a number of subtle differences are noticeable, confirming the obvious fact that, of course, not exactly the same populations are selected by avoidance behavior, attack latency, and apomorphine susceptibility. For instance, the data on feedback efficiency between the apo-sus and RHA animals do not match and require further study. Yet, the analysis of behavioral and neuroendocrine response patterns suggests that apo-sus, RHA animals, and SAL mice all represent the genetic selection of animals in the fight/flight, active, aggressive category. These subjects are characterized by highly offensive behavior in social confrontations, whereas their counterparts hardly display any aggression. Accordingly, a common genetic background of stress-reaction patterns, coping styles, and aggression is likely.

The two previous sections also emphasized enhanced postsynaptic nigrostriatal dopamine receptor and limbic serotonin receptor properties in aggression-prone rodents. In view of the genetic background of these altered amine receptor functions, it is of interest that, recently, knockout mice became available that had particular genes in amine signaling ablated. Mice with targeted disruption of the tyrosine hydroxylase gene (supplemented with L-dopa in utero) show impaired motor functions due to deficient nigrostriatal dopaminergic pathways, but no data on aggressive behavior are available in these mutants.[30]

Transgenic mice lacking monoamine oxidase (MAO)-A[31] or 5-HT1B gene expression[32] show increased aggressive behavior, reinforcing the notions on the genetic background related to the serotonin system in the manifestation of pathological aggression. Both mutants have in common that serotonergic transmission by way of postsynaptic 5-HT1A receptors is enhanced. This evidence from transgenesis is in line with the outcome of pharmacological and endocrine studies linking aggression with high serotonergic tone. The SAL mice have high limbic 5-HT1A receptor expression.[18] High stress-induced CORT levels enhance serotonergic transmission in limbic pathways.[33–35] Partial 5-HT1 agonists are anti-aggressive, and their action mechanism possibly involves postsynaptic 5-HT1A receptors.[22]

EARLY LIFE EVENTS ALTER BRAIN DEVELOPMENT

Collectively, the previous sections provided strong evidence for a genetic component in precipitation of aggressive behavior. Yet, another line of research has provided increasing evidence for a decisive role of early experience in programming of circuits underlying stress-response patterns in adult life. Below we first outline the features of the developing stress system, and next we will review the impact of early experience. The progress in this field is due to the pioneering studies of Seymour Levine.[36] More recently, the contributions of Michael Meaney and colleagues (this volume) have been important for linking the 5-HT system[38] with stress hormones in shaping the brain's ability to manage stress.[37]

Between postnatal days 4 and 14 the HPA axis in the rat is hyporesponsive to stress. During this stress-hyporesponsive period (SHRP) circulating CORT and ACTH levels are extremely low. Stressors that evoke a pronounced CORT response during adulthood are only weakly active in the infant. Corticosteroid-binding globulin (CBG) levels are not detectable during the SHRP, and the very low CORT levels are in the free form.[38]

The cause of the diminished responsiveness to stress during the SHRP appears to be multifactorial and depends on specific internal (endocrine, neural) and external (maternal) inputs to maintain overall quiescence. The major rate-limiting factors in HPA activation appear at the level of the brain and the adrenal.[39] Under most conditions, however, acutely elevated ACTH or exogenously administered ACTH do not trigger an adrenocortical response. The proximal cause of the SHRP lies, therefore, at the level of the adrenal due to reduced sensitivity to ACTH.

Studies using maternal separation have demonstrated that the mother regulates HPA responses in the infant. These HPA responses slowly develop as a function of time after maternal separation. A normally reared pup does not display CORT responses to saline, novelty, and acute maternal separation, unless maternal deprivation is prolonged for at least 8, and up to 24, hours. The phenomenon appears to involve priming (sensitization) of the adrenal to ACTH and stress. Besides duration, also the age of the infant exposed to maternal separation causes effects on HPA activity. The ACTH and CORT responses to ether, novelty, and saline injection immediately following 24 hours of maternal deprivation are larger at 9, 12, and 16 days of age, than at day 3.[36,40]

Maternal deprivation also revealed which factors actually are responsible for neonatal activation of the HPA axis during the SHRP. It appeared that tactile stimulation suppresses neural pathways involved in suppression of ACTH release. Feeding has yet other effects, which are predominantly peripheral, as demonstrated from the enhanced adrenocortical responsiveness following maternal deprivation.[36,41,42] Brief repeated daily separations (handling) followed by intensified sensory stimulation by the mother facilitates maturation of specific neural (limbic) pathways.[36,37] By contrast, a single 24-h period of maternal deprivation evokes, during the SHRP, increased CORT at a time the hormone level otherwise would be low and unperturbed.

PERMANENT STRESS SYSTEM EFFECTS OF EARLY EXPERIENCE

During development, maternal behavior ensures a quiescent stress response system in the newborn rat, which is characterized by low and constant CORT levels. There is now convincing evidence that altered mother-pup interaction has the ability to alter brain development and, subsequently, behavioral and physiological responses in later life. We have known for many years that enhanced sensory stimulation evoked by the handling procedure advances the maturation of the stress system.[43,44] During adulthood and senescence, handled animals show lower CORT levels in response to stress and improved cognitive functions in spatial learning.[45] By contrast, if daily separations are increased to 3 hours per day during the SHRP, the outcome for stress-induced HPA activation and cognition is the opposite. Such daily-deprived animals show hypercorticism and poor performance in spatial learning.[46]

As pointed out in the previous section, recent research using the 24-h deprivation paradigm has revealed some aspects of the underlying mechanism responsible for programming the stress system. The disruption of the SHRP causes inappropriate high levels of CORT, which are thought to interfere with normal brain development. Steroid hormones have profound and permanent effects on the differentiating nervous system. Such permanent steroid effects persist in adulthood and senescence. This is known for testosterone. Administration of testosterone during postnatal days 2 to 4 masculinizes brain and behavior[47] (after intracellular conversion to estradiol), which has profound effects on aggression.

During development CORT administration has permanent effects on growth and differentiation of the brain. The steroid inhibits protein synthesis, glucose uptake, neurogenesis, and gliogenesis. Neuronal "birthdays" are altered, and myelinogenesis, formation of dendritic spines, axonal growth, and synaptogenesis are retarded.[48] CORT is critical for neurotransmitter phenotype. For instance, without glucocorticoid receptors (GR) (in the homozygous mutant with targeted disruption of GR), the adrenal medulla is poorly developed.[49]

Thus, depending on the duration of maternal separation, the infant may experience changing effects of maternal sensory stimulation and/or CORT. As adults the consequence of short- and long-term maternal deprivation is strikingly different, inasmuch as emotional and adrenocortical reactivity seem oppositely affected. Other experiments have shown that the timing of the 24-h deprivation is also critical. The outcome of 24-h deprivation at three days of age is opposite of deprivation at 11 days, if ACTH levels at 20 days are taken as the index (van Oers, de Kloet, and Levine, manuscript in preparation). Deprivation at three days increases ACTH levels at 20 days.[50] As young adults (two months), the mother-deprived rats have reduced basal CRH mRNA expression. However, basal plasma ACTH and CORT levels are significantly elevated. Adrenal weight is also increased.[50]

Long-lasting effects of maternal deprivation have also been found on CORT receptor levels. Twenty-four hours of deprivation at postnatal day three resulted in reduced GR mRNA in PVN and anterior pituitary and reduced hippocampal GR binding in male adult rats. The reduced GR expression in the PVN is consistent with the feedback resistance, whereas the ensuing hypercorticism would explain GR down-regulation in the hippocampus due to overexposure to the steroid.[50] Interestingly, adult female rats showed the opposite effect, and an increased hippocampal GR number was found after deprivation on day three.[51] Sex differences were also noticed in rat pups exposed to endotoxin treatment on day three and analyzed as adults for basal and stress-induced HPA activation.[52]

DOES A TRAUMATIC EARLY LIFE EVENT PROGRAM AGGRESSIVE BEHAVIOR?

This section is short, because, to our knowledge, in rodents there are no data that have directly addressed the question on aggressive behavior precipitated by early life events. Yet, the animal experiments described above provide evidence, allowing some speculation. In our experiments we showed that male rat pups deprived at postnatal day three showed as adults increased susceptibility for apomorphine, as judged from the increased stereotyped behavior after administration of the drug. These animals showed hypercorticism and increased nigrostriatal dopamine responsiveness.[50,53] This finding raises the interesting point that the genetic selection for apomorphine susceptibility actually selects for a phenotype that is programmed by altered stress system activity due to the effect of early experience. Indeed, when the development of the nigrostriatal dopamine system and the HPA axis was examined in the apo-sus and unsus rat lines, HPA activity was increased after 20 days at a time dopamine was not affected.[53,54]

These data show that there is conclusive evidence from experiments in rats that the early experience of maternal deprivation permanently affects stress regulation.[45,50,55] The duration and frequency of the separation as well as the age and the sex of the pup appear to determine the outcome of the maternal deprivation procedures. The significance of these findings in relation to coping styles and aggressive behavior of the SAL, apo-sus, and RHA animals still needs to be explored.

CONCLUDING REMARKS

The idea that aggression may have a heritable basis touches upon fundamental scientific and social questions. The scientific questions concern the mechanisms of selection, the brain mechanisms involved, and the role of the developmental processes. The social questions concern strategies and time windows for prevention and intervention. It is generally assumed that aggressive behavior is caused by an interaction of biological, environmental, and social factors.[56] Therefore, it seems unlikely that a single gene would be responsible for the expression of aggressive behavior or that a particular gene would be exclusively involved in the expression of aggression. This concept is supported by the fact that selection on aggression also selects on active coping strategies accompanied by a typical endocrine phenotype in tree shrews,[4] monkeys,[5] and humans [6] and is described in detail here for mouse and rat lines.

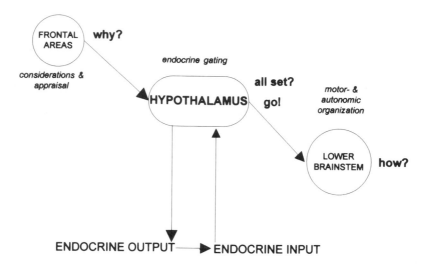

FIGURE 1. Functional integration scheme of the hypothalamus. The hypothalamus receives sensory input censored by the frontal areas, for example, frontal cortex, hippocampus, amygdala, septum, striatum, basal forebrain, and cerebral cortex. These areas contain neural circuits underlying appraisal of the sensory stimulus. The hypothalamus processes this information, and information processing depends on the neuroendocrine context. Lower brain-stem areas, for example, the substantia grisea centralis, ventral tegmental area, substantia nigra, formatio reticularis, and nucleus raphe anterior are involved in the organization of specific subroutines required for aggressive behavior.

In rats, very little work has been done on the HPA axis and aggression, as most work has concentrated on sex steroids and aggression.[47] However, it is known that CORT rises during fights in losers (intruders) and winners (residents)[16,56,57] but that winners show a much more effective termination of the CORT response.[16] Prolactin also rises, but mainly in losers, suggesting some defect in dopaminergic suppression (re, all aggressive mouse and rat lines had blunted prolactin responses). There is some evidence suggesting that CORT are involved in the expression of aggression in rats,[58,59] inasmuch as hypothalamic implants of CORT dramatically increase aggression in golden hamsters.[60] Taken together, these findings clearly suggest that studying aggression as a component of more general coping strategies may be worthwhile, conceptually as well as experimentally. This view calls for studies in the neuroendocrine context (FIG. 1).

The recent study on a so-called "aggression gene" in humans[61] can also be viewed as evidence for a linkage between aggressive behavior and general mechanisms involved in active coping with stressors. The males not only assault, but they are also rapists and arsonists. Moreover, the evidence presented shows that such aggressive episodes are often precipitated by failure to cope with perceived stressors.[61] Interestingly, the aggression gene encodes for an enzyme (MAO-A) breaking down serotonin and noradrenaline. As pointed out previously, mutant mice having the MAO-A gene ablated display aggressive behavior as well.[31]

Retrospective studies have clearly established the effects of childhood abuse and neglect on adult violent and criminal behavior in humans. Yet, despite slogans like "violence begets violence" or "the cycle of violence," the majority of abused and neglected children do not become violent.[62-64] How such individual differences arise is not clear (why some individuals are more vulnerable than others) and cannot be easily assessed in humans. Consequently, studies are few, and defining vulnerable populations and successful intervention programs has been difficult.[64] However, in a recent study, Scarpa and Kolko[65] found that children who "internalized" their abuse experiences were more likely to become aggressive. This was especially the case in those children who responded with increased cortisol in saliva following a provocative computer task. These findings suggest that aggressive behavior arises as a result of an interaction of biological and developmental factors.

Developmental studies on the effect of early neglect, violence, and stress on aggressive behavior and brain mechanisms later in life are rare. The available knowledge on aggressive brain mechanisms may not allow such studies yet. However, conceiving aggression as a component of a mechanism involved in active coping with stressors may open new ways to study interactions between genetic background and early experience in aggression. The much more extensive knowledge of the neuroendocrine mechanisms involved in the response to stressors has made it possible to define specific developmental factors that affect behavioral and endocrine responsiveness later in life.[36-44] A similar approach could be applied in aggression research, which would ultimately allow us to define windows of opportunity for more successful interventions and therapies.

ACKNOWLEDGMENT

We greatly appreciate the editorial assistance of Ms. Ellen M. Heidema.

REFERENCES

1. HENRY, J. P. & P. M. STEPHENS. 1977. Health and the environment: A sociobiological approach to medicine. Springer Verlag. Berlin, Germany.
2. ENGEL, G. L. & A. H. SCHMALE. 1972. Conservation-withdrawal: A primary regulatory process for organic homeostasis. *In* Physiology, Emotions and Psychosomatic Illness. R. Porter & J. Knight, Eds.: **8:** 57–76. CIBA Foundation Symposium. Elsevier Science Publishers. New York.
3. CANNON, W. B. 1915. Bodily changes in pain, hunger, fear and rage. Appelton. New York.
4. FUCHS, E., H. UNO & G. FLUGGE. 1995. Chronic psychosocial stress induces morphological alterations in hippocampal neurons of the tree shrew. Brain Res. **673:** 275–282.
5. BOTCHIN, M. B., J. R. KAPLAN, S. B. MANUCK & J. J. MANN. 1993. Low versus high prolactin responders to fenfluramine challenge: Marker of behavioural differences in adult male cynomolgus macaques. Neuropsychopharmacology **9**(3): 93–99.
6. COCCARO, E. F., L. J. SIEVER, H. M. KLAR, G. MAURER, K. COCHRANE, T. B. COOPER, R. C. MOHS & K. L. DAVIS. 1989. Serotonergic studies in patients with personality disorders. Arch. Gen. Psychiatry **46:** 587–599.
7. SIEVER, L. & R. L. TRESTMAN. 1993. The serotonin system and aggressive personality disorder. Int. Clin. Psychopharmacol. **8** suppl. 2: 33–39.
8. BOHUS, B., R. F. BENUS, D. S. FOKKEMA, J. M. KOOLHAAS, C. NYAKAS, G. A. VAN OORTMERSSEN, A. J. A. PRINS, A. J. H. DE RUITER, A. J. W. SCHEURINK & A. B. STEFFENS. 1987. Neuroendocrine states and behavioral and physiological responses. Progr. Brain Res. **72:** 57–71.

9. BOHUS, B. 1993. Physiological functions of vasopressin in behavioural and autonomic responses to stress. *In* Brain Functions of Neuropeptides: A Current View. J. P. H. Burbach & D. de Wied, Eds.: 15–41. The Parthenon Publishing Group. New York.
10. BENUS, R. F., B. BOHUS, J. M. KOOLHAAS & G. A. VAN OORTMERSSEN. 1989. Behavioral strategies of aggressive and non-aggressive male mice in active avoidance. Behav. Processes **20:** 1–12.
11. BENUS, R. F., B. BOHUS, J. M. KOOLHAAS & G. A. VAN OORTMERSSEN. 1991. Heritable variation for aggression as a reflection of individual coping strategies. Experientia **47:** 1008–1019.
12. BENUS, R. F., B. BOHUS, J. M. KOOLHAAS & G. A. VAN OORTMERSSEN. 1990. Behavioural strategies of aggressive and non-aggressive male mice in response to inescapable shock. Behav. Processes **21:** 127–141.
13. SLUYTER, F., S. M. KORTE, B. BOHUS & G. A. VAN OORTMERSSEN. 1996. Behavioral stress response of genetically selected aggressive and non-aggressive wild house mice in the shock-probe/defensive burying test. Pharmacol. Biochem. Behav. In press.
14. VAN OORTMERSSEN, G. A. & J. BUSSER. 1989. Studies in wild house mice. III: Disruptive selection on aggression as a possible force in evolution. *In* House Mouse Aggression: A model for understanding the evolution of social behavior. P. F. Brain, F. Mainardi & S. Parmigniani. Eds.: 87–116. Harwood Academic Publishers. London, U.K.
15. FOKKEMA, D. F., K. SMIT, J. VAN DER GUGTEN & J. M. KOOLHAAS. 1988. A coherent pattern among social behavior, blood pressure, corticosterone and catecholamine measures in individual male rats. Physiol. Behav. **42:** 485–489.
16. SCHUURMAN, T. 1980. Hormonal correlates of agonistic behavior in adult male rats. *In* Adaptive capabilities of the nervous system. P. S. McConnell, G. J. Boer, H. J. Romijn, N. E. van de Poll & M. A. Corner, Eds. Progress in Brain Research. Vol **53:** 415–420. Elsevier Science Publ. Amsterdam, the Netherlands.
17. SAPOLSKY, R. M. 1990. Stress in the wild. Sci. Am. **262:** 116–123.
18. KORTE, S. M., O. C. MEIJER, E. R. DE KLOET, B. BUWALDA, J. KEIJSER, F. SLUYTER, G. A. VAN OORTMERSSEN & B. BOHUS. Increased number of 5HT1A receptor mRNA and binding sites in dorsal hippocampus of aggressive house mice. Brain Res. In press.
19. KRUK, M. R. 1991. Ethology and pharmacology of hypothalamic aggression. Neurosci. Biobehav. Rev. **15:** 527–538.
20. OLIVIER, B., J. MOS & D. L. RASMUSSEN. 1990. Offensive aggressive paradigms. Rev. Drug Metab. Drug Interact. **8**(1–2): 34–55.
21. KRUK, M. R., A. M. VAN DER POEL, J. H. C. M. LAMMERS, TH. HAGG, A. M. D. M. DE HEY & S. OOSTWEGEL. 1987. Ethopharmacology of hypothalamic aggression in the rat. *In* Ethopharmacology of Agonistic Behaviour in Humans and Animals. B. Olivier, J. Mos & D. F. Brain, Eds.: 33–45. Martinus Nijhoff Publishers. Dordrecht, the Netherlands.
22. SIJBESMA, H., J. SCHIPPER, E. R. DE KLOET, J. MOS, H. VAN AKEN & B. OLIVIER. 1991. Post-synaptic 5-HT1 receptors and offensive aggression in rats: A combined behavioural and autoradiographic study of eltoprazine. Pharmacol. Biochem. Behav. **38:** 447–458.
23. BENUS, R. F., B. BOHUS, J. M. KOOLHAAS & G. A. VAN OORTMERSSEN. 1991. Behavioural differences between artificially selected aggressive and nonaggressive mice: Response to apomorphine. Behav. Brain Res. **43:** 203–208.
24. COOLS, A. R., R. BRACHTEN, D. HEEREN, A. WILLEMEN & A. ELLENBROEK. 1990. Search after neurobiological profile of individual-specific features of Wistar rats. Brain Res. Bull. **24:** 49–69.
25. ROTS, N. Y., A. R. COOLS, A. BÉROD, P. VOORN, W. ROSTÈNE & E. R. DE KLOET. 1996. Rats bred for enhanced apomorphine susceptibility have elevated tyrosine hydroxylase mRNA and dopamine D2 receptor binding sites in nigrostriatal and tuberoinfundibular dopamine system. Brain Res. **710:** 189–196.
26. ROTS, N. Y., A. R. COOLS, M. S. OITZL, J. DE JONG, W. SUTANTO & E. R. DE KLOET. 1996. Divergent prolactin and pituitary-adrenal activity in rats selectively bred for different dopamine responsiveness. Endocrinology **137:** 1678–1686.

27. ROTS, N. Y., A. R. COOLS, J. DE JONG & E. R. DE KLOET. 1995. Corticosteroid feedback resistance in rats genetically selected for increased dopamine responsiveness. J. Neuroendocrinol. **7:** 153–161.
28. SIEGEL, J., D. F. SISSON & P. DRISCOLL. 1993. Augmenting and reducing of visual evoked potentials in Roman high- and low avoidance rats. Physiol. Behav. **54:** 707–711.
29. WALKER, C. D., R. W. RIVEST, M. J. MEANEY & M. L. AUBERT. 1989. Differential activation of the pituitary-adrenocortical axis after stress in the rat: Use of two genetically selected lines (Roman low- and high-avoidance rats as model). J. Endocrinol. **123:** 477–485.
30. ZHOU-NATURE, Q.-Y., C. J. QUALFE & R. D. PALMITER. 1995. Targeted disruption of the tyrosine hydroxylase gene reveals that catecholamines are required for mouse fetal development. Nature **374:** 640–643.
31. CASES, O., I. SEIF, J. GRIMSBY, P. GASPAR, K. CHEN, S. POURNIN, U. MULLER, M. AQUET, C. BABINET, J. C. SHIH & E. DE MAEYER. 1995. Aggressive behavior and altered amounts of brain serotonin and norepinephrine in mice lacking MAO-A. Science **268:** 1763–1766.
32. SAUDOU, F., D. A. AMARA, A. DIERICH, M. LEMEUR, S. RAMBOZ, L. SEGU, M.-C. BUHOF & R. HEN. 1994. Enhanced aggressive behavior in mice lacking 5-HT1B receptor. Science **265:** 1875–1878.
33. DE KLOET, E. R., G. L. KOVÁCS, G. SZABO, G. TELEGDY, B. BOHUS & D. H. G. VERSTEEG. 1982. Decreased serotonin turnover shortly after adrenalectomy: Selective normalization after corticosterone substitution. Brain Res. **239:** 659–663.
34. JOËLS, M. & E. R. DE KLOET. 1992. Coordinative mineralocorticoid and glucocorticoid receptor-mediated control of responses to serotonin in rat hippocampus. Neuroendocrinology **55:** 344–350.
35. MEIJER, O. C. & E. R. DE KLOET. 1995. A role for the mineralocorticoid receptor in a rapid and transient suppression of hippocampal 5-HT1A receptor mRNA by corticosterone. J. Neuroendocrinol. **7:** 653–657.
36. LEVINE, S. 1994. The ontogeny of the hypothalamic-pituitary-adrenal axis: The influence of maternal factors. *In* Brain Corticosteroid Receptors: Studies on the Mechanism, Function, and Neurotoxicity of Corticosterone Action. E. R. de Kloet, E. C. Azmitia & P. W. Landfield, Eds.: **746:** 275–288. Annals of the New York Academy of Sciences. New York.
37. MEANEY, M. J., J. DORIO, D. FRANCIS, S. LAROQUE, D. O'DONNELL, J. W. SMYTHE, S. SHARMA & B. TANNENBAUM. 1994. Environmental regulation of the development of glucocorticoid receptor systems in the rat forebrain: The Role of Serotonin. E. R. de Kloet, E. C. Azmitia & P. W. Landfield, Eds.: **746:** 260–274. Annals of the New York Academy of Sciences. New York.
38. DE KLOET, E. R., P. ROSENFELD, J. A. M. VAN EEKELEN, W. SUTANTO & S. LEVINE. 1988. Stress, glucocorticoids and brain development. *In* Progress in Brain Research. G. J. Boer, M. G. P. Feenstra, M. Mirmiram & D. F. Swaab, Eds.: 101–120. Elsevier Science Publishers. Amsterdam, the Netherlands.
39. ROSENFELD, P., D. SUCHECKI & S. LEVINE. 1992. Multifactorial regulation of the hypothalamic-pituitary-adrenal axis during development. Neurosci. Biobehav. Rev. **16:** 353–368.
40. LEVINE, S., S. D. HUCHTON, S. G. WIENER & P. ROSENFELD. 1991. Time course of the effect of maternal deprivation on the hypothalamic-pituitary-adrenal axis in the infant rat. Dev. Psychobiol. **24:** 547–558.
41. ROSENFELD, P., J. EKSTRAND, E. OLSON, D. SUCHECKI & S. LEVINE. 1993. Maternal regulation of adrenocortical activity in the infant rat: Effects of feeding. Dev. Psychobiol. **26:** 261–277.
42. SUCHECKI, D., D. MOZZAFFARIAN, S. G. WIENER & P. ROSENFELD. 1994. Effects of maternal deprivation on the ACTH stress response in the infant rat. Neuroendocrinology **57:** 204–212.
43. LEVINE, S. 1957. Infantile experience and resistance to physiological stress. Science **126:** 405–406.

44. HOFER, M. 1983. On the relationship between attachment and separation processes in infancy. *In* Early Development. P. R. Emtion, Ed.: **99:** 199–219. Academic Press. New York.

45. ISSA, A. M., W. ROWE, S. GAUTHIER & M. J. MEANEY. 1992. Hypothalamic-pituitary-adrenal activity in aged, cognitively impaired, and unimpaired rats. J. Neurosci. **10:** 3247–3254.

46. PLOTSKY, P. & M. J. MEANEY. 1993. Early, postnatal experience alters hypothalamic corticotropin-releasing factor (CRF) mRNA, median eminence CRF content and stress-induced release in adult rats. Mol. Brain Res. **18:** 195–200.

47. SIMON, N., S. F. LU, S. E. MCKENNA, X. CHEN & A. C. CLIFFORD. 1993. Sexual dimorfisms in regulatory systems for aggression. *In* The Development of Sex Differences and Similarities in Behaviour. M. Haug *et al.*, Eds.: 389–408. Kluwer Academic Publishers. Dordrecht, the Netherlands.

48. BOHN, M. C. 1984. Glucocorticoid-induced teratologies of the nervous system. *In* Neurobehavioural Teratology. J. Yanai, Ed.: 365–387. Elsevier Science Publishers. New York.

49. COLE, T. J., J. A. BLENDY, A. P. MONAGHAN, K. KRIEGLSTEIN, W. SCHMID, A. GUZZI, G. FANTUZZI, E. HUMMLER, K. UNSICKER & G. SCHÜTZ. 1995. Targeted disruption of the glucocorticoid receptor gene blocks adrenergic chromaffin cell development and severely retards lung maturation. Genes & Dev. **9:** 1608–1621.

50. ROTS, N. Y., J. DE JONG, J. O. WORKEL, S. LEVINE, A. R. COOLS & E. R. DE KLOET. Neonatally deprived rats have as adults elevated basal pituitary-adrenal activity and enhanced susceptibility to apomorphine. J. Neuroendocrinol. In press.

51. SUTANTO, W., P. ROSENFELD, E. R. DE KLOET & S. LEVINE. 1996. Long-term effects of neonatal maternal deprivation and ACTH on hippocampal mineralocorticoid and glucocorticoid receptors. Dev. Brain Res. **92:** 156–163.

52. SHANKS, N., S. LAROCQUE & M. J. MEANEY. 1995. Neonatal endotoxin exposure alters the development of the hypothalamic-pituitary-adrenal axis: Early illness and later responsivity to stress. J. Neurosci. **15:** 376–384.

53. ROTS, N. Y. 1995. Dopamine and stress: Studies with genetically selected rat lines. PhD Thesis. Leiden University, the Netherlands.

54. ROTS, N. Y., J. O. WORKEL, A. R. COOLS & E. R. DE KLOET. 1996. Development of divergence in dopamine responsiveness in genetically selected rat lines is preceded by changes in hypothalamic-pituitary-adrenal activity. Dev. Brain Res. **92:** 164–171.

55. MACCARI, S., P. V. PIAZZA, M. KABBAJ, A. BARBAZANGES, H. SIMON & M. LEMOAL. 1995. Adoption reverses the long-term impairment in glucocorticoid feedback induced by prenatal stress. J. Neurosci. **15:** 110–116.

56. ERON, L. D. & N. GUERRA. Poverty and violence. *In* Human Aggression: Biological and Social Roots. S. Feshbach & J. Zagrodzka, Eds. Plenum Press. New York. In press.

57. DIJKSTRA, H., F. J. H. TILDERS, M. A. HIEHLE & P. G. SMELIK. 1992. Hormonal reactions to fighting in rat colonies: Prolactin rises during defense, not during offense. Physiol. Behav. **51:** 961–968.

58. HALLER, J. & I. BARNA. 1995. Hormonal and metabolic responses during psychosocial stimulation in aggressive and non-aggressive rats. Psychoneuroendocrinology **20:** 65–74.

59. HALLER, J., I. BARNA & J. L. KOVÁCS. 1994. Alpha-2 adrenoceptor blockade, pituitary hormones and agonistic interactions in rats. Psychopharmacology **115:** 478–484.

60. HAYDEN-HIXSON, D. M. & G. F. FERRIS. 1991. Steroid-specific regulation of agonistic responding in the anterior hypothalamus of male hamsters. Physiol. Behav. **50:** 793–799.

61. BRUNNER, H. G., M. R. NELEN, P. VAN ZANDVOORT, N. G. G. M. ABELING, A. H. VAN GENNIP, E. C. WOLTERS, M. A. KUIPER, H. H. ROPERS & B. A. VAN OOST. 1993. X-linked borderline mental retardation with prominent behavioural disturbance: Phenotype, genetic localization, and evidence for disturbed monoamine metabolism. Am. J. Hum. Genet. **52:** 1032–1039.

62. WIDOM, C. S. 1989. The cycle of violence. Science **244:** 160–166.

63. LUNZ, B. K. & C. S. WIDOM. 1994. Antisocial personality disorder in abused and neglected children grown-up. Am. J. Psychiatry **151**(50): 670–674.
64. GELLES, R. J. & J. R. CONTE. 1990. Domestic violence and sexual abuse of children: A review of research in the eighties. J. Marriage Fam. **52:** 1045–1058.
65. SCARPA, A. & D. J. KOLKO. 1996. Aggression in physically abused children: The role of distress-proneness. This volume.

Physically Aggressive Boys from Age 6 to 12 Years

Their Biopsychosocial Status at Puberty[a]

RICHARD E. TREMBLAY[b,d] AND BENOIST SCHAAL[c]

[b]Research Unit on Children's Psychosocial Maladjustment
University of Montreal
750 Gouin East
Montreal, H1C 1A6, Canada

[c]Laboratoire du comportement animal
Station de physiologie de la reproduction
CNRS URA 1291
37380 Nouzilly, France

Longitudinal studies of development during adolescence have generated similar growth curves for physical and psychosocial variables. According to Tanner,[1] the French naturalist, Buffon, published the first longitudinal study of the growth of a child in a supplement to his famous *Histoire Naturelle*. The data on growth in height was collected by Count de Montbeillard on his son from his birth (1759) to age 18 years. It showed the characteristic acceleration of growth in height from early to midadolescence, which has been labeled the "growth spurt." This acceleration is followed by a rapid deceleration until the end of physical growth around 18 years of age. More recently, a similar curve has been published for the prevalence of serious violence by males between 12 and 27 years of age in the United States. From a national longitudinal study of delinquent behavior, Elliott[2] shows that the frequency of serious violent behaviors increases sharply from age 12 to age 17 and then decreases as sharply from 17 to 22 years of age.

A number of investigators have suggested that these two curves are the product of the increase in testosterone levels during puberty.[3–5] Male plasma testosterone increases sharply from ages 12 to 18 years, and then levels off.[6] It is clear that testosterone has a direct impact on physical growth during adolescence;[7] however, the impact of testosterone on violent behavior is less clear. Although one study showed that testosterone levels during adolescence were correlated with self-reported responses to provocation,[8] there is no clear evidence that the increase in testosterone level during adolescence increases the likelihood of serious physically violent behavior.

[a] This work was made possible by Grants from the following sources: Quebec Council for Social Research (CQRS), Quebec City; Quebec Funds for Research Training and Research Support (FCAR), Quebec City; Social Sciences and Humanities Research Council of Canada (SSHRCC), Ottawa; The National Health Research and Development Program (NHRDP), Ottawa; and the Program on Human Development and Criminal Behavior at the Harvard School of Public Health, Cambridge, MA.

[d] Tel: (514) 385-2525; fax: (514) 385-5739; e-mail: gripret@ere.umontreal.ca.

To better understand the association between biological and psychosocial development during adolescence, we need to take into account the growth patterns of these different dimensions during childhood. It is clear that physically violent behaviors do not appear suddenly during adolescence. Longitudinal studies of aggressive behavior indicate that the relative level of physical aggression within samples of males are highly stable from 2 years of age to adulthood.[9-14] This stability is also highlighted by the weak impact of interventions aimed at disruptive children and delinquent youths.[15] To find effective interventions we need to understand the processes that foster this stability.

In addition to the lack of clear evidence that biological maturation during puberty increases the likelihood of physical aggression, there have been suggestions that psychosocial factors during childhood could have an impact on biological maturation during adolescence. Belsky et al.[16] and Susman et al.[17,18] have proposed that environmental conditions and behavioral patterns during childhood could have an impact on the onset of pubertal maturation. Interestingly, they predict completely opposite effects. Belsky et al. predict that stressful environments and behavior disorders during childhood will lead to early onset of puberty, whereas Susman et al. predict that the same conditions will lead to a late onset of puberty. Both acceleration and delay of pubertal maturation could, in turn, have negative or positive consequences on psychosocial adjustment during adolescence.[19]

The aim of this paper is to describe the developmental course, during puberty, of biological and psychosocial variables for groups of boys who showed extreme behavioral patterns from their entry into kindergarten to the end of elementary school, at the threshold of puberty. This description cannot confirm causal pathways, but it can indicate to what extent behavior patterns during childhood can predict specific developmental courses during adolescence, and to what extent the predictions are equally applicable to biological and psychosocial maturation.

Physical aggression and behavioral inhibition were chosen to categorize the behavioral patterns during childhood for two different reasons. First, they are both basic behavioral dimensions that have been shown to be highly stable during childhood and adolescence.[9,13,20,21] Second, in most personality theories these two dimensions are orthogonal;[22-24] thus, they may have different predictive values for later development. Susman et al. argue that childhood behavior problems should delay pubertal maturation because they activate adrenal hormones, which in turn inhibit gonadal hormones responsible for the onset of pubertal maturation. It can be hypothesized that this process would be most likely in boys who show high levels of behavioral inhibition during childhood. On the other hand, the hypothesis by Belsky et al., that behavioral problems would accelerate the onset of puberty, should be most likely in physically aggressive boys without behavioral inhibition. In this case, gonadal hormones would be stimulated without the inhibiting effect of adrenal hormones.

Physical aggression and behavioral inhibition during childhood have also been linked to different and sometimes similar psychosocial outcomes during adolescence and adulthood. For example, physical aggression during childhood has systematically been shown to predict later criminal behavior.[11,12,14] Behavioral inhibition, however, sometimes appears to be a protective factor for criminal behavior,[25,26] whereas at other times it appears to increase the likelihood of antisocial behavior.[27,28] The interplay between these two behavioral dimensions as precursors of biological and psychosocial processes during adolescence obviously needs to be clarified.

METHODS

Subjects

The subjects were selected from a longitudinal study of boys first assessed at the end of their kindergarten year in 1984 and followed since then with yearly assessments.[29] The kindergarten boys (N = 1161) were attending 53 schools in low socioeconomic areas of Montréal. To control for cultural effects, only those with parents born in Canada, Caucasian and French-speaking, were retained (N = 1037). Four groups of subjects with extreme behavioral patterns were created using teacher ratings of physical aggression and anxiety with the Social Behavior Questionnaire[30] at ages 6, 10, 11, and 12. Stable aggressive and inhibited (AI; N = 47) were rated above the 70th percentile on the physical aggression and anxiety scales at age 6 and on at least two of the three other years. Stable aggressive and not inhibited (ANI; N = 19) were rated above the 70th percentile on the physical aggression scale and below the 40th percentile on the anxiety scale at age 6, and for at least two of the three other years. Stable inhibited and not aggressive (INA; N = 52) were rated above the 70th percentile on the anxiety scale and below the 70th percentile on the physical aggression scale at age 6, and for at least two of the three other years. Finally, stable not aggressive and not inhibited (NANI; N = 57) were rated below the 70th percentile on the physical aggression scale and below the 40th percentile on the anxiety scale at age 6, and on at least two of the three other years. These four groups of boys were thus highly different in their behavioral patterns during elementary school. Although they were drawn from a socioeconomically and culturally homogeneous sample, there were also important differences in their family backgrounds. From TABLE 1 it can be seen that when the boys were in kindergarten the mothers and fathers of the inhibited boys had fewer years in school compared to the uninhibited, the fathers of the aggressive boys had fewer years in school compared to the nonaggressive boys, mothers of the aggressive boys were younger at the birth of their first child compared to the nonaggressive boys, and mothers of the ANI and NANI had higher occupational status jobs compared to mothers of the AI and INA. During their kindergarten year 31.6% of the boys were not living in intact families. Significantly more of the aggressive kindergarten boys were not living in intact families (AI = 45.7%; ANI = 57.9%) compared to the nonaggressive boys (INA = 20.4%; NANI = 12.3%). Overall, the aggressive boys and the inhibited boys were living in families with a higher adversity index (TABLE 1), as defined by the variables described above.[30] The AI had the highest level of family adversity and the NANI had the lowest level.

Instruments and Procedure

Teachers' Behavior Ratings

The Social Behavior Questionnaire (SBQ)[30] was used to obtain physical aggression and behavioral inhibition ratings from homeroom teachers at the end of the school year at ages 6, 10, 11, and 12 years. The physical aggression scale included three items: kicking, biting, or hiting other children; bullying other children; and fighting with other children (mean Cronbach's alpha = .85). The anxiety scale included five items: tended to be fearful or afraid of new things of new situations; worried about many things; cried easily; solitary; stared into space (mean Cron-

TABLE 1. Demographic Characteristics of Samples

Variables	Aggressive Inhibited (AI)	Aggressive Not Inhibited (ANI)	Not Aggressive Inhibited (INA)	Not Aggressive Not Inhibited (NANI)	Total Sample
Years in schools					
Mother[a,c]	9.4[d]	11.8	9.7	11.5	10.5
Father[a,b,c]	9.4	10.4	10.5	11.8	10.6
Occupational SES[e]					
Mother[a,c]	36.9	44.8	37.1	44.2	38.3
Father	37.2	35.1	37.9	42.9	39.3
Age at birth of first child					
Mother[a,b]	21.5	22.8	23.3	23.9	23.3
Father	26.1	26.6	26.8	25.1	26.5

[a] Significant effects, $p < 0.05$.
[b] Main aggressive effect.
[c] Main inhibition effect.
[d] N of subjects varies according to variables.
[e] SES = socioeconomic status.

bach's alpha = .77). The mean correlation between these two dimensions over the four years for the total sample was $r = .16$.

Classroom Status

Boys were considered to be progressing normally in school if at a given age they were in an age-appropriate regular classroom (A-ARC). The reasons for not being in the appropriate classroom could be that they were held back in a previous grade; that they were placed in a special class, or a special school; or placed in an institution. The data were obtained from the official records of the school boards and the ministry of education. Children who are placed out of their A-ARC are at high risk of not finishing high school,[31] whereas those who do not finish high school are at high risk of being in the lowest social classes during adulthood.[32] To some extent, being placed out of an A-ARC is a marker of low social status among your peer group.

Self-reported Delinquency and Sexual Intercourse

In the spring of each year, the boys were visited in school where they answered a questionnaire on school, family, friends, and leisure activities. This questionnaire included seven physically aggressive delinquency items (strong-arm force; gang fights; use of weapon in a fight; fist fights; beating up someone; carrying a weapon; throwing objects at persons; mean alpha = .78), 20 nonphysically aggressive delinquency items (stealing from school, from store, from home; keeping an object worth less than $10; stealing a bicycle; selling stolen goods; keeping an object worth between $10 and $100; stealing objects worth more than $100; breaking and entering; entering without paying; trespassing; taking drugs, alcohol; getting drunk; destroying school material, other material; vandalizing school; destroying objects at home; vandalizing a car; setting a fire; mean alpha = .86), and a question concerning the frequency of sexual intercourse. The delinquency questions were asked yearly from 12 to 16 years of age and referred to delinquent acts committed over the past 12 months. The sexual intercourse question was asked yearly from 13 to 16 years of age. At age 13 they were asked if they ever had sexual intercourse, and at what age. For the years that followed, the question referred to the past year.

Height and Pubertal Status

Each boy's height was measured by the research assistant who visited them at school in the spring of each year between ages 11 and 16 years. The questionnaire that they answered during that session included the questions from the Pubertal Development Scale.[33] The pubertal status is based on body and facial hair development, skin and voice changes, and growth spurt in height. The scale ranks the boys into five stages: prepuberty, beginning puberty, midpuberty, end of puberty, and postpuberty. The same questions were also asked of the mothers. The mean Spearman correlation between the boys' self-evaluations between 13 and 15 years of age and their mothers' was .46.

Family Adversity Index

The index is based on family status (intact, not intact), number of years of schooling for the parents, age of parents at the birth of their first child, and the occupational socioeconomic level of the parents.[30] Data for this index was obtained through a telephone interview with the mother at the end of each boy's kindergarten year.

Statistical Procedures

For dependent variables measured on a continuous scale (height and delinquency) the BMDP 5V procedure was used. For dependent variables measured on a dichotomous scale (classroom status, puberty status, sexual intercourse initiation), the SAS PRO CATMOD procedure was used. To control for differences in family background when the boys entered school, the family adversity index was used as a covariate with the BMDP 5V procedure. The PRO CATMOD procedure does not allow for covariates. Logistic regression was thus used when significant effects were obtained with the PRO CATMOD procedure to test if the significant effects were maintained after having included family adversity as a covariate.

RESULTS

Classroom Status

FIGURE 1 describes the percentage of boys from the total sample (N = 1037) and from each extreme group who were in an A-ARC each year from 7 to 16 years of age. From the total sample curve it is clear that with age more and more boys are placed out of their A-ARC. At age 12, when they should have been in their last year of elementary school, only 62% were in their A-ARC. When the four extreme groups were compared, between ages 12 and 14, with the SAS PRO CATMOD procedure, large significant effects were obtained for a physical aggression main effect (p = 0.004) and a behavioral inhibition main effect (p = 0.001), after having controlled for family adversity. Because these are additive effects, the NANI group had the best school performance, much higher than the average performance of the whole sample, whereas the AI group had the worst performance. Boys who were only aggressive (ANI) did a little better than the whole sample and the INA up to age 15 years.

Growth in Height

FIGURE 2A describes the growth curves for height from 11 to 16 years of age. It is very clear that inhibited boys as a group (AI, INA) were shorter than the mean of the whole sample throughout these early adolescent years, whereas the uninhibited boys as a group (NANI, ANI) were taller than the mean of the whole sample. This was confirmed by a significant main effect (p < 0.05) for inhibited behavior, after having controlled for family adversity. No main effect or interactions involving physical aggression were detected. FIGURE 2B describes the

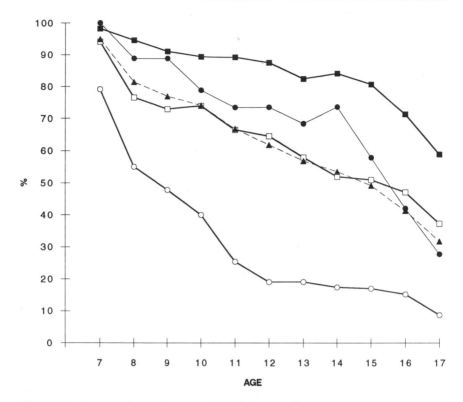

FIGURE 1. Percent who survive in A-ARC. Significant effects: age, aggression, and inhibition. —○—, AI; —●—, ANI; —□—, INA; —■—, NANI; ---▲---, total sample.

growth velocity (spurt) for height from 11 to 16 years of age. This curve represents the height increase (in cm) during a given year. It can be clearly seen that the largest gains in height were made during the boys' 13th and 14th years. The uninhibited boys (ANI, NANI) reached their peak velocity in growth during their thirteenth year, whereas the inhibited boys (AI, NAI) reached their peak velocity in growth one year later. A significant effect for the inhibited classification was obtained, $F(1,153) = 5.84$, $p < 0.02$, when the age at which the boys attained their peak velocity was used as the dependent variable in a 2×2 ANOVA. Family adversity in kindergarten was not significant when it was used as a covariate in an ANCOVA.

Pubertal Status

FIGURE 3 describes the percentages of boys who had reached the midpuberty stage between 11 and 14 years of age. At age 11 years only 26% of the total sample had reached the midpuberty stage, whereas 91% had reached that stage by 14 years of age. A significant interaction of behavioral inhibition by age was obtained from the PRO CATMOD procedure with the data at ages 12, 13, and 14. It can

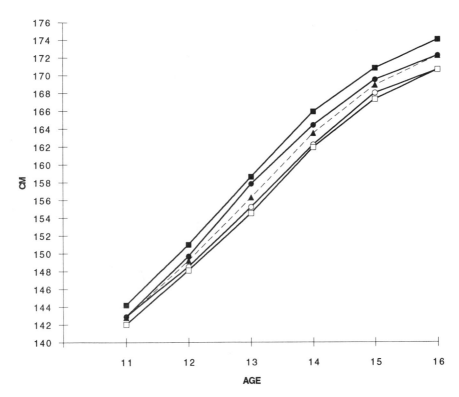

FIGURE 2A. Increase in height from ages 11 to 16 years. Significant effects: inhibition and age. —○—, AI; —●—, ANI; —□—, INA; —■—, NANI; ---▲---, total sample.

be seen from FIGURE 3 that 22% of the NANI boys changed pubertal status between ages 12 and 13 years, so that at age 13 more uninhibited subjects had reached midpuberty compared to inhibited subjects. These results indicate that boys with a history of behavioral inhibition during childhood tend to reach mid-puberty later than those without a history of behavioral inhibition. No significant effects were observed for the physical aggression classification. However, there was a trend for the ANI boys to reach midpuberty earlier than the rest of the sample.

Initiation of Sexual Intercourse

The percentages of boys who had their first sexual intercourse before age 17 are reported on FIGURE 4. It can be seen that 9% of the total sample had their first sexual intercourse before age 13; that percentage had reached 53% before age 17. A clear physical aggression effect can be observed (p < 0.01) from the PRO CATMOD procedure for ages. More boys with a history of physical aggression (ANI and AI) had an early onset of sexual intercourse compared to boys without a history of physical aggression. By 15 and 16 years of age the ANI group had

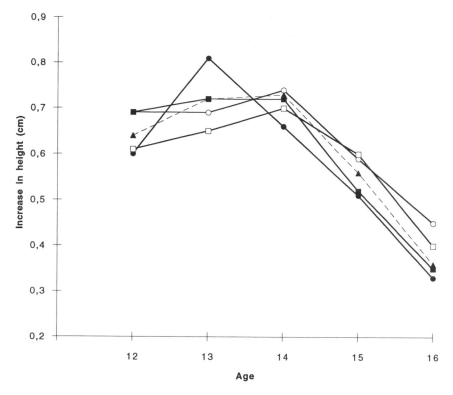

FIGURE 2B. Growth spurt. Significant effects: age and inhibition. Symbols as in FIG. 2A.

the largest percentage of boys who had initiated sexual intercourse. There were no significant effects for behavioral inhibition.

Nonphysically Aggressive Delinquency

FIGURE 5 describes nonphysically aggressive delinquency score means between 12 and 16 years of age for the total sample and the extreme groups. Significant main effects were obtained for the physically aggressive classification ($p < 0.0001$), for the behavioral inhibition classification ($p < 0.03$), and for age ($p < 0.0001$), after having controlled for family adversity when the boys entered kindergarten. As expected, the frequency of delinquent behavior increases from age 12 to age 16 years for the total sample, and for each extreme group. A history of physical aggression during elementary school increases the risk of nonphysically aggressive delinquency during adolescence, whereas a history of behavioral inhibition during elementary school decreases the risk of this type of delinquency during adolescence. As can be seen in FIGURE 5, these effects are additive: the ANI group reported the highest level of nonphysically aggressive delinquency from 12 to 16 years of age, whereas the NANI group reported the lowest levels during this age period.

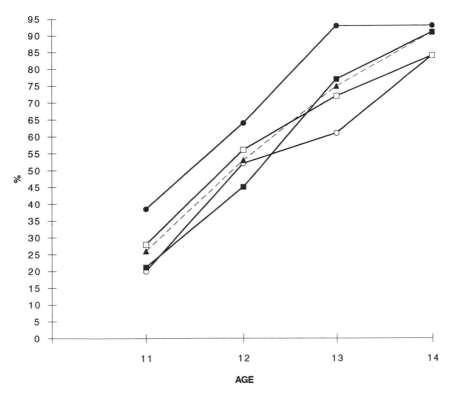

FIGURE 3. Percent who reached midpuberty between ages 11 and 14. Significant effect: inhibition × age. Symbols as in previous FIGURES.

Physically Aggressive Delinquency

Mean scores for self-reported physically aggressive delinquency between 12 and 16 years of age are presented in FIGURE 6. The level of this behavior remained relatively stable over time. A highly significant main effect for history of physically aggressive behavior was observed (p < 0.0001) after having controlled for family adversity, but there were no significant effects for history of behavioral inhibition. It can be clearly seen from FIGURE 6 that the ANI and AI groups systematically reported higher levels of physically aggressive delinquency than the total sample, whereas the NAI and NANI groups systematically reported lower levels of physically aggressive delinquency.

DISCUSSION

The aim of this study was to test with a community sample to what extent extreme patterns of physical aggression and behavioral inhibition during childhood could predict biological and psychosocial maturation during the first half of adolescence. Significant results were obtained for each of the six dependent variables: classroom status, height, pubertal status, initiation of sexual intercourse, nonphysically aggressive delinquency, and physically aggressive delinquency. However, the significant independent variables differed with respect to the types of dependent variables.

The two indices of biological maturation, height and pubertal status, were predicted only by age and behavioral inhibition. No significant effects were observed for the physical aggression classification. From the growth in height data and the pubertal status data, it appears relatively clear that a history of behavioral inhibition during childhood is a marker for slower pubertal maturation. These results give support to the delay of puberty hypothesis by Susman et al.[17,18] rather than the pubertal acceleration hypothesis of Belsky et al.[16] Thus, externalizing behavior problems during childhood, without internalizing behavior problems, would have no impact on the timing of puberty; on the other hand, internalizing behavior problems during childhood, with or without externalizing problems, would tend to delay the pubertal maturation process. This delay could be due to the inhibition of the gonadal hormones by the adrenal hormones.[17,18]

The four indices of psychosocial maturation (classroom status, initiation of sexual intercourse, physically aggressive delinquency, and nonphysically aggressive delinquency) were all predicted by age and the physical aggression classification. The behavioral inhibition classification had a significant impact in two cases,

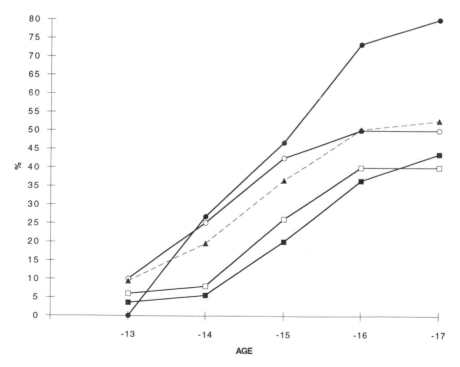

FIGURE 4. Percent with first sexual intercourse before age 17 years. Significant effects: aggression and age. Symbols as in previous FIGURES.

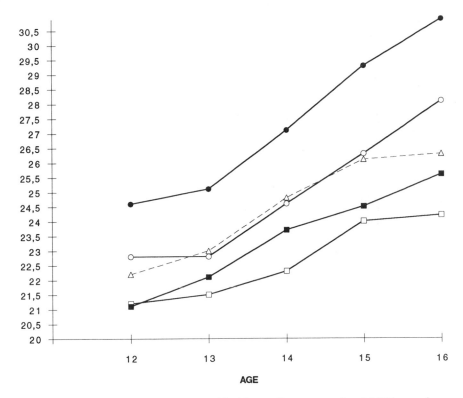

FIGURE 5. Nonaggressive delinquency. Significant effects: aggression, inhibition, and age. Symbols as in previous FIGURES.

classroom status and nonphysically aggressive delinquency. These four psychosocial dimensions vary with age as do the two biological dimensions, but the causal mechanisms appear somewhat different for each dimension.

First, with reference to classroom placement, the linear trend indicates that boys are more and more at risk of not "surviving" in an A-ARC as they grow older. This can be seen as the effect of the increased demands made by the social environment (the school system) as the boys grow older. Those less well equipped from a cognitive and a behavioral perspective are at greater risk of not surviving, and as they grow older the number of individuals who do not survive increases because the adaptive requirements have increased. This is clear from the additive main effects of age, physical aggression, and behavioral inhibition.

Second, with reference to initiation of sexual intercourse, the linear trend indicates, not surprisingly, that, as they grow older, boys will initiate sexual intercourse. This process is obviously dependent on biological maturation; but, although most of the boys had reached midpuberty by the age of 14 years, only half of the boys had initiated sexual intercourse before age 17 years. It is also important to note that, although behavioral inhibition appeared to delay pubertal maturation, it apparently had no significant impact on initiation of sexual intercourse. On the other hand, physical aggression, which had no impact on pubertal maturation, apparently had an impact on initiation of sexual intercourse. Thus, although behaviorally inhibited boys had a slower pubertal maturation, they still could show early initiation of sexual intercourse, especially if they had a history of physical aggression during childhood.

It is tempting to explain the association between physical aggression and early initiation of sexual intercourse by the role of testosterone in both processes, but it would then be hard to explain why AI show early initiation of sexual intercourse before age 13, although they had the lowest percentage of boys who had reached midpuberty at that age, and tended to be shorter in height. Schaal et al.[34] also showed that AI boys had the lowest levels of testosterone at 13 years of age. The results from this study, and those from a previous analysis with different subjects from the same sample,[35] indicate that early initiation of sexual intercourse by boys with externalizing behavior problems is not caused by early pubertal maturation. Boys need to have attained a given level of pubertal maturation to be biologically able to have sexual intercourse, but other factors will determine if and when they do start to have sexual intercourse. A number of such factors are suggested. The boys with externalizing behavior problems are more impulsive, they conform less to rules, and they are less supervised. They may also be more attractive to girls, at least to girls

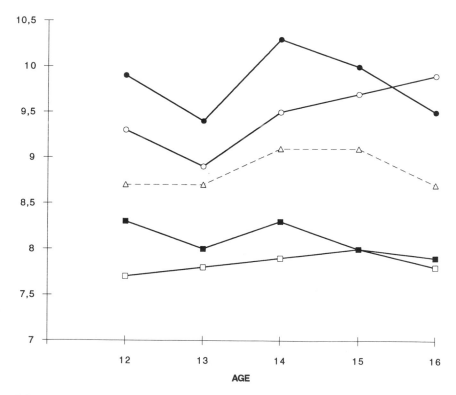

FIGURE 6. Physically aggressive delinquency from age 12 to 16 years. Significant effects: aggression and age. Symbols as in previous FIGURES.

who are also more impulsive, less conforming, and less supervised. Assortative mating would thus increase the likelihood that impulsive, nonconforming, and nonsupervised boys and girls would attract each other and initiate sexual intercourse in early adolescence.

Finally, with reference to delinquent behaviors, the results indicated that a history of aggressive behavior during childhood substantially increases the likelihood of aggressive and nonaggressive delinquency during adolescence. A history of behavioral inhibition acted as a protective factor, but only for nonphysically aggressive delinquency. It appears that boys who are behaviorally inhibited are less likely to take the risk of stealing, vandalizing, and using drugs. However, the inhibited boys who were also physically aggressive (AI) were as likely as the aggressive not inhibited (ANI) to be involved in physically aggressive delinquency. This is a puzzling finding. Why would behavioral inhibition protect from stealing, vandalism, and drug use but not from physical aggression? To answer this question we probably need to understand what leads the AI boys to aggressive behaviors.

It is of interest to note that the age curves for physically aggressive and nonphysically aggressive delinquency are quite different. The latter is much steeper than the former. In fact, although there was a significant age effect, the physically aggressive delinquency curve is almost flat compared to the nonphysically aggressive delinquency curve. These results do not support the hypothesis that the increase in testosterone levels during puberty leads to important increases in physically aggressive delinquency.[3-5] The boys who had the highest levels of physically aggressive delinquency from 12 to 16 years of age were those who already had a pattern of frequent physically aggresive behaviors from 6 to 12 years of age.

To find testosterone levels that have a causal relationship with levels of physical aggression during childhood and adolescence, one would probably need to look back at pre- and postbirth testosterone levels that could, through organizational effects on the neurological system, set behavioral tendencies during early childhood.[36,37] These behavioral tendencies (e.g., active and determined) would interact with the quality of the socializing environment (e.g., authoritative vs. negligent/abusive) and influence the child's ability to learn to control his physically aggressive behavior during the first three or four years of life. Those who do not learn to control would be propelled into a negative feedback loop (sibling, peer, teacher, and parent rejection), which would lead them to associate with similar deviant peers and reject most of the prevailing norms. The deviant behaviors during adolescence would thus be a product of a biopsychosocial developmental history that started during fetal life.

This study was an attempt to look at childhood behavioral precursors of biopsychosocial growth during puberty. The results indicate that most theoretical formulations to date do not anticipate the complexity of the developmental process. However, this study is limited by the fact that it started with kindergarten children. It becomes more and more obvious that the behavioral patterns we observe during childhood and adolescence have been set by processes that started during fetal development. Physical aggression appears during the first year of life[38] and may become a crystallized pattern of response by age two.[10] Longitudinal studies from prebirth to late adolescence, with controls for intergenerational biopsychosocial factors, are obviously needed to sort out the multiple factors that lead to these developmental pathways. Let us hope that the next generation of investigators will include individuals with the curiosity and the perseverance of Count de Montbeillard.

ACKNOWLEDGMENTS

We are grateful to Hélène Beauchesne and Lucille David for coordinating the data collection, to Lyse Desmarais-Gervais for coordinating the data management, to Maria Rosa for data analysis, to Minh Trinh and Sylvie Vézina for the documentation, and to Louise Leblanc for preparing the manuscript.

REFERENCES

1. TANNER, J. M. 1978. Education of physical growth (Second ed.). International Universities Press. New York.
2. ELLIOTT, D. S. 1994. Serious violent offenders: Onset, developmental course and termination: The American Society of Criminology 1993 Presidential Address. Criminology 32(1): 1–21.
3. ELLIS, L. & P. D. COONTZ. 1990. Androgens, brain functioning, and criminality: The neurohormonal foundations of antisociality. In Crime in Biological, Social and Moral Contexts. L. Ellis & H. Hoffman, Eds.: 162–193. Praeger. New York.
4. ARCHER, J. 1991. The influence of testosterone on human aggression. Br. J. Psychol. 82: 1–28.
5. REISS, A. J. & J. A. ROTH, Eds. 1993. Understanding and preventing violence. National Academy Press. Washington, D.C.
6. FOREST, M. G. 1989. Physiological changes in circulating androgens. In Androgens in Childhood: Biological, Physiological, Clinical and Therapeutic Aspects. M. G. Forest, Ed.: Vol. 19: 104–129. Karger. Basel.
7. MOWSZOWICZ, I. 1989. Physiological role of androgens. In Androgens in Childhood: Biological, Physiological, Clinical and Therapeutic Aspects. M. G. Forest, Ed.: Vol. 19: 84–97. Karger. Basel.
8. OLWEUS, D. 1986. Aggression and hormones: Behavioral relationship with testosterone and adrenaline. In Development of Antisocial and Prosocial Behavior: Research, Theories and Issues. D. Olweus, J. Block & M. Radke-Yarrow, Eds.: 51–72. Academic Press. Toronto.
9. CAIRNS, R. B., B. D. CAIRNS, H. J. NECKERMAN, L. L. FERGUSON & J. L. GARIÉPY. 1989. Growth and aggression: 1. Childhood to early adolescence. Dev. Psychol. 25(2): 320–330.
10. CUMMINGS, E. M., R. J. IANNOTTI & C. ZAHN-WAXLER. 1989. Aggression between peers in early childhood: Individual continuity and developmental change. Child Dev. 60(4): 887–895.
11. FARRINGTON, D. P. 1994. Childhood, adolescent, and adult features of violent males. In Aggressive Behavior: Current Perspectives. L. R. Huesmann, Ed.: 215–240. Plenum Press. New York.
12. HAAPASALO, J. & R. E. TREMBLAY. 1994. Physically aggressive boys from age 6 to 12: Family background, parenting behavior, and prediction of delinquency. J. Consult. Clin. Psychol. 62(5): 1044–1052.
13. HUESMANN, L. R., L. D. ERON, M. M. LEFKOWITZ & L. O. WALDER. 1984. Stability of aggression over time and generations. Dev. Psychol. 20(6): 1120–1134.
14. STATTIN, H. & D. MAGNUSSON. 1989. The role of early aggressive behavior in the frequency, seriousness and types of later crime. J. Consult. Clin. Psychol. 57(6): 710–718.
15. TREMBLAY, R. E. & W. CRAIG. 1995. Developmental crime prevention. In Building a Safer Society: Strategic Approaches to Crime. M. Tonry & D. P. Farrington, Eds.: 19: 151–236. The University of Chicago Press. Chicago.
16. BELSKY, J., L. STEINBERG & P. DRAPER. 1991. Childhood experience, interpersonal development and reproduction strategy: An evolutionary theory of socialization. Child Dev. 62: 647–670.
17. SUSMAN, E. J., L. D. DORN & G. P. CHROUSOS. 1991. Negative affect and hormone

levels in young adolescents: Concurrent and predictive perspectives. J. Youth and Adolesc. **20**(2): 167–190.

18. SUSMAN, E. J., G. INOFF-GERMAIN, E. D. NOTTELMANN, D. L. LORIAUX, G. B. CUTLER & G. P. CHROUSOS. 1987. Hormones, emotional dispositions, and aggressive attributes in young adolescents. Child Dev. **1987**(58): 1114–1134.

19. STATTIN, H. & D. MAGNUSSON. 1990. Pubertal motivation in female development. Lawrence Erlbaum. Hillsdale, N.J.

20. FOX, N. A. 1989. The psychophysiological correlates of emotional reactivity during the first year of life. Dev. Psychol. **25**: 364–372.

21. KAGAN, J., J. S. REZNICK & N. SNIDMAN. 1988. Biological bases of childhood shyness. Science **240**: 167–171.

22. EYSENCK, H. J. & G. H. GUDJONSSON. 1989. The causes and cures of criminality. Plenum. New York.

23. GRAY, J. A. 1982. The neuropsychology of anxiety. Oxford University Press. New York.

24. GRAY, J. A. 1990. Brain systems that mediate both emotion and cognition. Cognition Emotion **4**: 269–288.

25. BLUMSTEIN, A., D. P. FARRINGTON & S. MOITRA. 1985. Delinquent careers: innocents, desisters, and persisters. *In* Crime and Justice: An Annual Review. M. Tonry & N. Morris, Eds.: **6**: 187–219. University of Chicago Press. Chicago.

26. McCORD, J. 1987. Aggression and shyness as predictors of problems: A long term view. Biennial Meeting of the Society for Research in Child Development. Baltimore.

27. LAHEY, B. B., K. McBURNETT, R. LOEBER & E. L. HART. 1995. Psychobiology of conduct disorder. *In* Conduct Disorders in Children and Adolescents. G. P. Sholevar, Ed.: American Psychiatric Press. Washington, D.C.

28. MOSKOWITZ, D. S. & A. E. SCHWARTZMAN. 1989. Painting group portraits: Studying life outcomes for aggressive and withdrawn children. J. Pers. **57**(4): 723–746.

29. TREMBLAY, R. E., R. O. PIHL, F. VITARO & P. L. DOBKIN. 1994. Predicting early onset of male antisocial behavior from preschool behavior. Arch. Gen. Psychiatry **51**: 732–738.

30. TREMBLAY, R. E., R. LOEBER, C. GAGNON, P. CHARLEBOIS, S. LARIVÉE & M. LEBLANC. 1991. Disruptive boys with stable and unstable high fighting behavior patterns during junior elementary school. J. Abnorm. Child Psychol. **19**: 285–300.

31. ST-JACQUES, M. & R. DUSSAULT. 1994. Étude longitudinale sur le décrochage scolaire. Commission des Écoles Catholiques de Montréal. Montréal.

32. POWER, C., O. MANOR & J. FOX. 1991. Health and class: The early years. Chapman & Hall. London.

33. PETERSEN, A. C., L. CROCKETT, M. RICHARDS & A. BOXER. 1988. A self-report measure of pubertal status: reliability, validity, and initial norms. J. Youth Adolesc. **17**(2): 117–133.

34. SCHAAL, B., R. E. TREMBLAY, R. SOUSSIGNAN & E. J. SUSMAN. Male testosterone linked to high social dominance but low physical aggression in early adolescence. J. Am. Acad. Child Adolesc. Psychiatry. In press.

35. MALO, J. & R. E. TREMBLAY. The impact of paternal alcoholism and maternal social adjustment on pubertal maturation, sexual behavior, and school adjustment of early adolescent boys: A longitudinal perspective. J. Child Psychol. Psychiatry. In press.

36. JACKLIN, C. N., E. E. MACCOBY & C. H. DOERING. 1983. Neonatal sex steroid hormones and timidity in 6- to 18-month-old boys. Dev. Psychobiol. **16**: 163–168.

37. MONAGHAN, E. P. & S. E. GLICKMAN. 1992. Hormones and aggressive behavior. *In* Behavioral Endocrinology. J. B. Becker, S. M. Breedlove & D. Crews, Eds.: 261–285. The MIT Press. Cambridge, MA.

38. RESTOIN, A., H. MONTAGNER, D. RODRIGUEZ, J. J. GIRARDOT, D. LAURENT, F. KONTAR, V. ULLMANN, C. CASAGRANDE & B. TALPAIN. 1985. Chronologie des comportements de communication et profils de comportement chez le jeune enfant. *In* Ethologie et développement de l'enfant. R. E. Tremblay, M. A. Provost & F. F. Strayer, Eds.: 93–130. Editions Stock/Laurence Pernoud. Paris.

Disordered Views of Aggressive Children

A Late Twentieth Century Perspective[a]

JOHN E. RICHTERS[b]

Child and Adolescent Disorders Research Branch
National Institute of Mental Health
5600 Fishers Lane, Room 18C-17
Rockville, Maryland 20857

INTRODUCTION

American society made an unannounced site visit to the social and behavioral sciences recently in the midst of a rising national epidemic of youth violence.[1–3] The unusual visit took place in hundreds of public and private forums around the United States as major institutions of local, state, and federal government turned to individual researchers, their professional organizations, and their funding agencies for science-based insights and solutions to the violence crisis. Although unannounced in the conventional sense, the collective visit certainly was not unexpected. As the National Research Council's Committee on Basic Research in the Behavioral and Social Sciences concluded almost a decade ago, "few demands on the behavioral and social sciences are more insistent than the call for knowledge on how to reduce the threat of these dangerous acts."[4] Indeed, the United States has invested heavily during the past half century in scientific approaches to understanding, curbing, and preventing childhood aggression. Thus, the national violence crisis provided a natural occasion and very specific agenda for seeking a return on that investment.

Those in search for an *immediate* solution to the violence crisis found little guidance from the scientific community. What they did find, however, was a rich foundation of data useful for thinking about solutions on a longer time horizon. Emerging from decades of scientific evidence concerning risk factors, concurrent correlates, sequelae, and life course patterns of aggression and antisocial behavior, several robust trends stood out as particularly salient.[5,6] First, the majority of children engage in some form of aggressive and/or antisocial behavior during their adolescent years but desist following a limited period of experimentation. Second, the most persistent and severe patterns of antisocial and aggressive behavior often originate much earlier in life among a much smaller group of children. Third, these latter children are significantly more likely than the others to come from disadvantaged backgrounds characterized by multiple risk factors, and to perform less well on measures of cognitive, emotional, social, and nervous system functioning. Fourth, once the aggressive and antisocial lifestyles of these children develop and stabilize, they tend to be remarkably refractory to interventions. There remains

---

[a] Sections of this paper are based on a more elaborate discussion of the conduct disorder issue.[6]

[b] Tel: (301) 443-5944; e-mail: jrichter@nih.gov.

little in the way of scientific consensus about *why* some children become persistently aggressive and *why* their antisocial trajectories are so difficult to deflect once stabilized.[6] Nonetheless, for many within and outside the scientific community these general trends provided a rationale for investing in early childhood prevention initiatives, focusing especially on children at highest risk for developing persistent problems of aggression and antisocial behavior.

The Federal Violence Initiative Controversy

As the national dialogue turned to a consideration of specific strategies for prevention, however, a firestorm of protest erupted over allegations that the federal government intended to harness these general trends as justification for adopting a draconian biomedical approach to violence prevention.[7] While ignoring social influences such as poverty, racism, poor education, poor parenting, according to critics, the so-called federal Violence Initiative would focus on biological causes of violence by seeking to identify and treat "violence-prone" children on the basis of biological markers for aggression. Moreover, the government's justification for this approach would be a science-based interpretation of persistent childhood aggression as a form of mental disorder—conduct disorder.[8]

Not surprisingly, the allegations elicited images of Huxley's *Brave New World*, charges of racism, eugenics, coercive biological approaches to social control, and an immediate wave of public protest. Similar fears had been stirred almost 20 years ago when a medical advisor to President Richard Nixon recommended a government-sponsored mass screening of all 6- to 8-year-olds in the United States to detect and correct "violent and homicidal tendencies."[9] Even though Dr. Hutschecker's ill-fated proposal was rejected and harshly criticized at the time, it was soon dismissed in the public mind as misguided advice from an isolated individual who happened to have access to the president. The current proposal, however, could not be as easily dismissed. A detailed rationale for the disorder-based biomedical strategy had been put forward this time by the eminent biological psychiatrist Dr. Frederick Goodwin, the first scientist to demonstrate the therapeutic antidepressant effects of lithium and an internationally recognized expert on manic-depressive illness.[10] Even more important to critics, Goodwin was also the federal government's highest ranking psychiatrist and head of its lead agency for mental health policy, services, and research.[7] Thus, in contrast to Hutschnecker's memo, Goodwin's proposal seemed to carry the combined authority of government endorsement and scientific justification.

In reality, neither perception was true. Goodwin's proposal had not received serious consideration in government planning, and it was neither compelled nor justified in the eyes of other scientists by a dispassionate assessment of the scientific evidence. The so-called biological proposal outlined by Goodwin was very much his own initiative and had been put forward in an effort to win a more central role for his agency in the govenrment's violence prevention planning.[7] Moreover, as the Secretary of Health and Human Services would later acknowledge, the so-called Violence Initiative with a capital *V* and a capital *I* never existed.[11] What did exist was an earnest long-range planning effort—warranting only a lower case *v* and *i*—to better coordinate existing government programs and to determine whether additional programs were needed to stem the national tide of violence.

By the time this became clear to all but the most ardent of critics, however, considerable damage already had been done. The controversy stemming from

Goodwin's proposal had immediately sabotaged what had been a constructive national dialogue about science-based approaches to violence prevention strategies. Soon thereafter, it stirred a sufficient level of public tension to force postponement of a government-funded scientific conference on genetics and crime.[11] Finally, it triggered the appointment of a blue-ribbon panel to conduct an unprecedented assessment of the adequacy of NIH-funded violence-related research in addressing public health needs and to ensure that the research was being conducted in an ethically and socially responsible manner.[12]

The NIH Blue-ribbon Panel Review

The NIH panel's review did much to allay public fears about the alleged but nonexistent biomedically based federal Violence Initiative, but it was less effective in relieving public misgivings about the contemporary emphasis in scientific discourse on explanations of persistent childhood aggression as a form of mental disorder. The panel did, early in its deliberations, vigorously debate the controversial question of whether chronic childhood aggression is a medical disorder, a learned phenomenon, or multicomponent behavior. Some members found objectionable the claim that chronic and severe antisocial behavior in childhood and adolescence is necessarily evidence of an underlying mental disorder and raised concerns that it represented a counterproductive "medicalization" of a burgeoning and multidetermined social crisis (*i.e.*, antisocial behavior and violence) in the United States. No one on the NIH panel objected, in principle, to the notion that some chronic forms of violence and antisocial behavior might be products of underlying dysfunctions within individuals, warranting a mental disorder diagnosis and intervention. Rather, their comments stemmed from concerns about (1) the *overinclusiveness* of the criteria for conduct disorder, and (2) its potential for being misused to diagnose, label, and treat children and adolescents for a mental disorder when their behavior may instead be the product of deviant environments and/or subcultures. Some expressed the additional concern that the conduct disorder diagnosis and its consequences might be applied to disproportionate numbers of minority children.[12]

Far from arriving at anything approaching consensus on these concerns, the panel found itself mired in definitional ambiguities about the scientific meaning of terms, such as *psychopathology*, *mental disorder*, and *dysfunction*. One member even characterized the panel's debate as a "stroll through a semantic jungle"[12] (p. 78). In the end, the panel settled on expressing a more general concern about NIH-funded research focused narrowly on causes of aggression within the individual and recommended a shift toward more multidisciplinary research focusing on a broader range of relevant social influences, such as family, neighborhood, community, and culture.

OVERVIEW

It is customary following more traditional scientific site visits for investigators to engage in a period of debriefing, often focusing on the merits and implications of issues uncovered by the review. There was certainly nothing traditional about the recent site visit, either its unusual collective nature, its focus on the emotionally charged issue of mental disorder and aggression, or its concluding NIH panel review. Nonetheless, the issues it highlighted about the causes of childhood aggression and antisocial behavior are every bit as worthy of scientific debriefing. The discussion that follows is intended to initiate that process by reaching beyond the rhetoric and confusion of the recent controversy to consider the scientific merits of contemporary claims that persistent childhood aggression reflects an underlying mental disorder.

Before turning to that agenda, however, it is worth noting what the conduct disorder controversy is *not* about. Namely, there is no question that persistent aggression and antisocial behavior in childhood is objectionable and intolerable on social, ethical, moral, and public health grounds. It places children themselves at high risk for a disturbing array of harmful outcomes, ranging from tremendous personal distress and social-emotional problems, to physical danger, imprisonment, and even early death. Moreover, these harms tend to radiate outward and afflict all those who come into contact with antisocial children—individuals, families, neighborhoods, institutions, and ultimately society itself. Thus, there has never been controversy about the social, clinical, and public health significance of the childhood aggression problem, only about the validity and implications of claims that it is caused by a mental disorder. In fact, it is precisely because of the social and public health significance of childhood aggression that a proper understanding of its origins and causes is considered so important.[12]

THE ASCENDANCY OF CONDUCT DISORDER

The notion that persistent childhood aggression and antisocial behavior reflects an underlying mental disorder within the child has existed in the literature of psychiatry for more than 200 years.[13] Moreover, it has existed in one form or another in the scientific literature for most of the twentieth century, ranging from specific concepts of disorder to more general models of social-emotional maladjustment.[2] Its controversial claim to scientific and public health legitimacy, however, is of more recent origin, dating back only to 1980 when persistent childhood aggression was officially classified as *conduct disorder*, a mental disorder of childhood, by the American Psychiatric Association.[6,13]

Diagnostic Criteria

The significance of this event lies in the ambitious and dubious causal claim on which the conduct disorder diagnosis rests. According to the current edition of the APA's *Diagnostic and Statistical Manual of Mental Disorders* (DSM-IV), all children (under age 18) who engage in at least 3 of 15 antisocial behaviors over a 12-month period, with at least one during the past six months, resulting in clinically significant impairment in social, academic, or occupational functioning, suffer from *conduct disorder*, a major mental disorder of childhood.[8] If there is evidence that at least one of the 15 antisocial behaviors was present before age 10, the child is further classified as having *conduct disorder, childhood-onset type*; the remaining children are classified as having *conduct disorder, adolescent-onset type*. The diagnosis ignores all contextual information about the child as possible influences on and/or alternative explanations for the antisocial behavior, including personal and family background, previous experiences, and current circumstances. The fact that a child has engaged in a clinically significant pattern of antisocial behavior as defined by the behavioral diagnostic criteria is ipso facto evidence that he or she is suffering from a mental disorder. The DSM manual offers no defense or rationale for the disorder claim and does not specify exactly—or even generally—what has gone wrong within the child to cause the antisocial behavior. It is explicit only in claiming that the behavior pattern is a consequence of a dysfunction *within* the child.

Clinical Caveats

The DSM-IV diagnostic criteria reflect only modest changes from the criteria first published in 1980. In contrast to previous editions of the DSM, however, the DSM-IV included for the first time a vaguely worded but telling cautionary suggestion to clinicians: "It may be helpful for the clinician to consider the social and economic milieu in which undesirable behaviors occur before making a diagnosis."[8] The basis for this cautionary note, according to the manual, is that "concerns have been raised that the conduct disorder diagnosis may at times be applied to individuals in settings where patterns of undesirable behavior are sometimes viewed as protective (*e.g.*, threatening, impoverished, high crime)," further noting the example of "immigrant youth from war ravaged countries" (p. 88) whose behavior might have had survival value.[8] Despite the obvious intention of this "helpful suggestion," however, it is *only* a suggestion. It is not a requirement, it offers no guidelines for distinguishing between disordered and nondisorder variants of childhood antisocial behavior, and it is not reflected in the formal diagnostic criteria described above. Thus, whatever impact it may or may not have on the diagnostic decisions of practicing clinicians, it carries no weight in how the diagnosis is applied by researchers and epidemiologists, who study and estimate the prevalence and incidence of conduct disorder strictly on the basis of the formal criteria.

SCIENTIFIC AND PUBLIC HEALTH INFLUENCE

If the introduction of conduct disorder were simply a formalization of psychiatry's long-standing belief about the origins of childhood aggression, it might easily be ignored outside the narrow boundaries of the psychiatric profession. Since its introduction in 1980, however, the conduct disorder diagnosis has played an increasingly influential role in justifying, organizing, and interpreting government-funded research concerning risk factors, causes, preventions, and treatments for persistent childhood aggression. The magnitude of this impact is nowhere better reflected than in the change over two decades in the NIMH's posture concerning chronic aggression and mental disorder. In a 1968 statement, the NIMH conceptualized delinquent and criminal behaviors as "stemming from complex interactions of psychological, social, biological, and other factors," and specifically emphasized that the deviant behaviors warranted scientific study and not labels and definitions, such as *delinquency* and *mental disorder*[12] (p. 148). By 1990, by contrast, research concerning the causes, prevention, and treatment of conduct disorder was given a high priority in the *National Institute of Mental Health's National Plan for Research on Child and Adolescent Mental Disorders*.[15]

SIGNIFICANCE OF THE CONDUCT DISORDER CLAIM

There are a variety of reasons why the causal claim underlying the conduct disorder diagnosis warrants careful scientific scrutiny. First, as the recent controversy revealed, its current widespread usage in childhood aggression research is widely perceived as a tacit endorsement of the underlying causal claim. This perception in turn has considerable potential for inadvertently reinforcing stereotyped views of the causes of antisocial behavior that can restrict the range of intervention and prevention options considered by treatment providers and policy agencies. The Hutschnecker and Goodwin proposals were sobering reminders of how easily misguided solutions can spring from false beliefs about the causes of childhood aggression.

Second, as an ethical issue, the conduct disorder attribution carries with it the potential for long-term negative social consequences for those diagnosed. Two decades ago United States Senator Thomas Eagleton lost his bid for the vice presidency of the United States because of public concerns about his prior treatment for an affective disorder.[16] The comforting illusion that those days were well behind us was shattered again in 1996 when similar concerns were raised about the fact that the wife of General Colin Powell (retired) (himself a potential vice presidential nominee) had undergone treatment for an affective disorder. Unfortunately, stigmatization continues to play a significant role in the everyday lives of millions of Americans who are affected by mental disorders. These considerations are especially troubling at the close of the twentieth century, given the ever-expanding role of computer-aided access to information (including medical history) about the private lives of individuals. Ultimately, as in the case of all disorders, the most important question must be whether a diagnosis is scientifically valid and justified on the basis of its potential for conveying benefit to those diagnosed. That potential for benefit, however, must always be weighed against potential costs. It is not at all clear at present what those benefits are in the case of conduct disorder.

Third, as a social and public health issue, the conduct disorder attribution tends to focus attention on problems within the child and away from pathological conditions in the environment that may be largely responsible for his or her antisocial behavior. Finally, as a scientific matter, the assumption of underlying disorder tends also to have a powerful constraining influence on the questions that are asked and not asked by scientists about causes, treatments, and prevention strategies for childhood aggression.

IS PERSISTENT CHILDHOOD AGGRESSION A MENTAL DISORDER?

Negative Outcomes

By far, the most consistently cited justification for characterizing persistent childhood aggression as a form of mental disorder or psychopathology is the wealth of evidence showing that it is associated with significant levels of risk for a wide array of negative outcomes. For example, it has been amply demonstrated that, on average, children diagnosed with conduct disorder are much more likely to suffer from negative outcomes than children diagnosed with any of the other common behavioral syndromes and putative mental disorders of childhood. Beginning in preschool years, children who later display serious conduct problems have been shown to manifest significantly higher levels of impulsivity, irritability, and inattention than their peers—characteristics associated with negative interactions with parents, peers, and teachers.[17-19] During middle childhood, children with conduct problems are more likely to be rejected by their peers,[20] develop poor relationships with their teachers, engender less nurturance and support within the school setting,[18] and suffer from academic deficiencies.[21] These factors, in turn, have been shown to be associated with an increased likelihood of deviant peer group affiliations,[22] which itself has been implicated as a risk factor for both substance abuse,[23] dropping out of school,[24] and criminal behavior.[25,26]

In the clinical domain, children diagnosed with conduct disorder have been found to suffer from a range of emotional adjustment problems, including attention deficit hyperactivity disorder, oppositional defiant disorder,[27-29] anxiety, and depressive disorders.[30] Finally, it has been shown that approximately 31% of those who warrant the conduct disorder diagnosis as children remain sufficiently antisocial through adulthood to qualify for the diagnosis of antisocial personality disorder after age 18, and to suffer as adults from a wide range of negative social, emotional, and health outcomes.[31,32]

Internal Functioning Deficits

Researchers in the domains of developmental psychopathology have amassed a wealth of data over the years showing that, on average, aggressive children tend to differ from nonaggressive children on a variety of measures of impulsivity, cognitive functioning, learning skills, emotion regulation,[33-37] and problem solving.[38] The most frequently cited basis for claims of an underlying disorder, however, has been the evidence that persistent aggression tends to be associated with putative deficits in neurological, biological, and/or psychophysiological functioning.[5] These findings have been discussed in detail elsewhere.[6] For present purposes, it will suffice to describe briefly the kinds of evidence cited.

For example, mild neuropsychological deficits have been found in numerous studies to be associated with delinquent and aggressive behavior in childhood, including deficiencies in attention modulation,[39,40] self-control and impulsivity,[41] verbal skills, memory, IQ, and visual-motor integration.[42] In the biochemical domain, children and adolescents hospitalized for disruptive disorders (including conduct disorder) compared to matched controls have been shown to have significantly lower levels of the serotonin metabolite 5-hydroxyindoleacetic acid (CSF 5-HIAA).[43] Moreover, these findings are generally consistent with earlier reports of an association between lower CSF 5-HIAA and both impulsivity and aggression in adults,[44,45] and between CSF 5-HIAA and aggression in free-ranging rhesus monkeys living under naturalistic conditions.[46] Finally, several studies have reported that electrodermal responses to external stimuli, an index of sympathetic activity reflecting processes related to anxiety and inhibition, tend to be diminished in groups of aggressive children and adolescents.[47] So-called undersocialized aggressive children especially have been shown to be more likely than controls to perseverate to their disadvantage with previously rewarded behaviors in the face of punishment.[48,49] These data converge with similar findings based on adult samples of incarcerated psychopaths, and with theoretical models of the role played by passive avoidance learning deficits in acquiring antisocial behavior patterns.[50]

DISTINGUISHING BETWEEN DISORDER AND NONDISORDER

Plausible models and theories have been introduced over the years to account for how such characteristics might play direct and/or indirect causal roles in producing and/or sustaining antisocial behavior patterns, particularly those beginning in early childhood.[5] The crucial question, of course, is whether it is reasonable to interpret such descriptive findings as evidence for an underlying disorder or psychopathology. Many debates of the past concerning this question have been hampered both by limitations in the kinds of data available and by an absence of adequate theoretical models and frameworks for discriminating between disorder and nondisorder. During the past decade or so, however, there has been dramatic progress on both fronts. In the basic sciences there has been considerable progress in documenting and understanding the plasticity of the human nervous system, resulting in a much greater appreciation of the extent to which genetic, biological, and environmental factors interact in complex ways to influence human development.[51] Also, both reflecting and contributing to this progress, the hybrid discipline of developmental psychopathology has emerged as a powerful interdisciplinary framework for guiding research and theory concerning all aspects of human functioning and development.[52-54] Even more recently, there has been a resurgence of scholarly interest in defining the conceptual boundaries of mental disorder on the basis of evolutionary biology considerations.[55,56] Together, these developments provide a new foundation for thinking about the variety of factors that may lead ultimately to persistent childhood aggression, and for evaluating the scientific merits of claims that they reflect an underlying disorder within the child.

A Developmental Psychopathology Perspective

One of the most significant contributions of the developmental psychopathology perspective has been the heuristic power of its emphasis on the principle of equifinality drawn from systems theory.[57] Equifinality refers to the fundamental capacity of all open systems to achieve similar outcomes or behavior patterns through a variety of different causal pathways. Thus, not only may there be multiple contributors to the aggressive behavior of a given child, but the relevant causal processes may vary qualitatively between similar-appearing aggressive children. For one child the relevant causal influences may include a diathesis for impulsivity (inherited or acquired), poor self-esteem, a violent home environment and/or community, and minimal support or nurturance from caregivers.[58] For another child, however, the relevant factors may be positive characteristics, such as high intelligence and resourcefulness, in conjunction with conditions of poverty, poor parent monitoring, and/or a criminogenic neighborhood. Yet other children, for whom none of these factors is relevant, may develop persistent patterns of aggression and antisocial behavior primarily because they were socialized into a deviant value system, or as a strategy for coping in a hostile, dangerous environment. From this perspective, a major limitation of many efforts to identify and/or classify subtypes of aggressive children (including the conduct disorder classification) has been the reliance on behavioral similarities, *not* on the presumed or postulated underlying causal processes of ultimate interest to developmentalists.

Disorder as Harmful Dysfunction

The developmental psychopathology perspective is of tremendous heuristic value in conceptualizing, isolating, and understanding complex causal processes and their interactions. Judgments concerning whether and under what conditions a particular matrix of causal influences warrants the attribution of an underlying mental disorder, however, require the additional guidance of a coherent definition of disorder. The search for such a definition has led to a variety of proposals over the decades, the most notable of which have differentially emphasized suboptimal functioning, statistical deviance, unexpectable distress/disability, and/or biological disadvantage. Each of these, however, has been shown to possess severe limitations in its ability to accommodate noncontroversial disorders while excluding conditions that are widely considered *not* to be disorders. On the basis of a review and critique of these limitations, Wakefield recently proposed an overarching, hybrid, "harmful dysfunction" concept of disorder, with an associated set of criteria for distinguishing between disorder and nondisorder in the domains of both physical and mental functioning:

> A condition is a disorder if and only if (a) the condition causes some harm or deprivation of benefit to the person as judged by the standards of the person's culture . . . , and (b) the condition results from the inability of some internal mechanism to perform its natural function, wherein a natural function is an effect that is part of the evolutionary explanation of the existence and structure of the mechanism.[56]

By preserving the strengths and discarding the weaknesses of earlier proposals, the harmful dysfunction concept holds several advantages over its predecessors. First, it focuses on a broadly defined concept of internal mechanisms; it adopts an evolutionary biology approach that acknowledges the brain and its functions as legitimate manifestations of biological mechanisms developed through natural selection.[59] Although it assumes axiomatically that mental processes (*e.g.*, cognition, emotion, and perception) are ultimately traceable to underlying biological processes, it imposes no requirement to assess those processes at an anatomical or physiological level. Therefore, the harmful dysfunction concept is not yoked to the criterion of an identifiable physical lesion or any other single referent. Instead, those constructs may be postulated in psychological or biological terms, and may be indexed through biological and/or behavioral indicators at differing levels of abstraction. Consequently, the model is capable of accommodating both medical and mental disorders with equal ease.

Second, the harmful dysfunction concept emphasizes natural, evolved mechanisms within the individual that have gone awry. It therefore forces attention onto a specification of or reasoned speculation about those processes, and on the need to rule out alternative explanations in the form of normal functioning causal processes operating within, and environmental factors outside, the individual. It also minimizes the likelihood that conditions that are merely undesirable by social or political standards will be classified as disorders, as in the case of notable psychodiagnostic errors of the past such as "drapetomania" (the mental condition attributed to runaway slaves) and "childhood masturbation disorder" (see 56). Finally, the harmful dysfunction criterion places on a more solid scientific platform the basis for distinctions between disorder and other forms of human misery, unhappiness, and troubles.

Weaknesses in Existing Aggression-Disorder Claims

From the standpoint of the harmful dysfunction analysis, the correlates of persistent childhood aggression described earlier fall far short of meeting a reasonable standard for the disorder attribution. It is certainly true that most forms of persistent antisocial behavior in childhood are objectionable by conventional social and moral standards, and that parental concern over such behavior is often the basis for clinical referral. Moreover, there is a wealth of data demonstrating that aggressive children, particularly those whose antisocial behavior begins in early childhood, are at significant risk for a wide variety of harmful conditions and deprivations of benefit.[5] For a variety of methodological and conceptual reasons, however, the existing data do *not* provide adequate support for the claim that these behavior patterns are caused by dysfunctions of natural mechanisms within the child.

First, it is seldom clear whether identified differences between very aggressive and nonaggressive children on various indices of nervous system functioning reflect causes, spurious correlates, or consequences of the aggressive behavior. There is a regrettable bias in the literature toward strong causal interpretations of weak data patterns based on overly permissive scientific standards, frequently in the absence of any serious consideration of alternative, equally plausible explanations.[60,61] This is particularly troubling in light of the impressive evidence from the basic neurosciences showing the extent to which nervous system functioning at all levels can be influenced by environmental experiences. Second, most of the identified differences in nervous system functioning between groups of aggressive and nonaggressive children have been relatively modest, typically reflecting considerable overlap between groups. Third, even if a rigorous case *could* be made for the causal influence on aggressive behavior of some basic characteristic of nervous system functioning, this alone would not constitute evidence for an underlying dysfunction in the implicated mechanism. Given that all behaviors, harmful and beneficial alike, are reflected ultimately in underlying physiological processes, it is only a matter of time before we will be able to identify the physiological underpinnings of all manner of behavior. This is not to say that it is necessary, desirable, or even possible to adopt a reductionist approach to understanding human functioning. Rather, it is intended to underscore the obvious fact that equating internal causes of harmful behavior with dysfunctions in natural mechanisms is logically equivalent to attributing all harmful behaviors to underlying disorders. It is precisely for this reason that the harmful dysfunction concept directs attention to *dysfunctions* of *natural* mechanisms: the failure of natural mechanisms to function in the capacities for which they evolved, resulting in harm to the individual.

FUTURE CHALLENGES

The concept of harmful dysfunction only circumscribes the conceptual decisions that must be made in discriminating disorders from nondisorders. It does not specify how those decisions are to be made. These decisions necessarily require an admixture of complex scientific and value judgments. The identification of dysfunction, for example, requires scientific knowledge or theory about the natual mechanisms in question and their functional significance, as well as criteria for determining the dysfunctional status of those mechanisms or processes. Similarly, the harm requirement leaves open important questions concerning how to assess harmful effects, and how to discriminate between the *inability* of a mechanism to perform its natural function and a mere production deficit of an intact mechanism.

Although these decisions tend to be straightforward in the case of well-understood conditions, they become more controversial and subject to scientific dispute when the underlying mechanisms and processes are not yet well understood.[56] Thus, in the domain of mental disorders, tasks such as defining the domain of natural mechanisms, understanding the difference between normal variability and dysfunction, linking dysfunctions causally with harmful conditions, and even defining those harmful conditions are likely to be matters of considerable scientific dispute. These are not weaknesses, however, in the harmful dysfunction concept itself. Rather, they are burdens that must be shouldered within the substantive domains of developmental psychopathology, evolutionary biology, and related disciplines.[62] In the case of persistent childhood aggression, this burden is rendered especially difficult by limitations in our understanding of the relevant underlying mechanisms; the tentative, speculative nature of our knowledge about the causal status of variables that have been identified as correlates and/or risk factors; and our limited ability to operationalize and measure many of the constructs we believe to be most relevant.

Nondisordered Variants of Persistent Aggression

Just as the harmful dysfunction framework focuses attention on dysfunctions in natural mechanisms that might account for antisocial behavior, it also highlights the importance of considering how children might develop antisocial behavior patterns in the absence of internal dysfunctions. Their conduct problems instead may be caused by interactions between intact, normally functioning mechanisms and a variety of environmental influences. One obvious example might be children raised in criminogenic neighborhoods and/or families who engage in antisocial, even criminal actions because those are the behaviors modeled, expected, and/or rewarded by the major influences in their environments.[63] This is a particularly salient model to consider in the late twentieth century America, where in many major cities the allure of drug-related crime is ever present, and where gangs virtually control the social commerce and economic life of many neighborhoods. It is undeniably true that gang involvement places children at risk for an unimaginable array of negative outcomes, but from the perspective of many children living in those neighborhoods there are considerable physical and social risks as well in *not* joining a gang. Even beyond the issue of gangs, the short-term payoffs for participating in criminal and/or gang activity can be exceedingly attractive, especially to those who are disenfranchised, surrounded by violence and death, and who see no realistic chance of access to the opportunity/payoff matrix available to those in mainstream society. A reasonable case can be made that there may be many such children and youth for whom chronic antisocial behavior is, in our everyday sense of the word, a *choice* among alternatives; these children perform *willful* acts that are the products of deviant (from the mainstream) environments and/or value systems and are therefore *psychopathologically exculpable* in the sense that there is no underlying dysfunction in their natural mechanisms.

The potential seductiveness of antisocial and criminal lifestyles was illustrated recently in the biography of Henry Hill, a New York gangster now residing in the federal witness protection program, whose life was depicted in the recent American film *GoodFellas*. As a young child, Hill's family lived across the street from a local mob hangout, providing him with a vantage point afforded to few in the neighborhood:

> I was the luckiest kid in the world . . . I was fascinated by the place. I used to watch them from my window, and I dreamed of being like them. At the age of twelve my ambition was to be a gangster. To be a wiseguy. To me being a wiseguy was better than being president of the United States. It meant power among people who had no power. It meant perks in a working-class neighborhood that had no privileges. To be a wiseguy was to own the world. I dreamed about being a wiseguy the way other kids dreamed about being doctors or movie stars or firemen or ballplayers[64] (p. 13).

Hill's lifelong pattern of antisocial and criminal behavior was sufficiently pervasive to warrant the diagnosis of conduct disorder in childhood and antisocial personality disorder as an adult. The question raised by his circumstances and account, however, is whether it is necessary, useful, or justified to attribute his behavior to an underlying mental disorder. There is considerable room here for reasonable speculation about possible functioning deficits within Hill (*e.g.*, deficient learning mechanisms, underactive inhibition system) that may have accounted for why he was so attracted to the criminal element. There also is ample reason to be wary of Hill's own account of his motivations.[65] It is also easy to imagine, however, how a normally functioning child exposed to those temptations, especially in conjunction with poor parent monitoring, supervision, and discipline, might be drawn into an antisocial and/or criminal lifestyle with mental processes intact—that is, in the absence of underlying dysfunction in the sense defined by Wakefield. We cannot know, of course, and we need not know in Hill's case, but the questions raised by his account are provocative and warrant careful consideration in the case of tens of thousands of children living in equally seductive environments, often in conjunction with poor parenting and other social risk factors, whose antisocial and criminal behavior patterns are attributed by the DSM-IV to an underlying mental disorder.

CONCLUSION

The example of Henry Hill and others like him highlights an important question that invariably arises in discussions of chronically antisocial children: Isn't a prolonged pattern of inherently dangerous, self-destructive behavior ipso facto evidence that there is something fundamentally wrong with a child? The answer depends very much on what we mean by "wrong." If wrong means that we find the behavior misguided, regrettable, morally repugnant, and a source of our concern about the child's values and welfare, then the term wrong certainly applies. Harmful behavior, however, by itself is too broad a criterion for the attribution of an underlying mental disorder. There are numerous legal occupations that also place individuals at much higher than average risk for high levels of personal distress, physical harm, and even early death. Police officers, firefighters, rescue workers, soldiers, and missionaries are just a few notable examples of those who deliberately place themselves in harm's way on a regular basis. Yet we do not consider their behavior to be evidence of an underlying mental disorder. The reason is that we understand how the prevailing culture both values and rewards what they do; but this is no less true of the Henry Hills of the world. Mainstream society resists the notion that they can be fundamentally normally functioning human beings seduced by circumstance into deviant, antisocial lifestyles. As Nicholas Pileggi understood, however, the deviant (from mainstream) values and reward structures of subcultures can be every bit as coherent and powerful in their effects as those of the mainstream culture:

> For Henry and his wiseguy friends the world was golden. They lived in an environment awash in crime, and those who did not partake were simply viewed as prey. To live otherwise was foolish. Anyone who stood waiting his turn on the American pay line was beneath contempt. Those who did—who followed the rules, were stuck in low paying jobs, worried about their bills, put tiny amounts away for rainy days, kept their place, and crossed off workdays on their calendars like prisoners waiting their release—could only be considered fools . . . Henry and his pals had long ago dismissed the idea of security and the relative tranquility that went with obeying the law. They exulted in the pleasures that came from breaking it. Life was lived without a safety net. They wanted money, they wanted power, and they were willing to do anything necessary to achieve their ends[64] (p. 37).

We need not accept Hill's outlook and behavior to allow that these *may* be the characteristics of a normally functioning individual who has adopted and adapted to a different world view and set of values than those endorsed by the main culture.

It would be equally wrong, however, to assume that all antisocial children living in such high-risk environments arrive at their behavioral dispositions through normal processes. Indeed, much of what we know about the predictors and correlates of antisocial behavior suggests that there are probably numerous pathological pathways as well. The difficulty, of course, is that these very environments—those that are most likely to give rise to such psychopathologically exculpable behavior—are also among those with the most potential for producing dysfunctions in the Wakefieldian sense described earlier. The challenge for psychiatry and the developmental sciences is therefore to develop strategies and criteria for discriminating between what may be phenotypically similar though etiologically different forms of antisocial behavior. To assume instead that it always reflects an underlying mental disorder confuses different universes of discourse and frames of reference.[63] It blurs important distinctions between moral/social deviance and psychopathology, evaluative judgments of behavior and its underlying causes, and issues of public health and science. Moreover, a failure to maintain these distinctions jeopardizes any opportunity for constructing a meaningful concept of mental disorder and stands as an obstacle to achieving the level of scientific understanding necessary for guiding intervention efforts. This is particularly salient in the case of chronically antisocial and delinquent children and youth, for whom the collective efforts of science, psychology, psychiatry, criminology, juvenile justice, social work, and education have thus far failed to produce effective interventions.

REFERENCES

1. RICHTERS, J. E. 1993. Community violence and children's development: Toward a research agenda for the 1990's. Psychiatry **56:** 3–6.
2. RICHTERS, J. E. & P. E. MARTINEZ. 1993. Violent communities, family choices, and

children's chances; An algorithm for improving the odds. Dev. Psychopathol. **5:** 609–623.

3. RICHTERS, J. E. & P. MARTINEZ. 1993. The NIMH Community Violence Project: Children as victims and witnesses to violence. Psychiatry **56:** 7–21.

4. NATIONAL RESEARCH COUNCIL. 1988. The behavioral and social sciences: Achievements and opportunities. National Academy Press. Washington, DC.

5. MOFFITT, T. E. 1993. Adolescent-limited versus life-course persistent delinquency. Psychol. Rev. **100:** 674–701.

6. RICHTERS, J. E. & D. CICCHETTI. 1993. Mark Twain meets DSM-III-R: Conduct disorder, development, and the concept of harmful dysfunction. Dev. Psychopathol. **5:** 5–29.

7. WRIGHT, R. 1995. The biology of violence. The New Yorker (March 13).

8. AMERICAN PSYCHIATRIC ASSOCIATION. 1994. Diagnostic and Statistical Manual of Mental Disorders (4th ed.). American Psychiatric Association. Washington, D.C.

9. HUTSCHNECKER, A. 1969. A plan for prevention of crime. Memo to the President of the United States on the Eisenhower Commission on Crime.

10. GOODWIN, F. & K. JAMISON. 1990. Manic-depressive Illness. Oxford University Press. New York.

11. SULLIVAN, L. W. 1992. Remarks by the Secretary of Health and Human Services to the American Academy of Child and Adolescent Psychiatry. October 22. Washington, D.C.

12. NATIONAL INSTITUTES OF HEALTH. 1994. Report of the Panel on NIH Research on Antisocial, Aggressive, and Violence-related Behaviors and Their Consequences. National Institutes of Health. Rockville, Maryland.

13. LEWIS, D. O. 1996. Conduct disorder. In Child and Adolescent Psychiatry: A comprehensive textbook (2nd ed.). M. Lewis, Ed.: 564–577. Williams and Wilkins. New York.

14. AMERICAN PSYCHIATRIC ASSOCIATION. 1980. Diagnostic and Statistical Manual of Mental Disorders (3rd ed.). American Psychiatric Association. Washington, D.C.

15. NATIONAL ADVISORY MENTAL HEALTH COUNCIL. 1990. National Plan for Research on Child and Adolescent Mental Disorders. National Institute of Mental Health. Rockville, Maryland.

16. GARMEZY, N. 1978. Never mind the psychologists: Is it good for the children? Clin. Psychol. **31:** 1–6.

17. CAMPBELL, S. B., A. M. BREAUX, L. J. EWING & E. K. SZUMOWSKI. 1986. Correlates and prediction of hyperactivity and aggression: A longitudinal study of parent-referred problem preschoolers. J. Abnorm. Child Psychol. **14:** 217–234.

18. CAMPBELL, S. B. 1991. Longitudinal studies of active and aggressive preschoolers: Individual differences in early behavior and in outcome. In Rochester Symposium on Developmental Psychopathology, Volume 2: Internalizing and Externalizing Expressions of Dysfunction. D. Cicchetti & S. L. Toth, Eds.: 57–89. Lawrence Erlbaum Associates. Hillsdale, NJ.

19. PATTERSON, G. R., D. CAPALDI & L. BANK. 1991. An early starter model for predicting delinquency. In The Development and Treatment of Childhood Aggression. D. Pepler & K. H. Rubin, Eds.: 139–168. Lawrence Erlbaum Associates. Hillsdale, NJ.

20. LADD, G. S., J. M. PRICE & C. H. HART. 1990. Preschooler's behavioral orientations and patterns of peer control: Predictive of peer status? In Peer Rejection in Childhood. S. R. Asher & J. D. Coie, Eds.: 90–115. Cambridge University Press. Cambridge.

21. MELTZER, L. J., M. D. LEVINE, W. KARNISKI, J. S. PALFREG & S. CLAREK. 1984. An analysis of the learning style of adolescent delinquents. J. Learn. Disabil. **17:** 600–608.

22. DISHION, T. J., G. R. PATTERSON & M. S. SKINNER. 1989. April. A process model for the role of peers in adolescent social adjustment. Paper presented at the biennial meeting of the Society for Research in Child Development. Kansas City, MO.

23. DISHION, T. J. & R. LOEBER. 1985. Adolescent marijuana and alcohol use: The role of parents and peers revisited. Am. J. Drug Alcohol Abuse **11:** 11–15.

24. CAIRNS, R. B., B. D. CAIRNS & H. J. NECKERMAN. 1989. Early school dropout: Configurations and determinants. Child Dev. **60:** 1437–1452.

25. LOEBER, R. & T. J. DISHION. 1983. Early predictors of male delinquency: A review. Psychol. Bull. **74:** 68–99.
26. LOEBER, R. & M. STOUTHAMER-LOEBER. 1987. Prediction. *In* Handbook of Juvenile Delinquency. H. C. Quay, Ed.: 325–382. Wiley. New York.
27. FARAONE, S. V., J. BIEDERMAN, K. KEENAN & M. T. TSUANG. 1991. Separation of DSM-III attention deficit disorder and conduct disorder: Evidence from a family genetic study of American child psychiatry patients. Psychol. Med. **21:** 109–121.
28. LOEBER, R. 1988. Natural histories of conduct problems, delinquency, and associated substance use: Evidence for developmental progressions. *In* Advances in Clinical Child Psychology. B. B. Lahey & A. E. Kazdin, Eds.: **11:** 73–124. Plenum Press. New York.
29. WALKER, J. L., B. B. LAHEY, M. F. RUSSO, M. A. G. CHRIST, K. MCBURNETT, R. LOEBER, M. STOUTHAMER-LOEBER & S. M. GREEN. 1991. Anxiety, inhibition, and conduct disorder in children: Relations to social impairment. J. Am. Acad. Child Adolesc. Psychiatry **30:** 187–191.
30. ZOCCOLILLO, M. 1992. Co-occurrence of conduct disorder and its adult outcomes with depressive and anxiety disorders: A review. J. Am. Acad. Child Adolesc. Psychiatry **31:** 547–556.
31. ZOCCOLILLO, M., A. PICKLES, D. QUINTON & M. RUTTER. 1992. The outcome of childhood conduct disorder: Implications for defining adult personality disorder. Psychol. Med. **22:** 971–986.
32. ROBINS, L. N. 1966. Deviant Children Grown Up. Williams & Wilkins. Baltimore.
33. DODGE, K. A., J. BATES & G. S. PETTIT. 1990. Mechanisms in the cycle of violence. Science **250:** 1678–1683.
34. DODGE, K. A., G. S. PETTIT, C. L. MCCLASKEY & M. BROWN. 1986. Social competence in children. Monogr. Soc. Res. Child Dev. (Serial No. 213), Vol. 51, No. 2.
35. DODGE, K. A., R. R. MURPHY & K. BUCHSBAUM. 1984. The assessment of intention-cue detection skills in children: Implications for developmental psychopathology. Child Dev. **55:** 163–173.
36. LOCHMAN, J. E. 1987. Self and peer perceptions and attributional biases of aggressive and nonaggressive boys in dyadic interactions. J. Consult. Clin. Psychol. **55:** 404–410.
37. DODGE, K. A., J. D. COIE, G. S. PETTIT & J. M. PRICE. 1990. Peer status and aggression in boys' groups: Developmental and contextual analyses. Child Dev. **61:** 1289–1309.
38. ASARNOW, J. R. & J. W. CALLAN. 1985. Boys and with peer adjustment problems: Social cognitive processes. J. Consult. Clin. Psychol. **53:** 80–87.
39. NEWMAN, J. P. 1987. Reaction to punishment in extroverts and psychopaths: Implications for the impulsive behavior of disinhibited individuals. J. Res. Pers. **21:** 464–480.
40. NEWMAN, J. P. & E. HOWLAND. 1989. The effect of incentives on Wisconsin card sorting task performance in psychopaths. Unpublished manuscript. University of Wisconsin at Madison.
41. WHITE, J., T. E. MOFFITT, A. CASPI, D. J. NEEDLES & M. STOUTHAMER-LOEBER. Measuring impulsivity and examining its relationship to delinquency. *In* Conduct Disorders in Children and Adolescents: Assessments on Intervention. G. P. Sholeva, Ed. American Psychiatric Press. Washington, D.C.
42. MOFFITT, T. E. & P. A. SILVA. 1988. IQ and delinquency: A direct test of the differential detection hypothesis. J. Abnorm. Psychol. **97:** 330–333.
43. KRUESI, M. J. P., J. L. RAPOPORT, S. D. HAMBURGER, E. D. HIBBS, W. Z. POTTER, M. LENARE & G. L. BROWN. 1990. Cerebrospinal fluid monoamine metabolites, aggression, and impulsivity in disruptive behavior disorders of children and adolescents. Arch. Gen. Psychiatry **47:** 419–426.
44. BROWN, G. L., F. K. GOODWIN, J. C. BALLENGER, P. F. GOYER & L. F. MAJOR. 1979. Aggression in humans correlates with cerebrospinal fluid amine metabolites. Psychiatry Res. **1:** 131–139.
45. COCARRO, E. F., L. J. SIEVER, H. M. KLAR, G. MAURER, K. COCHRANE, T. B. COOPER, R. C. MOHS & K. L. DAVIS. 1989. Serotonergic studies in patients with affective and personality disorders: Correlates with suicidal and impulsive aggressive behavior. Arch. Gen. Psychiatry **46:** 587–599.

46. HIGLEY, J. D., P. T. MEHLMAN, D. M. TAUB, S. B. HIGLEY, S. J. SUOMI, M. LINNOILA & J. H. VICKERS. 1992. Cerebrospinal fluid monoamine and adrenal correlates of aggression in free-ranging rhesus monkeys. Arch. Gen. Psychiatry **49:** 436–441.
47. RAINE, A., P. H. VENABLES & M. A. WILLIAMS. 1990. Autonomic orienting responses in 15-year-old male subjects and criminal behavior at age 24. Am. J. Psychiatry **147:** 933–937.
48. DAUGHERTY, T. K. & H. C. QUAY. 1991. Response perseveration and delayed responding in childhood behavior disorders. J. Child Applied Discip. Psychol. **32:** 453–461.
49. SHAPIRO, S. K., H. C. QUAY, A. E. HOGAN & K. P. SCHWARTZ. 1988. Response perseveration and delayed responding in undersocialized aggressive conduct disorder. J. Abnorm. Psychol. **97:** 371–373.
50. NEWMAN, J. P. & D. S. KOSSON. 1986. Passive avoidance learning in psychopathic and nonpsychopathic offenders. J. Abnorm. Psychol. **95:** 257–263.
51. CICCHETTI, D. 1996. Regulatory processes. Special Issue. Dev. Psychopathol. **8:** 1–305.
52. CICCHETTI, D. 1984. The emergence of developmental psychopathology. Child Dev. **55:** 1–7.
53. CICCHETTI, D. 1990. Perspectives on the interface between normal and atypical development. Dev. Psychopathol. **2:** 329–333.
54. SROUFE, L. A. & M. RUTTER. 1984. The domain of developmental psychopathology. Child Dev. **55:** 17–29.
55. WAKEFIELD, J. C. 1992a. Disorder as harmful dysfunction: A conceptual critique of DSM-III-R's definition of mental disorder. Psychol. Rev. **99:** 232–247.
56. WAKEFIELD, J. C. 1992b. The concept of mental disorder: On the boundary between biological facts and social values. Am. Psychol. **47:** 373–388.
57. BERTALANFFY, L. VON. 1968. General System Theory. Braziller. New York.
58. CICCHETTI, D. & M. LYNCH. 1993. Toward an ecological/transactional model of community violence and child maltreatment: Consequences for children's development. Psychiatry **56:** 96–118.
59. BUSS, D. M. 1984. Evolutionary biology and personality psychology: Toward a conception of human nature and individual differences. Am. Psychol. **39:** 1135–1147.
60. MEEHL, P. E. 1978. Theoretical risks and tabular asterisks: Sir Karl, Sir Ronald, and the slow progress of soft psychology. J. Consult. Clin. Psychol. **46:** 806–834.
61. MALTZ, M. D. 1994. Deviating from the mean: The declining significance of significance. J. Res. Crime Delinquency **31:** 434–436.
62. RICHTERS, J. E. & D. CICCHETTI. 1993. Editorial: Toward a developmental perspective on conduct disorder. Dev. Psychopathol. **5:** 1–4.
63. McCORD, J. 1993. Conduct disorder and antisocial behavior: Some thoughts about processes. Dev. Psychopathol. **5:** 321–329.
64. PILEGGI, N. 1985. Wiseguy: Life in a Mafia Family. Pocket Books. New York.
65. FARRINGTON, D. P. 1993. Motivations for conduct disorder and delinquency. Dev. Psychopathol. **5:** 225–241.

A Prospective Examination
of Risk for Violence among
Abused and Neglected Children[a]

CATHY SPATZ WIDOM[b,d] AND MICHAEL G. MAXFIELD[c]

[b]School of Criminal Justice
The University at Albany (SUNY)
135 Western Avenue
Albany, New York 12222

[c]School of Public and Environmental Affairs
Indiana University
Bloomington, Indiana

INTRODUCTION

The idea that childhood victimization and violent behavior are linked has become firmly established in the minds of professionals as well as the general public. Over the last twenty years, numerous books and articles have described what has been referred to as the *cycle of violence* or the *intergenerational transmission of violence*.[1] However, despite tougher child abuse laws, increased public awareness, and an increase in social service agencies to deal with these problems, more than thirty years after Curtis[2] called attention to the intergenerational transmission of violence, our knowledge of the long-term consequences of abusive home environments remains limited. Because of a dearth of sound empirical information on the relationship between childhood abuse, neglect, and later violent criminal behavior, policy makers must operate on the basis of unsubstantiated assumptions and widespread beliefs.

One of the frequent observations in the criminology literature has been the association between child abuse and neglect and later delinquency, adult criminality, and violent criminal behavior. A number of studies have addressed this relationship.[3-10] Some studies provide support for the linkage between child abuse and neglect and later violent behavior, whereas others do not.[3,6] In some, abused delinquents were actually less likely to engage in later aggressive crimes.[5] Few studies have extended these investigations beyond adolescence and into adulthood.

In a review of the cycle of violence literature, Widom[1] concluded that "methodological problems play a major role in restricting our knowledge of the long-term consequences." With some exceptions, most studies have relied on retrospective, unsubstantiated reports of abuse and neglect, and most do not incorporate control groups into their designs. Because many of the same family and demographic

[a] This research was supported by Grants from the National Institute of Justice (86-IJ-CX-0033 and 93-IJ-CX-0031), Indiana University Research Committee (SO7 RR0731), and the Talley Foundation (Harvard University). Points of view are those of the authors and do not necessarily represent the position of the United States Department of Justice.
[d] Tel: (518) 442-5226; fax: (518) 442-5603.

characteristics found in abusive home environments also relate to delinquency and adult criminality, appropriate control groups are necessary to assess the independent effects of childhood victimization. Without control groups to provide rough estimates of such base rates, it has been difficult to assess the magnitude of these relationships or the independent contribution of childhood abuse and/or neglect. As Monahan[11] argued, the most important piece of information we can have in the prediction of violence is the base rate of violent behavior in the population with which we are dealing.

Research has begun to document the relationship between child abuse and neglect and later violent criminal behavior in a way that researchers, practitioners, and policy makers recognize and are willing to accept. In earlier reports,[12,13] children who were abused and neglected approximately 20 years ago were followed up through an examination of official criminal records and compared with a matched control group of children of the same age, sex, race, and approximate social class. Abused and neglected children overall had more arrests as juveniles (26 vs. 17%) and as adults (29 vs. 21%). Although physically abused children had the highest rates of arrest for violent criminal behavior (16%), neglected children had arrest rates for violence almost as high (13%). Importantly, the majority of these abused and neglected children did not become delinquents, adult criminals, or violent offenders, indicating that the linkage between childhood victimization and later antisocial and criminal behavior is far from inevitable. Thus, these earlier reports indicated that child abuse and neglect may predispose children toward a negative life trajectory, but they also emphasized that the relationship was by no means deterministic.

Widom's research was conducted in a metropolitan county in the Midwest, using cases of abuse and neglect that came to the attention of the courts during the years 1967 through 1971. Criminal history searches were conducted in 1987–1988. In a different geographic area of the country and a later time period, Thornberry and colleagues collected information about child abuse and neglect from the New York State Department of Social Services records as part of the Rochester Youth Development Study. Smith and Thornberry[14] reported significant relationships between child abuse and neglect (before the age of 11) and later delinquency, using self-reports as well as official arrest information. Similarly, using maltreated children and two court-aged, nonmaltreated comparison samples from Mecklenburg County, North Carolina, Zingraff, Leiter, Myers, and Johnsen[15] also found that maltreated children had higher rates of delinquency complaints than nonmaltreated school and impoverished children. The effects were diminished when the authors controlled for demographic and family structure variables.

Widom's[12,13] earlier research demonstrated convincingly that childhood victimization places children at increased risk for delinquency, adult criminality, and violent criminal behavior. That work was important as a first step in defining samples (abused and neglected subjects and a control group) and in answering basic questions about the relationship between childhood victimization and later violent behavior using official records. However, many unresolved issues and unanswered questions remain, including the assessment of risk for criminal violence through the peak years of risk for violent offending.

Official criminal histories were originally collected in 1987 and 1988. At that time, only 65% of the sample had passed through the peak years of offending (ages 20–25). Thus, the figures published to date on the child abuse, delinquency, and violence connections may be underestimates of lifetime arrest rates for violence, or the true extent of criminality and violence. Updated criminal histories were collected in 1994. In 1994, less than 1% of the sample was less than 25 years old. Thus, the vast majority of these individuals had reached or passed through the peak years of risk for violent offending.[16]

Purpose

There are five goals of this paper. The first goal is to document the prevalence of criminality and violence in this sample of previously abused and/or neglected children and controls using updated criminal history information. This new and updated criminal history information permits a more accurate and complete picture of the childhood victimization and violence relationship.

Second, a common assumption in the criminological literature is that once a person begins a delinquent career, the likelihood that they will continue is very high. The assumption is also made that once a person becomes a violent offender as a juvenile, there is a high probability that they will continue as a violent offender into adulthood. Earlier, we found no differences between abused and/or neglected and control subjects in the continuity of offending as a juvenile to offending as an adult.[17] Of those with juvenile offenses, roughly the same proportion of abused and neglected children and controls went on to commit offenses as adults, and, of those with violent offenses as juveniles, approximately the same proportion (about one third) of the abuse and neglect group was arrested for violence as adults as among the controls. Thus, despite major differences in the extent of involvement in criminal activity, nonabused and nonneglected subjects were just as likely as abused and neglected individuals to continue criminal activity and violent offending once they had begun.

Third, this paper also examines the extent to which there are gender differences in the relationship between childhood victimization and subsequent criminal and violent behavior. Earlier reports documented that experiencing child abuse or neglect had a substantial impact on criminal behavior, even on individuals with little likelihood of having an official record. The earlier work, however, suggested that the outcomes were not uniform across the sexes. Significant increases in violent offending were primarily found for males who had been abused and/or neglected in comparison to control males. The findings were different for females. Abused and/or neglected females were not more likely to commit a violent offense than nonabused females. Widom[13] speculated that the consequences of abuse and neglect in females might be directed inwardly, rather than through outward expressions of aggression, or in more subtle forms, such as self-destructive behavior or depression.

Another pervasive belief in the field of child abuse and neglect and among people who study violence is that violence begets violence. It is assumed that victims of violence themselves become violent victimizers when they grow up. How likely is it that today's victims of violence become tomorrow's perpetrators of violence? In its strictest sense, the notion that "violence begets violence" refers to the idea that physical abuse or physical punishment in childhood leads to later violence in adolescence and adulthood. Physically abusive parents are thought to serve as models for their children, who learn that such behavior is normative, acceptable as a means of relating interpersonally, and appropriate as a means of dealing with anger and conflict.[18] Thus, the fourth goal of this paper is to examine whether violence begets violence exclusively.

So far, this paper has focused on the role of childhood victimization as a risk factor for criminal violence. This paper also examines the role of one potential protective factor as a mediator of criminal violence. Not all abused and neglected children grow up to become delinquents, adult criminals, or violent criminal offenders. Although one can speculate on a number of reasons why child abuse and neglect lead to certain outcomes, it is possible that certain life experiences act as buffers against longterm negative consequences. Protective factors refer to attributes of persons, environments, situations, and events that appear to temper predictions of psychopathology or negative outcomes based on an individual's at-risk status. Protective factors provide resistance to risk, and are thought to ameliorate or buffer a person's response to constitutional risk factors or stressful life events.[19]

One of the factors that may act to protect abused and/or neglected children from more serious long-term consequences is placement outside the home. Scholars and practitioners have often criticized out-of-home placements (and foster care, in particular) for having deleterious consequences. Under certain circumstances, out-of-home placements may not necessarily lead to negative effects. On the other hand, children in foster care and other placement experiences are a particularly vulnerable group because they have experienced both a disturbed family situation and separation from their biological parents. Accordingly, child welfare policies today often seek to avoid removing the child from the home and instead mitigate negative family situations through counseling and related support. The fifth and final goal of this paper is to describe the role of out-of-home placement experiences as potential mediators of criminal violence among abused and neglected children.

METHODS

Design

This study used a specialized cohorts design to assess the effects of early childhood victimization on later criminal behavior. The design was a prospective one, based on a medical model with an experimental group and a matched control group, using specialized cohorts. All subjects were free of the "disease" in question (that is, delinquent, adult criminal, or violent criminal behavior) at the time they were chosen for the study (1967 through 1971). The groups differed, however, in the attribute of interest here (early childhood victimization in the form of substantiated cases of abuse or neglect). Cases were restricted to children who were aged 11 or under at the time of abuse, to avoid ambiguity in the temporal ordering of childhood victimization and offending. This design is particularly appropriate to yield findings with clear implications for developing primary prevention strategies and to suggest interventions to reduce long-term negative consequences.[20,21]

Case Selection

Cases of child abuse and neglect were identified from local juvenile court and adult criminal court records in a Midwest metropolitan area for the years 1967 through 1971. Physical abuse cases are those where an individual "knowingly and willfully inflicted unnecessarily severe corporal punishment" or "unnecessary physical suffering" upon a child. Physical abuse cases include injuries, such as bruises, welts, burns, abrasions, lacerations, wounds, cuts, bone and skull fractures, and other evidence of physical injury. Sexual abuse cases include a variety of charges, including "assault and battery with intent to gratify sexual desires," "fondling or touching in an obscene manner," sodomy, and incest. Neglect cases are those in which the court found a child to have no proper parental care or guardianship, to be destitute, homeless, or to be living in a physically dangerous environment. Neglect cases reflect the court's judgment that parents' deficiencies in child care were beyond those found acceptable by community and professional standards at the time.

Initially, all abuse and neglect cases filed in either juvenile court or adult criminal court were eligible for inclusion. Cases were excluded if the child was adopted, subject to involuntary neglect, or where the neglect charge involved only failure to pay child support. After exclusions, 908 victims of abuse or neglect remained.

Matched Control Group

Earlier studies of the consequences of child abuse often used clinical samples or other samples of convenience. Given that child abuse, delinquency, and adult criminal behavior have many common correlates, it is necessary to compare samples of abused or neglected cases to similarly situated children who have not been victims of abuse or neglect. Because a randomized design was not possible, cases of child abuse and neglect were matched with control subjects as closely as possible on age, race, sex, and approximate family social class.

Procedures for selecting matched controls for abuse and neglect cases varied by the subject's age. Children who were of school age at the time of abuse were matched with a control by sex, race, and date of birth ($\pm$ 6 months) who attended the same class in the same elementary school during the years 1967–1971, and who lived within a five-block radius of the abuse or neglect victim. Matches were found for 438 of 589 school-age children (74%). Children under school age were matched by sex, race, date of birth ($\pm$ 1 week), and hospital of birth. Of 319 subjects under school age, matches were located for 229 (72%). Although imperfect, these matching procedures produced controls for age, sex, race, and approximate family social class. The absence of school busing for racial integration helped produce homogeneous public schools in the study site. Similarly, the design assumed that persons of the same race, born in the same urban hospital within one week of each other in the late 1950s through 1970 were more similar with respect to income than were persons born in different urban hospitals at different times.

The prospective cohort design assumed that controls differed from subjects only in the experience of abuse or neglect. Official records were checked to determine if a proposed control subject had been abused or neglected. Records of abuse or neglect were discovered for 11 prospective matches who were subsequently excluded from the study and replaced with an alternate control subject.

Matches were found for 667 of the 908 abused and neglected subjects (73%), producing a total of 1575 subjects for analysis. As a group, abused and neglected children did not differ significantly from controls with respect to sex (49% and 50% male), race (35% and 31% black), and age (1994 mean ages were 32.6 and 32.5 years), respectively. Analyses reported here are based on all 1,575 subjects.

Detailed information about the abuse or neglect incident and family composition and characteristics were obtained from the files of the juvenile court and probation department, the authority responsible for cases of abused, neglected, or dependent and delinquent children. Juvenile court and probation department records were also examined for the control subjects. Searches also extended to the Bureau of

Motor Vehicles and (for all females) marriage license records to find social security numbers to assist in tracing subjects.

Criminal History Information

Records of three levels of law enforcement (local, state, and federal) agencies were searched for arrests. Initial criminal history searches were conducted in 1987 and 1988, and earlier publications[12,13,17] reflect that information. Updated criminal history searches were completed in June 1994. Violent offenses include arrests for the following crimes and attempts: assault, battery, robbery, manslaughter, murder, rape, and burglary with injury. Juvenile arrests refer to arrests for offenses committed while the person was less than 18 years of age. Adult arrests refer to arrests for (nontraffic) offenses committed by a person 18 years of age or older. Any violent arrest refers to any arrest for a violent offense (juvenile or adult).

RESULTS

Risk of Arrest for Criminal Violence

Abused and neglected children have a higher likelihood of arrests for delinquency, adult criminality, and violent criminal behavior than matched controls (see TABLE 1). The odds that an abused and/or neglected person will be arrested as a juvenile are 1.8 times higher than for a group of matched controls, 1.5 times higher for an arrest as an adult, and 1.35 times higher for an arrest for a violent crime. Furthermore, compared to controls, abused and neglected children are arrested earlier, commit more offenses, and more often become chronic or repeat offenders (data not shown). Overall, although the majority do not become delinquents, adult criminals, or violent criminals, for some subgroups of abused and neglected children (*e.g.*, males), the percent who become offenders is substantial and approaching the majority.

Gender Differences

Although males generally have higher rates of criminal behavior than females, TABLE 2 makes clear that being abused or neglected in childhood increases the

TABLE 1. Extent of Involvement in Delinquency, Adult Criminality, and Violent Criminal Behavior among Abused and/or Neglected (n = 908) and Control (n = 667) Subjects

Arrests (%)	Abuse/Neglect	Control	Odds Ratio	Confidence Interval
Juvenile	27.4	17.2***	1.80	1.41–2.31
Adult	41.6	32.5***	1.47	1.20–1.81
Any violent crime	18.1	13.9*	1.35	1.02–1.78

* p ≤ .05
** p ≤ .01
*** p ≤ .001

TABLE 2. Extent of Involvement in Delinquency, Adult Criminality, and Violent Criminal Behavior among Abused and/or Neglected and Control Groups by Gender

Arrests (%)	Abuse/Neglect	Control	Odds Ratio	Confidence Interval
Juvenile				
Male	35	23***	1.80	1.30–2.48
Female	20	11***	1.94	1.29–2.92
Adult				
Male	55	49[a]		
Female	28	16***	2.09	1.47–2.99
Violent Crime				
Male	28	24		
Female	8	4**	2.38	1.22–4.63

* $p \leq .05$
** $p \leq .01$
*** $p \leq .001$
[a] Significant at $p \leq 0.05$ level with one-tailed test.

risk of arrest for females. Thus, experiencing early child abuse or neglect has a substantial impact even on females who generally have little likelihood of engaging in officially recorded criminal behavior. The odds that abused and neglected females will be arrested as a juvenile, as an adult, and for a violent crime are about two times higher than for a matched group of control females. Interestingly, the odds that abused and neglected males will be arrested as adults and for violent crimes are not significantly higher than for control males. These findings are in contrast to earlier findings based on criminal history information collected through 1988.

Chronicity

Are abused and neglected children more likely to continue in a life of crime than other children? Roughly the same proportion of abused and neglected children and controls with juvenile arrests go on to have arrests as adults (71% versus 66%). This means that nonabused and nonneglected subjects are just as likely as abused and neglected individuals to continue criminal activity once they have begun, suggesting that early childhood victimization does not effect the likelihood that a person will continue in a life of crime. These findings also reinforce the notion of the stability of antisocial and aggressive behavior.[22] Once individuals begin to offend, there is a very high likelihood that they will continue to offend.

These findings point to the importance of distinguishing factors that may stimulate an individual to become involved in crime from factors that affect whether the person continues or desists in a criminal career. Although abuse and neglect may increase one's propensity to have an official criminal record and enter into delinquent acts, early childhood victimization does not appear to place one at increased risk for continuing in a life of crime over time.

Does Violence Beget Violence Exclusively?

In a direct test of the cycle of violence hypothesis, violent criminal behavior was examined as a function of the type of abuse or neglect experienced as a child.

TABLE 3. Does Violence Breed Violence? Arrest for Violence by Type of Abuse or Neglect[a]

Abuse Group	N	Arrest for Any Violent Offense (%)
Physical abuse only	76	21
Neglect only	609	20
Physical abuse and neglect	70	16
Sexual abuse and other abuse	28	11
Sexual abuse only	125	9
Controls	667	14

[a] chi square (5) = 16.04, p ≤ .01.

Defining a childhood history of violence as physical abuse only, the cycle of violence hypothesis would predict that compared to other types of abuse or neglect, individuals experiencing physical abuse as a child should show higher levels of violence. These findings indicate that being physically abused increases one's risk of criminal violence, but being neglected also increases the likelihood of violent behavior (see TABLE 3). Victims of sexual abuse were least likely to have an arrest for violence. However, this is somewhat misleading inasmuch as victims of sexual abuse were overwhelmingly female (84%), and females less often have official records for criminal violence.

Because different types of abuse and neglect are not distributed evenly across different age, sex, and race groups in our sample, these bivariate statistics (in TABLE 3) present a somewhat oversimplified picture. However, even after controlling for age, sex, and race, the physical abuse and neglect groups have a significantly higher likelihood of having an arrest for a violent crime than controls. Logistic regression analysis was used to examine the effects of predictor variables on the binomial response variable (having an arrest for violence). This technique was used to estimate the odds ratio (OR) of having an arrest for violence among subjects who exhibited a given characteristic, relative to subjects who did not have that characteristic. TABLE 4 presents the results of a logistic regression analysis that predicted any arrest for violence (juvenile or adult), showing sex, race, age in 1994, and the type of abuse or neglect. Group contrasts express

TABLE 4. Predictors of Arrest for Any Violent Crime (juvenile or adult): Logistic Regression Coefficients, Odds Ratios, and 95% Confidence Intervals (n = 1,460)

	B	Standard Error	Odds Ratio	Confidence Interval
Male	1.86***	.19	6.40	4.44–9.24
Black	1.41***	.16	4.09	3.00–5.57
Physical abuse	.65*	.33	1.91	1.00–3.68
Neglect	.43**	.17	1.55	1.12–2.14
Sexual abuse	.24	.38		
Age in 1994	.07**	.02	1.07	1.03–1.12

* p ≤ .05
** p ≤ .01
*** p ≤ .001

coefficients and ORs for each pure type of abuse (omitting cases of more than one type of abuse) relative to the control group.

The results of the multivariate analysis confirm the bivariate findings presented earlier in TABLE 3. Childhood victims of physical abuse and neglect were more likely to have been arrested for a violent crime, after controlling for age, sex, and race. Childhood victims of sexual abuse were not at significantly greater risk of arrest for violence, compared to the control subjects.

The Role of Out-of-Home Placement Experiences

Year-by-year information was available from official records of the juvenile court and probation department about placements, institutionalizations, and detentions for a subset of the larger sample of abuse and neglect cases, that is, 772 cases of children from the juvenile court. For these children, a variety of placement options was pursued, including foster care, guardian's home, and schools for the retarded or physically handicapped.[23] Only 14% of these court-substantiated cases of abuse and neglect had no record of having been placed up through age 18. The average amount of time in placement was about five years and sometimes lasted through childhood and adolescence.

As TABLE 5 shows, there was little difference between the arrest records of those who remained at home and those who were placed outside the home due to abuse and neglect. Abused and neglected children who were not placed outside the home and those placed only for abuse or neglect experiences had similar arrest outcomes, but both were strikingly different from children placed for abuse and neglect and for delinquency. At least for this sample, then, an out-of-home placement did not lead to negative effects on the arrest measure for those who were removed from their homes due only to abuse and neglect.

Looking at placement experiences for all abused and neglected children may also obscure important differences in outcome. There may be some children who benefit from out-of-home placement experiences and others for whom these experiences may not be beneficial. For example, a small group of abused and neglected children (6.8%) have notations in their files of behavior problems. These notes covered a wide spectrum of problem behaviors, including chronic fighting, fire setting, destructiveness, uncontrollable anger, sadistic tendencies (for example, aggressiveness toward weaker children), and extreme defiance of authority. Chil-

TABLE 5. Juvenile and Adult Arrests as a Function of Placement Experiences for Juvenile Court Cases Only (n = 772)

Type of Placement	N	Any Juvenile (n = 215)	Any Adult (n = 317)	Both Juvenile and Adult (n = 155)	Any Violent Crime (n = 148)
No placement	106	16.0	44.3	10.4	15.1
Abuse/neglect placement only	489	18.6	37.0	12.5	14.1
Delinquency placement plus abuse/neglect	96	92.7	78.1	71.9	53.1
		***	***	***	***

*** p < .001

dren with behavior problems in this sample were more likely to make frequent moves (an average of 4.0 moves) than children (1.4 moves) without indications of behavior problems in their records. Two thirds of these behavior problem children made three or more moves in various placements, as compared to only 16% of the other children in foster care with no behavior problems noted. Children who make more moves are at higher risk for later delinquency and adult criminality. Not surprisingly, children who have both of these characteristics (behavior problems and more frequent placement moves) have very high rates of delinquency, adult criminality, and violent criminal behavior.

CONCLUSIONS AND IMPLICATIONS

Childhood victimization represents a widespread, serious social problem. Earlier reports demonstrated that childhood abuse and neglect increases the likelihood of delinquency, adult criminality, and violent criminal behavior. These new, updated results make clear that the strength of these relationships continues to be potent. Although the majority of abused and neglected children continue not to have arrests, for some subgroups (males) the prevalence of criminal behavior approaches the majority.

The presence of gender differences in consequences of childhood victimization warrants some comment. These new, updated findings represent a change from earlier findings,[13] in which the abused and neglected females were not at increased risk for arrests for violent crimes. Females in general are less likely to be violent on the streets (and to be arrested for street violence), whereas they appear more often in statistics on violence in the home. One wonders whether the increase in risk of violence in the abused and neglected females in this further follow-up might be attributed to a different kind of violence (domestic violence, such as in child abuse or spouse abuse) that might develop later and that is also less likely to come to the attention of criminal justice officials. On the other hand, what some might have considered a weak finding in earlier research (*i.e.*, that abused and neglected females were significantly more likely to be arrested as *juveniles* for a violent crime than were control females) might have presaged a more enduring pattern of behavior that is more accurately depicted when subjects are traced through early adulthood, as we have done here. Further examination of these issues needs to be undertaken, as well as the provocative finding that abused and neglected males are not at increased risk of arrests for violence, compared to control males.

For females, the long-term consequences of child abuse and neglect may also be manifest in other ways. Abused females may be more likely to suffer depression and perhaps undergo psychiatric hospitalization as a consequence of early childhood experiences than to direct their aggression "outwardly." Because the type of abuse and neglect suffered by females and males differs (more females are sexually abused than males), this may influence differences in long-term outcomes. In addition, there is some evidence that depressed mothers have higher rates of abuse and neglect of their children than nondepressed mothers.[24,25] If childhood victimization leads to high rates of depression in women, then transmission across generations might be mediated by depression in mothers.

Some frequently held assumptions about childhood victimization and violent offending were supported by the findings of this study, but these results also seriously challenge some popular assumptions. If one were to answer the question posed earlier about the likelihood that today's abused and neglected children will become tomorrow's murderers and perpetrators of other violence, the answer is a complicated one. Children who are abused and neglected are subsequently at increased risk of being arrested for a violent crime, but by no means will all childhood victims of abuse and neglect become violent offenders. Although these children are at increased risk for violent offending, the relationship between early childhood victimization and later violent offending is not universal or deterministic, by any means.

However, these findings demonstrate a clear and direct link between neglect (as distinct from physical or sexual abuse) and later violent criminal behavior. There is also mounting evidence that many of the observed deficits in abused children may be attributed to neglect. Some researchers have suggested that neglect may be potentially more damaging to the development of the child than abuse (*i.e.*, if abuse is not associated with neurological impairment), particularly in the areas of language development,[26] psychosocial development,[27,28] and empathic responsiveness.[29] In one study of the influence of early malnutrition on subsequent behavioral development,[30] previously malnourished children had attention deficits, reduced social skills, and poorer emotional stability when compared to comparison children. These deficits were independent of IQ. Because neglected children are at significantly increased risk for becoming violent offenders, prevention efforts need to be expanded. Today's victims of neglect may well be defendants in tomorrow's violent criminal case.

These findings are also of particular concern inasmuch as the majority of official reports of child abuse and neglect are cases of neglect (15.9 per 1,000 children in 1986, as compared to 5.7 per 1,000 for physical abuse and 2.5 per 1,000 for sexual abuse).[31,32] Very little is known about the long-term consequences of childhood neglect. Evidence from the fields of developmental psychology and public health suggest serious long-term negative outcomes.

In contrast to today's practices, the vast majority of abused and neglected children in this sample were placed outside the home during some portion of their childhood. At present, it is unclear what proportion of children in foster care in the United States return home.[33] However, if it is determined that stability in placement is important, or that early placement under certain conditions is beneficial, then it may be necessary to make changes in the legal process to insure a greater degree of stability for the child. These findings challenge the assumption that it is necessarily unwise to remove children from negative family situations. Although stability of placement appears to be important, the potential damage of removing an abused and neglected child from the home did not include a higher likelihood of arrest for violent criminal behavior. At the same time, there may be certain conditions under which children are better served by remaining at home.

Although these findings offer insight into the role of placement experiences in mediating between childhood victimization and long-term criminal consequences, given the exclusive reliance on official records for both the independent and dependent variables, the time period investigated, and the geographic restrictiveness of this sample, caution is urged in interpreting and generalizing from these findings. Present-day abused and neglected foster care children may differ from the sample of children studied here and may come from more dysfunctional families, characterized by substance abuse, domestic violence, and homelessness.

This study focused on cases of early childhood abuse and neglect processed during the period 1967–1971, when out-of-home placements were a common intervention for abused and neglected children. The vast majority of these children were placed outside their home for an average of five years. This contrasts sharply with today's efforts to avoid out-of-home placement, on the assumption that separation may aggravate, rather than ameliorate, a child's problems. Yet, there was no evidence that those who were separated from their families fared any worse on the arrest measures than those who remained at home. Though these results are far from definitive, they do suggest that child protective policies in this area deserve close scrutiny. The assumption that removal from the home offers additional risk was not confirmed in this study. Policies founded on this assumption should be tested through contemporary studies of the consequences of out-of-home placement.

These findings suggest that interventions need to occur early so that they can affect early stages of development. Given the demonstrated increased risk associated with early childhood victimization, police, teachers, and health workers need to recognize signs of abuse and neglect and take action to intervene early. Later interventions should not be ignored, but the later the intervention in the child's life, the more labor intensive and more difficult the change process becomes. Particular attention needs to be paid to abused and neglected children with behavior problems noted early in their lives. These are likely to be the children who are at risk for becoming chronic runaways and at highest risk of becoming offenders and violent offenders. These children are likely to be the children who cycle through foster homes, not finding a stable home placement. Whether frequent moves reflects an early predisposition to antisocial behavior or, in part, a response to it, children with numerous placements are in need of special services. Policies that provide resources and specialized approaches for this small subgroup of abused and neglected children are needed.

These findings do not tell us about violent behavior in general, such as unrecorded or unreported family violence. In the past, there has been little attention paid to the overlap between criminal violence and family violence (violence toward children, spouses, siblings, or parents). The extent to which violence within the home extends to violence on the streets is unknown. Although there are suggestions in the literature that violence in one sphere of life tends to spill over into other spheres, fundamental questions remain about the proportion of families who are multiviolent as well as multiproblem.

Finally, there needs to be increased recognition that children are not doomed if their childhood includes abuse and/or neglect. Studies in the field of child abuse and neglect have begun to acknowledge that some substantial subset of physically or sexually abused or neglected children do not manifest psychopathology or criminal behavior. Not all children who grow up in abusive or neglectful homes become violent adults. Certainly there are a wide variety of environmental stresses, potential triggering mechanisms, and many other factors involved in that developmental process. There is an urgent need to learn more about the factors that protect children from the development of antisocial, delinquent, and adult criminal behavior and the factors that contribute to cessation of delinquent behavior once it has begun.

REFERENCES

1. WIDOM, C. S. 1989. Does violence beget violence? A critical examination of the literature. Psychol. Bull. **106**(1): 3–28.
2. CURTIS, G. C. 1963. Violence breeds violence—perhaps? Am. J. Psychiatry **120:** 386–387.
3. ALFARO, J. D. 1981. Report on the relationship between child abuse and neglect and later socially deviant behavior. R. J. Hunner & Y. B. Walker, Eds.: 175. In Exploring

the Relationship Between Child Abuse and Delinquency. Allanheld, Osmun. Montclair, NJ.

4. GELLER, M. & L. FORD-SOMMA. 1984. Violent homes, violent children: A study of violence in the families of juvenile offenders. New Jersey State Department of Corrections, Division of Juvenile Services, Trenton, N.J. (Prepared for the National Center on Child Abuse and Neglect.)

5. GUTIERRES, S. & J. A. REICH. 1981. A developmental perspective on runaway behavior: Its relationship to child abuse. Child Welfare 60: 89–94.

6. KRATCOSKI, P. C. 1982. Child abuse and violence against the family. Child Welfare 61: 435–444.

7. HARTSTONE, E. & K. V. HANSEN. 1984. The violent juvenile offender: An empirical portrait. R. A. Mathias, P. Demuro & R. S. Allinson, Eds.: 83. In Violent Juvenile Offenders: An Anthology. National Council on Crime and Delinquency. San Francisco.

8. LEWIS, D. O., S. S. SHANOK, J. H. PINCUS et al. 1979. Violent juvenile delinquents: Psychiatric, neurological, psychological, and abuse factors. J. Am. Acad. Child Psychiatry 18: 1161–1167.

9. LEWIS, D. O., M. FELDMAN & A. BARRENGOS. 1985. Race, health, and delinquency. J. Am. Acad. Child Psychiatry 24: 161–165.

10. McCORD, J. 1983. A forty-year perspective on effects of child abuse and neglect. Child Abuse & Neglect 7: 265–270.

11. MONAHAN, J. 1981. Predicting Violent Behavior: An Assessment of Clinical Techniques. Sage. Beverly Hills, CA.

12. WIDOM, C. S. 1989. Child abuse, neglect and adult behavior; Research design and findings on criminality, violence, and child abuse. Am. J. Orthopsychiatry 59: 355–367.

13. WIDOM, C. S. 1989. The cycle of violence. Science 244: 160–166.

14. SMITH, C. & T. P. THORNBERRY. 1995. The relationship between childhood maltreatment and adolescent involvement in delinquency. Criminology 33: 451–481.

15. ZINGRAFF, M. T., J. LEITER, K. A. MYERS et al. 1993. Child maltreatment and youthful problem behavior. Criminology 31: 173–202.

16. REISS, JR., A. I. &. J. A. ROTH, Eds. 1993. Understanding and Preventing Violence. National Academy Press. Washington, DC. pp. 73–74.

17. RIVERA, B. & C. S. WIDOM. 1990. Childhood victimization and violent offending. Violence Victims 5: 19–34.

18. STRAUS, M. A., R. J. GELLES & S. K. STEINMETZ. 1980. Behind Closed Doors: Violence in the American Family. Anchor Press, Garden City, NY.

19. RUTTER, M. 1979. Protective factors in children's response to stress and disadvantage. In Primary Prevention of Psychopathology: Social Competence in Children. M. W. Kent & J. E. Rolf, Eds. 3: 49. New England Press. Hanover, NH.

20. SCHULSINGER, F., S. A. MEDNICK & J. KNOP. 1981. Longitudinal Research: Methods and Uses in Behavioral Sciences. Martinus Nijhoff Publishers. Boston.

21. LEVENTHAL, J. M. 1982. Research strategies and methodologic standards in studies of risk factors for child abuse. Child Abuse & Neglect 6: 113–123.

22. ROBINS, L. N. 1978. Sturdy childhood predictors of adult antisocial behavior: Replications from longitudinal studies. Psychol. Med. 8: 611–622.

23. WIDOM, C. S. 1991. The role of placement experiences in mediating the criminal consequences of early childhood victimization. Am. J. Orthopsychiatry 6: 195–209.

24. DOWNEY, G., S. FELDMAN, J. KHURI et al. 1994. Maltreatment and childhood depression. In Handbook of Depression in Children and Adolescents. W. M. Reynolds & H. F. Johnson, Eds. Plenum Press. New York.

25. BRODY, G. H. & R. FOREHAND. 1986. Maternal perceptions of child maladjustment as a function of the combined influence of child behavior and maternal depression. J. Consult. Clin. Psychol. 54: 237–240.

26. ALLEN, R. E. & J. M. OLIVER. 1982. The effects of child maltreatment on language development. Child Abuse & Neglect 6: 299–305.

27. BOUSHA, D. M. & C. T. TWENTYMAN. 1984. Mother-child interactional style in abuse,

neglect and control groups: Naturalistic observations in the home. J. Abnorm. Psychol. **93:** 106–114.

28. EGELAND, B. E., L. A. SROUFE & M. ERICKSON. 1983. The developmental consequences of different patterns of maltreatment. Child Abuse & Neglect **7:** 459–469.

29. FRODI, A. & J. SMETANA. 1984. Abused , neglected, and nonmaltreated preschoolers' ability to discriminate emotions in others: The effects of IQ. Child Abuse & Neglect **8:** 459–465.

30. GALLER, J. R., F. RAMSEY, G. SOLIMANO *et al.* 1983. The influence of malnutrition on subsequent behavioral development. II. Classroom behavior. J. Am. Acad. Child Psychiatry **24:** 16–22.

31. WESTAT, I. 1988. Study Findings: Study of National Incidence and Prevalence of Child Abuse and Neglect: 1988. U.S. Department of Health and Human Services. Washington, DC.

32. SEDLAK, A. J. 1990. Technical amendments to the study findings—National Incidence and Prevalence of Child Abuse and Neglect. [NIS 2].

33. TATARA, T. 1989. Characteristics of children in foster care. Division of Child, Youth, and Family Services Newsletter **12:** 16–17.

Characteristics and Putative Mechanisms in Boys at Risk for Drug Abuse and Aggression

R. O. PIHL[a,c] AND J. PETERSON[b]

aDepartment of Psychology
McGill University
Stewart Biological Sciences Building
1205 Dr. Penfield Avenue
Montreal, Quebec, Canada H3A 1B1

bHarvard University
Cambridge, Massachusetts

The "at risk" paradigm is increasingly being used by researchers interested in understanding the reasons for the problematic behaviors of drug abuse and aggression. Mountains of descriptive statistics of characteristics of abusers and offenders exist, quantifying the extent of the problem. However, typically and unfortunately, this information does not clarify critically needed information regarding causes. This problem commonly emerges in studies of clinical populations, where the separation of cause from consequence is difficult. Drug abuse often results in bidirectional interactions, where the abuse leads to physiological changes and to new behaviors that are unrelated to and obscure important etiological mechanisms. This problem, and others, makes it necessary to study individuals who do not yet display the behaviors but are putatively at risk for developing them. The high-risk approach target also allows for the study of events as they occur, awareness of the multiplicity of potential outcomes, subdivision by age of onset, and developmental perspective of change over time. Furthermore, there exists the potential to observe complex circular-feedback mechanistic processes.

Risk factors in selecting target populations tend to be more focused in the area of drug abuse than aggression. Specifically, genetic models are common. Sons of male alcoholics, for example, are characterized by 4 to 9 times increased risk for developing alcoholism.[1] Offspring of aggressive individuals have been studied less often, although hereditary contributions to impulsivity and aggression have been reported[2] (as has risk information from numerous longitudinal studies).[3-7] Risk factors evident in populations of drug abusers and aggressors include gender; time of problem behavior onset; and various behavioral, social-psychological, biochemical, psychophysiological, and neuropsychological/cognitive factors. For example, boys develop drug abuse problems more frequently than girls and are more likely to have problems with physical aggression.[8] Furthermore, behavior patterns for both disorders differ between the sexes, and heritability of vulnerability may be sex linked. In addition, early onset of drinking problems is important in determining type and degree of abuse.[9] The same is true of aggression.[10] Finally, there appear to be clusters of characteristics in particular subpopulations that may relate to similarities in type of drug abuse and patterns of aggressive behavior.

c Tel: (514) 398-6100; fax: (514) 398-4896.

The focus of the first part of this paper is on the commonalities in individual characteristics between the groups. The second part of the paper presents a speculative explanation of why these phenomena may occur together.

BEHAVIORAL CHARACTERISTICS

Boys at risk for either or both drug abuse and aggression are impulsive, hyperactive, and attentionally deficient.[11,12] These conditions appear in frequent association with early onset of aggression and possible diagnosis of conduct disorder. It is true that families of these individuals are often overtly unstable. Nonetheless, occurrence of these associated behaviors has been reported for boys at risk for drug abuse, with environmental factors controlled.[13] A fundamental problem in behavioral regulation apparently forms a core of vulnerability. A related issue is the frequently debated overlap between attention deficit hyperactivity disorder (ADHD) and conduct disorder.[14] Although, important differences between the two conditions exist, commonalities abound. Children afflicted with conduct disorder and ADHD both manifest problematic attention, poor control of motor behavior in structured situations, and a proclivity to respond with aggression. It is additionally clear that individuals beset with both problems suffer the worst consequences.[14] Sons of male alcoholics, for example, constitute one population frequently characterized by this specific pair of problems.[11]

Youth at risk for drug abuse have been described as emotionally reactive,[15] particularly to negative affect,[16] and as characterized by high levels of anxiety.[17] "Hot tempered,"[18] "callous," "unemotional," and "ubiquitously impulsive,"[19] by contrast, are terms commonly applied to highly aggressive adolescents. The application of a multidimensional view of personality to individuals genetically at risk for alcoholism has resulted in the creation of two typologies: a male-limited, more severe, early-onset variant often with prior antisocial personality (ASP) (type II), and a less severe, late-developing heterogenous disorder (type I).[9] Young males at risk for type II alcoholism are characterized as low in harm avoidance (anxiety), high in novelty seeking (impulsivity), and low in reward dependence (detached, tough minded). Each of these characteristics has been linked theoretically to postulated different brain systems.[9] Although data have been far from confirmatory (there are, for example, individuals clearly impulsive and anxious and even mixed impulsive-anxious in the type II sample), these characteristics also emerge in models of conduct disorder.[20,21] Such models often borrow from Gray's[22,23] ideas of a behavioral activation incentive reward system, a behavioral inhibition system (anxiety), and a fight/flight system (response to punishment). We[24] recently tested Cloninger's model on a large sample of boys assessed for temperament in kindergarten, and at age 13 for delinquency. The strongest predictor of delinquency was novelty seeking/impulsivity, followed by the relatively weaker predictors of low anxiety and low-reward dependence. Further, at age 13, 71% of the boys who were early-onset delinquent reported having been drunk, compared to 25% of the remainder of the sample.

SOCIAL-PSYCHOLOGICAL FACTORS

The willingness to try a drug and its effect appears powerfully affected by the expectation one has of that drug's effect. For example, it is the case that different alcoholic beverages seem to result in differential proclivities to aggression (at identical blood alcohol levels).[25] Similarly, group-specific expectations seem to dictate the saliency of provocative stimuli and thus the probability of aggression.

At the familial level, individuals at risk for drug abuse are exemplified by high levels of family adversity.[26] A similar pattern is commonly noted in individuals at risk for aggression.[27] Of course, most individuals from such backgrounds do not become drug abusers or aggressors. It thus becomes important to first recognize this fact and second explore how abuse and neglect interact to increase risk status. For example, Cadoret and Stewart's[2] adoption study showed that socioeconomic status and adoptive family pathology interacted with biological parent antisociality to predict aggressiveness in 283 male adoptees. Family stress, variously defined, is implicated in the development of both drug and aggression problems. Consequently, calls for promoting family and parental competence are frequently heard (with target age of intervention, "the younger the better").

Peer influences similarly are of profound import for both problems. They are among the strongest predictors of drug use among the young.[28] An absence of strong peer relationships, in fact poor social skills and rejection, seems to characterize highly aggressive children.[29] This is particularly true if the aggressive behavior is highly condemned. However, where the behavior is viewed ambiguously or even expected, peer influence can provide powerful reinforcement for aggression.

BIOCHEMICAL CHARACTERISTICS: THE SEROTONIN (5-HT) STORY

It seems that almost every neurotransmitter, neuromodulator, and neurohormone has been implicated as important in determining risk for both drug abuse and aggression. However, comparisons between specific populations remain difficult, due to the lack of a critical mass of study for a particular chemical and a lack of study comparability. Where findings generally do concur, other methodological issues unfortunately become relevant. Regarding low platelet monoamine oxidase activity, for example, a rather recurrent finding in both populations, the measurement often lacks both specificity and accuracy when assessing central functioning.[11]

The study of 5-HT levels and functioning has drawn a great deal of recent attention, and, in consequence, the preceding caveats have become somewhat less applicable. Two recent reviews of clinical[30] and animal studies[31] have detailed the role of 5-HT in alcohol intake, abuse, and dependence. These reviews conclude that decreased 5-HT levels appear to increase alcohol intake, whereas increased 5-HT levels decrease intake. There also exists substantial support for the idea that some alcoholics have lowered central 5-HT neurotransmission. A small number of studies of high-risk individuals have been completed. These individuals also appear characterized by reduced 5-HT neurotransmission.[32,33]

A growing volume of human and animal studies have similarly implicated reduced 5-HT functioning in violent behavior. In humans, reduced cerebrospinal-fluid (CSF) 5-HIAAA (a major metabolite of 5-HT) characterizes a number of impulsive and aggressive populations, including children who display severe cruelty toward animals (and who are otherwise aggressive),[34] men with poor impulse control,[35] criminal recidivists who commit violent crimes,[36] and successful suicide victims.[37] One technique used to study 5-HT effects on behavior is to manipulate the 5-HT precursor, tryptophan. In one study we completed[38] male and female vervet monkeys were fed tryptophan-supplemented, -balanced or -depleted diets.

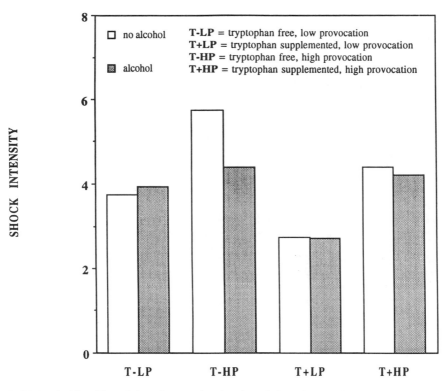

FIGURE 1. The effect of altered tryptophan levels and alcohol under high and low provocation on the intensity of shock administered to subjects.

Tryptophan depletion increased aggression among males, particularly during social interactions (such as competition during feeding), which tend to naturally elicit aggression. In another study,[39] using a similar procedure with humans, the tryptophan manipulation was crossed with alcohol, and subjects were then tested on a competitive laboratory aggression task under two levels of provocation. FIGURE 1 illustrates the results of this study. Tryptophan depletion and alcohol significantly increased the intensity of shock delivered to an opponent.[39] These results offer laboratory support to the idea that low 5-HT levels may be related to increased aggression.

The general conclusion of a number of reviews[40,41] is that 5-HT plays a constraining or governance role on the CNS. We have previously[42] compared the ascending serotonergic projections to a conductor of an orchestra, who is responsible for the organization and control of the orchestra's sometimes fractious instrumental sections (composed of talented but individualistic soloists). As "conductor," the serotonergic system seems to regulate the CNS in at least three primary ways. These are portrayed schematically in FIGURE 2. First, the 5-HT system appears to modify sensitivity to incoming sensory stimuli. The system is densely innervated in cortical areas devoted to primary sensory processing. Furthermore, it has been shown that reductions in 5-HT potentiate startle to the unexpected and theoretically dangerous.[43] This startle may serve as a nonspecific primer, enhancing CNS capability to select and engage in specific behaviors. Reductions in 5-HT appear to decrease the focus but increase the breadth of sensory response. Second, a decrease in the functioning of the 5-HT system seems to decrease control and extend duration of psychomotor response (frequency and amplitude to primary reinforcers).[41] The 5-HT and dopaminergic psychomotor systems interact in determining response to incoming sensory information and appear to engage in reciprocal homeostatic modulation. Dopaminergic activity, for example, in the nucleus accumbens, appears to facilitate behavior motivated by relevant sensory input by reward, punishment, and signals of reward. Decreased 5-HT enhances, and increased 5-HT constrains, this facilitation. Furthermore, 5-HT depletion appears to maintain reward-driven behavior for longer periods of time regardless of variations and external contingencies. Thus, it appears that decreased 5-HT concentrations increase sensory, affective, and behavioral sensitivity to (unconditioned) stimuli that drive reward and punishment-driven behavior. Third, the functioning of the 5-HT system seems to modulate sensitivity to cues that regulate driven behavior (such as cues of punishment defined as threat). High levels of 5-HT in primates are associated with social potency, low levels with decreased dominance and heightened aggression.[44] Decreases in 5-HT activity may alter the sensitivity to signals that normally suppress social behaviors; therefore, abnormally low levels of 5-HT may be associated with inappropriate social behavior. 5-HT reduction similarly reduces decreased inhibition of social interaction in

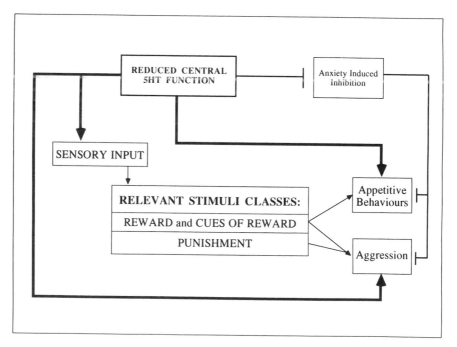

FIGURE 2. A speculative model of how reduced central 5-HT function effects appetitive behaviors and aggression.

novel, brightly lit, and thus fear-inducing environments and shares characteristics with a number of GABA agonists, including benzodiazepines, barbiturates, and alcohol. However, the effect of GABA potentiation and 5-HT depletion are far from identical. It appears possible that potentiated GABA inhibition inhibits anxiety at the affective level, whereas reduced 5-HT activity reduces the inhibitory control of anxiety on behavior (without necessarily reducing the affective aspect of anxiety).

Analysis of the role serotonin plays in modulating motivational states can help clear up a pervasive mystery: How is it that impulsive/substance-abusing children can be simultaneously anxious and impulsive? The different motivational systems that make up the human psyche might be considered analogous to motors. The systems responsible, respectively, for response to punishment, consummatory reward, threat, and incentive reward each can gain access to motor output and capacity for abstraction. What one system wants, so to speak, is not necessarily what is best for another: an object may be simultaneously threatening and promising, or rewarding in the short-term and punishing over the longer course. The ancient serotonergic system appears capable of moderating and integrating the operation of the different "motors," insuring that the person is not working at cross-purposes. Low levels of 5-HT appear associated with the independent working of the different motivational systems, and with their increased activation; higher levels are associated with harmonization and less activation. An individual characterized by low serotonin can therefore be simultaneously anxious, in terms of experienced emotional state, and impulsive, in terms of behavioral output, because he/she cannot use anxiety to govern behavior. It is interesting to note—and relevant to the latter sections of this paper—that the frontal cortex and the ascending serotonergic systems are mutually regulating, and that the abstract capacity of the anterior portion of the brain is actively involved in the processes that underly the serotonergic system's ability to modulate and control the intensity and direction of motivational drive.

PSYCHOPHYSIOLOGICAL CHARACTERISTICS

Sons of alcoholics display, when sober, a distinctive cortical evoked-potential response (EPR), which is a brief waveform to a specific stimulus derived from the electroencephalogram by signal-averaging techniques. Polich et al.[45] in a meta-analytic review of this literature found that overall these individuals displayed smaller P300 waveform amplitudes than controls. This was particularly true on tasks that used visual stimuli and were more difficult. This response, which has predictive value, has also been shown to be heritable, that is, found in approximately one third of boys genetically at high risk for alcoholism, although only in one fifth of genetically at-risk girls. An increased incidence of alcohol and drug abuse characterizes individuals who manifest abnormal EPR response at young ages.[46] This abnormal response pattern might be associated with reduced frontal lobe functioning.[47] Similarly, EPR studies in individuals at risk for aggression have found the characteristic reduced amplitudes.[48,49] Recent studies[50] have looked at frontal P300 decrements and examined EPR correlates of selective attention in aggressive subjects and concluded that, as in the studies of alcoholics' sons, frontal lobe dysfunction is likely.

A second psychophysiological characteristic typical of individuals at risk for alcohol and drug abuse is heightened autonomic response to novel, threatening, and rewarding stimuli, all of which might be considered motivationally significant. Logically, this response has been particularly noted in individuals at risk for the abuse of depressants and anxyiolytics, because reactivity is often dampened by ingestion of these drugs. This phenomenon has been labeled "stress dampening"[51] and is negatively reinforcing.[11] Dampening appears to be associated only with the rising limb of the drug response curve[52] and appears dose dependent.[53] There is some lack of consistency in the literature regarding dampening, which could be accounted for by time of assessment, dose effects, and population and expectancy differences.[54] It is interesting to note, and may be relevant, that certain strains of animals sensitive to alcohol (*e.g.*, high alcohol–sensitive rats and the long-sleep mice) are differentially sensitive to the sedative effects of alcohol.[55]

The arousal response of individuals at risk for aggression has also been studied, with varied results. Both hypo- and hyperarousal have been reported. Findings of hypoarousal support the notion that a deficient inhibition system typifies psycho-pathic adults and antisocial children.[56] The idea of general hypoarousal, however, does not seem consistent, as conduct disordered children who were nonreactive to neutral high intensity stimuli have been shown to exhibit increased reactivity to pleasant stimuli.[57] Furthermore, disruptive children (antisocial, noncooperative, disobedient, aggressive) are characterized by higher resting heart rate[58] and can be divided into anxious and nonanxious subgroups. FIGURE 3 illustrates the heart rate response of such subdivided boys to a math stress test involving both wins and losses.[59] The marked reactivity of the anxious disruptive subjects is apparent.

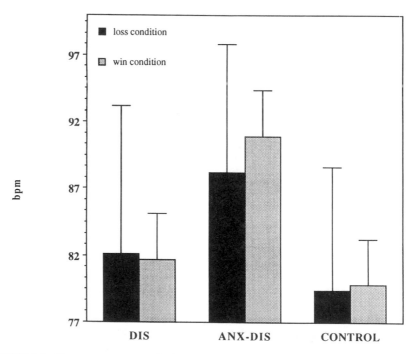

FIGURE 3. Heart-rate response in beats per minute to wins and losses in disruptive, anxious-disruptive, and control 10-year-old boys.

SELF ORDERED POINTING

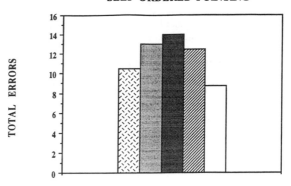

FIGURE 4. Scores on the Self-Ordered Pointing and Word Fluency neuropsychological tests for stable and unstable aggressive and control boys, and for boys with family histories of male-limited alcoholism (FH+) and those with negative family histories (FH−). ▨, nonfighters; □, unstable fighters; ■, stable fighters; ▨, FH+; □, FH−.

WORD FLUENCY

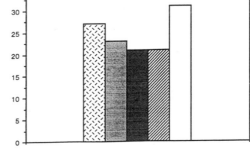

In this context, it is worth noting that animals most reactive to stress are most aggressive[60] and that aggressive outbursts are often seen in cardioreactive humans.[61]

COGNITIVE/NEUROPSYCHOLOGICAL CHARACTERISTICS

Distinctive aspects of cognitive functioning of males at high risk for the development of alcoholism have been reported. There have been two types of relevant studies: those that focus on school performance and academic variables and those that rely on specific, primarily neuropsychological, testing. FIGURE 4 schematically portrays a pattern of deficient performance for sons of male alcoholics between the ages of 8 to 15, with IQ controlled.[59] This FIGURE demonstrates their deficiency in cognitive abilities known to be mediated by the prefrontal cortex. The specific tests illustrated have been shown both in clinical populations following lesions and in normal populations on MRI/pet studies to involve differential areas of the frontal lobes.[62] The performance of 13-year-old individuals with stable histories of aggression existent over an 8-year period is also portrayed.[62] The similarity between the two at-risk populations is striking. The idea that a general neuropsychological deficit can alter the regulation of aggressive behavior has growing acceptance.[10,63] The presence of a specific neuropsychological deficit, however, and the precise nature of such a deficit has remained debatable. Peterson and Pihl[64] have theorized that the cognitive deficit, partially illustrated in the data in FIGURE 4, is central to the behavioral, psychophysiological, and increased risk for drug abuse characteristic of sons of multigenerational male alcoholics. This dysfunction is thought to be primarily reflected in atypical psychophysiological reactivity to threat and novelty and increased exploration. We have previously postulated a basic problem in classification of the meaning of stimulus events and associated difficulties in verbal reasoning, abstraction, and problem solving. These deficits are also seen as leading to a decreased likelihood of responding to nonintrinsic, nonindividually, relevant stimuli and to an increased likelihood of responding affectively to nonspecific novelty and threat. This situation likely stems from a problem in assigning specific affective relevance to these latter events. There is some evidence that alcohol dampens this system in some individuals at risk for alcoholism and concomitantly reduces aggression[25] from comparatively high sober levels. This model seems just as applicable to aggressive individuals per se who display similar cognitive characteristics.

POTENTIAL COMMONALITIES AND MECHANISMS

FIGURE 5 is a schematic model of the interrelationship of three possible explanatory mechanisms as they relate to the high correlation to being violent and intoxicated by alcohol. Over 50% of murders, assaults, and rapes occur when the perpetrator (and, almost as frequently, when the victim) is intoxicated.[65] The model also has applicability to understanding commonalities in risk for both drug abuse and aggression. Specifically, the model postulates that drugs alter at least three systems that modulate the likelihood of aggressive behavior. The hypothesized systems are the threat system, the exploratory system, and the cognitive control system. These systems in turn each act on what is called a general expectancy set, which is a socioculturally determined theoretical dynamic encompassing all existent expectancies, providing the context in which objective stimuli are individually interpreted.[66,67] The fundamental assumptions of the model are that (1) threat, specifically threat of punishment for one's own aggressive behavior, is soluble in alcohol (thus the inhibition of aggression in specifically retaliatory situations is reduced), (2) increased exploration subsequent to alcohol intake increases the likelihood of aggressive contact, along with increased sensitivity to cues for positive reinforcement and thus increased instrumental aggression; and that (3) cognitive control reduced by intoxication not only modulates the previous two systems but in itself can readily produce or fail to produce alternative solutions to a singular aggressive response. We have detailed elsewhere,[25] evidence supporting how each of these systems is involved in this alcohol/aggression relationship. What follows is an attempt to argue how these systems are simultaneously involved in increasing the risk for both drug abuse and/or aggressive behavior.

THE THREAT SYSTEM

This motivational system responds to cues of punishment and inhibits ongoing behavior in the presence of information, indicating that punishment is about to

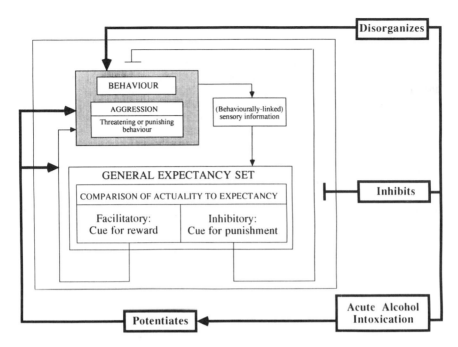

FIGURE 5. The effects of acute alcohol intoxication on aggression: inhibition of fear, potentiation of reward, and the disorganization of behavior.

take place. The operation of this system produces anxiety, an annoying state we are motivated to avoid. Individuals with a high threshold for anxiety are likely to engage in motivationally significant (satisfying or promising) activities that others might regard as too dangerous to be fun. Drugs with high abuse potential, such as alcohol, dissolve anxiety, and their capacity to do so allows individuals to engage in behaviors that might, for example, result in their own demise. The fundamental survival of the organism depends on identifying and responding to stimuli previously associated with danger, or possessing the possibility of representing danger. To avoid calamity or hurt, threat inhibits ongoing behavior. The affective component can be specific (fear) or general (anxiety). The importance of the amygdala, hippocampus, and prefrontal cortex in this system has been detailed. Sensory experience becomes labeled as threatening or promising through amygdaloid functions[68] unless obviated by other systems involved in imaginative or verbally mediated memory. Individual variability within the threat system may be a function of structure and/or level of naturally occurring endogenous anxiolytics or anxiogenics. GABAergic neurotransmission seems to modulate these systems and is readily potentiated by alcohol, benzodiazepines, and barbiturates. The increased behavioral sensitivity to these drugs in certain animal strains has been shown to be related to increased sensitivity to ethanol-potentiated chloride-ion influx at GABA A receptors.[69]

The abuse of drugs that readily dampen this threat system intuitively explains the high level of abuse found in patients with panic disorders,[42] as well as in individuals with anxiety sensitivity.[42] Stress dampening is also characteristic of sons of alcoholics when intoxicated[11] (however, just what is being dampened is not as apparent). Reactivity dampening and reduced aggression in these sons of alcoholics when intoxicated have lead us to theorize that the drug is somehow reducing the consequences of their sober cognitively mediated dysfunction in the classification of stimuli. This particular sober cognitive problem appears quite unlike the cognitive content problem characteristic of individuals who are anxiety or panic sensitive.[42] In fact, when not intoxicated, the cognitive problem in sons of alcoholics is seen as resulting in increased aggression and the other academic and behavioral difficulties displayed by these subjects.

If appropriately socialized, one's own aggressive behavior is a cue for punishment, and even contemplation of aggression in a nonwarranted situation evokes in such individuals fear and anxiety. Unfortunately, this system is poorly developed in many individuals where the definition of unwarranted is very narrow or nonexistent. The usual culprits for this condition, a cacophony of values, a lack of socialization training, and the absence of meaningful external controls, particularly during periods of natural developmental rebellion, likely contribute heavily. In a sense, it is not so much that aggression is learned but rather that control of aggression is not learned and does not become a fixture of one's general expectancy set.

THE PSYCHOMOTOR EXPLORATORY SYSTEM

The motivational system that responds to cues of reward is also activated, directly, by the more addictive substances. Drugs that activate this system potentiate motivated behavior; if the motivation is towards aggression, it is aggressive behavior that may be potentiated. Individuals who are temperamentally predisposed to respond to cues of reward (e.g., sensation seekers) are more likely to abuse abusable substances. This proclivity is likely enhanced if they are simultaneously immune to anxiety.

The effect of activating the psychomotor system, primarily dopaminergically innervated, is to promote exploration and interaction with biologically relevant stimuli in the environment.[70] Direct stimulation of this system through the implantation of electrodes or cannula is intrinsically motivating, as other potent reinforcers will be ignored and second order learning easily occurs.[71] This effect is dependent on the density of dopamine neurons and is blocked by dopamine antagonists. Drugs that activate this system by various means may heighten sensitivity to cues of reward. Indeed, given this effect, the question should be not why these drugs are abused but why not?

Stimulants such as cocaine and amphetamines, and alcohol (at moderate dosages on the rising limb of the curve) produce a reverse tolerance, which means that the use of one drug makes the others operate more effectively on the psychomotor exploratory system.[70] This may explain why their is such a high comorbidity among certain classes of drug abuse. For example, 84% of cocaine abusers also abuse alcohol.[72] Yet, contrary to the general stereotype, there appears to be a great deal of individual variability in the stimulating effect of these drugs. Two rat strains, high alcohol drinking and P alcohol preferring, have been shown to have unusually dense GABA innervation (inhibitory function) of the dopaminergic system.[73] This state may account for the heightened alcohol preference that would stimulate this system. These rats after being administered alcohol, for example, manifest more locomotor activity,[74] maintain bar pressing longer, and are more sensitive to alcohol-induced sedation.[75] Perhaps representing a similar effect, alcoholics suffer intense craving when alcohol is withdrawn, and sons of male alcoholics display a heightened heart rate response to the ingestion of alcohol.[42] Heavy drinking sons of male alcoholics, in fact, peak faster on the blood alcohol curve than heavy drinking nongenetically related individuals[42] and display EEG wave forms associated with states of well being and pleasure.[76]

Individuals at risk for aggression are often described as seekers of highly stimulating situations, a behavior pattern that conforms to basal low arousal theories of psychopathy. As stated previously, this is true of some highly aggressive individuals, but probably not even the majority. For example, most of the aggressive subjects in the Montreal longitudinal study are both anxious and aggressive. An intriguing question remains: Does this differentiation, based on the presence or absence of anxiety, account for differential typologies of aggressive youth, for example, lifetime resistant versus adolescent limited[10] and/or later adult diagnoses of ASP and/or psychopathy?

THE COGNITIVE CONTROL SYSTEM

A major function of the prefrontal cortex is to deal with abstractions and, more significantly, to help us make abstractions and to allow us to use our abstractions to govern our behavior. Furthermore, its operations are critical to our capacity to generate and consider alternatives, and to understand how we might successfully avoid those places where unpleasant things are most likely to happen. Impairments in this system produce disinhibited, aggressive, short-term-motivated behavior. Such impairments may occur as a consequence of endogenous events; alternatively, they may be drug induced. The neuropsychological deficits often found in both individuals at risk for alcohol and drug abuse, and aggression are highly suggestive of just such a problem. We have referred to this as a deficit in classification-oriented cognitive processing.[64] The deficits in these populations of voluntary attention, particularly under conditions of social demand, verbal reasoning, abstraction, problem solving, regulation of response to threat and novelty, and amount of exploratory behavior place the individual in a position of diminished control. This of course need not be independent of a reduced sensitivity to cues of punishment or heightened sensitivity to cues of reward that could well be additive.

Particular frontal cortical and limbic structures are implicated in these deficits based on neuropsychological and electrophysiological findings. Bidirectional interconnections between these areas and other brain areas, such as sensory association areas, however, counsels reserve in specifying which structures may be involved. Basically, the prefrontal cortex appears involved in the human capacity to make the abstract meaningful,[77] so that the individual is capable of attaching emotional significance to distal stimuli and using that stimuli to govern motivated behavior in the present. We generally describe this ability as empathy, which is the capacity to "feel the pain" of the abstract other, and to behave accordingly, or to use the (hypothetical) consequences of our actions to govern our actions. Empathy and the capacity to identify with a potential future self appear as capacities that are integrally related. In this perspective, the antisocial personality can neither empathize with the person one will become nor with the others one constantly encounters. These functions of the prefrontal cortex are thus involved in the construction of verbal and motor responses to novelty and/or threat and provide strategies that become the building blocks of the general expectancy set. Consequently, both the production and the inhibition of a response is affected.

Recent findings are relevant. Certain individuals at risk for aggression and drug abuse are highly reactive, and this reactivity is linked to a cognitive problem.[62,78] One concomitant of this problem may be a change in saliency of stimuli so that sensitivity is heightened. It has recently been shown that sons of alcoholics, like alcoholics, are more sensitive to pain or threat of pain (electric shock) than controls that are dampened by alcohol.[79] Stable aggressive boys with high cognitive functioning show a more complex picture in their response to pain. Central processing is also important in response to inhibition. The characteristics of impulsivity for both at-risk groups have been previously detailed. Recently, we[80] assessed individuals who scored high and low on a putative frontal test and then ran these subjects on an aggression task under inhibited and noninhibited conditions. Notably, low cognitive functioners did not inhibit their level of aggression even under high response cost conditions. In another study,[81] high functioners were also paid for reduced aggression and clearly were able to inhibit even when intoxicated, unlike low functioners. It would seem important to learn how these individuals preserved control and what methodologies might produce a similar response in those we now know to be vulnerable to responding with aggression.

CONCLUSIONS

There are profound similarities in the characteristics of boys at risk for drug abuse and boys at risk for aggression. These are found in behavioral, social, psychological, biochemical, and neuropsychological/cognitive measures. The patterns of overlapping characteristics suggest that there are a number of at-risk groups for both drug abuse and aggression, likely because of divergent etiologies. Differential mechanisms that may be operative include a diminished response to threat, an accelerated exploratory system, and lessened cognitive control. It appears the functioning of these, not necessarily independent, systems contributes markedly to risk.

REFERENCES

1. GOODWIN, D. W. 1985. Arch. Gen. Psychiatry **42:** 171–174.
2. CADORET, R. & M. STEWART. 1991. Comp. Psychiatry **32:** 73–82.
3. FARRINGTON, D. 1991. The Psychologist **4:** 389–394.
4. HUESMANN, L., L. ERON, M. ELFKOWITZ & L. WALDER. 1984. Dev. Psychol. **20:** 1120–1134.
5. McCORD, J. 1978. Am. Psychol. **33:** 284–289.
6. STATTIN, H. & D. MAGNUSSON. 1989. J. Consult. Clin. Psychol. **57:** 710–718.
7. TREMBLAY, R., B. MASSE, D. PERRON, M. LeBLANC, A. SCHWARTZMAN & J. LEDINGHAM. 1992. J. Consult. Clin. Psychol. **60:** 64–72.
8. OFFORD, D., M. BOYLE, J. FLEMING, H. BLUM & N. GRANT. 1989. Can. J. Psychiatry **34:** 483–491.
9. CLONINGER, C. 1987. J. Abnorm. Psychol. **100:** 427–448.
10. MOFFITT, T. 1993. Psychol. Rev. **100:** 674–701.
11. PIHL, R. O., J. B. PETERSON & P. R. FINN. 1990. J. Abnorm. Psychol. **99:** 291–301.
12. PIHL, R. & J. PETERSON. 1991. Alcohol Health Res. World **15:** 25–31.
13. CADORET, R. J. & A. GATH. 1978. Br. J. Psychiatry **132:** 252–258.
14. HINSHAW, S. P. 1987. Psychol. Bull. **101:** 443–463.
15. SHER, K. J., K. S. WALITZER, P. K. WOOD & E. BRENT. 1991. J. Abnorm. Psychol. **100:** 427–448.

16. CHASSIN, L., D. PILLOW, P. CURRAN, B. MOLINA & M. BARRERA. 1993. J. Abnorm. Psychol. **102:** 3–19.
17. TARTER, R., M. KABENE, E. ESCALLIER, S. LAIRD & T. JACOB. 1990. Alcoholism Clin. Exp. Res. **14:** 380–382.
18. OLWEUS, D. 1980. Dev. Psychol. **16:** 644–660.
19. FRICK, P., B. O'BRIEN, J. WOOTTON & K. MCBURNETT. 1994. J. Abnorm. Psychol. **103:** 700–707.
20. QUAY, H. 1993. Dev. Psychopathol. **5:** 165–180.
21. NEWMAN, J. 1987. J. Res. Pers. **21:** 464–480.
22. GRAY, J. A. 1982. The Neuropsychology of Anxiety: An Enquiry into the Function of the Septal-Hippocampal System. Oxford University Press. Oxford.
23. GRAY, J. A. 1987. The Psychology of Fear and Stress. Cambridge University Press. Cambridge.
24. TREMBLAY, R., R. PIHL, F. VITARO & P. DOBKIN. 1994. Arch. Gen. Psychiatry **51:** 732–739.
25. PIHL, R., J. PETERSON & M. LAU. 1993. J. Stud. Alcohol (Suppl.). **11:** 123–139.
26. KNOP, J., T. W. TEASDALE, F. SCHULSINGER & D. W. GOODWIN. 1985. J. Stud. Alcohol. **46:** 273–278.
27. ROUTHBAUM, F. & J. WEISZ. 1994. Psychol. Bull. **116:** 55–74.
28. HAWKINS, J., R. ATALANO & J. MILLER. 1992. Psychol. Bull. **112:** 64–105.
29. NEWCOMB, A., W. BUKOWSKI & L. PATTEE. 1993. Psychol. Bull. **113:** 99–128.
30. LEMARQUAND, D., R. PIHL & C. BENKELFAT. 1994. Biol. Psychiatry **36:** 326–337.
31. LEMARQUAND, D., R. PIHL & C. BENKELFAT. 1994. Biol. Psychiatry **36:** 395–421.
32. RAUSCH, J., M. MONTEIRO & M. A. SCHUCKIT. 1991. Neuropsychopharmacology **4:** 83–86.
33. ERNOUF, D., P. COMPAGNON, P. LOTHION, G. NARCISSE, J. BENARD & M. DAOUST. 1993. Life Sci. **52:** 989–995.
34. KRUESI, M., J. RAPPOPORT, S. HANBERGER, E. HIBBS, W. POTTER, M. LEVANE & G. BROWN. 1990. Arch. Gen. Psychiatry **47:** 419–426.
35. LINNOILA, M., M. VIRKKUNEN, M. SCHEININ, A. NUNTILA, R. RINON & F. GOODWIN. 1983. Life Sci. **33:** 2609–2614.
36. VIRKKUNEN, M. & M. LINNOILA. 1993. J. Stud. Alcohol (Suppl.). **11:** 163–169.
37. MANN, J. J., V. ARANGO & M. D. UNDERWOOD. 1990. Ann. N. Y. Acad. Sci. **600:** 476–485.
38. CHAMBERLAIN, B., F. ERVIN, R. PIHL & S. YOUNG. 1987. Psychopharm. Biochem. Behav. **28:** 503–510.
39. PIHL, R., S. YOUNG, P. HARDEN, S. PLOTNICK, B. CHAMBERLAIN & F. ERVIN. 1995. Psychopharm. **119:** 353–360.
40. SOUBRIE, P. 1986. Behav. Brain Sci. **9:** 319–364.
41. SPOONT, M. R. 1992. Psychol. Bull. **12:** 330–350.
42. PIHL, R. & J. PETERSON. 1995. J. Psychiat. Neurosci. **20:** 372–396.
43. DAVIS, M. 1980. Neurosci. Biobehav. Rev. **4:** 241–263.
44. RALEIGH, M., G. BRAMMER, A. YUWILER, J. FLANNERY, M. McGUIRE & E. GELLER. 1980. Exp. Neurol. **68:** 322–334.
45. POLICH, J., V. POLLOCK & F. BLOOM. 1994. Psychol. Bull. **115:** 55–73.
46. HILL, S. & S. STEINHAUER. 1993. J. Stud. Alcohol. **54:** 350–358.
47. BAUER, L., S. O'CONNOR & V. HESSELBROCK. 1994. Alcohol. Clin. Exp. Res. **18:** 1300–1305.
48. BLACKWOOD, D., D. ST. CLAIR & S. KUTCHEN. 1986. Biopsychiatry **21:** 557–560.
49. DRAKE, M., B. PHILLIPS & A. PAKALMIS. 1991. Clin. Electroencephalogr. **22:** 188–192.
50. STEIN, D., J. TOWEY & E. HOLLANDER. 1995. In Impulsivity and Aggression. E. Hollander & D. Stein, Eds.: 91–105. Wiley. New York.
51. SHER, K. J., K. S. WALITZER, P. K. WOOD & E. BRENT. 1991. J. Abnorm. Psychol. **100:** 427–448.
52. NEWLIN, D. & J. THOMPSON. 1991. Alcoholism Clin. Exp. Res. **15:** 399–405.
53. STEWART, S., P. FINN & R. PIHL. 1992. J. Stud. Alcohol **53:** 499–506.
54. EARLEYWINE, M. 1994. Alcoholism Clin. Exp. Res. **18:** 711–714.

55. CRABBE, J., J. BELKNAP & K. BUCK. 1994. Science **264:** 1715–1723.
56. RAINE, A. & P. VENABLES. 1984. Biol. Psychiatry **18:** 123–132.
57. GERRALDA, E., J. CONNELL & D. TAYLOR. 1991. Psychol. Bull. **21:** 947–957.
58. ZAHN, T. & M. KRUESI. 1993. Psychophysiology **30:** 605–614.
59. HARDEN, P., R. O. PIHL, F. VITARO, P. GENDREAU & R. TREMBLAY. 1995. J. Emotion Behav. Dis. **3:** 183–190.
60. MANUCK, S., J. KAPLAN, T. CLARKSON, M. ADAMS & C. SHIVELY. 1992. *In* Hostility, Coping and Health. American Psychological Association. H. S. Freedman, Ed.: 99–106. Washington, D.C.
61. DEMBROWSKI, T. & R. WILLIAMS. 1989. *In* Handbook of Research Methods in Cardiovascular Behavior Medicine. N. Schneiderman *et al.*, Eds.: 553–569. Plenum. New York.
62. SÉGUIN, J., R. PIHL, P. HARDEN & R. TREMBLAY. 1995. J. Abnorm. Psychol. **104:** 614–624.
63. KANDEL, E. & D. FREED. 1989. J. Clin. Psychol. **45:** 404–413.
64. PETERSON, J. & R. PIHL. 1990. Neuropsychol. Rev. **1:** 343–369.
65. MURDOCH, D., R. O. PIHL & D. ROSS. 1990. Int. J. Addiction **25:** 1065–1981.
66. LURIA, A. R. 1980. Higher cortical functions in man. Moscow University Press. Moscow.
67. SOKOLOV, E. N. 1969. In Handbook of Contemporary Society Psychology. I. Maltzman & K. Coles, Eds.: 671–704. Basic Books. New York.
68. KLING, A. S. & L. A. BROTHERS. 1992. *In* The Amygdala. J. P. Aggleton, Eds.: 353–377. Wiley-Liss. New York.
69. HARRIS, R. & A. ALLAN. 1989. FASEB J. **3:** 1689–1694.
70. WISE, R. A. 1988. Ann. N. Y. Acad. Sci. **537:** 228–234.
71. FIBIGER, H. C. & A. G. PHILLIPS. 1988. Ann. N. Y. Acad. Sci. **537:** 206–215.
72. HELZER, J. E. & T. R. PRYZBECK. 1988. J. Stud. Alcohol. **49:** 219–224.
73. MCBRIDE, W. J., J. M. MURPHY, L. LUMENG & T. K. LI. 1990. Alcohol **7:** 199–205.
74. KRIMMER, E. C. & M. D. SCHECHTER. 1992. Alcohol **9:** 71–74.
75. SCHWARZ-STEVENS, K., H. H. SAMSON, G. A. TOLLIVER, L. LUMENG & T. K. LI. 1991. Alcoholism Clin. Exp. Res. **15:** 277–285.
76. POLLOCK, V. E., J. VOLAVKA, D. W. GOODWIN, S. A. MEDNICK, W. F. GABRIELLI, J. KNOP & F. SCHULSIGER. 1983. Arch. Gen. Psychiatry **40:** 857–861.
77. DAMASIO, A. 1994. Decartes' Error. Putnam. New York.
78. HARDEN, P. & R. O. PIHL. 1995. J. Abnorm. Psychol. **104:** 94–103.
79. STEWART, S., P. FINN, R. PIHL. 1995. PSYCHOPHARMACOLOGY **119:** 261–267.
80. LAU, M. & R. PIHL. Unpublished manuscript. McGill University.
81. HOAKEN, P., J. M. ASSAAD & R. PIHL. Unpublished manuscript. McGill University.

Considerations Regarding Biosocial Foundations of Personality and Aggression

JOAN McCORD[a]

Department of Criminal Justice
Temple University
Philadelphia, Pennsylvania 19122

We stub a toe and feel pain. We see a friend enter the room and rise to greet her. These are ordinary actions that exemplify the interaction between thoughts (mind) and biological processes (body). Nevertheless, the notion that biological and social or mental processes interact has tended to produce more heat than light when the actions in question pertain to aggressive behavior in children.

Much of the heat has been generated by the mistaken view that biological processes determine outcomes. This view is wrong. A tulip cannot be a tulip without an appropriate bulb; but neither will any bulb become a tulip without sufficient light and water. Similarly, to be an outstanding athlete requires certain biological propensities; but the propensities will not result in superior athletic performance without adequate environmental and mental conditions.

It would be foolish to assign a number representing the degree to which biological factors determine variation in plant or human health, though biology is clearly influential. The degree to which biological processes determine outcomes varies in relation to environmental conditions as well as the variability in biological factors being considered.

Variance is a measure of groups, changing in relation to what and how objects are measured. The degree to which a set of properties (*e.g.*, genetic factors) accounts for the variance among groups does not explain why individuals have particular characteristics. An emphasis on evaluating the proportion of variance attributable to genetics has tended to divert attention away from necessary studies of the way in which different environments interact with various biologically differentiated individuals.

In order to understand how bulbs grow to become healthy plants, horticulturists study varieties of bulbs under varying conditions. They do not expect all plants to respond similarly to direct sunlight or torrential rains. Nor should behavioral scientists expect that all people will be similarly responsive to the same environmental stimuli.

What is important about the interactions between biology and social or mental conditions is understanding how these affect development. Craig Ferris and Thomas Grisso organized a conference designed to stimulate discussions about these interactions. That conference incorporated reports by biologists and social scientists. Often, they talked past one another. Yet the knowledge conveyed by the biologists had tremendous potential for understanding development of antisocial behavior, a social classification.

[a] Address for correspondence: 623 Broadacres Road, Narberth, PA 19072. Tel: (610) 667-6197; fax: (610) 667-0568; e-mail: mccord@vm.temple.edu.

Reporting on work with monkeys and rodents, as well as humans, for example, the biologists showed that inhibition of aggression is related to serotonin (5-HT), with low serotonin related to aggression. They showed that fluoxetine tends to increase the concentration of extracellular serotonin. Intriguingly, hamsters' responses to injections of arginine vasopressin, an aggression facilitator, were related to their dominance.

Probably more than hamsters, babies differ from each other neuroanatomically and biochemically. It is reasonable to suppose that these differences result in differential responses even to early environmental stimuli like noises, lights, hunger, and touch. Perinatal stress probably affects the infant's neuroendocrine system. It seems likely, therefore, that high levels of arginine vasopressin and/or low levels of 5-HT can result from either heritable or environmental processes. Whether interventions to reduce a tendency toward aggressive responses differ as a function of source (as heritable or environmental) is an empirical question.

In addition to fearing biological determinism, people oppose investigation of the biological underpinnings of aggression on the mistaken view that if biological processes influence outcomes, biological interventions (e.g., eugenics) are necessary. Yet, clearly, social interventions have biological consequents and biological interventions have social consequents. At the most obvious level, teachers and books transmit sometimes necessary information about how to operate machines and fix cars. Cocktail parties increase the probability of alcohol-related physiological changes. Perhaps more relevantly, transmission of AIDS has been influenced by mating policies, and high blood pressure can be altered by changing daily routines or practicing yoga.

There is reason to believe that aggression could be reduced by social programs whether or not aggressiveness is rightly attributed to biological processes. Perhaps, for some people, reducing the probability of violence is more difficult than for others. There is no evidence, however, that it is more difficult to effect change if a cause is biological than if it is social. Epileptic seizures, for example, can be prevented by ingesting phenobarbital. Diabetic coma can be prevented through control of diet. Surely discovery of appropriate interventions is not advanced by refusing to learn how biological and psychological processes interact in the production of violence.

There are three contexts in which research involving interactions between biological and psychosocial processes would be particularly welcome.

(1) Animal models should be used to advance understanding of how various social conditions influence biological processes. Biological effects of parental loss have been studied with rhesus monkeys. These studies have the advantage of being able to control conditions that, in humans, would present insurmountable statistical problems related to collinearity. We need to learn about conditions under which stress tends to produce neurotransmitters conducive to aggression. In humans, stress is related to poverty, exposure to violence, poor health, and other conditions that might explain the biological concomitants of aggression. We should investigate the impact of social isolation on biological processes. We need to study the impact of touch, as a representation of affection, on serotonin production. We should learn whether habituation to deprivation involves decreased serotonin or increased arginine vasopressin or other, perhaps yet unknown, neuroendocrine activity.

(2) Longitudinal studies of newborns and their mothers should include information about biological, psychological, and social conditions. We do not know whether sucking behavior influences maternal responsiveness or the quality of the mother's milk. We have only a little information to suggest that it makes a

difference whether infants receive attention when they are content or discontent. Yet if newborns learn to cry from experience, they may become less attractive than they would have been had alternative caretaking techniques been used. If neglect or mistreatment results, the seeds of antisocial behavior may be planted at an early age.

We do not know whether babies of different temperaments respond similarly to being encased in blankets that could be described as "binding" or as "secure." Nor do we know whether babies differing biochemically respond to changes in light, heat, and noise in different ways. Plausibly, neonates with low (or high) testosterone or serotonin benefit from stimulation, whereas their peers do not.

(3) We should study the interaction between biological manifestations of the aging process and psychosocial responses. Testosterone at birth appears to have different consequences than testosterone during adolescence. There may be important age-related biosocial differences in responses to control, affection, and predictability. These could be related to habituation. Knowledge about effects of age and habituation can be expected to be valuable in understanding why so many intervention programs fail to have the desired effects.

SUMMARY

I have suggested that research into biosocial processes has been impeded because of two mistaken opinions. The first pertains to a belief that biological processes are determinative. I have tried to show that they are potentiating. The second pertains to a belief that if biology contributes to aggression, biological interventions are necessary. I have demonstrated that social processes can alter biological conditions. I have also suggested that biosocial research can make important contributions through animal models and longitudinal studies.

Integrating Social-skills Training Interventions with Parent Training and Family-focused Support to Prevent Conduct Disorder in High-risk Populations

The Fast Track Multisite Demonstration Project[a]

KAREN L. BIERMAN[c] AND THE CONDUCT PROBLEMS
PREVENTION RESEARCH GROUP[b]

Department of Psychology
The Pennsylvania State University
522 Moore Building
University Park, Pennsylvania 16802

Conduct disorder is one of the most prevalent and most intractable mental health problems of childhood and adolescence. Although some childhood conduct problems remit by adolescence, rarely do adolescent cases of conduct disorder or adult cases of antisocial personality disorder begin without warning signs in early childhood.[1,2] "Early starting" patterns of conduct disorder are notoriously difficult to treat in adolescence. Once the disorder has progressed from oppositional behavior to aggressive behavior and then to antisocial behaviors, and once the disorder has spread from the home to school and peer-group contexts, it becomes very stable developmentally and difficult to treat effectively. For these reasons, clinical researchers have turned increasingly to prevention programs, hoping that, by catching the precursors to conduct disorder in early or middle childhood, the negative developmental trajectory might be averted.

Numerous short-term prevention efforts have been directed at young children who show high rates of aggressive or impulsive behavior. In general, the results of such efforts have been promising in the short run but disappointing in the long run.[3,4] Often some posttest change is evident, but it has been difficult to document long-term improvements and to promote changes across both home and school settings. No known study to date has been successful in the long-term prevention of conduct disorder.

[a] This work was supported in part by National Institute of Mental Health Grants R18MH48083, R18MH50951, R18MH50952, and R18MH50953. The Center for Substance Abuse Prevention also has provided support for Fast Track through a memorandum of support with the NIMH. Support has also come from the Department of Education Grant S184430002 and NIMH Grants K05MH00797 and K05MH01027.

[b] Members of CPPRG (in alphabetical order) are Karen L. Bierman (Pennsylvania State University), John D. Coie (Duke University), Kenneth A. Dodge (Vanderbilt University), Mark T. Greenberg (University of Washington), John E. Lochman (Duke University), and Robert J. McMahon (University of Washington).

[c] Tel: (814) 863-1733; fax: (814) 231-8764; e-mail: kb2@psuvm.psu.edu.

A review of developmental research on the emergence of aggressive behavior problems provides some insight into the apparent difficulties associated with the prevention of conduct disorders. Developmentally, it is clear that aggressive behavior and later conduct disorders are multiply determined and multifaceted. The development of children who show early aggression and go on to develop conduct disorders is compromised in a number of ways. Their aggressive behavior is only one symptomatic pattern in a developmental picture that typically includes deficits in other core capacities for emotion regulation, self-control, cognitive functioning, and social interaction. In addition, conduct disorders do not emerge as an intrapersonal process within a child, but require and reflect interpersonal "training," opportunities, and influences.[2,5,6] It is important to examine the complex developmental processes associated with conduct disorders in order to design comprehensive prevention programs that recognize both the multiple domains of child deficits and the contextual and interpersonal processes that must be addressed.

THE DEVELOPMENT OF CONDUCT DISORDER

In the more serious and long-term cases (the "early starter" developmental course), conduct disorders emerge early in the child's development and follow an escalating course.[6] Problems typically first become evident during the preschool years, when children begin to show high rates of noncompliance, temper tantrums, and power struggles with their parents. The child's temperamental characteristics, such as irritability, high levels of activity, and inattention, may increase the likelihood that negative parent-child interactions will emerge in these early years.[7] Parental reactions to, and treatment of, their young child have a marked impact on the child's developmental trajectory.[2]

During infancy and early childhood, the quality of the parent-child attachment may affect the development of the child's emotional regulatory capabilities and behavioral control, as well as serve as a "template" or model for the child's later expectancies and affect in interpersonal relationships.[8] Parents who are able to provide sensitive and responsive caregiving during these early years facilitate the adaptive development of their youngster's emotional and behavioral control capabilities. By contrast, infants and young children who have parents who are unavailable, nonresponsive, or intrusive in their responding are more likely to develop insecure relationships and to show more disorganized and less focused emotional reactions and environmental exploration.[8]

During the preschool years, parental disciplinary practices begin to play a role in the development of the child's conduct problems. Inconsistent and punitive disciplinary strategies can lead to escalating cycles of coercive interaction, in which parents and children model and reinforce each other for increasingly aversive interpersonal demands.[8] Exposure to and participation in coercive family interactions train the child in a style of interpersonal interaction that includes aggressive, oppositional, and coercive behavior. In addition, exposure to high rates of hostile interactions is demoralizing for children and parents, contributing to feelings of depression, anxiety, anger, and hostile interpersonal beliefs.[9] Conditions of psychosocial adversity, such as financial stress, poverty, marital discord, single parenting, and maternal depression may stress parents and increase the likelihood of coercive family interactions.[2]

By the early grade-school years, the child's behavior problems may include physical and verbal aggression and hostile interpersonal behavior that generalizes from home to school settings. For the children involved, the consequences of developing a confrontational attitude toward interpersonal interactions is that they may elicit more hostility from adults and peers, as well as prevent or reduce opportunities for positive socialization. Hence, children who enter school with many conduct problems often show additional difficulties in the area of poor academic readiness, deficient language skills, and attentional difficulties, which increase their risk for academic failure and peer rejection.[10] Aggressive children who are ostracized from the mainstream peer group at school may drift into (or seek out) affiliations with deviant peer groups, where their hostile interpersonal beliefs and beliefs in the effectiveness of aggression are reinforced.[11] Unfortunately, children at high-risk for aggression often attend schools in which there are many other children at high-risk,[12] creating a difficult teaching environment and an increased exposure to the modeling and escalation of conduct problems. In addition, children who are particularly stressed cognitively and behaviorally by the academic demands of school, such as those with attentional deficits or hyperactive behaviors, may be at increased risk for negative interactional experiences in the school setting.[13]

By adolescence, full conduct disorder often emerges, as children become alienated from the mainstream culture; adopt antisocial goals, values and affiliations; disengage from school; and begin more serious criminal behavior. Parent-child relations of conduct-disordered children have often deteriorated completely by adolescence, and parents give up their unsuccessful attempts at control and become demoralized and alienated from their child.[1]

A developmental perspective on conduct disorders makes it clear that the problems faced by these children go beyond their aggressive behavior. Correspondingly, the model suggests that intervention efforts focused solely on the reduction of aggressive behavior are unlikely to change a child's long-term developmental trajectories. Instead, by early grade school, the developmental capabilities of "early starters" are compromised, deficient, and distorted in a number of ways. Stable aggressive behavior problems are typically accompanied by social skill deficits; academic deficits; and difficulties with self-control, emotion regulation, and interpersonal relationships. It follows that these multiple skill deficits may need to be addressed in preventive interventions, along with efforts to reduce aggressive behavior.

In addition, the developmental trajectory associated with conduct disorders often emerges from and promotes a growing range of contextual support deficits, starting with parental difficulties with discipline and extending to deterioration of other aspects of the parent-child relationship. In addition, negative interactions with teachers and with peers may promote deviant peer affiliations, which, in turn, support antisocial behavior and diminish bonding to positive social institutions and goals.

IMPLICATIONS FOR PREVENTIVE INTERVENTION DESIGN

The developmental model of conduct disorder has several important implications for intervention design. First, the developmental model suggests that preventive interventions designed for children at-risk for conduct disorder must focus on more than simply the reduction of aggressive behaviors, but must also address the interpersonal, cognitive, and emotional deficits (or distortions) that contribute to the broad array of social adjustment problems faced by these children. Preventive interventions should target multiple skill domains for the child, including skills needed for enhancing emotional/behavioral regulation, sustaining adaptive interpersonal relationships, and promoting academic achievement.

Second, it is clear that aggressive behavior develops in interpersonal contexts that must be addressed to affect long-term developmental changes. That is, interventions must address the supportive socializing agents of parents, peers, and teachers, facilitating effective parental discipline guidance and support, positive peer group support, and effective classroom management and support by the teacher.

Third, conduct disorders are developmental disorders that are very difficult to remedy due to their overdetermined nature. The risk factors change with development. Hence, effective interventions should be sustained, cross-situational, and well integrated to provide sufficient opportunities for the remediation and development of critical child competencies, adaptive system changes in family and school domains, and the establishment of effective working collaborations and networks of support across the socialization domains of family and school.

THE FAST TRACK PREVENTION PROGRAM

The Fast Track prevention program was designed, based upon a developmental model of conduct disorders, to test the effectiveness of a comprehensive, multifaceted, and long-term set of prevention activities for children at risk for conduct disorders.[5] The program involves a series of controlled field trials currently underway in four areas of the country, which were selected to represent a range of geographical areas and demographic characteristics: rural Pennsylvania; Seattle, Washington; Durham, North Carolina; and Nashville, Tennessee. At each of these sites, three cohorts of children were identified as at risk for the development of conduct disorders based upon teacher and parent ratings of behavior problems in kindergarten.[5] Schools were randomly assigned to intervention or control conditions. Hence, depending upon the child's school in first grade, half of the families of high-risk children were recruited into the intervention and the others continued to participate in a developmental study that constituted the comparison group.

The total intervention program involves a six-year span of prevention activities, covering the important developmental transitions of school entry and the transition to middle school. The school entry program (grades 1 and 2) consists of seven integrated components, including parent training, home visiting, parent-child relationship enhancement, and academic tutoring components, as well as three social skills training components focused on strengthening social-cognitive skills, emotional regulation capabilities, and interpersonal competencies of high-risk children. Skills-training components include a universal prevention curriculum used by teachers, a social-skills training group program for targeted high-risk children, and a peer-pairing program, all designed to build social skills and enhance positive peer relationships.

Although a complete description of the Fast Track program is beyond the scope of this paper, in the next section, the social-skills training program components and the corresponding family support program components used in the first phase of intervention (at school entry in grades 1 and 2) will be described briefly. For further details about the intervention program, see Bierman, Greenberg, and the CPPRG;[14] and McMahon, Slough, and the CPPRG.[15]

The Social-skills Training Program Components

The Fast Track social-skills training programs contain both universal and selective levels of intervention.[16] The universal intervention is a primary prevention strategy directed at all first-grade children in targeted schools and implemented in regular education classrooms by classroom teachers. With training and consultation provided by Fast Track staff, classroom teachers teach the PATHS (Promoting Alternative Thinking Strategies) curriculum.[17] In addition to enhancing the skills of all children in the classroom, the PATHS curriculum is also designed to improve the manageability and positivity of the classroom climate, by increasing the compliance and on-task behavior of all children, reducing the distractions that may stimulate inappropriate behavior of risk children, and increasing peer and teacher support for the display of self-control and nonaggressive solutions to peer problems. Teaching strategies include direct instruction, discussion, the use of modeling stories or videos, role-playing activities, and problem-solving meetings. Teachers are also encouraged to generalize their use of PATHS concepts across the school day and to other settings of the school outside the classroom, to help children become adept at using the skills in their ongoing school and peer interactions.

Although universal interventions can be quite effective, children with severe behavior problems may fail to benefit from this level of intervention alone. Hence, the Fast Track program includes a second level of more intensive remedial intervention for those children most at risk for conduct problems: a series of extracurricular social skills training "friendship groups" and corresponding school-based "peer-pairing" sessions. The selective levels of intervention are aimed at children who demonstrated behavior problems in kindergarten and thus were considered at risk for school adjustment problems in first grade and beyond. In the Fast Track program, the universal and selective interventions complement each other, with all children receiving some social skills training in the classroom and at-risk children receiving additional extracurricular and in-school social skills training and social support.

Extracurricular groups contain five to six children and focus on remedying child deficits in prosocial and play skills[18] as well as providing extended practice employing self-control, anger coping, and interpersonal problem–solving skills in the context of peer interactions.[19] In-school peer-pairing sessions promote the generalization of positive social skills to the school setting by giving each target child opportunities for guided play sessions during the school day with a classroom peer partner who rotates during the course of the school year. In these sessions, the dyad completes activities (games, art, and crafts activities) designed to allow the target child to display improved social skills to the classroom peer and to foster mutually rewarding exchanges between the target child and a variety of classmates.

At school entry, the universal and selective levels of social-skills training address skills in six domains: (a) social participation (*e.g.*, joining activities, paying attention, being part of a group), (b) prosocial behavior (*e.g.*, cooperating, sharing, taking turns, helping), (c) communication skills (*e.g.*, expressing one's point of view and feelings clearly, listening to another's point of view), (d) self-control (*e.g.*, inhibiting impulsive reactivity in the face of frustration and negative arousal, taking the time to think about an appropriate response), (e) regulating oneself in rule-based interactions (*e.g.*, following rules in the classroom and in games with peers), and (f) social problem–solving skills (*e.g.*, identifying problems, generating and evaluating solutions, making and executing a plan).

Academic Tutoring

In addition to the social skills training children receive in the Fast Track program, academic tutoring is provided to support the development of reading skills during the initial school years. Learning difficulties and academic failure frequently accompany social and behavioral problems at school and lead to poor adjustment outcomes.[6] Hence, academic tutoring is provided to all identified high-risk children during their first-grade year and occurs parallel to the peer-pairing and friendship group sessions. Paraprofessionals are trained to administer an individualized tutoring program that emphasizes a phonics-based, mastery-oriented approach toward the development of initial reading skills.[20] This program is designed to promote phonemic-awareness skills in young children who might otherwise have difficulty learning to read, and has been demonstrated to bring low-readiness children from disadvantaged backgrounds up to grade-expected reading skill levels in the first year of school. The paraprofessional tutors are also trained in positive behavioral support strategies designed to promote the development of the social and self-control skills the children need for successful adaptation at school. By using the same paraprofessionals to provide tutoring in reading skills and to direct the peer-pairing sesions, both of which occur in the school setting, high-risk children are provided with a supportive adult who they see on a regular basis throughout the year. In first grade, tutors work with children for three half hour sessions each week. After the first-grade year, academic tutoring is continued on an as-needed basis for those children who continue to struggle with reading skills.

Family-focused Intervention Components

There are three family-focused intervention components at school entry: parent group training, parent-child sharing sessions, and home visiting. All of these components share the goal of assisting parents in helping their children reduce negative behaviors and improve in their ability to succeed at school.

The parent group training program occurs at the same time as the child social-skills training program. The group training focuses on improving family-school relationships, parental self-control, developmentally appropriate expectations for the child's behavior, and parenting skills to improve parent-child interaction and decrease acting-out behaviors. Parents learn a problem-solving approach to parenting, with an emphasis on problem analysis and identification, consideration of various potential solutions, and a selection of the optimal parental response for various child problems.

A half-hour session of parent-child sharing time is held following the parent and child groups. The goals of the parent-child sharing program are to promote positive parent-child relationships through cooperative activities and to provide an opportunity for parents to practice their newly acquired parenting skills with their children, with support from the Fast Track staff.

The home visiting component of the intervention allows staff to provide individualized attention to the specific needs of particular parents and families. The goals are to develop trusting relationships with the entire family system, promote generalization of newly acquired parenting skills to the home, promote parental support for the child's school adjustment, and promote parental problem–solving, coping, and goal-setting as a means of dealing with many stressful life events (*e.g.*, marital conflict, substance use, social isolation, housing issues) that at-risk families often experience. A problem-solving approach, promoting parental empowerment and self-efficacy, is used by the home visiting staff. Fast Track staff make biweekly home visits and have weekly contact with families during the first year of the program. In later grades, home visits may occur less frequently, depending upon the needs and progress of various families and children.

Intervention-program Structure

In first grade, friendship groups and parent groups of five to six children and their families meet weekly for 22 weeks across the course of the year. These group sessions are two hours long and are held at local elementary schools. During the initial hour, children meet in friendship groups while parents meet in parent groups. Following these training sessions, children and parents spend a half hour together in parent-child sharing, and parents observe a tutor working with their child on academic skills for a half hour. Siblings are cared for in a separate part of the program during these sessions. The same basic format characterizes the groups during second grade. However, groups meet biweekly rather than weekly (for 14 sessions during the year), groups may be somewhat larger (*e.g.*, six to seven children), and group sessions are 90 minutes in duration. In second grade, some children "graduate" from academic tutoring; hence, tutoring is no longer conducted during the extracurricular enrichment sessions.

EVALUATION PLANS

The field trial to evaluate the Fast Track program is currently underway, and results are not yet available. However, some of the planned evaluation strategies will be described below, along with examples of preliminary analyses that illustrate the value of the field trial for testing models of intervention effects as well as for assessing outcomes. With regard to assessing outcomes, the basic hypothesis to be tested in the Fast Track program is the extent to which this set of comprehensive prevention efforts carried out during the elementary school years can reduce the emergence and severity of adolescent conduct disorder. The research design includes an assessment of the various behavioral manifestations of conduct problems and includes multiple methods of measurement (*e.g.*, parent and teacher ratings, behavioral observations, peer sociometric ratings, and interviews with the child). Comparisons between at-risk children who are receiving the intervention and at-risk children who are in a comparison group will allow us to estimate the nature and degree of intervention impact over time. In addition, developmental data is being collected on a representative normative sample at each site, so that the progress made by at-risk children in the intervention group may be compared over time to developmental norms established at each site.

In addition to assessing outcomes, we will also be able to examine the patterns of change that occur and to test aspects of the developmental model. For example, we plan to examine qualitative data from this study to acquire a more comprehensive understanding of how family ecology and school/community context contribute to the development (or increase resistance to the development) of conduct disorders and how family/school/community context variables may affect or mediate the impact of this preventive intervention.

We also plan to test different models of intervention effects to extend our assessment beyond the straightforward question Did it work? and to address questions, such as For whom did it work?, How did it work?, and What factors facilitated or inhibited intervention effectiveness? For example, the developmental model of conduct disorder presented in this paper suggests that the child's social-cognitive and emotion-regulation skills play a key role in the development of conduct problems. Therefore, three types of social-skills training programs (e.g., the PATHS curriculum, the friendship group program, and the peer-pairing program) were included in the program in order to foster the development of adaptive child social-cognitive and emotion-regulation skills. In addition, the developmental model suggests that parental practices have a marked impact on child development; positive parental support of the child's skill development and school adjustment may reduce risk for escalating conduct problems. Hence, parenting practices and positive parental support for school adjustment were included as target skills in three additional program components: the parent group, parent-child sharing, and home visiting components of the Fast Track program. In order to evaluate the degree to which patterns of change support the developmental model, analyses will include regression models. Developmentally, we anticipate that improvements in child social-cognitive skills (problem-solving skills, emotional regulation skills, academic skills) and increases in positive parental practices (positive discipline practices, involvement, and support for the child's school performance) will have a positive impact on a child's behavioral and social adjustment, which in turn will reduce risk for later conduct disorder. Hence, we will conduct regression analyses to determine the extent to which improvements in child behavioral and social adjustment are predicted by changes in the child's social-cognitive skills and parenting practices and, in turn, whether reduced rates of conduct disorders in later years are predicted by child behavior and social adjustment improvements in earlier years. Our preliminary analyses suggest that the improvements we are seeing after one year of intervention lend support to this developmental model of change.[21]

Based on the developmental model, limited effects are expected for the first year of intervention. Future analyses will examine the cumulative and longer-term effects of the Fast Track intervention program as it is continued over the elementary school years and into the transition to middle school. In addition, long-term follow-up of the children and families involved is planned, to determine how intervention affects outcomes in later adolescence.

CONCLUSIONS

From a developmental standpoint, conduct disorder is multiply determined. Effective prevention efforts must be comprehensive in nature and extend over the formative years.[3] Hence, the Fast Track program was designed to supplement social-skills training programs with family-focused interventions designed to improve parenting, parent-teacher relationships, and child academic skills. The Fast Track program is designed to continue intervention into the later elementary school years when the transition into middle school marks a second important developmental risk point for the escalation of conduct disorders. The structure and focus of the program shift somewhat in these later years to address the developmental issues and additional risk factors for conduct problems that emerge in preadolescence.

One of the long-term goals of the Fast Track program is to determine the effects of sustained, comprehensive, and integrated prevention activity. It is hoped that by addressing multiple socialization contexts (family and school), focusing on multiple skill domains (social, emotional, and cognitive/academic), and continuing intervention support across the elementary and preadolescent years, significant reductions in conduct disorders and significant improvements in adaptive outcomes will be attained.

REFERENCES

1. LOEBER, R. 1990. Clin. Psychol. Rev. **10:** 1–41.
2. PATTERSON, G. R. 1982. Coercive Family Processes. Castalia. Eugene, OR.
3. KAZDIN, A. E. 1987. Psychol. Bull. **102:** 187–203.
4. LYTTON, H. 1990. Dev. Psychol. **26:** 683–697.
5. Conduct Problems Prevention Research Group. 1992. Dev. Psychopathol. **4:** 509–528.
6. MOFFITT, T. E. 1990. Child Dev. **61:** 893–910.
7. CAMPBELL, S. B. 1990. The socialization and social development of hyperactive children. *In* Handbook of Developmental Psychopathology. M. Lewis & S. M. Miller, Eds.: 77–92. Plenum. New York.
8. GREENBERG, M. T., C. A. KUSCHE & M. SPELTZ. 1991. Emotional regulation, self-control and psychopathology: The role of relationships in early childhood. *In* Rochester Symposium on Developmental Psychopathology: Internalizing and Externalizing Expressions of Dysfunction. D. Cicchetti & S. Toth, Eds.: **2:** 21–56. Erlbaum. Hillsdale, N.J.
9. DODGE, K. A., J. E. BATES & G. S. PETTIT. 1990. Science **250:** 1678–1683.
10. BIERMAN, K. L., D. L. SMOOT & K. A. AUMILLER. 1993. Child Dev. **64:** 139–151.
11. COIE, J. D., K. A. DODGE & J. KUPERSMIDT. 1990. Peer group behavior and social status. *In* Peer Rejection in Childhood. S. R. Asher & J. D. Coie, Eds.: 17–59. Cambridge University Press. New York.
12. RUTTER, M., B. MAUGHAN, P. MORTIMORE, J. OUSTON & A. SMITH. 1979. Fifteen Thousand Hours: Secondary Schools and their Effects on Children. Harvard University Press. Cambridge, MA.
13. MOFFITT, T. E. & P. A. SILVA. 1988. J. Abnorm. Child Psychol. **16:** 553–569.
14. BIERMAN, K. L., M. T. GREENBERG & THE CONDUCT PROBLEMS PREVENTION RESEARCH GROUP. Social skill training in the Fast Track program. *In* Prevention and Early Intervention: Childhood Disorders, Substance Abuse, and Delinquency. R. DeV. Peters & R. J. McMahon, Eds. Sage. Newbury Park, CA. In press.
15. MCMAHON, R. J., N. SLOUGH & THE CONDUCT PROBLEMS PREVENTION RESEARCH GROUP. Family-based intervention in the Fast Track Program. *In* Prevention and Early Intervention: Childhood Disorders, Substance Use, and Delinquency. R. DeV. Peters & R. J. McMahon, Eds. Sage. Newbury Park, CA. In press.
16. MRAZEK, P. J. & R. J. HAGGERTY, Eds. 1994. Reducing Risks for Mental Disorders: Frontiers for Preventive Intervention Research. National Academy Press. Washington, D.C.
17. GREENBERG, M. T. & C. A. KUSCHE. 1993. Promoting Social and Emotional Development in Deaf Children: The PATHS Project. University of Washington Press. Seattle, WA.
18. BIERMAN, K. L., C. M. MILLER & S. STABB. 1987. J. Consult. Clin. Psychol. **55:** 194–200.
19. LOCHMAN, J. E., P. R. BURCH, J. F. CURRY & L. B. LAMPRON. 1984. J. Consult. Clin. Psychol. **52:** 915–916.
20. WALLACH, M. A. & L. WALLACH. 1976. Teaching All Children to Read. University of Chicago Press. Chicago, IL.
21. THE CONDUCT PROBLEMS PREVENTION RESEARCH GROUP. March, 1993. Effects of intervention on children at high risk for conduct problems. Paper presented as part of a symposium at the Biennial meeting of the Society for Research in Child Development, New Orleans.

Bullying at School

Knowledge Base and an Effective Intervention Program[a]

DAN OLWEUS[b]

Research Center for Health Promotion (HEMIL)
University of Bergen
Øisteinsgate 3, N-5007
Bergen, Norway

"For two years, Johnny, a quiet 13 year old, was a human plaything for some of his classmates. The teenagers badgered Johnny for money, forced him to swallow weeds and drink milk mixed with detergent, beat him up in the rest room and tied a string around his neck, leading him around as a "pet." When Johnny's torturers were interrogated about the bullying, they said they pursued their victim because it was fun" (newspaper clipping presented in ref. 1).

Bullying among schoolchildren is certainly a very old phenomenon. The fact that some children are frequently and systematically harassed and attacked by other children has been described in literary works, and many adults have personal experience of it from their own school days. Though many people are acquainted with the bully/victim problem, it was not until fairly recently, in the early 1970s, that the phenomenon was made the object of more systematic research.[2,3] For a number of years, these efforts were largely confined to Scandinavia. In the 1980s and early 1990s, however, bullying among school children has also attracted attention in Great Britain, Japan, the Netherlands, Australia, Canada, and the United States. There are now clear indications of an increasing societal as well as research interest into bully/victim problems in several parts of the world.[1,4]

DEFINITION OF BULLYING

I define bullying or victimization in the following general way: A student is being bullied or victimized when he or she is exposed, repeatedly and over time, to negative actions on the part of one or more other students. It is a negative action when someone intentionally inflicts injury or discomfort upon another—basically what is implied in the definition of aggressive behavior. Negative actions can be carried out by physical contact, by words, or in other ways, such as making faces or mean gestures, and intentional exclusion from a group.

[a] The research reported in this chapter was supported by Grants from the William T. Grant Foundation, the Norwegian Research Council for Social Research (NAVF), the Swedish Delegation for Social Research (DSF), and in earlier phases, from the Norwegian Ministry of Education, which is gratefully acknowledged.

[b] Tel: +4755212327; fax: +4755902556; e-mail: olweus@psych.uib.no.

In order to use the term *bullying,* there should also be an imbalance in strength (an asymmetric power relationship): the student who is exposed to the negative actions has difficulty defending him/herself and is somewhat helpless against the student or students who harass.

In my definition, the phenomenon of bullying is thus characterized by the following criteria: it is aggressive behavior or intentional "harmdoing," which is carried out repeatedly and over time in an interpersonal relationship characterized by an imbalance of power. One might add that the bullying behavior often occurs without apparent provocation. This definition makes it clear that bullying can be considered a form of abuse, and I sometimes use the term *peer abuse* as a label of the phenomenon. What sets it apart from other forms of abuse, such as child abuse and wife abuse, is the context in which it occurs and the relationship characteristics of the interacting parties.

It is useful to distinguish between direct bullying/victimization, with relatively open attacks on the victim, and indirect bullying/victimization, in the form of social isolation and intentional exclusion from a group.

BASIC FACTS ABOUT BULLYING

Prevalence

On the basis of a survey of more than 130,000 Norwegian students with my Bully/Victim Questionnaire carried out in connection with a nationwide campaign against bullying,[1] one can estimate that some 15% of the students in elementary and secondary/junior high schools (grades 1 through 9, roughly corresponding to ages 7 through 16) in Norway were involved in bully/victim problems with some regularity (autumn 1983), as bullies or victims. This percentage represents one student out of seven, or 84,000 students (out of a total of 568,000 students). Approximately 9% were victims, and 7% bullied other students. Some 9,000 students were both victim and bully (1.6% of the total or 17% of the victims). A total of some 5% of the students were involved in more serious bullying problems (as bullies or victims or bully/victim), occurring about once a week or more frequently. Very likely, these figures represent underestimates of the number of students involved in these problems during a whole year.

It is apparent, then, that bullying is a considerable problem in Norwegian schools, a problem that affects a very large number of students. Data (in large measure collected with my Bully/Victim Questionnaire) from a number of other countries, including Sweden, Finland, Great Britain, the Netherlands, Ireland, Japan, Australia, Canada and the United States, indicate that this problem certainly exists also outside Norway, with similar or even higher prevalence rates (see ref. 5 for references).

There are many more boys than girls who bully other students, and a relatively large percentage of girls report that they are mainly bullied by boys. Also, there is a somewhat higher percentage of boys who are victims of bullying. Although (direct) bullying is thus a greater problem among boys, a good deal of bullying occurs among girls as well. Bullying with physical means is less common among girls, however; girls typically use more subtle and indirect ways of harassment, such as slandering, spreading of rumors, intentional exclusion from the group, and manipulation of friendship relations. Such forms of bullying may be more difficult to detect for adults. We have also found that it is the younger and weaker students who are most exposed to bullying. Although most bullying occurs among students at the same grade level, a good deal of bullying is also carried out by older students towards younger ones (see ref. 1 for more details).

There is a good deal of evidence to indicate that the behavior patterns involved in bully/victim problems are fairly stable over time: this means that being a bully or a victim is something that is likely to continue for substantial periods of time, unless systematic efforts are made to change the situation.[3,6,7]

Three Common "Myths" about Bullying

A common view holds that the bully/victim problem is a consequence of large classes and/or schools: the larger the class or the school, the higher the level of bully/victim problems. Closer analysis of this hypothesis, making use of the Norwegian survey data from more than 700 schools and several thousand classes, gave clear-cut results: there were no positive associations between level of bully/victim problems and class or school size. Thus, the size of the class or school appears to be of negligible importance for the relative frequency or level of bully/victim problems. Nor was there anything in the data to suggest that it was easier to do something about bullying in a small school or a small class, within the relatively wide ranges represented in the study.

Second, in the general debate it has been commonly maintained that bullying is a consequence of competition and striving for grades in school. More specifically, it has been argued that the aggressive behavior of the bullies toward their environment can be explained as a reaction to failures and frustrations in school. Also, this hypothesis failed to receive support from a detailed LISREL analysis of 444 boys followed from grade 6 through grade 9. Although there were moderate negative correlations between grades (grade point averages) and aggressive behavior at both time points, there was nothing in the results to suggest that the behavior of the aggressive boys was a consequence of poor grades and failure in school.[8]

Third, a widely held view explains victimization as caused by external deviations. It is argued that students who, for example, are fat, are red-haired, wear glasses, or speak with an unusual dialect are particularly likely to become victims of bullying. This explanation seems to be quite common among students.

This hypothesis also received no support from empirical data. It was concluded that external deviations play a much smaller role in the origin of bully/victim problems than generally assumed. However, in spite of the lack of empirical support for this hypothesis, it still seems to enjoy considerable popularity. Some probable reasons why this is so have been advanced, and the interested reader is referred to this discussion.[1]

All of these hypotheses have thus failed to receive support from empirical data. Accordingly, one must look for other factors to find the origins of these problems. The research collected so far clearly suggests that personality characteristics/typical reaction patterns, in combination with physical strength or weakness, in the case of boys, play a major role in the development of these problems in individual students. At the same time, other factors, such as the teachers' attitudes, routines, and behavior, play a major role in determining the extent to which the problems will manifest themselves in a classroom or a school.

Characteristics of Typical Victims

A relatively clear picture of both the typical victims and the typical bullies has emerged from research.[1,3,4,5,9,10] By and large, this picture seems to apply to both boys and girls; it must be acknowledged, however, that clearly less research has, so far, been done on bullying among girls.

The typical victims are more anxious and insecure than students in general. Further, they are often cautious, sensitive, and quiet. When attacked by other students, they commonly react by crying (at least in the lower grades) and withdrawal. Also, victims suffer from low self-esteem; they have a negative view of themselves and their situation. They often look upon themselves as failures and feel stupid, ashamed, and unattractive.

The victims are lonely and abandoned at school. As a rule, they do not have a single good friend in their class. They are not aggressive or teasing in their behavior, however, and, accordingly, one cannot explain the bullying as a consequence of the victims themselves being provocative to their peers (see below). Also, these children often have a negative attitude toward violence and use of violent means. If they are boys, they are likely to be physically weaker than boys in general.[3]

I have labeled this type of victim *the passive or submissive* victim, as opposed to the far less common type described below. In summary, it seems that the behavior and attitude of the passive/submissive victims signal to others that they are insecure and worthless individuals who will not retaliate if they are attacked or insulted. A slightly different way of describing these victims is to say that they are characterized by an anxious or submissive reaction pattern combined (in the case of boys) with physical weakness.

In-depth interviews with parents of victimized boys indicate that these boys are characterized by a certain cautiousness and sensitivity from an early age. Boys with such characteristics (maybe combined with physical weakness) are likely to have had difficulty in asserting themselves in the peer group and may have been somewhat disliked by their age-mates. There are thus good reasons to believe that these characteristics contributed to making them victims of bullying (see also ref. 11). At the same time, it is obvious that the repeated harassment by peers must have considerably increased their anxiety, insecurity, and general negative evaluation of themselves.

As mentioned, there is also another, clearly smaller group of victims, *the provocative victims*, who are characterized by a combination of both anxious and aggressive reaction patterns. These students often have problems with concentration and behave in ways that may cause irritation and tension around them. Some of these students can be characterized as hyperactive. It is not uncommon that their behavior is irritating to many students in the class, thus resulting in negative reactions from all, or a large part of, the class. The dynamics of bully/victim problems in a class with provocative victims differ in part from problems in a class with passive victims.[3]

A follow-up study of two groups of boys[12] who had or had not been victimized by their peers in school (from grades 6 through 9) shows that the former victims had "normalized" in many ways as young adults, at age 23. This was seen as an indication that the boys, after having left school, had considerably greater freedom to choose their own social and physical environments. In two respects, however, the former victims fared much worse than their nonvictimized peers: they were more likely to be depressed and had poorer self-esteem. The pattern of findings clearly suggested that this was a consequence of the earlier, persistent victimization that thus had left its scars on their minds.

Characteristics of Typical Bullies

A distinctive characteristic of the typical bullies is their aggression toward peers; this is implied in the definition of a bully. Bullies, however, are often aggressive toward adults as well, both teachers and parents. Generally, bullies have a more positive attitude toward violence and use of violent means than students in general. Further, they are often characterized by impulsivity and strong needs to dominate others. They have little empathy with victims of bullying. If they are boys, they are likely to be physically stronger than boys, in general, and the victims, in particular.[1,3]

A commonly held view among psychologists and psychiatrists is that individuals with an aggressive and tough behavior pattern are actually anxious and insecure "under the surface." The assumption that the bullies have an underlying insecurity has been tested in several of my own studies and with a number of different methods, including indirect methods, such as projective techniques and the use of stress hormones (adrenaline and noradrenaline). There was nothing in the results to support the common view; they rather pointed in the opposite direction: the bullies had unusually little anxiety and insecurity, or were roughly average on such dimensions.[13,14] They did not suffer from poor self-esteem.

It should also be emphasized that there are students who participate in bullying but who do not usually take the initiative; these may be labeled passive bullies, followers, or henchmen. A group of passive bullies is likely to be fairly mixed and can also contain insecure and anxious students.

In summary, the typical bullies can be described as having an aggressive reaction pattern, combined (in the case of boys) with physical strength.

As regards the possible psychological sources underlying bullying behavior, the pattern of empirical findings suggests at least three partly interrelated motives (in particular in boys, who have been studied more extensively than girls). First, the bullies have unusually strong needs for power and dominance; they seem to enjoy being "in control" and subduing others. Second, in light of the family conditions under which many of them have been reared (below), it is natural to assume that they have developed a certain degree of hostility towards the environment; such feelings and impulses may make them derive satisfaction from inflicting injury and suffering upon other individuals. Finally, there is an "instrumental or benefit component" to their behavior. The bullies often coerce their victims to provide them with money, cigarettes, beer, and other things of value. In addition, it is obvious that aggressive behavior is in many situations rewarded with prestige.

Bullying can also be viewed as a component of a more general antisocial and rule-breaking ("conduct-disordered") behavior pattern.[7,15] In my follow-up studies we have found strong support for this view. Approximately 60% of boys who were characterized as bullies in grades 6 through 9 had been convicted of at least one officially registered crime by the age of 24. Even more dramatically, as much as 35–40% of the former bullies had three or more convictions by this age, whereas this was true of only 10% of the control boys (those who were neither bullies nor victims in grades 6 through 9). Thus, as young adults, the former school bullies had a fourfold increase in the level of relatively serious, recidivist criminality as documented in official crime records. It may be mentioned, that the former victims had an average or somewhat below average level of criminality in young adulthood.

Development of an Aggressive Reaction Pattern

In light of the characterization of the bullies as having an aggressive reaction pattern, that is, they display aggressive behavior in many different situations, it becomes important to examine the question, What kind of rearing and other conditions during childhood are conducive to the development of an aggressive reaction pattern? Very briefly, the following four factors have turned out to be particularly important (based chiefly on research with boys[16]). The first factor is the basic emotional attitude of the primary caretaker(s) toward the child during early years (usually the mother). A negative emotional attitude, characterized by lack of warmth and involvement, increases the risk that the child will later become aggressive and hostile toward others. Factor two is the permissiveness for aggressive behavior by the child. If the primary caretaker is generally permissive and "tolerant," without setting clear limits to aggressive behavior toward peers, siblings, and adults, the child's aggression level is likely to increase. The third factor is the use of power-assertive child-rearing methods, such as physical punishment and violent emotional outbursts. Children of parents who make frequent use of these methods are likely to become more aggressive than the average child. "Violence begets violence." We can summarize these results by stating that too little love and care and too much "freedom" in childhood are conditions that contribute strongly to the development of an aggressive reaction pattern. The final factor is the temperament of the child. A child with an active and hot-headed temperament is more likely to develop into an aggressive youngster than a child with an ordinary or more quiet temperament. The effect of this factor is less powerful than the first two factors

The factors listed above are important for both younger and somewhat older children. For adolescents, it is also very important whether or not the parents supervise their child's activities outside school, checking on what they are doing, and with whom.[17]

It should also be pointed out that the aggression levels of the boys participating in the analyses above were not related to socioeconomic conditions of their families, measured in several different ways. Similarly, there was basically no relationship between the four childhood factors discussed and the socioeconomic conditions of the family. This lack of relationship may, to some degree, be a consequence of the relative homogeneity of the Scandinavian countries in this respect. Accordingly, it is quite possible that studies from other countries, with greater socioeconomic inequalities, for example, the United States or Great Britain, will show somewhat stronger associations between the presence of bully/victim problems in the child and the socioeconomic conditions of the family.

A Question of Fundamental Democratic Rights

The victims of bullying constitute a large number of students who tend to be virtually neglected by their schools. We have shown that many of these youngsters are the targets of bullying for long periods of time, often for many years. It does not require much imagination to understand what it is to go through the school year in a state of more or less permanent anxiety, insecurity, and poor self-esteem.

It is not surprising that the victims' devaluation of themselves sometimes becomes so overwhelming that they see suicide as the only possible solution.

Bully/victim problems in school really speak to some of our basic values and principles. For a long time, I have argued that it is a fundamental democratic right for a child to feel safe in school and to be spared the oppression and repeated, intentional humiliation implied in bullying. No student should be afraid of going to school for fear of being harassed or degraded, and no parent should need to worry about such things happening to his or her child!

In 1981, I proposed the passage of a new law against bullying in school. At that time, there was little political support for the idea. In 1994, however, this suggestion was followed up in Sweden with a new school law, including formulations that are very similar to those expressed above. The law places responsibility for realization of these goals, including development of an intervention program against bullying for the individual school, with the principal. At present, a similar law is being discussed in Norway, and there seems to be considerable political support for this proposal.

EFFECTS OF A SCHOOL-BASED INTERVENTION PROGRAM

Against this background, I will now briefly describe the effects of the intervention program that I developed and evaluated in connection with the campaign against bully/victim problems in Norwegian schools. For more details about the program and its evaluation, the reader is referred to the book *Bullying at school: What We Know and What We Can Do*[1] as well as to other sources.[5,18-20,c] The major goals of the program were to reduce as much as possible existing bully/victim problems and to prevent the development of new problems.

Evaluation of the effects of the intervention program was based on data from approximately 2500 students originally belonging to 112 grade 4 through 7 classes in 42 primary and secondary/junior high schools in Bergen, Norway. The subjects of the study were followed over a period of 2.5 years. Each of the four grade/age cohorts consisted of 600–700 subjects with a roughly equal distribution of boys and girls. The first data collection (time 1) was in late May 1983, approximately four months before introduction of the intervention program. New measurements were taken in May 1984 (time 2) and May 1985 (time 3). The design employed is usually called a selection-cohorts or age-cohort design, making use of time-lagged contrasts between age-equivalent groups.

The main findings of the analyses can be summarized as follows: (1) There were marked reductions, by 50% or more, in the levels of bully/victim problems (for both direct and indirect bullying, and for bullying others) for the periods studied, 8 and 20 months of intervention, respectively. By and large, reductions were obtained for both boys and girls across all cohorts compared. See FIGURE 1 for the effects after 8 months of intervention on a variable representing a combination of direct and indirect bullying. (2) Similar reductions were obtained for the

---

[c] The "package" related to the intervention program consists of the Bully/Victim Questionnaire (can be ordered from the author), a 20-minute video cassette showing scenes from the everyday lives of two bullied children (with English subtitles; can be ordered from the author), and the book *Bullying at School: What We Know and What We Can Do* (ref. 1), which describes in detail the program and its implementation.

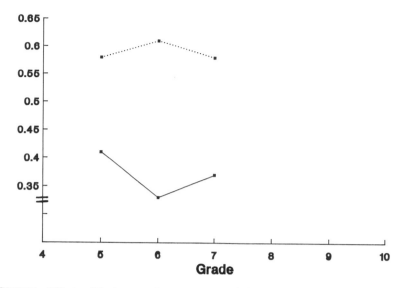

FIGURE 1. Effects of the intervention program on "being bullied by other students" (being exposed to direct as well as indirect bullying) for boys and girls combined. Upper curve shows baseline data (at time 1, before intervention) for the grade 5, 6, and 7 (or years 12, 13, and 14) cohorts, whereas the lower curve displays data for corresponding age-equivalent cohorts (grades 4, 5, and 6, or year 11, 12, and 13 cohorts) at time 2 (one year later), when they had been exposed to the intervention program for 8 months.

aggregated peer rating variables, "number of students being bullied in the class" and "number of students in the class bullying other students." There was thus consensual agreement in the classes that bully/victim problems had decreased considerably during the periods studied. (3) There was no displacement of bullying on the way to, and from, school. There were reductions or no change in bully/victim problems on the way to, and from, school. (4) There were also clear reductions in general antisocial behavior, such as vandalism, pilfering, fighting, drunkenness, and truancy. (5) In addition, we registered a marked improvement in various aspects of the social climate of the class: improved order and structure, more positive social relationships, and a more positive attitude to schoolwork and the school. There was an increase in student satisfaction with school life. (6) For several of the variables, the effects of the intervention program were more marked after 20 months than after 8 months. (7) The intervention program not only affected already existing victimization problems but also reduced the number (and percentage) of new victims.

In the majority of comparisons for which reductions were reported above, the differences between baseline and intervention groups were significant/highly significant, with medium, large, or even very large effect sizes (d-values of more than 1.0 for several variables[25]).

A detailed analysis of the quality of the data and the possibility of alternative interpretations of the findings led to the following general statements:[18] It is very difficult to explain the results obtained as a consequence of underreporting by the students, gradual changes in the students' attitudes regarding bully/victim problems, repeated measurement, and concomitant changes in other factors, including general time trends. All in all, it was concluded that the changes in bully/

victim problems and related behavior patterns were likely to be mainly a consequence of the intervention program and not of some other "irrelevant" factor. It was also noted that self-reports, which were implicated in most of the analyses, were probably the best data source for the purposes of this study.[d] At the same time, largely parallel results were obtained for the peer-rating variables mentioned above and for teacher ratings of bully/victim problems at the class level. In the latter case, however, the effects were somewhat weaker.

BRIEF COMMENTS

The reported effects of the intervention program must be considered quite positive, in particular because many previous attempts to systematically reduce aggressive and antisocial behavior in preadolescents and adolescents have been relatively unsuccessful.[21-23]

The importance of the results is further accentuated by the fact that there has been a disturbing increase in the prevalence of violence and other antisocial behavior in most industrialized societies in the last decades. In the Scandinavian countries, for instances, various forms of registered criminality have typically increased by 300–600 percent since the 1950s or 1960s. Similar changes have occurred in most Western, industrialized societies, including the United States.

As mentioned above, we estimate that approximately 80,000 students in Norwegian elementary and secondary/junior high schools were involved in bully/victim problems (in 1983). On the basis of the reported results, the following conclusion can be drawn: If all elementary and secondary/junior high schools in Norway used the intervention program the way it was used in Bergen, the number of students involved in bully/victim problems would be reduced by 40,000 or more in a relatively short period of time. Effective use of the intervention program would probably also result in lower levels of vandalism, pilfering, and other antisocial behavior saving society large amounts of money.

BASIC PRINCIPLES

The intervention program is built on a limited set of key principles derived chiefly from research on the development and modification of the implicated problem behaviors, in particular, aggressive behavior. It is thus important to try to create a school (and ideally, also a home) environment characterized by warmth,

---

[d] With regard to the validity of self-reports on variables related to bully/victim problems, in the early Swedish studies (ref. 3), composites of 3–5 self-report items on being bullied or bullying and attacking others, respectively, correlated in the 0.40–0.60 range (Pearson's correlation) with reliable peer ratings on related dimensions. Similarly, Perry, Kusel & Perry (Dev. Psychol. **24:** 807–814) reported a correlation of 0.42 between a self-report scale of three victimization items and a reliable measure of peer nominations of victimization in elementary schoolchildren. In the intervention study, we also found class-aggregated student rating estimates of the number of students in the class who were bullied or who bullied others during the reference period to be highly correlated with class-aggregated estimates derived from the students' own reports of being bullied or bullying others. Correlations were in the 0.60–0.70 range (see reference 14 for details).

TABLE 1. Overview of Core Program

	General Prerequisites
$++^a$	Awareness and involvement on the part of adults
	Measures at the School Level
$++$	Questionnaire
$++$	School conference day
$++$	Better supervision during recess and lunch time
$+^b$	Formation of coordinating group
	Measures at the Class Level
$++$	Class rules against bullying
$++$	Regular class meetings with students
$+$	Class PTA meetings
	Measures at the Individual Level
$++$	Serious talks with bullies and victims
$++$	Serious talks with parents of involved students
$+$	Teacher and parent use of imagination

[a] $++$, Core component.
[b] $+$, Highly desirable component.

positive interest, and involvement from adults, on the one hand, and firm limits to unacceptable behavior ("We don't accept bullying in our school"), on the other. Also, in cases of violations of limits and rules, nonhostile, nonphysical sanctions should be applied consistently. Implied in the latter two principles is also a certain degree of monitoring and surveillance of the students' activities in and out of school. Finally, adults, both at school and home, should act as authorities, at least in some respects.

The principles listed above were "translated" into a number of specific measures to be used at the school, class, and individual levels. It is considered important to work on all of these levels, if possible. TABLE 1 lists a set of core components that are considered, on the basis of statistical analyses and our experience with the program, to be particularly important in any implementation of the program.

With regard to implementation and execution, the program is mainly based on the use of the existing social environment: teachers and other school personnel, students, and parents. Non–mental health professionals thus play a major role in the desired restructuring of the social environment. Experts, such as school psychologists, counsellors, and social workers, also serve important functions as planners and coordinators, in counseling teachers and parents (groups), and in handling more serious cases.

Possible reasons for the effectiveness of this nontraditional intervention approach have been discussed in some detail.[19] They include changes in the "opportunity" and "reward structures" for bullying behavior (resulting in fewer opportunities and rewards for bullying). It is also emphasized that bully/victim problems can be seen as an excellent entry point for dealing with a variety of problems that plague our schools. Furthermore, one can view the program from the perspective of planned organizational change (with quite specific goals) and in this way link it with the current lively work on school effectiveness and school improvement.

This core program in many ways represents what is often called "a whole-school policy approach to bullying" in the recent English literature. It consists of a set of routines, rules, and strategies of communication and action for dealing with existing and future bullying problems in the school.

This antibullying program is now in use or in the process of being implemented in a considerable number of schools in Europe and North America. Although there have been few research-based attempts, beyond the study in Bergen, to evaluate the effects of the program unsystematic information and reports indicate that the general approach is well received by parents, teachers, and administrators and that the program (with or without cultural adaptations or additions of culture-specific components) works well under varying cultural conditions, including ethnic diversity. Recently, there has, however, been one large-scale evaluation of the basic approach, containing most of the score elements of the program and with a research design similar to that of the Bergen study. Also in this project,[24] comprising 23 schools (with a good deal of ethnic diversity) in Sheffield, United Kingdom, the results were quite encouraging (though fewer behavioral aspects were studied). It can be argued that the robustness and possible generalizability of the program is not really surprising, inasmuch as the existing evidence seems to indicate that the factors and principles affecting the development and modification of aggressive, antisocial behavior are fairly similar across cultural contexts, at least within the Western, industrialized part of the world.

FINAL WORDS

The basic message of our findings is quite clear: With a suitable intervention program, it is definitely possible to dramatically reduce bully/victim problems and related problem behaviors in school. This antibullying program can be implemented with relatively simple means and without major costs; it is, above all, a question of changing attitudes, behavior, and routines in school life. Introduction of the program is likely to have a number of other positive effects as well.

REFERENCES

1. OLWEUS, D. 1993. Bullying at School: What We Know and What We Can Do. Blackwell Publishers. Cambridge, MA. (Oxford, U.K.).
2. OLWEUS, D. 1973. Hackkycklingar och Översittare. Forskning om skolmobbning. Almqvist & Wicksell. Stockholm.
3. OLWEUS, D. 1978. Aggression in the schools. Bullies and Whipping Boys. Hemisphere Press (Wiley). Washington, D.C.
4. FARRINGTON, D. 1993. Understanding and preventing bullying. In Crime and Justice: A Review of Research. M. Tonry, Ed.: Vol. 17. University of Chicago Press. Chicago, IL.
5. OLWEUS, D. 1994. Annotation: Bullying at school: Basic facts and effects of a school based intervention program. J. Child Psychol. Psychiatry 35: 1171–1190.
6. OLWEUS, D. 1977. Aggression and peer acceptance in adolescent boys: Two short-term longitudinal studies of ratings. Child Dev. 48: 1301–1313.
7. OLWEUS, D. 1979. Stability of aggressive reaction patterns in males: A review. Psychol. Bull. 86: 852–875.
8. OLWEUS, D. 1983. Low school achievement and aggressive behavior in adolescent boys. In Human Development. An Interactional Perspective. D. Magnusson & V. Allen, Eds. Academic Press. New York.

9. BJÖRKQVIST, K., K. EKMAN & K. LAGERSPETZ. 1982. Bullies and victims: Their ego picture, ideal ego picture and normative ego picture. Scand. J. Psychol. 23: 307–313.
10. PERRY, D., S. J. KUSEL & L. C. PERRY. 1988. Victims of peer aggression. Dev. Psychol. 24: 807–814.
11. SCHWARTZ, D., K. DODGE & J. COIE. 1993. The emergence of chronic peer victimization in boys' play groups. Child Dev. 64: 1755–1772.
12. OLWEUS, D. 1993. Victimization by peers: Antecedents and long-term outcomes. In Social Withdrawal, Inhibition, and Shyness in Childhood. K. H. Rubin & J. B. Asendorf, Eds. Erlbaum. Hillsdale, NJ.
13. OLWEUS, D. 1981. Bullying among school-boys. In Children and Violence. N. Cantwell, Ed. Akademilitteratur. Stockholm.
14. PULKKINEN, L. & R. E. TREMBLAY. 1992. Patterns of boys' social adjustment in two cultures and at different ages: A longitudinal perspective. Int. J. Behav. Dev. 15: 527–553.
15. LOEBER, R. & T. DISHION. 1983. Early predictors of male delinquency: A review. Psychol. Bull. 94: 69–99.
16. OLWEUS, D. 1980. Familial and temperamental determinants of aggressive behavior in adolescent boys: A causal analysis. Dev. Psychol. 16: 644–660.
17. PATTERSON, G. R. 1986. Performance models for antisocial boys. Am. Psychol. 41: 432–444.
18. OLWEUS, D. 1991. Bully/victim problems among schoolchildren: Basic facts and effects of a school based intervention program. In The Development and Treatment of Childhood Aggression. D. Pepler & K. Rubin, Eds. Erlbaum. Hillsdale, NJ.
19. OLWEUS, D. 1992. Bullying among schoolchildren: Intervention and prevention. In Aggression and Violence Throughout the Life Span. R. D. Peters, R. J. McMahon & V. L. Quincy, Eds. Sage. Newbury Park, CA.
20. OLWEUS, D. & F. D. ALSAKER. 1991. Assessing change in a cohort longitudinal study with hierarchical data. In Problems and Methods in Longitudinal Research. D. Magnusson, L. Bergman, G. Rudinger & B. Törestad, Eds. Cambridge University Press. New York.
21. DUMAS, J. E. 1989. Treating antisocial behavior in children: Child and family approaches. Clin. Psychol. Rev. 9: 197–222.
22. KAZDIN, A. E. 1987. Treatment of antisocial behavior in children: Current status and future directions. Psychol. Bull. 102: 187–203.
23. GOTTFREDSON, G. D. 1987. Peer group interventions to reduce the risk of delinquent behavior: A selective review and a new evaluation. Criminology 25: 671–714.
24. SMITH, P. K. & S. SHARP. 1994. School Bullying: Insights and Perspectives. Routledge. London.
25. COHEN, J. 1977. Statistical Power Analysis for the Behavioral Sciences. 2nd rev. edition. Academic Press. New York.

Preliminary Findings of an Early Intervention Program with Aggressive Hyperactive Children

RUSSELL A. BARKLEY,[a] TERRI L. SHELTON,
CHERYL CROSSWAIT, MAUREEN MOOREHOUSE,
KENNETH FLETCHER, SUSAN BARRETT,
LUCY JENKINS, AND LORI METEVIA

Departments of Psychiatry and Neurology
University of Massachusetts Medical Center
and
Worcester Public Schools
Worcester, Massachusetts

Studies of hyperactive children, or those diagnosed as having attention-deficit hyperactivity disorder (ADHD), have found that approximately 40 to 70% experience coexisting problems with social aggression, or oppositional defiant disorder (ODD).[1-4] This subgroup manifests a considerably higher likelihood of experiencing a variety of psychological, academic, emotional, and social difficulties than do hyperactive children without such comorbid aggression.[3,5-7] Research following hyperactive children into adolescence documents a markedly higher risk for conduct disorder; delinquent or criminal activities; academic achievement deficits; school behavioral problems and disciplinary actions; and substance experimentation, use, and abuse.[5,8-13] Likewise, research on conduct-disordered youth finds that the combination of early hyperactive-impulsive behavior with aggression in childhood is associated with significantly earlier onset of conduct disorder and antisocial behavior, greater diversity of delinquent activities, greater persistence of conduct disorder during adolescence, and a greater risk for substance use and abuse in adolescence.[14-17]

Aggression in hyperactive children has been associated with increased family dysfunction as well. Greater psychopathology, marital discord, and divorce have been documented in parents of these comorbid children relative to the parents of nonaggressive hyperactive children.[3,18,19] Not surprisingly, parent-child conflict has been found to be substantially higher in families of aggressive hyperactive children, or those with combined ADHD and ODD, in contrast to the parent-child interactions of purely hyperactive or ADHD children.[2,18,20]

Hyperactive children have been found to demonstrate a larger-than-normal amount of service utilization within schools and community health care, and within mental health and social service agencies.[21] This seems to be especially so for those with comorbid aggression or conduct problems.[2,12] The expense to society of attempting to manage the numerous problems posed by these children is considerable.

[a] Address correspondence to Russell A. Barkley, Ph.D., Department of Psychiatry, University of Massachusetts Medical Center, 55 Lake Avenue North, Worcester, MA 01655. Tel: (508) 856-5843; fax: (508) 856-6426; e-mail: RBarkley@BANGATE1.ummed.edu.

The substantial risks posed for young children with comorbid hyperactivity (ADHD) and aggression (ODD) and their high likelihood of failure upon entering school led to the development of an early intervention project for these high-risk children. Children were to be detected as being aggressive-hyperactive-impulsive (AHI) at registration for public school kindergarten (ages 4.5–6 yrs), and their families were to be invited to participate in a randomized trial of various behavioral, psychosocial, and academic interventions aimed at reducing the risk for negative outcomes for these children. The treatments chosen for inclusion in this project were based upon research conducted up until 1990 that indicated or implied promising results for such treatments when applied to hyperactive or ADHD children. At that time, these interventions appeared to be parent training in child behavior management methods, behavior modification used in the classroom, self-control training in the classroom, social skills training, and anger-control training.[22–28] Although stimulant medication had shown promise in reducing aggressive behavior in hyperactive or ADHD children by that time,[29,30] it was not considered advisable or socially acceptable for use in children below age 6 years who had been detected as high risk simply through a community screening procedure as opposed to being clinically referred. Thus, medication was not included as a treatment component for this early intervention project.

The present paper outlines some of the preliminary findings of the project, particularly as regards the area of childhood aggression and the impact of treatment upon this domain of functioning. The study is not yet complete, given that each child is being followed up for two years after leaving the active treatment programs, and these follow-up evaluations have yet to be completed for all children. The results to be presented here pertain only to some of the initial differences among the groups in the study and a selection of some of the immediate treatment effects (pre- to posttreatment comparisons). Full reports of the findings of the project will be published elsewhere in scientific journals.

SUMMARY OF PROJECT METHODS

The project has spanned five years (1991–96). In the spring of 1991, the Worcester Public Schools (WPS) granted permission for research staff to participate in the registration process of all kindergarten-age children entering WPS for the fall kindergarten. The screening of children for high levels of hyperactivity and coexisting aggression was permitted only if it could be done within a brief period (10 minutes) during the already hectic kindergarten registration process. This registration occurs at a central location in Worcester, MA, a city of nearly 170,000 residents having an annual enrollment of approximately 1,200 to 1,600 preschool children per year for kindergarten.

A parent-completed rating scale was used to achieve this screening and identification of high-risk hyperactive-aggressive youngsters. Parents were invited to complete the questionnaire but were not required to do so to register their children. As a result, a sizable minority of parents (up to 20%) declined to complete the scale. Children who did not speak English or whose parents were not sufficiently familiar with English to complete the screening questionnaire were excluded from the project. This had the effect of eliminating non–English speaking Hispanic and Asian families each year from the screening process. In the end, approximately 65% of those children registering for kindergarten, or approximately 800 to 1,100 children per year, were ultimately screened for the presence of high levels of both hyperactive-impulsive behavior and social aggression.

The screening scale contained the 14 symptom items for ADHD and 8 symptom items for ODD from the DSM-III-R as well as the nonredundant hyperactive-impulsive factor items and conduct problem factor items from the Conners Parent Rating Scale-Revised.[31] To be identified as hyperactive-aggressive, parents had to rate their children as placing above the 93rd percentile on either the ADHD or Conner's Parent Rating Scale (CPRS) hyperactive-impulsive items and above the 93rd percentile for the ODD or CPRS conduct-problem items. Consequently, scores on both the hyperactive-impulsive-inattentive dimension and the aggression dimension had to place the child in the top 7 percent of normal children. During the first year of screening, norms published for these items were employed.[31,32] During the second and third year of screening, the actual local norms derived from more than 1000 children screened in year one were employed. The adjustments made to the initial published thresholds for subject selection based on the local norms were slightly downward from those calculated from the published norms, however, insuring that the subjects in cohort 1 were as deviant as those in cohorts 2 and 3. Approximately 3100 children registering for kindergarten were screened across the first three years of the project. Of those identified as high risk and solicited to be in the project, approximately 70% accepted the invitation.

During each of the first three years of the project (1991–93), an annual cohort of hyperactive-aggressive children were recruited from this screening process. Before contacting parents concerning participation, the names of the identified children were randomly assigned to participate in one of four treatment groups: (1) parent training only; (2) treatment classroom only; (3) parent training and treatment classroom; and (4) no treatment control group. Randomization within gender was done to insure that relatively equal numbers of each sex were assigned to each treatment group. Parents of these high-risk children were then contacted and invited to participate in the treatment program to which they had been assigned. Those who declined to be in their assigned treatment program were not informed about nor given an opportunity to shift to any other program. However, randomization had to be violated in several cases each year for two reasons: (1) to insure that several sets of twins or siblings of subjects participating in an earlier cohort were assigned to the same treatment group; and (2) to accommodate children where busing could not be provided in the special kindergarten class. The latter children were assigned to the no-treatment control group or, if initially offered parent-training with the special classroom, to the parent-training only group.

A normal community control group was chosen by selecting every fifth child's name falling within one standard deviation of the mean on both the hyperactive and aggressive items of the screening scale. These families were not provided with any interventions but received the same free psychological evaluations each year, described below, as the high-risk children.

In the summer months of each of the first three years, before that cohort started treatment, the high-risk and normal children received a lengthy battery of structured psychiatric interviews, psychological and academic tests, parent behavior rating scales, and direct behavioral observation. In late September, before any treatments were initiated, the behavior of all children was observed and coded in their kindergarten classrooms. Teachers completed behavior rating scales. These observations were repeated again in January and May of that academic year. A packet of behavior rating scales was completed by both the teachers and parents at these times as well. The annual summer testing battery was repeated at the end of kindergarten (posttreatment) and at the end of first and second grade (1 and 2 years posttreatment, respectively). Thus, three cohorts of high-risk and normal children were screened, identified, and invited to participate in the project.

This resulted in a total of 158 AHI children and 47 normal control children enlisting in the project and completing the initial evaluation. An additional 12 high-risk children and their parents volunteered to participate in the project but were either determined to be ineligible during the more intensive summer pretreatment evaluation or their families withdrew from the project before kindergarten began.

The parent training program used in treatment was identical to that published by Barkley[33] and was provided to parents in a group format over 10 weekly sessions beginning in October of each year. Following these weekly sessions, monthly booster sessions were offered to these parents each month from January to May of the kindergarten year. All parent training groups were conducted by the same child psychologist who was trained by the principal investigator and who had three years of experience in this treatment program.

The two special treatment classrooms were located in two Worcester Public School (WPS) locations, one on the east side and the other on the west side of town. Approximately 14–16 high-risk children were assigned to each of these special kindergarten classes each year, and busing was provided to these children to the classrooms by the project. Each classroom was outfitted with the same equipment as a standard kindergarten classroom in the WPS. A teacher and teacher aide were hired from an eligible pool of WPS teachers and aides to work in each classroom. The behavioral interventions used in these classrooms were modeled on those in use at the University of California, Irvine (UCI) special school for ADHD children developed by James Swanson, Ph.D., and colleagues (Linda Pfiffner, Ph.D. and Keith McBurnett, Ph.D.) (see Pfiffner & Barkley for a description[27]). The project was most fortunate to be able to hire a master teacher from the University of California, Irvine with special expertise in the behavioral interventions used there for kindergarten children. This master teacher trained the teachers in the behavioral treatments and worked a half day in each classroom each school day to supervise the teachers, insure consistency in the curriculum and behavioral interventions across the classrooms, individually tutor the children in reading and math skills, and fill in when teachers and aides were absent due to illness. An experienced child psychologist with special expertise in early intervention programs (Terri Shelton, Ph.D.) also trained the teachers and aides, supervised the classroom intervention program, spot-checked each classroom several times per week for adherence to the program, and met weekly for supervision with the teachers, aides, and master teacher. The teachers and aides hired to be in the project received extensive training from this master teacher and child psychologist in these behavioral methods and the special treatment curriculum during the summer months prior to starting the first cohort's treatment program. They were retrained each summer in the behavioral treatments.

The multiple behavioral interventions used in the project classrooms were (1) an intensive token system (started in October); (2) response cost, overcorrection, and time-out from reinforcement (started in October); (3) group cognitive-behavioral self-control training (started in November); (4) group social skills training, comprised mainly of the skill streaming program by Goldstein and that used in the UCI program (started in November); (5) group anger-control training adapted from the program developed by Stephen Hinshaw, Ph.D., and colleagues at UCLA and UC, Berkeley (started in January); and (6) a daily school report card with home-based reinforcement (started in May of kindergarten). Behavior modification programs were also developed by the classroom staff for disruptive recess or bus-ride behaviors, as needed. In addition to this intensive behavioral training program, an accelerated curriculum was designed, such that the standard WPS kindergarten curriculum was covered within three months, after which greater emphasis was placed on early academic skills, such as reading, spelling, math skills, and hand-writing. Children in each class also had access to two personal computers for weekly sessions of skill drills using educational software for math, reading, and logic skills.

Children who had participated in these special treatment kindergartens were then provided with follow-up consultations to their first-grade teachers upon returning to their neighborhood schools for their first grade year. These first grade teachers received consultations from the master teacher and child psychologist during the late summer and early fall. This was done to educate the first grade teachers above the behavioral methods used in the kindergarten that might be helpful to extend into first grade, about the academic strengths and weaknesses of the student that might require attention from this teacher, and about what special educational services the children might be eligible for upon their return to their neighborhood school. Therefore, some effort was provided to program for generalization and maintenance of the special classroom treatment gains into the first grade year. Thereafter, all interventions with the subjects by project staff ceased.

PRELIMINARY RESULTS AND DISCUSSION

Two groups of children participated at the start of the current project: 158 AHI children and 47 normal community control children. The AHI children were subdivided into four treatment groups to which they were randomly assigned prior to kindergarten entry: (a) no-treatment control (n = 42), (b) parent training only (n = 39), (c) special treatment, classroom only (n =37), and (d) parent training combined with special classroom (n = 40). The first results to be presented below deal with the initial differences prior to treatment between the 158 AHI children and the 47 control children.

Group Differences

Complete detailed analyses comparing the AHI and normal control children before the intervention began will be described in a later publication. These analyses found that the brief behavior rating scale completed by parents at the children's kindergarten registration identified a group of children later found to have numerous behavioral, emotional, cognitive, academic, and social problems on an extensive multimethod, multisource battery of measures relative to a community control group. Behavior ratings by parents and teachers, direct observations taken in the children's classes, psychological tests, and observations taken of the children in a clinical setting all identified a number of problems that the AHI children were experiencing. These findings clearly underscore the high-risk nature of this sample of AHI children and support the need for efforts at early intervention and prevention, as was undertaken in this project.

Some of these group differences in the areas of child development and family functioning are shown in TABLE 1. The groups were not significantly different in age of the children but did differ in the age of their mothers. Mothers of the AHI children were significantly younger than mothers of the control children. The groups did not differ in the age of their fathers. Both the mothers and fathers of the AHI children were significantly less educated than mothers and fathers of the control children. Nevertheless, the socioeconomic status of the parents did not

TABLE 1. Demographic Information by Group and Statistical Test Results

	AHI Group		Control Group			
Measure	Mean	SD	Mean	SD[a]	t[b]	p[c]
Child's Age (years)						
Child's PPVT-R[d] IQ	91.8	15.5	99.1	14.8	2.85	.005
Mother's age (years)	29.4	4.9	32.6	5.4	3.85	.001
Father's age (years)	33.2	6.6	34.9	6.0	1.54	—
Mother's education (years)	12.6	2.2	13.7	2.3	3.04	.003
Father's education (years)	12.6	2.5	13.8	3.0	2.45	.017
Mother's economic status[e]	30.2	24.2	36.1	26.1	1.30	—
Father's economic status	43.6	23.4	49.0	23.0	1.25	—

[a] Standard deviation.
[b] Results for the t-test.
[c] Probability value for the t-test, if significant.
[d] Peabody picture vocabulary test, revised.
[e] Economic status based on the Hollingshead two-factor index of social position.

differ between the groups either for mothers or fathers based on the Hollingshead two-factor index of social position. The gender representation was equivalent in both groups of subjects given that efforts were made to equate groups on this variable. For the control group, 38% were female, and 62% were male. For the AHI group, 34% were female, and 66% were male.

The ethnic representation of the groups was also not significantly different, with the AHI group composed of 78% Caucasian, 10% African-American, 7% Puerto Rican, < 1% Asian, 1% Native American, and 3% various other groups. For the control group, the representation was 89% Caucasian, 4% African-American, 4% Puerto Rican, 2% Asian, and no Native Americans.

Significantly more of the custodial parents in the AHI group were currently separated or divorced from the other biological parent of the child than in the control group (40% vs. 19%), $\chi^2 = 7.2$, p <.008. The age of the children at the time of their parents' divorce was not significantly different between groups (2.2 yrs vs. 2.1 yrs). The percentage of mothers and fathers in each group working more than 20 hours per week was not significantly different between these groups (mothers: 45% AHI vs. 53%; fathers: 86% AHI vs. 92%). However, more families of AHI children were receiving public assistance (welfare) than in the control group (39% vs. 15%), $\chi^2 = 11.62$, p <.003.

The parents were interviewed using the diagnostic interview schedule for children (parent form) (DISC-P) for DSM-III-R and DSM-IV disorders. They also completed several behavior-rating scales about their children. The results are shown in TABLE 2. Both the parents' ratings of global functioning of the AHI children and those given by the interviewers were significantly lower than those of the control group. Children with AHI also had more symptoms of ODD and conduct disorder (CD) endorsed by their parents during this clinical interview than did control children. These findings serve to validate the initial screening measure used to select these AHI children during their kindergarten registration several months prior to this interview being conducted. Not surprisingly, then, 67% of the AHI children received a DSM-IV diagnosis of ADHD, and 64% received a diagnosis of ODD. Despite their young age (pre-kindergarten), 18% met criteria for a diagnosis of conduct disorder. None of the children in the control group met criteria for these disruptive behavior disorders.

Parents of the AHI children rated them as having significantly more problems on the aggression and delinquency scales of the child behavior checklist as well as on the Conners parent rating scale (revised) than parents of the children in the control group.

Kindergarten teachers for all of the subjects were asked to complete several rating scales dealing with classroom behavior, self-control, and social skills. In addition, observers visited the classroom and observed each subject for one hour, after which they completed the child behavior checklist direct observation form. The results for some of these rating scales are displayed in TABLE 3. Teachers rated the AHI group as having significantly more problems on the Conner's teacher rating scale (revised) than the control children. On the CBCL-teacher report form (TRF) scales of aggression and delinquency, teachers rated the AHI children as having significantly more behavioral problems than children in the control group. Such findings are important from the standpoint that they corroborate the parent reports of similar problems in the home and community setting. They also serve to further validate the screening instrument used to select the children as AHI and high risk during the brief kindergarten screening.

Treatment Effects

The complete results from the extensive and detailed analyses of treatment effects will also be described in a later publication.

As noted earlier, the AHI children were subdivided into four treatment groups to which they were randomly assigned prior to kindergarten entry: (a) no-treatment control (n = 42), (b) parent training only (n = 39), (c) special treatment, classroom only (n = 37), and (d) parent training combined with special classroom (n = 40). However, up to a third of those families assigned to the two-parent training programs and who had volunteered for these treatments failed to attend any of

TABLE 2. Parent Reports of Child Behavior by Group and Statistical Test Results

Measure	AHI Group		Control Group			
	Mean	SD	Mean	SD	t	p
DISC[a] functioning, parent	69.9	13.7	89.8	4.9	15.24	.001
DISC functioning, examiner	63.4	14.6	87.9	5.3	17.53	.001
DISC ODD symptoms, number	7.0	3.2	1.4	1.6	15.95	.001
DISC CD symptoms, number	1.8	2.3	0.2	0.4	8.28	.001
Parent Report						
Delinquent behavior (CBCL[b])	62.4	8.3	51.8	3.2	13.06	.001
Aggressive behavior (CBCL)	67.3	10.4	51.8	3.7	15.67	.001
CPRS[c] total score	44.1	18.6	11.9	9.1	16.21	.001
Teacher Report						
Delinquent behavior (CBCL)	56.6	7.2	51.9	4.2	5.52	.001
Aggressive behavior (CBCL)	60.6	10.4	52.9	5.1	6.82	.001
CTRS[d] total score	24.7	19.7	9.1	13.1	6.29	.001

[a] Diagnostic Interview Schedule for Children.
[b] Child behavior checklist.
[c] Conner's Parent Rating Scale, revised.
[d] Conner's Teacher Rating Scale, revised.

TABLE 3. Means and Standard Deviations for Symptoms of ADHD, ODD, and CD from the Structured Parental Psychiatric Interview by Treatment Group for Pre- and Posttreatment Evaluations

| | Treatment Groups | | | | | | | |
| | No Tx[a] | | Parent Trng[b] | | Classroom[c] | | Combined[d] | |
Measure	Mean	SD	Mean	SD	Mean	SD	Mean	SD
DISC–Oppositional Defiant Disorder (ODD)								
Pretreatment	6.4	3.3	7.4	2.9	7.6	3.2	6.4	3.1
Posttreatment	5.5	3.3	6.0	3.3	5.1	2.9	5.9	3.0
DISC–Conduct Disorder (CD): (T[e], PT × T[f], SCT × T[g])								
Pretreatment	1.4	2.3	1.6	2.1	2.7	2.7	1.4	1.9
Posttreatment	1.2	2.2	1.6	1.8	1.0	1.5	1.3	2.1
Parent CBCL delinquency: (T)								
Pretreatment	61.2	8.2	62.8	8.4	64.3	8.2	62.5	8.8
Posttreatment	58.5	8.3	62.3	11.2	59.5	7.4	59.2	9.9
Parent CBCL aggression: (T)								
Pretreatment	64.1	10.4	69.4	10.1	70.4	11.5	69.0	9.4
Posttreatment	59.7	8.5	65.9	12.9	62.0	11.1	62.6	10.0
Teacher CBCL delinquency: (SCT, T, SCT × T)								
Pretreatment	54.0	6.2	54.5	6.0	58.1	8.1	59.0	7.5
Posttreatment	54.6	6.4	55.5	5.6	54.3	5.3	55.7	6.4
Teacher CBCL aggression: (SCT, T, SCT × T)								
Pretreatment	56.6	7.9	58.1	11.2	62.5	11.0	64.5	10.2
Posttreatment	56.2	8.3	58.3	10.8	56.9	5.8	58.7	6.9

[a] No treatment, control group.
[b] Parent training–only group.
[c] Special classroom treatment–only group.
[d] Parent training combined with special classroom treatment group.
[e] Main effect for time was significant.
[f] Interaction of parent training with time was significant.
[g] Interaction of special classroom treatment × time was significant.

the parent training classes, even though they had participated in the pre- and posttreatment evaluations. These nonattenders were in addition to those 5% who dropped out of the study entirely. We removed these nonattenders from both of the parent training groups for the analysis of treatment effects, given that they essentially received no treatment. This reduced the two-parent training groups to the following sample sizes for the analysis of treatment effects: (1) parent training only (n = 24) and (2) parent training with special classroom (n = 27).

To analyze the effects of treatment having maximum statistical power, we used a 2 (special classroom, no special classroom) × 2 (parent training, no parent training) × 2 (occasions of assessment) factorial design with repeated measures on the last factor and multivariate analysis of variances (MANOVAs) on conceptually related sets of measures. The parent and teacher ratings obtained on three occasions were analyzed using a similar 2 × 2 × 3 design and the same statistical analyses. All MANOVAs reported below are of the 2 × 2 × 2 type unless otherwise specified. It should be borne in mind, in such a design, that it is the interaction of each treatment type with time (occasion of assessment) that indicates treatment effects and not the main effect for either treatment type. A main effect for time would indicate that all groups improved significantly as a function of time (development?), regardless of treatment type. Nonattenders in both parent training groups were excluded from these analyses of treatment effects described below.

In doing so, we realized that children in the combined treatment program whose parents did not attend parent training still received the special classroom treatment program and thus should not go unanalyzed for treatment effects of the classroom on their behavior. However, reassigning them into the special classroom only treatment group would mean that 25% of the members of that treatment would not have been assigned at random to that group, violating the assumption of randomness in treatment assignments. We have chosen to exclude this group from the present analyses but plan to conduct separate analyses of these children later by contrasting them to the no-treatment control group to determine if special classroom treatment resulted in improvements on any measures. Because of the reduction in sample sizes from removing the parent-training nonattenders and the commensurate reduction in statistical power, particularly for the interaction terms, we have set $p < .05$ as the level of significance in this report of our findings so as to reduce the likelihood of type II errors.

Parents were interviewed pre- and posttreatment on the DISC-P. From this structured psychiatric interview, we extracted the number of symptoms endorsed for each childhood disorder. For this report, we have analyzed the results for the symptoms of ODD and CD as they are most pertinent to the aims of this early intervention program (reduction of disruptive behavior problems). The means and standard deviations for these scores are shown in TABLE 3.

The MANOVA conducted on these scores revealed no significant main effects for parent training (PT) or the special classroom treatment (SCT), nor was the interaction of the two significant. There was a significant main effect for time (T), $F = 8.02$, $df = 3/118$, $p < .001$. Inspection of the univariate tests indicated that all groups improved in symptoms of all three disorders between pre- and posttreatment evaluations. However, there were several significant interactions of treatment condition with time that must qualify this main effect. There was a significant interaction of PT × T, $F = 2.91$, $df = 3/118$, $p = .037$. The univariate tests showed that this interaction was significant for symptoms of CD but not for symptoms of ODD. There was also a significant interaction of SCT × T, $F = 2.76$, $df = 3/118$, $p = .045$. This effect was likewise significant on the univariate tests for CD symptoms but not for ODD symptoms. Even these interaction terms may need to be interpreted cautiously, as the three-way interaction (PT × SCT × T) was marginally significant, $F = 2.48$, $df = 3/118$, $p = .065$. Inspection of the means for these groups indicates that the effects of treatment appear mainly to have occurred in the group receiving the SCT only treatment program, whereas those in the other treatment groups appear to have changed little from pre- to posttreatment.

Parents completed the CBCL before and after treatment. The CBCL subscale T scores were analyzed by MANOVA. The means and standard deviations for two of the externalizing scales appear in TABLE 3. The main effect for PT and SCT were not significant, whereas that for time was significant, $F = 6.47$, $df = 9/112$, $p < .001$. Inspection of the univariate analyses revealed significant main effects for time on these two scales. Again, this indicates that all groups appeared to improve with time on the majority of these measures, particularly those pertaining to disruptive or externalizing behavior. The interaction of PT × SCT approached significance, $F = 1.95$, $df = 9/112$, $p = .052$. Neither the interaction of PT with time nor SCT with time was significant, nor was the three-way interaction (PT × SCT × T). Thus, there were no significant effects of treatment demonstrated on this parent-completed scale.

Teacher ratings on the CBCL-TRF were collected at pre- and posttreatment.

The means and standard deviations for two of the externalizing scales by group for each of these assessments are displayed in TABLE 3. The results indicated a significant main effect for SCT, $F = 4.21$, $df = 8/114$, p $<.001$; and for time, $F = 3.73$, $df = 8/114$, p $<.001$; as well as a significant interaction of SCT $\times$ T, $F = 3.33$, $df = 8/114$, p $<.002$. Examination of the univariate analyses indicated that this interaction was significant for the delinquency and aggression scales. An inspection of the means indicates that those who received the special classroom program showed significantly greater declines over the course of treatment on these scales than those who did not. No other interaction terms were significant.

The results to date indicate that the parent training program was ineffective in producing significant improvements in child behavior problems, academic achievement, and school behavioral problems. The problem with this parent training program was not its effectiveness, as this program has been shown, in past studies of clinic-referred children, to produce significant improvements in the majority of families receiving training. The problem was that the present families were not clinic referred, and many lacked the motivation to attend the free training program offered to them. Of those who attended, many did not attend all sessions and so investment in the training program by many of the parents must be considered modest at best. This study does show that screening children at kindergarten entry for behavioral problems and academic risks and then offering their parents a free parent-training program is unlikely to be very practical, as many families will fail to take advantage of the program. Those who do not participate fully in the program can expect little benefit for themselves or their high-risk children.

Cunningham et al.[34] report similar disheartening results when training is offered in a hospital/medical school but more optimistic results when it is provided through neighborhood schools. As others have reported recently (Henggeler et al.;[35] Nye, Zucker and Fitzgerald[36]), providing the training program in the homes of the families insures fewer dropouts, more parental investment in the training program, and greater success of the intervention program as a result.

These results do show that the special behavioral treatment classroom program was effective in reducing children's inattentive, hyperactive, impulsive, and aggressive behaviors; reducing the pervasiveness and severity of their school behavioral difficulties; and improving their self-control and social skills relative to high-risk AHI children who attended their regular neighborhood kindergartens. Such improvements were documented both through the teacher ratings of these behavioral domains as well as by observers coding the children's class behavior during the kindergarten year. Unfortunately, these behavioral and social improvements were limited to the school setting, with almost no evidence of any generalization of treatment effects from these special classes to the home setting. The only exception to this was a trend toward greater improvements in adaptive behavior in the home as reported by parents of the children in the special classes relative to parents whose children attended regular kindergarten. Also disappointing was the failure to demonstrate any greater improvements in academic skills in the children attending the special classes than in children who did not receive these classes, despite providing a more academically accelerated curriculum for children in the special classes. This was not only found in the results of the academic tests but also in the teacher ratings of academic competence as obtained on the social skills rating scale.

Similarly disappointing results using this same test battery are just now being reported by the multisite early intervention program for conduct-disorder children (Coie, Dodge, Bierman, and McMahon). Although it is possible that problems with the sensitivity of the measure may play some role in these discouraging results, as Bierman (personal communication, October 2, 1995) has suggested, the fact remains that most of the tests were able to demonstrate significant improvements with development over the course of kindergarten for all children, regardless of group.

If the treatment effects of the special classroom program on disruptive, aggressive, and antisocial behaviors can be sustained over time, now that the children have returned to their regular neighborhood public schools, it would suggest that this program may reduce later risks for conduct disorder, school disciplinary actions, delinquency, and possibly substance experimentation and abuse. The maintenance of these treatment effects after treatment termination will be examined later this winter when the measures for the one-year posttreatment (end of first grade) are completely scored, verified, and double-entered in our data base, so that they may be analyzed.

Meanwhile, these initial results are encouraging, at least for the special classroom treatment program. These findings also suggest that if the treatment outcomes from the special classroom intervention persist after treatment, they may result in a reduction of later academic risks as well as the risks for oppositional defiant disorder and conduct disorder, and perhaps their associated risks for substance use and abuse.

REFERENCES

1. BARKLEY, R. A., G. J. DUPAUL & M. B. MCMURRAY. 1990. A comprehensive evaluation of attention deficit disorder with and without hyperactivity. J. Consult. Clin. Psychol. **58:** 775–789.
2. BARKLEY, R. A., M. FISCHER, C. S. EDELBROCK & L. SMALLISH. 1991. The adolescent outcome of hyperactive children diagnosed by research criteria. III. Mother-child interactions, parenting stress, and maternal psychopathology. J. Abnorm. Child Psychol. **20:** 180–195.
3. HINSHAW, S. P. 1987. On the distinction between attentional deficits/hyperactivity and conduct problems/aggression in child psychopathology. Psychol. Bull. **101:** 443–447.
4. LONEY, J. & R. MILICH. 1982. Hyperactivity, inattention, and aggression in clinical practice. *In* Advances in Developmental and Behavioral Pediatrics. D. K. Routh & M. Wolraich, Eds. **3:** 113–147. Greenwich, CT. JAI.
5. PELHAM, W. E. & R. MILICH. 1984. Peer relations in children with hyperactivity/attention deficit disorder. J. Learn. Disabil. **17:** 560–567.
6. PELHAM, W. E. & R. MILICH. 1984. Peer relations in children with hyperactivity/attention deficit disorder. J. Learn. Disabil. **17:** 560–567.
7. TAYLOR, E., S. SANDBERG, G. THORLEY & S. GILES. 1991. The Epidemiology of Childhood Hyperactivity. Institute of Psychiatry. London.
8. FISCHER, M., R. A. BARKLEY, C. S. EDELBROCK & L. SMALLISH. 1990. The adolescent outcome of hyperactive children diagnosed by research criteria. II. Academic, attentional, and neuropsychological status. J. Consult. Clin. Psychol. **58:** 580–588.
9. GITTELMAN, R., S. MANNUZZA, R. SHENKER & N. BONAGURA. 1985. Hyperactive boys almost grown up. Arch. Gen. Psychiatry **42:** 937–947.
10. LONEY, J., J. KRAMER & R. MILICH. 1981. The hyperkinetic child grows up: Predictors of symptoms, delinquency, and achievement at follow-up. *In* Psychosocial Aspects of Drug Treatment for Hyperactivity. K. Gadow & J. Loney, Eds. Westview Press. Boulder, CO.
11. SATTERFIELD, J. H., C. M. HOPPE & A. M. SCHELL. 1982. A prospective study of delinquency in 110 adolescent boys with attention deficit disorder and 88 normal adolescent boys. Am. J. Psychiatry **139:** 795–798.
12. WALKER, J. L., B. B. LAHEY, G. HYND & C. FRAME. 1987. Comparison of specific patterns of antisocial behavior in children with conduct disorder with and without coexisting hyperactivity. J. Consult. Clin. Psychol. **55:** 910–913.

13. WEISS, G. & L. T. HECHTMAN. 1993. Hyperactive Children Grown Up (2nd Ed.) Guilford Press. New York.
14. HINSHAW, S. & C. ANDERSON. 1996. Oppositional and conduct disorder. *In* Child Psychopathology. E. J. Mash & R. A. Barkley, Eds.: 113–152. Guilford Press. New York.
15. LOEBER, R. 1990. Development and risk factors of juvenile antisocial behavior and delinquency. Clin. Psychol. Rev. **10:** 1–42.
16. MOFFITT, T. E. 1990. Juvenile delinquency and attention deficit disorder: Boys' developmental trajectories from age 3 to 15. Child Dev. **61:** 893–910.
17. PATTERSON, G. R., T. DISHION & J. REID. 1992. Antisocial boys. Castalia. Eugene, OR.
18. BARKLEY, R. A., A. D. ANASTOPOULOS, D. G. GUEVREMONT & K. F. FLETCHER. 1991. Adolescents with attention deficit hyperactivity disorder: Patterns of behavioral adjustment, academic functioning, and treatment utilization. J. Am. Acad. Child Adolesc. Psychiatry **30:** 752–761.
19. LAHEY, B. B., J. C. PIACENTINI, K. MCBURNETT, P. STONE, S. HARTDAGEN & G. HYND. 1988. Psychopathology in the parents of children with conduct disorder and hyperactivity. J. Am. Acad. Child Adolesc. Psychiatry **27:** 163–170.
20. TALLMADGE, J., C. PATERNITE, & M. GORDON. 1989. Hyperactivity and aggression in parent-child interactions: Test of a two-factor theory. Paper presented at the Society for Research in Child Development. Kansas City, MO.
21. SZATMARI, P., D. R. OFFORD & M. H. BOYLE. 1989. Correlates, associated impairments, and patterns of service utilization of children with attention deficit disorders: Findings from the Ontario Child Healty Study. J. Child Psychol. Psychiatry **30:** 203–217.
22. BARKLEY, R. A. 1989. Attention deficit hyperactivity disorder. *In* Treatment of Childhood Disorders. E. J. Mash & R. A. Barkley, Eds. Guilford. New York.
23. GUEVREMONT, D. G. 1990. Social skills training. *In* Attention Deficit Hyperactivity Disorder: A Handbook for Diagnosis and Treatment. R. A. Barkley, Ed. Guilford Press. New York.
24. HINSHAW, S. P., B. HENKER & C. K. WHALEN. 1984. Cognitive behavioral and pharmacological interventions for hyperactive boys: Comparative and combined effects. J. Consult. Clin. Psychol. **52:** 739–749.
25. KENDALL, P. C. & L. BRASWELL. 1984. Cognitive-behavioral therapy for impulsive children. Guilford. New York.
26. KENDALL, P. C. & L. E. WILCOX. 1980. Cognitive-behavioral treatment for impulsivity: Concrete versus conceptual training in non-self-controlled problem children. J. Consult. Clin. Psychol. **48:** 80–91.
27. PFIFFNER, L. & R. A. BARKLEY. 1990. Educational management. *In* Attention Deficit Hyperactivity Disorder: A Handbook for Diagnosis and Treatment. R. A. Barkley, Ed. Guilford. New York.
28. PISTERMAN, S. J., P. MCGRATH, P. FIRESTONE, J. T. & GOODMAN. 1989. Outcome of parent-mediated treatment of preschoolers with attention deficit disorder. J. Consult. Clin. Psychol. **57:** 628–635.
29. BARKLEY, R. A., M. B. MCMURRAY, C. S. EDELBROCK & K. ROBBINS. 1989. The response of aggressive and nonaggressive ADHD children to two doses of methylphenidate. J. Am. Acad. Child Adolesc. Psychiatry **28:** 873–881.
30. PELHAM, W. E., J. STURGIS, B. HOZA *et al.* 1987. Sustained release and standard methylphenidate effects on cognitive and social behavior in children with attention deficit disorder. Pediatrics **4:** 491–501.
31. GOYETTE, C. H., C. K. CONNERS & R. F. ULRICH. 1978. Normative data on Revised Conners Parent and Teacher Rating Scales. J. Abnorm. Child Psychol. **6:** 221–236.
32. DUPAUL, G. J. 1991. Parent and teacher ratings of ADHD symptoms: Psychometric properties in a community-based sample. J. Clin. Child Psychol. **20:** 245–253.
33. BARKLEY, R. A. 1987. The assessment of attention deficit hyperactivity disorders. Behav. Assess. **5:** 207–233.
34. CUNNINGHAM, C. E., R. BREMMER & M. BOYLE. 1995. Large group community based parenting programs for families of preschoolers at risk for disruptive behavior

disorders: Utilization, cost effectiveness, and outcome. J. Child Psychol. Psychiatry **36:** 1141–1159.
35. BORDUIN, C. M., B. J. MANN, L. T. CONE, S. HENGGELER, B. R. FUCCI, D. M. BLASKE & R. A. WILLIAMS. 1995. Multisystemic treatment of serious juvenile offenders: Long-term prevention of criminality and violence. J. Consult. Clin. Psychol. **63:** 569–578.
36. NYE, C. L., R. L. ZUCKER & H. E. FITZGERALD. 1995. Early intervention in the path to alcohol problems through conduct problems: Treatment involvement and child behavior change. J. Consult. Clin. Psychol. **63:** 831–840.

A Clinical Approach to the Pharmacotherapy of Aggression in Children and Adolescents

DANIEL F. CONNOR[a,c] AND RONALD J. STEINGARD[b]

[a]Pediatric Psychopharmacology
University of Massachusetts Medical Center
Worcester, Massachusetts

[b]Pediatric Psychopharmacology
Children's Hospital
Harvard University
Boston, Massachusetts

Aggression in children and adolescents may be defined as destructive behavior with intent to inflict harm or physical damage to others, self, or property. To be considered inappropriate and excessive, the destructive behavior must not only cause risk to others but also cause impairment in the child's development, interpersonal relationships, and achievements at home, school, or in the community. The aggressive behavior must be overt and can include physical aggression, verbal threats of aggression, explosive outbursts of property destruction in the context of frustration or aversive stimulation, and self-injurious behavior (SIB). This definition excludes aggression in the service of competition, assertiveness, or striving for a desired goal and thus does not include the positive role that aggression may play for children or adolescents in society.[1] Furthermore, this definition does not include more covert antisocial behaviors such as lying or stealing.

This type of behavior is common in children and adolescents referred for psychiatric treatment. When populations of nonreferred 4- to 16-year-old children are compared to groups of children referred for mental health services, rates of aggressive and assaultive behaviors are found to be higher in the referred group compared to the nonreferred group.[2,3] Assaultive threats and attempts are also found to be highly prevalent among children and adolescents admitted to inpatient psychiatric units.[4,5] Aggressive behavior, conduct problems, and antisocial behaviors encompass one third to one half of all child and adolescent psychiatric clinic referrals.[6]

Clinically, excessive aggression is a problem with a heterogeneous etiology and requires a multimodal approach to treatment. Multiple family, behavioral, and community treatment strategies exist.[6] Preclinical research investigating the underlying neurobiologic mechanisms of aggression[7] and clinical studies investigating possible effective pharmacologic interventions in adults[8] have created an increased interest in the pharmacologic treatment of excessive aggression in psychiatrically referred children and adolescents.

Historically, a nonspecific approach has been used in the pharmacologic treat-

[c] Address correspondence to Daniel F. Connor, M.D., Division of Child and Adolescent Psychiatry, Room S7-828, University of Massachusetts Medical Center, 55 Lake Ave. North, Worcester, MA 01655. Tel: (508) 856-4094; fax: (508) 856-6426.

ment of aggression in children. Aggression has been defined as the target symptom for intervention, regardless of underlying etiology or diagnosis. As a result, anecdotal experience has led to the clinical use of many medications. Although this experience was successful for some children, this inherent lack of specificity has led to relatively unfocused clinical interventions wherein outcome expectations and results are unclear, increasing the possibility of adverse side effects.

This generic approach also fails to lead to a clearer understanding of the underlying pathophysiology of aggression in children. Ideally, pharmacotherapy should be based upon a lucid understanding of the underlying neurobiology of behavioral symptoms or psychiatric disorder. This would create the possibility of developing clinical interventions possessing greater specificity and reduced risk of adverse events. Presently, our understanding of the neurobiology of aggression is incomplete and limited in its ability to determine specific pharmacologic interventions.

In an attempt to increase the specificity of treatment, alternative clinical approaches to the pharmacotherapy of aggression have been developed. The most salient of these alternatives involves the use of careful descriptive diagnoses in an attempt to define primary or co-occurring psychiatric or medical/neurologic disorders that may have an etiologic relationship to aggressive behavior. Therefore, the target of intervention is not aggression per se, but the underlying or co-occurring disorder, with the intent of reducing aggression as an associated symptom. Although this approach is not ideal and remains phenomenologically driven, it has somewhat greater specificity than what has historically been practiced and lends itself to the posssibility of more specific clinical treatment.

This paper reviews the literature on psychopharmacologic interventions for excessive aggression in ten psychiatric diagnoses associated with aggressive behavior in children and adolescents. Although the focus is on youth, occasional reference will be made to the adult literature where appropriate. Suggestions are made with the hope of better clarifying which psychiatrically referred child or adolescent with aggression might be helped by psychopharmacologic intervention.

ATTENTION-DEFICIT HYPERACTIVITY DISORDER

Attention-deficit hyperactivity disorder (ADHD)[9] is a chronic, etiologically heterogeneous disorder characterized by excessive inattention, impulsivity, and gross motor overactivity that cause impairment in the child's development both at home and school. ADHD is common, with a prevalence rate varying between 2.0% to 9.5% among children and adolescents.[10] Although aggression is not a specific criteria for diagnosis, there exists a large overlap between attentional deficits/hyperactivity and conduct problems/aggression.[11] Inasmuch as ADHD and conduct disorder (CD) co-occur in 30% to 50% of cases,[12] it is common to find aggression as a chief clinical complaint in children presenting for psychiatric evaluation with underlying ADHD.

Stimulant medications (methylphenidate, dextroamphetamine, and pemoline) are the medications of choice in the treatment of ADHD, with improvement noted in 70% to 75% of children.[13] Recently, a number of controlled studies have reported reductions in aggressive behavior in ADHD children treated with stimulants. Stimulant drug-induced improvements in aggression have been shown from both parent and teacher rating scales as well as direct observation studies in a variety of settings, including outpatient and inpatient psychiatric units and public school classrooms.[14-19]

Nonstimulant medications have also been studied in aggressive ADHD children with comorbid oppositional defiant disorder (ODD) or CD. Clonidine, a centrally acting alpha$_2$-noradrenergic receptor agonist, acts on presynaptic neurons to inhibit release of norepinephrine from the locus caeruleus. Controlled studies have reported efficacy for clonidine in treating children and adolescents diagnosed with ADHD.[20] The best responders to clonidine appear to have early-onset ADHD, overaroused behavior, extreme hyperactivity, uninhibited impulsivity, with concomitant aggression.[21]

Several medications have been reported to improve symptoms of low-frustration tolerance and irritability that can contribute to excessive aggression in children with ADHD and comorbid disorders. Guanfacine, a more selective and less sedating noradrenergic antagonist, was reported helpful in diminishing conduct-disordered behaviors in 13 children diagnosed with ADHD.[22] The addition of fluoxetine to ongoing methylphenidate was successful in alleviating chronic irritability and conduct problems in 32 ADHD children with comorbid depression and disruptive behavioral disorders.[23]

Bupropion, a nontricyclic antidepressant, has been reported to show significant improvement in 30 prepubertal ADHD children with prominent symptoms of conduct disorder and aggression.[24] Tricyclic antidepressants have been shown to be efficacious for ADHD, although their effects on aggression have not specifically been studied.[25]

Controlled studies of neuroleptics have documented efficacy for thioridazine, chlorpromazine, and haloperidol in reducing aggression in children who meet criteria for ADHD. However, studies comparing antipsychotics with stimulants generally find stimulants to be significantly more effective. In addition, neuroleptics possess an adverse risk profile that generally limits their use in a chronic condition, such as ADHD.[26]

In summary, ADHD children presenting for psychiatric evaluation often have excessive aggression. Coexisting aggression does not appear to attenuate an ADHD response to stimulants. Aggression within the context of ADHD may be improved by stimulant medication. Clonidine, guanfacine, and antidepressants may also help aggression in ADHD, although further controlled research is needed. The routine use of neuroleptic medication to treat aggression in ADHD should be discouraged.

CONDUCT DISORDER

Children with CD represent the most common group of patients referred for psychiatric services.[27] CD is characterized by a repetitive and persistent pattern of behavior in which the basic rights of others or major age-appropriate societal norms or rules are violated. Aggression in referred youth is thought to occur most commonly with this condition. Other maladaptive activities include covert behaviors, such as lying and stealing, and norm violations, such as school truancy. Associated symptoms include impulsivity, hyperactivity, learning problems (especially reading), and poor social skills.[9]

Conduct disorder is a prevalent disorder with reported rates of 6–16% in males and 2–9% for females under age 18.[9] There exists substantial comorbidity with ADHD:[28] unipolar depression,[29] bipolar depression,[30,31] learning disorders,[9] and psychotic disorders, especially paranoid thinking.[32] Current research does not support the efficacy of pharmacotherapy alone in the treatment of CD. Comprehensive treatment planning using psychosocial, behavioral, educational, and community interventions is necessary. Pharmacotherapy is adjunctive and appropriate for aggression accompanied by an affective component such as explosiveness and rage.[33] An overall goal of pharmacotherapy is the down-regulation of irritable, explosive, impulsive aggression to allow the conduct-disordered patient to be more responsive to psychosocial therapies. A further goal is treatment of any comorbid disorders. New learning can then take place, and treatment can shift from containment of behavior to rehabilitation.

Clinical research suggests that several psychotropic medications are effective for the management of aggression when it occurs in the context of conduct disorder. Neuroleptics are the most commonly used drugs for the treatment of aggressive children and adolescents. Controlled studies support haloperidol (mean dose 2.95 mg/d),[34] molindone (mean dose 26.8 mg),[35] thioridazine (mean dose 169.9 mg/d), and chlorpromazine (mean dose 150 mg/d)[36] as effective in reducing aggressive behavior in CD. However, the adverse side-effect profile associated with neuroleptics, including sedation (which can interfere with learning), acute dystonic reactions, parkinsonian side effects, and tardive and withdrawal dyskinesias (TD), create a need to investigate alternative medication options.

Three controlled studies have demonstrated that lithium is as efficacious as either chlorpromazine or haloperidol and significantly better than placebo in the treatment of impulsive aggression in CD.[34,36,37] Optimal doses of lithium ranged between 500–2000 mg/d, with serum levels between 0.32–1.79 mEq/L. Lithium was associated with fewer side effects than haloperidol.

Open pilot research has found the anticonvulsant carbamazepine to be effective in hospitalized aggressive children with CD who were free of seizure disorder.[38] Other anticonvulsants, such as diphenylhydantoin, have not shown superiority over placebo in reducing aggression in conduct disorder.[39]

Stimulants, such as d-amphetamine and methylphenidate, have shown mixed results in CD without comorbid ADHD.[33] Although benzodiazepines have shown differential effects on aggression, the possibility of worsening aggression[40] and the risk of drug dependence have limited their use in pediatric psychopharmacology. Trazodone, an antidepressant with a more selective serotonergic action, has been reported effective in improving symptons of impulsivity and aggression in hospitalized children with CD or ODD.[41] Propranolol and clonidine have also been reported effective in case reports and pilot studies for the treatment of severe aggression in CD.[42,43]

Unipolar depression can be an important comorbid diagnosis of conduct disorder[29] and can often precede the onset of CD.[44] An open study of 13 children with depression and CD found 11 had remission of aggression and conduct symptoms following successful antidepressant treatment of depression.[44] ADHD is also highly comorbid with CD. When they occur together, methylphenidate has been found to significantly reduce aggression.[15]

In summary, nonpharmacologic treatment strategies remain most important in CD. Pharmacotherapy of aggression is generally adjunctive to a comprehensive treatment plan. In the evaluation of aggression in CD, it is important to first assess comorbid unipolar depression, bipolar depression (especially in conduct-disordered adolescents), and ADHD. Antidepressants, lithium, and stimulants may be specifically helpful in these subgroups. For nonspecific treatment of aggression in this disorder, controlled studies support the use of neuroleptics and lithium as effective. Carbamazepine, trazodone, clonidine, and beta blockers may be effective, but more controlled research is needed. Aggressiveness associated with explosiveness and impulsivity may be more responsive than premeditated planned aggression. Covert behaviors such as lying, cheating, and stealing may not be helped by medication.

PSYCHOTIC DISORDERS

Although most children and adolescents who suffer from psychotic disorders are not violent, there is much evidence to support a connection between psychosis and violence.[32,45] A study of 51 hospitalized adolescent schizophrenics found 66% to have histories of serious assaultive behavior against others.[46] In a study of children residing in a state correctional school, the more violent children were more likely to demonstrate psychotic symptomatology, including paranoid ideation and rambling associations.[32] Paranoia has been found to be a predictor of dangerousness in adult hospitalized schizophrenics.[47] Paranoid patients believe others are threatening or trying to harm them. Violence is a reaction to these perceived threats. As a systematized delusional system, paranoia can be quite stable over time. Paranoid and persecutory delusions were common in a study of 20 psychotic children.[48] The prevalence of delusions rises precipitously in psychotic adolescents, especially after age 17.[49] Psychotic symptoms can be found in schizophrenia, affective disorders, and in highly traumatized children.

Although few controlled treatment studies of schizophrenic children and adolescents have been completed to date and no controlled studies of psychotropic medication specifically for aggression in this population have been reported, neuroleptics remain the pharmacologic treatment of choice in aggressive psychotic youth. Aggressive behavior in the context of delusions, hallucinations, formal thought disorder, and disorganized behavior remain indications for neuroleptic treatment.[50] Those studies that have been done show that haloperidol (1–6 mg/d), thioridazine (50–300 mg/d), chlorpromazine (100–200 mg/d), loxapine (150–200 mg/d), and thiothixene (0.2 mg/kg/d) are effective in controlling psychotic symptoms and result in improvement on ratings of behavior.[50] However, aggressive symptoms were not specifically addressed in these studies. As noted previously, the risks of extrapyramidal side effects (EPS), TD, sedation, dysphoria, and possible adverse effects on learning[50] support the investigation of alternative medications.

One small controlled study found lithium helpful in decreasing aggression and explosive outbursts in 10 disturbed children, six of whom carried a schizophrenic diagnosis.[51] There are a few open studies of adolescents with childhood onset schizophrenia treated with clozapine, 300–400 mg/d. In addition to improvement in psychotic symptoms, aggressive behavior is reported to respond as well.[52] Although the risk of EPS and TD appear much less with clozaril, serious side effects, such as agranulocytosis and increased incidence of seizures, limit use in the pediatric population and require close clinical monitoring. Open studies report efficacy of low-dose risperidone for aggression in children and adolescents. Risk of EPS and other side effects appear minimal.[53] Although controlled research is necessary, risperidone may represent a safer alternative than traditional neuroleptics for the acute treatment of excessive aggression.

In summary, neuroleptics remain the pharmacologic treatment of choice in the aggressive psychotic child and adolescent. However, controlled research has not yet established their efficacy; many children may not respond; and concern about long-term toxicity, such as tardive dyskinesia, limit their use in the pediatric age range. Careful monitoring of side effects over time and the use of a standardized assessment for detecting tardive dyskinesia are mandatory. Further research is needed to develop or assess medications with less potential toxicity that may be effective for aggression in this population.

TRAUMATIC BRAIN INJURY

Traumatic brain injury (TBI) is a prevalent health problem in children and adolescents. Five million children sustain head injuries each year in the United States and 2000–5000 remain severely handicapped.[54] The peak age for TBI is 18–24 years.[55] Neuropsychiatric disturbance is associated with both the acute and chronic phase of TBI.

The most important predictor of neuropsychiatric sequelae is severity of injury, defined as a posttraumatic amnesia period that exceeds 7 days.[56] The neuropsychiatric consequences of TBI are determined by multiple factors, including the extent and type of injury. Frontal lobe dysfunction is characterized by irritability, aggressive outbursts, impaired judgement, disinhibition, and affective lability.[57] Damage to temporal lobes can result in impulsivity, hostility, and inappropriate behavior.[58] Depression, ADHD, and psychotic symptoms have been described after TBI.[59] Behavior subsequent to TBI is also influenced by preinjury behavior. Those children with persistent behavior problems after TBI were found to have pretrauma behavior disturbances and families with marital conflicts, psychiatric disturbance, and social disadvantage.[56]

Aggressiveness, explosive outbursts, and irritability are highly associated with TBI and a major source of stress to families. Aggression is often triggered by trivial stimuli, does not usually involve premeditation, serves no clear goal, is explosive in quality, and intermittent in frequency.[57]

The pharmacotherapy of aggression and impulse dyscontrol in TBI children is currently not well developed. Studies are largely uncontrolled, and recommendations are empiric. Neuroleptics are probably the most commonly used agents to manage aggression in this population.[60] However, with the exception of aggression associated with psychotic symptoms, their antiaggressive properties are not specific, and clinical response is probably related to overall sedation. The use of neuroleptics in TBI is associated with many risks. There is evidence from preclinical studies of motor neuron injury in animals that haloperidol has a detrimental effect on neuronal recovery and may be contraindicated during acute recovery from brain injury.[61] Chronic use of neuroleptics place children at risk for tardive dyskinesia[62] and can lower the seizure threshold in patients suffering from epilepsy.[63] If neuroleptics are used in this population, high potency agents, such as haloperidol, seem to be best tolerated by children.[64] They should be used in the smallest effective doses and for the shortest length of time necessary.[60]

Controlled studies have demonstrated the efficacy and safety of beta-adrenergic blocking agents, such as propranolol, in the empirical treatment of aggression in adults with a variety of organic mental disorders, including TBI.[65] No controlled studies have yet been conducted in children. A recent review summarized the literature on beta blockers for aggression in 66 children and adolescents described in 11 case reports and case series.[43] Most, but not all, of these children exhibited aggressive behavior in the context of an existing organic mental disorder, including TBI. Overall, 75–82% were reported improved regarding aggression and behavioral dyscontrol. Doses ranged between 50–960 mg/day, with most children receiving 80 to 320 mg/day. Time to improvement was up to 12 weeks.[43]

Other case reports have described successful outcomes for trazodone,[66] buspirone,[59] and stimulants[67] in the treatment of excessive aggression in TBI. Although further research is needed, these agents may offer an alternative to neuroleptics.

SEIZURE DISORDER

The relationship between aggressive behavior and epilepsy remains controversial. The frontal cortex, amygdala, hippocampus, and hypothalamus are all involved in the regulation of aggression in humans. Seizure activity involving these structures could result in violent behavior.[68] The Isle of Wight study, an epidemiologic study of the rates of childhood psychiatric disorder from a single geographical area, found a 29% prevalence of psychiatric disorder in children with idiopathic epilepsy. This was a much higher rate of behavior disorder than control groups of children with physical disorders not involving the brain (12%) and children free of physical disease (7%) but less than children with structural brain disease, such as cerebral palsy (44%).[69] Among children with uncomplicated epilepsy, temporal lobe epilepsy carried the greatest risk for psychiatric disorder. However, these psychiatric disorders were generally nonspecific, not related to specific seizure type, and not necessarily manifested by aggressive behavior.[69]

A positive association between epilepsy and aggression in children has been supported by several studies. Nuffield found children with temporal lobe epilepsy to have aggression rating scores four times higher than children with petit mal epilepsy.[70] In a longitudinal study of 100 children with temporal lobe epilepsy, Ounsted found 36 to have outbursts of catastrophic rage.[71] Aggression occurring during a seizure (ictal aggression) has been found to occur rarely. Lewis *et al.* found psychomotor epilepsy in 18 of 97 incarcerated adolescent boys. Five of these patients with definite psychomotor seizures had ictal aggression. The number of psychomotor symptoms in this sample correlated with the degree of violence.[72]

However, the association between aggression and seizure disorder diminishes when co-occurring psychosocial and neurologic risk factors are controlled.[73] In the study by Ounsted[71] most of the children with aggressive outbursts suffered their first seizure early in life, exhibited hyperkinetic behavior, and had cognitive delays. Children with temporal lobe epilepsy alone, without other evidence of neurologic dysfunction, did not exhibit rage attacks. In the study by Lewis *et al.*, psychomotor epileptic signs also correlated independently with the presence of psychotic symptoms, including hallucinations, thought disorder, and paranoid ideation. These symptoms may have impaired impulse control and contributed to aggression.

Aggression is complex, with multiple determinants, and is typically not caused by a single factor, such as a seizure disorder. A relationship between aggressive behavior and epilepsy probably does exist, but the nature of the association is not clear. The relationship is most likely due to nonspecific risk factors that are common to patients with both aggressive behavior and epilepsy. Brain damage may be the most significant of these factors, perhaps leading to a reduction in inhibition or an increase in irritability.[68]

The pharmacologic treatment of ictal aggression remains seizure control with anticonvulsant medication. The existence of interictal aggressive behavior has been described in adults with temporal lobe epilepsy.[74] The existence of sudden, explosive rage to minor provocation in patients with subtle neurologic and EEG abnormalities, the episodic dyscontrol syndrome, has also been described.[75] However, the validity of interictal aggression and episodic dyscontrol remains controversial. Treatment is also unclear. The antiaggressive effects of anticonvulsants have been most studied in this population, although research in children generally remains uncontrolled.

Recent reviews of the literature have supported the empiric use of carbamazepine for symptoms of aggression, hyperactivity, and diminished concentration, independent of diagnosis, presence of brain disorder, or EEG abnormalities.[76,77] However, caution is advised, because case reports have described paradoxical increases in aggression, worsening of seizure control, and development of manic and psychotic symptoms in some children treated with anticonvulsants for aggression.[78,79] When carbamazepine is used, the rare risk of blood dyscrasias requires monitoring. Tricyclic antidepressants, neuroleptics, and lithium should be used very cautiously in children with epilepsy, as they may lower seizure threshold.[80]

MENTAL RETARDATION

Mental retardation is defined by significantly subaverage intelligence (IQ < 70) and significant impairments in adaptive functioning, with an onset before age 18.[9] Compared to persons of normal intelligence, disruptive behaviors, characterized by aggression, property destruction, impulsivity, hyperactivity, and SIB, are more common in mentally retarded (MR) individuals.[81] The MR represent an overmedicated and psychiatrically underdiagnosed group. In a survey identifying 55,438 MR individuals younger than age 22 living in public residential facilities, 31% were receiving psychotropic medication. Neuroleptics were given to 20% and stimulants to 0.7 percent.[82] Although the MR population has a 4- to 6-fold increased frequency of all psychiatric disorders, relative to the general population,[83] most are treated in a nonspecific fashion for aggression and gross behavior disturbance. Careful evaluation of any underlying psychiatric illness that may be contributing to aggression and may respond to standard psychiatric treatment is essential. Should no specific treatable etiology for aggression be found, empiric treatment may be pursued. Initial interventions should emphasize behavioral therapy. If these fail and aggression continues to significantly impair daily functioning, an adjunctive pharmacologic trial may be warranted.

Neuroleptics are most often used to treat aggressive behavior in the MR population.[84] Controlled studies of chlorpromazine, thioridazine, haloperidol, and pimozide have reported modest improvements in target symptoms, including reductions in stereotypies, hyperactivity, conduct problems, irritability, and SIB, all of which may lower frustration tolerance and contribute to aggression.[84] However, low potency, strongly anticholinergic neuroleptics (chlorpromazine, thioridazine) may cause sedation, impair memory and cognition, and interfere with learning in this vulnerable population. The prevalence of tardive dyskinesia in MR children and adolescents receiving neuroleptics has been found to be as high as 34 percent.[85] As a result, neuroleptics are increasingly considered a treatment of last resort. Other agents are being explored for excessive aggression in this population.

Methylphenidate (MPH) has been found effective in a controlled study for improving hyperactivity, motor excess, irritability, and conduct problems in children with mild mental retardation.[86] Beause of an increased risk of idiosyncratic drug response, caution is advised with stimulant use in the more severely MR child. Fenfluramine, a serotonin-depleting agent, has been found effective in reducing symptoms of inattention, irritability, and aggression in more severely MR children.[86] However, chronic use of fenfluramine has been found to reduce CNS catecholamines; use can also worsen preexisting psychiatric illness.

Open studies have examined beta-blocking agents for aggression in the MR population. A recent review of 62 patients with mental retardation found 81% improved in aggression when receiving either propranolol or nadolol. Rage outbursts, verbal and physical assault, and agitation were improved, and patients showed increased frustration tolerance. Children and adolescents with mental retardation appeared to respond to propranolol in doses of less than 150 mg/day.[87]

Other open studies and case reports have suggested that lithium[88] and carbamazepine[89] may be helpful as antiaggression agents in mentally retarded youth. Agents that affect the serotonergic nervous system, such as buspirone[90] and fluoxetine,[91] may also be effective for aggression and SIB.

In summary, an accurate assessment and diagnosis is the first step in managing the aggressive MR child or adolescent. If a treatable underlying etiology causing aggression is not found, empiric treatment may be indicated. Although the antiaggressive properties of neuroleptics are presently supported by the most methodologically controlled research in the MR population, their adverse risk profile and negative effects on cognition make one hesitant to recommend them initially. Stimulants may be helpful for a subgroup of mild MR aggressive children with prominent symptoms of ADHD. Although further research is needed, beta blockers, especially for the organically brain-damaged MR child; buspirone; selective serotonin reuptake-inhibiting antidepressants, such as fluoxetine; and lithium deserve consideration. Medication should always be adjunctive to a comprehensive treatment plan. Pharmacology should be accompanied by careful monitoring of side effects in this vulnerable population and be time limited with periodic reassessment of risk versus benefit and need for ongoing medication treatment.

PERVASIVE DEVELOPMENTAL DISORDERS

The pervasive developmental disorders (PDD) are a heterogeneous group of conditions characterized by severe and pervasive impairment in reciprocal social interaction, verbal and nonverbal communication, or the presence of rigid stereotyped behavior and activities relative to the child's developmental level or mental age.[9] Associated features often include mental retardation, seizures, and disruptive behaviors, including excessive aggression, impulsivity, temper outbursts, and SIB. Autism, the prototypic pervasive developmental disorder, has a prevalence of 2–5 cases per 10,000 individuals in epidemiologic studies.[9]

No rational pharmacologic treatment exists that can undo the core features of social and communication deviance or associated cognitive dysfunction in PDD. A major goal of psychopharmacologic research is to find effective medication that can decrease maladaptive target behaviors without side effects or excessive sedation that can interfere with learning. Current treatment for excessive aggression in PDD emphasizes behavioral modification.[92] Psychopharmacology remains adjunctive to a multidisciplinary psychoeducational treatment plan when aggression, impulsivity, hyperactivity, or SIB remain treatment resistant and significantly interfere with rehabilitation.

Neuroleptics are probably the most common medications used for the symptom of aggression in PDD. Trifluoperazine, fluphenazine, thiothixene, and molindone have been investigated.[93] Haloperidol is probably the most well studied.[94] Controlled studies have shown target symptoms of excessive aggression, temper tantrums, hyperactivity, and angry affect to be reduced on haloperidol, 0.5 to 3.0 mg/day.[95] Although positive effects on discrimination learning in a laboratory have not been shown, low dose haloperidol has not been reported to adversely affect learning.[94] Minimal side effects have been reported at these doses.[95]

However, studies reporting minimal side effects to low dose neuroleptics have not commented specifically on tardive and withdrawal dyskinesia in this population. In a prospective study of movement disorders in 82 autistic children treated with haloperidol, 0.25 to 10.5 mg/day, and studied from 1 to 78 months, 24 developed withdrawal (N = 19) or tardive dyskinesia (N = 5).[96] Duration of dyskinetic movements was 7 to 225 days. Fortunately no irreversible dyskinesias were observed after medication was stopped. This toxicity of neuroleptics has prompted a search for alternative medications in the PDD population.

Agents that affect serotonergic functioning may be beneficial for certain target behaviors in PDD children. In a controlled investigation of clomipramine, a selective serotonin reuptake inhibitor, significant improvement in anger attacks and ritualized behavior in 12 autistic children was shown compared to placebo and desipramine (a predominantly noradrenergic reuptake inhibitor).[97] Open studies have reported improvement in aggression, SIB, and impulsivity with fluoxetine[98] and buspirone.[99]

In empiric trials, medications that down-regulate noradrenergic functioning have also been reported beneficial for irritability and aggression in these children. Clonidine has been shown to diminish irritability and hyperactivity in a small group of autistic children.[100] Open case studies have reported propranolol[101] and nadolol[102] helpful for impulsive aggressive behaviors in this population.

It has been suggested that abnormalities of the endogenous opiate system underlie some of the maladaptive behaviors associated with autism.[103] Naltrexone is an opiate antagonist. In a controlled study of 41 disruptive autistic children, naltrexone, 1 mg/kg/day, significantly improved only hyperactivity. There was a trend for SIB to improve. No affects on aggression were found.[104]

Stimulants have been considered contraindicated in autism because of reports of increased irritability and stereotyped movements. However, several open studies have reported the safety and utility of stimulants in autistic children with comorbid hyperactivity, impulsivity, and aggression.[105,106]

In summary, low dose haloperidol remains the best-studied drug for aggression in PDD children. Alternative medications include clomipramine or other selective serotonin reuptake inhibitors, especially if ritualistic behavior accompanies anger attacks. The cautious use of stimulants for a subgroup of hyperactive, aggressive PDD children may be indicated, although further research is needed. Buspirone, clonidine, beta blockers, and naltrexone also deserve further research as alternatives to neuroleptic medication.

DEPRESSION

Depression is increasingly recognized as occurring in children and adolescents.[107] There is consensus that the phenomenology of depression is similar in children and adolescents as well as in adults.[108] Rates of depression among psychiatrically referred children and adolescents vary between 7%–30% and become more frequent with advancing age.[109] Irritability and aggression can be a common symptom of depression, especially in males.[110] In depressed adults, discrete anger attacks have been described.[111] Depressed patients with anger attacks may have a greater serotonin dysregulation than depressed patients without such attacks.[112] In children, high rates of comorbidity with conduct disorder and ADHD have been found[113] and contribute to the possibility of excessive aggression. The clinician should carefully assess psychiatrically referred aggressive youth for the presence of depressive disorder.

To date, controlled trials of tricyclic antidepressants (TCA), such as imipramine, desipramine, amitriptyline, and nortriptyline, have not supported their efficacy over placebo in pediatric depression.[114] Aggression has not been specifically addressed in these studies. Newer-generation antidepressants, such as the selective serotonin-reuptake inhibitors (SSRIs) fluoxetine, sertraline, and paroxetine; the atypical antidepressant, bupropion; and the monoamine oxidase inhibitors are only beginning to be studied in childhood depression.[107] Given the complex relationships between aggression and depression, a comprehensive multidisciplinary treatment plan emphasizing psychosocial therapies is first recommended. However, with a number of open antidepressant trials reporting positive results in pediatric depressive disorders, TCA and SSRIs (which have a safer side-effect profile) should be empirically considered if initial therapeutic interventions fail.[114,107]

BIPOLAR DISORDER

There is evidence that the phenomenology of bipolar depressive illness (BDI) is similar in childhood, adolescence, and adulthood.[115] Current diagnostic criteria are similar for children and adults.[9] The diagnosis of adolescent-onset BDI is well established, with 25% of adult bipolar patients reporting onset between ages 15 and 19 years.[116] The lifetime prevalence of bipolar depressive spectrum disorders in 14- to 18-year-old adolescents has been reported to approximate 1% in epidemiologically studied community populations.[117] Although BDI has been described in children younger than age 12,[118] diagnosis in the prepubertal years remains controversial.[119] Childhood onset may describe a more chronic, nonepisodic, and severe form of the disorder.[115] Psychotic symptoms, aggression, irritability, and hostility may be more pronounced in early-onset BDI as compared to adult onset.[120,121] In adolescence, differentiation of BDI from schizophrenia and conduct disorder is important. In prepuberty, manic agitation can be mistaken for ADHD. The distinction is important, as stimulants (the common treatment for ADHD) have been reported to induce mania in children.[122]

The effectiveness of lithium carbonate in the treatment of adolescent BDI and aggression has been reported in several open studies.[123] Lithium treatment of prepubertal children suspected of BDI is less certain. A study reported positive benefits of lithium in ten hospitalized 6- to 12-year-old children diagnosed with BDI who were highly aggressive. All ten improved.[120] Long-term lithium treatment of a heterogeneous group of children with a mix of disorders, including BDI and aggression, found the usefulness of lithium was related to diagnosis. Children with BDI, behavior disorders, and affective-aggressive symptoms, who also had lithium-responsive parents, seemed to respond best over a decade of lithium treatment.[124] Recently, these indications have been expanded to also include aggression with repeated episodes of mood disorder and a biologic family history of lithium-responsive affective disorders; severe depression with hypomanic symptoms; and depression with acute onset, psychomotor retardation, and psychotic features.[125]

In summary, lithium has not yet been systematically studied in the pediatric age range. However, a trial of lithium in conjunction with other treatment modalities seems reasonable in children and adolescents who present with excessive aggression in the context of bipolar features; a family history of bipolar disorder; a history of lithium-responsive parents; or a mix of affective, psychotic, and aggressive symptoms. There is one small (N = 11) uncontrolled study reporting efficacy of valproate in adolescent mania in which aggression also improved.[126] Carbamazepine and valproate have also not been systematically studied in childhood BDI.

POSTTRAUMATIC STRESS DISORDER

The core symptoms of posttraumatic stress disorder (PTSD) include the experience of an extreme traumatic stressor in which death or serious injury to self or another occurs; and a feeling of intense fear and helplessness to escape, accompanied by persistent reexperiencing of the traumatic event, avoidance of stimuli associated with the event, and sympathetic nervous system (SNS) hyperarousal.[9] With some symptomatic differences, the core features of PTSD are similar in children, adolescents, and adults.[9] Precipitants can include events such as kidnapping,[127] natural disaster,[128] or sexual abuse.[129]

A hallmark of PTSD is SNS hyperarousal that is associated with symptoms of anxiety, exaggerated startle reaction, hyperactivity, flashbacks, and sleep disturbance.[130] This can also be associated with risk for impulsivity, hostility, irritability, and vulnerability to excessive aggression in traumatized children.[131]

The pharmacotherapy of childhood PTSD is not well studied. Interest has centered on medications that can reduce SNS hyperarousal. Propranolol, a beta-adrenergic antagonist, has been found in a five-week open trial to reduce aggression in 11 children with acute PTSD.[132]

In the absence of controlled studies, the pharmacotherapy of PTSD should be adjunctive to a comprehensive treatment plan that emphasizes environmental safety. Although further research is needed, medications that down-regulate adrenergic overarousal may prove helpful when symptoms of excessive aggression, hyperactivity, and impulsivity complicate the clinical presentation of PTSD.

SUMMARY

Overt aggression in its various forms is the most prevalent symptom presenting to pediatric mental health providers, regardless of setting. It is a behavior with a heterogeneous etiology and requires a comprehensive approach to evaluation and treatment. Evaluation of the aggressive child must assess medical, neurologic, psychiatric, psychosocial, familial, and/or educational contributions to behavioral dyscontrol. Multimodal treatment is generally required.

At present, there is no single medication to recommend for the treatment of aggressive behavior. Multiple medications have clinically been used in a nonspecific fashion to target excessive childhood aggression. Although successful for some, this approach increases risk for ineffective interventions accompanied by side effects.

Until a scientific understanding of the developmental neurobiology of aggression leads to more specific treatment, this review suggests the use of a diagnostic-based approach to the pharmacology of aggression (FIG. 1). Descriptive diagnostic techniques should be used to define the presence of any primary or comorbid psychiatric disorder that presents with aggression as an associated symptom. Treating aggression in the context of these psychiatric syndromes appears to be the most direct approach. Aggression occurring in the context of a medication-responsive psychiatric diagnosis appears most sensitive to pharmacologic intervention. Presently, evidence for efficacy is strongest for aggression in the context of ADHD, psychotic disorder, adolescent-onset bipolar disorder, and ictal aggression (FIG. 1).

TABLE 1. Efficacy of Clinical Pharmacologic Trials for Pediatric Aggression

Aggression in (condition)	Efficacy in at Least One Controlled Trial	Efficacy in Open Trials
ADHD	stimulants clonidine bupropion neuroleptics	fluoxetine guanfacine
Conduct disorder	neuroleptics lithium	clonidine trazodone carbamazepine propranolol
Psychotic disorders	lithium	neuroleptics
TBI		neuroleptics propranolol trazodone buspirone stimulants
Seizure disorder		carbamazepine
MR	neuroleptics stimulants fenfluramine	propranolol nadolol lithium carbamazepine buspirone fluoxetine
PDD	neuroleptics clomipramine clonidine	fluoxetine buspirone propranolol nadolol stimulants naltrexone
Unipolar depression		SSRI TCA
Bipolar depression		lithium valproic acid (adolescents)
PTSD		propranolol

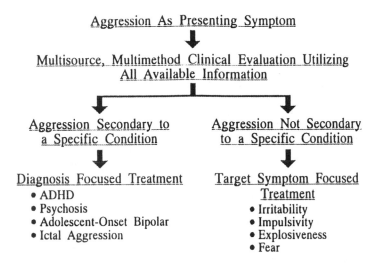

FIGURE 1. A clinical approach to the pharmacology of aggression.

It remains less clear that medication can help aggression when it occurs independently of a pharmacologically treatable comorbid psychiatric disorder. Aggression may respond to a target symptom approach where discrete behavioral symptoms that contribute to aggression, such as irritability, explosiveness, fear, or impulsivity, may be modified by medication intervention (FIG. 1). When treatment is approached in this fashion, it is standard practice to use the least toxic and safest intervention first. Behavioral treatment based on contingency management principles could be initially recommended. Medication trials should first use medications that have demonstrated empiric efficacy in reducing aggression (TABLE 1) and that have a favorable safety profile.

Neuroleptics to treat aggression in nonpsychotic psychiatrically referred youth should be kept to a minimum, secondary to their significant adverse risk profile. Alternative medications, such as selective serotonin reuptake-inhibiting antidepressants, buspirone, lithium, anticonvulsants, opiate blocking agents, propranolol, nadolol, and clonidine, deserve more clinical research in pediatric aggression. These medications may offer effective and less toxic alternatives in the pharmacologic treatment of inappropriate excessive childhood aggression.

REFERENCES

1. VOLAVKA, J. 1995. Neurobiology of Violence. American Psychiatric Press, Inc. Washington, DC.
2. ACHENBACH, T. M. & C. S. EDELBROCK. 1981. Monogr. Soc. Res. Child Dev. **46** (Serial No. 188).
3. PFEFFER, C. R., R. PLUTCHIK, M. S. MIZRUCHI & R. LIPKINS. 1987. J. Am. Acad. Child Adolesc. Psychiatry **26:** 256–261.
4. GARRISON, W. T., B. ECKER, M. FRIEDMAN, R. DAVIDOFF, K. HAEBERLE & M. WAGNER. 1990. J. Am. Acad. Child Adolesc. Psychiatry **29:** 242–250.
5. PFEFFER, C. R., G. SOLOMON, R. PLUTCHIK, M. S. MIZRUCHI & A. WEINER. 1985. J. Am. Acad. Child Adolesc. Psychiatry **24:** 775–780.

6. KAZDIN, A. E. 1987. Psychol. Bull. **102:** 187–203.
7. MICZEK, K. A. 1987. The psychopharmacology of aggression. *In* Handbook of Psychopharmacology. L. L. Iverson, S. Iverson & S. H. Snyder, Eds. Vol. **19:** 183–328. Plenum Press. New York.
8. EICHELMAN, B. 1988. Hosp. Community Psychiatry **39:** 31–39.
9. American Psychiatric Association, Committee on Nomenclature and Statistics. 1994. Diagnostic and Statistical Manual of Mental Disorders, 4th edit. American Psychiatric Association. Washington, DC.
10. BAUERMIESTER, J. J., G. CANINO & H. BIRD. 1994. Child Adolesc. Psychiatr. Clin. N. Am. **3:** 177–194.
11. HINSHAW, S. P. 1987. Psychopharmacol. Bull. **101:** 443–463.
12. BIEDERMAN, J., S. V. FARAONE & K. LAPEY. 1992. Child Adolesc. Psychiatr. Clin. N. Am. **1:** 335–360.
13. BARKLEY, R. A. 1977. J. Child Psychol. Psychiatry **18:** 137–165.
14. GADOW, K. D. 1992. J. Child Psychol. Psychiatry **33:** 153–195.
15. KAPLAN, S. L., J. BUSNER, S. KUPIETZ, E. WASSERMANN & B. SEGAL. 1990. J. Am. Acad. Child Adolesc. Psychiatry **29:** 719–723.
16. BARKLEY, R. A., M. B. McMURRAY, C. S. EDELBROCK & K. ROBBINS. 1989. J. Am. Acad. Child Adolesc. Psychiatry **28:** 873–881.
17. GADOW, K. D., E. E. NOLAN, J. SVERD, J. SPRAFKIN & L. PAOLICELLI. 1990. J. Am. Acad. Child Adolesc. Psychiatry **29:** 710–718.
18. GADOW, K. D., L. M. PAOLICELLI, E. E. NOLAN, J. SCHWARTZ, J. SPRAFKIN & J. SVERD. 1992. J. Child Adolesc. Psychopharmacol. **2:** 49–61.
19. HINSHAW, S. P. 1991. J. Clin. Child Psychol. **20:** 301–312.
20. HUNT, R. D., R. B. MINDERAA & D. J. COHEN. 1985. J. Am. Acad. Child Adolesc. Psychiatry **24:** 617–629.
21. HUNT, R. D., L. CAPPER & P. O'CONNELL. 1990. J. Child Adolesc. Psychopharmacol. **1:** 87–102.
22. HUNT, R. D., A. F. T. ARNSTEN & M. D. ASBELL. 1995. J. Am. Acad. Child Adolesc. Psychiatry **34:** 50–54.
23. GAMMON, G. D. & T. E. BROWN. 1993. J. Child Adolesc. Psychopharmacol. **3:** 1–10.
24. CLAY, T. H., C. T. GUALTIERI, R. W. EVANS & C. M. GULLION. 1988. Psychopharmacol. Bull. **24:** 143–148.
25. BIEDERMAN, J., R. J. BALDESSARINI, V. WRIGHT, D. KNEE & J. S. HARMATZ. 1989. J. Am. Acad. Child Adolesc. Psychiatry **28:** 777–784.
26. GREEN, W. H. 1992. Child Adolesc. Psychiatr. Clin. N. Am. **1:** 458–460.
27. KAZDIN, A. E. 1987. Conduct Disorder in Childhood and Adolescence. Sage Publications. London.
28. NEWCORN, J. H. & J. M. HALPERIN. 1994. Child Adolesc. Psychiatr. Clin. N. Am. **3:** 227–252.
29. CARLSON, G. & D. CANTWELL. 1980. Am. J. Psychiatry **137:** 445–449.
30. KOVACS, M. & M. POLLOCK. 1995. Am. J. Child Adolesc. Psychiatry **34:** 715–723.
31. ARRENDONDO, A. E. & S. F. BUTLER. 1994. J. Child Adolesc. Psychopharmacol. **4:** 151–158.
32. PINCUS, J. H. & D. O. LEWIS. 1991. Semin. Neurol. **11:** 146–154.
33. CAMPBELL, M., N. M. GONZALEZ & R. R. SILVA. 1992. Psychol. Clin. N. Am. **15:** 69–85.
34. CAMPBELL, M., A. M. SMALL, W. H. GREEN, S. J. JENNINGS, R. PERRY, W. G. BENNETT & L. ANDERSON. 1984. Arch. Gen. Psychiatry **41:** 650–656.
35. GREENHILL, L. L., M. SOLOMON, R. PLEAK & P. AMBROSINI. 1985. J. Clin. Psychiatry **46:** 20–25.
36. CAMPBELL, M., I. L. COHEN & A. M. SMALL. 1982. J. Am. Acad. Child Adolesc. Psychiatry **21:** 107–117.
37. CAMPBELL, M., P. B. ADAMS, A. M. SMALL, V. KAFANTARIS, R. R. SILVA, J. SHELL, R. PERRY & J. E. OVERALL. 1995. J. Am. Acad. Child Adolesc. Psychiatry **34:** 445–453.
38. KAFANTARIS, V., M. CAMPBELL, M. V. PADRON-GAYOL, A. M. SMALL, J. J. LOCASIO & C. R. ROSENBERG. 1992. Psychopharmacol. Bull. **28:** 193–199.

39. CONNERS, C. K., R. KRAMER, G. H. ROTHSCHILD, L. SCHWARTZ & A. STONE. 1971. Arch. Gen. Psychiatry 24: 156–160.
40. PETTI, T. A., B. FISH, T. SHAPIRO, I. L. COHEN & M. CAMPBELL. 1982. J. Clin. Psychopharmacol. 2: 270–273.
41. ZUBIETA, J. K & N. E. ALESSI. 1992. J. Clin. Psychopharmacol. 12: 346–351.
42. KEMPH, J. P., C. L. DEVANE, G. M. LEVIN, R. JARECKE & R. L. MILLER. 1993. J. Am. Acad. Child Adolesc. Psychiatry 32: 577–581.
43. CONNOR, D. F. 1993. J. Child Adolesc. Psychopharmacol. 3: 99–114.
44. PUIG-ANTICH, J. 1982. J. Am. Acad. Child Adolesc. Psychiatry 21: 118–128.
45. WESSELY, S. 1993. Violence and psychosis. In Violence: Basic and Clinical Science. C. Thompson & P. Cowen, Eds.: 119–134. Butterworth-Heineman. Oxford.
46. INAMDAR, S. C., D. O. LEWIS, G. SIOMOPOULOS, S. S. SHANAK & M. LAMELA. 1982. Am. J. Psychiatry 139: 932–935.
47. YESAVAGE, J. A. 1984. J. Psychiatr. Res. 18: 225–231.
48. GARRALDA, M. E. 1984. Psychol. Med. 14: 589–596.
49. BETTES, B. A. & E. WALKER. 1987. J. Child Psychol. Psychiatry 28: 555–568.
50. WHITAKER, A. & U. RAO. 1992. Psychiatr. Clin. N. Am. 15: 243–276.
51. CAMPBELL, M., B. FISH, J. KOREIN, T. SHAPIRO, P. COLLINS & C. KOH. 1972. J. Austism Child. Schizophr. 2: 234–263.
52. FRAZIER, J. A., C. GORDON, K. MCKENNA, M. C. LENCINE, D. JIH & J. L. RAPOPORT. 1994. J. Am. Acad. Child Adolesc. Psychiatry 33: 658–663.
53. SIMEON, J. G., N. J. CARREY, D. M. WIGGINS, R. P. MILIN & S. N. HOSENBOCUS. 1995. J. Child Adolesc. Psychopharmacol. 5: 69–79.
54. RAPHAELY, R. C., D. B. SWEDLOW, J. J. DOWNES & D. A. BRUCE. 1980. Pediatr. Clin. N. Am. 27: 715–727.
55. GUALTIERI, T. C. 1990. J. Child Adolesc. Psychopharmacol. 1: 149–152.
56. BROWN, G., O. CHADWICK, D. SHAFFER, M. RUTTER & M. TRAUB. 1981. Psychol. Med. 11: 63–78.
57. SILVER, J. M. & S. C. YUDOFSKY. 1994. Aggressive disorders. In Neuropsychiatry of Traumatic Brain Injury. J. M. Silver, S. C. Yudofsky & R. E. Hales, Eds.: 313–353. American Psychiatric Press. Washington, DC.
58. BLUMMER, D. & D. F. BENSON. 1975. Personality changes with frontal and temporal lobe lesions. In Psychiatric Aspects of Neurologic Disease. D. F. Benson & D. Blume, Eds.: 151–170. Grune & Stratton. New York.
59. MANDOKI, M. 1994. J. Child Adolesc. Psychopharmacol. 4: 129–139.
60. STEWART, J. T., W. C. MYERS, R. C. BURKETT & W. B. LYLES. 1990. J. Am. Acad. Child Adolesc. Psychiatry 29: 269–277.
61. FEENY, D. M., A. GONZALEZ & W. A. LAW. 1982. Science 217: 855–857.
62. CAMPBELL, M., D. M. GREGA, W. H. GREEN & W. G. BENNETT. 1983. Clin. Neuro-pharmacol. 6: 207–222.
63. JAMES, D. H. 1986. J. Ment. Defic. Res. 30: 185–189.
64. CAMPBELL, M. 1985. Psychiatr. Ann. 15: 105–107.
65. BROOKE, N. M., D. R. PATTERSON, K. A. QUESTAD, D. CARDENAS & L. FARREL-ROBERTS. 1992. Arch. Phys. Med. Rehabil. 73: 917–921.
66. PARMELEE, D. X. 1989. Psychiatr. Med. 7: 11–16.
67. GUALTIERI, C. T. & R. W. EVANS. 1988. Brain Inj. 2: 273–290.
68. FENWICK, P. 1993. Aggression and epilepsy. In Violence: Basic and Clinical Science. C. Thompson & P. Cohen, Eds.: 76–98. Butterworth-Heinemann. Oxford.
69. RUTTER, M., P. GRAHAM & W. YULE. 1970. Clinics in Developmental Medicine (35/36). SIMP/Heinemann. London.
70. NUFFIELD, E. 1961. J. Ment. Sci. 107: 438–461.
71. OUNSTED, C. 1969. J. Psychosom. Res. 13: 237–242.
72. LEWIS, D. O., J. H. PINCUS, S. S. SHANOK & G. H. GLASER. 1982. Am. J. Psychiatry 139: 882–887.
73. HERZBERG, J. L. & P. B. C. FENWICK. 1980. Br. J. Psychiatry 153: 50–55.
74. DEVINSKY, O. & D. BEAR. 1984. Am. J. Psychiatry 141: 651–656.
75. ELLIOT, F. A. 1990. Semin. Neurol. 10: 303–312.

76. ELPHICK, M. 1989. Psychol. Med. **19:** 591–604.
77. EVANS, R. W., T. H. CLAY & C. T. GUALTIERI. 1987. J. Am. Acad. Child Adolesc. Psychiatry **26:** 2–8.
78. PLEAK, R. R., B. BIRMAHER, A. GAURILESCU, C. ABLCHANDANI & D. T. WILLIAMS. 1988. J. Am. Acad. Child Adolesc. Psychiatry **27:** 500–503.
79. BHATARA, V. S. & J. CARRERA. 1994. J. Am. Acad. Child Adolesc. Psychiatry (letter). **33:** 282.
80. BALDESSARINI, R. J. 1984. Antipsychotic agents. *In* The Somatic Therapies: Part I. The American Psychiatric Association Commission on Psychiatric Therapies. T. B. Karasu, Ed.: 119–170. American Psychiatric Association Press. Washington, DC.
81. ROJAHN, J., S. A. BORTHWICK-DUFFY & J. W. JACKSON. 1993. Ann. Clin. Psychiatry **5:** 163–170.
82. HILL, B., E. A. BALOW & R. H. BRUININKS. 1985. Psychopharmacol. Bull. **21:** 279–284.
83. MATSON, J. L. 1985. Psychopharmacol. Bull. **21:** 258–261.
84. CAMPBELL, M., N. M. GONZALEZ, M. ERNST, R. R. SILVA & J. S. WERRY. 1993. Antipsychotics. *In* Practitioner's Guide to Psychoactive Drugs for Children and Adolescents. J. S. Werry & M. G. Aman, Eds.: 269–296. Plenum Press. New York.
85. GUALTIERI, G. T., S. R. SCHROEDER, R. E. HICKS & D. QUADE. 1986. Arch. Gen. Psychiatry **43:** 335–340.
86. AMAN, M. G., R. A. KERN, D. E. MCGHEE & E. L. ARNOLD. 1993. J. Am. Acad. Child Adolesc. Psychiatry **32:** 851–859.
87. ARNOLD, L. E. & M. G. AMAN. 1991. J. Child Adolesc. Psychopharmacol. **1:** 361–373.
88. DOSTAL, T. & P. ZVOLSKY. 1970. Int. Pharmacopsychiatry **5:** 203–207.
89. RAPOPORT, M. D., W. A. SONIS, M. J. FIALKOV, J. L. MATSON & A. E. KAZDIN. 1983. Behav. Modif. **7:** 255–265.
90. RATEY, J. J., R. SOVNER, E. MIKKELSEN & H. E. CHMIELINSKI. 1989. J. Clin. Psychiatry **50:** 382–384.
91. RICKETS, R., A. B. GOZA, C. R. ELLIS, Y. N. SINGH, N. N. SINGH & J. C. COOKE. 1993. J. Am. Acad. Child Adolesc. Psychiatry **32:** 865–869.
92. RUTTER, M. 1986. Infantile autism and other pervasive developmental disorders. *In* Child and Adolescent Psychiatry, Modern Approaches. M. Rutter & L. Hersov, Eds.: 545–566. Blackwell Scientific. Oxford.
93. SOLOMON, L. 1991. Psychiatr. Clin. N. Am. **14:** 165–182.
94. ANDERSON, L. T., M. CAMPBELL, P. ADAMS, A. SMALL. R. PERRY & J. SHELL. 1989. J. Autism Dev. Disord. **19:** 227–255.
95. JOSHI, P. T., J. A. CAPOZZOLI & J. T. COYLE. 1988. Am. J. Psychiatry **145:** 335–338.
96. CAMPBELL, M., P. ADAMS, R. PERRY, E. K. SPENCER & J. E. OVERALL. 1988. Psychopharmacol. Bull. **24:** 251–255.
97. GORDON, C. T., R. C. STATE, J. E. NELSON, S. D. HAMBURGER & J. L. RAPOPORT. 1993. Arch. Gen. Psychiatry **50:** 441–447.
98. COOK, E. H., R. ROWLETT, C. JASELSKIS & B. L. LEVENTHAL. 1992. J. Am. Acad. Child Adolesc. Psychiatry **31:** 739–745.
99. REALMUTO, G. M., G. J. AUGUST & B. D. GARFINKEL. 1989. J. Clin. Psychopharmacol. **9:** 122–125.
100. JASELSKIS, C. A., E. H. COOK, K. E. FLETCHER & B. L. LEVENTHAL. 1992. J. Clin. Psychopharmacol. **12:** 322–327.
101. WILLIAMS, D. T., R. MEHL, S. YUDOFSKY, D. ADAMS & B. ROSEMAN. 1982. J. Am. Acad. Child Adolesc. Psychiatry **21:** 129–135.
102. CONNOR, D. F. 1994. J. Child Adolesc. Psychopharmacol. **4:** 101–111.
103. HERMANN, H. H. 1991. Effects of opiate antagonists in the treatment of autism and self-injurious behavior. *In* Mental Retardation: Developing Pharmacotherapies. J. J. Ratey, Ed.: 107–137. American Psychiatric Press. Washington, DC.
104. CAMPBELL, M., L. T. ANDERSON, A. M. SMALL, P. ADAMS & N. M. GONZALEZ. 1993. J. Am. Acad. Child Adolesc. Psychiatry **32:** 1283–1291.
105. GELLER, B., L. B. GUTTMACHER & M. BLEEG. 1981. Am. J. Psychiatry **138:** 388–389.
106. BIRMAHER, B., H. QUINTANA & L. GREENHILL. 1988. J. Am. Acad. Child. Adolesc. Psychiatry **27:** 248–251.

107. STEINGARD, R. J., D. R. DeMASO, S. J. GOLDMAN, K. L. SHORROCK & J. P. BUCCI. 1995. Harv. Rev. Psychiatry **2:** 313–326.
108. MITCHELL, J., E. McCAULEY, P. BURKE & S. MOSS. 1988. J. Am. Acad. Child Adolesc. Psychiatry **27:** 12–20.
109. McCRACKEN, J. T. 1992. Child Adolesc. Psychiatr. Clin. N. Am. **1:** 53–72.
110. KASHANI, J. H., J. M. DAHLMEIER, C. M. BORDUIN, S. SOLTYS & J. C. REID. 1995. J. Am. Acad. Child Adolesc. Psychiatry **34:** 322–326.
111. FAVA, M., J. F. ROSENBAUM, J. A. PAVA, M. K. McCARTHY, R. J. STEINGARD & E. BOUFFIDES. 1993. Am. J. Psychiatry **150:** 1158–1163.
112. ROSENBAUM, J. F., M. FAVA, J. A. PAVA, M. K. McCARTHY, R. J. STEINGARD & E. BOUFFIDES. 1993. Am. J. Psychiatry **150:** 1164–1168.
113. ANGOLD, A. & E. J. COSTELLO. 1992. Child Adolesc. Psychiatr. Clin. N. Am. **1:** 31–51.
114. AMBROSINI, P. J., M. D. BIANCHI, H. RABINOVICH & J. ELIA. 1993. J. Am. Acad. Child Adolesc. Psychiatry **32:** 1–6.
115. DWYER, J. T. & G. R. DeLONG. 1987. J. Am. Acad. Child Adolesc. Psychiatry **26:** 176–180.
116. JOYCE, P. R. 1984. Psychol. Med. **14:** 145–149.
117. LEWINSOHN, D. E., D. N. KLEIN & J. R. SEELEY. 1995. J. Am. Acad. Child Adolesc. Psychiatry **34:** 454–463.
118. WOZNIAK, J., J. BIEDERMAN, K. KIELY, J. S. ABLON, S. V. FARAONE, E. MUNDY & D. MENNIN. 1995. J. Am. Acad. Child Adolesc. Psychiatry **34:** 867–876.
119. FRISTAD, M. A., E. B. WELLER & R. A. WELLER. 1992. Child Adolesc. Psychiatr. Clin. N. Am. **1:** 13–29.
120. VARANKA, T. M., R. A. WELLER, E. B. WELLER & M. A. FRISTAD. 1988. Am. J. Psychiatry **145:** 1557–1559.
121. McGLASHAN, T. H. 1988. Am. J. Psychiatry **145:** 221–223.
122. KOEHLER-TROY, C., M. STROBER & R. MALENBAUM. 1986. J. Clin. Psychiatry **47:** 566–567.
123. ALESSI, N., M. W. NAYLOR, M. GHAZIUDDIN & J. K. ZUBIETA. 1994. J. Am. Acad. Child Adolesc. Psychiatry **33:** 291–304.
124. DeLONG, G. R. & A. L. ALDERSHOF. 1987. J. Am. Acad. Child Adolesc. Psychiatry **26:** 389–394.
125. WELLER, E. B., R. A. WELLER & M. A. FRISTAD. 1995. J. Am. Acad. Child Adolesc. Psychiatry **34:** 709–714.
126. WEST, S. A., P. E. KECK JR., S. L. McELROY, S. M. STRAKOWSKI, K. L. MINNERY, B. J. McCONVILLE & M. T. SORTER. 1994. J. Child Adolesc. Psychopharmacol. **4:** 263–267.
127. TERR, L. C. 1982. Annu. Prog. Child Psychiatry Child Dev. 383–396.
128. BURKE, J. D., J. F. BORUS, B. J. BURNS, K. H. MILLSTEIN & M. C. BEASLEY. 1982. Am. J. Psychiatry **139:** 1010–1014.
129. McLEER, S. V., M. CALLAGHAN, D. HENRY & J. WALLEN. 1994. J. Am. Acad. Child Adolesc. Psychiatry **33:** 313–319.
130. CHARNEY, D. S., A. Y. DEUTCH, J. H. KRYSTAL, S. M. SOUTHWICK & M. DAVIS. 1993. Arch. Gen. Psychiatry **50:** 294–305.
131. ARMSWORTH, M. W. & M. HOLADAY. 1993. J. Counsel. Dev. **72:** 49–56.
132. FAMULARO, R., R. KINSCHERFF & T. FENTON. 1988. Am. J. Dis. Child. **142:** 1244–1247.

Intervention with Excessively Aggressive Children

Conceptual and Ethical Issues

JEFFREY BLUSTEIN[a]

Department of Epidemiology and Social Medicine
Albert Einstein College of Medicine
Bronx, New York 10461

Barnard College
Columbia University
New York, New York 10027-6598

INTRODUCTION

News reports these days are increasingly filled with accounts of children as young as 11 and 12 committing violent crimes. In the not-so-distant past, antisocial behavior among young people usually took less extreme forms: stealing, vandalism, truancy, and the like. In recent years, however, there has been an escalation in both the frequency and severity of such behavior. According to a new report issued by the National Center for Juvenile Justice, the arrest rates for juveniles between the ages of 10 and 17 jumped 100% between 1983 and 1992.[1] Accounts of muggings, beatings, rapes, and even killings, carried out by youngsters singly or in groups, initially inspire incomprehension and horror. They challenge our assumptions about childhood innocence. What sort of children are they? we ask. Why do they do it? Do they suffer from a mental disorder, do they have violent and abusive parents, or are they just spoiled brats? Is there a general dulling and desensitization toward violence among the young, due in no small measure to the casual and widespread depiction of violence on television and in the movies? In addition to these efforts at understanding the etiology of childhood violence, and to some extent pulling against them, there has been increased public pressure for tougher treatment of juvenile offenders. In the view of many in our society, the juvenile justice system, operating with a philosophy of rehabilitation, has treated youthful offenders too leniently and has failed to safeguard the rights of law-abiding citizens. Moreover, as part of the social response to the rising tide of juvenile crime, questions have been raised about whether children, simply because they are children, are really less responsible for their crimes than adults are.

I will have no more to say here about whether the state should start treating young people who commit adult crimes as adults (for more information, see ref. 2). I am interested rather in some of the problems connected with designing effective intervention strategies to prevent aggressive or violent behavior in children and treating children who have already shown a propensity to behave in these ways. To do this, clearly, we first need to identify the causes or correlates

[a] Address for correspondence: Weiler Hospital, 1825 Eastchester Road, Bronx, NY 10461. Tel: (718) 904-2299; fax: (718) 904-3498; e-mail: blustein@aecom.yu.edu.

of the behavior we are trying to minimize. Ethical concerns arise at three points: identification of the causes or correlates, development of intervention strategies, and implementation of the strategies. I will say something about ethical issues pertaining to each of these stages later in this paper.

It would not be sensible, however, to leap into a discussion of these matters without first taking up some conceptual issues. Because the term "aggression" is ambiguous, denoting both positive and negative behaviors, it is not aggressive behavior per se, or the prospect of aggressive behavior per se, that motivates the interest in intervention strategies. It is rather what might be called "excessive" or "inappropriate" aggression. These adjectives, however, express value judgments, and values can be questioned and attacked. Another conceptual issue has to do with the classification of inappropriate, excessive aggression in children as a mental disorder. Much hinges, as we shall see, on whether we view a child's pathway to aggressive behavior as "normal," that is, a normal response to adverse circumstances, or as pathological, the product of some internal dysfunction.

DEFINING THE PROBLEM

Aggression: Positive and Negative

Behavioral scientists differ in their theories about aggression. Freudians, for example, believe that aggression, like sexuality, is an innate drive or instinct (or group of drives) in each of us. Others theorize that it is not an inborn drive but a response to frustrations that every human being experiences almost from birth. Whatever the source of aggressive energy in human motivation, it would be wrong to think of it entirely in negative terms. A certain amount of aggression is necessary throughout childhood and adolescence, both to assert oneself and take initiative within the home, as well as to master the environment, establish and reestablish one's identity, and engage in cooperative and competitive activities with one's peers. Channeled in the proper direction, human aggression is the force that enables a person to be healthfully self-assertive and independent and to achieve mastery of the environment and the self.

What is judged to be healthful self-assertion in any given society is influenced by prevailing cultural norms and role expectations, and these may be criticized on moral and other grounds. For example, in the days before the modern feminist movement, there was the clear expectation that men would take the initiative in courtship and sexual relations: women who did so tended to be branded as "unladylike," brazen, or licentious. It is one thing, however, to challenge the particular ways in which individuals have been socialized to express their aggressive energy—as I would do in this case—and quite another to claim that aggression is necessarily a pernicious force in human affairs.

Although there may be social conditions and ethical imperatives that sometimes justify destructive acts, in the context of child development, aggression is improperly channeled when it is directed toward destructive ends. The objects of these destructive impulses may be other persons, property, and even the self. These aggressive acts interfere with healthy child development by upsetting the parent-child relationship and preventing the formation of friendships with peers. Being rejected because you are hitting or kicking others leads to low self-esteem, which, in a vicious cycle, leads to more destructiveness. Even if, as an adolescent, the youngster becomes part of a gang where he is accorded some social recognition because of his antisocial behavior, the underlying feelings of inferiority and inadequacy remain.

Although there are cases of violent behavior in children that clearly cannot be tolerated in any civilized society, for example, murder and rape, attributions of inappropriate excessive aggression may become more controversial as we move away from these core paradigm cases. Judgments of aggressiveness reflect the values and interests of those doing the judging, and these in turn are influenced by the class, race, ethnicity, and gender of the judge. Behaviors might be labeled dangerous, hence socially unacceptable, merely because they are offensive to middle-class sensibilities, for example, or because they challenge or upset an immoral or unjust status quo. Moreover, which youngsters get identified as excessively aggressive in the core sense of causing or threatening physical injury may be more reflective of social stereotyping than objective assessment of the individual child's conduct and propensities.

Children who are judged to be excessively aggressive often come from poor and fragmented communities and belong to minority groups that have suffered from racial and economic discrimination and negative social stereotyping. In these circumstances, it would not be surprising if, say, a white middle-class teacher were to assess the behavior of a white middle-class youth very differently from that of a black, inner-city youth, to the latter's detriment. What is judged merely bothersome or annoying, when the former does it, may be judged intolerable and even dangerous when done by the latter. Intervention strategies that target children on the basis of membership in some racial or ethnic group, however, are invidiously discriminatory: they are merely thinly disguised efforts at social control and injurious to many children identified as problematic.

Aggression in Childhood as a Disorder

Questions raised in the 1970s about the use of psychotropic drugs to treat children said to have minimal brain dysfunction provide a number of instructive parallels to the issues I am discussing in this paper. One area of concern had to do with what some saw as a misguided attempt to apply the medical treatment model to certain kinds of social behavior. Sometimes, it was argued, certain kinds of behavior that appear to be violations of community standards are normal responses to very destructive situations. In particular, youngsters who act out and are hyperactive may not be exhibiting signs of pathology but may be expressing their frustration with a situation that is persistently unresponsive to their needs. What is wrong with the medical treatment model, these critics said, is that it leads us to locate the problem within the individual and diverts attention from the pursuit of environmental remedies.[3]

Similar concerns arise with respect to the treatment and prevention of aggression in children. Is excessive aggression in children primarily a problem of individual or environmental pathology? When does chronic and serious antisocial behavior in childhood reflect an underlying mental disorder?

By the standards of contemporary psychiatry, a sustained pattern of antisocial behavior in children warrants a diagnosis of *conduct disorder*. First introduced as a formal diagnostic category in 1980, the term *conduct disorder* is used generically to refer to a constellation of symptoms, including aggression, lying, stealing, truancy, running away, and other behaviors. However, the mere presence of this set of symptoms is not sufficient ground for concluding that a given child suffers from a mental disorder. Although there is compelling evidence in the extant literature that some children who engage in the criterial behaviors of conduct disorder suffer from certain types of underlying mental disorders, and that these disorders play an important role in the maintenance of their chronic antisocial behavior, we should not assume that an explanation of such behaviors in terms of underlying mental disorder is always warranted.[b]

These remarks presuppose a conception of disorder, and so I need to make explicit how I am using this term. Wakefield offers the following definition, which is intended to encompass both physical and mental disorders:

> A condition is a disorder if and only if (a) the condition causes some harm or deprivation of benefit to the person as judged by the standards of the person's culture . . . , and (b) the condition results from the inability of some internal mechanism to perform its natural function, wherein a natural function is an effect that is part of the evolutionary explanation of the existence and structure of the mechanism.[4]

Though this definition raises a number of questions of its own that I cannot examine here,[c] it nonetheless provides a useful framework for thinking about the plausibility of different explanatory models of antisocial behavior in children. As noted earlier, chronic antisocial behavior in childhood interferes with normal development and is harmful to the individual who engages in it, both while growing up and later in adulthood. This is the case whatever the etiology of the behavior. In order to establish that the harmful behavior syndrome results from a disorder, according to Wakefield's definition, we have to be able to demonstrate that this is a direct or indirect consequence of some dysfunction of natural processes within the individual child.

I do not wish to claim that the cluster of symptoms associated with conduct disorder is never due to a disorder in Wakefield's sense. Indeed, recent work in the field of neurobiology makes a strong case that brain dysfunction, specifically a decreased metabolism of serotonin in the brain, plays a role in the explanation of violent antisocial behavior in some individuals.[d] It would be equally wrong to assume, however, that all chronically antisocial children become and remain antisocial entirely or even partly because of some internal dysfunction. Indeed, inasmuch as the introduction of the concept of a disorder has important consequences for the ways we think about and frame our questions about antisocial behavior in children and for the strategies we devise to respond to it, we need to be especially on our guard against misapplications of this concept.

One reason we should be wary of attributing antisocial behavior in children to an underlying mental disorder is that it tends to carry with it significant, long-term negative consequences for the children themselves. Though a diagnosis of mental disorder can lead to treatment interventions that may benefit some children, there is the attendant concern that those who are classified as suffering from a mental disorder are often stigmatized because of this. Among the young, particu-

---

[b] Richters and Cicchetti criticize the DSM-III-R for making this assumption. RICHTERS, J. E. & D. CICCHETTI. 1993. Mark Twain meets DSM-III-R: Conduct disorder, development, and the concept of harmful dysfunction. Dev. Psychopathol. **5:** 5–29.

[c] For example, there are questions about how to discriminate between the inability of a mechanism to perform its natural function and a mere failure of an intact mechanism to function normally, and about how to distinguish between normal variability and dysfunction.

[d] For a review of the vast literature on the relationship between the neurotransmitter serotonin and aggressive behavior, see E. F. Coccaro. 1989. Central serotonin and impulsive aggression. Br. J. Psychiatry **155:** 52–62.

larly, the impact on the sense of self-worth and psychological functioning can be devastating. Second, stigmatization tends to further entrench the behavior that we are trying to combat. The child so labeled may come to identify himself as a "troubled youth," and in a misguided effort to win, if not respect, then at least acknowledgement from others, act out the part with even greater intensity.

A third reason for caution is that the mental disorder attribution may inadvertently serve to reinforce prejudiced views about those who commit antisocial acts, thereby further deepening social divisions and perpetuating discriminatory treatment of disadvantaged groups in our society.

A final risk of the mental disorder attribution has to do with its impact on the range of treatment and prevention options considered by treatment providers and policy agencies. A point earlier critics made about the application of the medical treatment model to hyperactive children has a parallel here: attributing behavior to an underlying mental disorder tends to focus attention away from problems in the environment that might account for antisocial behavior in children. Many children raised in communities and/or families where a lot of crime exists, for example, engage in antisocial, even criminal, behaviors because these are the behaviors modeled, expected, and/or rewarded by the major influences in their environment. What is more, beyond one's immediate community or family, the glorification of violence in our society, its promotion of violence as the way to deal with conflicts and to achieve social status, no doubt contributes significantly to the occurrence of aggressive behavior among the young.

The dangers I have mentioned—stigmatization, entrenchment of antisocial behavior, exacerbation of social injustice, diversion of attention from environmental factors—may not provide sufficient reason to call a halt to research on the biological causes or correlates of antisocial behavior in children, as some have urged. The costs, however, for the individuals who are labeled as suffering from a disorder, for the potential victims of their aggression, and for society at large are neither unlikely nor trivial, and they should not be discounted. At the very least, what this requires of researchers is that they be alert to the danger of moral judgment masquerading as clinical diagnosis. The classification of chronically antisocial behavior as a disorder may be dictated more by the researchers' ideological biases than by scientifically credible evidence. Beyond this, the study of aggression in children should not ignore other explanations and modes of treatment. Equal attention should be devoted to the possibility that factors other than, or in addition to, biological ones play an important role in causing antisocial behavior among the young.

ETHICAL ISSUES IN RESEARCH AND TREATMENT

Like all research involving human subjects, human research on the biological bases of antisocial aggression and the psychopharmacology of aggressive behavior must be conducted according to strict ethical guidelines. The guidelines that specify the conditions under which it is ethically acceptable to perform research on adult human subjects are encoded in federal regulation and are well-known to everyone in the research community. First is the informed consent requirement, which is founded on the moral principle of autonomy. The subjects of the research must be adequately informed of the aims, methods, and potential benefits, hazards, and discomforts of the proposed research, and of their right to abstain from participation and to withdraw their consent to participation at any time. The consent must also be voluntary, that is, not the result of coercion, duress, manipulation, and the like. Second is the requirement of a favorable risk/benefit ratio, which is founded on the moral principle of beneficence. In assessing a particular research protocol, we attempt to balance these two requirements. For example, research that poses a minimal risk to the individual subject and that presents the prospect of direct benefit to the subject, and that has voluntary and informed consent, is relatively uncontroversial. There may be research protocols, however, that present such an unfavorable risk/benefit ratio that we should not permit the research to go forward, even with the participants' informed and free consent. (Other requirements are that the proposed research be properly designed and that it not violate principles of justice, but I shall say no more about these here.)

Research involving minors introduces a number of complications, however. Young children may be able to assent to participation, that is, they may be able to affirmatively agree; with a few exceptions, the assent of the child should be secured before proceeding with the research. Assent, however, is not consent. For various reasons, young children (in the early adolescent years or younger) should normally not be accorded the sort of decisional authority that the principle of informed consent entails. They typically lack the capacity to adequately understand the nature of the risks and benefits of their participation and to weigh them against one another. Studies of cognitive development indicate that formal operational thinking, that is, the ability to problem solve using abstract concepts, to perform inductive and deductive operations or hypothetical reasoning, and to predict future consequences of action, first appears at about the age of 11 or 12, and that by midadolescence reasoning ability is as good as that seen in adulthood and involves the same flaws. The maturity of these young people, however, might still be challenged on the ground that they are not able to exercise reasonable or sound judgment. Further, in order for informed consent to morally authorize intervention, the consent must be voluntarily given, and voluntariness appears to be limited among children younger than about 14 years of age because of a reluctance to resist authority figures such as parents and doctors.[e]

Some adolescents may be functionally indistinguishable from young adults and exhibit comparable levels of cognition, judgment, independence, and responsibility. Nevertheless, because adolescents mature at varying rates, an individualized assessment of capacity is appropriate whenever risky research involving older children is contemplated. Even when adolescents are judged capable of consenting on their own to participation in research, if it involves greater than minimal risk, researchers should work with them to identify a supportive and responsible adult who will assist in decision making. Though minors who are capable of giving an informed consent do not ethically require the consent of a parent or guardian to participate in research, it would not be wise to proceed without the involvement

---

[e] This summary of the empirical findings is drawn from the following sources: GRISSO, T. & L. VIERLING. 1978. Minors' consent to treatment: A developmental perspective. Prof. Psychol. 9: 412–427; LEIKEN, S. 1982. Minor's assent or dissent in medical treatment. President's Commission for the Study of Ethical Problems in Medicine, Making Health Care Decisions, Volume III: Appendices. U.S. Government Printing Office, Washington, D.C., pp. 175–191; LEWIS, C. E. 1983. Decision making related to health: When could/should children act responsibly? In Children's Competence to Consent. G. B. Melton, G. P. Koocher & M. J. Saks, Eds.: 75–91. Plenum Press. New York; Weithorn, L. A. & S. B. Campbell. 1982. The competency of children and adolescents to make informed treatment decisions. Child Dev. 53: 1589–1598.

and emotional support of an adult who understands the adolescent's situation and is committed to his or her well-being.*f*

Plainly, much research on children would be ethically impermissible if informed consent had to be obtained from them. Traditionally, however, we have relied on a principle of proxy consent to satisfy the informed consent requirement. The ones to whom we turn for consent are normally the child's parents, for at least two reasons. First, parents are presumed to have authority over minors by virtue of the parents' role within the family and their general responsibility for the care and custody of their children. Second, parents have a deep emotional commitment to their children and therefore can be trusted to make decisions that are in their children's best interests. Parents, however, are not always the appropriate proxy decision makers, morally speaking, and the presumptions we make about the parent-child relationship can be rebutted in particular cases. Moreover, children might not live with their parents, but might be institutionalized or in group homes, or literally or functionally alone. Proxy consent presents special problems in this population: who ought to give consent for such children to participate in research, and what mechanisms exist for ensuring that the children's interests are protected?

There is a particular worry connected with parents' giving permission for their child to participate in clinical research on aggression. Children who engage in severe antisocial behavior, including aggression, are also normally extremely difficult to manage at home. Parents complain of "impossible" children, of children they are incapable of disciplining who make family life intolerable. As well, parents are stigmatized by others and criticized for not being able to control their own children. Under these circumstances, the normal assumption that parents can be trusted to safeguard the well-being of their children in research settings may be challenged. Parents might give permission for their children to participate in morally questionable research out of a sense of shame, helplessness, and despair.

Turning now to the second requirement, the risk/benefit calculation must be sensitive to the particular risks and discomforts that children face as participants in research. Some factors that deserve special attention in the case of children are fear of a procedure, pain, and separation from parents or familiar surroundings. In the light of these factors, what is minimally risky or unpleasant to an adult may not be so to a child or younger adolescent. Risks and harms must also be assessed against the background of the child's emerging sense of self. Adolescence, in particular, is a period of psychological upheaval in which the young person experiments with different social roles in different relationships in the search for a satisfying sense of self. Risks and discomforts that might be manageable for adults might be magnified for adolescents because of the possible detrimental impact of research on the process of general identity formation that adolescents are undergoing. Further, the age/maturity of the subjects also has a bearing on what is an acceptable risk/benefit ratio. Among competent adults, research that presents significantly greater than minimal risk and no prospect of direct benefit to the participants may be morally allowable. Because of their particular vulnerability and inability to independently consent to participate as research subjects, however, children need extra protection against undue risks. We fail to provide this protection if we allow children to participate in research of this sort, even if they have their parents' permission to do so.

---

f This follows the recent Guidelines for Adolescent Health Research, which grew out of a national consensus process sponsored by the Society for Adolescent Medicine. See J. Adolesc. Health **17:** 264–269.

Informed consent, of course, is not only a requirement of ethically valid research, but of treatment as well, and what I said earlier also applies in this context. Here too we must distinguish between minors with a developing capacity to participate in decision making and minors who have achieved the capacity to make some or all health-care decisions. The former require others to consent for them, but respect for them as persons requires involving them in decision making to the extent that they are capable of participating. Here too, for reasons given earlier, reliance on parental consent raises ethical concerns. Among other things, because parents have to live with the disruptive consequences of their child's aggressive behavior, they may not be sufficiently disinterested to make sound treatment decisions on his or her behalf. For those minors who have decisional capacity comparable to that of competent adults, their informed consent must be sought and obtained. Further, there are sound reasons for adopting a sliding scale in assessing consents to, and refusals of, treatment by mature minors, as with adults. That is, as the consequences of the individual's decision become more consequential, the standard of capacity becomes more demanding.[5]

In discussing treatments for aggressive behavior in children and adolescents, stage of development is important not only because of its relevance to the question of decisional capacity, but because it also bears on the question of whether and when it is appropriate to offer treatment. Behavior that is "problematic" among older children may be relatively common among younger ones, and problem behaviors may disappear with maturation and socialization. Further, whether or not youngsters have the cognitive ability and maturity of judgment to decide on their own about treatment, treatment cannot be entirely effective in the long run if they are noncompliant. However, because so much of normal adolescent development has to do with control issues, the treatment itself may become a focal point of contention between the adolescent and his adult caretakers. To help ensure compliance, it is necessary to convince the adolescent that the treatment supports and promotes his own goals, not those of adults who may have their own agendas.

THE POLITICS OF AGGRESSION RESEARCH

Even if research on the biological roots and pharmacologic treatment of aggressive behavior satisfies the informed consent requirement and does not expose participants to excessive risk, there is an additional consequentialist argument that some have advanced against it, namely, that such research is far more likely to be used against minority groups than against other perpetrators of violent acts. This comment by the International Committee against Racism, aimed specifically at a federal research agenda known as the Violence Initiative, is representative:

> [The Violence Initiative] ties directly into the ruling class strategy for maintaining "law and order" in a society coming apart at the seams due to social conflicts stemming from extreme racism and economic injustice.[6]

Such research should be halted, the argument goes, because, given the society in which we live, it will only play into the hands of those who wish to promote racist ideals and thinking, and so further isolate, oppress, and dehumanize minority groups. I would like to say a few words in closing about this sort of criticism.

Rational decision making about the ethics of conducting a certain line of research necessarily involves an appeal to the consequences of conducting the research. We consider various possible outcomes of doing the research and not doing it, the values to be assigned to the different projected outcomes, and the probabilities of their occurring.[7] In some cases, we may know a good deal about the probability of alternative outcomes, but there may be significant disagreement about the utilities to be assigned to them. In other cases, although there may be little controversy about whether the projected outcomes are desirable or not, we may not have enough knowledge to be able to assign probabilities to them with any degree of confidence. There may also be some types of research that we all agree should not go forward because the probability of undesirable outcomes occurring is extremely high and the probability of desirable ones extremely low: these are the easiest cases.

What can we say about biological and drug research on aggression? What are the potential benefits and potential dangers, what are their probabilities, and is it ethically proper to go ahead with the research in the light of what we know about these factors? Those who share the views of the International Committee against Racism not only believe that certain possible outcomes of this research are undesirable—oppression and dehumanization—but also that, being possible outcomes, the research ought to be halted. That these outcomes are undesirable few would dispute. What may be questioned, however, is the inference that is drawn from this. Do we know enough about the probability of these racist outcomes to be able to confidently assert that such research is unethical and should be stopped? The critic will respond that this sets up too high a standard and that unless we are willing to give the scientific community the license to do anything that in its eyes seems beneficial, we must take a stand against some types of research, even if the probability of harm is not known.

On the other hand, we need to consider the possible beneficial outcomes of biological and pharmacological research on aggression. Perhaps, despite the potential dangers, this research ought to go forward because it holds out the prospect of significant benefits for those who participate, as well as for others. Again, the critics will not be impressed, for even if they do not question the motives of individual researchers, they will maintain that under current social conditions there is good reason to doubt that the research will actually have the benefits proponents anticipate. Given the potential dangers and the dubious benefits, the critics conclude, the research should be condemned.

How shall we proceed? The claim that freedom of scientific inquiry takes precedence over all other values, I take it, is not a morally tenable response to the critic, nor is a position of neutrality on the question of the acceptability of this sort of research a satisfactory one for society to adopt. Scientists who do biological and drug research on aggression are not neutral with respect to the value of their activities, and human subjects research committees that monitor what the research community is doing must reach a verdict about proposals that come before them. They need normative guidance, and policy decisions need to be made now about whether this research should continue, in the light of the best knowledge we currently possess about risks and benefits. Because many considerations of different types should be included in these policy decisions, ultimately they should be societal ones and should be the product of open public discussion and debate. Researchers can and should play an important role in this process, by providing information about the possible benefits of this research for children, families, and society. The larger question, however, which they alone cannot answer, is this: Are we as a society willing to support research that may give us a better understanding of human aggression, its treatment, and prevention, despite the possible misuse of this knowledge?

ACKNOWLEDGMENTS

Early discussions with Peter Leone, Ruth Macklin, David Osher, and Trina Osher helped orient my thinking on the issues explored in this paper, and I thank them for their generous assistance. Thanks are also due to Craig Ferris and Thomas Grisso for comments on an earlier draft.

REFERENCES

1. THE NEW YORK TIMES. "Grim Forecast Is Offered on Rising Juvenile Crime." September 8, 1995.
2. BLUSTEIN, J. 1985. Adolescence and criminal responsibility. Int. J. Appl. Philos. **2:** 1–17.
3. STEINFELS, M. & L. DACH, Eds. 1976. MBD, drug research and the schools. Hastings Cent. Rep. June(Suppl.): 1–22.
4. WAKEFIELD, J. C. 1992. The concept of mental disorder: On the boundary between biological facts and social values. Am. Psychol. **47:** 384.
5. DRANE, J. 1985. The many faces of competency. Hastings Cent. Rep. **15:** 17–21.
6. A position paper of the International Committee against Racism. Biological Determinism Feeds Fascism. p. 12.
7. MACKLIN, R. 1977. On the ethics of *not* doing research. Hastings Cent. Rep. **7:** 11–13.

Summary: Cultivating Violence

CRAIG F. FERRIS

Program in Neuropsychiatric Sciences
Department of Psychiatry
University of Massachusetts Medical Center
55 Lake Avenue North
Worcester, Massachusetts 01655

ENVIRONMENT VERSUS BIOLOGY

With the escalation of violence around the world, health professionals and policy makers alike are looking for factors contributing to violent behavior and how to remedy the problem. Yet no subject raises more concern and does more to divide the scientific and political communities than the topic of violence in society. The battle lines are usually drawn around the issues of environment and biology.

At one extreme, the "pure environmentalist" claims all behavioral problems are learned and can be resolved with better guidance from primary caregivers and education. Some might even claim that all biological studies on violence are racist and should be stopped immediately.[1] At the other extreme, is the view that most individual violence is due to an uncontrollable biology. Over two decades ago, there was much written on violence that was due to brain damage.[2] Those so afflicted could not be helped by learning but could be saved by brain surgery. This extreme biological position was abandoned but in recent years has resurfaced under the guise of molecular biology as we look for genes controlling criminal and violent behavior.[3] Unfortunately, there is a pervading feeling that molecular biology may be the solution to our social problems. Children who display inappropriate, excessive aggression are sometimes believed to be genetically predisposed to behave as such, captive to their genes.

Biologists, physicians, and social scientists came to the meeting, the contents of which are recorded in this *Annals*, to discuss inappropriate, excessive aggression in children as the consequence of environmental and biological interactions. The extreme positions noted above were not represented. All participants recognized that a child's behavior is due to a continuous interaction between environment and biology throughout the development of the individual. Indeed, this interactive model found support in many of our presentations and discussions.

As a biologist, I thought it imperative to understand the methods and findings of social scientists studying the environment in which these children live. I was equally compelled to learn about the problems faced by physicians working with the most intractable cases in a clinical setting. Only by melding all three points of view does one arrive at a better understanding of the psychosocial and biological antecedents of inappropriate, excessive aggression in children and the potential for improved intervention strategies. The passages that follow are a biologist's perspective on the meeting. In this summary, I tried to incorporate ideas from as many talks as possible. Not all the works are included, and for this I apologize to my colleagues. All of the presentations were exceptional, and my failure to integrate each is due to my own inability to synthesize the many facets of this complex problem.

THE SPECTRUM OF AGGRESSION

As I sat and listened to the presentations and talked with the participants, I recognized that there is a spectrum of inappropriate, excessive aggressive behavior as defined by the severity of the condition and its responsiveness to learning and/or psychopharmacological interventions. At one end of the spectrum there is aggressive behavior associated with psychiatric illness in children. At the other end, there is societal aggression cultivated in children by deplorable living conditions, substandard nutrition and education, and emotional and physical abuse.

Inappropriate Excessive Aggression in Psychiatric Illness

Let me start by sharing my thoughts on those children that are often hospitalized for their uncontrollable behavior. Children with a history of mental illness may be predisposed to impulsive and aggressive outbursts. Many health professionals responsible for the care of these mentally ill children maintain that their aggressive behavior is secondary to the primary disorder and a possible symptom of any childhood neuropsychiatric illness. Thus a small percentage of children that suffer from such conditions as mental retardation, autism, Tourette's syndrome, and attention deficit/hyperactivity disorder (ADHD) may also display impulsive, aggressive behavior. Mentally retarded and autistic children may direct their aggression toward themselves, biting and lacerating their hands and arms, and smashing their heads against walls. A child with a history of untreatable Tourette's with ADHD may uncontrollably strike out at an individual much larger than themselves.

What triggers their aggressive outbursts? Several studies raised the possibility that loss in cognitive abilities, altered perception, changes in endocrine responsivity to stress, and diminished tolerance to excitatory stimuli may all contribute to antisocial behavior and the possibility for inappropriate excessive aggression when exposed to certain environments. Inasmuch as all of the mental illnesses noted above have a strong biological predilection and in some cases are hereditary, the role of genetic influences cannot be ignored. However, although these children may suffer from a dysfunction in brain biology, their affliction is not caused by the inheritance of "genes for violence" or "normal aggression genes" gone awry. These children with a history of psychiatric illness have an underlying neuropsychiatric problem contributing to their impulsive aggressive behavior. Most of these children are not neglected or abused. They are loved and cared for by attentive parents and primary caregivers. These children and their families deserve our compassion and understanding.

The problems faced by pediatric psychiatrists treating children with inappropriate, excessive aggression were exemplified in a case history provided by Dr. Joseph Gartner. A child was admitted to the hospital with uncontrollable rage. The child had been placed in five foster homes, was rejected from all, and was diagnosed as ADHD with conduct disorder. Efforts to control her behavior in the hospital through calm but firm discussion or by simplifying her environment to eliminate any potential threats or sources of aggravation were ineffective. On the day of admission, all drug treatments used to control her behavior were stopped. For the next two weeks, the child's behavior improved considerably with behavioral techniques that rewarded prosocial behavior but withheld privileges or assigned "time-outs" for bad behavior. In addition, psychotherapy was introduced to get the child to verbalize and to understand the social effects of her behavior. Despite these efforts and the noticeable improvement in general behavior, the child still exploded, attacking and hitting the health professionals working with her. Consequently, the child was given a stimulant to decrease her impulsivity and to treat the ADHD. Her aggressive behavior was not altered, so a drug that stimulates the serotonin system was added. With this last medication on board, her violent behavior was controlled.

This multimodal approach of combining behavioral modification and psychotherapy with one or more drugs is the most efficacious treatment strategy for these children. Dr. Daniel Connor agreed with the multimodal approach but was concerned that the treatment regimens were not scientifically grounded, as the developmental neurobiology of violence in clinically referred children is not understood. "How did these kids get this way, how are these drugs acting to improve their behavior, and what are these drugs doing to an immature nervous system?" he asked. "We lack a comprehensive definition of aggression in children that would help clinicians around the world have a clearer picture of the problem. More research is needed to examine the characteristics of aggression and the factors that contribute to the problem. Almost all of the research is on adult psychiatric patients, and the findings trickle down to kids. We know so little about the biological consequences of using drugs in children that were developed and tested for adult psychiatric illness. Despite the overwhelming negative impact of this behavior on the lives of these kids and their families, these children remain research orphans when it comes to understanding and treating their inappropriate, excessive aggression."

The pediatric clinicians in attendance all agreed that they would like more time to observe these children and assess the full benefit of behavioral modification and psychotherapies but that they were handicapped by the shrinking health dollar. With the advent of managed health care, a child may only be covered for four to seven days in the hospital. Outpatients may only be covered for four to six visits. Managed health care is pressuring the clinician for a quick fix, a solution that can only be found in psychopharmacology. This is an ethical dilemma for pediatric psychiatrists. Biologists and clinicians know so little about the developmental consequences of using psychoactive drugs on children to treat impulsive aggressive behavior. Yet the government and the pharmaceutical industry are hesitant to invest in this area of research. There is no public outcry to develop safe, selective, effective drugs to ameliorate inappropriate excessive aggression in clinically referred children while sparing other normal behavior. We are in need of drugs that will allow those with violent behavior associated with psychiatric illness to return to their home life and schools without endangering themselves, educators, health professionals, or the families that care for them.

Inappropriate Excessive Aggression in Society

Violence associated with a clearly defined mental illness accounts for a small fraction of the inappropriate, excessive aggression displayed by children. Instead, normal healthy babies subjected to early emotional and environmental insult may be pushed down a pathway where the risk of violent behavior is increased. Young children identified as impulsive, highly aggressive, and disruptive in school track for social failure. Their behavior, often classified under the rubric of "conduct disorder," is very consistent during childhood and throughout adolescence. Many of these children are at risk for future truancy, delinquency, drug abuse, depression, suicide, and violence. There is a long litany of psychosocial and environmental factors, such as prenatal exposure to drugs, parental criminality and inadequate parental care, illiteracy, unemployment, peer pressure, drug abuse, and poverty, that may contribute to their disruptive, antisocial behavior.

EARLY ABUSE AND NEGLECT

One area that has drawn particular attention is early abuse and neglect. Dr. Cathy Spatz Widom reported on children from court-substantiated cases of physical abuse and neglect. Abuse cases included injury from bruises, welts, or burns, and neglect cases reflected a judgment by the courts that the parent's deficiencies in child care were beyond those found acceptable by professional and community standards at the time. For example, neglect would be extreme failure to provide food, clothing, shelter, or medical attention. Dr. Widom found that victimized children are more likely to grow up with antisocial personality disorder. Interestingly, the prevalence of inappropriate, excessive aggression in neglected children is as high as that observed in children with a history of physical abuse. Although it is true that neglected and abused children have higher rates of violent crime when they grow up, existing evidence suggests that parents abused as children are not predetermined to be abusive caregivers themselves.

At least some abusive caregivers are afflicted with many of the same problems they pass on to their children. Poverty, unemployment, illiteracy, the dissolution of the family, teenage and unwanted pregnancies, deficient prenatal and postnatal health care, and parental drug use and addiction are the swaddling clothes they use to wrap their babies. The intergenerational transmission of antisocial behavior appears to contribute to the cycle of violence, supporting the popular maxim that violence begets violence. Is there no hope for abused and neglected children? Is there an endless cycle of antisocial behavior and risk for violence? The lives of a majority of children earmarked as troublemakers in school do not end in crime and violence. Indeed, many children are resilient, immune to the deleterious effects of childhood victimization. Is there a biological predisposition that saves many but fails some? Although we know much about the factors that contribute to vulnerability, we know nothing about the factors that contribute to resilience.

PSYCHOSOCIAL INTERVENTION

Intensive efforts to intercede in this cycle of social failure that may predispose a child to impulsive and potentially violent behavior has met with frustration, as intervention strategies do not generalize from one environmental condition to another. For example, although there may be some positive results in the classroom and playground, behavioral modification may not carry over to the home or the street. In a five-year study directed by Dr. Russell Barkley in the Worcester Massachusetts Public Schools, kindergarten children identified as ADHD and displaying inappropriate excessive aggression were targeted for intense behavioral training with an accelerated school curriculum. Efforts to incorporate parental training into the intervention strategy were ineffective and not practical, as the parents of many of these children were uncommitted to the program. However, the special behavioral treatment classroom program helped reduce much of the hyperactive, impulsive, and aggressive behavior displayed in the school setting. Unfortunately these improvements did not carry over to the home setting. Furthermore, the accelerated curriculum failed to demonstrate any improvement in academic skills in these high-risk children.

What is "learned can be unlearned," was a phrase I heard spoken by many social scientists. Biologists studying the molecular bases of learning and memory agreed, but they argued that there are periods in neural development that are more critical in their responsivity and plasticity than others. The behavior and biology of school-age children become more recalcitrant with each passing year. "Perhaps we should be looking earlier into the lives of these children, between the ages of 1 and 3," suggested Dr. Richard Tremblay, research director for a twelve-year longitudinal study on boys at risk in the Montreal school system. Starting in kindergarten, boys are followed until the ages of 17 to 18. Boys rated as high fighters at the age of 5 to 6 continue to show inappropriate excessive aggression into adolescence that is unaffected by psychosocial intervention strategies, like counseling, behavioral therapy, and educational and community programs. "It is likely that only very powerful interventions can change the course of their behavior."

Teaching children how to behave is not a simple task. Learning requires a healthy neuronal substrate to achieve optimal results. Many children with histories of neglect and abuse have severe learning disabilities. They lack the cognitive and social skills to successfully interact with the environment. They fail to read the feelings of others. Many cannot empathize with the pain and suffering of others, perhaps as a coping mechanism for their own childhood anguish. Because they are unable to recognize the emotional disposition of peers, these children may exacerbate potentially aggressive social encounters and precipitate violent interactions. Efforts to teach coping skills during early school years are not easy when the child lacks the tools necessary for healthy interpersonal relationships. Concern for cognitive and social skills was incorporated into a multifaceted intervention program reported by Dr. Bierman. Entitled Fast Track, this six-year program covers critical developmental periods and transitions in a child's life. The program aims at fostering increased parental care, a positive home environment, increased cognitive and social skills, and successful peer relationships. Because this is an ongoing six-year program, it is still too early to know whether these many preventive activities can decrease social failure in children and lessen the risk of future violence.

BIOLOGICAL AND BEHAVIORAL CONSEQUENCES OF EARLY ABUSE AND NEGLECT

Chronic abuse and neglect have pervasive effects on the psychology and biology of children. In the absence of a reliable and consistent primary caregiver, like a parent or a substitute parent, children are at risk of developing problems in controlling their feelings and behavioral responses to external stressors. A child's attachment to the primary caregiver helps regulate arousal. The love and physical contact of the caregiver can channel the normal sensory agitation of the infant into a state of calm and well-being. Without the loving, physical attention of the caregiver, the infant/child may cope by rocking, self-clasping, and other stereotyped motor behavior that serve to self-stimulate. These children withdraw and gaze into space in response to neglect, ignoring sensory stimulation as a means of managing. These behavioral consequences of early neglect were poignantly described in the work of Drs. Felton Earls and Mary Carlson.[4] In Romania, thousands of orphan children are raised in institutions called *leaganes* ("cradles"). Although many of these children are provided a clean environment where their physical needs are met, they are not routinely held or loved. Does this severe tactile and social deprivation impact on the development of the nervous system? Based upon preclinical studies, Drs. Earls and Carlson are convinced that neuronal development is altered in these children, together with their perception and response to environmental stress.

Behavioral and biological evidence attesting to the devastating effects of early maternal deprivation are told in the work of Harry Harlow in studies of nonhuman primates.[5] To study the development of learning, Harlow and co-workers at the University of Wisconsin Primate Laboratory and Regional Primate Research Center bred rhesus monkeys and separated the babies at birth from their mothers. In studies conducted over at least two decades, monkeys raised in partial or complete social isolation for six months to a year derived their nutritional needs from human caretakers. Emotional needs were unmet, as these monkeys did not establish attachments or "bonds" with a mother or other monkeys.

Monkeys with complete social isolation perform equally well as control monkeys on numerous simple learning tasks, like concurrent object discrimination, but perform below normal as the learning tasks become more complex, like oddity discrimination. For example, they are presented with two objects and are rewarded for choosing one and not the other. This is done with twenty-five different pairs of objects presented in series. The experimental and control monkeys can both learn a list of twenty-five objects, a task referred to as concurrent object discrimination. However, when presented with two blue balls and one red ball, it is more difficult for monkeys with a history of early social isolation to learn to identify the different ball, a task called oddity discrimination.

Careful attention to their social behavior later in life after varying periods of isolation reveals a much greater problem. Monkeys raised in partial social isolation (visual and physical contact with humans) show exaggerated oral behavior like thumb and toe sucking, self-clutching, rocking, and stereotyped motor activities not unlike those observed in emotionally neglected children. Self-mutilation is common, as monkeys appear to dissociate from an arm or leg and attack the disembodied appendage as if it were an intruder in their environment. When introduced into a social setting with other infant/preadolescent monkeys, they are very impulsive, fearful, and aggressive. Over time, animals with a history of early neglect can assimilate into a monkey group and appear normal; however, when confronted with a stressful situation like the introduction of a strange monkey to the group, they revert to the withdrawal, excessive aggression, or stereotyped motor behaviors that were common during their time in isolation. Hence, the dormant seed of antisocial behavior planted during early development can sprout later in life during social stress.

The social consequences of total isolation are more devastating than partial isolation. Monkeys denied any social or visual contact with monkeys or humans for the first six months of life show permanent alterations in psychosocial behavior. It is extraordinarily difficult to habituate these monkeys into social groups. The social behaviors that typically emerge are fear, impulsivity, and inappropriate aggression, as animals with a history of early isolation will inexplicably attack infants as well as larger adult males. Without early maternal care, and unable to learn from peers, these animals do not respond normally to physical or vocal communication. Females show no sexual activity. When artificially impregnated, these mothers, at best, reject and ignore their babies; they commonly attack their offspring and may physically injure or kill them.

Drs. Gary Kraemer and A. Susan Clarke continue the scientific legacy of Harlow at the University of Wisconsin primate laboratories. They and their co-workers have discovered still another insidious consequence of early social isolation: predispositions toward drug abuse and increased sensitivity to amphetamines. Monkeys with a history of early neglect prefer sweetened alcoholic beverages over nonalcoholic beverages and consume more alcohol as adults than group-reared peers. In addition, monkeys isolated at birth but successfully assimilated into a monkey group may appear to be normal as noted above, but their early neglect has left an indelible mark on their neurochemistry. Low doses of amphetamine that have no obvious behavioral effects on group-reared monkeys transform neglected animals into killers. Following amphetamine treatment, animals with a history of early isolation become wild and violent, attacking and killing peers in their group. The extrapolation of these findings to human behavior is frightening. Neglected and abused children are more prone toward antisocial behavior, including drug abuse. Perhaps these children take drugs to self-medicate and alleviate the hostility, depression, and suicidal ideation that fill their minds. As if taking the drugs is not bad enough, their nervous system may be programmed to respond adversely, precipitating extreme, unpredictable behavior.

USING ANIMAL MODELS TO IDENTIFY CHANGES IN THE NERVOUS SYSTEM CAUSED BY EARLY ENVIRONMENTAL STIMULI

Can studies on laboratory rodents provide insights into the long-term biological and behavioral consequences of early environmental and emotional insults such as abuse and neglect? In an elegant series of studies, Dr. Michael Meaney and co-workers traced the individual stress response of adult rats back to a cascade of molecular events triggered by early neonatal handling. Isolating or gently handling pups for fifteen minutes each day from postnatal day two to postnatal day fourteen permanently alters the responsiveness of the hypothalamic-pituitary-adrenal axis during stress. Activation of this "stress axis" results in the release of glucocorticoids or stress hormones that have a permissive effect on numerous physiological processes that promote health. However, in excess these stress hormones can contribute to neuropathology, heart disease, and immunosuppression. Animals with a history of neonatal handling are better able to control their stress response than nonhandled animals. Handling increases serotonin activity during early development that appears to be responsible for facilitating glucocorticoid receptor expression in the hippocampus and the frontal cortex. An increase in glucocorticoid receptors translates into better feedback regulation of the stress axis and control of stress hormones. The net result is longer life expectancy, a better immune system, and less neuropathology, as rats are better able to cope with exposure to acute and chronic stress. This work provides evidence that environmental events during critical developmental windows can permanently alter neural mechanisms that affect an individual's perception and response to stress over their lifetime.

If something as benign as gentle handling of neonates can shape future biology and behavior, what would be the consequences of perinatal exposure to drugs? For instance, recent surveys indicate that 17% of women in the United States smoke during pregnancy, exposing the developing fetus to high quantities of nicotine. Dr. Jean King reported that prenatal and early postnatal exposure to nicotine in rats leads to changes in the development of the serotonin system, a neurotransmitter instrumental in the control of aggressive behavior. This animal study appears to translate to the human condition. Children of mothers that smoked one or more packs of cigarettes each day during and/or after pregnancy are more likely to have behavioral problems as compared to children of mothers that did not smoke.[6]

Drs. Yvon Delville and Richard Melloni and I at the University of Massachusetts Medical Center developed an animal model for assessing the behavioral and biological consequences of physical and emotional abuse during adolescence. In humans, adolescence is defined as a period of pronounced physical, cognitive, and emotional growth. This period usually begins just before puberty and ends in early adulthood with sexual maturity, social awareness, and independence. In the golden hamster there is a developmental period analogous to adolescence. In the wild, hamsters wean around postnatal day 25 (P-25), leave the home nest, forage on their own, establish nest sites, and defend their territory. Hamsters can begin to establish dominance hierarchies as early as P-35 and have a minimal breeding age of 42 days. Androgen levels start to rise dramatically between P-28 and P-35. Thus between P-25 and P-42, as hamsters achieve independence from the maternal nest, they double their weight and size, reach full sexual maturity and reproductive competence, and establish social relationships. We designate this period between P-25 and P-42 as "adolescence" in golden hamsters.

On P-25, adolescent hamsters are placed into the home cage of an adult hamster experienced in fighting. This encounter lasts for one hour and is repeated each day for fourteen consecutive days. During this daily bout of social subjugation, the adolescent intruder is chased, nipped, and threatened by the resident. The stress of attack and threat is unremitting because each day the adolescent is introduced to a different resident. During early adulthood, days after cessation of physical and emotional abuse, animals are tested for agonistic behavior. In one case, animals with a history of abuse are introduced to a smaller, younger, more timid hamster, whereas in a second, they are introduced to a peer of equal weight and size. Placing a smaller intruder into the home cage of previously abused hamsters elicits a greater number of biting attacks and a shorter latency to attack from the resident than that of the littermates raised under control conditions. Although adult hamsters routinely challenge and attack an intruder that invades their territory, the level of aggression displayed by animals with a history of abuse toward smaller, weaker opponents is excessive. Interestingly, these same animals when confronted by an intruder of equal weight and size are much less aggressive than their control littermates and are themselves often very timid. Much like bullies on a playground, animals with a history of early abuse are highly aggressive toward a potential victim but run from more worthy opponents. Interestingly, these animals with a history of early abuse show significant changes in their serotonin and vasopressin innervation of the anterior hypothalamus, an area involved in the regulation of agonistic behavior.

This context-dependent agonistic behavior, which is extreme in its implementation, can be mimicked by administration of glucocorticoids directly into the hypothalamus of hamsters.[7] Dominant adult male hamsters are implanted with crystalline pellets of cortisol or control pellets of cholesterol. On the following day, animals from each experimental condition are matched by weight in a Plexiglas-neutral arena and scored for agonistic behavior. All animals implanted with cortisol in the anterior hypothalamus flee from their cholesterol-treated opponent. However, when these same cortisol-treated animals are matched with a previously identified submissive animal, they promptly attack the victim. Artificially elevating cortisol in the hypothalamus would appear to affect perception and assessment of risk leading to exaggerated agonistic responding. Fearfulness, hypervigilance, and the misinterpretation of threats are a volatile mix that can lead to inappropriate excessive aggression.

Stress would appear to play a critical role in the development of inappropriate, excessive aggression. Hamsters that are continuously subjugated and lose fights against stronger opponents have a disrupted stress axis. As a result, losers have exaggerated, sustained elevations in blood levels of glucocorticoids following a stressful conflict as compared to winners. The effect of early environmental and emotional insults on the disruption of the negative feedback control and regulation of stress hormones appears to be a common theme across many species. Dr. Elizabeth J. Susman argued that it is not testosterone that correlates with increased aggressive behavior in adolescence, but adrenal androgens and glucocorticoids. The endocrine milieu contributing to the developmental onset of aggressive behavior in children may better reflect the activation of the adrenal glands than the gonads.

NEUROCHEMICAL REGULATION OF AGGRESSION

Is aggression under neurochemical regulation? Dr. Ray Fuller, one of the key senior scientists at Eli Lilly, responsible for the discovery of fluoxetine (Prozac), a serotonin-specific reuptake inhibitor, reported on a vast literature indicating an inverse relationship between serotonin levels in the brain and aggressive behavior in many species, including humans. Diminishing the activity of serotonin in the brain or eliminating certain classes of serotonin receptors results in elevated attack behavior in many species. Conversely, attacks and bites can be significantly reduced with pharmacological manipulations that increase serotonin levels or stimulate serotonin receptors. In my own laboratory, I have found that resident hamsters do not attack or bit an intruder when treated with fluoxetine.

On the opposite side of the aggression coin, my co-workers and I have discovered that injecting vasopressin directly into the hypothalamus of male hamsters increases their aggression toward intruders placed into their home cage. Blocking the vasopressin receptors in the hypothalamus inhibits attacks and bites against intruders without altering other social behaviors or sexual activity. The action of vasopressin is not confined to the hypothalamus and is not specific to the golden hamster. Other rodent species are similarly stimulated to attack by injection of vasopressin into different parts of the brain. The ability of vasopressin to affect aggression at multiple sites in the central nervous system is evidence that this neurochemical may have a broad physiological role in enhancing arousal during social conflict.

There are data supporting the notion that vasopressin promotes aggression and dominant behavior by enhancing the activity of the neural network controlling agonistic behavior that is normally restrained by serotonin. Vasopressin and serotonin receptors are found in the same critical areas of the brain that comprise the neural network regulating aggression. Vasopressin neurons are innervated by serotonin terminals. Pretreating animals with fluoxetine diminishes the activity of the vasopressin system by inhibiting its release and blocking its action to facilitate aggression. These preclinical studies examining the interaction between vasopressin and serotonin are particularly exciting, inasmuch as a recent clinical study by Dr. Emil Coccaro indicates a similar relationship between these neurotransmitters in human studies. Personality-disordered subjects with a history of fighting and assault show a negative correlation for prolactin release in response to

d-fenfluramine challenge, an indication of a hyposensitive serotonin system. More-over, these same subjects show a positive correlation between cerebrospinal fluid levels of vasopressin and aggression. Thus, in humans, a hyposensitive serotonin system may result in enhanced central nervous system levels of vasopressin and the facilitation of aggressive behavior.

RETHINKING THE ENVIRONMENT/BIOLOGY CONTROVERSY

Are people with a history of early abuse and neglect predisposed to impulsive and potentially violent behavior? Based upon all of the data presented at the meeting, the possibility cannot be ignored that early environmental and emotional insults can trigger changes in the stress response in humans and perhaps the interplay between multiple neurotransmitter systems that safeguard against violent behavior. The argument about what percentage of behavior is environmental and what percentage is genetic is spurious. We are 100% of both. The two are insepara-ble. There is a constant interaction between the environment and the genetic expression of behavior. Altering behavior alters the perception and interaction of the organism with its environment. The interaction is not in a single direction from environment to biology, but circular. As Dr. McCord noted, "social interven-tions have biological consequents and biological interventions have social conse-quents." Some argue that we are slaves to our genes. Considering the long-term biological and behavioral consequences of early abuse and neglect, the opposite extreme could be argued: for critical periods in our life, we may be slaves to our environment.

ATTENDING TO THE NEEDS OF THE NEWBORN

We should be in the business of building resilience not vulnerability in children. Our typical approach is to correct, stop, or fix the problem. We attend to the problem after it becomes a problem. It intuitively makes more sense to "improve," "grow," and "nourish" our babies so that they are more resilient to the insults they will face through childhood and adolescence. As the public health dollar continues to shrink, where should we invest? When asked this question at the conference, clinicians and social scientists alike answered, without hesitation, "prenatal and postnatal health care and early parental care." Dr. Eichelman and A. C. Hartwig best summarized this opinion in their advice to a concerned mother. They advised her "to carry her child to term in an environment/society that treasures its young and provides a supportive, nutritional, and medically super-vised environment with reduced stress and protection against maternal separation for its most precious 'product,' its children."

REFERENCES

1. BREGGIN, P. R. & G. R. ST. BREGGIN. 1994. The War Against Children. Martin's Press. New York.
2. MARK, V. H. & F. R. ERVIN. 1970. Violence and the Brain. Harper & Row. New York.
3. DILALLA, L. F. & I. I. GOTTESMAN. 1991. Biological and genetic contributors to vio-lence—Widom's untold tale. Psychol. Bull. **109:** 125–129.
4. CARLSON, M. & F. EARLS. 1996. Psychological and neuroendocrinological sequelae of

early social deprivation in institutionalized children in Romania. Ann. N. Y. Acad. Sci. In press.

5. HARLOW, H. F., M. K. HARLOW & S. J. SUOMI. 1971. From thought to therapy: Lessons from a primate laboratory. Am. Sci. **59:** 538–549.
6. WEITZMAN, M., S. GORTMAKER & A. SOBOL. 1992. Maternal smoking and behavior problems of children. Pediatrics **90:** 342–349.
7. HAYDEN-HIXSON, D. M. & C. F. FERRIS. 1991. Cortisol exerts site-, context-, and dose-specific effects on the agonistic behaviors of male golden hamsters. J. Neuroendocrinol. **3:** 613–622.

Beliefs about Aggressive Feelings and Actions

JOHN ARCHER[a] AND ANADELLE HAIGH

Department of Psychology
University of Central Lancashire
Preston, Lancashire
PR1 2HE United Kingdom

INTRODUCTION AND METHODS

Campbell and Muncer[1] set out a theory concerning how people think and feel about an aggressive incident in which they have been involved. The researchers distinguished between instrumental and expressive beliefs, which were subsequently measured by a 20-item forced-choice questionnaire, the EXPAGG.[2] These two ways of construing an aggressive incident were held to be characteristic of men and women, respectively, and this was confirmed by consistent sex differences on the questionnaire.

In study 1 (n = 130), we redesigned the EXPAGG as a 40-item questionnaire by casting the alternative responses for each item as separate statements to be judged along a 5-point Likert scale (TABLE 1); we also inquired about the type of aggressive incident the person was thinking of when completing the questionnaire. We tested two hypotheses implicit in the original questionnaire: first, that expressive and instrumental responses are necessarily alternatives to one another; and second, that women and men have equivalent referents when answering questions about their feelings and actions following an aggressive incident. We also examined sex differences and the factor structure of the questionnaire.

In study 2, the same questionnaire was used on another sample of young adults (n = 200) to assess the association between beliefs about aggression and self-reported aggression, using the aggression questionnaire.[3]

RESULTS

In both samples, we found the following: (1) The instrumental and expressive beliefs were only moderately correlated (r = −.35), and their separation into 20-item scales showed a clearer factor structure than when all 40 items were combined. (2) Men showed higher instrumental scores, whereas women showed higher expressive scores (FIG. 1): in study 1, factor analysis revealed one major factor in each case on which items showing the highest sex differences were concentrated. (3) Women were equally likely to be thinking of an aggressive episode with a same-sex opponent as with an opposite-sex partner; men nearly always were thinking of an aggressive episode with another man. Neither instrumental nor

[a] Tel: 01772-893430; fax: 01772-892925; e-mail: j.archer@uclan.ac.uk.

TABLE 1. Examples of Items from the 40-item Modified EXPAGG

Expressive
1. If I hit someone and hurt them, I feel guilty.
2. After a physical fight, I feel drained and guilty.
3. In an argument, I feel more annoyed with myself if I hit the other person than if I cry.
4. If I hit someone and hurt them, I feel guilty.
5. The worst thing about physical aggression is that it hurts another person.

Instrumental
1. I believe that physical aggression is necessary to get through to some people.
2. After I lash out physically at another person, I like to make sure they never annoy me again.
3. The best thing about acting aggressively is that it makes the other person get in line.
4. When I hit someone and hurt them, I feel as if they were asking for it.
5. I believe my aggression comes from being pushed too far by obnoxious people.

expressive scores were affected by whether a woman was thinking of a partner or a same-sex opponent. In study 2, we found the following: (1) Instrumental beliefs were highly correlated with physical aggression ($r = .53$), and to a lesser extent with hostility ($r = .40$), verbal aggression ($r = .31$), and anger ($r = .30$). (2) Expressive beliefs showed much lower correlations with all four measures. (3) Instrumental beliefs were endorsed more strongly at younger ages for both sexes.

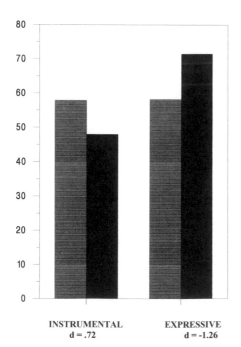

FIGURE 1. Sex differences in beliefs about aggression (study 2). ■, males; ■, females. d values are effect sizes, a negative sign indicating higher female values.

CONCLUSIONS

Instrumental and expressive beliefs about aggression were only moderately related to one another, rather than being alternatives, with women showing higher expressive scores and men showing higher instrumental scores. Instrumental but not expressive beliefs were highly correlated with physical aggression, and to a lesser extent with hostility, anger, and verbal aggression. Men nearly always had in mind an aggressive exchange with another man, a finding consistent with social disapproval of men's physical aggression towards women.

REFERENCES

1. CAMPBELL, A. & S. MUNCER. 1987. Models of anger and aggression in the social talk of women and men. J. Theory Soc. Behav. **17:** 489–511.
2. CAMPBELL, A., S. MUNCER & E. COYLE. 1992. Social representations of aggression as an explanation of gender differences: A preliminary study. Aggressive Behav. **18:** 95–108.
3. BUSS, A. H. & M. PERRY. 1992. The aggression questionnaire. J. Personality and Social Psychol. **63:** 452–459.

Stable Perseveration

Predictors and Correlates

L. ARSENEAULT,[a] R. E. TREMBLAY,
AND B. BOULERICE

Research Unit on Children's Psychosocial Maladjustment
University of Montreal
750 East Gouin Boulevard
Montreal, Quebec H2C 1A6, Canada

One of the maladaptive aspects of persistent antisocial behavior is the failure to modify its course in response to changing circumstances.[1] That characteristic corresponds to response perseveration, which is an inability to hold back a response that has been previously associated with punishment. Response perseveration is reported in conduct-disordered children,[2,3] as well as in psychopaths,[4] and is part of the disinhibition syndrome.[5] It might express executive-function deficits, such as inattention and impulsivity, and possibly have roots early in life.[1] To verify this hypothesis, we examined the links between various disinhibited behaviors at age 6 and stable perseveration during adolescence. This report was also conducted to determine the association between stable perseveration and specific delinquent behaviors at ages 13 and 14.

The subjects were French-Canadian boys who had been participating in the Montreal longitudinal study[6] since the age of 6. Disinhibited behaviors, such as physical aggression, inattention, and hyperactivity, were rated by teachers with subscales from the Preschool Behavior Questionnaire[7] when the boys were 6 years old. The Jesness Inventory[8] was used to assess self-reported delinquent personality (manifest aggression, delinquent value orientation, and social maladjustment). Self-reports of delinquent behaviors, such as robbery, drug use, physical aggression, and destructiveness, were also obtained.[6] The increase in delinquent behav-

TABLE 1. Predictors of Stable Perseveration Behavior between 13 and 14 Years of Age

Variables	B	Wald	df	p	Odds Ratio
Inattention at age 6	.42	8.28	1	.0040	1.5173
Physical aggression increase from ages 13 to 14	.36	3.98	1	.0461	1.4263

When inattention scores at age 6 were not forced:

Variables	B	Wald	df	p	Odds Ratio
Social maladjustment at age 14	.07	5.53	1	.0187	1.0759

[a] Tel: (514) 385-2525; fax: (514) 385-5739; e-mail: arseneal@ere.umontreal.ca.

TABLE 2. The Disinhibition Index at Age 6 as a Predictor of Stable Perseveration Behavior between 13 and 14 Years of Age

Variables	B	Wald	df	p	Odds Ratio
Disinhibition index at age 6	.13	5.89	1	.0154	1.1352

iors from 13 to 14 years of age was used to represent a difficulty to inhibit a reprehensible behavior. Boys were classified as stable perseverant (n = 35) if they played more than 80 cards in the card playing task[4] at 13 and 14, and stable nonperseverant (n = 34) if they played less than 80 cards at both ages. Backward stepwise logistic regressions were used to verify prediction power and concurrent association.

Results indicate that stable perseveration can be predicted from the age of 6 with attention-deficit ratings by teachers (TABLE 1). The self-reported physical aggression increase from the age of 13 to 14 was associated with stable perseveration during adolescence (TABLE 1). The interaction between inattention at age 6 and increase in physical aggression from the age of 13 to 14 was not significant. When the inattention score at age 6 was not forced in the first step of the regression, social maladjustment at age 14 was associated with perseveration (TABLE 1). Results also indicate that a disinhibited behavior index, computed with physical aggression, inattention, and hyperactivity scales significantly predicted perseveration during adolescence (TABLE 2).

This report is consistent with previous studies showing that perseveration behavior is associated with maladaptive behaviors, more specifically with an increase in physical aggression during adolescence. Moreover, the results suggest that stable perseveration mechanisms might be in place as early as during the preschool years. These would involve inattention, which may reflect an executive-function deficit. Results also suggest that inattention during preschool years and social maladjustment at age 14 share common variance in explaining perseveration behavior. Further studies using a multimethod and multisource assessment of perseveration behavior are needed to support those results.

REFERENCES

1. MOFFITT, T. 1993. Psychol. Rev. **100**: 674–701.
2. SHAPIRO, S. K., H. C. QUAY, A. E. HOGAN & K. P. SCHWARTZ. 1988. J. Abnorm. Psychol. **97**(3): 371–373.
3. DAUGHERTY, T. K. & H. C. QUAY. 1991. J. Child Psychol. Psychiatry Allied Discip. **32**(3): 453–461.
4. NEWMAN, J. P., C. M. PATTERSON & D. S. KOSSON. 1987. J. Abnorm. Psychol. **96**(2): 145–148.
5. GORENSTEIN, E. E. & J. P. NEWMAN. 1980. Psychol. Rev. **87**(3): 301–315.
6. TREMBLAY, R. E., R. O. PHIL, F. VITARO & P. DOBKIN. 1994. Arch. Gen. Psychiatry **51**: 732–739.
7. BEHAR L. & S. STRINGFIELD. 1974. Dev. Psychol. **10**: 601–610.
8. JESNESS. 1983. The Jessness Inventory. Consulting Psychologists Press. Palo Alto, CA.

Criminality and Morbidity in Young Victims of Firearm Injuries

A Follow-up Study

B. BERGMAN,[a,d] S. PONZER,[b] AND B. BRISMAR[c]

[a]Departments of Psychiatry
and
[b]Orthopedic Surgery
[c]Disaster and Emergency Medical Center
Huddinge Hospital and Stockholm Söder Hospital
Karolinska Institute
Stockholm, Sweden

Our aim was to study psychiatric and somatic morbidity and criminality in young victims of firearm injuries.

MATERIAL

All patients (n = 96; 86.5% were males) treated in public hospitals due to firearm injuries between 1972 and 1993 in Stockholm, Sweden and born in 1970 or later were studied through register data concerning criminality and morbidity. According to the ICD-9 classification, there were 77 cases of accidental firearm injuries, eight cases of murder/attempted murder, two cases of suicide/attempted suicide, and seven undetermined cases. The patients were compared with 96 age- and sex-matched controls, none of whom had been a victim of firearm injury, as all such patients were already included in the patient group. The mean age for the 96 patients when shot was 13.9 years (SD 4.5; range 1–22 years), and 64 were 15 years or younger. At the end of the follow-up period, December 1993, the mean age of the 192 patients and controls was 19.1 years (SD 3.4; range 7–23 years), 160 of whom were 15 years or older.

METHOD

Data on patients and controls was collected from the police register of past sentences and the Stockholm county council computer files on inpatient care covering the period 1972–1993.

RESULTS

Thirty-one of the patients (32.3%) compared to seven (7.3%) of the controls had been sentenced for a criminal offense. This difference was most pronounced concerning crimes of violence. When all episodes of care caused by the firearm injury were excluded, 53 patients and 36 controls had been admitted as inpatients

[d] Tel: +46 8 7461000; fax: +46 8 7795416.

during the study period. When the diagnoses were divided into three groups, somatic diseases, psychiatric disorders, and trauma, the distribution of inpatient care episodes among the patients was 60.0%, 16.4%, and 23.6%, respectively. The corresponding figures for the controls were 82.9%, 1.2%, and 15.9%.

CONCLUSION

Young victims of firearm injuries constitute a high-risk group for criminality; their morbidity is raised, and these risk factors appear at relatively young ages. The risk for injuries in general is high, and psychiatric disorders are common. This indicates that young victims of firearm injuries constitute a psychosocially disadvantaged group, which may be potentially costly for society. This makes preventive measures necessary, not only from a societal point of view, but also to avoid individual suffering in this high-risk group of youngsters.

During the study period in question, a total of 820 patients were treated due to firearm injuries. Data on criminality and morbidity in this group have been reported.[1,2]

REFERENCES

1. PONZER, S., B. BERGMAN & B. BRISMAR. 1995. J. Trauma **38:** 845–850.
2. PONZER, S., B. BERGMAN & B. BRISMAR. 1996. J. Public Health. **110:** 41–46.

Peer Perceptions of Aggression and Bullying Behavior in Primary Schools in Northern Ireland

KATRINA COLLINS[a] AND ROB BELL

School of Psychology
The Queen's University of Belfast
Keir Building, Malone Road
Belfast, BT7 1NN, Northern Ireland

INTRODUCTION

Research into bullying behavior in schools has increased over the last 10 years, with considerable bullying being reported by schoolchildren in Scandinavia, and in Britain, Ireland, Australia, Japan, and the United States. Methodology originating from pioneering work in Scandinavia[1] has been modified and used in Britain and Ireland. The Olweus Bullying Questionnaire[2] is a self-report measure that identifies children involved and the frequency of involvement. However, Ahmad and Smith[3] found the combination of self-reports and peer nominations to be the best method of identifying bully-victim problems in schools.

The Olweus Questionnaire was used in this study. The social reputation of children was also measured using the Revised Class Play (RCP) method.[4] Peer nominations for sociability-leadership, aggressive-disruptive, and sensitive-isolated characteristics were calculated, and the social reputation scores of children identified as bullies, victims, bully-victims, and noninvolved were compared. The behavioral descriptions that children were nominated for may provide information about the characteristics associated with certain groups. The characteristics examined in the present study may add to the existing evidence on the behavioral traits of bullies, victims, and noninvolved children.[5] The Self-Perception Profile for Children[6] has been used extensively to examine how bullying and victimization effects self-esteem.[7] The Harter Scale was used in this study to examine the effect of involvement or noninvolvement in the bullying situation. Differences between the groups were discussed.

METHOD

One hundred eighteen (58 boys and 60 girls) children, 8–10 years old from three primary schools in Belfast, were administered the Olweus Questionnaire, the RCP test, and the Self-Perception Profile for Children in groups at different times.

RESULTS

Twenty-four percent (18% boys and 6% girls) of 118 school children were identified as bullies. A significant positive relationship was found between self-

[a] Tel: 44 1232 245133 ext. 5445; fax: 44 1232 664144; e-mail: psychology@qub.ac.uk.

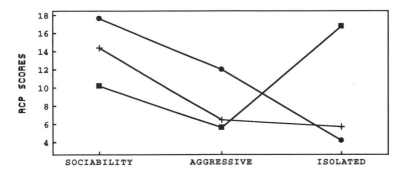

FIGURE 1. Graph showing interaction between status on the bullying questionnaire and scores on RCP. ●—●, bully; ■—■, victim; +—+, noninvolved.

reported aggression on the Olweus Questionnaire and peer nominations given to bullies of aggressive-disruptive behavior on the RCP test ($r = .4223$). ANOVA also revealed a significant interaction between these scores; $F(7.015) = .0000$, $p < 0.05$ (FIG. 1). Bullies scored higher on all categories of the Harter Scale except on behavioral conduct self-competence (FIG. 2).

CONCLUSIONS

The number of bully-victim problems found in this study highlights the need for more research into the extent of bullying in schools throughout Northern Ireland. Few studies to date have examined this issue. Peer nominations on the RCP test found that bullies had the highest sociability-leadership score, a high aggressive-disruptive score, with lowest scores for sensitive-isolated traits. Peer awareness and sensitivity of school situations may provide invaluable information about how bullies and victims are perceived within the group and how that status affects social reputation and feelings about themselves. Victims in this study had

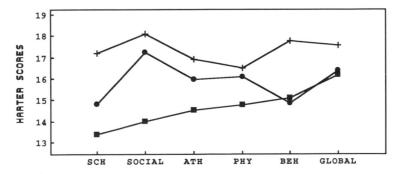

FIGURE 2. Graph showing interaction between status and scores on the Harter Scale. For symbols, see FIG. 1. SCH, scholastic; ATH, athletic; PHY, physical; BEH, behavioral.

low levels of self-esteem on all categories of the Harter Scale. Bullies displayed a pattern similar to children identified as noninvolved but scored lowest on the behavioral conduct category. They may be aware of their behavioral improprieties but are unable to change their behavior or attribute it to external sources, for example, provocative peers. The stability of patterns found in this study will be addressed longitudinally over the next year.

REFERENCES

1. OLWENS, D. 1978. Aggression in the Schools: Bullies and Whipping Boys. John Wiley (Hemisphere Press). Washington.
2. OLWEUS, D. 1989. The Bullying Questionnaire. Bergen University.
3. AHMAD, Y. & P. K. SMITH. 1990. Behavioural measures: Bullying in schools. Newsl. Assoc. Child Psychol. Psychiatry 12: 26–27.
4. MASTEN, A. S., P. MORISON & D. S. PELLEGRINI. 1985. A revised class play method of peer assessment. Dev. Psychol. 21(3): 523–533.
5. BESAG, V. 1989. Bullies and Victims. Open University Press. Milton Keynes.
6. HARTER, S. 1985. Manual for the Self-perception Profile for Children. University of Denver. Denver, CO.
7. BOULTON, M. J. & P. K. SMITH. 1994. Bully/victim problems in middle-school children: Stability, self-perceived competence, peer perceptions and peer acceptance. Br. J. Dev. Psychol. 12: 315–329.

Effects of Serotonergic$_{1A}$ and $_{1B}$ Agonists in Androgenic versus Estrogenic Systems for Aggression[a]

A. COLOGER-CLIFFORD, S. A. SMOLUK,
AND N. G. SIMON[b]

Department of Biological Sciences
Lehigh University
Bethlehem, Pennsylvania 18015

Mixed serotonergic$_{1A}$ and $_{1B}$ agonists reduce offensive aggression in male rodents without producing sedating effects.[1] The specificity of these drugs suggest that 5-HT$_{1A}$ and 5-HT$_{1B}$ receptors are involved in the regulation of intermale aggression. However, the relative contribution of each receptor to the attenuation of aggression and the neuroanatomical localization of the effects are not well understood. In addition, testosterone-induced aggression in mice can be regulated by either an estrogen-sensitive or an androgen-sensitive system, with the functional pathway determined by genotype.[2] Therefore, serotonergics are acting in the presence of either an estrogen-mediated or an androgen-mediated regulatory pathway.

The present study examined whether the ability of 5-HT$_{1A}$ (8-OH-DPAT), 5-HT$_{1B}$ (CGS12066B), or combined 5-HT$_{1A/1B}$ treatments to decrease the display of aggression was modulated by specific androgenic or estrogenic stimulation of gonadectomized male mice. In addition, a preliminary microinjection study examined the behavioral effects of these serotonergic agents after administration into the medial preoptic area in the presence of androgen or estrogen.

Gonadectomized CF-1 male mice were housed in groups of 4–5 and screened for aggression against an olfactory bulbectomized male intruder. Nonfighters were subcutaneously implanted with either DES (estrogen), DHT or R1881 (nonaromatizeable androgens), or TP (an aromatizeable androgen stimulating estrogenic and androgenic systems). Two weeks later, they were individually housed with a female and screened again. Males that showed at least five biting attacks were randomly assigned to experimental treatments. During drug testing, females were removed from the home cage, and a bulbectomized male was introduced. The frequency of the following behaviors were scored for 10 minutes: (1) biting attacks, lateral threats, and tail rattling (combined to provide a composite aggression score), and (2) locomotion and rearing (composite motor behavior score).

Systemic drug effects (see Fig. 1) suggested that estrogen and androgen differentially affected the sensitivity of 5-HT$_{1A}$ and 5-HT$_{1B}$ receptors. In the presence of estrogens, only activation of 5-HT$_{1A}$ receptors by DPAT (1.0 mg/kg given alone or in combination with CGS, 4.0 mg/kg) reduced aggression, whereas CGS given alone had no effect. This is in contrast to drug effects produced in the presence

[a] This research was supported in part by the Harry F. Guggenheim Foundation and the National Institutes of Health, 2NGS.

[b] Address for correspondence: Department of Biological Sciences, Iacocca Hall 111, Lehigh University, Bethlehem, PA 18015. Tel: (610) 758-3680; fax: (610) 758-4004; e-mail: ngs0@lehigh.edu.

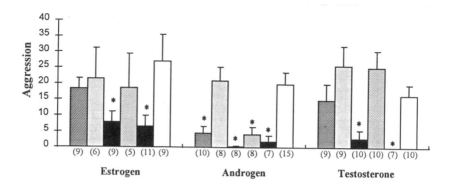

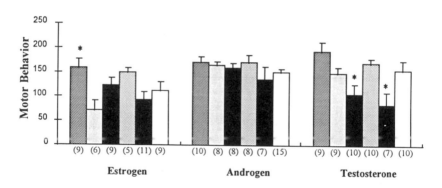

Steroid System

FIGURE 1. Effects of 5-HT$_{1A}$ (8-OH-DPAT) and 5-HT$_{1B}$ (CGS12066B) agonists on aggression and motor behavior in CF-1 male mice treated with either DES (estrogen), DHT or R1881 (androgen), or TP (estrogen and androgen). Data for aggression are expressed as the mean frequency of (biting attacks and lateral threats and tail rattling) ± SE$_m$. Data for motor behavior are expressed as the mean frequency of (locomotion and rearing) ± SE$_m$. The number of mice for each condition are shown in parentheses. *Significantly different from saline (p <0.05).

of androgens, where 5-HT$_{1A}$, 5-HT$_{1B}$, or combined 5-HT$_{1A/1B}$ activation reduced aggression. These drug effects were specific to aggression because they were not accompanied by changes in motor behavior. However, when both androgens and estrogens were present, only DPAT reduced aggression, along with a reduction in motor behavior. This nonspecific effect suggests that combined androgenic and estrogenic stimulation alters the sensitivity of 5-HT$_{1A}$ receptors, perhaps in regions involved in motor function. The lack of 5-HT$_{1B}$ agonist effect in the combined

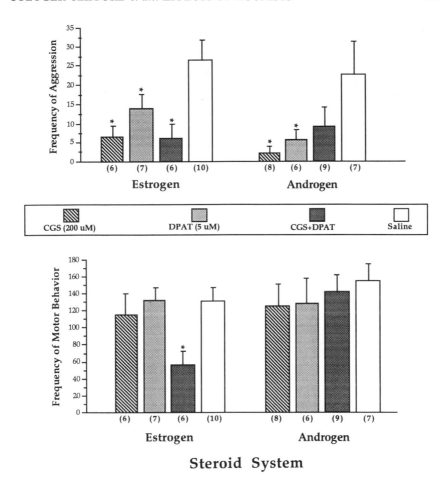

FIGURE 2. Effects of microinjections of 5-HT$_{1A}$ (8-OH-DPAT) and 5-HT$_{1B}$ (CGS12066B) agonists into the MPO of CF-1 male mice treated with either DES (estrogen) or DHT (androgen). Data for aggression are expressed as the mean frequency of (biting attacks and lateral threats and tail rattling) $\pm$ SE$_m$. Data for motor behavior are expressed as the mean frequency of (locomotion and rearing) $\pm$ SE$_m$. The number of mice for each condition are shown in parentheses. *Significantly different from saline (p <0.05).

steroid system suggests that estrogenic action and/or housing conditions may affect 5-HT$_{1B}$ receptor sensitivity.

Medial preoptic area (MPO) microinjections of CGS (200 μM) and DPAT (5 μM) in estrogen- and androgen-treated males significantly reduced aggressive behaviors without affecting motor behavior. This suggests that the MPO is an active site for the regulation of offensive aggression (see Fig. 2).

The discrepancy between systemic and microinjection effects of CGS in the presence of estrogens suggests that other brain regions may contribute to the expression of aggressive behaviors. We are currently exploring serotonergic effects in the regulation of steroid-mediated aggression in different regions of the mouse brain.

REFERENCES

1. OLIVIER, B., J. MOS, M. RAGHOEBAR, P. DE KONING & M. MAK. 1994. Prog. Drug Res. **42:** 167–308.
2. SIMON, N. G., S. F. LU, S. E. MCKENNA, X. CHEN & A. C. CLIFFORD. 1993. *In* The Development of Sex Differences and Similarities in Behavior. M. Haug *et al.*, Eds.: 389–403. Kluwer Academic Publishers. the Netherlands.

Attachment and Aggression among Children of the Working Poor[a]

JOHN N. CONSTANTINO[b]

Departments of Psychiatry and Pediatrics
Washington University School of Medicine
Saint Louis, Missouri

Across studies in a variety of environmental settings, secure attachment relationships appear to protect impoverished children who are at risk from deviant outcome in the hostile-aggressive domain.[1,2] A recently established measure of parents' mental representations of their own early attachment relationships, the Adult Attachment Interview (AAI),[3,4] yields adult attachment classifications that are analogous to the categories for infant attachment classification (as derived from the Ainsworth Strange Situation[5]) and predicts the four-category classification of the attachment relationship that is obtained when that parent and his or her child are observed in the Strange Situation (SS). This holds true when the two measures are done concordantly,[6] when the AAI is done five years after the SS,[7] and when the AAI is performed prenatally and correlated with SS classifications at one year of age.[8–10] There has been only one previous study correlating parents' AAI classifications with behavior problems in their children;[11] it showed that 90% of mothers of young children referred to a child psychiatric clinic were classified as "insecure" on the AAI, compared to 58% in a middle-class control group of children in two-parent families. The present study is the first to correlate behavioral profiles of impoverished children of single working parents with their parents' classifications on the AAI.

Maternal AAIs of 10 abnormally aggressive preschoolers (mean externalizing T-score on the Child Behavior Checklist (CBCL) = 76) from two low-income day care centers were compared with those of 10 age-, race-, sex-, and center-matched controls (mean externalizing T-score = 45). Children were excluded from the study if they had ever had any caregiver (other than their single mothers) with whom they had spent more than 20 hours per week for a period of more than one year. All of the children were enrolled in full-time care at the time of the study; none of the children had been enrolled in their current day care center before the age of 18 months, and both day care centers move children to new classrooms with new teachers on a yearly basis. The results are shown in FIGURE 1: all aggressive children had parents classified as insecure on the AAI; parents of all but one of the controls were classified as secure on the AAI (p <.001). Videotaped observations of parents and their children in free-play sessions demonstrated maternal-child relationship qualities that supported the AAI classifications. Relevant sample characteristics are summarized in TABLE 1: family income, disciplinary practices, parents' histories of abuse, and time in day care did not distinguish the two groups.

[a] This work was supported by a Grant from the Johann Jacobs Foundation.

[b] Address for correspondence: John N. Constantino, M.D., Department of Psychiatry, Washington University School of Medicine, 4940 Children's Place, Saint Louis, Missouri 63110. Tel: (314) 362-9430; fax: (314) 362-4294 (attention: John Constantino); e-mail: johnc @sironald.wustl.edu.

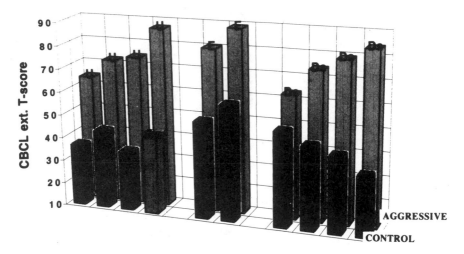

FIGURE 1. CBCL externalizing scores and maternal AAI classifications of matched pairs of subjects. ■, Secure (autonomous); ▣, insecure, U: insecure-unresolved; E: insecure-entangled/preoccupied; Ds: insecure-dismissing.

A single secure attachment relationship may be one component of what Scarr[12] and others have referred to as a "good enough" rearing environment for children to express their genetic potential for normal social development. The presence or absence of such a relationship in early childhood may be an important factor in the transmission or discontinuation of intergenerational patterns of antisocial behavior (the "cycle of violence"). The AAI may be a useful intergenerational predictor of antisocial and resilient outcome among children whose single parents are their only resource for long-standing attachment relationships. Further studies are needed to determine whether specific interventions that have been shown to enhance the quality of attachment relationships between infants and their parents[13] might serve to prevent antisocial development. Alternatively, the provision of an

TABLE 1. Selected Sample Characteristics

	Aggressive Subjects	Controls
*Mean Internalizing T-score on CBCL	64.7 ± 18.4	45.7 ± 7.4
Family income ($/yr)	17,200 ± 6350	19,200 ± 3419
Number of siblings	1.6 ± 0.7	0.7 ± .9
Years of maternal education	13 ± 1.5	12.8 ± 1.2
Number of first and second degree relatives with antisocial disorder	2.0 ± 1.7	3.1 ± 2.4
Percent of parents abused in their childhood	30%	40%
Percent of children abused by caregivers other than mother	20%	20%
Pregnancy with subject unplanned	80%	80%
Months enrolled in current day care center	20.3 ± 11	22.0 ± 14

* p < .005

emotionally available caregiver other than the parent (*e.g.*, a day care provider) who maintains regular contact with the child in the caregiving context and thereby represents an attachment resource for some critical early period (perhaps longer than the conventional one-year school term that has been adopted by most day care centers) could be tested as an early intervention to prevent antisocial development.

REFERENCES

1. LYONS-RUTH, K., L. ALPERN & B. REPACHOLI. 1993. Child Dev. **64:** 572–585.
2. CONSTANTINO, J. N. 1995. Harv. Rev. Psychiatry **2:** 259–273.
3. MAIN, M., N. KAPLAN & J. CASSIDY. 1985. Monogr. Soc. Res. Child Dev. **50:** 66–106.
4. BAKERMANS-KRANENBURG, M. J. & M. H. VAN IJZENDOORN. 1993. Dev. Psychol. **29:** 870–879.
5. AINSWORTH, M. D. S., M. C. BLEHAR & E. WATERS. 1978. Patterns of Attachment: A Psychological Study of the Strange Situation. Erlbaum. Hillsdale, NJ.
6. ZEANAH, C. H., D. BENOIT, M. BARTON, C. REGAN, L. M. HIRSHBERG & L. P. LIPSITT. 1995. J. Am. Acad. Child. Adolesc. Psychiatry **32:** 278–286.
7. HINDE, R. A. & J. STEVENSON-HINDE, Eds. 1988. Relations within Families. Oxford University press. Oxford.
8. FONAGY, P., H. STEELE & M. STEELE. 1991. Child Dev. **62:** 891–905.
9. BENOIT, D. & K. C. H. PARKER. 1994. Child Dev. **65:** 1444–1456.
10. WARD, M. J. & E. A. CARLSON. 1995. Child Dev. **66:** 69–75.
11. CROWELL, J. & S. FELDMAN. 1988. Child Dev. **59:** 1273–1285.
12. SCARR, S. 1992. Child Dev. **63:** 1–19.
13. VAN DEN BOOM, D. C. 1994. Child Dev. **65:** 1457–1477.

Aggression, Attachment, and Depression among School-age Children at High Social Risk

M. ANN EASTERBROOKS[a] AND GRETCHEN BIESECKER

Eliot-Pearson Department of Child Development
Tufts University
105 College Avenue
Medford, Massachusetts 02155

Support was provided for the hypothesized relations between (1) aggression and attachment, and (2) aggression and depression. Children who exhibited insecure attachment behavior and representations, particularly the D insecure controlling classification, were reported to exhibit more aggressive behavior at home and school. Children with other attachment patterns (A, insecure avoidant; B, secure; C, insecure ambivalent) displayed less aggressive behavior (FIGURES 1 and 2).

It is suggested that attachment relationships are one vehicle through which children form internal working models of the self, relationships, and the world. These representations then guide how children approach their world, regulate their own behavior and emotions, as well as the manner in which they interpret others' behavior. Children with insecure controlling attachment representations, in particular, may represent the world as hostile and adopt aggressive behavior as a regulatory strategy.

In addition to links with attachment, depressive symptomatology was greater among aggressive children and their mothers. Children's self-reports of depression (self-blame, low energy, negative mood, low self-worth) were correlated with mothers' reports ($r = .33$) and teachers' reports of child aggression ($r = .46$). Maternal depressive symptomatology also was associated with aggressive behavior ($r = .34$ both mother and teacher report). Further, aggressive children were reported by their mothers and teachers to also exhibit more internalizing difficulties ($r = .64$ mother, .59 teacher), less happiness ($r = -.58$), less learning ($r = -.38$), and poorer performance ($r = -.36$) in school. In this sample, aggressive behavior problems were not related to the family structure (presence of father in home), but a composite measure of psychosocial environmental risk (indexing income, legal problems, child maltreatment reports, and school difficulties) was related to mother- and teacher-reported aggression.

According to ethological attachment theory,[1] one of the functions of secure child-mother attachment bonds is the facilitation of emotional and behavioral regulation. Children with secure attachments are confident that their caregivers will be sensitively responsive; this is reflected in their behavioral orientation toward the world. In some children with conduct disorder, the attachment system fails to provide the structure for behavioral regulation. The purpose of the present study was to examine the relation between aggression, attachment, and depression

[a] Tel: (617) 627-3355; fax: (617) 627-3503; e-mail: aeasterb@pearl.tufts.edu.

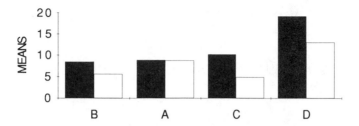

FIGURE 1. Separation anxiety test classifications. ■, Mother CBCL; aggression, time 1 (T1). □, Teacher CBCL; aggression, T1.

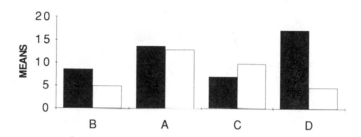

FIGURE 2. Reunion classification, T1. (See FIG. 1 for definition of symbols.)

in a sample of 45 school-age children at high social risk due to poverty and caregiving difficulties.

At ages 7 and 8, two techniques were used to assess attachment in a laboratory playroom: (a) child reunion behavior following an hour-long separation from mother,[2] and (b) assessment of attachment representations, using the Separation Anxiety Test,[3] a technique that elicits verbal representations in response to pictured separation situations. Aggressive behavior was assessed through mothers' and teachers' reports on the Child Behavior Checklist (CBCL).[4] Child depressive symptomatology was evaluated using the Dimensions of Depression Profile;[5] maternal depression was indexed using the Center for Epidemiological Studies Depression Scale.[6]

REFERENCES

1. BOWLBY, J. 1969. Attachment. Basic Books. New York.
2. MAIN, M. & J. CASSIDY. 1987. Classification of attachment in 5- to 7-year olds. Unpublished manual. University of California, Berkeley.
3. KLAGSBRUN, M. & J. BOWLBY. 1976. Responses to separation from parents: A clinical test for young children. Br. J. Projective Psychol. **21:** 7–21.
4. ACHENBACH, T. 1991. Manual for the Child Behavior Checklist/4-18 and 1991 Profile. University of Vermont Department of Psychiatry. Burlington, VT.
5. HARTER, S. & M. NOWAKOWSKI. 1987. The Dimensions of Depression Profile for Children and Adolescents. Unpublished manual. University of Denver. Denver, CO.
6. RADLOFF, M. 1977. The CES-D scale: A self-report depression scale for research in the general population. Appl. Psychol. Meas. **3:** 385–401.

Adolescent Stress Alters Ethanol Ingestion and Agonistic Behavior in the Male Golden Hamster

CRAIG F. FERRIS[a] AND JUDE BREWER

Program in Neuropsychiatric Sciences
Department of Psychiatry
University of Massachusetts Medical Center
55 Lake Avenue North
Worcester, Massachusetts 01655

INTRODUCTION

Exposure to ethanol (ETOH) can affect aggressive responding in many species.[1,2] One species, golden hamsters (*Mesocricetus auratus*), are a good animal to study because they readily ingest ETOH[3,4] and routinely show robust fighting behavior in different laboratory settings.[5,6] In a previous study, Brewer *et al.*[7] characterized the voluntary ingestion of ETOH in adolescent male golden hamsters. It was observed that when allowed a free choice, adolescent hamsters readily drank ETOH and drank in bouts that occurred primarily during the dark phase of the L : D cycle. The blood ETOH concentration in hamsters voluntarily ingesting ethanol was 20 ± mg/dL and ranged between 9 and 57 mg/dL. When tested for agonistic behavior as young adults, animals exposed to ETOH during adolescence were no more or less aggressive than controls. The present studies were performed to test the notion that stress can alter ETOH ingestion during adolescence and affect agonistic behavior in early adulthood.

In the wild, hamsters wean around postnatal day 25 (P-25), leave the home nest, forage on their own, establish nest sites, and defend their territory.[8] Hamsters begin to establish dominance hierarchies as early as P-35 and have a minimal breeding age of 42 days.[8,9] Androgen levels start to rise dramatically between P-28 and P-35.[9] Thus, between P-25 and P-42, hamsters achieve independence from the maternal nest, double their weight and size, reach full sexual maturity and reproductive competence, and establish social relationships. For our purposes, this period is defined as adolescence in this species.

RESULTS

Does stress affect ETOH ingestion during adolescence? Shown in FIGURE 1 are data on the daily voluntary intake of 30% ETOH in adolescent male hamsters subjected to shock (n = 9) or isolation (n = 9) stress. Starting on P-22, hamsters were individually housed and allowed free access to a 30% ETOH solution in addition to water and standard laboratory chow provided *ad libitum*. Starting on

[a] Tel: (508) 856-5530; fax: (508) 856-6426; e-mail: craig.ferris@banyan.ummed.edu.

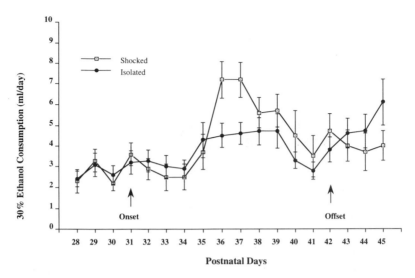

FIGURE 1. Altered ETOH ingestion during adolescence in response to the stress of electrical shock or isolation in a novel environment. Vertical lines denote SEM.

P-31 (onset), animals were subjected to daily 10-min episodes of isolation stress or shock stress for eleven consecutive days (offset). Shock consisted of eight unpredictable/uncontrollable 0.15 mA pulses/min in a shock box. Animals subjected to isolation were placed into a novel clean cage each day. The pattern of drinking was significantly different across days and between conditions ($p < .001$). Vertical bars denote SEM.

Does stress and ETOH in adolescence affect agonistic behavior in early adulthood? Shown in FIGURE 2 are data on agonistic behavior collected on P-45 from four different groups of hamsters subjected to different treatments (see legend) during adolescence. On the day of testing, a smaller, younger male hamster was placed into the home cage of the experimental animal. The resident was scored for latency to bite, total bites, and total contact time toward the intruder over a 10-min test period. Six out of nine animals tested from the ETOH plus shock group bit their intruder, whereas no more than three such incidents occurred in any of the other three groups. Although there was a trend toward higher aggression scores for animals exposed to ETOH and shock stress during adolescence, due to the high variance, these data were not significantly different from the other groups. Conversely, there was a trend toward low aggression in animals presented with water and shock during adolescence. In fact, only one out of eight animals in this group bit the intruder. In many of the cases, animals with shock stress alone were timid and avoided the intruder, as noted by the significantly ($p < 0.006$) less time spent in contact with the intruder.

SUMMARY

These data suggest that shock stress during adolescence increases ETOH consumption and may contribute to an increase in aggression in early adulthood.

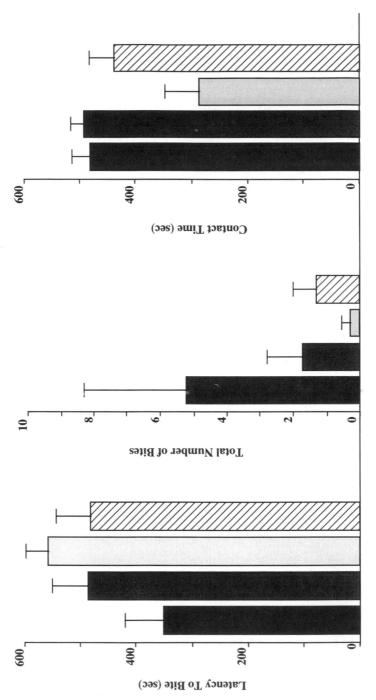

FIGURE 2. Aggressive behaviors towards intruders. Animals with a history of adolescent stress and ETOH ingestion show altered aggressive behavior as young adults. Vertical lines denote SEM. ■, EtOH + shock; ■, EtOH + isolation; □, water + shock; ◨, water + isolation.

Interestingly, shock stress without ETOH results in timid behavior in early adulthood. One might speculate that adolescent hamsters "self-medicate" to deal with continuous stress. However, because of the variability between experimental groups, it is necessary to replicate these studies with larger numbers of animals and expand the findings to include blood ETOH concentrations.

REFERENCES

1. MICZEK, K. A., J. T. WINSLOW & J. F. DEBOLD. 1984. Heightened aggressive behavior by animals interacting with alcohol-treated conspecifics: Studies with mice, rats and squirrel monkeys. Pharmacol. Biochem. Behav. **20:** 349–353.
2. EVERILL, B. & M. S. BERRY. 1987. Effects of ethanol on aggression in three inbred strains of mice. Physiol. & Behav. **39**(1): 45–51.
3. ARVOLA, A. & O. FORSANDER. 1961. Comparison between water and alcohol consumption in six animal species in free-choice experiments. Nature **4790:** 819–820.
4. McCOY, G. D., A. D. HAISLEY, P. POWCHIK & P. C. TAMBONE. 1981. Ethanol consumption by Syrian golden hamsters. J. Stud. Alcohol **42**(5): 508–513.
5. FERRIS, C. F. & M. POTEGAL. 1988. Vasopressin receptor blockade in the anterior hypothalamus suppresses aggression in hamsters. Physiol. & Behav. **44:** 235–239.
6. POTEGAL, M. & C. F. FERRIS. 1990. Intraspecific aggression in male hamsters is inhibited by vasopressin receptor antagonists. Aggressive Behav. **15:** 311–320.
7. BREWER, J. A., R. C. McKENNA & C. F. FERRIS. 1996. Voluntary ingestion of ethanol in adolescent male golden hamsters. Physiol. & Behav. Consideration for publication following revision.
8. FESTING, M. F. W. 1972. Hamsters. *In* the UFAW Handbook on the Care and Management of Laboratory Animals. 4th edition. Universities Federation for Animal Welfare, Ed.: 242–256. Williams and Wilkens. Baltimore, MD.
9. VOMACHKA, A. J. & G. S. GREENWALD. 1979. The development of gonadotropin and steroid hormone patterns in male and female hamsters from birth to puberty. Endocrinology **105:** 960–966.

Cholesterol, Serotonin, and Behavior in Young Monkeys

M. BABETTE FONTENOT,[a,d] JAY R. KAPLAN,[a]
CAROL A. SHIVELY,[a] STEPHEN B. MANUCK,[b]
AND J. JOHN MANN[c]

[a]Department of Comparative Medicine
Bowman Gray School of Medicine of Wake Forest University
Medical Center Boulevard
Winston-Salem, North Carolina 27157-1040

[b]Department of Psychology
506 Old Engineering Hall
4015 O'Hara Street
University of Pittsburgh
Pittsburgh, Pennsylvania 15260

[c]Department of Neuroscience
New York State Psychiatric Institute
and Department of Psychiatry
Columbia Presbyterian Medical Center
722 West 168th Street
New York, New York 10032

Naturally low or clinically reduced plasma cholesterol concentrations are associated with increased mortality resulting from suicides and accidents.[1-5] Aggressive and suicidal behavior also has been associated with low central serotonergic activity.[6,7] We have found that low cholesterol intake and low plasma cholesterol concentrations are associated with low central serotonergic activity and with aggressive and antisocial behavior in adult male macaques.[8,9] The extent to which our findings can be generalized to females and across the life cycle is unknown. Therefore, we evaluated the effects of dietary cholesterol on behavior and monoaminergic activity in male and female juvenile monkeys consuming diets high in fat and either high or low in cholesterol.

The subjects were 17 *Macaca fascicularis* (TABLE 1) housed in two social groups corresponding to their dietary condition. At approximately eight months of age, after weaning, all animals consumed a diet relatively high in fat (40% of calories, with 12% saturated, 13% polyunsaturated, and 15% monounsaturated). Monkeys in the high-cholesterol condition consumed 0.08 mg cholesterol per kilocalorie, and monkeys were fed 0.03 mg cholesterol per kilocalorie in the low-cholesterol condition. After the animals had consumed the diet for approximately four months, the social behavior of each animal was observed for ten minutes twice per week using a focal sampling procedure.[10] On two occasions, ten weeks apart, after the animals had consumed the experimental diet for approximately six months, the animals were anesthetized with ketamine HCl (15 mg/kg im), and

[d] Tel: (910) 716-7045; fax: (910) 764-5818; e-mail: bfontenot@cpm.bgsm.edu.

TABLE 1. Characteristics of Animals[12]

	Low Cholesterol	High Cholesterol	p Value
Preexperimental Characteristics[a]			
Sex	4 M, 4 F	5 M, 4 F	NS
Age	250 (17)[b]	243 (17)	NS
Total plasma cholesterol (mg/dL)	211 (31)	238 (32)	NS
High-density lipoprotein cholesterol (mg/dL)	82 (11)	84 (9)	NS
Postexperimental characteristics[c]			
Total plasma cholesterol (mg/dL)	235 (23)	623 (34)	<0.001
High-density lipoprotein cholesterol (mg/dL)	58.8 (5.2)	27.6 (2.8)	<0.001
Weight (kg)	1.35 (0.08)	1.31 (0.08)	NS

[a] Comparisons, except for sex, by one-factor (diet condition$_{low,high}$) analysis of variance.
[b] Standard error in parentheses.
[c] All data were the mean of two samples. Analyses were by one-factor (diet condition$_{low,high}$) analysis of variance with repeated measures (sample$_{1,2}$). NS, not significant.

a 1–2 mL sample of cerebrospinal fluid (CSF) was obtained from the cisterna magna. Using previously described methods,[11] concentrations of CNS metabolites of serotonin (5-hydroxyindoleacetic acid [5-HIAA]), norepinephrine (3-methoxy-4-hydroxyphenylglycol [MHPG]), and dopamine (homovanillic acid [HVA]) were determined. One week later, the anesthetization procedure was repeated, and a 5.0 mL sample was taken by femoral venipuncture for determination of total plasma cholesterol and high-density lipoprotein cholesterol concentrations (TABLE 1).

The monkeys consuming the low-cholesterol diet were more aggressive, less social (p's < 0.01), and had lower CSF concentrations of the serotonergic metabolite 5-HIAA (p < 0.001) than did monkeys consuming high-cholesterol diets (FIG. 1).

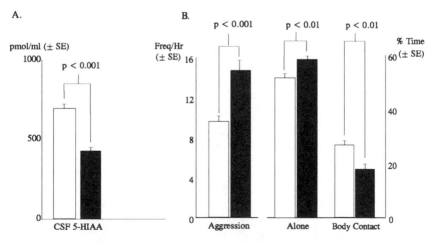

FIGURE 1. A: Effects of dietary cholesterol consumption on CSF 5-HIAA concentrations. **B:** Effects of dietary cholesterol consumption on aggressive, antisocial (time spent alone), and social (body contact) behavior. Open bars: high-cholesterol condition; black bars: low-cholesterol condition.[12]

These data provide evidence of an association among low-plasma cholesterol concentrations, reduced central serotonergic activity, and increased aggressive and antisocial behavior in juvenile monkeys. During this study, the young monkeys were at the age during which macaques typically learn to express appropriate aggressive behavior and engage in positive social interactions. These findings suggest that, in prepubertal monkeys, the patterning and frequency of aggression and the balance of prosocial to antisocial behavior may be altered by the level of dietary cholesterol.

REFERENCES

1. MULDOON, M. S. F., S. B. MANUCK & K. A. MATTHEWS. 1990. Br. Med. J. **301:** 309–314.
2. ENGLEBERG, H. 1992. Lancet **339:** 727–729.
3. SMITH, G. D. & J. PEKKANEN. 1992. Br. Med. J. **304:** 431–434.
4. LINDBERG, G., L. RÅSTAM, B. GULLBERG & G. A. EKLUND. 1992. Br. Med. J. **305:** 277–279.
5. MORGAN, R. E., L. A. PALINKAS, E. BARRETT-CONNOR & D. WINGARD. 1993. Lancet **341:** 75–79.
6. ROY, A., J. DEJONG & M. LINNOILA. 1989. Arch. Gen. Psychiatry **46:** 609–612.
7. VIRKKUNEN, M., J. DEJONG, J. BARTKO & M. LINNOILA. 1989. Arch. Gen. Psychiatry **46:** 604–606.
8. KAPLAN, J. R., S. B. MANUCK & C. A. SHIVELY. 1991. Psychosom. Med. **53:** 634–642.
9. MULDOON, M. F., J. R. KAPLAN, S. B. MANUCK & J. J. MANN. 1992. Biol. Psychiatry **31:** 739–742.
10. ALTMANN, J. 1974. Behaviour **49:** 221–226.
11. SCHEININ, M., W-H. CHANG, K. L. KIRK & M. LINNOILA. 1983. Anal. Biochem. **131:** 246–253.
12. KAPLAN, J. R., C. A. SHIVELY, M. B. FONTENOT, T. M. MORGAN, S. M. HOWELL, S. B. MANUCK, M. F. MULDOON & J. J. MANN. 1994. Psychosom. Med. **56:** 479–484.

Friendship Networks and Bullying in Schools

ARJA HUTTUNEN,[a] CHRISTINA SALMIVALLI,[b] AND
KIRSTI M. J. LAGERSPETZ[c]

Department of Psychology
University of Turku
Turku, Finland

INTRODUCTION

There are certain similarities among children who make friends, and stay friends. Gender, age, and race, for instance, are factors that have an effect in the formation of friendship networks.[1] Behavioral similarities between friends occur as well. For example, aggressive children tend to affiliate with aggressive peers. In addition, there is evidence that aggressive pupils have quantitatively bigger, but less intimate, friendship networks than nonaggressive ones.[2]

In the bullying process, children may act in several different ways: they may have a participant role of bully, victim, reinforcer, assistant, defender, or outsider.[3] The aim of this study was to find out whether children with similar behavioral tendencies, in regard to bullying, form friendship networks with each other. We also investigated whether children in different participant roles have quantitatively or qualitatively different friendship networks.

SUBJECTS AND METHOD

Subjects

The children taking part in the study were 459 sixth-grade children (218 girls, 241 boys) from 18 school classes in Finland. The mean class size was 25.5. The data were collected in the form of a questionnaire. The same pupils had participated in a larger research project of bullying in schools. On the basis of the previous data analyses in that project, we had certain background information about the subjects. The procedures to generate that information have been presented in detail elsewhere.[3,4]

Background Information about the Subjects

The pupils' scores on five subscales (bully, reinforcer, assistant, defender, and outsider scales), describing their peer-evaluated bullying-situation behavior, were available. On the basis of their scores on these scales, and a separate peer-nomination procedure to identify the victims, participant roles of bully, victim,

[a] Tel: (+) 358-21-250 5449; fax: (+) 358-21-333 5060.
[b] Tel: (+) 358-21-333 5423; fax: (+) 358-21-333 5060; e-mail: tiina.salmivalli@ra.abo.fi.
[c] Tel: (+) 358-21-333 5421; fax: (+) 358-21-333 5060; e-mail: kirsti.lagerspetz@utu.fi.

reinforcer, assistant, defender, and outsider had been assigned to the subjects. In addition, we knew the most liked classmate of each subject.

Defining the Friendship Networks

The pupils were asked to draw a social map of their class, in which they indicated friendship groups. From these drawings, we constructed matrices for further analyses. A child was considered to belong in the same friendship network with another child if at least 30% of the same-sex classmates had mentioned them in the same group.

Behavior of the Friendship Network Members

For each child, we counted indexes to indicate how many of his/her friends (*i.e.*, the members in his/her network) were engaged in bullying, reinforcing the bully, assisting the bully, defending the victim, and staying outside the bullying situations. These indexes were simply the means of the scores of the child's friendship network members on the corresponding scales.

Mutuality of Friendships

A child was considered to have a friendship relation with mutual liking if his/her "first choice" (the classmate he/she liked the most) had reciprocally chosen the child as his/her most-liked classmate.

RESULTS

Behavior of the Child and His/Her Network Members

The correlations between individual children's scores on the bully, reinforcer, assistant, defender, and outsider scales, and the corresponding friendship network behavioral indexes can be seen in TABLE 1. The similarities between a child's and his/her network members' behavior are evident.

Quantitative Differences in Friendship Networks

There were significant differences between the sizes of the friendship networks of children in different participant roles (F(5) = 11.67, p < .0001). Assistants, reinforcers, and bullies had the largest networks, whereas the networks of outsiders, defenders, and victims were smaller. The friendship networks of the girls were smaller than those of the boys (FIG. 1).

Qualitative Differences in Friendship Networks

Mutuality was assumed to be one aspect distinguishing qualitatively different relationships from each other. However, the most striking differences in this

TABLE 1. Correlations between Individual Children's Scores on the Bully, Reinforcer, Assistant, Defender, and Outsider Scales, and the Corresponding Friendship Network Behavioral Indexes

		Behavior of the Friendship Network Members			
	Bullying	Reinforcing Bully	Assisting Bully	Defending Victim	Staying Outside
Behavior of individual child					
Bullying	.51***	.50***	.36***	−.29***	−.29***
Reinforcing bully	.60***	.74***	.53***	−.44***	−.45***
Assisting bully	.59***	.62***	.46***	−.36***	−.37***
Defending victim	−.36***	−.45***	−.41***	.73***	.43***
Staying outside	−.53***	−.67***	−.57***	.47***	.65***

*** = p < .001.

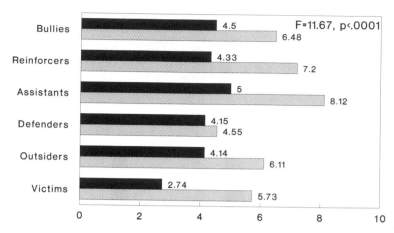

FIGURE 1. Mean sizes of the friendship networks of children in different participant roles. ■ , girls; ▨, boys.

respect occurred between the sexes, not between the children with different behavioral tendencies. Girls' friendships ("like most" choices) were significantly more often reciprocal than those of the boys ($\chi^2(1) = 16.10$, p < .0001). The majority of girls, in all participant roles, had a relationship with mutual liking, except the girl victims: 64% of them did not have this kind of relationship. The boys, however, usually did not have a reciprocal relationship with mutual liking. This was true for boys in all participant roles, with the only exception of the boys in the role of defender: 62.5% of them did have a reciprocal friendship relation.

CONCLUSIONS

Children with similar behavioral tendencies with regard to bullying formed friendship networks with each other. Behavior in bullying situations can thus be said to be one feature around which the friendship networks in a school class are organized. This can be explained referring both to selection and socialization effects. For instance, a child who bullies others joins other children who do the same, or who reinforce his/her behavior. Once this kind of subgroup is formed, the members further socialize each other in the same direction.

Children with tendencies toward bullying behavior, either as bullies, reinforcers, or assistants, had larger friendship networks (in fact, they can be assumed to form these networks with each other) than more prosocial children (defenders and outsiders). Also the victims' friendship networks were relatively small (or they did not belong to a friendship network at all).

Many girl victims seemed to lack the intimate, reciprocal friendship relationship usually typical for girls of this age. Interestingly, the boys who took sides with the victim (defenders) often did have a reciprocal relationship, which was not so typical among the boys in general.

REFERENCES

1. HARTUP, W. 1992. Friendships and their developmental significance. *In* Childhood Social Development: Contemporary Perspectives. H. McGurk, Ed. Lawrence Erlbaum. Hillsdale, NJ.
2. CAIRNS, R., B. CAIRNS, H. NECKERMAN, S. GEST & J-L. GARIEPY. 1988. Social networks and aggressive behavior: Peer support or peer rejection? Dev. Psychol. **24:** 815–823.
3. SALMIVALLI, C., K. M. J. LAGERSPETZ, K. BJÖRKQVIST, K. ÖSTERMAN & A. KAUKIAINEN. 1996. Bullying as a group process: Participant roles and their relations to social status within the group. Aggressive Behav. **22:** 1–15.
4. SALMIVALLI, C., J. KARHUNEN & K. M. J. LAGERSPETZ. 1996. How do the victims respond to bullying? Aggressive Behav. **22:** 99–109.

Suggested Theoretical Model for Interventions to Stop Group-based or Group-motivated Adolescent Aggressive Behavior

KEN JACOBSON[a]

Department of Anthropology
Brandeis University
Waltham, Massachusetts 02154

Franz Boas, credited as being the father of modern American anthropology observed:

> The reaction of a member of a society to the outer world may be twofold. He may act as a member of a crowd, in which case his activities are immediately determined by imitation of the activities of his fellows; or he may act as an individual; then the influence of the society of which he is a member will make itself felt by the habits of action and thought of the individual.[1]

There is an extensive literature that suggests that aggressive behavior in children is as much group behavior, or at least group-motivated behavior, as behavior motivated by individual predispositions (although those predispositions certainly may be present).[2]

Emile Durkheim (whose seminal insights inspired both sociology and anthropology) argued that social problems require social solutions. I am arguing that youthful aggression is mostly group behavior (*i.e.*, social). Accordingly, interventions may need to be aimed, where practical, at the motivating groups, as well as at "aggressive" individuals, especially because groups tend to continue to exist regardless of the individual members. Some groups are reproducing organisms. It is clear that trivializing an individual's problem with long-term drug therapy or incarceration predictably will not stop the undesired behavior: others continue it. However, not all groups are well-ordered street gangs. In those cases, interventions may need to be more structural in nature.

Further, those groups may well view their "aggression" as, at worst, defensive. Animal studies have documented the distinction between defensive and offensive aggression.[3] Although it is comfortable to think of human aggressive behavior as more cognitive or willed than animal behavior, that distinction is problematic.[b] It

---

[a] Tel: (617) 277-0684; fax (617) 277-5268.

[b] The concept of "sham rage" may be useful here. A cat whose forebrain is severed will express rage but be unable to attack.[5] Clearly, then, aggression does have a cognitive component. Just as importantly, the triggering mechanism is in the limbic system. This architectural structuring makes survival sense. Too much "thinking" might result in a dead cat (or human), and survival is, for most people, the ultimate motivator. Accordingly, defensive aggression is socially acceptable. It is possible, therefore, that the prefrontal lobes in humans act more to direct effective aggression (or effective flight) than to decide whether to fight or flee, although culture might program the degree of response. For example, if culture mediates rage, some groups might sustain rage longer, which might partially explain why groups of people slaughter other groups of people.

has been shown that hormonal cascades can result in either fight or flight in humans. However, a marker has yet to be found that definitively labels fight from flight behavior, and the exact biochemical triggering device has not been found.[4,c]

I suggest that those cascades are not self-triggering. The triggering mechanisms may very well be a perceived environmental condition, which I am arguing will be culturally mediated. That is, if an individual reacts to a person (or to a group or to a situation) as threatening, the nature of that reaction is probably influenced by that individual's society/culture (or subsociety/subculture).

This is not to imply that a model that might accurately predict an individual's aggressive tendencies would be unilinear. Individual aggressive behavior probably varies depending on circumstances, not the least of which is whether or not the individual is in a group, and especially who is in that particular group.[2]

I would argue that both individual and group behaviors are probabilistic.[d] Statistics, therefore, should map the probabilities of various behavior possibilities. Statistics that speak of mean behaviors may be less useful and may chart behaviors that never actually occur. Further, correlations of statistical behavioral findings require a hypothesis that explains underlying casual mechanisms.[6] In the case of

---

Even though all organisms must act within the parameters of their biological capacities, those capacities are so plastic that extreme variability is seen. Group behavior is, likewise, plastic, and plasticity can work in two directions. Either we may see different groups react differently to similar stimuli, or we may, as Boas suggested, see similar group behaviors in reaction to entirely different stimuli. Is there a limit to plasticity, however? More research is needed on the social/cultural and biological mechanisms by which survival anxiety leads to terror and terror to either uncontrolled rage or panic: Are there limits to social control? What is the role of the prefrontal lobes when an individual is experiencing rage or panic? At what point does survival anxiety become self-destructive? Does the individual perceive their behavior as self-destructive?

[c] Further, it has not been shown that, except for very rare mutations, any sizable population of humans is more genetically prone to aggression (or passivity) than any other sizable population.

[d] The term "norm" is widely used in the literature. Norms are theoretical concepts imputed from behavior. Classically, norms represent rules or expectations within a particular group that lead to individual statuses (rights and obligations) and roles (ways of behaving). It may be that norms are probabilistic: that they represent ranges of acceptable behaviors; that those ranges are not fixed but vary with ecological conditions; that where an individual falls in the range of any particular time (that is how a role is acted) may vary with circumstances and with whom the individual is in contact. If this view is correct, some normalized behaviors will be more radical than others; aggression to the extent it is socially/culturally mediated will then be probabilistic. Some aggressive behavior, although still within the group's acceptable range for defensive aggression, may be perceived by those outside the group as inappropriately aggressive.

It is in this process of trying to distinguish the probabilities of particular actions from among the range of acceptable actions that a chemical marker would be particularly useful. If our prediction is that a group of people will perceive and react to particular environmental conditions (e.g., fight or flight) in a similar way, then a chemical marker would allow an experimental test of the hypothesis. All similarly encultured people should release the same chemical under the same conditions. Our further prediction would be that relative quantities of marker produced (controlling for individual physiological differences) would vary with individuals within a probabilistic range. So one group should show a marker, although another group does not; but the quantity of marker in individuals would vary within normalized ranges.

a child's aggressive behavior, that hypothesis should explain the child's perceptions at the time of the behavior.

Ethnocentricity, a pejorative concept, judgmentally imposes one set of cultural values on another. If most aggressive behavior is culturally mediated, it is ethnocentric to characterize that behavior as wrong, deviant, or antisocial. The people behaving aggressively probably do not view their behavior as wrong, even though if caught in their "deviance" they may decide to apologize for their behavior in order to mitigate the potential punishment. There probably are (as anthropologist Richard Shweder recently said at a talk at Harvard) no moral universals. To think otherwise leads too readily to racism. Accordingly, not only is it suggested that interventions against excessively aggressive behavior might be effective on the group level, but that the effectiveness will be increased if interventions are nonjudgmental.

CONCLUSION

I have suggested that biological mechanisms are not the causes of aggression in humans, although they direct all aggressive behaviors: biological mechanisms are not self-triggering. Rather, I have argued that socially/culturally mediated perceptions are the triggers that set off biochemical cascades leading to aggression or flight. I further argue that it is ethnocentric to characterize any set of cultural perceptions (beliefs) as wrong, even if those beliefs lead to behaviors that from another culture's perspective are inappropriately aggressive. Inasmuch as survival behaviors are, by this model, culturally mediated, one group's defensive aggression may be perceived by another group as excessive offensive aggression. Interventions that focus on individuals alone, and/or that focus on conditions assumed to be predisposing to individual excessive aggression, may not be as effective as ones that, recognizing group reproductiveness, also focus on motivating individual behaviors through the group. Those group (cultural) interventions must be nonjudgmental (nonethnocentric). Given the probabilistic nature of behavior, further research is needed to find methodologies that will sort out radical normalized behaviors from more mainstream ones. That search might show that the socially acceptable defensive aggression of the majority of a group's members can be distinguished from the excessive defensive aggression of a few of the group's members. Negotiations would focus on inducing the majority to control the minority, on the premise that excessive defensive aggression is, in fact, that and not required for group survival.

REFERENCES

1. BOAS, FRANZ. 1974. Psychological problems in anthropology. *In* The Shaping of American Anthropology, 1883–1911. G. W. Stocking, Jr., Ed.: 243–254. Basic Books Inc. New York.
2. WARR, MARK. 1996. Organization and Instigation in Delinquent Groups. Criminology **30:** 11–37.
3. FERRIS, C. F. 1996. Serotonin diminishes aggression by suppressing the activity of the vasopressin system. Ann. N.Y. Acad. Sci. This volume.
4. KING, J. A. 1996. Perinatal stress and impairment of the stress response: Possible link to nonoptimal behavior. Ann. N.Y. Acad. Sci. This volume.

5. SHEPARD, GORDON M. 1994. Neurobiology. 606–608. Oxford University Press. New York.
6. LITTLE, DANIEL. 1991. Varieties of Social Explanation. 38. Westview Press. Boulder, CO.

Social Intelligence and Empathy as Antecedents of Different Types of Aggression

A. KAUKIAINEN,[a,c] K. BJÖRKQVIST,[b] K. ÖSTERMAN,[b]
AND K. M. J. LAGERSPETZ[a]

[a]Department of Psychology
University of Turku
Turku, Finland

[b]Department of Social Sciences
Åbo Akademi University
Vaasa, Finland

Aggressiveness changes during a person's life span. Among young children lacking verbal skills, aggression is predominantly physical. When verbal skills develop, they are used not only for peaceful communication, but also for aggressive purposes. When social intelligence, empathy, and other social skills are developing, they facilitate the use of even more sophisticated strategies of aggression, namely indirect aggression. A typical strategy of indirect aggression is hurting the other person in a disguised, manipulative way in a social context.[1] On the other hand, empathy has been found to be an inhibitor of aggressive behavior.[2]

It was hypothesized that indirect aggression and direct verbal aggression require a certain level of social intelligence, so both of these were expected to correlate with social intelligence. Instead, we have found that the use of direct physical aggression does not depend on social intelligence to the same extent. Accordingly, the correlation between them is negative. Further, a high level of empathy might be incompatible with aggression. Empathizing with a person may inhibit the wish to hurt him or her. Empathy could thus be expected to have a negative correlation with all types of aggression.

METHODS

Subjects in two age groups, 10- and 12-year-old adolescents (N = 73), participated in the study. Aggression was measured with peer estimations using the direct-indirect aggression scale (DIAS). The indirect aggression scale consisted of 12 items (alpha = .88), for example, becoming friends with another as revenge, ignoring someone, and gossiping. The verbal aggression scale consisted of five items (alpha = .85), for example, yelling, insulting, and name calling. The physical aggression scale consisted of seven items (alpha = .90), for example, hitting, kicking, pushing, and pulling.

Social intelligence was measured with the peer-estimated social intelligence (PESI) scale. The PESI scale consisted of 30 items (alpha = .96). Examples of the items were, "sees easily what others mean and intend," and "adapts well to new situations and new classmates."

[c] Tel: +358 2 333 5423; fax: +358 2 333 5060; e-mail: ari.kaukiainen@utu.fi.

TABLE 1. Pearson's Product Moment Correlation Coefficients between Different Peer-estimated Types of Aggression, and Social Intelligence and Self-estimated Empathy

| | Type of Aggression | | |
	Indirect	Verbal	Physical
Social intelligence	.36**	.11	.07
Empathy	−.05	−.12	−.23

** = $p < .01$

Empathy was measured with self-estimations and consisted of seven items (alpha = .75). Examples included "I become sad when I see a lonely person in a group," and "I get emotional when my friend has problems."

RESULTS

TABLE 1 shows the correlations between different types of aggression, and social intelligence and empathy. There was a statistically significant correlation between indirect aggression and social intelligence. In the case of empathy, the correlations were negative, but they did not reach the level of significance.

TABLE 2 shows correlation coefficients for 10- and 12-year-old cohorts. Only in the case of 12-year-old children were there significant correlations between indirect aggression and social intelligence, and physical aggression and empathy.

CONCLUSIONS

Previous studies have shown that indirect aggression is quite common in children and adolescents, and it can be traced by peer ratings.[1,4] The present study was an attempt to explore antecedents of different types of aggression: social intelligence and lack of empathy. It was found that social intelligence is connected to the use of indirect aggression and that empathy had a negative correlation to physical aggression. These were true only in the case of 12-year-old subjects.

TABLE 2. Pearson's Product Moment Correlation Coefficients for 10- and 12-Year-Old Subjects between Different Peer-Estimated Types of Aggression, and Social Intelligence and Self-estimated Empathy

| | Type of Aggression | | |
	Indirect	Verbal	Physical
Age 10 (n = 38)			
Social intelligence	.27	.11	.05
Empathy	.19	−.01	.05
Age 12 (n = 33)			
Social intelligence	.47**	.10	.06
Empathy	−.15	−.11	−.50**

** = $p < .01$

Perhaps the older subjects' ratings are more reliable because they may have had more skills to rate rather complicated psychological traits, such as social intelligence and indirect aggression.[3]

However, we do not want to argue that empathy has no role in the use of verbal and indirect aggression. One reason for the lack of connection might be that the variables were measured by different methods: empathy was measured using self-estimations, whereas social intelligence and aggression were measured by peer ratings. Presently, we are developing a peer-rating scale of empathy.

This study was based on a relatively small number of subjects. This fact makes us regard the results as somewhat tentative. A replication study with a larger sample is in progress.

REFERENCES

1. BJÖRKQVIST, K., K. ÖSTERMAN & A. KAUKIAINEN. 1992. The development of direct and indirect aggressive strategies in males and females. In Of Mice and Woman. Aspects of Female Aggression. K. Björkqvist & P. Niemelä, Eds.: 51–64. Academic Press. New York.
2. RICHARDSON, R. D., S. G. HAMMOCK, M. S. W. GARDNER & M. SIGNO. 1994. Empathy as a cognitive inhibitor of interpersonal aggression. Aggressive Behav. 4: 275–289.
3. R. SELMAN. 1980. The Growth of Interpersonal Understanding. Academic Press. New York.
4. LAGERSPETZ, K. M. J., K. BJÖRKQVIST & T. PELTONEN. 1988. Is indirect aggression typical of females? Gender differences in aggressiveness in 11- to 12-year-old children. Aggressive Behav. 14: 403–414.

Disruptiveness, Inhibition, and Withdrawal as Predictors of Boys' Delinquency and Depression

MARGARET KERR,[a] RICHARD E. TREMBLAY, LINDA
PAGANI-KURTZ, AND FRANK VITARO

Gannon University
University Square
Erie, Pennsylvania 16541-0001

University of Montreal
Montreal, Quebec, Canada

Childhood aggression and hyperactivity increase the risk of later delinquency.[1–3] Dimensions such as anxiety, shyness, and withdrawal, on the other hand, might protect against future delinquency. However, in some studies these constructs have appeared to protect against delinquency;[4,5] in others they have appeared to increase the risk.[6,7] We argue that one element common to all these constructs, behavioral inhibition, is the protective factor, but in previous research it has been confounded with behaviorally similar constructs that are not protective. We used longitudinal data to discover whether (1) behavioral inhibition protects against future delinquency when it is distinguished from social withdrawal; (2) comorbidity of aggression with inhibition or withdrawal increases the risk of negative outcomes; and whether (3) inhibition might increase risk for later depressive symptoms.

Subjects were 778 white, French-speaking, native-born Canadian boys whose parents were mostly unskilled workers.[1] Ratings from the peer evaluation inventory[8] were used to classify boys on disruptiveness, inhibition, and withdrawal for ages 10, 11, and 12. We dichotomized mean (10-, 11-, and 12-year) measures using 70th percentile cutoffs. Age 15 self-reported depressive symptoms from the childhood depression inventory[9,10] provided the depression measure, and self-reports of behavior over one-year periods prior to the 13-, 14-, and 15-year assessments provided the delinquency measure. These variables were also dichotomized using 70th percentile cutoffs. Eight predictor groups were formed to represent all possible combinations of disruptiveness, inhibition, and withdrawal. Four outcome groups were formed to represent all possible combinations of delinquency and depression. We then used EXACON[11] to identify significant types (predictor-outcome combinations for which there were more subjects than would be expected by chance) and significant antitypes (predictor-outcome combinations for which there were fewer subjects than would be expected by chance).

Results suggest that inhibition is a protective factor. Two predictor profiles were significantly linked to delinquent outcomes—the two disruptive profiles that did not include inhibition. The two disruptive profiles that did include inhibition were not linked to delinquent outcomes. Additionally, inhibited-only boys were significantly less likely than chance to become delinquent. Withdrawal, on the

[a] Tel: (814) 871-7537; fax: (814) 871-5889; e-mail: kerr_m@cluster.gannon.edu.

other hand, was not a protective factor. Furthermore, comorbidity of inhibition and aggression did not increase risk of negative outcomes, whereas comorbidity of withdrawal and aggression did increase risk. Finally, withdrawal, not inhibition, with comorbid disruptiveness increased the risk of later depressive symptoms.

These results are consistent with Cloninger's[12,13] tridimentional theory: if withdrawal is compared with lack of social-reward dependence in Cloninger's model, behavioral inhibition is compared with harm-avoidance anxiety, and disruptiveness is compared with novelty seeking. Cloninger[13] postulates that harm avoidance (behavioral inhibition) modulates novelty-seeking (aggressive-hyperactive) tendencies, whereas low reward dependence (withdrawal) potentiates those tendencies. These results also suggest that behavioral inhibition should be distinguished from other constructs, however conceptually and behaviorally similar they might be.

REFERENCES

1. TREMBLAY, R. E., R. O. PIHL, F. VITARO & P. L. DOBKIN. 1994. Predicting early onset of male antisocial behavior from preschool behavior. Arch. Gen. Psychiatry **51:** 732–739.
2. WHITE, J. L., T. E. MOFFITT, F. EARLS, L. ROBINS & P. A. SILVA. 1990. How early can we tell? Predictors of childhood conduct disorder and adolescent delinquency. Criminology **28:** 507–533.
3. FARRINGTON, D. P., R. LOEBER & W. B. VAN KAMMEN. 1990. The long term criminal outcomes of conduct problem boys with or without impulsive-inattentive behavior. *In* Straight and devious pathways from childhood to adulthood. L. N. Robins & M. Rutter, Eds.: 62–81. Cambridge University Press. New York.
4. ENSMINGER, M. E., S. G. KELLAM & B. R. RUBIN. 1983. School and family origins of delinquency: Comparisons by sex. *In* Prospective Studies of Crime and Delinquency. K. T. Van Dusen & S. A. Mednick, Eds.: 73–97. Kluwer-Nifhoff. Boston, MA.
5. BLUMSTEIN, A., D. P. FARRINGTON & S. MOITRA. 1984. Delinquency careers: Innocents, amateurs, and persisters. Crime and Justice: A Review of Research **6:** 187–219.
6. McCORD, J. 1987. Aggression and shyness as predictors of problems: A long term view. Biennial meeting of the Society for Research in Child Development. Baltimore.
7. MOSKOWITZ, D. S. & A. E. SCHWARTZMAN. 1989. Painting group portraits: Studying life outcomes for aggressive and withdrawn children. J. Pers. **57:** 723–746.
8. PEKARIK, E. G., R. J. PRINZ, D. E. LIEBERT, S. WEINTRAUB & J. M. NEALE. 1976. The pupil evaluation inventory—A sociometric technique for assessing children's social behavior. J. Abnorm. Child Psychol. **1:** 83–97.
9. KOVACS, M. 1983. The Children's Depression Inventory: A self-rated depression scale for school-aged youngsters. Unpublished Manuscript. University of Pittsburg, Pittsburgh, PA.
10. KOVACS, M. 1985. The Children's Depression Inventory (CDI). Psychopharmacol. Bull. **21:** 995–998.
11. BERGMAN, L. & B. EL-KHOURI. 1987. EXACON: A FORTRAN 77 program for the exact analysis of single cells in a contingency table. Educ. Psychol. Measurement **47:** 155–161.
12. CLONINGER, C. R. 1986. A unified biosocial theory of personality and its role in the development of anxiety states. Psychiatric Developments **3:** 167–226.
13. CLONINGER, C. R. 1987. A systematic method for clinical description and classification of personality variants. Arch. Gen. Psychiatry **44:** 573–588.

Gender Differences in the Prolactin Response to Fenfluramine Challenge in Children with Disruptive Behavior Disorders

VIVIAN H. KODA, JEFFREY M. HALPERIN,[a]
JEFFREY H. NEWCORN, SUSAN T. SCHWARTZ,
AND KATHLEEN E. McKAY

Queens College
City University of New York
and
Mount Sinai Medical Center
One Gustave Levy Place
New York, New York 10029-6574

Recent studies have begun to elucidate the neurobiological substrates of disruptive behavior disorders (DBDs) in children. These studies have suggested a role for central serotonergic (5-HT) function in the manifestation of impulsive/aggressive behavior.[1-4] However, virtually all of these studies have been conducted with male populations, leaving unexamined the question whether disruptive behavior in females is similarly related to these neurochemical substrates. This relative neglect is due in part to the higher prevalence of DBDs in boys and the desire to focus statistical power on more homogenous male samples. Yet, as many as 9% of school-age girls may present with DBDs,[5] and the limited data available suggest that many go on to develop more severe academic, social, and psychiatric disturbances.[6]

This preliminary study of gender differences in children compared the prolactin (PRL) response to fenfluramine (FEN), a dynamic measure of central 5-HT function in the hypothalamic-pituitary axis,[7-9] in three prepubertal girls (ages 8–9), presenting with DBDs, to closely age- and behavior-matched boys (N = 6). All children were rated by their parents (child behavior checklist, CBCL)[10] and teachers (Iowa Conners teacher rating scale)[11] on measures of aggression and hyperactivity. Despite cognitive and behavioral similarities (see TABLE 1), the girls had a significantly greater PRL response to FEN challenge than the boys (mean for girls = 18.3, SD, 5.6; mean for boys = 8.6, SD, 2.1; $p < .01$; see FIG. 1). Girls did not differ from boys in the plasma levels of the catecholamine metabolites 3-methoxy-4-hydroxyphenylglycol (MHPG) and homovanillic acid (HVA), but they had lower levels of platelet 5-HT ($p < .05$).

These data are consistent with those in adults, indicating an enhanced PRL response to FEN in women as compared to men. However, it has been suggested that the enhanced PRL response seen in adult females may reflect variability in

[a] Address for corresondence: The City University of New York, 65-30 Kissena Boulevard, Flushing, NY 11367-1597. Tel: (718) 997-3754; fax: (212) 289-7872; e-mail: Jeffrey_Halperin@qc.edu.

TABLE 1. Comparison of Prepubertal Girls and Boys on Descriptive and Neurochemical Measures

	Girls (N = 3)		Boys (N = 6)			
	Mean	SD	Mean	SD	t	p
Age	8.7	0.2	8.7	0.1	0.25	—
FSIQ[a]	92.0	9.8	96.8	14.5	0.51	—
CBCL Hyperactivity	74.3	12.1	73.0	11.5	0.16	—
CBCL Aggression	68.3	7.6	68.3	15.6	0.00	—
Iowa Conners I/O[b]	13.0	1.0	10.3	3.3	1.32	—
Iowa Conners aggressive scale	5.3	5.5	6.3	5.0	0.28	—
Delta PRL	18.3	5.6	8.6	2.1	3.93	<.01
HVA	7.7	1.6	8.9	2.6	0.70	—
MHPG	3.0	1.1	3.8	0.9	1.09	—
Platelet 5-HT	0.11	0.1	0.30	0.1	3.64	<.05

[a] Full-scale intelligence quotient.
[b] Intelligence/overactivity.

the secretory capacity of the pituitary lactotroph and may not reflect enhanced CNS serotonergic responsivity in adult females.[12] Other studies have suggested that observed variations in PRL responses to FEN throughout the menstrual cycle occur as the result of an estradiol effect at 5-HT receptors, or a more general effect at the level of the lactotroph.[13] Our data suggest that gender-associated differences in serotonergic responsivity or serotonin-mediated neuroendocrine responses occur in prepubertal children. Further investigation with a larger cohort will address whether (1) prepubertal girls and boys with DBDs differ in central 5-HT

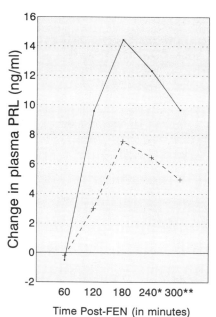

FIGURE 1. PRL response to fenfluramine (FEN) challenge in girls and boys. −□−, girls; −+−, boys. *p < .05; **p = .055.

function, (2) neurochemical correlates of aggressive and other DBD behaviors are similar in girls and boys, and (3) gender differences in behaviors can be accounted for, in part, by gender differences in neurochemistry.

REFERENCES

1. KRUESI, M. J. P. *et al.* 1990. Arch. Gen. Psychiatry **47:** 419–426.
2. KRUESI, M. J. P. *et al.* 1992. Arch. Gen. Psychiatry **49:** 429–435.
3. CASTELLANOS, F. X. *et al.* 1994. Psychiatry Res. **52:** 305–316.
4. HALPERIN, J. M. *et al.* 1994. Am. J. Psychiatry **151:** 243–248.
5. AMERICAN PSYCHIATRIC ASSOCIATION. 1994. Diagnostic and Statistical Manual of Mental Disorders. Fourth Edition.
6. ROBINS, L. N. & R. K. PRICE. 1991. Psychol. Res. **54:** 116–131.
7. QUATTRONE, A. *et al.* 1978. Eur. J. Pharmacol. **49:** 163–168.
8. ROWLAND, N. E. & J. CARLTON. 1986. J. Prog. Neurobiol. **27:** 13–62.
9. COCCARO, E. F. *et al.* 1989. Arch. Gen. Psychiatry **46:** 587–599.
10. ACHENBACH, T. M. *et al.* 1983. Manual for the Child Behavior Checklist and Revised Child Behavior Profile.
11. PELHAM, W. E. *et al.* 1989. J. Clin. Child Psychol. **3:** 259–262.
12. McBRIDE, P. A. *et al.* 1990. Biol. Psychiatry **27:** 1143–1155.
13. O'KEANE, V. *et al.* 1991. Clin. Endocrinol. **34:** 289–292.

Adolescent Anabolic Steroid Use and Aggressive Behavior in Golden Hamsters

RICHARD H. MELLONI JR.[a,b,c] AND CRAIG F. FERRIS[b]

aMolecular Neurobiology Laboratory
bProgram in Neuropsychiatric Sciences
Department of Psychiatry
University of Massachusetts Medical Center
55 Lake Avenue North
Worcester, Massachusetts 01655

INTRODUCTION

The naturally occurring male hormone, testosterone, and its synthetic derivatives (collectively termed anabolic-androgenic steroids [AAS]) have been used by athletes and bodybuilders for more than two decades to improve athletic performance and enhance overall physical strength and muscle mass.[1–3] Despite various educational programs and legal prohibitions placed on these substances by the Federal Drug Administration, the illicit use of AAS is rising and appears to have reached near epidemic proportions.[4–7] This pattern of abuse appears to be particularly relevant in adolescence. Several studies have reported an increased incidence of AAS abuse among adolescent teenagers.[8–13] These studies have found that as many as 11% of males and 2.5% of female adolescents have used or are using AAS.[8–10] Recent data from several national surveys indicate that the illicit use of AAS may be more entrenched in the male adolescent population than previously reported and that the increased incidence of adolescent AAS abuse equals or exceeds that of all other age groups.[8,10,12,14,15] Indeed, it has been suggested that if the incidence of AAS abuse in this group is applicable to the national population, about 700,000 high school students use AAS, constituting a serious drug problem within the adolescent population.[12]

Anabolic androgenic steroid abuse by adolescents represents a significant health-care risk due to the potential for long-term negative physical and behavioral sequelae. By far the most consistently cited behavioral sequelae of AAS abuse in adult clinical populations and experimental animals is increased aggressive behavior.[16–25] The purpose of the present study was to examine, in a hamster model system, the behavioral consequences of high-dose AAS exposure during a developmental period that is physiologically similar to adolescence in humans.

RESULTS

Does exposure to AAS during adolescence affect aggressive behavior in early adulthood? Shown in FIGURES 1 and 2 are data on aggressive behavior collected

[c] Tel: (508) 856-6580; fax: (508) 856-6426; e-mail: richard.melloni@banyan.ummed.edu.

on postnatal day 45 (P-45) from intact male hamsters (n = 11) treated daily for 14 consecutive days (P-27–42) with subcutaneous (sc) injections of either a cocktail of AAS, consisting of 2 mg/kg testosterone cypionate, 2 mg/kg nandrolone decanoate, and 1 mg/kg boldenone undecylenate (Sigma Chemical Co., St. Louis, MO) suspended in sesame oil, or sesame oil alone. On the day of testing, an intruder of equal size and weight was placed into the home cage of the experimental animal. The resident was scored for latency to bite, total bites and attacks, and total contact time toward the intruder over a 10-min test period.

Animals treated with high doses of AAS during their adolescent development showed significantly heightened measures of offensive aggression. Hamsters treated with AAS showed a significant increase in the total number of attacks (p < 0.01) and bites (p < 0.01) over vehicle-treated control animals (FIG. 1). These components of aggression were clustered in AAS-treated hamsters. In highly aggressive hamsters (attacks/bites ≥ 12 each, *i.e.*, 3 times the maximum value for vehicle-treated animals), the number of attacks/bites per aggressive encounter was each greater than four.

In addition, AAS-treated hamsters displayed a significantly quicker aggressive response towards intruders (latency to bite, $t(21) = 4.03$, p < 0.01) than did sesame oil (vehicle)-treated control animals (FIG. 2). As evidenced by the bite latency data, the aggressive response of the AAS-treated residents was not immediate. In fact, the aggressive behaviors of AAS-treated hamsters occurred within roughly the last half of the test period. Typically, hamsters treated with AAS generally would not begin attacking the intruder until approximately 5 minutes into the 10-minute test period, in comparison to vehicle-treated control animals whose

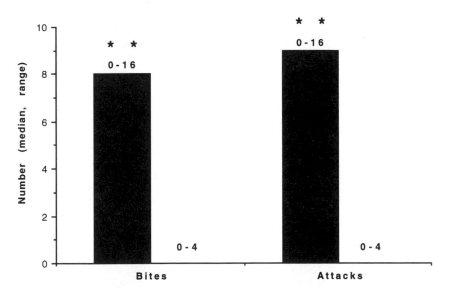

FIGURE 1. Anabolic-androgenic steroids increase offensive aggression. Number of bites and attacks in anabolic-androgenic steroid and vehicle-treated residents. ■, treated with AAS. Bars denote SEM.

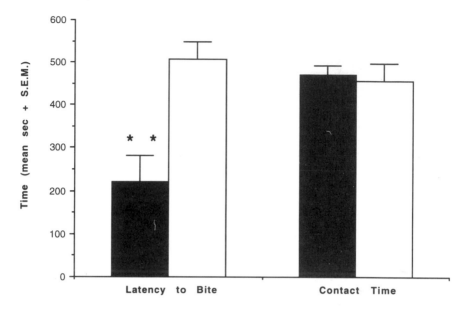

FIGURE 2. Anabolic-androgenic steroids increase aggressive responding. Mean latencies to first bite and total contact time in anabolic-androgenic steroid and vehicle-treated residents. ■, treated with AAS; □, vehicle. Bars denote SEM.

first aggressive response was displayed towards the end of the test period (approximately 9 minutes into the test). Finally, although AAS-treated animals showed heightened levels of aggressive behavior, no significant changes were observed ($t(21) = 0.273$, p > 0.1) in the total contact time measured between the AAS-treated and vehicle-treated animals (FIG. 2).

SUMMARY

In the present study, the ability of high-dose androgens, namely AAS, administered during adolescence to facilitate aggressive behavior in experimental animals was examined. Data from these studies show clearly that exposure to high doses of multiple AAS during adolescent development can predispose animals to intense bouts of aggressive behavior during young adulthood. Specifically, young adult hamsters treated with high doses of AAS throughout adolescence were more likely to attack and bite intruders placed in their home cage than sesame oil (vehicle)-treated control animals. Further, AAS-treated animals displayed a higher intensity of attack during the test period, exhibiting greater than four times the number of attacks/bites of control animals. Given the recent reports of increased incidence of AAS abuse in the adolescent population and the documented stimulatory effects of AAS on aggressive behavior, the study of the behavioral and neurobiological effects of prolonged exposure to AAS during critical phases of development such as adolescence warrants further investigation.

REFERENCES

1. DYMENT, P. G. 1987. The adolescent athlete and ergogenic acids. J. Adolesc. Health Care **8:** 68–73.
2. STRAUSS, R. H. 1987. Anabolic steroids. *In* Drugs and Performance in Sports. R. H. Strauss, Ed.: 59–67. W. B. Saunders. Philadelphia.
3. YESALIS, C., N. KENNEDY, A. DOPSTEIN & M. BAHRKE. 1993. Anabolic-androgenic steroid use in the United States. J. Am. Med. Assoc. **270:** 1217–1221.
4. ANDERSON, W. & D. MCKEAG. 1985. The substance use and abuse habits of college student athletes. Research paper #2. National Collegiate Athletic Association. Mission, Kansas.
5. WRIGHT, J. 1989. Anabolic Steroids in Sports. Science Consultants. Natick, MA.
6. EDITORIAL. 1987. Some predict increased steroid use in sports despite drug testing crackdown on suppliers. J. Am. Med. Assoc. **257:** 3025–3029.
7. YESALIS, C., R. HERRICK, W. BUCKLEY, K. E. FRIEDL, D. BRANNON & J. E. WRIGHT. 1988. Estimated incidence of anabolic steroid use among elite powerlifters. Physician Sportsmed. **16:** 91–100.
8. BUCKLEY, W. E., C. E. YESALIS III, D. E. FREIDL, W. A. ANDERSON, A. L. STREIT & J. E. WRIGHT. 1988. Estimated prevalence of anabolic steroid use among male high school seniors. J. Am. Med. Assoc. **260:** 3441–3445.
9. COMMITTEE ON THE JUDICIARY, U.S. SENATE. 1989. Drug misuse: Steroids and human growth hormone: Report to the chairman. Washington, D.C.: Government Printing Office, Publication no. GAO/HRD-89-109.
10. JOHNSON, M. D., M. S. JAY, B. SHOUP & V. I. RICKERT. 1989. Anabolic steroid use by male adolescents. Pediatrics **83:** 921–924.
11. JOHNSON, M. D. 1990. Anabolic steroid use in adolescent athletes. Pediatr. Clin. North Am. **37:** 1111–1123.
12. TERNEY, R. & L. G. MCLAIN. 1990. The use of anabolic steroids in high school students. Am. J. Dis. Child. **144:** 99–103.
13. WINDSOR, R. & D. DUMITRU. 1989. Prevalence of anabolic steroid use by male and female adolescents. Med. Sci. Sports Exercise **21:** 494–497.
14. CORDER, B., T. DEZELSKY & J. TOOHEY. 1975. Trends in drug use behavior at ten central Arizona high schools. Ariz. J. Health, Phys. Educ., Recreat. Dance. **18:** 10–11.
15. NEWMAN, M. 1986. Michigan Consortium of School Student Survey. Hazelden Research Services. Minneapolis, MN.
16. CLARK, A. S. & D. M. BARBER. 1994. Anabolic-androgenic steroids and aggression in castrated male rats. Physiol. & Behav. **56:** 1107–1113.
17. LONG, S. F. & W. M. DAVIS. 1994. Cocaine and nandrolone increase aggression in male rats. J. Neurosci. Abst. p. 594.
18. LUMIA, A. R., K. M. THORNER & M. Y. MCGINNIS. 1994. Effects of chronically high doses of the anabolic steroid, testosterone, on internal aggression and sexual behavior in male rats. Physiol. & Behav. **55:** 331–335.
19. POPE, H. G. & D. L. KATZ. 1987. Bodybuilders' psychosis. Lancet 863.
20. POPE, H. G., D. L. KATZ & R. CHAMPOUX. 1988. Anabolic-androgenic steroid use among 1010 college men. Physician Sportsmed. **16:** 75–81.
21. POPE, H. G. & D. L. KATZ. 1994. Psychiatric and medical effects of anabolic-androgenic steroid use. Arch. Gen. Psychiatry **51:** 375–382.
22. REJESKI, W. J., P. H. BRUBAKER, R. A. HERB, J. R. KAPLAN & D. KORITNIK. 1988. Anabolic steroids and aggressive behavior in cynomolgus monkeys. J. Behav. Med. **11:** 95–105.
23. ROSE, R. M., I. S. BERNSTEIN & J. W. HOLIDAY. 1971. Plasma testosterone, dominance rank, and aggressive behavior in a group of male rhesus monkeys. Nature **231:** 366–368.
24. STRAUSS, R. H., J. E. WRIGHT & G. A. M. FINERMAN. 1983. Side-effects of anabolic steroids in weight trained men. Physician Sportsmed. **11:** 87–96.
25. SU, T., M. PAGLIARO, P. J. SCHMIDT, D. PICKAR, O. WOLKOWITZ & D. R. RUBINOW. 1993. Neuropsychiatric effects of anabolic steroids in male normal volunteers. J. Am. Med. Assoc. **269:** 2760–2764.

Relationship of Aggression and Anxiety to Autonomic Regulation of Heart Rate Variability in Adolescent Males

ENRICO MEZZACAPPA,[a,f] RICHARD E. TREMBLAY,[b]
DANIEL KINDLON,[c] J. PHILIP SAUL,[d]
LOUISE ARSENEAULT,[b] ROBERT O. PIHL,[b,e]
AND FELTON EARLS[c]

[a]Judge Baker Children's Center
Harvard University
Boston, Massachusetts

[b]Research Unit on Children's Psychosocial Maladjustment
University of Montreal
Montreal, Canada

[c]Division of Maternal and Child Health
Harvard School of Public Health
Harvard University
Boston, Massachusetts

[d]Division of Cardiology
The Children's Hospital
Harvard University
Boston, Massachusetts

[e]Department of Psychology
McGill University
Montreal, Canada

BACKGROUND

In order to explore autonomic nervous system–behavioral relationships, we studied aggression and anxiety in relation to heart rate (HR), and to the effects of postural and respiratory change on HR variability, in 15-year-old, Caucasian, French-Canadian boys of lower socioeconomic status (n = 175).[1] Previous investigators have identified lower HR in subjects with aggression or conduct disorder, and higher HR in inhibited subjects.[2–4] In addition to replicating these findings, we determined if aggression was associated with evidence for increased vagal mediation of respiratory-driven HR variability, and if anxiety was associated with evidence for increased sympathetic mediation of HR variability due to postural change.

[f] Address for correspondence: The Judge Baker Children's Center, 295 Longwood Avenue, Boston, MA 02115. Tel: (617) 232-8390, ext. 2603. Fax: (617) 232-8399; e-mail: mezzacappa@a1.tch.harvard.edu.

376

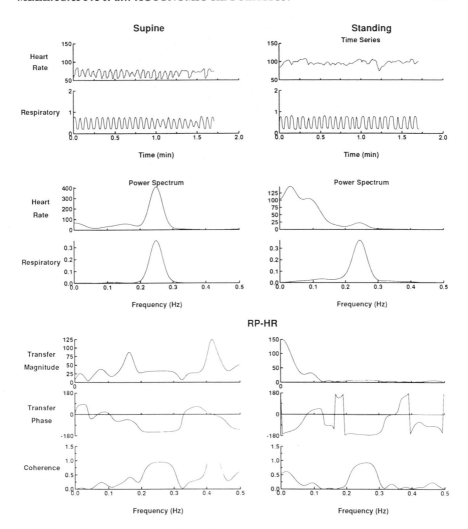

FIGURE 1. Supine and standing HR and respiratory time series, power spectra, and respiratory-to-HR transfer functions in a 15-year-old male breathing at 15 respirations per minute (0.25 hertz). Note the correspondence between the HR and respiratory power spectra around the breathing frequency, the changes in the HR time series and power spectra, and respiratory-to-HR transfer functions related to postural change. Note the drop in HR variability at the respiratory frequency despite preservation of respiratory variability and the emergence of a spectral peak around 0.10 hertz, due to the HR response to blood pressure regulation following postural change. Transfer of respiratory-to-HR variability (transfer magnitude or gain) and transfer timing (phase) also diminish in relation to postural change. Coherence (closeness and reliability) of the respiratory-HR relationship remains relatively constant with postural change in this subject but frequently decreases under these circumstances as well.

TABLE 1. Units of Measure and Group Means for Specific Cardiac-behavioral Relationships (see text)

Cardiac Index	Aggressive Subjects (n = 7)	Anxious Subjects (n = 6)	Controls (n = 8)
Supine HR (bpm)	61.5	75.5	70.1
Standing HR (bpm)	86.7	108.9	95.8
Supine RSA (bpm²/hertz)	4.0	12.0	18.4
Standing RSA (bpm²/hertz)	2.3	1.6	3.1
Supine phase (degrees)	−8.1	−38.0	−30.7
Standing phase (degrees)	−18.2 (n = 5)[a]	−40.5 (n = 4)[a]	−92.6 (n = 5)[a]

[a] Unreliable estimates were eliminated because of low coherence between respiration and HR.

METHODS

Longitudinal histories of aggression towards persons, and social anxiety were derived from self-reports, obtained yearly from age 10 through 15,[1,5] and converted to composite scores representing stable behavioral traits. Applying the criteria of two standard deviations from the composite means, homogenous groups of controls (n = 8), anxious (n = 6), and aggressive (n = 7) subjects were identified. Subjects performed rhythmic breathing and underwent orthostatic (supine to standing) postural change while HR and respiratory volume were continuously recorded. Heart rate variability and transfer relations between respiratory and HR variability were quantified and broken down into components of known origin, using spectral analytic techniques (see FIG. 1).[6,7] Where bivariate relationships indicated, the effects of height, weight, pubertal status, and physical conditioning were included in the ANOVAs comparing the cardiac indices across groups. Repeated-measures ANOVA, with posture as the repeated within-subjects factor, were also performed, and are reported were contributory.

RESULTS

Anxious subjects showed higher HR in the supine posture than did aggressive subjects ($F = 4.12$, df = 20, $p < .04$, $r^2 = .31$), and higher HR in the standing posture than both control and aggressive subjects ($F = 6.91$, df = 20, $p < .006$, $r^2 = .43$). Both anxious and aggressive subjects showed less delayed timing of transfer (phase) of respiratory to HR variability in the standing posture when compared with controls ($F = 4.80$, df 13, $p < .03$, $r^2 = .47$). Aggressive subjects demonstrated an unexpected trend towards reduction of vagally mediated, respiratory-driven HR variability (respiratory sinus arrhythmia or RSA) in the supine posture ($F = 3.22$, df = 20, $p < .07$, $r^2 = .26$), not accounted for by a reduction in respiratory drive. Repeated-measures ANOVA revealed significant main effects for group ($F = 7.35$, $p < .02$) and posture ($F = 14.41$, $p < .002$), and a group by posture interaction ($F = 5.82$, $p < .03$) for this component of HR variability (see TABLE 1).

CONCLUSIONS

Our findings concerning the relationship between HR and behavior are consistent with those of previous investigators. Our findings further suggest that aggression is associated with disruption of the ordinarily robust relationship between HR and respiratory activity, mediated predominantly by phasic vagal activity. The significance of the altered transfer phase in anxious and aggressive subjects is uncertain. These findings require replication in larger samples, and in those differing in age, sex, racial, ethnic, and socioeconomic composition.

REFERENCES

1. TREMBLAY, R. E., R. O. PIHL, F. VITARO & P. I. DOBKIN. 1994. Predicting early onset of male antisocial behavior from preschool behavior. Arch. Gen. Psychiatry **51:** 732–739.
2. KINDLON, D., R. E. TREMBLAY, E. MEZZACAPPA, F. EARLS, D. LAURENT & B. SCHAAL. 1995. Longitudinal patterns of heart rate and fighting behavior in 9- to 12-year-old boys. J. Am. Acad. Child Adolesc. Psychiatry **34:** 371–377.
3. RAINE, A., P. H. VENABLES & M. WILLIAMS. 1990. Autonomic orienting responses in 15-year-old male subjects and criminal behavior at age 24. Am. J. Psychiatry **147:** 933–937.
4. KAGAN, J., J. S. REZNICK & N. C. SNIDMAN. 1987. The physiology and psychology of behavioral inhibition in children. Child Dev. **58:** 1459–1473.
5. JESNESS, C. F. 1983. The Jesness Inventory of Adolescent Personality (revised ed.). Multi Health Systems. North Tonawanda, NY.
6. APPEL, M. L., R. D. BERGER, J. P. SAUL, J. M. SMITH & R. J. COHEN. 1989. Beat to beat variability in cardiovascular variables: Noise or music? J. Am. Coll. Cardiol. **14:** 1139–1148.
7. MEZZACAPPA, E., D. KINDLON, J. P. SAUL & F. EARLS. 1994. The utility of spectral analytic techniques in the study of the autonomic regulation of beat-to-beat heart rate variability. Int. J. Methods Psychiatric Res. **4:** 29–44.

Television Violence Viewing and Aggression in Females

JESSICA F. MOISE AND L. ROWELL HUESMANN[a]

The Institute for Social Research
The University of Michigan
P.O. Box 1248
Ann Arbor, Michigan 48109-1248

Although the literature on the long-term effects of television violence viewing on aggression has demonstrated unambiguously that for boys early exposure to media violence increases the risk for later aggressive behavior, the results for girls have been less clear. In the 1960s, laboratory studies showed short-term effects for girls, but little evidence could be found for long-term effects on girls or young women in field studies.[1] More recently, however, one three-year field study, which was started in the 1970s, did find a relationship between violence viewing in the first year of the study and aggression two years later for girls, ages 6 to 11.[2] It may be that recent increases in violence in the media and in societal acceptance of aggression by girls are changing the magnitude of the effect for females. The major purpose of the current study is to examine the long-term effects of early violence viewing on later aggressive behavior on girls during the 1980s and 1990s.

METHOD

The current report examines these relationships in girls with data from a 15-year follow-up of 384 girls who were originally assessed in 1977 (when they were in either first or third grade). Two hundred and eleven of these girls were reinterviewed 14–16 years later. The procedure for the child interviews has been described in detail in Huesmann and Eron.[2] For the follow-up study, subjects either came into the University of Illinois, Chicago and completed an interview using a computer (N = 154), or the subject completed a combination phone and mail version of the interview (N = 57).

In the initial study, children were asked about their favorite TV programs (which were then coded for violence level) and how often they watched them, about how much they thought they were "like" aggressive TV characters, and about how much they fantasized about aggression. Children's aggressive behavior was measured using the peer-nominated aggression index. For a complete description of these measures, see Huesmann and Eron.[2] In the follow-up study, we remeasured each of these variables using procedures very similar to those described for the early waves, except the questions were adapted to an adult sample. To measure adult aggression, we asked them to report their frequency of engaging in indirect aggression and mild physical aggression,[3] self-rated aggressive

[a] Tel: (313) 763-4844; fax: (313) 763-1202; e-mail: jmoise@umich.edu.

TABLE 1. Correlations of Girls' TV Habits with Their Aggressive Behaviors (N = 211)[a]

| | Child TV Measures | | | Adult TV Measures | | | |
| | | Identification with Aggressive TV Characters | | Violence Viewing | | Identification with Aggressive TV Characters | |
	TV Violence Viewing	Female	Male	TV	Movie	Female	Male
Child aggression measures							
Fantasy aggression	.11	—	.14*	—	—	—	—
Peer-nominated aggression	.38***	.13*	.12+	—	—	.10	.18*
Adult aggression measures							
Fantasy aggression	.14*	.18**	.12+	.19**	.15*	.23**	—
Aggressive personality	.23**	.27***	.28***	.16*	.21**	.23**	.17*
Indirect aggression	.18*	.18*	.16*	—	—	.12+	.14
Self-rated aggressive behavior	.16*	.22**	.16*	.22**	.17*	.29***	.11
Self-reported mild physical aggression	—	.13+	—	—	—	.12	—
Severe physical aggression	.17*	—	—	—	.16*	.15*	—
Frequency of criminal behavior	.17*	.14*	—	.31***	.20**	.29***	.17*

[a] +p < .10
* p < .05
** p < .01
*** p < .001. Note: correlations less than .10 are not reported.

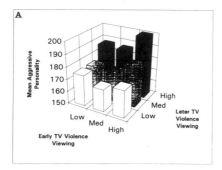

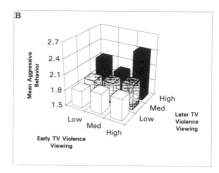

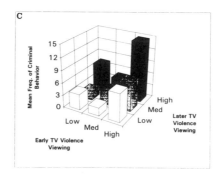

FIGURE 1. **A.** Aggressive personality (MMPI F + 4 + 9) as a function of early and later TV violence viewing. $F(2,185) = 6.50$, $p < .01$ for early TV violence viewing; $F(2,185) = 2.99$, $p = .05$ for later TV violence viewing. **B.** Frequency of self-rated aggressive behavior as a function of early and later TV violence viewing. $F(2,193) = 4.60$, $p < .05$ for early TV violence viewing; $F(2,193) = 2.93$, $p < .10$ for later TV violence viewing. **C.** Frequency of criminal behavior as a function of early and later TV violence viewing. $F(2,193) = 4.15$, $p < .05$ for early TV violence viewing; $F(2,193) = 8.81$, $p < .001$ for later TV violence viewing.

behavior,[2] severe physical aggression,[2] and criminal behavior.[4] In addition, subjects were given the MMPI, and the F, 4, and 9 scales were combined as a measure of aggressive personality.[5]

RESULTS

As TABLE 1 reveals, for females, watching violent media and identification with aggressive TV characters (especially female characters) are significantly correlated with aggression and with fantasy about aggression, both in childhood and in adulthood. In addition, childhood television variables are significantly correlated with many adult aggression variables, but the reverse does not hold true. That is, childhood aggression variables for the most part are not correlated with adult TV violence viewing. Although the correlations are not large, many of them are significant, indicating that early TV violence viewing and identification with aggressive TV characters are related to later aggression and fantasizing about aggression.

We also examined the differences in mean scores on these measures for those who were high TV violence viewers both as children and as adults compared to those who were low or medium TV violence viewers. The results, shown in FIGURE 1, indicate that both early and later TV violence viewing independently have a significant main effect on aggression.

DISCUSSION

The results of this sudy indicate that there now does exist a relationship between television violence viewing and aggression for females—in childhood, in adulthood, and across time. Although this preliminary analysis does not test causality, the results in conjunction with the large body of literature supporting a causal model for boys suggest that it is plausible to conclude that viewing television violence can lead to the development of aggression for girls as well as for boys. Moreover, the results suggest that this relationship is exacerbated by identification with aggressive television characters and fantasizing about aggression.

REFERENCES

1. ERON, L. D., L. R. HUESMANN, M. M. LEFKOWITZ & O. WALDER. 1972. Does television violence cause aggression? Am. Psychol. **27:** 253–263.
2. HUESMANN, L. R. & L. D. ERON. 1986. Television and the Aggression Child: A Cross-National Comparison. Erlbaum. Hillsdale, NJ.
3. BJORKQVIST, K., K. OYSTERMAN & A. KAUKIAINEN. 1992. The development of direct and indirect aggressive strategies in males and females. *In* Of Mice and Women: Aspects of Female Aggression. K. Bjorkqvist & P. Niemela, Eds. Academic Press. New York.
4. ELLIOT, D. S., F. W. DUNFORD & D. H. HUIZINGA. 1987. The identification and prediction of career offenders utilizing self-reported and official data. *In* Prevention of Delinquent Behavior. J. D. Burchard & S. N. Burchard, Eds. Sage. Newbury Park.
5. HUESMANN, L. R., M. M. LEFKOWITZ & L. D. ERON. 1978. Sum of MMPI Scales F, 4, 9 as a measure of aggression. J. Consult. Clin. Psychol. **46:** 1071–1078.

Aggressive Behaviors of Transgenic Estrogen-receptor Knockout Male Mice[a]

SONOKO OGAWA,[b,e] DENNIS B. LUBAHN,[c]
KENNETH S. KORACH,[d] AND DONALD W. PFAFF[b]

[b]Laboratory of Neurobiology and Behavior
The Rockefeller University
New York, New York 10021

[c]Department of Biochemistry and Child Health
University of Missouri-Columbia
Columbia, Missouri 65211

[d]Laboratory of Reproductive and Developmental Toxicology
National Institute of Environmental Health Sciences
Research Triangle Park, North Carolina 27709

Aggressive behaviors of male mice have been shown to be regulated by both androgen receptor–dependent and estrogen receptor (ER)–dependent brain mechanisms. In the present study, the role of ER activation by endogenous estrogen on aggressive behaviors was determined using transgenic estrogen receptor knockout (ERKO) mice,[1,2] which lack functional estrogen receptors.

ERKO and age-matched wild-type (WT) male mice (16–22 weeks old, gonadally intact) were individually housed for at least 14 days. They were then tested twice in their home cages against a group-housed olfactory bulbectomized (OBX) male intruder mouse (Swiss Webster) for 15 minutes. OBX mice are known to reliably elicit aggression from the resident mouse, but neither initiate aggression nor respond to the aggression of the resident mouse.[3] All behavioral tests were done during the dark phase of the light/dark cycle under white lights and videotaped for further analysis. An aggressive bout was defined as a continuous series of behavioral interactions, including at least one aggressive behavioral act. Aggressive behavior bouts were classified either as (1) aggression without attacks and biting (i.e., aggressive behavior bouts with only chasing, tail rattling, and boxing) or (2) aggression with attacks (bouts consisting of severe attacks, biting, and wrestling in addition to chasing, tail rattling, and boxing). Cumulative duration of each, as well as latency to the first aggressive act, were recorded for each test.

It was found that the cumulative duration of both kinds of aggressive behavior bouts were significantly less in ERKO mice compared to WT mice. ERKO mice occasionally showed mild aggressive acts, such as biting, chasing, or tail rattling (0.93 ± 0.72 s, mean ± SEM vs. 16.71 ± 3.81 s in WT mice, p < 0.01) but never showed aggressive behaviors with attacks, severe biting, and wrestling to an intruder opponent mouse. WT mice, on the other hand, exhibited vigorous offen-

[a] This study was supported partially by a Harry Frank Guggenheim Research Grant to S. Ogawa.

[e] Address correspondence to Sonoko Ogawa, Box 275, the Rockefeller University, 1230 York Avenue, New York, NY 10021. Tel: (212) 327-8667; fax: (212) 327-7974; E-mail: ogawa@rockvax.rockefeller.edu.

sive attacks, and cumulative duration of such aggression reached about 91.8 $\pm$ 17.8 s in 15-min behavioral tests (p $<$ 0.01, vs. ERKO mice). The latency to the first attack was also much longer in ERKO mice (805.07 $\pm$ 50.94 s) compared to WT mice (260.93 $\pm$ 66.41 s, p $<$ 0.001 vs. ERKO mice).

It can be stated that reduced levels of aggression were not due to a decrease in general locomotor activity or physical weakness in ERKO mice. ERKO mice were more active than WT mice in open-field and elevated plus-maze tests. ERKO mice also appeared normal in their general responsiveness to other mice. During aggression tests, they engaged in social investigation, such as nose sniffing or genital licking of the opponent mouse. Moreover, ERKO mice often showed attempted mounts toward an opponent male mouse. It was also found that ERKO mice showed mounts towards a sexually receptive female mouse, although ERKO mice rarely ejaculated. Finally, our preliminary immunocytochemical studies revealed that no conventional strong ER immunoreactive cells were apparent in adult male ERKO mice in any brain region in which abundant ER-positive cells were found in WT mice. Despite the loss of functional ER protein, however, ERKO mice seem to have equivalent levels of brain androgen receptor as well as aromatase-immunoreactive cells. Moreover, serum testosterone levels were not different between ERKO and WT male mice.

Collectively, these findings suggest the relative importance of ER activation in the regulation of aggressive behaviors in male mice. Studies are in progress to ask whether ERKO mice could show aggression toward different types of opponents or in different testing environments, which might affect the levels of aggression in male mice.[4]

REFERENCES

1. KORACH, K. S. 1994. Insights from the study of animals lacking functional estrogen receptor. Science **266:** 1524–1527.
2. LUBAHN, D. B., J. S. MOYER, T. S. GOLDING, J. F. COUSE, K. S. KORACH & O. SMITHIES. 1993. Alternation of reproductive function but not prenatal sexual development after insertional disruption of the mouse estrogen receptor gene. Proc. Natl. Acad. Sci. USA **90:** 11162–11166.
3. OGAWA, S., A. ROBBINS, N. KUMAR, D. W. PFAFF, K. SUNDARAM & C. W. BARDIN. 1996. Effects of testosterone and 7α-methyl-19-nortestosterone (MENT) on sexual and aggressive behaviors in two inbred strains of male mice. Horm. Behav. **30:** 74–84.
4. MAXSON, S. C., A. DIDIER-ERICKSON & S. OGAWA. 1989. The Y chromosomes, social signals, and aggression in mice (*Mus musculus*). Behav. Neural Biol. **52:** 251–259.

The Effects of Marital Transition on Children's Aggressive Behavior

A Prospective Design[a]

LINDA PAGANI-KURTZ,[b] BERNARD BOULERICE,
RICHARD E. TREMBLAY, AND FRANK VITARO

Research Unit on Children's Psychosocial Maladjustment
University of Montreal
Montreal, Quebec, Canada H2C 1A6

Using an autoregressive modeling technique with a time-invariant random effect,[1] we examine the effects of divorce and remarriage on children's disruptive behavior and social competence at school using a population-based sample of children who were followed longitudinally from kindergarten. Although most children were living in intact families at age 6, some had already experienced one (*i.e.*, divorce) or two (*i.e.*, remarriage) marital transitions during early childhood (see TABLE 1). We expected that[2] children who experienced divorce early in life would exhibit comparatively more disturbance than their peers, whose parents divorced later; and that remarriage would not have a significant impact on children's behavioral development once the legacy of previous family experiences was controlled for in the analyses.

The Quebec Longitudinal Study represents a random sample of 3013 French-speaking children followed from the end of kindergarten (mean = 6.15, SD = 0.46) to the beginning of adolescence (mean = 12.15, SD = 0.46). For this study, 632 boys and 684 girls were selected, based on the following criteria: (1) covariates (maternal education and age at birth of target child) had to be available at age 6; (2) data could not be missing for two consecutive years; (3) no child could have experienced more than two marital transitions (*i.e.*, divorce and then remarriage). This study examined children's social competence with a form completed by teachers at ages 6, 8, 10, and 12 that assessed disruptive behavior (13 items, alpha = 0.82) and prosocial behavior (10 items, alpha = 0.90).[3]

We used a basic autoregressive model, with a time-invariant random effect representing the typical evolution of behavior, regardless of the effects of external events, such as divorce and remarriage. It consisted of a random unobserved, time-invariant factor (*i.e.*, a latent variable), measuring individual behavioral predispositions.[1] Time-invariant group characteristics, such as sex of the child, maternal age at birth of the target child, and education were then entered as explanatory variables for this latent predisposition. The effects of life events (*i.e.*, divorce or remarriage) on behavior at a given time were measured beyond the persisting

[a] This study was supported by Quebec's funding agencies: FCAR, FRSQ, CQRS, and Canada's SSHRC.

[b] Address for correspondence: L. Pagani-Kurtz, Ph.D., Research Unit on Children's Psychosocial Maladjustment, University of Montreal, 750 Gouin Blvd. East, Montreal, Quebec, Canada H2C 1A6. Tel: (514) 251-4015 ext. 2349; e-mail: paganikl@brise.ere.umontreal.ca.

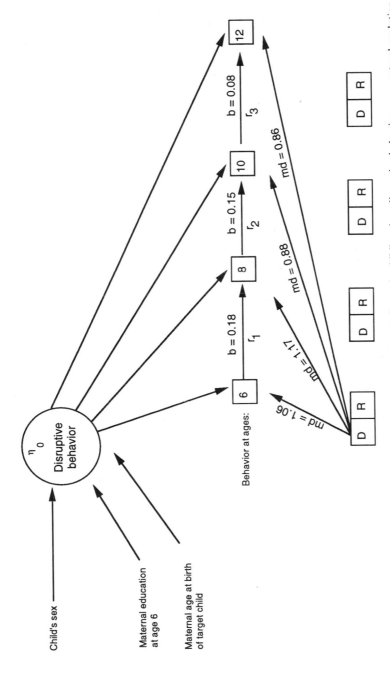

FIGURE 1. The short- and long-term effects of a parental divorce occurring during early childhood on disruptive behavior. η_0 = natural evolution of behavior; md = mean differences; D = divorce occurring; R = remarriage occurring; r = indirect pathway; b = beta.

TABLE 1. Number of Divorces and Remarriages Occurring between Assessment Waves[1] and Number of Subjects in Divorced, Remarried, and Intact Family Configurations at each Assessment Wave[2,a]

Family Status	Age 6	Age 8	Age 10	Age 12
Divorced[1]	85	23	38	54
Remarried[1]	32	25	30	54
Divorced[2]	85	83	91	119
Remarried[2]	32	57	87	113
Intact	1199	1176	1138	1084

[a] The two parts of this table are dependent on one another and should be read in a dynamic manner. (For example, at age 6, 85 children had already experienced parental divorce. At age 8, 23 divorces and 25 remarriages took place; hence 85 + 23 − 25 = 83 subjects from divorced homes at age 8.)

effect of other changes prior to the event. This model makes an implicit assumption that the effects of age are a shared component by all individuals at a given time and thus must be reflected in the mean structure.

The model for disruptive behavior had a very good fit. The covariates explained approximately 16% of the variance in the latent predisposition and were all significant. As shown in FIGURE 1, departures from the latent predisposition in disruptive behavior were significant and less persistent with age. We observed a significant short- and long-term negative effect of parental divorce on disruptiveness when it occurred during early childhood. All mean differences (boys from divorced versus intact families) were significant when divorce occurred prior to age 6, beyond any persistent effects that would be expected in the basic model. As hypothesized, the enduring negative effects of divorce that occurred before age 6 did not appear to be affected by remarriage. As expected, these results support the notion[2] of a "vulnerable period," whereby marital disruption can have a detrimental effect on a child's sociobehavioral development. There are several explanations that are consistent with this concept. First, perhaps the experience of parental divorce early in life may disrupt attachment processes in the parent-child relationship. Second, it might be that when children are younger and a divorce occurs, parents encounter more economic hardship and social isolation. A strained parent-child relationship would thus contribute to disrupted parent-child interactions. Unexpectedly, the results for prosocial behavior revealed no significant effects of divorce and remarriage.

ACKNOWLEDGMENTS

The authors thank Hélène Beauchesne and Lucille David for coordinating the data collection, Lyse Desmarais-Gervais and Nicole Thériault for creating the data bank, and Minh Trinh for the documentation.

REFERENCES

1. MUTHÉN, B. O. 1991. Analysis of longitudinal data using latent variable models with varying parameters. *In* Best Methods for the Analysis of Change: Recent Advances,

Unanswered Questions, Future Directions. L. M. Collins & L. H. Horn, Eds.: 1–25. American Psychological Association. Washington, DC.

2. HETHERINGTON, E. M. 1989. Coping with family transition: Winners, losers, and survivors. Child Dev. **60**(1): 1–14.

3. TREMBLAY, R. E., R. LOEBER, C. GAGNON, P. CHARLEBOIS, S. LARIVÉE & M. LEBLANC. 1991. Disruptive boys with stable and unstable high fighting behavior patterns during junior elementary school. J. Abnorm. Child Psychol. **19**: 285–300.

Stress, Anger, and Hostility Felt by Students as a Consequence of Subabusive Violence by the Teacher

ANNA PIEKARSKA

Faculty of Psychology
Warsaw University
Stawki 5/7, Warsaw, Poland

The main subject of these two research studies was the condition and consequences of the stress felt by students in the Polish public schools, where subabusive violent attitudes and behaviors from teachers towards students frequently occur.

The first study was conducted in six Warsaw primary schools. Two hundred seventy-one students, ages 13–14, were examined, using six questionnaires. The main goal of the study was to establish the psychological stress factors and the coping strategies used by the children. Nervous system resistance, understood here not only as the level of stimulation, but also as the level of inhibition and mobility of nervous processes, was shown to be a significant, complex correlate of the intensity of stress.

Subabusive behavior of teachers towards students, mostly related to the giving of examinations, was detected as the most frequent cause of stress. The kinds of coping strategies used by the students and the resultant outcomes were determined by the levels of stress and anxiety, and nervous system resistance. This study demonstrated the psychological mechanism of overloading a child's nervous system through using a high level of stress, mostly related to subabusive violence by the teacher.

The second study was conducted in two Warsaw secondary schools. One hundred fifty 16-year-old students were the subjects of the research. Five tests were used to obtain data on the most frequent school-related stressors; the intensity of subjective stress, anxiety, and mood states; and on psychosomatic complaints.

The main goal of this study was to establish a relationship between stress in school and their mood, such as tension/anxiety, depression/dejection, anger/hostility, vigor/activity, fatigue/inertia, and confusion/bewilderment. The study also examined psychosomatic feelings and subjective states of health.

The results of this study, as was shown in the first study, proved and confirmed the role of the teacher's behavior as an important stress factor for students. As a consequence, the level of the students' anger and hostility was high and significantly connected with the frequency and intensity of stress in school. The students' levels of anxiety, depression, and fatigue were also connected with their psychosomatic complaints and subjective feelings of health.

Although, in the tested sample, school achievements, measured by grades, were not negatively connected with stress and depression, they seemed to be negatively influenced by the health of the students. Thus, more than one third of tested students had been ill during the month preceding the study, and more than two thirds of them had not felt well. Nearly one third of subjects pretended to be ill to avoid school, but one fifth of the sample actually had to stay in bed for several days because of an illness. The sample mean of absent school days in the last month was nearly three days.

Serotonergic and Cardiac Correlates of Aggression in Children[a]

DANIEL S. PINE,[b] GAIL WASSERMAN,
JEREMY COPLAN, JANE FRIED, RICHARD SLOAN,
MICHAEL MYERS, LAURENCE GREENHILL,
DAVID SHAFFER, AND BRUCE PARSONS

Division of Child and Adolescent Psychiatry
New York State Psychiatric Institute and
the College of Physicians & Surgeons of Columbia University
722 West 168th Street
New York, New York 10032

INTRODUCTION

The relationship between aggression and biological profiles measured in the serotonergic and cardiac systems may developmentally vary. For serotonergic measures, aggressive adults exhibit a blunted prolactin response to fenfluramine, whereas aggressive children exhibit an enhanced prolactin response.[1,2] For cardiac measures, hostile or aggressive adults exhibit elevated blood pressure and reduced heart period variability, whereas aggressive children exhibit low resting heart rate.[3-5] The current study, using a sample of boys at risk for aggression, examines associations between aggression and both serotonergic and cardiac measures.

METHODS

A group of 126 younger brothers of convicted delinquents in New York City was identified in 1992. From impoverished families, they were 8.5 ± 2 years old and were 55% African-American, 45% Hispanic, and 5% Caucasian. These boys received psychiatric assessments with the Child Behavior Checklist (CBCL) and Diagnostic Interview Schedule for Children (DISC) in both 1992–1993 (time 1) and 1994–1995 (time 2). At time 1, these boys received a physical exam (n = 120) during which routine cardiac indices and platelet 5-HT_2 receptor patterns were assessed. At time 2, they received a more extensive biological assessment (FIG. 1). In brief, cardiac profiles were assessed through an analysis of heart period variability (HPV)[3] during orthostatic challenge (n = 99). Serotonergic profile was assessed using the fenfluramine challenge procedure and an assessment of platelet 5-HT_2 receptor patterns.[2]

[a] This work was supported by a Grant from the Leon Lowenstein Foundation, NIMH Research Training Grant MH-16432, and NIMH Center Grant MH-43878 to the Center to Study Youth Anxiety, Suicide, and Depression.
[b] Tel: (212) 960-2389; fax: (212) 568-8856; e-mail: pined@child.cpmc.columbia.edu.

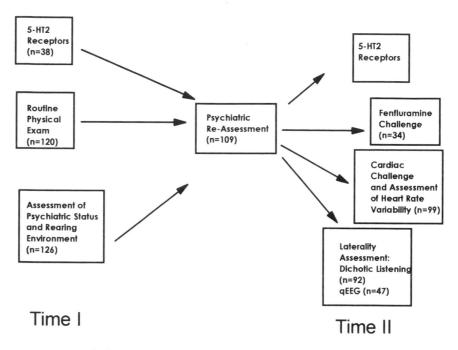

FIGURE 1. Timeline for biological assessment protocol.

RESULTS

As we will present in detail elsewhere, this study found broad associations between disruptive psychopathology and both cardiac and serotonergic indices. Associations between psychopathology and cardiac indices were most consistent with prior studies in adults. As discussed elsewhere,[6] at time 1, an elevated score on the CBCL delinquency scale was associated with three risk factors for ischemic cardiac disease: elevated blood pressure, obesity, and a family history of hypertension. Although only preliminary data are available from time 2, an elevated CBCL externalizing score was associated with reduced high frequency (0.15–0.50 Hz) HPV in the 55 boys with available data. However, there was considerable comorbidity between the externalizing score and an anxiety diagnosis on the DISC, which also predicted reduced high-frequency HPV. This is also consistent with studies examining cardiovascular correlates of both hostility and anxiety disorders among adults.[3,7] By contrast, associations between aggression and serotonergic measures were consistent with prior studies in children but not adults. The 10 boys with oppositional defiant or conduct disorder exhibited an augmented prolactin response to fenfluramine relative to other boys with available data (n = 13).

DISCUSSION

Consistent with studies among aggressive adults, disruptive children exhibited elevated blood pressure and reduced HPV, though the association with reduced

HPV was partially mediated by comorbid anxiety. This is also consistent with studies in adults.[7] In contrast to studies among adults, but consistent with Halperin *et al.*,[2] aggressive children exhibited enhanced prolactin responses to fenfluramine challenge.

REFERENCES

1. COCCARO, E. F., L. J. SIEVER, H. KLAR *et al.* 1989. Arch. Gen. Psychiatry **43:** 587–599.
2. HALPERIN, J. M., V. SHARMA, L. J. SIEVER *et al.* 1994. Am. J. Psychiatry **52:** 305–316.
3. SLOAN, R. P., P. A. SHAPIRO, E. BAGIELLA *et al.* 1994. Am. J. Cardiol. **74:** 298–300.
4. SMITH, T. W. 1992. Health Psychol. **11:** 139–150.
5. RAINE, A. 1993. The Psychopathology of Crime. Academic Press. New York.
6. PINE, D. S., G. WASSERMAN, J. S. COPLAN *et al.* Psychosom. Med. In press.
7. YERGANI, V. K., K. SRINIVASA, R. BALON *et al.* 1994. Am. J. Psychiatry **151:** 1226–1228.

Outcomes of Childhood Aggression in Women

CHERYL-LYNN PODOLSKI
AND L. ROWELL HUESMANN[a]

The Institute for Social Research
The University of Michigan
P.O. Box 1248
Ann Arbor, Michigan 48109-1248

Research has shown that early aggression predicts late aggression for both males and females.[1] However, it appears that there are some sex differences in the long-term effects of childhood aggression. Whereas aggressive boys have increased rates of "externalizing" disorders as they grow up, aggressive girls have increased rates of both "externalizing" and "internalizing" disorders.[2] Hence, it appears that childhood aggression in females may lead to adult depression.

The current study investigates the relationship between aggression and depression with a specific focus on sex differences in development. Whereas early aggression is expected to be positively correlated with adult aggression in both males and females, it is hypothesized that early aggression will also be positively correlated with adult depression only in females.

METHOD

The subjects consisted of 211 women and 195 men who were part of a longitudinal study of aggressive behavior. Subjects were interviewed during their first or third year of grade school (ages 6–8 or 8–10) and again during their early twenties. The procedures for the early waves of data collection are described in Huesmann and Eron.[3] The follow-up interview 15 years later was conducted in person (N = 300) or by phone (N = 106). An "other" person who knew the subject well was also interviewed in 356 cases.

In the early waves, a peer-nominated aggression score and a measure of aggressive fantasy were obtained.[3] In the late wave, measures of aggression included an aggressive personality score (MMPI F + 4 + 9),[4] self-reported indirect aggression,[5] self- and other-reported mild physical aggression,[5] self-reported severe physical aggression,[3] and self- and other-reported criminal behavior.[6] Depression was measured using the MMPI Depression Scale,[7] the Beck depression inventory,[8] and a global dysphoria measure.[9] Normative beliefs about aggression were measured using a self-report measure about whether it was OK to perform certain aggressive behaviors.[10]

---

[a] Tel: (313) 764-8385; fax: (313) 763-1202; e-mail: chp@umich.edu.

TABLE 1. Correlations between Early Aggression and Adult Criterion Measures

Adult Criterion Measures	Early Aggression			
	Females (N = 206)		Males (N = 187)	
	Peer-Nominated Aggression	Fantasy Aggression	Peer-Nominated Aggression	Fantasy Aggression
Adult aggression				
Aggressive personality	.18*	.12+	.13+	.12
Self-reported indirect aggression	.15*	—	.21**	—
Self-reported mild physical aggression	.11	—	.14*	—
Other-reported mild physical aggression	—	—	.08	.21**
Self-reported severe physical aggression	.11	—	.11	—
Self-reported criminal behavior	.12+	—	.15*	—
Other-reported criminal behavior	.13+	—	.20*	.16*
Adult depression				
MMPI depression scale	.14+	.07	−.19*	—
Beck depression inventory	.19**	.17*	—	—
Global dysphoria	.15*	—	—	—

+ p < .10
* p < .05
** p < .01. Note: Correlations smaller than .10 are not reported here.

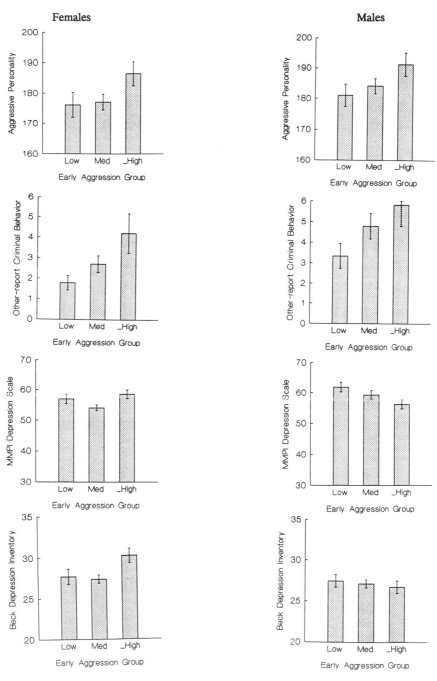

FIGURE 1. Mean adult aggression and depression scores by early aggression group for males and females.

RESULTS

As TABLE 1 shows, for both males and females, childhood aggression is positively correlated with adult aggression. However, childhood aggression is positively correlated with adult depression in females and negatively correlated with adult depression in males. In FIGURE 1 these relations are illustrated with graphs that plot mean scores on adult aggression and depression for subjects who were low, medium, and high in childhood aggression. It may be that these sex differences are due to differential approval of aggression in males and females. In fact, we found that young females disapprove more of aggression than do young males (t = −4.13, df = 366.58, p < .000).

DISCUSSION

Early aggression was found to be positively correlated with adult depression for females but negatively for males. These findings confirm earlier studies that illustrate sex difference in the long-term effects of early aggression. Early aggressive behavior seems to lead to later externalizing and internalizing behaviors in females but only externalizing behaviors in males. These findings are consistent with Eron's[11] theory that differential socialization may lead to the translation of aggression into "internalizing" disorders for females. Consistent with this theory was the finding that females have stronger beliefs prohibiting the use of aggression than do males. An alternative explanation for the current findings may be that girls who learn aggressive scripts are learning behaviors that result in peer isolation. It may be that this isolation results in lack of social support that in turn leads to adult depression. Future research that investigates the accuracy of these explanations needs to be conducted.

REFERENCES

1. HUESMANN, L. R., L. D. ERON, M. M. LEFKOWITZ & L. O. WALDER. 1984. Stability of aggression over time and generations. Dev. Psychol. 20(6): 1120–1134.
2. ROBINS, L. N. 1986. The consequences of conduct disorder in girls. In Development of Antisocial and Prosocial Behavior. D. Olweus, J. Black & M. Radke-Jarrow, Eds. Academic Press. New York.
3. HUESMANN, L. R. & L. D. ERON. 1986. Television and the Aggressive Child: A Cross-National Comparison. Lawrence Erlbaum Associates. Hillsdale, NJ.
4. HUESMANN, L. R., M. M. LEFKOWITZ & L. D. ERON. 1978. Sum of MMPI Scales F, 4, and 9 as a measure of aggression. J. Consult. Clin. Psychol. 46: 1071–1078.
5. BJORKQVIST, K., K. OYSTERMAN & A. KAUKIAINEN. 1992. The development of direct and indirect aggressive strategies in males and females. In Of Mice and Women: Aspects of Female Aggression. K. Bjorkqvist & P. Niemela, Eds. Academic Press. New York.
6. ELLIOT, D. S., F. W. DUNFORD & D. HUIZINGA. 1987. The identification and prediction of career offenders utilizing self-reporting and official data. In Prevention of Delinquent Behavior. J. D. Burchard & S. N. Burchard, Eds.: 90–121. Sage Publications. Newbury Park.
7. DAHLSTROM, W. G. & G. S. WELSH. 1960. An MMPI Handbook. University of Minnesota Press. Minneapolis, MN.
8. BECK, A. T., C. H. WARD, M. MENDELSON, J. MOCK & J. ERBAUGH. 1961. An inventory for measuring depression. Arch. Gen. Psychiatry 4: 561–571.

9. ANDREWS, F. M. & S. B. WITHEY. 1976. Social indicators of well-being. Plenum. New York.
10. HUESMANN, L. R. & N. G. GUERRA. Children's normative beliefs about aggression and aggressive behavior. J. Pers. Soc. Psychol. In press.
11. ERON, L. D. 1992. Gender differences in violence: Biology and/or socialization? *In* Of Mice and Women: Aspects of Female Aggression. K. Bjorkqvist & P. Niemela, Eds.: 89–97. Academic Press. New York.

The Effect of a Short, Intensive Intervention upon Bullying in Four Classes in a Czech Town

PAVEL ŘÍČAN,[a] KATEŘINA ONDROVÁ,[b]
AND JIŘÍ SVATOŠ[c]

[a]Institute of Psychology
Czech Academy of Sciences
Prague, Czechoslovakia

[b]Department of Education
University of Olomouc
Olomouc, Czechoslovakia

[c]Department of Mathematics
Charles University
Prague, Czechoslovakia

Inspired by the ideas of Dan Olweus,[1] the pioneer in the field of bullying research and author of numerous books and articles since the 1970s, we assessed the effect of a set of measures used to counter bullying among school children.

METHOD

Sample

Eight fourth-grade elementary school classes (median age 10 years) were used, half of them as an experimental group, the other half as a control.

Measurement Techniques

The Olweus questionnaire of bullying was used to measure several aspects of bullying, first, during November 1994, and again about four months later. A peer-nomination technique was also used, yielding bully and victim scores for each child as well as his or her popularity within the class. Results of the peer nomination were used to improve the teachers' knowledge of the classes, which was part of the intervention described below.

Intervention Methods

(1) The most important component of intervention, according to Olweus, is raising awareness of the problem of bullying at the particular school (in the particular class). This was done by sharing with teachers the results of the Olweus questionnaire as well as of the peer-nomination technique and by discussing with them possibilities of an individual approach to the bullies as well as to the victims.

TABLE 1. Percentages of Bullies and Victims Before and After a Short-term Antibullying Intervention, according to the Olweus Questionnaire

	Experimental classes		Control classes			
	Before (N = 100)	After (N = 98)	Before (N = 98)	After (N = 98)	U	P
Victims						
Broader criterion	18.0	7.1	16.3	14.3	1.90	0.029
Narrower criterion	5.0	1.0	7.1	3.1	−0.04	N.S.
Bullies						
Broader criterion	19.0	7.1	13.3	11.2	2.09	0.019
Narrower criterion	10.0	2.0	3.1	2.0	2.09	0.018

(2) The teachers were instructed to introduce relevant ethical aspects into all elements of the curriculum where possible. The ideal of knighthood was suggested for history classes. For literature and grammer classes, the idea of consideration towards the weak was introduced in sentences used for dictation and analysis. (3) A method called "class charter" was used: Children were asked to name desirable behavioral features of teachers towards students, of students towards teachers, and of students among themselves, with the goal of agreeing on a set of ten or so important rules. The experimenter then showed the children a list of principles that she had chosen. The principle "the strong defends the weak" was included. Children were given a chance to sign the list that finally was placed on the wall in the classroom. (4) The Olweus videocassette on bullying, showing several types of bullying characteristic to Norwegian schools, was presented to the children and discussed with them.

RESULTS

The improvement shown in TABLE 1 is somewhat greater than that achieved by Olweus,[1] probably because our intervention, although similar in nature, was more intensive.

REFERENCE

1. OLWEUS, D. 1993. Bullying at School: What We Know and What We Can Do. Blackwell Publishers. Oxford.

Bullying in Schools

Main Results of the Research Project

C. SALMIVALLI[a] AND K. M. J. LAGERSPETZ[b]

Department of Psychology
University of Turku
Turku, Finland

INTRODUCTION

In this study, the following issues were addressed: (1) What do the other children do when the bully is harassing the victim, that is, what kind of participant roles, in addition to the traditionally studied roles of bully and victim, do the children have in the bullying process? (2) How is the participant role related to a child's social status within the group? (3) How do the victims respond to bullying? and (4) What kind of behavior on the part of the victims is perceived as provoking bullying, or, on the other hand, diminishing bullying or putting an end to it?

METHOD

The subjects were 573 sixth-grade children (286 girls, 287 boys) from 23 school classes in Finland. The data were collected by a peer-rating questionnaire.

Participant Roles

The subjects evaluated how well each classmate fit 50 descriptions of their behavior in a situation when someone was bullied. From these items, four subscales describing tendencies to act as bully, reinforcer of the bully, assistant of the bully, defender of the victim, and outsider were formed. Corresponding participant roles of the children were derived from these scales, except the role of victim: the victims were nominated separately by the subjects. If at least 30% of the classmates nominated a child as a victim, that was considered to be his or her role.

Victim Behavior

The subjects evaluated how each victim responded to bullying. From the 29 items describing the victims' responses, three subscales of victim behavior were formed: counteraggression, helplessness, and nonchalance. In addition, the subjects named the victim(s) who behaved in a way that (a) made others start or continue the bullying or (b) diminished the bullying or put an end to it.

[a] Tel: (+) 358-21-333 5423; fax: (+) 358-21-333 5060; e-mail: tiina.salmivalli@ra.abo.fi.
[b] Tel: (+) 358-21-333 5421; fax: (+) 358-21-333 5060; e-mail: kirsti.lagerspetz@utu.fi.

Sociometry

The pupils in each class nominated the three girls and the three boys from their class whom they liked the most and the least. On the basis of these nominations, each child's scores for social acceptance (SA) and social rejection (SR) were counted. For details about the methods and the procedures, see Salmivalli et al.[1,2]

RESULTS

Participant Roles

The participant roles assigned to the subjects were bully, victim, reinforcer, assistant, defender, and outsider. There was a statistically significant sex difference ($\chi^2(5) = 239.5$, $p < .001$) in the distribution of the participant roles. Boys were more frequently bullies, reinforcers, and assistants, whereas the most frequent roles for the girls were those of defender and outsider (FIG. 1).

Status Differences

Both male and female victims scored low on social acceptance (SA) and high on social rejection (SR); they were clearly rejected children. Male bullies, as well as female reinforcers and assistants, had a similar pattern (low SA, high SR). Female bullies, however, scored above average both on social rejection and social acceptance. Male reinforcers had a profile of popular children (high SA, low SR), whereas male assistants scored near average on both SA and SR. The most popular children of all were the defenders of the victim (high SA, low SR). This was true

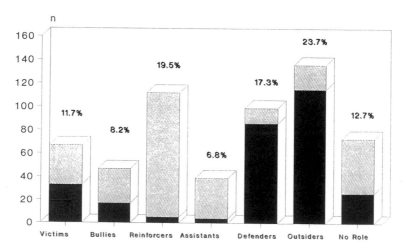

FIGURE 1. Percentage distribution of the subjects between the different participant roles. ■, girls; ▨, boys.

for both sexes. The outsiders (both male and female) scored below average on both SA and SR.

The Victims' Responses to Bullying

Boy victims tended to react with counteraggression significantly more than girl victims (t(65) = 2.45, p < .05). Girl victims scored higher than boys on helplessness, although the difference was not significant. However, for both boy and girl victims, the most typical response was to show nonchalance when they were bullied.

What Provokes the Bullying? What Makes It Stop?

According to multiple stepwise regression analyses, counteraggression in the case of boy victims and helplessness in the case of girl victims were perceived as provoking the bullying. Nonchalance, as well as the absence of the above-mentioned provocative responses, was effective in making the bullying diminish or stop (TABLE 1).

CONCLUSIONS

The results support the notion that bullying may be regarded as a group phenomenon in which most children in a school class have a definable participant role.

TABLE 1. Multiple Stepwise Regression Analyses: What Kind of Behavior of Girl and Boy Victims Makes the Bullying Start or Continue? What Kind of Behavior Makes It Diminish or Stop?

What Makes the Bullying Start or Continue?	R	R^2	R^2 Change	F	Beta
Variables entered					
Girl victims					
Helplessness	.46	.21		8.12**	.51
Counteraggression	.59	.35	.14	7.99**	.38
Boy victims					
Counteraggression	.73	.53		35.85***	.73

What Makes the Bullying Diminish or Stop?	R	R^2	R^2 Change	F	Beta
Variables entered					
Girl victims					
Helplessness	.42	.18		6.78*	−.42
Boy victims					
Counteraggression	.46	.21		8.69**	−.46
Nonchalance	.59	.35	.14	8.46**	.38

* p < .05.
** p < .01.
*** p < .001.

Boys were more actively involved in bullying than girls. One explanation for this might be that for boys aggressive ways of being together are more approved of and even expected. Girls are expected to behave in more prosocial and helping ways—it is a part of the female social role. A further explanation for the difference might be the girls' better developed ability for empathy.

Among both boys and girls, victims had a lower status than the other groups. Their unpopularity can be seen both as a cause and as a result of continuous bullying. One reason for their being picked on and harassed in the first place may have been their original unpopularity within the group. On the other hand, as Olweus[3] has pointed out, there are gradual cognitive changes in the perceptions of the victims by the peers. As the bullying continues, they start to see the victim as worthless, almost deserving to be harassed. Along with these cognitive changes, the victim becomes even more unpopular. It becomes a social norm of the group not to like him or her.

Defenders of the victim had the highest status. Two interpretations are conceivable: (1) Defenders have high status just because they react to bullying in that particular way: defending the victim is appreciated by the peers; (2) children who already have high status do not have to be afraid of being victimized themselves, even if they take sides with the victim. High status enables defending the victim.

Male bullies were clearly low-status children. Female bullies, on the other hand, formed an exceptional group; they scored above the mean in both social acceptance and social rejection.

Nonchalant victims were perceived as most able to diminish the bullying or to put an end to it. This suggests that for a victim, a good response is not to respond. Both helplessness (especially for girls) and counteraggression (especially for boys) were perceived as provoking the bullying.

In our view, interventions against bullying should be directed towards the whole group. Children in different participant roles, for example, outsiders or reinforcers, should be made use of when trying to put an end to bullying. Their behavior may be easier to change than the aggressive behavior of the bullies. Through these changes, even the behavior of the bullies might be affected.

REFERENCES

1. SALMIVALLI, C., K. M. J. LAGERSPETZ, K. BJÖRKQVIST, K. ÖSTERMAN & A. KAUKI-AINEN. 1996. Bullying as a group process: Participant roles and their relations to social status within the group. Aggressive Behav. **22:** 1–15.
2. SALMIVALLI, C., J. KARHUNEN & K. M. J. LAGERSPETZ. 1996. How do the victims respond to bullying? Aggressive Behav. **22:** 99–109.
3. OLWEUS, D. 1978. Aggression in the schools. Bullies and whipping boys. Hemisphere Press (John Wiley). Washington D.C.

Aggression in Physically Abused Children

The Role of Distress Proneness

ANGELA SCARPA[a,c] AND DAVID J. KOLKO[b]

[a]Department of Psychology
Eastern Washington University
Cheney, Washington 99004-2431

[b]Western Psychiatric Institute and Clinic
University of Pittsburgh Medical Center
Pittsburgh, Pennsylvania

Although the phenomenon of physical abuse in children is related to a heightened risk of aggression, the majority of abused children do not become aggressive.[1] Factors that put some physically abused children at increased risk for aggressive behavior remain to be clarified. A transactional, biopsychosocial model of development suggests that aggressive behavioral problems arise when intrinsic child vulnerabilities interact with a nonoptimal environment.[2] Internalizing problems, such as anxiety and depression, have been found to be markedly higher in youth with conduct disorder.[3] This suggests that vulnerability to emotional distress (*i.e.,* distress proneness) may be one intrinsic child vulnerability related to later aggression. This preliminary study examined the influence of distress proneness on aggression in physically abused children. In line with the transactional model of development, it was hypothesized that the experience of physical abuse in children will interact with distress proneness to heighten the risk of their involvement in aggression. In other words, this study was conducted to test the hypothesis that the relationship between abuse and aggression will be strongest in the presence of distress proneness, using data from two consecutive summer treatment programs for 7- to 15-year-old children with disruptive behavior disorders.

METHOD AND RESULTS

In the first program, the parent report of internalizing behavior was used to measure distress proneness, and aggressive behavior was rated independently by parents, teachers, and clinic staff for 52 children (45 boys, 7 girls; 38 African-American, 14 Caucasian). According to all three sources, the highest reports of aggressive behavior occurred in children who had been both abused and rated with high internalizing behavior ($t(48) = 7.17$, $p < .000$ for parents; $t(30) = 2.15$, $p < .02$ for teachers; $t(45) = 1.44$, $p < .08$ for staff, relative to abused children rated with low internaling behavior). See FIGURE 1 for an illustration of these results.

[c] Address for correspondence: Department of Psychology, Rm. 139, University of Georgia, Baldwin Street, Athens, GA 30602-3013. Tel: (706) 542-0307; fax: (706) 542-3275; e-mail: ascarpa@uga.cc.uga.edu.

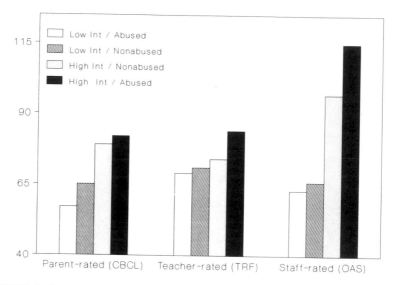

FIGURE 1. Parent, teacher, and staff ratings of aggression for physically abused and nonabused children divided into high versus low internalizers. CBCL, Child Behavior Checklist; TRF, Teacher's Report Form; OAS, Overt Aggression Scale; Int, internalizer.

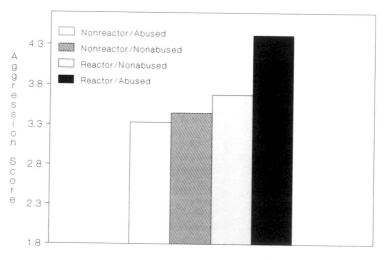

FIGURE 2. Staff (Overt Aggression Scale) ratings of aggression for physically abused and nonabused children divided into cortisol reactors versus nonreactors.

In the second program, salivary cortisol reactivity after a provocation task was measured as a physiological index of distress proneness for 19 children (17 boys, 2 girls; 14 African-American, 5 Caucasian). Children were divided into reactors (*i.e.*, cortisol levels increased after the task) and nonreactors (*i.e.*, cortisol levels remained the same or decreased after the task). Staff reports of aggression were analyzed, and a trend was found showing the highest rates were reported in children who were both abused and classified as cortisol reactors ($t(15) = 1.45$, p < .084; see FIG. 2) relative to abused children classified as cortisol nonreactors. This replicated the same pattern of aggression scores as found in the first program sample.

CONCLUSIONS

In both samples, a similar pattern emerged in which disruptive children who have a cooccurring physical abuse history and distress proneness showed the highest levels of aggressive behavior. This pattern of results is consistent with the transactional model of aggression, suggesting that aggressive behavior problems arise when child vulnerabilities are coupled with an adverse family environment. Thus, vulnerability to emotional distress may be seen as one factor related to the increased risk of aggression in some physically abused children.

REFERENCES

1. WIDOM, C. S. 1989. Psychol. Bull. **106:** 3–28.
2. SANSON, A. V., D. SMART, M. PRIOR & F. OBERKLAID. 1993. J. Am. Acad. Child Adolesc. Psychiatry **32:** 1207–1216.
3. HINSHAW, S. P., B. B. LAHEY & E. L. HART. 1993. Dev. Psychopathol. **5:** 31–49.

Low Pain Sensitivity and Stability of Physical Aggression in Boys

J. R. SÉGUIN,[a] R. O. PIHL,[b] B. BOULERICE,
R. E. TREMBLAY, AND P. W. HARDEN

Stewart Biological Sciences Building
McGill University
1205 Dr. Penfield Avenue
Montreal, Quebec, Canada H3A 1B1
and
University of Montreal
Montreal, Quebec, Canada

It has been proposed that psychopaths are characterized by low pain sensitivity[1,2] and, alternately, that pain and other aversive conditions could reliably elicit aggression.[3] In this latter case it is possible that high pain sensitivity mediates aggressive behavior. A first question addressed whether stably aggressive boys would be characterized by high or low pain sensitivity. A second question examined the putative role of the frontal lobes in pain modulation and its association with physically aggressive behavior. From the observation that pain perception was affected by frontal lobe lesions[4] and that psychopaths and violent criminals were also reported as having impairments in frontal lobe activity,[5] Schalling[6] and Petrie[7] proposed that if low pain sensitivity and psychopathy were associated, they might both be associated with low frontal lobe functioning.

Adolescent boys (N = 177), in which teacher-rated physical aggression, teacher-rated anxiety, and preschool family adversity had been assessed since kindergarten formed three groups that differed in stability of physical aggression: stable, unstable, and nonaggressive. We derived a measure of frontal lobe function from validated tests of executive functions.[8] These tests putatively measure dorsolateral frontal lobe abilities. Pain sensitivity was measured with a 400 *g* version of a modified finger pressure pain stimulation device.[9] We found that stable aggressive boys were the least pain sensitive, whereas unstable aggressive boys were the most pain sensitive. Aggression categories and executive functions both overlapped with pain sensitivity but not completely with one another. To clarify this overlap, an interaction between aggression categories and executive functions revealed that at low levels of executive functioning, pain sensitivity could not be distinguished between the aggressive groups. However, relative to their low executive counterpart, at high levels, unstable aggressive boys reported even more pain, whereas stable aggressive boys reported even less pain (see FIG. 1). The reporting of pain by high executive function aggressive boys may be the result of the use of strategies. Psychopaths had already been thought to deceptively underreport pain.[2] Why such deception would have been used in the context of our study is unclear.

High sensitivity to pain may explain why some aggressive boys have not been stable in their aggression. Stable aggressive boys with low pain sensitivity would

---

[a] Tel: (514) 398-6100; fax: (514) 398-4896; e-mail: seguinj@ere.umontreal.ca.
[b] Author to whom correspondence should be addressed.

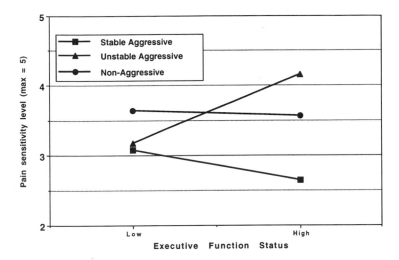

FIGURE 1. Pain sensitivity levels as a function of high and low executive functions by groups at 3 minutes.

be at a different risk for criminal behavior as a function of their executive functions status. Those who have lower executive functioning would presumably commit more impulsive crimes,[5,10] whereas their more cognitively proficient counterpart would likely commit more elaborate crimes and be less likely to get caught.

Secondary results on covariables indicate that variations in anxiety had strong positive associations with pain sensitivity in unstable aggressive boys. Finally, the relation between pain sensitivity and family adversity had a quadratic shape; high pain ratings were found in boys who had a moderate level of family adversity, and low pain ratings were found in boys with low or high adversity. Although the family adversity measure is a crude estimate of social interactions in a family, it appears sensitive enough. It is possible that at moderate levels of adversity, some families encourage or react strongly to expressions of pain,[11] and that a toughening (*i.e.,* counterconditioning) effect occurs in high-adversity families.[12]

REFERENCES

1. HARE, R. D. 1968. J. Abnorm. Psychol. **73:** 268–272.
2. HARE, R. D. 1966. J. Abnorm. Psychol. **71:** 25–29.
3. BERKOWITZ, L. 1993. Motiv. Emotion **17:** 277–293.
4. BOUCKOMS, A. J. 1994. Limbic surgery for pain. *In* Textbook of Pain. P. D. Wald & R. Melzack, Eds.: 1171–1186. 3rd edit. Churchill Livingstone. Edinburgh.
5. RAINE, A., M. S. BUCHSBAUM, J. STANLEY, S. LOTTENBERG, L. ABEL & J. STODDARD. 1994. Biol. Psychiatry **36:** 365–373.
6. SCHALLING, D. 1978. Psychopathy-related personality variables and the psychophysiology of socialization. *In* Psychopathic Behaviour: Approaches to Research. R. D. Hare & D. Schalling, Eds.: 85–106. Wiley. New York.
7. PETRIE, A. 1978. Individuality in Pain and Suffering. 2nd edit. University of Chicago Press. Chicago.

8. SÉGUIN, J. R., R. O. PIHL, P. W. HARDEN, R. E. TREMBLAY & B. BOULERICE. 1995. J. Abnorm. Psychol. **104:** 614–624.
9. BRUEHL, S., C. R. CARLSON & J. A. MCCUBBIN. 1992. Pain **48:** 463–467.
10. MOFFITT, T. E. & B. HENRY. 1989. Dev. Psychopathol. **1:** 105–118.
11. MELZACK, R. & P. WALL. 1988. The Challenge of Pain. 2nd edit. Penguin. London.
12. GRAY, J. A. 1987. The Psychology of Fear and Stress. 2nd edit. Cambridge University Press. Cambridge, Britain.

Fighting as a Function of Personality and Neuropsychological Measures

KRISTIN E. VICKERS,[a,d] JORDAN B. PETERSON,[a]
CHRISTOPHER D. HORNIG,[a] ROBERT O. PIHL,[b]
JEAN SÉGUIN,[b] AND RICHARD E. TREMBLAY[c]

[a]Harvard University
33 Kirkland Street
Cambridge, Massachusetts 02138

[b]McGill University
Montreal, Quebec, Canada H3A 1B1

[c]University of Montreal
Montreal, Quebec, Canada H2C 1A6

Violence among young people has surpassed communicable disease as the primary cause of mortality in young people.[1] A complete understanding of what causes aggression remains elusive, but it is likely that the probability of exhibiting violent behavior is dependent upon interactive, multifactorial mechanisms.[2] Greater magnitude of familial adversity has been linked to increased likelihood of aggressive behavior.[3,4] Personality profiles in kindergarten have been shown to predict antisocial behavior in adolescence,[5] and deficits in neuropsychological function have been used to discriminate between levels of aggression.[6] In this study, the subjects, 143 Caucasian boys derived from a community sample of 53 schools with the lowest socioeconomic status (SES) in Montreal, were rated for fighting behavior by their teachers at ages 6, 10, 11, and 12 using the Preschool Behavior Questionnaire (PBQ).[7] These fighting scores were used to divide the sample into three groups: stable fighters (n = 52), above the 70th percentile on the fighting scale of the PBQ at age 6 and at one more assessment; stable nonfighters (n = 47), who were below the 70th percentile at all assessments; and unstable fighters (n = 44), not otherwise classifiable. Neuropsychological and personality instruments were administered, and teacher-rated anxiety and mother-rated familial adversity measures were obtained. The best fit multiple linear regression equation contained 13 variables, including neuropsychological and pesonality measures, as well as teacher-rated anxiety (R^2 = proportion of variance explained = 0.49). The best fit logistic regression equation comparing stable fighters versus stable nonfighters contained 15 variables and obtained a classification accuracy hit rate of 92% for identifying members of both groups. A four-variable logistic regression model containing the neuropsychological factors of verbal learning and executive functions,[7] plus the Eysenck Junior Personality Questionnaire Anxiety Scale and the NEO-PIR Agreeableness Scale, had a hit rate of 90% for stable fighters and 83% for stable nonfighters. Two of the three a priori hypotheses were supported, as neuropsychological and personality measures were included in the

---

[d] Address correspondence to Kristin E. Vickers, Harvard University, c/o 435 Washington Street, #402, Somerville, MA 02143. Tel: (617) 576-9294; fax: (617) 495-3728; e-mail: kristin@wjh.harvard.edu.

411

best-fit prediction models. Familial adversity was not significant in any of these analyses, possibly due to restriction of range in this low SES sample.

REFERENCES

1. BLUM, R. 1987. Contemporary threats to adolescent health in the United States. J. Am. Med. Assoc. **257:** 3390–3395.
2. RAINE, A. 1993. The Psychopathology of Crime: Criminal Behavior as a Clinical Disorder. Academic Press. San Diego, CA.
3. PATTERSON, G. R., B. D. DEBARYSHE & E. RAMSEY. 1989. A developmental perspective on antisocial behavior. Am. Psychol. **44:** 329–335.
4. VITARO, F., R. E. TREMBLAY & C. GAGNON. 1992. Adversité famiale et troubles du comportement au début de la période de fréquentation scolaire. Rev. Can. Sante Mentale. **11:** 45–62.
5. TREMBLAY, R. E., R. O. PIHL, F. VITARO & P. L. DOBKIN. 1994. Predicting early onset of male antisocial behavior from preschool behavior. Arch. Gen. Psychiatry **51:** 732–739.
6. SEGUIN, J. R., R. O. PIHL, P. W. HARDEN & R. E. TREMBLAY. 1995. Cognitive and neuropsychological characteristics of physically aggressive boys. J. Abnorm. Psychol. **104:** 614–624.
7. TREMBLAY, R. E., L. DESMARAIS-GERVAIS, C. GAGNON & P. CHARLEBOIS. 1987. The preschool behavior questionnaire: Stability of its factor structure between cultures, sexes, ages and socioeconomic classes. Int. J. Behav. Dev. **10:** 467–484.

Persistence of Aggressive and Nonaggressive Delinquency in Relation to Neuropsychological Functioning [a]

HELENE RASKIN WHITE [b] AND MARSHA E. BATES

Center of Alcohol Studies
Rutgers University
P.O. Box 969
Smithers Hall
Piscataway, New Jersey 08855-0969

Recent research in delinquency has identified several types of adolescent delinquents based on the content of the behavior (*e.g.*, covert/nonaggressive delinquents vs. overt/aggressive delinquents)[1] or the stability of the behavior over time (*e.g.*, life-course-persistent vs. adolescence-limited delinquents).[2] These varying groups of delinquents may differ in etiological risk factors. Moffit[2] suggests that persistent as compared to adolescence-limited delinquents are more likely to exhibit neuropsychological deficits, especially in verbal skills and executive functions. We examined differences in neuropsychological functioning and related school performance across three groups based on the persistence of aggressive behavior (*e.g.*, assault) and three groups based on persistence of nonaggressive behavior (*e.g.*, theft) from adolescence into adulthood.

METHOD

A subsample of 406 male subjects from the Rutgers Health and Human Development Project was included in the analyses.[3] These subjects were tested four times; attrition was less than 10% at any test occasion. At time 1 (T1) subjects were age 12 (young cohort) or 15 (middle cohort), and at T4 they were ages 25 and 28, respectively. The sample was primarily white, middle and working class.

Self-report data were used to define three aggressive and three nonaggressive delinquency groups: nondelinquents (NON); adolescence-limited (AL) delinquents; and persistent (PER) delinquents (see TABLE 1). Three domains of neuropsychological functioning were assessed at T3 and T4: general intelligence/abstraction (INTELL), immediate memory (MEM), and spatial relations/visuoperceptive skills.[3] We also assessed fourth-grade performance and average grades in the last three years in English and math.

RESULTS

In the young cohort, AL and PER aggressive delinquents scored significantly lower than nondelinquents on INTELL and MEM at T3 (age 18); however, there

[a] Preparation of this paper was supported in part by Grants from the National Institute on Drug Abuse (#DA/AA-03395) and the Alcoholic Beverage Medical Research Foundation.
[b] Tel: (908) 445-3579; fax: (908) 445-3500; e-mail: hewhite@rci.rutgers.edu.

TABLE 1. Number and Percent of Subjects in Delinquency Groups by Cohort[a]

	Nondelinquent	Adolescence-limited	Persistent
Aggressive delinquency groups			
Young Cohort			
Number	134	41	15
Percent[b]	66.3	20.3	7.4
Middle Cohort			
Number	143	40	14
Percent	70.1	19.6	6.9
Nonaggressive delinquency groups			
Young Cohort			
Number	128	52	15
Percent	63.4	25.7	7.4
Middle Cohort			
Number	144	39	13
Percent	70.1	19.1	6.4

[a] For aggressive delinquency groups: NON scored low (bottom 85%) on aggression during adolescence and adulthood; AL aggressive delinquents scored high (top 15%) during adolescence, but low in adulthood; and PER aggressive delinquents scored high both in adolescence and adulthood. Nonaggressive delinquency groups were developed in the same manner.

[b] Percentages do not add to 100% because a fourth group of late onset delinquents (who scored low in adolescence, but high in adulthood) were excluded from the analyses due to small numbers.

were no reliable differences at T4 (see TABLE 2). In the middle cohort, spatial scores were significantly lower for AL and PER aggressive delinquents than for NON at T3 (age 21), but only lower for AL at T4 (age 28). In addition, AL aggressive delinquents reported significantly lower grades than NON in English at ages 15 (both cohorts) and 18 (middle cohort only). No significant differences were found between AL and PER aggressive delinquents in neuropsychological or school performance (although most means on the neuropsychological measures were in the predicted direction).

AL and PER nonaggressive delinquents were not reliably different from each other, or from NON on any of the neuropsychological measures (not shown). AL nonaggressive delinquents performed significantly worse than NON in English at ages 15 and 18 (both cohorts) and math at age 18 (middle cohort only).

DISCUSSION

The significant differences between aggressive delinquents and nondelinquents in neuropsychological functioning were not replicated across time or cohort. Further, there were no significant differences on any of the neuropsychological measures among nonaggressive delinquency groups. The one consistent finding across cohorts and delinquency types was that AL delinquents reported lower grades in English in middle and late adolescence than NON. This result supports previous findings that delinquents have lower verbal skills and reading abilities than nondelinquents.[2]

Contrary to expectations, there were no significant differences between AL and PER delinquents on any of the cognitive measures. Although these findings

TABLE 2. ANOVA Results for Aggressive Delinquency Groups and Mean Differences on Neuropsychological Functioning and School Performance (Standardized Means Presented)[a]

Young cohort

| Measures | Aggressive Delinquency Groups | | | F value |
	Nondelinquent	Adolescence-limited	Persistent	
INTELL3[b,c]	3.78	−8.47	−14.46	5.85*
INTELL4	1.52	−4.06	−0.65	1.40
MEMORY3[b,c]	0.80	−1.91	−3.86	8.42*
MEMORY4	0.45	−1.20	−2.83	3.62
SPATIAL3	4.07	−6.27	−11.92	3.48
SPATIAL4	3.29	−4.71	−4.73	1.26
4th Grade	−0.03	0	0.26	0.75
ENGLISH 12	−0.06	−0.03	0.69	1.72
ENGLISH 15[b]	−0.29	0.70	0.62	7.83*
ENGLISH 18	−0.22	0.40	0.81	4.70*
MATH 12	−0.04	0.40	−0.70	2.51
MATH 15	−0.19	0.36	0.66	3.02
MATH 18	−0.17	0.19	0.70	2.52

Middle cohort

| Measures | Aggressive Delinquency Groups | | | F value |
	Nondelinquent	Adolescence-limited	Persistent	
INTELL3	2.36	−2.57	−11.20	1.94
INTELL4	1.69	−3.49	−7.46	2.50
MEMORY3	0.54	−0.70	−2.79	2.85
MEMORY4	0.30	−0.64	−1.38	0.96
SPATIAL[b,c]	5.61	−10.44	−24.22	6.81*
SPATIAL[b]	4.71	−12.67	−14.80	5.41
4th Grade	−0.07	0.17	0.10	1.19
ENGLISH 15[b]	−0.24	0.66	0.37	5.36*
ENGLISH 18[b]	−0.29	0.68	0.66	7.64*
MATH 15	−0.15	0.33	0.33	1.64
MATH 18	−0.19	0.40	0.32	1.99

[a] Higher scores on the neuropsychological measures indicate better performance. Lower scores on the school performance measures indicate better performance.

[b] Based on Scheffe tests, nondelinquents are significantly ($p < .05$) different from adolescence-limited aggressive delinquents.

[c] Based on Scheffe tests, nondelinquents are significantly ($p < .05$) different from persistent aggressive delinquents.

* $p < .01$.

are consistent with those of Nagin,[4] they conflict with those reviewed by Moffitt.[2] There are several reasons why our findings may differ: (1) the amount of aggressive and nonaggressive delinquency was minimal in this sample and was often restricted to trivial events; (2) the small number of subjects in the PER group limited the power to find significant differences; (3) the neuropsychological tests that we used and the way they were grouped were somewhat different than those used in other studies; and (4) our measures of neuropsychological functioning were assessed in late adolescence and adulthood. Perhaps as delinquents age, compensatory processes mask neuropsychological deficits.[3] Alternatively, the apparent deficits in young delinquents may primarily represent developmental lags or cognitive delays. Nevertheless, in our sample, preadolescent and early adolescent school grades did not differentiate between delinquents and nondelinquents, or between AL and PER delinquents. A more extensive examination of single cognitive test performance and replications across samples varying in age and delinquency severity may help address these issues.

REFERENCES

1. LOEBER, R. 1988. *In* Advances in Clinical Child Psychology. B. B. Lahey & A. E. Kazdin, Eds.: **11:** 73–124. Plenum. New York.
2. MOFFITT, T. E. 1993. Psychol. Rev. **100**(4): 674–701.
3. TRACY, J. I. & M. E. BATES. 1994. J. Stud. Alcohol **55:** 726–738.
4. NAGIN, D. S., D. P. FARRINGTON & T. E. MOFFITT. 1995. Criminology **33**(1): 111–139.

Subject Index

Index of Contributors